Fodor's

BOSTON

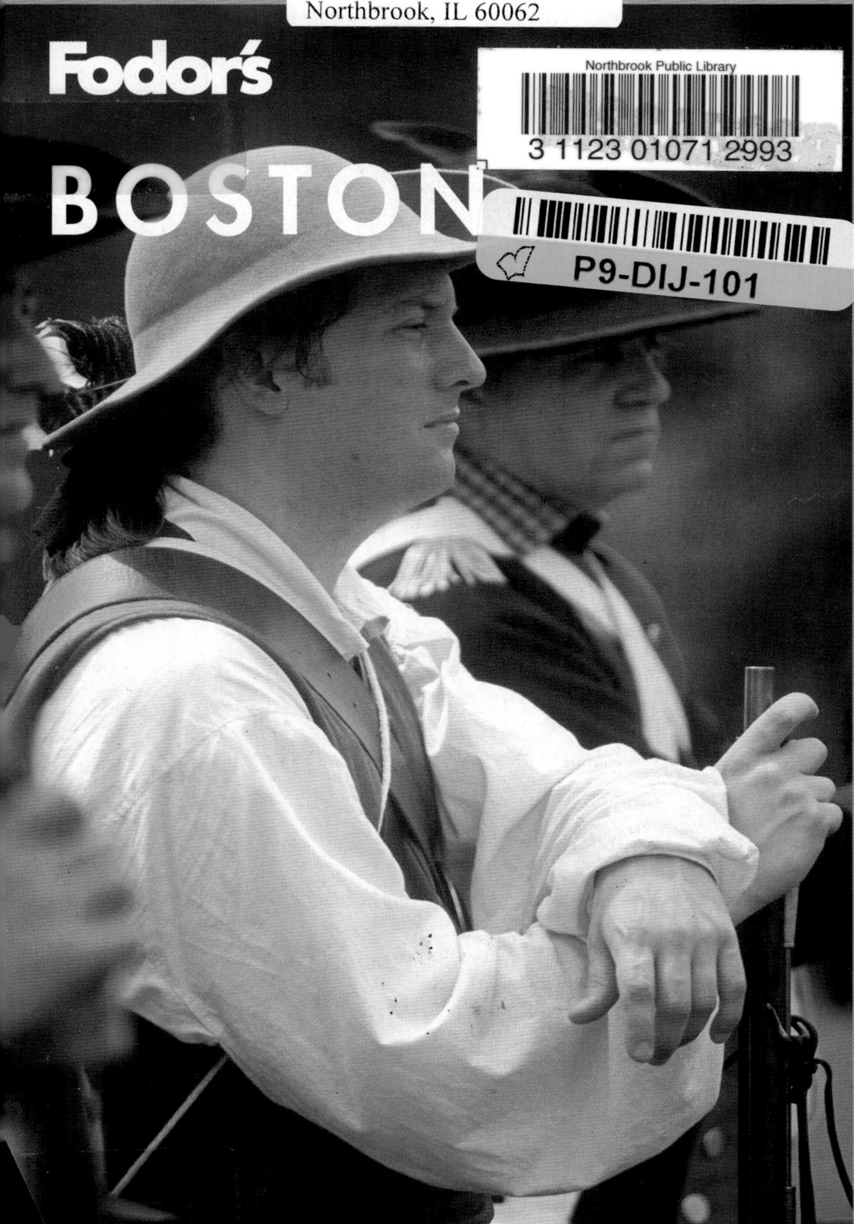

WELCOME TO BOSTON

Bursting with Yankee pride, Boston attracts visitors for its rich past and vibrant present. From Boston Common to Faneuil Hall to Fenway Park, the city is a hub of American history and culture. Buzzing neighborhoods such as the North End, Beacon Hill, and Back Bay mix venerable landmarks and lively street life. On the other side of the Charles River is bustling Cambridge, home of Harvard University and MIT. Wherever you choose to explore, Boston's locavore restaurants, chic galleries, and tempting shops are all easily accessible on satisfying strolls.

TOP REASONS TO GO

★ **Historic Icons:** The Freedom Trail links sites from the American Revolution's start.

★ **The Charles:** The river's bridges and esplanade reward exploration by foot or boat.

★ **Great Museums:** The Museum of Fine Arts and New England Aquarium satisfy curious minds.

★ **Stylish Shopping:** Newbury and Boylston Streets give shopaholics a boutique buzz.

★ **Cuisine:** Seafood restaurants and chef-led hotspots fuel a booming restaurant scene.

★ **Parks and Squares:** Boston Public Garden and Copley Square have prime people-watching.

Fodor's BOSTON

Publisher: Amanda D'Acierno, *Senior Vice President*

Editorial: Arabella Bowen, *Editor in Chief*; Linda Cabasin, *Editorial Director*

Design: Fabrizio La Rocca, *Vice President, Creative Director*; Tina Malaney, *Associate Art Director*; Chie Ushio, *Senior Designer*; Ann McBride, *Production Designer*

Photography: Melanie Marin, *Associate Director of Photography*; Jessica Parkhill and Jennifer Romains, *Researchers*

Maps: Rebecca Baer, *Senior Map Editor*; Mark Stroud and Harry Colomb, Moon Street Cartography; David Lindroth, Inc.; Mapping Specialists, *Cartographers*

Production: Linda Schmidt, *Managing Editor*; Evangelos Vasilakis, *Associate Managing Editor*; Angela L. McLean, *Senior Production Manager*

Sales: Jacqueline Lebow, *Sales Director*

Marketing & Publicity: Heather Dalton, *Marketing Director*; Katherine Fleming, *Senior Publicist*

Business & Operations: Susan Livingston, *Vice President, Strategic Business Planning*; Sue Daulton, *Vice President, Operations*

Fodors.com: Megan Bell, *Executive Director, Revenue & Business Development*; Yasmin Marinaro, *Senior Director, Marketing & Partnerships*

Writers: Fred Bouchard, Frances Folsom, Kim Foley MacKinnon, Victoria Abbott Riccardi

Editor: Kristan Schiller

Production Editor: Evangelos Vasilakis

28th Edition

ISBN 978-0-8041-4208-3

ISSN 0882-0074

PRINTED IN COLOMBIA

10 9 8 7 6 5 4 3 2 1

CONTENTS

Fodor's Features

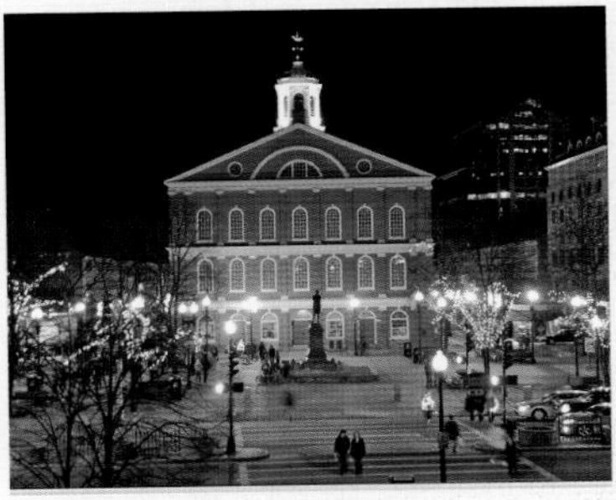

CONTENTS

MAPS

ABOUT THIS GUIDE

Fodor's Recommendations

Everything in this guide is worth doing—we don't cover what isn't—but exceptional sights, hotels, and restaurants are recognized with additional accolades. Fodor'sChoice★ indicates our top recommendations; and **Best Bets** call attention to notable hotels and restaurants in various categories. Care to nominate a new place? Visit Fodors.com/contact-us.

Trip Costs

We list prices wherever possible to help you budget well. Hotel and restaurant price categories from **$** to **$$$$** are noted alongside each recommendation. For hotels, we include the lowest cost of a standard double room in high season. For restaurants, we cite the average price of a main course at dinner or, if dinner isn't served, at lunch. For attractions, we always list adult admission fees; discounts are usually available for children, students, and senior citizens.

Hotels

Our local writers vet every hotel to recommend the best overnights in each price category, from budget to expensive. Unless otherwise specified, you can expect private bath, phone, and TV in your room. For expanded hotel reviews, facilities, and deals, visit Fodors.com.

Restaurants

Unless we state otherwise, restaurants are open for lunch and dinner daily. We mention dress code only when there's a specific requirement and reservations only when they're essential or not accepted. To make restaurant reservations, visit Fodors.com.

Credit Cards

The hotels and restaurants in this guide typically accept credit cards. If not, we'll say so.

Top Picks

★ Fodor'sChoice

Listings

- ✉ Address
- Branch address
- ☏ Telephone
- Fax
- Website
- E-mail
- Admission fee
- Open/closed times
- Ⓜ Subway
- Directions or Map coordinates

Hotels & Restaurants

- Hotel
- Number of rooms
- Meal plans
- ✕ Restaurant
- Reservations
- Dress code
- No credit cards
- $ Price

Other

- ⇨ See also
- ☞ Take note
- Golf facilities

EXPERIENCE BOSTON

BOSTON TODAY

Boston is the undisputed epicenter of American history. Much of the political ferment that spawned the nation took place here, and visitors are often awed by the dense concentration of sites. Locals, on the other hand, take them in stride. Sure, they revere Revere as much as the next guy. Yet Bostonians refuse to see their hometown as some sort of frozen-in-time memorial to the days of yore. This is a living city—not a museum—and, as such, it continues to evolve.

Enshrining Art

Although no one refers to Boston as "The Athens of America" anymore, appreciating art seems to be as characteristic of folks here as dropping "R's" and taking the "T." That explains why the Museum of Fine Arts renovated its I. M. Pei building and reopened it as the Linde Family Wing for Contemporary Art in 2011—less than a year after the ribbon was cut on its new Art of the Americas wing. The latter, boasting 53 galleries on four floors, an auditorium, and soaring central courtyard, increased MFA's size by almost a third. Not to be outdone, in 2012 the Isabella Stewart Gardner Museum unveiled its own stunning new complex—entry, concert hall, glassed garden, and gallery—by architect Renzo Piano. He's also the serene genius behind Harvard Art Museums' $400-million reinvention, set to debut in late 2014.

Harboring Hope

This city has long been defined by its harbor: the first colonists were largely drawn here because of it, and local commerce has been inextricably bound to the water ever since. Over time, development obscured the view, and what was visible wasn't always pretty. (Suffice it to say that more than British tea and molasses got dumped in it!) Nevertheless, a decades-long, $3.8-billion clean-up effort has paid off. See for yourself on HarborWalk, a 45-mile-long path linking Columbus Park to the New England Aquarium, Seaport, and Fan Pier, with harborside sites, picturesque piers, parks, working wharves, hotel lounges, and urban beaches. New attractions keep popping up on it, like Liberty Wharf, with four restaurants (notably a Legal Sea Foods complex), a water-view plaza, and public marina.

Communing with Kennedys

The year 2013 marked the 50th anniversary of the assassination of John F. Kennedy, and the memory of Boston's beloved native son lingers on. As proof, witness a 90-minute walking tour covering sites associated with JFK or the inauguration of a 30,000-square foot wing at the John F. Kennedy Presidential Library & Museum, with archival space and a gallery for temporary exhibits relating to his 1,000 days in office. The legacy of brother Ted is equally apparent next door at the $60-million Edward F. Kennedy Institute. Slated to open in autumn 2014, it will host public programs and house a replica of the Senator's Capitol Hill office. The late family matriarch hasn't been forgotten, of course: the Rose Fitzgerald Kennedy Greenway, a lively linear park threading through Downtown, is named in her honor.

Exercising Options

There are lots of ways to get around Beantown: foot, cab, bus, ferry, subway, trolley, water taxi. Factor in cool conveyances aimed at vacationers, which run the gamut from Segways to World War II–style amphibious craft, and the list

lengthens. But these days there's another eminently practical way for travelers to be transported: three-speed bicycle. Begun in 2011, the Hubway bike-sharing program makes it easy because pedal pushers can cheaply access one of 1,000 cycles from more than 100 self-service "docks" citywide. (⇨ *Read how it works in the Travel Smart section.*)

Seeing Stars

Lights! Camera! Action! Those words are being heard a lot lately, because a state tax credit for film producers has translated into a moviemaking boom. As a result, playing "spot the star" is a popular pastime. Big-screen names like Leonardo DiCaprio, Rooney Mara, Denzel Washington, and homegrown celebs Ben Affleck and Mark Wahlberg (raised in Cambridge and Dorchester respectively) have all worked here recently. Ditto for emerging talents such as Jesse Eisenberg, Mila Kunis, and Anna Faris. Interested in an entirely different type of star? No problem. The Museum of Science is more stellar than ever thanks to the 2011 unveiling of its renovated Charles Hayden Planetarium, the centerpiece of which is a $2-million Zeiss Starmaster Projector. Free Friday night stargazing sessions, March through November, light its rooftop observatory.

Changing the Channel

Revitalization of the Fort Point Channel neighborhood has been ongoing for a decade: the dynamic Boston Convention & Exhibition Center, the brazen Institute of Contemporary Art, the expanded Children's Museum (by the monster Hood milk bottle, now celebrating its centennial), and the opening of Atlantic and Liberty wharves. The area's new high-water marks aren't beside the channel but rather in it: the Boston Tea Party Ships (a trio of replicas with a matching museum) stand by the Congress Street Bridge, with guides in period garb. On-the-water recreational options allow tour boats, kayaks, and floating restaurants and entertainment barges in the mile-long channel.

Eating Wicked Good Food

Yes, do try traditional dishes like baked beans, codfish cakes, and slabs of roast beef at Yankee haunts like Durgin-Park. But Boston lays claim to a long line of innovative chefs. M. Sanzian's invention of Boston cream pie in 1856 made quite a stir among Parker House patrons; and a century later, Julia Child launched a culinary revolution from her Cambridge kitchen. Today, top chefs such as Jodi Adams, Gordon Hamersley, Joanne Chang, Barbara Lynch, Ken Oringer, Michael Schlow, Lydia Shire, Ming Tsai, Jason Bond, Ana Sortun, Tim Wiechmann, and Tony Maws make dining out a gastronomic adventure. These hometown favorites have created a thriving independent restaurant scene; an ideal time to taste their creations—and those of up-and-coming sous-chefs or competitors—is during Restaurant Week. The biannual event (March and August) sees more than 200 eateries serving three-course prix-fixe dinners for as little as $33.

WHAT'S WHERE

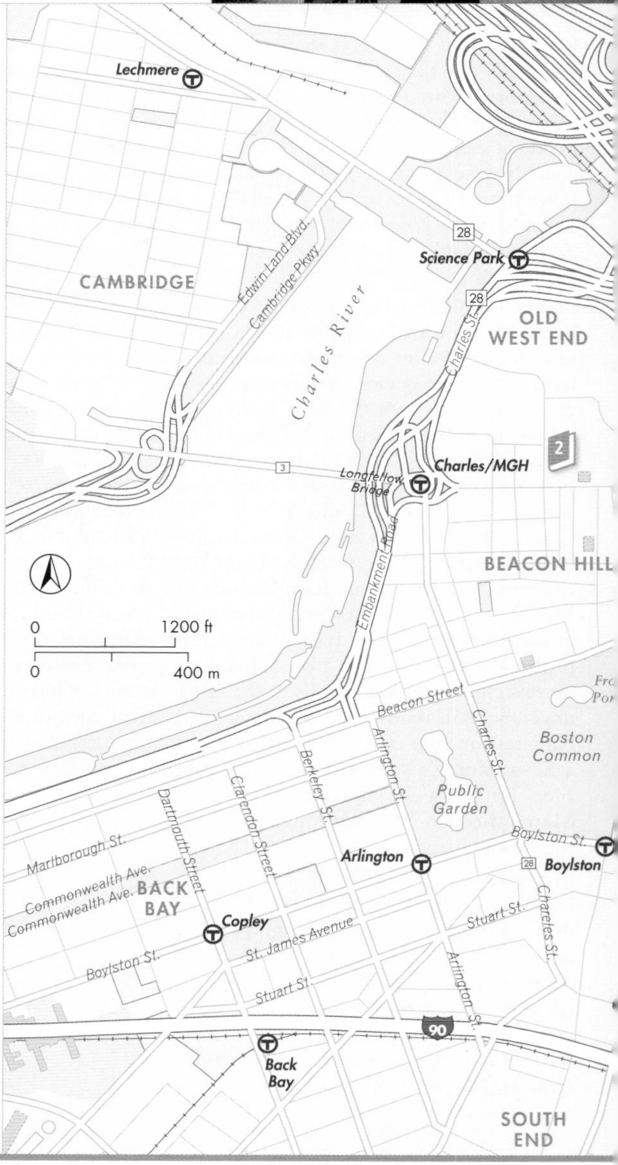

The following numbers refer to chapters in the book.

2 Beacon Hill, Boston Common, and the Old West End. If you follow the Freedom Trail you'll start up on Beacon Hill. The gas-lighted streets behind the gold-domed State House, lined with Federal townhomes, make this a wonderful place to walk. Below Beacon Hill lies Boston Common (a popular hangout—first for cows, then for people—since 1634); off to the North in the Old West End the big draws are the Museum of Science and TD Garden, home to the Bruins and Celtics, Boston's pro hockey and basketball teams.

3 Government Center and the North End. Architecture buffs may admire Government Center's brutalist structures, but most out-of-towners scurry past the plaza en route to Faneuil Hall and the trio of restored brick warehouses that share its name. Faneuil Hall Marketplace (Quincy Market) is chock-a-block with boutiques, bars, and a food court, while on the cobbled street, performers and souvenir vendors vie for your attention. Just across the Greenway stands the North End, which welcomed waves of 19th-century immigrants (the Italians arrived last, so it still seems like Little Italy.) Copp's Hill Burying Ground attests to a

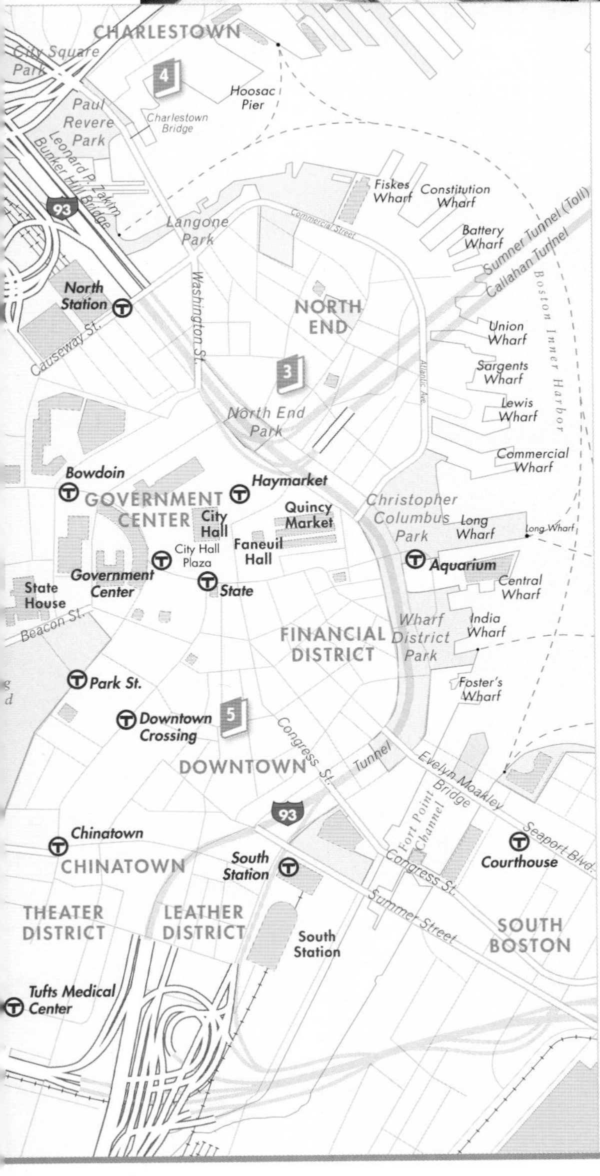

Puritan past, and Paul Revere House and Old North Church evoke the Revolutionary era.

4 Charlestown. Poised on the banks of Boston Harbor and the Mystic River, Charlestown's top sights can't be missed—literally. The Bunker Hill Monument is a towering tribute to one of the pivotal battles of 1775; the USS *Constitution*, America's Ship of State, flies a taut tangle of masts and rigging. Gentrification began here 40 years ago, when *Old Ironsides'* home was transformed from a hardscrabble naval yard into a National Historic Site. Now locals live in restored shipbuilders' houses and area restaurateurs no longer cater to a "hardtack-and-grog" crowd.

5 Downtown. This maze-like section of central Boston scores points for diversity. Freedom Trail walkers come to see sights like the Old South Meeting House and Old State House, wedged incongruously between office towers. Families are drawn by the Aquarium and Children's Museum or strolling the Greenway. Playgoers flock to the Theater District. There is an interesting mishmash of other districts as well, among them Downtown Crossing (one of Boston's main retail zones), Chinatown's pan-Asian exotica, and the loft-y Leather District.

WHAT'S WHERE

6 The Back Bay and South End. In chic Back Bay stand the city's most impressive skyscrapers (Prudential Center and John Hancock Tower) and arguably its most beautiful building, majestic Trinity Church. Streets are laid out in orderly fashion, making it easy to eye the well-dressed residents. Given the concentration of high-end shops around Newbury Street, you may emulate their couture—if your pockets are deep. More shopping, as well as dining, await in the South End, beyond the south side of Huntington Avenue. Handsomely rebuilt bowfront houses in this rehab housing heaven earned the area a spot in the National Register of Historic Places and enough style to win Boston's "hippest hood" award.

7 The Fenway. Baseball fans, art aficionados, and intellectuals meet head on in the Fens: a meandering green space that serves as the first "jewel" in Boston's Emerald Necklace. Fenway Park, a veritable shrine to the Boston Red Sox, is just northwest of the Fens. To the south sit the Museum of Fine Arts and Isabella Stewart Gardner Museum. Academic institutions in the neighborhood include Museum School, Mass College of Art, Northeastern University, and Harvard Medical School.

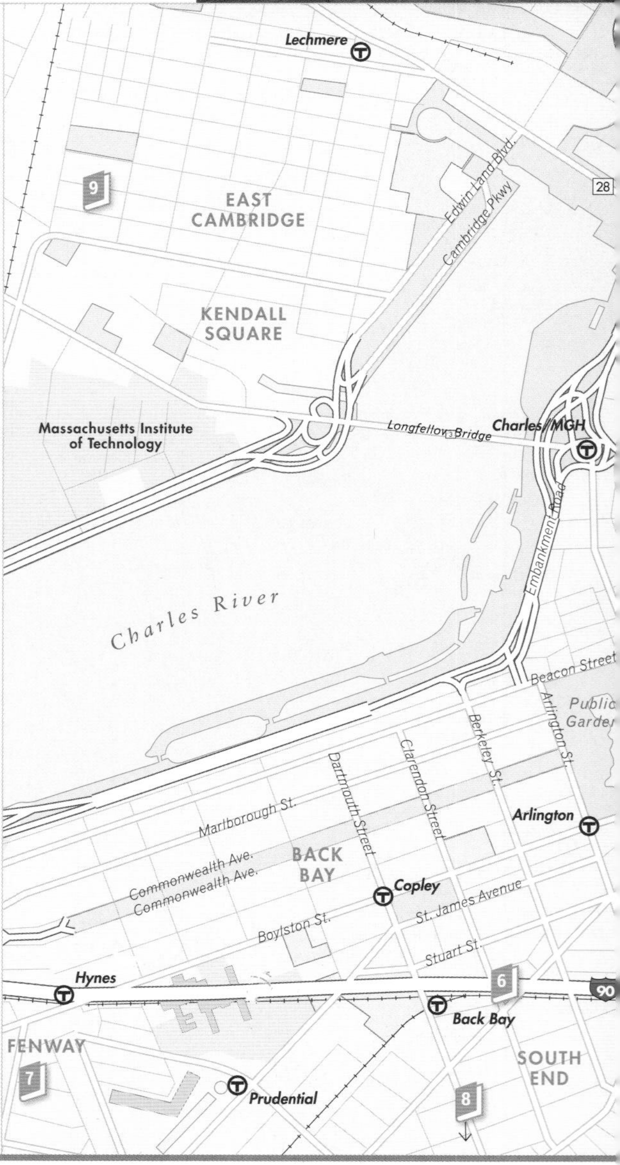

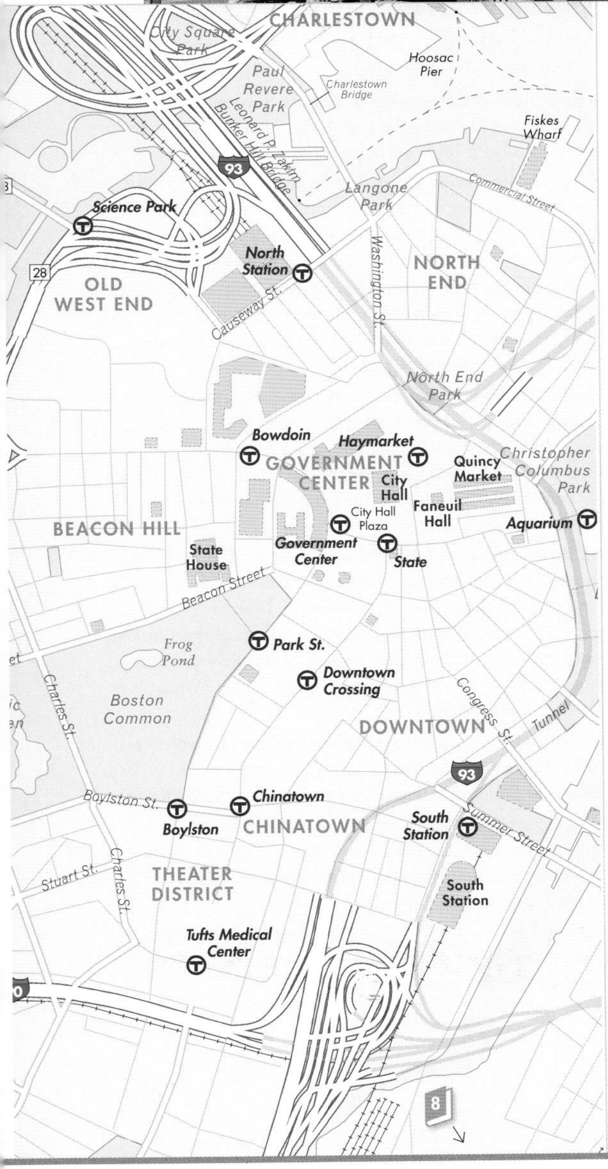

8 Boston Outskirts. South Boston (not the South End) was once a working-class Irish enclave. Its Seaport District is the poster child for waterfront revitalization, thanks to developments like the Boston Convention and Exhibition Center, the Institute of Contemporary Art, and Liberty Wharf. South of "Southie" are the Streetcar Suburbs, including Dorchester and Jamaica Plain. The former is home to the John F. Kennedy Presidential Library & Museum and University of Massachusetts. Jamaica Plain (J.P.) lays claim to the Arnold Arboretum, Jamaica Pond, and multicultural Centre Street.

9 Cambridge. The "People's Republic of Cambridge," a separate city across the Charles River, has long been a haven for writers, academics, and iconoclasts. Although largely working class, it is famed for its largest landowners, Harvard University and M.I.T. While the universities manage campuses, housing, and affiliated museums, their faculty and students, conversely, support a mix of stores and services. So, despite increasing gentrification in Harvard, Kendall, and Porter Squares, Cambridge features a fair share of quirky cafés, independent bookstores, galleries, and shops.

BOSTON PLANNER

When to Go

Weather-wise, late spring and fall are the optimal times for a visit. Aside from mild temperatures, May offers blooming gardens throughout the city and October finds the surrounding countryside ablaze with colorful foliage. At both times, however, expect hordes of visitors.

More than 250,000 students flood into the area each September, then pull out again in May and June. So hotels and restaurants fill up especially fast on move-in, move-out, and graduation weekends.

The good news is that Boston is a four-season destination. Along with the most reliable sunshine, summer brings sailboats to Boston Harbor, concerts to the Esplanade, and café tables to sidewalks. Summer is prime time for a shore vacation, but advance planning is imperative.

Even winter has its pleasures. The cultural season heats up when it's cold, and Boston gets a holiday glow, thanks to the thousands of lights strung around the Common, Public Garden, and Commonwealth Avenue Mall. During the post-Christmas lull, temperatures fall, but lodging prices do, too. You're only two to three hours south of quality ski slopes.

Mark Your Calendar

Greater Boston Convention & Visitors Bureau. Kiosks can be found at Prudential Center and Boston Common. ☎ *888/733–2678* 🌐 *www.bostonusa.com.*

Winter Boston Wine Expo. The Boston Wine Expo features tasting seminars and a Grand Cru Wine Lounge. ✉ *Seaport World Trade Center, 200 Seaport Blvd., Downtown/Seaport District, Boston* 🌐 *www.wine-expos.com.*

Spring Boston Marathon. Runners race 26.2 miles on Patriot's Day (🌐 *www.bostonmarathon.org*) from Hopkinton to Boylston Street, and horsemen reenact **Paul Revere's Ride** (🌐 *www.nationallancers.org.*)

Summer Boston Pops Concert & Fireworks Display. Independence Day is capped off with pyrotechnics, real and musical. ✉ *DCR Hatch Shell on the Esplanade, Beacon Hill, Boston* 🌐 *www.July4th.org.* **Harborfest.** Boston's Fourth of July celebration sponsors more than 200 events. 🌐 *www.bostonharborfest.com.*

Fall Boston Film Festival. The weeklong festival features independent film premieres with frequent attendance by directors and actors. ✉ *200 Stuart St., Theater District, Boston* 🌐 *www.bostonfilmfestival.org.* **Head of the Charles Regatta.** The world's largest rowing event draws rowers from across the world. ✉ *Banks of the Charles River, Cambridge* 🌐 *www.hocr.org.*

Fall Outside the City Working Waterfront Festival. New Bedford's commercial anglers showcase their skills. ✉ *State Pier, New Bedford* 🌐 *www.workingwaterfrontfestival.org.*

Essex County's **Topsfield Fair** (🌐 *www.topsfieldfair.org*), happens in October; Salem hosts witch trial reenactments and other **Haunted Happenings** (🌐 *www.hauntedhappenings.com*).

Celebrate turkey day at Plymouth's **Thanksgiving Parade** (🌐 *www.usathanksgiving.com*), or with dinner at **Plimoth Plantation** (🌐 *www.plimoth.org*).

Getting Around

"America's Walking City," with all its historic nooks and crannies, is best explored on foot. But when hoofing it around town seems too arduous, there are alternatives.

By Car

In a place where roads evolved from cow paths and colonial lanes, driving is no simple task. One-way streets, inconsistent signage and aggressive local drivers add to the confusion. Nevertheless, having your own car is helpful, especially if you're taking side trips.

If you would rather leave the driving to someone else, you can call a cab or hail one on the street 24/7: they wait outside major hotels and line up near hot spots like Harvard Square, South Station, Faneuil Hall, Long Wharf, and the Theater District. Rides within the city cost $2.60 for the first 1/7 mile and 40¢ for each 1/7 mile thereafter (tolls, where applicable, are extra).

By Public Transit

The "T," as the subway system is affectionately nicknamed, is the cornerstone of a far-reaching public transit network that also includes aboveground trains, buses, and ferries. Its five color-coded lines will put you within a block of virtually anywhere. Subways operate from 5 am to 1 am (schedules vary by line). The same goes for buses, which crisscross the city and suburbia.

A standard adult subway fare is $2 with a CharlieCard or $2.50 with a ticket or cash. For buses it's $1.50 with a CharlieCard or $2 with a ticket or cash (more for an Inner or Outer Express bus). Commuter rail and ferry fares depend on the route. For details on schedules, routes, and rates, contact the **MBTA** (☎ *617/222–3200 or 800/392–6100* 🌐 *www.mbta.com*).

CHARLIEPASS AND THE CHARLIECARD

Retro music fans recall the 1959 Kingston Trio hit about a fellow named Charlie, who, unable to pay his fare, "never returned" from Boston's subway system. Charlie lives on as the mascot of the MBTA's ticketing scheme. There are two stored-value options: a plastic CharlieCard or paper CharlieTicket, both of which are reusable and reloadable with cash, credit or debit cards. At a station, obtain a CharlieCard from an attendant or a CharlieTicket from a machine. CharlieCards can't yet be used on commuter rail, commuter boats, or Inner Harbor ferries. For most visitors, the best deal will be the unlimited one-day ($11) or one-week ($18) LinkPass.

Quick Forecasts

Check the coded lights atop the Berkeley Building overlooking Copley Square: *Steady blue means clear view; flashing blue, clouds due; steady red, rain ahead; flashing red, snow instead*... except in baseball season, when red means the Sox game is canceled!

Visitor Centers

Cambridge Tourism Office. The kiosk in the epicenter of Harvard Square is open 9 am to 5 pm daily. Volunteers know Cambridge well and recommend walks and tours. A hotline is available for other questions and planning tours. ✉ *4 Brattle St., Cambridge* ☎ *800/862–5678 hotline* 🌐 *www.cambridge-usa.org.*

Greater Boston Convention & Visitors Bureau. The bureau operates visitor information centers at Boston Common and the Shops at Prudential. ☎ *888/733–2678* 🌐 *www.bostonusa.com.*

Harvard Square Visitor Information Booth ✉ *Outside main T entrance, Harvard Sq., Boston* ☎ *617/497–1630* ⏲ *Daily 9–5.*

Massachusetts Office of Travel and Tourism. The office staff and website can help visitors plan side trips outside metropolitan Boston. ✉ *10 Park Plaza, Ste. #4510, Downtown, Boston* ☎ *800/227–6277, 617/973–8500* 🌐 *www.massvacation.com.*

BOSTON TOP ATTRACTIONS

USS *Constitution*

(A) The world's oldest commissioned warship, dubbed "*Old Ironsides*" for its seemingly impenetrable oak hull, was launched in 1797. See hulking masts, 52 brass cannons, and below-deck quarters on free tours led by active-duty sailors then visit the free museum next door.

Boston Public Garden

(B) Built on a reclaimed marsh in the 19th century, America's first botanical garden combines broad lawns and ornamental flower beds. At its heart on a 4-acre lagoon, Swan Boats (floating fixtures since 1877) circle from mid-April to mid-September with the resident mallards and pigeons. Once autumn arrives, the willow, beech, oak, and maple trees burst with color.

The Museum of Fine Arts

(C) This world-class institution includes Byzantine mosaics, Native American pottery, impressionist paintings, contemporary photos, and Egyptian and American art. Allot time to explore a few of the MFA's 450,000 objets d'art. Mull them over at one of four restaurants or Japanese gardens.

The New England Aquarium

(D) The aquarium's signature exhibit—a multistory Ocean Tank with a thousand fish and its queen, a massive sea turtle named Myrtle—has been enlarged and made sustainable with divers collecting eggs. Additions like the shark-and-ray touch tank, "Take a Dip with the Seals" marine mammal exhibit, and a coral reef keep it fresh. Ditto for the daily animal shows and IMAX films.

Faneuil Hall Marketplace

(E) Faneuil Hall Marketplace (aka Quincy Market) is always packed. Souvenir sellers coupled with buskers, mimes, drummers, and jugglers, create a Disneyesque atmosphere some disdain. But the rest of

us recognize fun when we see it. Browse the 1826 complex's restored stalls; then jostle in the food court to sample Boston's edible holy trinity: lobster, clams, and "chowdah."

Boston Harbor Islands

(F) The 34 islands of this National Recreation Area boasts a pre–Civil War fort, vintage lighthouses, hiking trails, swimming beaches, camping, and picnic spots. The islands represent one of the city's top values. May through October, the round-trip Harbor Islands Express ferry from Long Wharf to Georges Island provides a day of fun for just $14.

Harvard University

(G) Massachusetts reportedly has the world's highest concentration of colleges and universities. None, however, is more venerable than Harvard, a Cambridge institution since 1636. Visitors can enter the ivory tower without having to pay tuition. Students lead complimentary hour-long campus tours; find details on the university website (🌐 *www.harvard.edu*).

Mount Auburn Cemetery

(H) Inspired by Paris's Pere Lachaise Cemetery, America's first garden cemetery, circa 1831, offers urbanites 175 acres of "country-in the-city" a bus ride from Harvard Square. Guided tours focus on historical personages buried here, artistic gravestones and crypts, the 700 carefully cultivated tree species, and thousands of shrubs and herbaceous plants. As a well-known flyway for migratory birds, it's frequented by birders at early hours, especially in April and May.

GREAT ITINERARIES

BOSTON IN 4 DAYS

Clearly every traveler moves at a different pace. One might be content to snap a pic of the Bunker Hill Monument and push on; another might insist on climbing the obelisk's 294 spiraling steps and studying the adjacent museum's military dioramas. Nevertheless, in four days you should be able to see the city highlights without feeling rushed. With more time, explore nearby communities.

Day 1: Hit the Trail

About 3 million visitors walk the Freedom Trail every year—and there's a good reason why: taken together, the route's 16 designated sites offer a crash course in colonial history. That makes the trail a must, so tackle it sooner rather than later. Linger wherever you like, leaving ample time to lunch amid magicians and mimes in Faneuil Hall Marketplace or buy fresh fruit from Haymarket's street vendors. Next, cross into the North End via the Rose F. Kennedy Greenway. Though hemmed in by water on three sides, this bustling neighborhood is crammed full of history. Don't miss Old North Church and Paul Revere's former home (Boston's oldest house, constructed almost 100 years prior to his arrival); then, after wandering the narrow Italianate streets, fortify yourself with espresso or gelato and cross the Charlestown Bridge. See the USS *Constitution* and climb the Bunker Hill Monument (a breathtaking site in more ways than one) before catching the MBTA water shuttle back to Downtown.

Day 2: Head for the Hill

Named for the signal light that topped it in the 1800s, Beacon Hill originally stood a bit taller until locals dug earth off its summit and used it as landfill nearby. Now its shady, gas-lighted streets, brick sidewalks, tidy mews, and stately Brahmin brownstones evoke a bygone Boston. (Lovely Mt. Vernon Street opens onto leafy Louisburg Square, where Louisa May Alcott once lived.) When soaking up the ambience, take in some of Beacon Hill's major sites from Boston's various theme trails: gold-domed Massachusetts State House, Boston Athenaeum, Granary Burying Ground, and newly restored African Meeting House. Afterward, stroll to the Common and Public Garden. Both promise greenery and great people-watching. If shopping's your bag, cruise for antiques along Charles Street, the thoroughfare that separates them. In the evening, feast on stir-fry noodles in pan-Asian Chinatown or go upscale at an übertrendy restaurant (Pigalle, Troquet) in the Theater District where restorations in recent years have been, well, dramatic.

Day 3: Get an Overview

From the Back Bay you can cover a lot of Boston's attractions in a single day. Start at the top (literally) by ogling 360-degree views from the Prudential Center's Skywalk Observatory. (Or end it with a drink at Top of the Hub upstairs). Once you understand the lay of the land, plot a route based on your interests. Architecture aficionados can hit the ground running at the neoclassical Public Library and Romanesque Trinity Church. Shoppers can opt for stores along Newbury Street and in Copley Place, a high-end mall anchored by Neiman Marcus. Farther west in the Fens, other choices await. Art connoisseurs might view the collections at the Museum of Fine Arts or Isabella Stewart Gardner Museum, both recently expanded and beautified. Carnival-like Fenway Park beckons baseball fans to the other side of the Fens. Depending on your taste—and ticket availability—cap

the day with a Symphony Hall concert or a Red Sox game.

Day 4: On the Waterfront

A spate of openings and reopenings in recent years has transformed the Seaport District into a magnet for museum hoppers. Begin your day artfully at the Institute of Contemporary Art (ICA) on Fan Pier. The mod museum's bold cantilevered design (computer printer?) makes the most of its waterside location. It makes the most of its art collection, too, by offering programs and exhibits that appeal to little tykes and hard-to-please teens. Keep tiny tots engaged with a run to the Children's Museum and its innovative exhibits; then relive a turning point in American history at the Boston Tea Party Ships & Museum's three authentic-looking vessels and interpretive center. From there, continue on to that waterfront favorite, the New England Aquarium. Highlights include the Giant Ocean Tank, hands-on tidal pools, a seal-training tutorial, and a new 25,000-gallon touch tank brimming with sharks and rays. On the wharf, sign up for a harbor cruise, whale-watch boat trip, or ferry ride to the beckoning Boston Harbor Islands.

BEYOND BOSTON PROPER

Day 1: Explore Cambridge

From pre-Revolutionary times, Boston was the region's commercial center and Cambridge was the burbs: a retreat more residential than mercantile, with plenty of room to build the nation's first English-style, redbrick university. The heart of the community—geographically and practically—is still Harvard Square. It's easy enough to while away a day here browsing the shops, lounging at a café, then wandering to the riverbank to watch crew teams practice. But Harvard Square is also the starting point for free student-led campus tours, as well as for strolls along Brattle Street's "Tory Row" (No. 105 was occupied by both Washington and Longfellow!). Fine museums include the family-friendly Museum of Natural History, loaded with dinosaur bones, gemstones, and 21 million stuffed critters. The Harvard Art Museum is another must. If you're visiting before Renzo Piano's newly reimagined facility has opened on the site of the original Fogg building, view a "greatest hits" collection across the street at the Sackler Building. End your day in true Cantabrigian style by taking in a concert or lecture at handsome Sanders Theatre.

Day 2: Step Back in Time

You only have to travel a short distance to visit historic places you read about in grade school. For a side trip to the 17th century, head 35 miles southeast to Plymouth. The famed rock doesn't live up to its hype, but Plimoth Plantation (an open-air museum re-creating life among Pilgrims) and the *Mayflower II* are well worth the trip. A second option is to veer northwest to explore Revolutionary-era sites in handsome, suburban Lexington. Start at the National Heritage Museum for a recap of the events that kicked off the whole shebang; then proceed to Battle Green, where "the shot heard round the world" was fired. After stopping by Minute Man National Historic Park, continue to Concord to tour the homes of literary luminaries like Ralph Waldo Emerson, Louisa May Alcott, and Nathaniel Hawthorne. Conclude your novel excursion with a walk around Walden Pond, where Henry David Thoreau wrote one of the founding documents of the environmental movement.

TIPS

Getting your mitts on Red Sox tickets may be tricky. Savvy spectators reserve online as soon as tickets become available. Procrastinators may get lucky at the ticket office next to Gate A, which opens at 10 am. If you strike out, a limited number are sold at Gate E two hours before game time. As a last resort, sidle up to that guy holding up tickets just after the opening pitch and haggle—or watch the action at Game On!, a sports bar attached to Fenway Park.

Think you need a car to venture beyond Boston? Think again. Grayline affiliate Brush Hill Tours (☎ *800/343–1328 or 781/986–6100* 🌐 *www.brushhilltours.com*) offers coach excursions for Boston-based day-trippers to Lexington, Concord, Salem, and Plymouth. In autumn, foliage-themed tours are available, too.

Diehard sightseers may want to buy a pass. The "Go Boston" Pass (☎ *866/628–9027* 🌐 *www.smartdestinations.com*) covers more than 70 attractions, tours, and excursions and is sold in one-day to one-week increments from $59.99; CityPass (☎ *888/330–5008* 🌐 *www.citypass.com*) covers five key sites for $51/$36 (adults/kids $3/$11).

Day 3: A Shore Thing

Anyone eager to taste the salt air or feel the surge of the sea should take a day trip to the North Shore towns of Salem and Gloucester. The former has a Maritime National Historic Site—complete with vintage wharves and warehouses—that proves there is more to the notorious town than just witchcraft.

Prefer to just sun yourself? Year-round nature lovers flock to Crane Beach in Ipswich, about an hour north of Boston. Part of a 1,200-acre wildlife refuge, it includes 4 miles of sand rimmed by scenic dunes. For a quick sand-in-every-crevice experience, take either the MBTA's Harbor Express ferry south to Nantasket Beach in Hull or the commuter train north to Manchester-by-the-Sea's Singing Beach, where the sand has such a high silica content that it actually sings (or at least squeaks) when you walk on it.

LIKE A LOCAL

Be a Sport

Locals mark off the seasons by checking the sports lineup. The "Boys of Summer" arrive each spring, and the Bruins come out of hibernation in the fall. But sports fans can get a fix here any time of year.

When the Red Sox play at home, ball fans are out braving the throngs along Yawkey Way, munching a Fenway Frank or sausage sub, and bellowing "Sweet Caroline" during the seventh inning stretch. Sweet indeed.

Next stop, TD Garden (in Bostonese that's "Gah-din"). Even if you can't score tickets to watch the Bruins or Celtics, you can see their arena via the Sports Museum. Come early on game day and you might catch players warming up.

Football fans get a kick out of Gillette Stadium in Foxborough. It is home turf for the Super Bowl–winning New England Patriots; nearby is the sprawling Patriot Place, a complex that houses the team's high-tech Hall of Fame.

Book It to the Library

Think libraries are boring? Proper Bostonians will beg to differ. Boston is a hotbed of authors (John Updike, Junot Diaz, Robert Parker) and poets (Robert Pinsky, Sylvia Plath, Mary Oliver), and the city remains a haven for readers. Poetry slams are popular features in colleges, coffeehouses, and clubs, and libraries draw record attendances.

Bookworms adore the Boston Public Library, just as Ralph Waldo Emerson and his literary buddies did in the 1800s. The building is beautiful, and one may freely browse its vast collection, reading halls, and courtyard.

The Mary Baker Eddy Library isn't merely full of books. It includes the **Mapparium** (a mammoth walk-in glass globe, the interior of which is spanned by a 30-foot bridge) plus a virtual fountain that spews famous quotations.

Even in this age of political cynicism, folks cherish the memory of JFK. So the John F. Kennedy Presidential Library & Museum in Dorchester feels like hallowed ground. Memorabilia and multimedia displays chronicle his term.

Join the Festivities

The Brits who founded Boston get a lot of attention. Yet they were only the first of many immigrant groups who helped shape this city. Locals applaud the others' colorful legacy through equally colorful celebrations.

Irish eyes are always smiling on the Sunday closest to March 17. That's when the St. Patrick's Day Parade passes through Southie, thus proving that all Boston Celtics are not basketball players.

In America's third-largest Chinatown, dragon parades and firecrackers mark Chinese New Year, while the August Moon Festival features lion dancing, lanterns, and moon cakes. Events center on Gateway Arch.

Each summer the North End hosts weekend street festivals, honoring Italy's patron saints on their name days with processions, brass bands, and Italian delicacies like *zeppoli* (fried dough), pizza, and pasta creations. St. Anthony of Padua's is the biggie, going three days in late August.

FAMILY FAVORITES

Costs add up when you're traveling with kids, so do your wallet a favor and download a "Family Friendly ValuePass" (🌐 *www.bostonusa.com/greatdeals*). You can use it to snag discounts for more than 75 shops, eateries, tours, and attractions.

Follow the Redbrick Road

Wannabe time travelers will have a blast on the Freedom Trail. To make the most of the walk, have your kids sign up for the free NPS Junior Ranger program, which adds treasure hunts to the history lesson. Most trail takers go south to north, but the reverse works best for families: this allows you to start with *Old Ironsides* and the Bunker Hill Monument (star attractions in young eyes) and end in Boston Common (an ideal place to unwind after a long trek). ⇨ *See "Follow the Redbrick Road" at the end of this chapter.*

Enjoy Fowl Play

For the quintessential Boston experience, treat your family to a Swan Boat ride around the Public Garden lagoon. Afterward, check out the pair of real swans (Romeo and Juliet); then waddle over to the nearby Duckling sculpture to see Mrs. Mallard and the rest of the quacking clan from Robert McCloskey's 1941 book, *Make Way for Ducklings.*

Kid Around

Established in 1913, the Boston Children's Museum is one of the oldest facilities of its kind. Highlights include art studios, a full-size replica of Arthur the Aardvark's cartoon realm, and a hands-on construction zone. Some kiddies, though, may not want to leave the multistory climbing structure that dominates the lobby.

Yell "Eureka"

No place does gizmos and gadgets like the Museum of Science, where almost everything is meant to be pushed, pulled, or otherwise maneuvered. Like its interactive displays, the live demos are over the top or hair-raising (think lightning bolts manufactured in an air-insulated Van de Graaff generator). The result is so entertaining children won't believe it's educational.

Find Nemo

The New England Aquarium features endless exhibits, including touch tanks that give children a real feel for marine life. On top of the activities covered by the ticket price, there are in-the-water animal encounters and behind-the-scene tours for visitors willing to pay extra. The aquarium also organizes whale-watching trips to Stellwagen Bank, April to October.

Have a Ball

Small but mighty Fenway, the oldest Major League Baseball ballpark, is a pilgrimage site for baseball fans of all ages, and daily 50-minute tours provide the ultimate insider's view. You'll get a firsthand look at the press box, Pesky's Pole, and (schedule permitting) the Green Monster. This is as close as anyone gets to the fabled field without being drafted into the MLB.

Tour the Town

Want your little people to get the big picture? **Boston By Foot** (☎ *617/367–2345* 🌐 *www.bostonbyfoot.org*) has guided walks aimed at the 6-to-12-year-old crowd. **Old Town Trolley** (☎ *888/910–8687* 🌐 *www.trolleytours.com*) offers hop-on, hop-off tours for anyone who would rather ride than walk; and **Boston Duck Tours** operates fun amphibious vehicles (☎ *617/267–3825* 🌐 *www.bostonducktours.com*).

FREE OR ALMOST FREE

Let Freebies Ring

Freedom may not be free, but the **Freedom Trail** is. So are 13 of the 16 attractions lining its route. The **Massachusetts State House,** for instance, schedules complimentary tours weekdays, 10 to 4. The **USS Constitution, meanwhile,** conducts tours Tuesday to Sunday, from 10 to 6, April through September; Tuesday to Sunday, from 10 to 4 in October; and Tuesday to Sunday, from 10 to 4, November through March. Mid-April through November, you're also welcome to join a free **National Park Service Tour** of the trail. Check with the Boston National Historical Park for details.

Try a Different Trail

The Freedom Trail's success has spawned other no-cost routes, including the **Black Heritage Trail** (⇨ *Box in the Beacon Hill, Boston Common, and Old West End chapter)* and the **Walk to the Sea**, which traces four centuries of civic development. The **Irish Heritage Trail** and **Boston Women's Heritage Trail** are other options. The former covers sites relating to Irish-Americans from John Hancock to John F. Kennedy as well as the 1840s Potato Famine. The latter pays tribute to ladies who gained fame as suffragettes and artists.

Artsy Alternatives

Symphony Hall (a Victorian showpiece with superb acoustics) and the historic **Boston Public Library** both run free tours. Moreover, the **Museum of Fine Arts** and **Institute of Contemporary Art** waive admission on Wednesday and Thursday evenings respectively. It's worth noting as well that the **Isabella Stewart Gardner Museum** is always free for those under 18—and anyone named Isabella! Penny pinchers should also watch for events such as the Fenway Cultural District's **Opening Our Doors Day.** Held each Columbus Day, it sponsors concerts, lectures, and tours at some of Boston's finest arts institutions.

Enjoy Free Parking

When you're ready for a rest, remember that relaxing in Boston's parks doesn't cost a dime. If you have already visited the **Public Garden** and **Boston Common**, check out the **Emerald Necklace.** In 1878 landscape architect Frederick Law Olmsted began work on six pocket parks strung together by a greenway, resembling jewels on a necklace. Linked to the Common and Public Garden by the Commonwealth Avenue Mall, the Necklace extends over 7 miles from Downtown through Arnold Arboretum in Jamaica Plain to Franklin Park in Dorchester.

Feeling Indecisive?

HarborWalk (🌐 *www.bostonharborwalk.com*) offers visitors a bit of everything on its interconnected 45 miles of waterside trails and pathways. Aside from scenic viewpoints (some with free binoculars), amenities range from parks, public art installations, and interpretative panels to a pocket Maritime Museum at the Fairmont Battery Wharf Hotel. HarborWalk also provides a glimpse at paid attractions like the New England Aquarium's Marine Mammal Center. Traversing the trail could take days. Download a free audio guide from the website and enjoy a narrated stroll from Christopher Columbus Park to Fan Pier.

BACK BAY ART AND ARCHITECTURE WALK

In the folklore of American neighborhoods, Boston's Back Bay stands alongside New York's Park Avenue as a symbol of chic. In the 1850s, Boston's power brokers built Victorian mansions amidst lush green spaces and by the time the Great Depression hit, Back Bay was the city's poshest address.

Copley Square

Back Bay's hub, embraces a range of architectural styles from Romanesque Revival to Bauhaus-inspired skyscrapers. Fairmount Copley Plaza Hotel's Oak Long Bar and Kitchen, with its catbird seats, offers a perfect place to begin your walk. Designed in 1912 by Henry Hardenbergh, five years after his famed Plaza Hotel in Manhattan, the hotel underwent a $20-million centenary renovation. Boston Public Library, housing 9 million books, was conceived by architects Mead, McKim, and White, who opted for an Italian Renaissance palazzo. Modern architect Philip Johnson's 1972 wing respectfully reflects the original.

The Pru and Commonwealth Avenue

Heading up Boylston Street with the Library on your left, you'll find the 52-story Prudential Tower, built in the 1960s, and affectionately dubbed "The Pru." On a clear day from the top-floor Skywalk, you'll see sweeping vistas of Boston. With the Pru behind you, take Gloucester Street across Newbury to Commonwealth Avenue, turn left, and cross Massachusetts Avenue to 395 Commonwealth, where you'll see Louis Comfort Tiffany's famous Ayer Mansion.

Boston Public Garden

At the bronze statue of George Washington at the foot of Commonwealth Avenue, enter Boston Public Garden, America's oldest botanical garden sheltering 24 acres of weeping willow, elm, spruce, and dawn redwood. The garden pond is spanned by a faux-suspension bridge while the garden itself abuts Boston Common. Exit with Washington behind you, walk one block to Newbury Street, turn right and head towards the Gothic Revival Church of the Covenant, on Newbury Street at Berkeley, built in 1867.

Trinity Church and Hancock Tower

Take Berkeley one block to Boylston Street then head back up Boylston to Copley Square to visit its crowning centerpiece, Trinity Church. This 1877 Romanesque Revival masterpiece conceived by Henry Hobson Richardson exhibits sumptuously carved interior woodwork, ornamented ceilings, and intricate stained glass. Another architectural award winner is the John Hancock Tower, behind Trinity Church on St. James Street. Architect Henry Cobb managed to construct this modernist 58-story building without disrupting the square's scale and proportion in part by having the glass panels mirror Trinity Church.

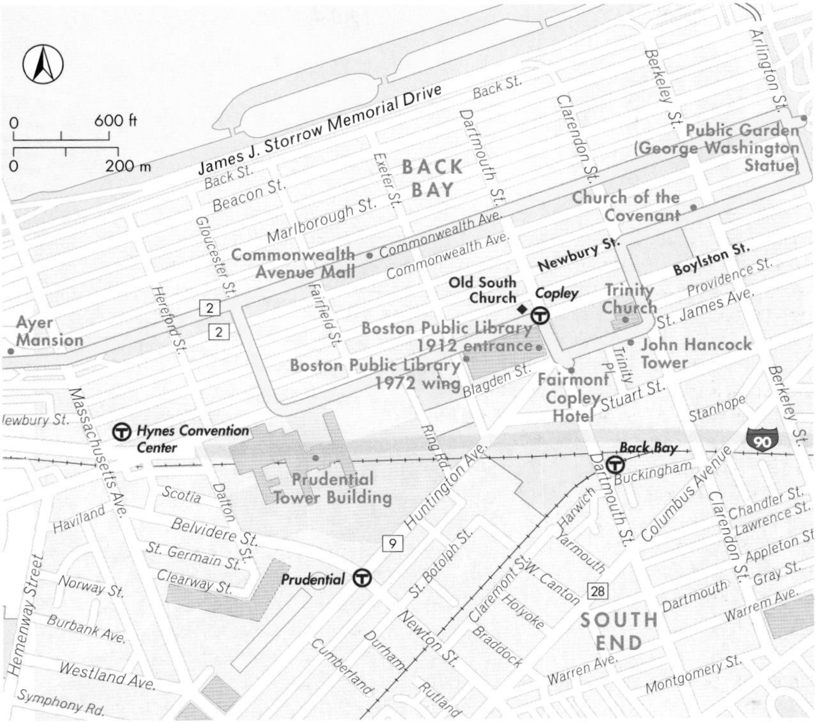

Highlights	Copley Square's handsome ensemble of church, park, library, and sky-scraper; Boston Public Garden
Where to Start	Oak Bar in Fairmont Copley Square Hotel
Length	2.6 km (1.6 miles) or about 1.5 hours with brief stops
Where to End	Back where you started, people-watching from an Oak Bar settee or a bench facing the library or Trinity Church
Best Time to Go	Any time when you can see all the sights in daylight
Worst Time to Go	Rush hour or when it's raining or very cold
Editor's Choice	Strolling the mall in the snow, tiny cloister garden behind Trinity Church, George Washington with his attendant pigeons

FOLLOW THE REDBRICK ROAD

BOSTON'S FREEDOM TRAIL

by Mike Nalepa

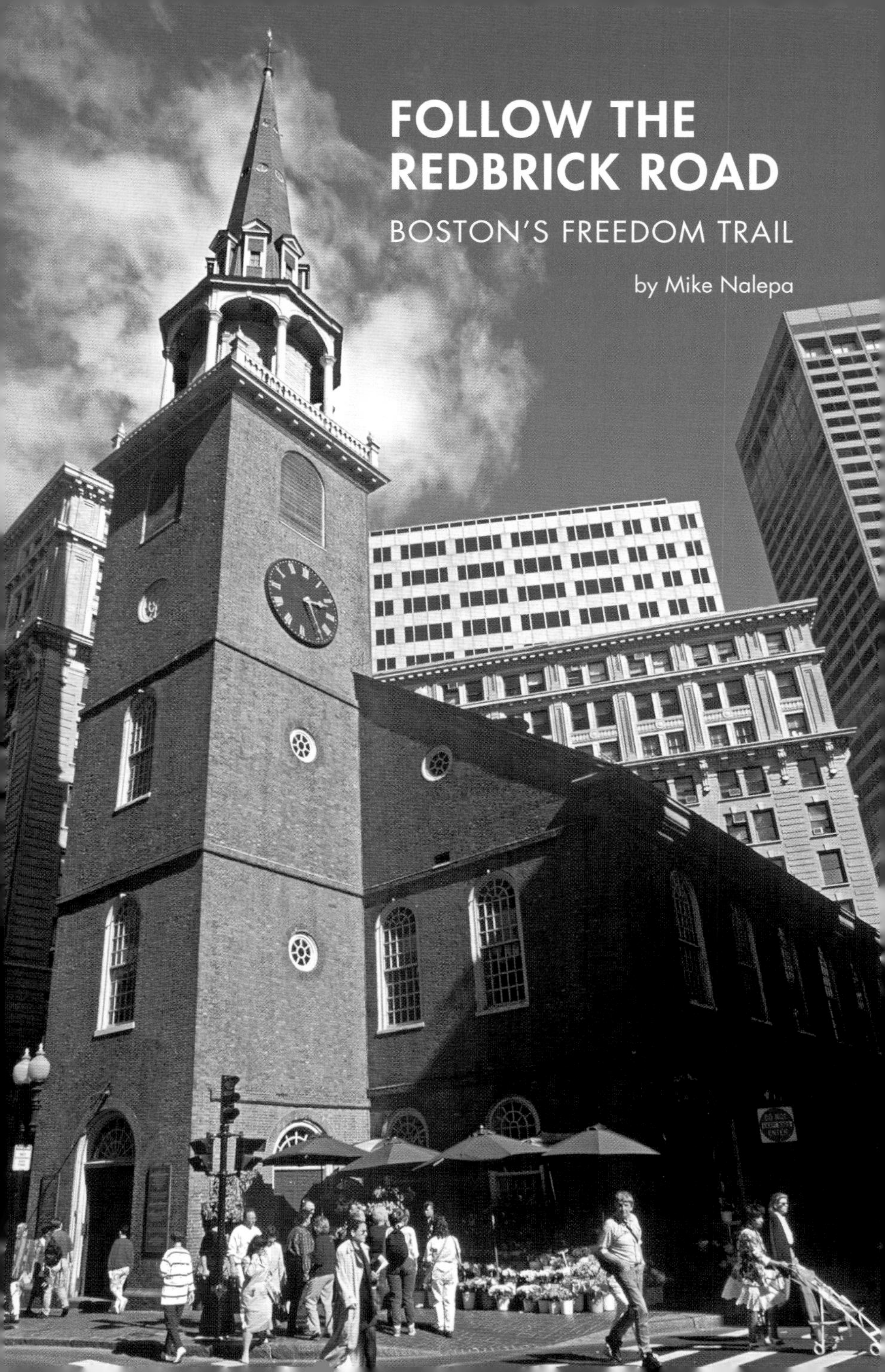

Paul Revere

Paul Revere's ride

Benjamin Franklin

Samuel Adams

John Hancock

The Freedom Trail is more than a collection of historic sites related to the American Revolution or a suggested itinerary connecting Boston's unique neighborhoods. It's a chance to walk in the footsteps of our forefathers—literally, by following a crimson path on public sidewalks—and pay tribute to the figures all school kids know, like Paul Revere, John Hancock, and Ben Franklin. In history-proud Boston, past and present intersect before your eyes not as a re-creation but as living history accessible to all.

Boston played a key role in the dramatic events leading up to the American Revolution. Many of the founding fathers called the city home, and many of the initial meetings and actions that sparked the fight against the British took place here. In one day, you can visit Faneuil Hall—the "Cradle of Liberty"—where outraged colonial radicals met to oppose British authority; the site of the incendiary Boston Massacre; and the Old North Church, where lanterns hung to signal Paul Revere on his thrilling midnight ride. Colonists may have originally landed in Jamestown and Plymouth, but if you really want to see where America began, come to Boston.

Boston Common, Founder's Statue

www.nps.gov/bost
www.thefreedomtrail.org

617/242–5642

Admission to the Freedom Trail itself is free. Several museum sites charge for admission. However, most attractions are free monuments, parks, and landmarks.

The 1729 Old South Meeting House, where many protesters gathered during the American Revolution.

PLANNING YOUR TRAIL TRIP

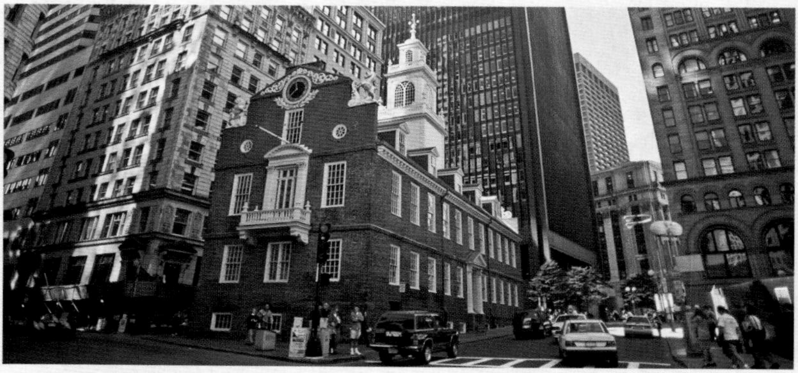

THE ROUTE

The 2½-mi Freedom Trail begins at Boston Common, winds through Downtown, Government Center, and the North End, and ends in Charlestown at the USS *Constitution*. The entire Freedom Trail is marked by a red line on the sidewalk; it's made of paint or brick at various points on the Trail. ⇨ *For more information on Freedom Trail sites, see listings in Neighborhood chapters.*

GETTING HERE AND BACK

The route starts near the Park Street T stop. When you've completed the Freedom Trail, head for the nearby Charlestown water shuttle, which goes directly to the downtown area. For schedules and maps, visit *www.mbta.com*.

TIMING

If you're stopping at a few (or all) of the 16 sites, it takes a full day to complete the route comfortably. **TIP→ If you have children in tow, you may want to split the trail into two or more days.**

VISITOR CENTERS

There are Freedom Trail information centers in Boston Common (Tremont Street), at 15 State Street (near the Old State House), and at the Charlestown Navy Yard Visitor Center (in Building 5).

TOURS

The National Park Service's free 90-minute Freedom Trail walking tours begin at the Boston National Historical Park Visitor Center at 15 State Street and cover sites from the Old South Meeting House to the Old North Church. Check online for times; it's a good idea to show up at least 30 minutes early, as the popular tours are limited to 30 people.

Half-hour tours of the USS *Constitution* are offered Tuesday through Sunday. Note that visitors to the ship must go through security screening.

FUEL UP

The trail winds through the heart of Downtown Boston, so finding a quick bite or a nice sit-down meal isn't difficult. Quincy Market, near Faneuil Hall, is packed with cafés and eateries. Another good lunch choice is one of the North End's wonderful Italian restaurants.

WHAT'S NEARBY

For a short break from revolutionary history, be sure to check out the major attractions nearby, including the Boston Public Garden, New England Aquarium, and Union Oyster House.

Above: In front of the Old State House a cobblestone circle marks the site of the Boston Massacre.

TOP SIGHTS

Benjamin Franklin Statue

Boston Common

The Granary Burial Grounds

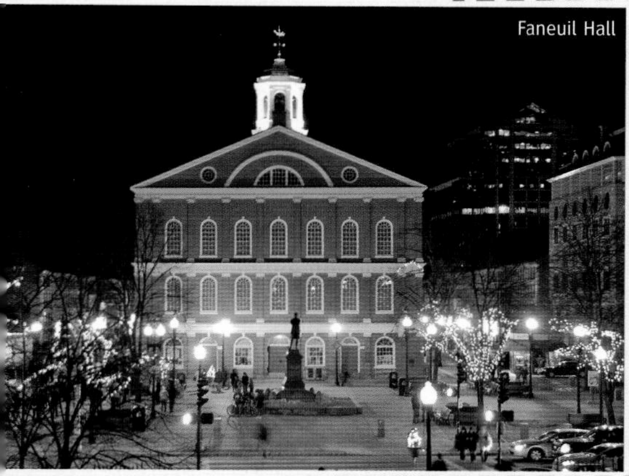
Faneuil Hall

Park Street Church

Old North Church

Bunker Hill Monument

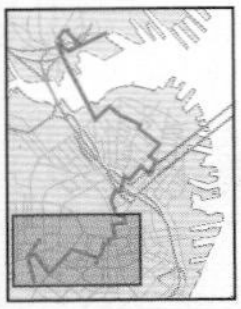

BOSTON COMMON TO FANEUIL HALL

Old State House

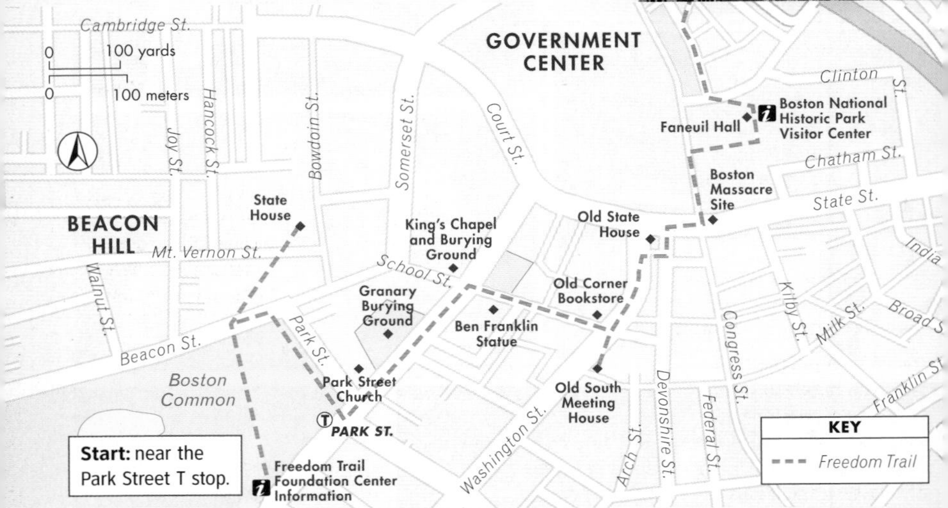

Many of the Freedom Trail sites between Boston Common and the North End are close together. Walking this 1-mile segment of the trail makes for a pleasant morning.

THE ROUTE

Begin at ★ **Boston Common,** then head for the **State House,** Boston's finest example of Federal architecture. Several blocks away is the **Park Street Church,** whose 217-foot steeple is considered to be the most beautiful in New England. The church was actually founded in 1809, and it played a key role in the movement to abolish slavery.

Reposing in the church's shadows is the ★ **Granary Burying Ground,** final resting place of Samuel Adams, John Hancock, and Paul Revere. A short stroll to Downtown brings you to **King's Chapel,** founded in 1686 by King James II for the Church of England.

Follow the trail past the **Benjamin Franklin statue** to the **Old Corner Bookstore** site, where Hawthorne, Emerson, and Longfellow were published. Nearby is the **Old South Meeting House,** where arguments in 1773 led to the Boston Tea Party. Overlooking the site of the Boston Massacre is the city's oldest public building, the **Old State House,** a Georgian beauty.

In 1770 the Boston Massacre occurred directly in front of here—look for the commemorative stone circle.

Cross the plaza to ★ **Faneuil Hall** and explore where Samuel Adams railed against "taxation without representation." **TIP→ A good mid-trail break is the shops and eateries of Faneuil Hall Marketplace, which includes Quincy Market.**

Old Corner Book Store Site

★ = Fodor's Choice ★ = Highly Recommended = Family Friendly

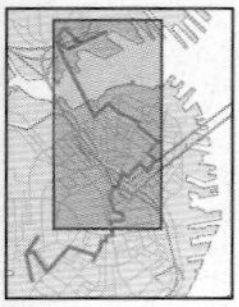

NORTH END TO CHARLESTOWN

USS *Constitution*

Freedom Trail sites between Faneuil Hall and Charlestown are more spread out along 1½ miles. The sites here, though more difficult to reach, are certainly worth the walk.

THE ROUTE

When you depart Faneuil Hall, follow the red stripe to the North End, Boston's Little Italy.

The **Paul Revere House** takes you back 200 years—here are the hero's own saddlebags, a toddy warmer, and a pine cradle made from a molasses cask. It's also air-conditioned in the summer, so try to stop here in mid-afternoon to escape the heat. Next to the Paul Revere House is one of the city's oldest brick buildings, the **Pierce-Hichborn House.**

Next, peek inside a place guaranteed to trigger a wave of patriotism: the ★ **Old North Church** of "One if by land, two if by sea" fame. Then head toward **Copp's Hill Burying Ground,** where you can view graves from the late 17th century through the early 19th century. Afterward, cross the bridge over the Charles and check out that revered icon, the **USS *Constitution*,** "Old Ironsides." It's open until 6 PM (4 PM November through March), and you'll need about an hour for a visit, so plan accordingly.

The perfect ending to the trail? A walk to the top of the **Bunker Hill Monument** for the incomparable vistas. The hill was the site of one of the first battles of the Revolutionary War. Though the colonial rebels actually lost, they inflicted large casualties on the better-trained British, proving themselves against the empire.

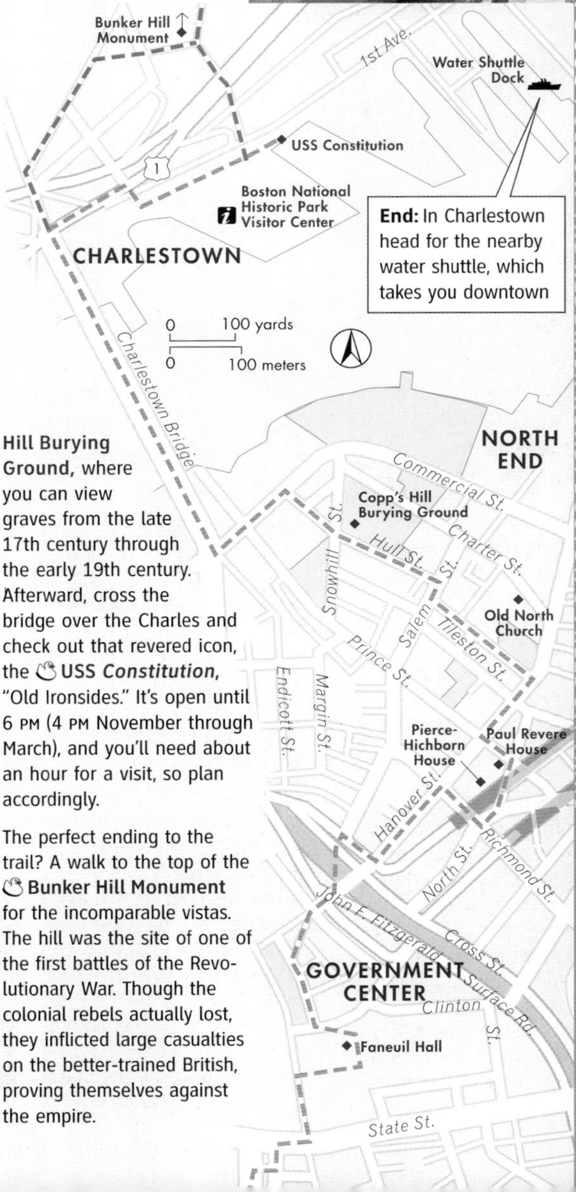

Paul Revere House

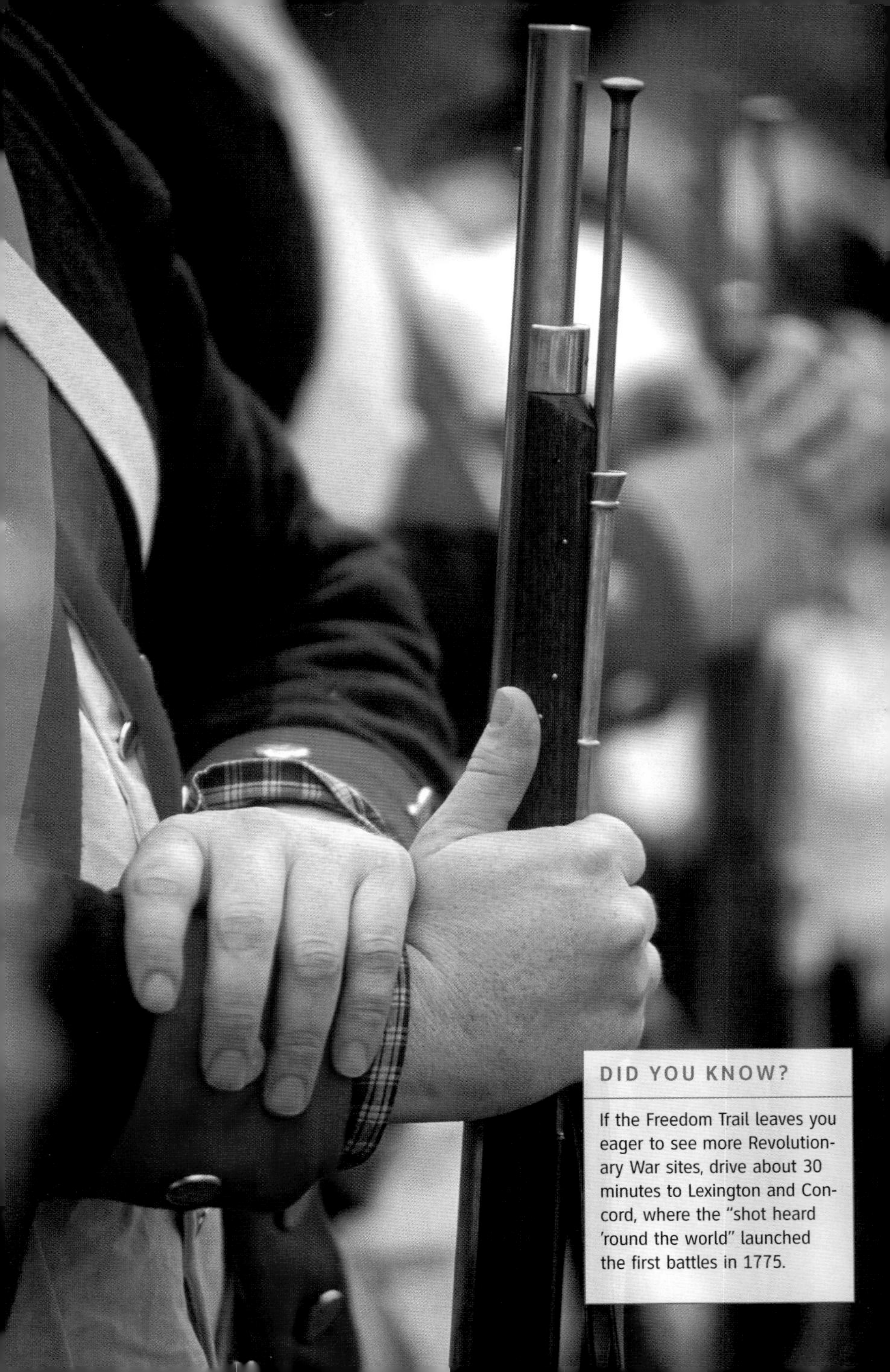

DID YOU KNOW?

If the Freedom Trail leaves you eager to see more Revolutionary War sites, drive about 30 minutes to Lexington and Concord, where the "shot heard 'round the world" launched the first battles in 1775.

BEACON HILL, BOSTON COMMON, AND THE OLD WEST END

GETTING ORIENTED

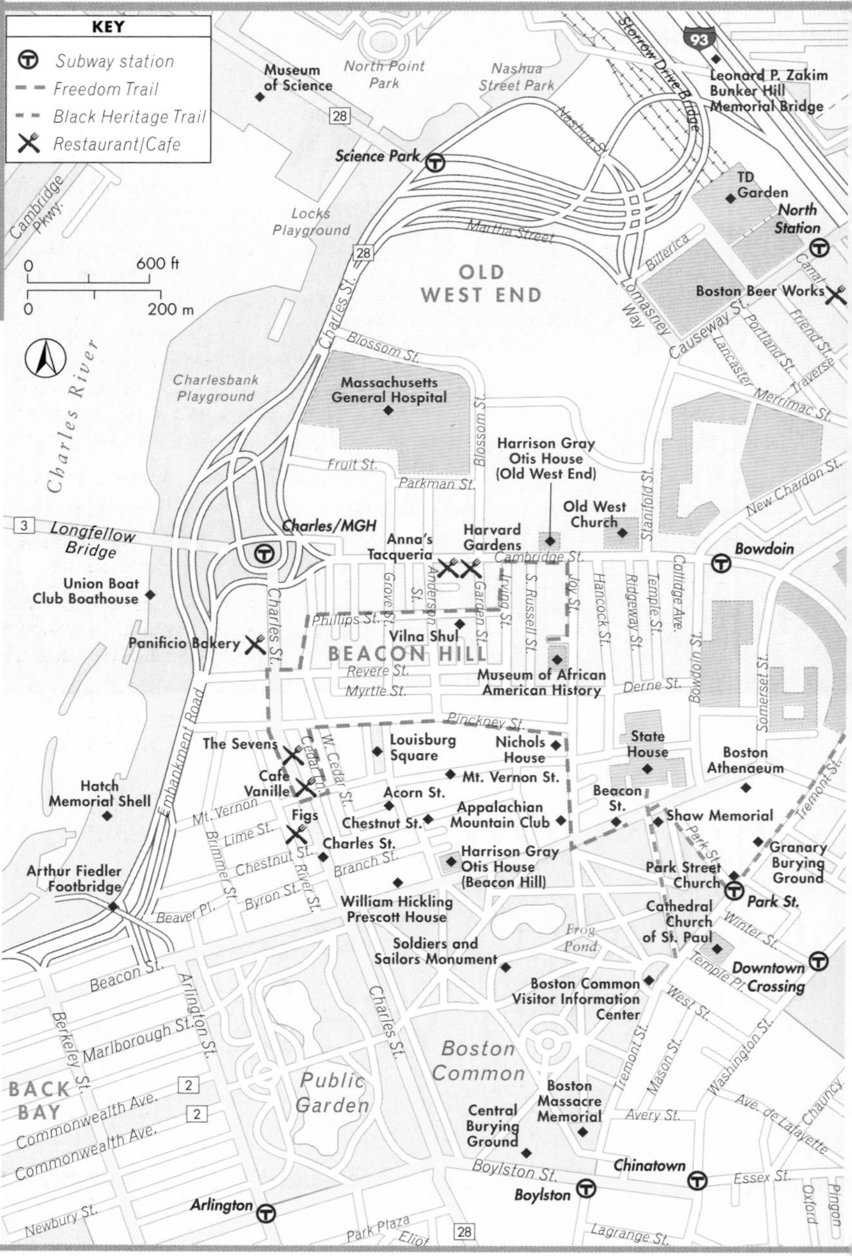
KEY
Subway station
Freedom Trail
Black Heritage Trail
Restaurant/Cafe
0
600 ft
0
200 m
Museum of Science
North Point Park
Nashua Street Park
Storrow Drive Bridge
93
Leonard P. Zakim Bunker Hill Memorial Bridge
28
Nashua St.
Science Park
Cambridge Pkwy.
Locks Playground
Martha Street
TD Garden
North Station
OLD WEST END
Billerica
Lomasney Way
Canal
Boston Beer Works
Causeway St.
Portland St.
Friend St.
Lancaster
Traverse
Merrimac St.
Charles St.
Blossom St.
Charles River
Charlesbank Playground
Massachusetts General Hospital
Blossom St.
Harrison Gray Otis House (Old West End)
Fruit St.
Parkman St.
Staniford St.
New Chardon St.
3
Longfellow Bridge
Charles/MGH
Anna's Tacqueria
Harvard Gardens
Old West Church
Cambridge St.
Bowdoin
Union Boat Club Boathouse
Grove St.
Anderson St.
Garden St.
Irving St.
S. Russell St.
Joy St.
Hancock St.
Ridgeway St.
Temple St.
Coltidge Ave.
Phillips St.
Vilna Shul
Panificio Bakery
BEACON HILL
Revere St.
Myrtle St.
Museum of African American History
Derne St.
Bowdoin St.
Somerset St.
Embankment Road
Pinckney St.
The Sevens
Cedar Ln.
W. Cedar St.
Louisburg Square
Nichols House
State House
Boston Athenaeum
Mt. Vernon St.
Cafe Vanille
Acorn St.
Hatch Memorial Shell
Mt. Vernon
Figs
Chestnut St.
Appalachian Mountain Club
Beacon St.
Shaw Memorial
Tremont St.
Lime St.
Charles St.
Granary Burying Ground
Brimmer St.
Chestnut St.
River St.
Branch St.
Harrison Gray Otis House (Beacon Hill)
Park St.
Park Street Church
Arthur Fiedler Footbridge
Byron St.
Park St.
Beaver Pl.
William Hickling Prescott House
Cathedral Church of St. Paul
Winter St.
Soldiers and Sailors Monument
Frog Pond
Temple Pl.
Downtown Crossing
Beacon St.
Arlington St.
Boston Common Visitor Information Center
West St.
Berkeley St.
Marlborough St.
Charles St.
Tremont St.
Mason St.
Washington St.
Boston Common
BACK BAY
2
Public Garden
Boston Massacre Memorial
Chauncy
Commonwealth Ave.
Central Burying Ground
Avery St.
Ave. de Lafayette
Commonwealth Ave.
Boylston St.
Chinatown
Essex St.
Boylston
Oxford
Pingon
Arlington
Newbury St.
Park Plaza
Eliot
Lagrange St.

GETTING HERE AND AROUND

Bounded by Cambridge Street on the north, Beacon Street on the south, the Charles River Esplanade on the west, and Bowdoin Street on the east, the small neighborhood of Beacon Hill is best experienced on foot. Take the Green Line to the Park Street stop, and walk through the Common toward Beacon Street; the Red Line to the Charles/MGH stop and stroll past the shops on Charles Street; or the Blue Line to Bowdoin Street and head toward the State House.

The Old West End is accessible by T: jump off the Red Line at the Charles/MGH stop to reach the Esplanade; get off the Green Line at Science Park for the Museum of Science and a view of the Leonard P. Zakim Bunker Hill Bridge; and exit the Green Line at North Station for the Garden or for commuter trains to the northern suburbs.

TIMING AND SAFETY

Beacon Hill can be easily explored in an afternoon; add an extra few hours if you wish to linger on the Common and in the shops on Charles Street or tour the Black Heritage Trail. For the most part, the Old West End can be covered in a few hours. Extend your visit to a full day to take in the Museum of Science and an IMAX movie, check out the Sports Museum, and catch a game at the Garden.

At night, stay in well-lighted areas and avoid remote corners of the Common. Also be cautious walking late at night on Causeway Street—on nongame nights this area can be a bit deserted.

BEACON HILL QUICK BITES

Try a wood fire–grilled pizza at Todd English's **Figs** (✉ *42 Charles St., between Chestnut and Mt. Vernon Sts.*) or pub grub at **Sevens Ale House** (✉ *77 Charles St., between Pinckney and Mt. Vernon Sts.*). Grab a cappuccino and croissant at **Cafe Vanille** (✉ *70 Charles St., at Mt. Vernon St.*).

TOP REASONS TO GO

- Tour the State House and experience colonial history.
- Discover the history of Boston's African American community on the Black Heritage Trail.
- Explore the picture-perfect brownstones lining cobblestone streets.
- Meander through the Common and check out the Granary Burying Ground, the final resting place of Sam Adams, John Hancock, and Paul Revere.
- Window-shop for antiques on Charles Street.
- Enjoy the thrill of discovery at the Museum of Science.
- Catch a glimpse of the Leonard P. Zakim Bunker Hill Bridge at night awash in blue lights.
- Root for the home team (Celtics or Bruins) or check out the Sports Museum at the TD Garden.

FREEDOM TRAIL SIGHTS

- Boston Common
- The State House
- Park Street Church
- Granary Burying Ground

OLD WEST END QUICK BITES

In the Old West End follow the locals to **Anna's Taqueria** (✉ *242 Cambridge St.*) for the yummiest Mexican takeout around. Sample a local microbrew and side of sour-cream-and-chive fries at **Boston Beer Works** (✉ *110 Canal St.*).

Sightseeing ★★★★
Dining ★★★
Lodging ★★★
Shopping ★★★★
Nightlife ★★★

Past and present home of the old-money elite, contender for the "Most Beautiful" award among the city's neighborhoods, and hallowed address for many literary lights, Beacon Hill is Boston at its most Bostonian. The redbrick elegance of its narrow streets sends you back to the 19th century just as surely as if you had stumbled into a time machine. But Beacon Hill residents would never make the social faux pas of being out of date. The neighborhood is home to hip boutiques and trendy restaurants, frequented by young, affluent professionals rather than DAR (Daughters of the American Revolution) matrons.

BEACON HILL AND BOSTON COMMON

Updated by Kim Foley MacKinnon

Once the seat of the Commonwealth's government, Beacon Hill was called "Trimountain" and later "Tremont" by early colonists because of its three summits, Pemberton, Mt. Vernon Hill, and Beacon Hill, and named for the warning light set on its peak in 1634. In 1799 settlers leveled out the ground for residences, using it to create what is now Charles Street; by the early 19th century the crests of the other two hills were also lowered.

When the fashionable families decamped for the new development of the Back Bay starting in the 1850s, enough residents remained to ensure that the south slope of the Hill never lost its Brahmin character.

By the mid-20th century, most of the multistory single-family dwellings on Beacon Hill were converted to condominiums and apartments, which are today among the most expensive in the city.

A good place to begin an exploration of Beacon Hill is at the Boston Common Visitor Information Center (⇨ *below*), where you can buy a map or a complete guide to the Freedom Trail.

2

TOP ATTRACTIONS

Acorn Street. Surely the most photographed street in the city, Acorn is Ye Olde Colonial Boston at its best. Leave the car behind, as the cobblestone street may be Boston's roughest ride (and so narrow that only one car can squeeze through at a time). Delicate row houses line one side, and on the other are the doors to Mt. Vernon's hidden gardens. Once the homes of 19th-century artisans and tradespeople, these little jewels are now every bit as prestigious as their larger neighbors on Chestnut and Mt. Vernon streets. ✉ *Beacon Hill.*

FAMILY Fodor's Choice ★ **Boston Common.** Nothing is more central to Boston than the Common, the oldest public park in the United States and undoubtedly the largest and most famous of the town commons around which New England settlements were traditionally arranged. Dating from 1634, Boston Common started as 50 acres where the freemen of Boston could graze their cattle. (Cows were banned in 1830.) Latin names are affixed to many of the Common's trees; it was once expected that proper Boston schoolchildren be able to translate them.

On Tremont Street near Boylston stands the 1888 **Boston Massacre Memorial**; the sculpted hand of one of the victims has a distinct shine from years of sightseers' caresses. The Common's highest ground, near the park's Parkman Bandstand, was once called Flagstaff Hill. It's now surmounted by the **Soldiers and Sailors Monument,** honoring Civil War troops. The Common's only body of water is the **Frog Pond,** a tame and frog-free concrete depression used as a children's wading pool during steamy summer days and for ice-skating in winter. It marks the original site of a natural pond that inspired Edgar Allan Poe to call Bostonians "Frogpondians." In 1848 a gushing fountain of piped-in water was created to inaugurate Boston's municipal water system.

On the Beacon Street side of the Common sits the splendidly restored **Robert Gould Shaw 54th Regiment Memorial,** executed in deep-relief bronze by Augustus Saint-Gaudens in 1897. It commemorates the 54th Massachusetts Regiment, the first Civil War unit made up of free black people, led by the young Brahmin Robert Gould Shaw. He and half of his troops died in an assault on South Carolina's Fort Wagner; their story inspired the 1989 movie *Glory.* The monument—first intended to depict only Shaw until his abolitionist family demanded it honor his regiment as well—figures in works by the poets John Berryman and Robert Lowell, both of whom lived on the north slope of Beacon Hill in the 1940s. This magnificent memorial makes a fitting first stop on the Black Heritage Trail (⇨ *The Black Heritage Trail box, below).* ✉ *Bounded by Beacon, Charles, Tremont, and Park Sts., Beacon Hill* Ⓜ *Park St., Boylston.*

Central Burying Ground. The Central Burying Ground may seem an odd feature for a public park, but remember that in 1756, when the land was set aside, this was a lonely corner of the Common. It's the final resting place of Tories and Patriots alike, as well as many British casualties of the Battle of Bunker Hill. The most famous person buried here is Gilbert Stuart, the portraitist best known for his likenesses of George and Martha Washington; he died a poor man in 1828. The Burying Ground is open daily 9–5. ✉ *Boylston St. near Tremont, Beacon Hill* 🌐 *www.cityofboston.gov/parks/hbgi/CentralBuryingCentral.asp* Ⓜ *Park St., Boylston.*

Boston Common Visitor Information Center. This center, run by the Greater Boston Convention and Visitors Bureau, is on the Tremont Street side of Boston Common. It's well supplied with stacks of free pamphlets about Boston, including a useful guide to the Freedom Trail, which begins in the Common. ✉ *148 Tremont St., Beacon Hill* ☎ *888/733–2678* 🌐 *www.bostonusa.com* 🕒 *Mon.–Fri. 8:30–5, Sat.–Sun. 9–5* Ⓜ *Park St.*

SECRET GARDENS

Hidden Gardens of Beacon Hill tour. Strolling through Beacon Hill, you might be sorely tempted to sneak a peek into those glorious private gardens that are just barely visible behind sheltering walls and wrought-iron gates. Rather than risk arrest, time your visit for the third Thursday in May, when about a dozen of them open to the public for the Hidden Gardens of Beacon Hill tour, an event that's happened annually since 1929. It costs $35 if you purchase tickets in advance. ☎ *617/227–4392* 🌐 *www.beaconhillgardenclub.org.*

Fodor's Choice ★ **Granary Burying Ground.** "It is a fine thing to die in Boston," A. C. Lyons, an essayist and Old Boston wit, once remarked, alluding to the city's cemeteries, among the most picturesque and historic in America. If you found a resting place here at the Old Granary, as it's called, chances are your headstone would have been elaborately ornamented with skeletons and winged skulls. Your neighbors would have been impressive, too: among them are Samuel Adams, John Hancock, Paul Revere, and Benjamin Franklin's parents. Note the winged hourglasses carved into the stone gateway of the burial ground; they are a 19th-century addition, made more than 150 years after this small plot began receiving the earthly remains of colonial Bostonians. ✉ *Entrance on Tremont St., Beacon Hill* 🕒 *Daily 9–5* Ⓜ *Park St.*

Louisburg Square. One of Beacon Hill's most charming corners, Louisburg Square (proper Bostonians always pronounce the "s") was an 1840s model for a townhouse development that was never built on the Hill because of space restrictions. Today, the grassy square, enclosed by a wrought-iron fence, belongs collectively to the owners of the houses facing it. The statue at the north end of the green is of Columbus, the one at the south end of Aristides the Just; both were donated in 1850 by a Greek merchant who lived on the square. The houses, most of which are now divided into apartments and condominiums, have seen their share of famous tenants, including author and critic William Dean Howells at Nos. 4 and 16, and the Alcotts at No. 10 (Louisa May not only lived but also died here, on the day of her father's funeral). In 1852 the singer Jenny Lind was married in the parlor of No. 20. Louisburg Square is also the current home of U.S. Secretary of State John Kerry.

Several Founding Fathers rest at the Granary Burial Ground, a picturesque Freedom Trail stop.

There's a legend that Louisburg Square was the location of the Rev. William Blaxton's spring, although there's no water there today. Blaxton, or Blackstone, was one of the first Bostonians, having come to the Shawmut Peninsula in the mid-1620s. When the Puritans, who had settled in Charlestown, found their water supply inadequate, Blaxton invited them to move across the river, where he assured them they would find an "excellent spring." Just a few years later, he sold them all but 6 acres of the peninsula he had bought from the Native Americans and decamped to Rhode Island, seeking greater seclusion; a plaque at 50 Beacon Street commemorates him. ⊠ *Between Mt. Vernon and Pickney Sts., Beacon Hill* Ⓜ *Park St.*

FAMILY Fodor's Choice ★ **Museum of African American History.** Ever since runaway slave Crispus Attucks became one of the famous victims of the Boston Massacre of 1770, the African American community of Boston has played an important part in the city's history. Throughout the 19th century, abolition was the cause célèbre for Boston's intellectual elite, and during that time, blacks came to thrive in neighborhoods throughout the city. The Museum of African American History was established in 1964 to promote this history. The umbrella organization includes a trio of historic sites: the Abiel Smith School, the first public school in the nation built specifically for black children; the African Meeting House, where in 1832 the New England Anti-Slavery Society was formed under the leadership of William Lloyd Garrison; and the African Meeting House on the island of Nantucket, off the coast of Cape Cod. Park Service personnel continue to lead tours of the **Black Heritage Trail** *(⇨ The Black Heritage Trail box)*, starting from the Shaw Memorial. The museum is the site of activities, including lectures, children's storytelling, and concerts focusing on black composers. ✉ *46 Joy St., Beacon Hill* ☎ *617/725–0022* 🌐 *www.afroammuseum.org* 🎫 *$5* 🕒 *Mon.–Sat. 10–4* Ⓜ *Park St.*

WORTH NOTING

Appalachian Mountain Club. The bowfront mansion that serves as the headquarters of one of New England's oldest environmental institutions draws nature lovers from all over the world. The club is a reliable source of useful information on outdoor recreation throughout the region, including cross-country skiing and hiking. (You don't have to be a member to use its resources.) Architecturally, the building is notable for its carved cornices and oriel window decorated with vines and gargoyles. You can buy guidebooks and maps here. ✉ *5 Joy St., Beacon Hill* ☎ *617/523–0655* 🌐 *www.amcboston.org* 🕒 *Weekdays 9–4:30* Ⓜ *Park St.*

Beacon Street. Some New Englanders believe that wealth is a burden to be borne with a minimum of display. Happily, the early residents of Beacon Street were not among them. They erected many fine architectural statements, from the magnificent State House to grand patrician mansions. Here are some of the most important buildings of Charles Bulfinch, the ultimate designer of the Federal style in America: dozens of bowfront row houses, the Somerset Club, and the glorious Harrison Gray Otis House. (⇨ *"Touring Beacon Street" box for a walking tour of the area.*)

Boston Athenaeum. It was William Tudor, one of the cofounders of the Boston Athenaeum, who first compared Boston with Athens because of its many cultural and educational institutions; Bostonians now jealously guard the title "Athens of America." One of the oldest libraries in the country, the Athenaeum was founded in 1807 from the seeds sown by the Anthology Club (headed by Ralph Waldo Emerson's father) and moved to its present imposing quarters—modeled after Palladio's Palazzo da Porta Festa in Vicenza, Italy—in 1849. Only 1,049 proprietary shares exist for membership in this cathedral of scholarship, and most have been passed down for generations; the Athenaeum is, however, open for use by qualified scholars, and yearly memberships are open to all by application.

The first floor is open to the public and houses an art gallery with rotating exhibits, marble busts, porcelain vases, lush oil paintings, and books. The children's room is also open for the public to browse or read a story in secluded nooks overlooking the Granary Burying

HISTORIC BY LAW

The classic face of Beacon Hill comes from its brick row houses, nearly all built between 1800 and 1850. Even the sidewalks are brick, and will remain so by public fiat; in the 1940s, residents staged an uncharacteristic sit-in to prevent conventional paving. Since then, public law, the Beacon Hill Civic Association, and the Beacon Hill Architectural Commission have maintained tight control over everything from the gas lamps to the colors of front doors.

TOURING BEACON STREET

After the **Boston Athenaeum,** Beacon Street highlights begin at No. 34, originally the Cabot family residence and until 1996 the headquarters of Little, Brown and Company, once a mainstay of Boston's publishing trade. At 33 Beacon Street is the **George Parkman House,** its gracious facade hiding more than a few secrets. One of the first sensational "trials of the century" involved the murder of Dr. George Parkman, a wealthy landlord and Harvard benefactor. He was bludgeoned to death in 1849 by Dr. John Webster, a Harvard medical professor and neighborhood acquaintance who allegedly became enraged by Parkman's demands that he repay a personal loan. At the conclusion of the trial, the professor was hanged; he's buried in an unmarked grave on Copp's Hill in the North End. Parkman's son lived in seclusion in this house overlooking the Common until he died in 1908. The building is now used for civic functions.

Notice the windows of the twin **Appleton-Parker Houses,** built by the pioneering textile merchant Nathan Appleton and a partner at Nos. 39 and 40. These are the celebrated purple panes of Beacon Hill; only a few buildings have them, and they are incredibly valuable. Their amethystine mauve color was the result of the action of the sun's ultraviolet light on the imperfections in a shipment of glass sent to Boston around 1820. The mansions aren't open to the public.

The quintessential snob has always been a Bostonian—and the **Somerset Club,** at 42 Beacon Street, has always been the inner sanctum of blue-nose Cabots, Lowells, and Lodges. The mansion is a rare intrusion of the granite Greek Revival style into Beacon Hill. The older of its two buildings was erected in 1819 by David Sears and designed by Alexander Parris, the architect of Quincy Market. A few doors down is the grandest of the three houses Harrison Gray Otis built for himself during Boston's golden age.

Ground. Take the guided tour to spy one of the most marvelous sights in the world of Boston academe, the fifth-floor Reading Room. With two levels of antique books, comfortable reading chairs, high windows, and assorted art, the room appears straight out of a period movie, rather than a modern scholarly institution. **TIP→ Only eight people can fit in the tiny elevator to the fifth floor, so call at least 24 hours in advance to reserve your spot on the tour.** Among the Athenaeum's holdings are most of George Washington's private library and the King's Chapel Library, sent from England by William III in 1698. With a nod to the information age, an online catalog contains records for more than 600,000 volumes. The Athenaeum extends into 14 Beacon Street. ✉ *10½ Beacon St., Beacon Hill* ☎ *617/227–0270* 🌐 *www.bostonathenaeum.org* *Free* ⏲ *Mon.–Wed. 9–8; Thurs. and Fri. 9–5:30; Sat. 9–4. Tours Tues. and Thurs. at 3* Ⓜ *Park St.*

Cathedral Church of St. Paul. Though it looks a bit like a bank, St. Paul's is actually the first Boston structure built in the Greek Revival style (1820). It was established by a group of wealthy and influential patriots

CLOSE UP

The Black Heritage Trail

Until the end of the 19th century, the north side of opulent Beacon Hill contained a vibrant free black community—more than 8,000 at its peak—who built houses, schools, and churches that stand to this day. In the African Meeting House, once called the Black Faneuil Hall, orators rallied against slavery. The streets were lined with black-owned businesses. The black community has since shifted to other parts of Boston, but visitors can rediscover this 19th-century legacy on the Black Heritage Trail.

Established in the late 1960s, the self-guiding trail stitches together 14 sites along a 1½-mile walk. Park rangers give daily tours Monday through Saturday, Memorial Day through Labor Day, at 10 am, noon, and 2 pm, and from Labor Day to Memorial Day at 2 pm, starting from the Shaw Memorial in Boston Common. To tour on your own, pick up brochures from the **Museum of African American History** (✉ *46 Joy St.*), the **National Park Service Visitor Center** (✉ *15 State St.*), or download one online at 🌐 *www.afroammuseum.org/trail.htm.*

Start at the stirring **Robert Gould Shaw 54th Regiment Memorial** in Boston Common. Shaw, a young white officer from a prominent Boston abolitionist family, led the first black regiment to be recruited in the North during the Civil War. From here, walk up Joy Street to 5–7 Pinckney Street to see the 1797 **George Middleton House,** Beacon Hill's oldest existing home built by blacks. Nearby, the **Phillips School** at Anderson and Pinckney streets was one of Boston's first integrated schools. The **John J. Smith House,** at 86 Pinckney, was a rendezvous point for abolitionists and escaping slaves, and the **Charles Street Meeting House,** at Mt. Vernon and Charles streets, was once a white Baptist church and later a black church and community center. In 1876 the building became the site of the **African Methodist Episcopal Church,** which was the last black institution to leave Beacon Hill, in 1939. The **Lewis and Harriet Hayden House** at 66 Phillips Street, the home of freed slaves turned abolitionists, was a stop on the Underground Railroad. Harriet Beecher Stowe, author of *Uncle Tom's Cabin,* visited here in 1853 for her first glimpse of fugitive slaves. The Haydens reportedly kept a barrel of gunpowder under the front step, saying they'd blow up the house before they'd surrender a single slave. At **2 Phillips Street,** John Coburn, cofounder of a black military company, ran a gaming house, described as a "private place for gentlemen."

The five residences on **Smith Court** are typical of African American Bostonian homes of the 1800s, including No. 3, the 1799 clapboard house where William C. Nell, America's first published black historian and a crusader for school integration, boarded from 1851 to 1865. At the corner of Joy Street and Smith Court is **Abiel Smith School,** the city's first public school for black children. The school's exhibits interpret the ongoing struggle started in the 1830s for equal school rights. Next door is the venerable **African Meeting House,** which was the community's center of social, educational, and political activity. The ground level houses a gallery; in the airy upstairs, you can imagine the fiery sermons that once rattled the upper pews.

who wanted a wholly American Episcopal parish—the two existing Episcopal churches, Christ Church (Old North) and Trinity, were both founded before the Revolution—that would contrast with the existing colonial and "gothick" structures around town. The building was to be topped with an entablature showing St. Paul preaching to the Corinthians—but the pediment remained uncarved for 190 years. Finally, in 2012, Philadelphia-based sculptor Donald Lipski, chosen out of a field of 150 artists, inscribed a nautilus shell into the pediment on a blue background, making for a contemporary and striking monument. ✉ *138 Tremont St., Beacon Hill* ☎ *617/482–5800* 🌐 *www.stpaulboston.org* ⏲ *Weekdays 9–5. Services Sun. at 8 am and 10 am; Mon. at 1; Tue. at 12:15.* Ⓜ *Park St.*

DID YOU KNOW?

Beacon Hill's north slope played a key part in African American history. A community of free blacks lived here in the 1800s; many worshipped at the African Meeting House, established in 1805 and still standing. It came to be known as the "Black Faneuil Hall" for the fervent antislavery activism that started within its walls.

Charles Street. Chockablock with antiques shops, clothing boutiques, small restaurants, and flower shops, Charles Street more than makes up for the general lack of commercial development on Beacon Hill. You won't see any glaring neon; in keeping with the historic character of the area, even the 7-Eleven has been made to conform to the prevailing aesthetic standards. Notice the old-fashioned signs hanging from storefronts—the bakery's loaf of bread, the florist's topiary, the tailor's spool of thread, and the chiropractor's human spine. Once the home of Oliver Wendell Holmes and the publisher James T. Fields (of the famed Bostonian firm of Ticknor and Fields), Charles Street sparkles at dusk from gas-fueled lamps, making it a romantic place for an evening stroll. ✉ *Beacon Hill.*

Chestnut Street. Delicacy and grace characterize virtually every structure on this street, from the fanlights above the entryways to the wrought-iron boot scrapers on the steps. Author and explorer Francis Parkman lived here, as did the lawyer Richard Henry Dana (who wrote *Two Years Before the Mast*), and 19th-century actor Edwin Booth, brother of John Wilkes Booth. Edwin Booth's sometime residence, No. 29A, dates from 1800, and is the oldest house on the south slope of the hill. Also note the **Swan Houses,** at Nos. 13, 15, and 17, commissioned from Charles Bulfinch by Hepzibah Swan as dowry gifts for her three daughters. Complete with Adam-style entrances, marble columns, and recessed arches, they are Chestnut Street at its most beautiful.

Harrison Gray Otis House. Harrison Gray Otis, a U.S. senator, Boston's third mayor, and one of the Mt. Vernon Proprietors (a group of prosperous Boston investors), built in rapid succession three of the city's most splendidly ostentatious Federal-era houses, all designed by Charles Bulfinch and all still standing. This, the third Harrison Gray Otis House, was the grandest. Now the headquarters of the American Meteorological Society, the house was once freestanding and surrounded by English-style gardens. The second Otis house, built in 1800 at 85 Mt. Vernon

Street, is now a private home. The first Otis house, built in 1796 on Cambridge Street, is the only one open to the public *(⇨ Old West End)*. Otis moved into 45 Beacon Street in 1805, and stayed until his death in 1848. His tenure thus extended from the first days of Beacon Hill's residential development almost to the time when many of the Hill's prominent families decamped for the Back Bay, which was just beginning to be filled at the time of Otis's death. ✉ *45 Beacon St., Beacon Hill.*

Mt. Vernon Street. Mt. Vernon Street, along with Chestnut Street, has some of Beacon Hill's most distinguished addresses. Mt. Vernon is the grander of the two, however, with houses set back farther and rising taller; it even has a freestanding mansion, the second Harrison Gray Otis House, at No. 85. Henry James once wrote that Mt. Vernon Street was "the only respectable street in America," and he must have known, as he lived with his brother William at No. 131 in the 1860s. He was just one of many literary luminaries who resided here, including Julia Ward Howe, who composed "The Battle Hymn of the Republic" and lived at No. 32, and the poet Robert Frost, who lived at No. 88. ✉ *Beacon Hill.*

Nichols House. The only Mt. Vernon Street home open to the public, the Nichols House was built in 1804 and is attributed to Charles Bulfinch. It became the lifelong home of Rose Standish Nichols (1872–1960), Beacon Hill eccentric, philanthropist, peace advocate, and one of the first female landscape designers. Although Miss Nichols inherited the Victorian furnishings, she added a number of colonial-style pieces to the mix, such as an American Empire rosewood sideboard and a bonnet-top Chippendale highboy. The result is a delightful mélange of styles. Nichols made arrangements in her will for the house to become a museum, and knowledgeable volunteers from the neighborhood have been playing host since then. To see the house, you must take a tour (included in the price of admission). Check the website for special events and exhibits. ✉ *55 Mt. Vernon St., Beacon Hill* ☎ *617/227–6993* 🌐 *www.nicholshousemuseum.org* 🎫 *$8* 🕒 *Apr.–Oct., Tues.–Sat. 11–4; Nov.–Mar., Thurs.–Sat. 11–4. First tour at 11, tours on ½ hr thereafter; last tour starts at 4* Ⓜ *Park St.*

Park Street Church. If this Congregationalist church at the corner of Tremont and Park streets could sing, what joyful noise it would be. Samuel Smith's hymn "America" was first sung inside the church, which was designed by Peter Banner and erected in 1809–10, on July 4, 1831. The country's oldest musical organization, the Handel & Haydn Society, was founded here in 1815. In 1829 William Lloyd Garrison began his long public campaign for the abolition of slavery here. The distinguished steeple is considered by many critics to be the most beautiful in New England. Just outside the church, at the intersection of Park and Tremont streets (and the main subway crossroads of the city) is **Brimstone Corner.** Whether the name refers to the fervent thunder of the church's preachers, the gunpowder that was once stored in the church's crypt, or the burning sulfur that preachers once scattered on the pavement to attract potential churchgoers, we'll never know—historians simply can't agree. ✉ *1 Park St., Beacon Hill* ☎ *617/523–3383*

🌐 *www.parkstreet.org* ⏲ *Tours mid-June–Aug., Tues.–Sat. 9:30–3. Sun. services at 8:30, 11, and 4* Ⓜ *Park St.*

Park Street Station. One of the first four stops on the first subway in America, Park Street Station was part of the line that originally ran only as far as the present-day Boylston stop. It was opened for service in 1897, against the warnings of those convinced it would make buildings along Tremont Street collapse. The copper-roof kiosks are National Historic Landmarks—outside them cluster flower vendors, street musicians, and partisans of causes and beliefs ranging from Irish nationalism to Krishna Consciousness. The station is the center of Boston's subway system; "inbound" trains are always traveling toward Park Street. ✉ *Park and Tremont Sts., Beacon Hill.*

NEED A BREAK?

Panificio Bakery. While window-shopping on Charles Street, stop in at the Panificio Bakery, a cozy neighborhood hangout and old-fashioned Italian café. Soups and pizzas are made on the premises; for quick fortification, go for one of the Mediterranean sandwiches, or satisfy your sweet tooth with a raspberry turnover and a cappuccino. ✉ *144 Charles St., Beacon Hill* ☎ *617/227–4340* 🌐 *www.panificioboston.com.*

State House. On July 4, 1795, the surviving fathers of the Revolution were on hand to enshrine the ideals of their new Commonwealth in a graceful seat of government designed by Charles Bulfinch. Governor Samuel Adams and Paul Revere laid the cornerstone; Revere would later roll the copper sheathing for the dome.

Bulfinch's neoclassical design is poised between Georgian and Federal; its finest features are the delicate Corinthian columns of the portico, the graceful pediment and window arches, and the vast yet visually weightless golden dome (gilded in 1874 and again in 1997). During World War II the dome was painted gray so that it would not reflect moonlight during blackouts and thereby offer a target to anticipated Axis bombers. It's capped with a pinecone, a symbol of the importance of pinewood, which was integral to the construction of Boston's early houses and churches; it also serves as a reminder of the state's early connection to Maine, once part of Massachusetts.

Inside the building are Doric Hall, with its statuary and portraits; the Hall of Flags, where an exhibit shows the battle flags from all the wars in which Massachusetts regiments have participated; the Great Hall, an open space used for state functions that houses 351 flags from the cities and towns of Massachusetts; the governor's office; and the chambers of the House and Senate. The Great Hall contains a giant, modernistic clock designed by New York artist R. M. Fischer. Its installation in 1986 at a cost of $100,000 was roundly slammed as a symbol of legislative extravagance. There's also a wealth of statuary, including figures of Horace Mann, Daniel Webster, and a youthful-looking President John F. Kennedy in full stride. Just outside Doric Hall is *Hear Us,* a series of six bronze busts honoring the contributions of women to public life in Massachusetts. But perhaps the best-known piece of artwork in the building is the carved wooden *Sacred Cod,* mounted in the Old State House in 1784 as a symbol of the Commonwealth's maritime wealth.

It was moved, with much fanfare, to Bulfinch's structure in 1798. By 1895, when it was hung in the new House chambers, the representatives had begun to consider the Cod their unofficial mascot—so much so that when *Harvard Lampoon* wags "codnapped" it in 1933, the House refused to meet in session until the fish was returned, three days later. You can take a guided tour or do a self-guided tour. ✉ *Beacon St. between Hancock and Bowdoin Sts., Beacon Hill* ☎ *617/727–3676* 🌐 *www.sec.state.ma.us/trs/trsidx.htm* 🎫 *Free* 🕒 *Weekdays 8:45–5. 30-minute guided tours 10–3:30. Advance reservations requested* Ⓜ *Park St.*

> **FRUGAL FUN**
>
> The Boston Parks and Recreation department offers year-round free activities all over the city, including live performances and participatory arts programs in the summer at local parks and autumn kayaking. Contact the Boston Parks and Recreation for a full schedule (☎ *617/635–4505* 🌐 *www.cityofboston.gov/parks*).

Vilna Shul. This historic treasure, one of the oldest synagogues in the region, is the focus of both renovation and research. The two-story brick building was completed in 1919 by Jews from Vilna (or Vilnius), the capital of present-day Lithuania. Modeled after the great synagogue of Vilna, it's the last remaining immigrant era synagogue in Boston and stands in a neighborhood that was once deeply Jewish. The building, abandoned in 1985 after the congregation dropped to a single member, was bought by the Boston Center for Jewish Culture, which is overseeing its restoration. Above the doorway gleams renewed gilded Hebrew lettering; the hand-carved ark and the stained-glass Star of David are worth a peek; and murals depicting traditional themes are being uncovered from beneath seven layers of paint. Three skylights flood the space with natural light. Guided tours are available; call ahead to arrange. ✉ *14–18 Phillips St., Beacon Hill* ☎ *617/523–2324* 🌐 *www.vilnashul.org* 🎫 *Donations accepted* 🕒 *Wed., Thurs., and Fri. 11–5, Sun. 1–5* Ⓜ *Charles/MGH.*

William Hickling Prescott House. Now a modest but engaging house museum, this 1808 Federal structure was designed by Asher Benjamin, and was the home of noted historian William Hickling Prescott from 1845 to 1859. Today, in addition to the museum, it's the headquarters for the Massachusetts Society of Colonial Dames of America, which offers tours. Some rooms are furnished with period furniture, including the former study with Prescott's desk and "noctograph," which helped the nearly blind scholar write. (He was blinded in one eye by a flying crust of bread during a food fight at Harvard.) Ask about Prescott's secret staircase, which allowed him to escape into his study when bored by guests in the parlor. The house also has a fine costume collection. ✉ *55 Beacon St., Beacon Hill* ☎ *617/742–3190* 🌐 *www.nscda.org/ma/prescott_house.php* 🎫 *$7* 🕒 *Tours June–Aug., Wed., Thurs., and Sat. noon–4 and Sept.–May, Thurs. and Sat. noon–4* Ⓜ *Park St., Charles/MGH.*

THE OLD WEST END

There are just a few reminders here of what was once the Old West End: a few brick tenements and a handful of monuments, including the first house built for Harrison Gray Otis. What once was a tangled web of streets housing myriad ethnic groups succumbed to a vast urban renewal project in the 1960s designed by I. M. Pei. The biggest surviving structures in the Old West End with any real history are two public institutions, Massachusetts General Hospital and the former Suffolk County Jail, which dates from 1849 and was designed by Gridley Bryant. The onetime prison is now part of the luxurious, and wryly named, Liberty Hotel.

Behind Massachusetts General and the sprawling Charles River Park apartment complex (famous among Storrow Drive commuters as the place with signs reading "If you lived here, you'd be home now") is a small grid of streets recalling an older Boston. Here are furniture and electric-supply stores, a discount camping-supply house (Hilton's Tent City), and many of the city's most popular watering holes. The main drag here is Causeway Street. North Station and the area around it, on Causeway between Haverhill and Canal streets, provide service to commuters from the northern suburbs and cheap brews to local barflies, and can be jammed when there's a game at the TD Garden, home of the Bruins and Celtics.

In addition to the Garden, the innovative Museum of Science is one of the more modern attractions of the Old West End. The newest addition to the area's skyline is the Leonard P. Zakim Bunker Hill Bridge, which spans the Charles River just across from the TD Garden.

TOP ATTRACTIONS

FAMILY Fodor's Choice ★ **Museum of Science.**
See highlighted listing in this chapter.

WORTH NOTING

Harrison Gray Otis House. If the name sounds familiar, it's because a Beacon Hill home bears the same name. This is the first of three houses built for Harrison Gray Otis, Boston's third mayor and a prominent citizen and developer. It's owned and operated by Historic New England, an organization that owns and maintains dozens of properties throughout the region. The furnishings, textiles, wall coverings, and even the interior paint, specially mixed to match old samples, are faithful to the Federal period, circa 1790–1810. You may be surprised to see the bright and vivid colors favored in those days. Otis lived here only four years before moving to more sumptuous digs, also designed by Charles Bulfinch, on Beacon Hill. A second-floor room brings to life the home's days as a late-19th-century boardinghouse, and a display describes the "champoo baths" of former resident Mrs. Mott. From May through October, Historic New England runs a Beacon Hill walking tour from the house. It highlights the two sides of Beacon Hill,

MUSEUM OF SCIENCE

Science Park at Charles River Dam, Old West End 617/723–2500 www.mos.org $23 July 5–Labor Day, Sat.–Thurs. 9–7, Fri. 9–9; after Labor Day–July 4, Sat.–Thurs. 9–5, Fri. 9–9 M Science Park.

TIPS

- The planetarium is best for children older than five.
- After touring the museum, refuel the family at one of the six eateries in the Riverview Cafe located in the Red Wing on the first level.
- From April through November, you can catch a Duck Tour from the first level of the museum. You'll need a reservation, so plan ahead. You might be in the mood to sit and tour the city after spending a morning on your feet walking through the exhibit halls.
- Combine your admission with tickets to either the planetarium or Omni Theater and save $5 overall.

With 15-foot lightning bolts in the Theater of Electricity and a 20-foot-long *Tyrannosaurus rex* model, this is just the place to ignite any child's scientific curiosity. Located just north of Massachusetts General Hospital, the museum sits astride the Charles River Dam. More than 550 exhibits cover astronomy, astrophysics, anthropology, medical progress, computers, the organic and inorganic earth sciences, and much more. The emphasis is on hands-on education.

Highlights

At the "Investigate!" exhibit, there are no wrong answers, only discoveries. Children explore such scientific principles as gravity by balancing objects. They learn the physics behind everyday play activities such as swinging and bumping up and down on a teeter-totter in the "Science in the Park" exhibit. Other displays include "Light House," where you can experiment with color and light, and the perennial favorite, "Dinosaurs: Modeling the Mesozoic," which lets kids become paleontologists and examine dinosaur bones, fossils, and tracks.

The Charles Hayden Planetarium, with its sophisticated multimedia system based on a Zeiss planetarium projector, produces exciting programs on astronomical discoveries. Laser light shows, with laser graphics and computer animation, are scheduled Thursday through Sunday evenings. The museum also includes the Mugar Omni Theater, a five-story dome screen. The theater's state-of-the-art sound system provides extra-sharp acoustics, and the huge projection allows the audience to practically experience the action on-screen. Try to get tickets in advance online or by phone; call or check the museum's website for showtimes.

2

taking visitors past grandiose mansions and more modest townhomes. Along the way, you'll pass the African Meeting House, Louisburg Square, and the Boston Common. The $12 price includes admission to the Otis house. ✉ *141 Cambridge St., Old West End* ☎ *617/994–5920* 🌐 *www.historicnewengland.org* 🎫 *$8* ⏲ *Tours on hr and ½ hr Wed.–Sun. 11–4:30* Ⓜ *Charles/MGH, Bowdoin.*

NEED A BREAK?

Harvard Gardens. Harvard Gardens, a Beacon Hill legend, was the first bar in the city to get its liquor license after the repeal of Prohibition. It opened in 1930, and was owned by the same family until the 1990s. Once considered a dive bar, it's much more upscale today, with a menu of gourmet pizzas and sandwiches and scrumptious brunch fare, including a spectacular Bloody Mary. Their classic Reuben provides a solid start to a day's exploring. The place is often packed with doctors and nurses enjoying post-shift drinks. ✉ ***316 Cambridge St., Old West End*** ☎ ***617/523–2727*** 🌐 ***www.harvardgardens.com.***

DUCK TOURS

Boston Duck Tours is a Boston fixture, taking more than half a million people every year on unique amphibious tours: Boylston Street, Tremont Street, and the River Charles, all in one 80-minute trip. Tours depart from the Prudential Center and the Museum of Science, and run seven days a week, rain or shine, from late March to late November (all ducks are heated). Tickets are $34 for adults, $23 for kids ages 3–11, and $10.50 for kids ages 2 and under. Reserve tickets early. A shorter tour (65 minutes) is offered from the New England Aquarium (☎ *617/267–3825* 🌐 *www.bostonducktours.com*).

Leonard P. Zakim Bunker Hill Memorial Bridge. The crown jewel of the "Big Dig" construction project, the 1,432-foot-long Leonard P. Zakim Bunker Hill Memorial Bridge (or Zakim Bridge, for short), was designed by Swiss bridge architect Christian Menn and is one of the widest cable-stayed hybrid bridges ever built, and the first to use an asymmetrical design. The towers evoke the Bunker Hill Monument, and the distinctive fan shape of the cables gives the bridge a modern flair. The bridge was named for both Lenny Zakim, a local civil-rights activist who headed the New England Region of the Anti-Defamation League (and died of cancer in 1999) and the Battle of Bunker Hill, a defining moment in U.S. history. One of the best spots to view the bridge is from the Charlestown waterfront across the river. The best viewing is at night, when the illuminated bridge glows blue; sometimes other colors are used, like pink, to commemorate breast cancer awareness month. ✉ *Old West End* 🌐 *www.leonardpzakimbunkerhillbridge.org.*

Massachusetts General Hospital (MGH). Incorporated in 1811, MGH has traditionally been regarded as the nation's premier general hospital. The domed, granite **Bulfinch Building** was designed in 1818 by Boston's leading architect, Charles Bulfinch. Harvard Medical School was once on the grounds of Massachusetts General, and today the hospital is the school's oldest teaching affiliate. ✉ *55 Fruit St., Old West End* ☎ *617/726–2000* 🌐 *www.mgh.harvard.edu* Ⓜ *Charles/MGH.*

Amphitheater. It was in the hospital's amphitheater that, on October 16, 1846, Dr. John Collins Warren performed the first public demonstration of a patient being anesthetized using ether; the place was promptly nicknamed the "Ether Dome." You may visit the amphitheater today when it's not in use (admission free; open daily 9–5) and see the fourth-floor display describing the procedure that made modern surgery possible. ✉ *Main entrance on N. Grove St.; turn right after coffee shop.*

Old West Church. Built in 1806 using the design of builder and architect Asher Benjamin, this imposing United Methodist church stands, along with the Harrison Gray Otis House next door, as a reminder of the area's more fashionable days. The church was a stop on the Underground Railroad, and it was the first integrated congregation in the country, giving open seating to blacks and whites alike just before 1820. The building narrowly escaped demolition in the 1950s, when most of the West End was razed; thankfully it was saved and was named a historic landmark in 1971. ✉ *131 Cambridge St., Old West End* ☎ *617/227–5088* 🌐 *www.oldwestchurch.org* ⏲ *Tues.–Fri. 10–3. Sun. services at 11 am* Ⓜ *Bowdoin, Government Center.*

FAMILY **TD Garden.** Diehards still moan about the loss of the old Boston Garden, a much more intimate venue than this mammoth facility, which opened in 1995. Regardless, the home of the Celtics (basketball) and Bruins (hockey) is still known as the good old "Gah-den," and its air-conditioning, comfier seats, improved food selection, 1,200-vehicle parking garage, and nearly double number of bathrooms, has won grudging acceptance. The Garden also serves as a concert venue, featuring big-name acts, like Justin Timberlake and Nine Inch Nails. On occasion, there are public-skating events in winter; call ahead for information. ✉ *100 Legends Way, Old West End* ☎ *617/624–1050* 🌐 *www.tdbanknorthgarden.com* Ⓜ *North Station.*

Sports Museum of New England. The fifth and sixth levels of the TD Garden house the Sports Museum of New England, where displays of memorabilia and photographs showcase local sports history and legends. Take a tour of the locker and interview rooms (off-season only), test your sports knowledge with interactive games, and see how you stand up to life-size statues of heroes Carl Yastrzemski and Larry Bird. The museum is generally open daily 10–4, but call ahead to confirm. Admission is $10. ✉ *Use west premium seating entrance* ☎ *617/624–1234* 🌐 *www.sportsmuseum.org* 🎟 *$10.*

3

GOVERNMENT CENTER AND THE NORTH END

GETTING ORIENTED

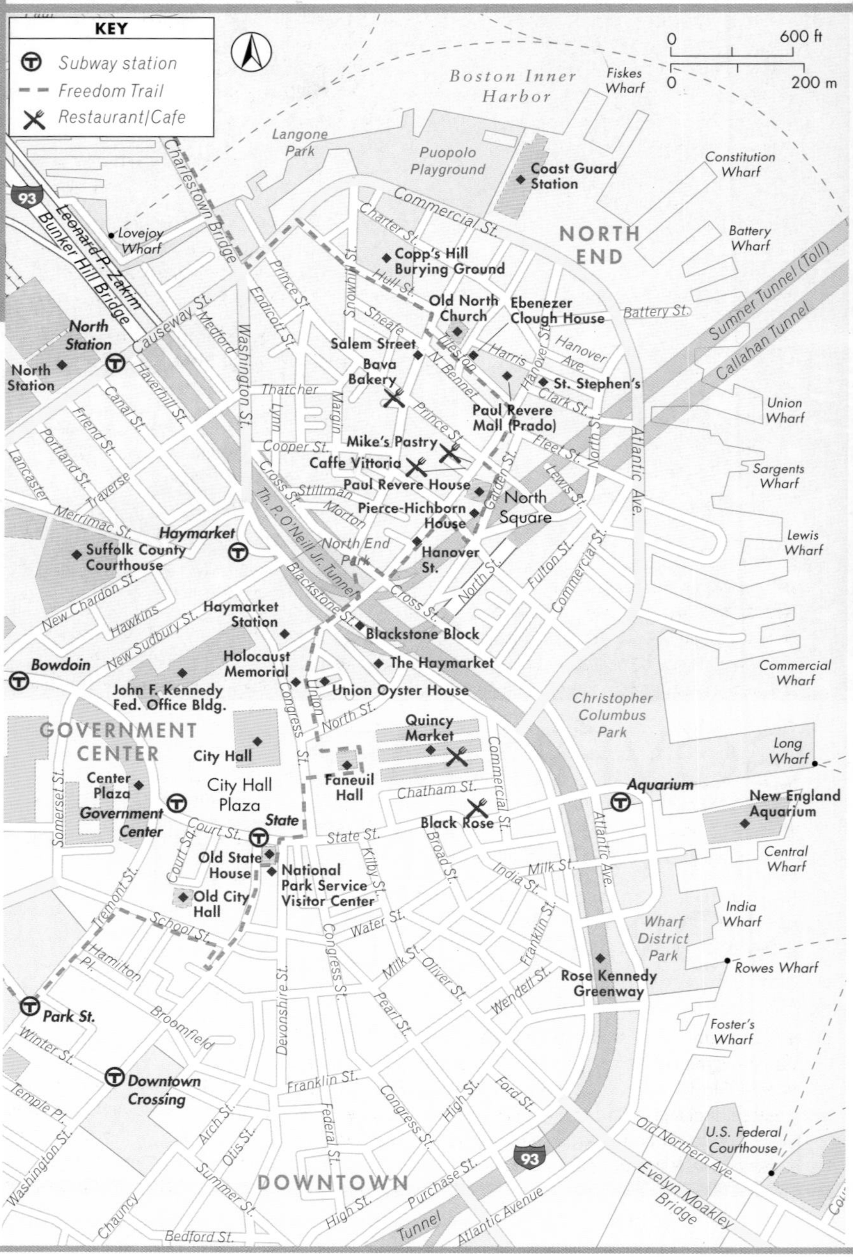

TOP REASONS TO GO

- Shop 'til you drop at the North and South markets of Quincy Marketplace.
- Imagine the debates of old during a tour of historic Faneuil Hall.
- Grab a slice of Pizzeria Regina's cheesy best on the way through Quincy Market.
- Enjoy a pint with a side of live Irish music at the Black Rose.
- Come hungry, leave happy! Enjoy the delicious Italian fare in the North End, Boston's Little Italy.
- Visit Old North Church and relive the night of Paul Revere's Ride.
- Visit Paul Revere's house, the oldest standing home in Boston, to experience colonial life in Boston.

GETTING HERE AND AROUND

Government Center is perfect for walking. If you arrive via the T, jump off the Green Line at Government Center, the Blue Line at State Street, or the Orange Line at Haymarket to explore. The T is your best bet for accessing the North End. Get off the Orange Line at Haymarket and walk southeast to Hanover Street; take a left there to enter the North End. Alternatively, exit the Blue Line at Aquarium and walk northeast on Atlantic Avenue, past Christopher Columbus Park to access the North End.

TIMING AND SAFETY

You can easily spend several hours hitting the stores, boutiques, and historic sites of the Faneuil Hall and Quincy Market complex. On Friday and Saturday join crowds at the Haymarket farmers' market (wear good walking shoes, as the cobblestones get slippery with trampled produce).

Allow two hours for a walk through the North End, longer if you plan on dawdling in a café. This part of town is made for strolling, day or night. Many people like to spend part of a day at Quincy Market, then head over to the North End for dinner—the district has an impressive selection of traditional and contemporary Italian restaurants.

Be cautious in the Government Center area late at night. The North End is a relatively safe neighborhood; you'll have plenty of company day or night.

GOVERNMENT CENTER QUICK BITES

You can't do any better for quick bites than **Quincy Market** near Government Center. The hall is filled with stalls of every imaginable food from chowder and lobster rolls to pizza, Chinese, Indian, Italian pastries, ice cream, and candy. Grab your grub to go and enjoy a meal outside on the benches between the North or South markets.

FREEDOM TRAIL SIGHTS

- Boston Massacre Site
- Copp's Hill Burying Ground
- Faneuil Hall
- Old North Church
- The Old State House
- Paul Revere House

NORTH END QUICK BITES

For a quick bite and a classic North End experience, head to **Mike's Pastry** (✉ *300 Hanover St.*) for cappuccino, cannoli, and people-watching in this bustling café.

Sightseeing ★★★★
Dining ★★★★★
Lodging ★★★★
Shopping ★★★★
Nightlife ★★★★★

Government Center is a section of town Bostonians love to hate. Not only does it house what they can't fight—City Hall—but it also contains some of the bleakest architecture since the advent of poured concrete. But though the stark, treeless plain surrounding City Hall has been roundly jeered for its user-unfriendly aura, the expanse is enlivened by feisty political rallies, free summer concerts, and the occasional festival. On the corner of Tremont and Court streets the landmark Steaming Kettle, a gilded kettle cast in 1873 that once boiled around the clock, lightens the mood a bit. (It now marks a Starbucks.) More historic buildings are just a little farther on: 18th-century Faneuil Hall and the frenzied Quincy Market.

GOVERNMENT CENTER

Updated by Kim Foley MacKinnon

The curving six-story Center Plaza building, across from the Government Center T stop and the broad brick desert of City Hall Plaza, echoes the much older Sears Crescent, a curved commercial block next to the Government Center T stop. The Center Plaza building separates Tremont Street from Pemberton Square and the old and "new" courthouses to the west.

The warren of small streets on the northeast side of Government Center is the North End. For visitors, Government Center is usually just a way station to get to Faneuil Hall, Quincy Market, and other downtown attractions, unless there happens to be a festival scheduled. Come during the annual Jimmy Fund Scooper Bowl ice cream event in June or

A GOOD WALK

The modern, stark expanse of Boston's **City Hall** and the twin towers of the **John F. Kennedy Federal Office Building** are an introduction to Boston in its urban-renewal stage. But just across Congress Street is **Faneuil Hall**, a site of political speech making since Revolutionary times, and just beyond that is **Quincy Market**, where you can shop (and eat) until you drop. For more Bostonian fare, walk back toward Congress Street to the **Blackstone Block** and the city's oldest restaurant, the **Union Oyster House**. (Fashionable ladies take note: The cobblestones are treacherous if you're wearing heels.) Near the restaurant is the **Holocaust Memorial**, a six-tower construction of glass and steel. Follow Marshall Street north and turn right onto Blackstone Street to pass the **Haymarket**, a flurry of activity on Friday and Saturday, with open-air stalls selling produce and other foodstuffs. To sample Italian goodies, make your way to the North End via the pedestrian walkways that lead to Salem and Hanover streets.

3

during the city's Fourth of July festival, and you'll find bleak City Hall Plaza a bustling, jubilant spot.

TOP ATTRACTIONS

Blackstone Block. Between North and Hanover streets, near the Haymarket, lies the Blackstone Block, now visited mostly for its culinary landmark the **Union Oyster House.** Named for one of Boston's first settlers, William Blaxton, or Blackstone, it's the city's oldest commercial block, for decades dominated by the butcher trade. As a tiny remnant of Old Boston, the Blackstone Block remains the city's "family attic"—to use the winning metaphor of critic Donlyn Lyndon: more than three centuries of architecture are on view, ranging from the 18th-century Capen House to the modern Bostonian Hotel. A colonial-period warren of winding lanes surrounds the block.

Facing the Blackstone Block, in tiny **Union Park,** framed by Congress Street and Dock Square, are two bronze figures, one seated on a bench and the other standing eye to eye with passersby. Both represent James Michael Curley, the quintessential Boston pol and a questionable role model for urban bosses. It's just as well that he has no pedestal. Also known as "the Rascal King" or "the Mayor of the Poor," and dramatized by Spencer Tracy in *The Last Hurrah* (1958), the charismatic Curley was beloved by the city's dominant working-class Irish for bringing them libraries, hospitals, bathhouses, and other public-works projects. His career got off to a promising start in 1903, when he ran—and won—a campaign for alderman from the Charles Street Jail, where he was serving time for taking someone else's civil-service exam.

Over the next 50 years he dominated Boston politics, serving four nonconsecutive terms as mayor, one term as governor, and four terms as congressman. No one seemed to mind the slight glitch created when his office moved, in 1946, to the federal penitentiary, where he served five

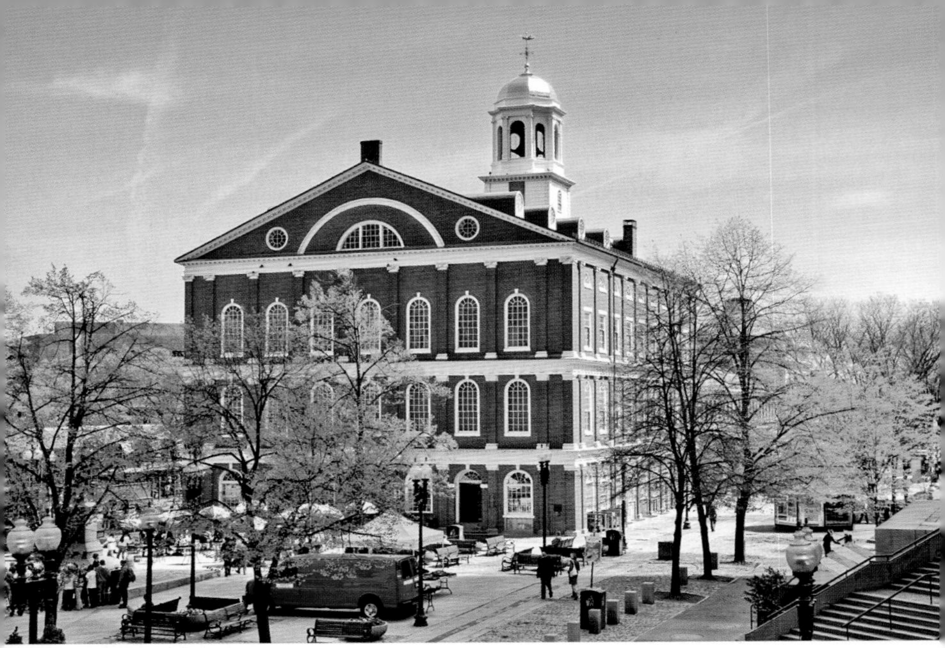
Imagine Samuel Adams stoking the fires of revolution at Faneuil Hall.

months of a 6- to 18-month sentence for mail fraud: he was pardoned by President Truman and returned to his people a hero.

Faneuil Hall. The single building facing Congress Street is the real Faneuil Hall, though locals often give that name to all five buildings in this shopping complex. Bostonians pronounce it *Fan*-yoo'uhl or *Fan*-yuhl. Like other Boston landmarks, Faneuil Hall has evolved over many years. It was erected in 1742, the gift of wealthy merchant Peter Faneuil, who wanted the hall to serve as both a place for town meetings and a public market. It burned in 1761 and was immediately reconstructed according to the original plan of its designer, the Scottish portrait painter John Smibert (who lies in the Granary Burying Ground). In 1763 the political leader James Otis helped inaugurate the era that culminated in American independence when he dedicated the rebuilt hall to the cause of liberty.

In 1772 Samuel Adams stood here and first suggested that Massachusetts and the other colonies organize a Committee of Correspondence to maintain semiclandestine lines of communication in the face of hardening British repression. In later years the hall again lived up to Otis's dedication when the abolitionists Wendell Phillips and Charles Sumner pleaded for support from its podium. The tradition continues to this day: in presidential-election years the hall is the site of debates between contenders in the Massachusetts primary.

Faneuil Hall was substantially enlarged and remodeled in 1805 according to a Greek Revival design of the noted architect Charles Bulfinch; this is the building you see today. Its purposes remain the same: the balconied Great Hall is available to citizens' groups on presentation of a request signed by a required number of responsible parties; it also plays host to regular concerts.

Inside Faneuil Hall are dozens of paintings of famous Americans, including the mural *Webster's Reply to Hayne* and Gilbert Stuart's portrait of Washington at Dorchester Heights. Park rangers give informational talks about the history and importance of Faneuil Hall every half hour. There are interactive displays about Boston sights and National Park Service rangers at the visitor center on the first floor can provide maps and other information.

Faneuil Hall has always sat in the middle of Boston's main marketplace. When such men as Andrew Jackson and Daniel Webster debated the future of the Republic here, the fragrances of bacon and snuff—sold by merchants in **Quincy Market** across the road—greeted their noses. Today the aroma of coffee wafts through the hall from a snack bar. The shops at ground level sell New England bric-a-brac. ✉ *Faneuil Hall Sq., Government Center* ☎ *617/523–1300* 🌐 *www.cityofboston.gov/freedomtrail/faneuilhall.asp* 🎫 *Free* ⏲ *Great Hall daily 9–5; informational talks every ½ hr. Shops Mon.–Sat. 10 am–9 pm, Sun. 11 am–6 pm. Visitor center daily 9–5* Ⓜ *Government Center, Aquarium, State.*

Ancient & Honorable Artillery Company of Massachusetts. On the building's top floors are the headquarters and museum of the Ancient & Honorable Artillery Company of Massachusetts. Founded in 1638, it's the oldest militia in the Western Hemisphere, and the third oldest in the world, after the Swiss Guard and the Honorable Artillery Company of London. Its status is now strictly ceremonial, but it's justly proud of the arms, uniforms, and other artifacts on display. Admission is free. The museum is open weekdays 9 to 3. ☎ *617/227–1638* 🌐 *www.ahac.us.com*

Fodor's Choice ★

Holocaust Memorial. At night its six 50-foot-high glass-and-steel towers glow like ghosts. During the day the monument seems at odds with the 18th-century streetscape of Blackstone Square behind it. Shoehorned into the north end of Union Park, the Holocaust Memorial is the work of Stanley Saitowitz, whose design was selected through an international competition; the finished memorial was dedicated in 1995. Recollections by Holocaust survivors are set into the glass-and-granite walls; the upper levels of the towers are etched with 6 million numbers in random sequence, symbolizing the Jewish victims of the Nazi horror. Manufactured steam from grates in the granite base makes for a particularly haunting scene after dark. ✉ *Union St. near Hanover St., Government Center* ☎ *617/457–8755* 🌐 *www.nehm.org.*

Quincy Market. Not everyone likes Quincy Market, also known as Faneuil Hall Marketplace; some people prefer grit to polish, and disdain the shiny cafés and boutiques. But there's no denying that this pioneer effort at urban recycling set the tone for many similar projects throughout the country, and that it has brought tremendous vitality to a once-tired corner of Boston. Quincy Market continues to attract huge crowds of tourists and locals throughout the year. In the early '70s, demolition was a distinct possibility for the decrepit buildings. Fortunately, with the participation of the Boston Redevelopment Authority,

The haunting Holocaust Memorial sits at the north end of Union Park.

architect Benjamin Thompson planned a renovation of Quincy Market, and the Rouse Corporation of Baltimore undertook its restoration, which was completed in 1976. Try to look beyond the shop windows to the grand design of the market buildings themselves; they represent a vision of the market as urban centerpiece, an idea whose time has certainly come again.

The market consists of three block-long annexes: **Quincy Market, North Market,** and **South Market,** each 535 feet long and across a plaza from Faneuil Hall. The structures were designed in 1826 by Alexander Parris as part of a public-works project instituted by Boston's second mayor, Josiah Quincy, to alleviate the cramped conditions of Faneuil Hall and clean up the refuse that collected in Town Dock, the pond behind it. The central structure, made of granite, with a Doric colonnade at either end and topped by a classical dome and rotunda, has kept its traditional market-stall layout, but the stalls now purvey international and specialty foods: sushi, frozen yogurt, bagels, calzones, sausage-on-a-stick, Chinese noodles, barbecue, and baklava, plus all the boutique chocolate-chip cookies your heart desires. This is perhaps Boston's best locale for grazing.

Along the arcades on either side of the Central Market are vendors selling sweatshirts, photographs of Boston, and arts and crafts—some schlocky, some not—alongside a couple of patioed bars and restaurants. The North and South markets house a mixture of chain stores and specialty boutiques. Quintessential Boston remains here only in Durgin Park, opened in 1826 and known for its plain interior, brassy waitresses, and large portions of traditional New England fare.

A greenhouse flower market on the north side of Faneuil Hall provides a splash of color; during the winter holidays, trees along the cobblestone walks are strung with thousands of sparkling lights. In summer up to 50,000 people a day descend on the market; the outdoor cafés are an excellent spot to watch the hordes if you can find a seat. Year-round the pedestrian walkways draw street performers, and rings of strollers form around magicians and musicians. ✉ *Bordered by Clinton, Commercial, and Chatham Sts., Government Center* ☎ *617/523–1300* 🌐 *www.faneuilhallmarketplace.com* 🕑 *Mon.–Sat. 10–9, Sun. 11–6. Restaurants and bars generally open daily 11 am–2 am; food stalls open earlier* Ⓜ *Government Center, Aquarium, State.*

PAHK YOUR CAH

Government Center and the North End are best seen on foot, but if you must bring a car, here are some tips. There is parking near Government Center at 75 State Street. Be sure to ask for the $3-off parking coupon when purchasing anything at Quincy Market or Faneuil Hall.

The North End barely has enough parking for residents let alone visitors. The closest parking garages to Hanover Street (the North End's main thoroughfare) are the Dock Square Garage (✉ *20 Clinton St.*) and Parcel 7 Garage (✉ *136 Blackstone St.*).

3

Union Oyster House. Billed as the oldest restaurant in continuous service in the United States, the Union Oyster House first opened its doors as the Atwood & Bacon Oyster House in 1826. Charles Forster of Maine was the first American to use the curious invention of the toothpick on these premises. And John F. Kennedy was also among its patrons; his favorite booth has been dedicated to his memory. The charming facade is constructed of Flemish bond brick and adorned with Victorian-style signage. With its scallop, clam, and lobster dishes—as well as the de rigueur oyster—the menu hasn't changed much since the restaurant's early days (though the prices have). ✉ *41 Union St., Government Center* ☎ *617/227–2750* 🌐 *www.unionoysterhouse.com* 🕑 *Sun.–Thurs. 11–9:30, Fri. and Sat. 11–10; bar open until midnight* Ⓜ *Haymarket.*

NEED A BREAK?

Black Rose. If all that snacking has you craving something more substantial, you might want to sample the cuisine of Boston's Irish at the Black Rose; take a right at the far end of the South Market. The bar-restaurant features traditional Irish fare and live music seven nights a week. ✉ ***160 State St., Government Center*** ☎ ***617/742–2286*** 🌐 ***www.blackroseboston.com.***

WORTH NOTING

City Hall. Over the years, various plans—involving gardens, restaurants, music, and hotels—have been floated to make this a more people-friendly site. Possibly the only thing that would ameliorate Bostonians' collective distaste for the chilly Government Center is tearing it down. But for the moment, City Hall, an upside-down ziggurat design on a brutalist redbrick plaza remains in commission. The design, by

Kallman, McKinnell, and Knowles, confines administrative functions to the upper floors and places offices that deal with the public at street level. ✉ *One City Hall Sq., Government Center* Ⓜ *Government Center.*

The Haymarket. Loud, self-promoting vendors pack this exuberant maze of a marketplace at Marshall and Blackstone streets on Friday and Saturday from dawn to dusk (most vendors are usually gone by 5). Pushcart vendors hawk fruits and vegetables against a backdrop of fish, meat, and cheese shops. The accumulation of debris left every evening has been celebrated in a whimsical 1976 public-arts project—Mags Harries's *Asaroton,* a Greek word meaning "unswept floors"—consisting of bronze fruit peels and other detritus smashed into pavement. Another Harries piece, a bronze depiction of a gathering of stray gloves, tumbles down between the escalators in the Porter Square T station in Cambridge. At Creek Square, near the Haymarket, is the **Boston Stone.** Set into a brick wall, this was allegedly a marker used as milepost zero in measuring distances from Boston. ✉ *Marshall and Blackstone Sts., Government Center* ⏲ *Fri. and Sat. 7 am–mid-afternoon* Ⓜ *Government Center.*

John F. Kennedy Federal Office Building. Looming at the northwest edge of City Hall Plaza, these twin towers are noted structures for architecture aficionados: they were designed by the founder of the Bauhaus movement, Walter Gropius, who taught at Harvard toward the end of his illustrious career. Gropius's house, designed by him in textbook Bauhaus style, is in nearby suburban Lincoln. ✉ *15 New Sudbury St., Government Center.*

THE NORTH END

On the northeast side of Government Center is the North End, Boston's Little Italy. In the 17th century the North End *was* Boston, as much of the rest of the peninsula was still under water or had yet to be cleared. Here the town bustled and grew rich for a century and a half before the birth of American independence. Now visitors can get a glimpse into Revolutionary times while filling up on some of the most scrumptious pastries and pastas to be found in modern Boston.

Today's North End is almost entirely a creation of the late 19th century, when brick tenements began to fill up with European immigrants—first the Irish, then Central European Jews, then the Portuguese, and finally the Italians. For more than 60 years, the North End attracted an Italian population base, so much so that one wonders whether wandering Puritan shades might scowl at the concentration of Mediterranean verve, volubility, and Roman Catholicism here. This is Boston's haven not only for Italian restaurants but also for Italian groceries, bakeries, boccie courts, churches, social clubs, cafés, and street-corner debates over home-team soccer games. **TIP→ July and August are highlighted by a series of street festivals, or feste, honoring various saints, and by local community events that draw people from all over the city. A statue of St. Agrippina di Mineo—which is covered with money when it's paraded through the streets—is a crowd favorite.**

TWO WAYS TO EXPLORE THE NORTH END

LA DOLCE VITA

Known as Boston's Little Italy, the North End has, in addition to an abundance of top-notch Italian eateries, many deliciously authentic Italian bakeries and cafés. Take a stroll down **Hanover Street,** the main thoroughfare, and you'll find all the cannoli and cappuccinos your heart could desire. On this street alone you'll find Caffe Paradiso at 255, Caffe Pompei at 278, and Caffe Vittoria at 290. Have a seat in any of these to relax, have a small snack, and take in the scene. Hanover Street is almost always crowded on weekend afternoons and nights, so it's an excellent place to people-watch. If you're looking to take a piece of the North End home with you in a little cardboard box tied up with string, visit one of Hanover's excellent bakeries: Modern Pastry Shop at 257, Mike's Pastry at 300, or Bova's Bakery at 134 Salem Street. Bova's claim to fame is that it is open 24 hours a day, so it is at your service no matter when the craving strikes.

RELIVE REVOLUTIONARY HISTORY

Since the North End was Boston at the time of the Revolution, some of the city's most historic buildings reside here. Visit the **Paul Revere House,** the oldest home in Boston, and learn how this legendary patriot made his historic midnight ride to warn of the oncoming British troops. The **Pierce-Hitchborn house** next door was owned by some of Revere's relatives and provides a peek into 18th-century middle-class life. Also in the North End is **Old North Church,** where Paul Revere hung two lanterns to signal that the British troops would depart by sea. Finally, stroll the **Prado,** or Paul Revere Mall, to see the bronze statue that commemorates Revere's famous ride.

Although hordes of visitors follow the redbrick ribbon of the Freedom Trail through the North End, the jumbled streets retain a neighborhood feeling, from the grandmothers gossiping on fire escapes to the laundry strung on back porches. Gentrification diluted the quarter's ethnic character some, but linger for a moment along Salem or Hanover streets and you can still hear people speaking with Abruzzese accents. If you wish to study up on this fascinating district, head for the North End branch of the Boston Public Library on Parmenter Street, where a bust of Dante acknowledges local cultural pride.

TOP ATTRACTIONS

Copp's Hill Burying Ground. An ancient and melancholy air hovers like a fine mist over this colonial-era burial ground. The North End graveyard incorporates four cemeteries established between 1660 and 1819. Near the Charter Street gate is the tomb of the Mather family, the dynasty of church divines (Cotton and Increase were the most famous sons) who held sway in Boston during the heyday of the old theocracy. Also buried here is Robert Newman, who crept into the steeple of the Old North Church to hang the lanterns warning of the British attack the night of Paul Revere's ride. Look for the tombstone of Captain Daniel Malcolm;

it's pockmarked with musket-ball fire from British soldiers, who used the stones for target practice. Across the street at 44 Hull is the **narrowest house in Boston**—it's a mere 10 feet across. ✉ *Intersection of Hull and Snowhill Sts., North End* 🌐 *www.cityofboston.gov/freedomtrail/coppshill.asp* 🕒 *Daily 9–5* Ⓜ *North Station.*

DID YOU KNOW?

Longfellow's poem aside, the Old North Church lanterns were not a signal *to* Paul Revere but *from* him to Charlestown across the harbor.

Hanover Street. This is the North End's main thoroughfare, along with the smaller and narrower Salem Street. It was named for the ruling dynasty of 18th- and 19th-century England; the label was retained after the Revolution, despite a flurry of patriotic renaming (King Street became State Street, for example). Hanover's business center is thick with restaurants, pastry shops, and Italian cafés; on weekends, Italian immigrants who have moved to the suburbs return to share an espresso with old friends and maybe catch a soccer game broadcast via satellite. Hanover is one of Boston's oldest public roads, once the site of the residences of the Rev. Cotton Mather and the colonial-era patriot Dr. Joseph Warren, as well as a small dry-goods store run by Eben D. Jordan—who went on to launch the Jordan Marsh department stores. ✉ *North End.*

NEED A BREAK?

Caffe Vittoria. Caffe Vittoria is rightfully known as Boston's most traditional Italian café. Gleaming brass, marble tabletops, and one of the city's best selections of grappa keep the place packed with locals. ✉ ***290–296 Hanover St., North End*** ☎ ***617/227-7606*** 🌐 ***www.vittoriacaffe.com.***

Fodor's Choice ★

Old North Church. At one end of the **Paul Revere Mall** is a church famous not only for being the oldest standing church building in Boston (built in 1723) but for housing the two lanterns that glimmered from its steeple on the night of April 18, 1775. This is Christ, or Old North, Church, where Paul Revere and the young sexton Robert Newman managed that night to signal the departure by water of the British regulars to Lexington and Concord.

Although William Price designed the structure after studying Christopher Wren's London churches, Old North—which still has an active Episcopal congregation (including descendants of the Reveres)—is an impressive building in its own right. Inside, note the gallery and the graceful arrangement of pews; the bust of George Washington, pronounced by the Marquis de Lafayette to be the truest likeness of the general he ever saw; the brass chandeliers, made in Amsterdam in 1700 and installed here in 1724; and the clock, the oldest still running in an American public building. The pews—No. 54 belonged to the Revere family—have the tallest walls in the United States because of the little charcoal-burning foot warmers. Try to visit when changes are rung on the bells, after the 11 am Sunday service; they bear the inscription, "We are the first ring of bells cast for the British Empire in North America." On the Sunday closest to April 18, descendants of the patriots reenact

The statue of Paul Revere outside the Old North Church commemorates his famous ride.

the raising of the lanterns in the church belfry during a special evening service. Visitors are welcome to drop in, but to see the bell-ringing chamber and the crypts, take the 30-minute behind-the-scenes tour offered Monday to Saturday.

Behind the church is the **Washington Memorial Garden,** where volunteers cultivate a plot devoted to plants and flowers favored in the 18th century. The garden is studded with several unusual commemorative plaques, including one for the Rev. George Burrough, who was hanged in the Salem witch trials in 1692; Robert Newman was his great-grandson. In another niche hangs the "Third Lantern," dedicated in 1976 to mark the country's bicentennial celebration. ✉ *193 Salem St., North End* ☎ *617/523–6676* 🌐 *www.oldnorth.com* 🕒 *Jan. and Feb., Tues.–Sun. 10–4; Mar.–May, daily 9–5; June–Oct., daily 9–6; Nov. and Dec., daily 10–5. Sun. services at 9 and 11 am* Ⓜ *Haymarket, North Station.*

WORTH NOTING

Ebenezer Clough House. Built in 1712, this house is now the only local survivor of its era aside from Old North Church, which stands nearby. Picture the streets lined with houses such as this, with an occasional grander Georgian mansion and some modest wooden-frame survivors of Old Boston's many fires—this is what the North End looked like when Paul Revere was young. Today, the lower rooms serve as the Old North gift shop, with Captain Jackson's Colonial Chocolate Shop and the Printing Office of Edes & Gill, which offer an interactive look into the past. Watch a chocolate demonstration (and get a taste) and then learn how printers worked in the colonial era. ✉ *21 Unity St., North*

CLOSE UP

Paul Revere's Ride

Test: Paul Revere was (1) a patriot whose midnight ride helped ignite the American Revolution; (2) a part-time dentist; (3) a silversmith who crafted tea services; (4) a printer who engraved the first Massachusetts state currency; or (5) a talented metallurgist who cast cannons and bells. The only correct response is "all of the above." But there's much more to this outsize Revolutionary hero—bell ringer for the Old North Church, founder of the copper mills that still bear his name, and father of 16 children.

Although his life spanned eight decades (1734–1818), Revere is most famous for that one night, April 18, 1775, when he became America's most celebrated Pony Express rider. *"Listen, my children, and you shall hear / Of the midnight ride of Paul Revere"* are the opening lines of Henry Wadsworth Longfellow's poem, which placed the event at the center of American folklore. Longfellow may have been an effective evangelist for Revere, but he was an indifferent historian.

Revere wasn't the only midnight rider. As part of the system set in motion by Revere and William Dawes Jr., also dispatched from Boston, there were at least several dozen riders, so that the capture of any one of them wouldn't keep the alarm from being sounded. It's also known that Revere never looked for the lantern signal from Charlestown. He told Robert Newman to hang two lanterns from Old North's belfry since the Redcoats were on the move by water, but by that time Revere was already being rowed across the Charles River to begin his famous ride.

Revere and Dawes set out on separate routes, but had the same mission: to warn patriot leaders Samuel Adams and John Hancock that British regular troops were marching to arrest them, and alarm the countryside along the way. The riders didn't risk capture by shouting the news through the streets—and they never uttered the famous cry "The British are coming!," since Bostonians still considered themselves British. When Revere arrived in Lexington a few minutes past midnight and approached the house where Adams and Hancock were lodged, a sentry challenged him, requesting that he not make so much noise. "Noise!" Revere replied. "You'll have noise enough before long."

Despite Longfellow's assertion, Revere never raised the alarm in Concord, because he was captured en route. He was held and questioned by the British patrol, and eventually released, without his horse, to walk back to Lexington in time to witness part of the battle on Lexington Green.

Poetic license aside, this tale has become part of the collective American spirit. Americans dote on hearing that Revere forgot his spurs, only to retrieve them by tying a note to his dog's collar, then awaiting its return with the spurs attached. The resourcefulness he showed in using a lady's petticoat to muffle the sounds of his oars while crossing the Charles is greatly appreciated. Little wonder that these tales resonate in the hearts and imagination of America's citizenry, as well as in Boston's streets on the third Monday of every April, Patriots' Day, when Revere's ride is reenacted—in daylight—to the cheers of thousands of onlookers.

3

End ☎ *617/523–4848* ⏲ *Chocolate and printing shops open April 15–June 14 weekends 11–5, June 15–Oct. 31 daily 11–5. Gift shop open year-round; call for hours.*

FAMILY **Paul Revere House.** Originally on the site was the parsonage of the Second Church of Boston, home to the Rev. Increase Mather, the Second Church's minister. Mather's house burned in the great fire of 1676, and the house that Revere was to occupy was built on its location about four years later, nearly a hundred years before Revere's 1775 midnight ride through Middlesex County. Revere owned it from 1770 until 1800, although he lived there for only 10 years and rented it out for the next two decades. Pre-1900 photographs show it as a shabby warren of storefronts and apartments. The clapboard sheathing is a replacement, but 90% of the framework is original; note the Elizabethan-style overhang and leaded windowpanes. A few Revere furnishings are on display here, and just gazing at his silverwork—much more of which is displayed at the Museum of Fine Arts—brings the man alive. **TIP→ Special events are scheduled throughout the year, many designed with children in mind.**

The immediate neighborhood also has Revere associations. The little park in North Square is named after Rachel Revere, his second wife, and the adjacent brick **Pierce-Hichborn House** once belonged to relatives of Revere. The garden connecting the Revere house and the Pierce-Hichborn House is planted with flowers and medicinal herbs favored in Revere's day. ✉ *19 North Sq., North End* ☎ *617/523–2338* 🌐 *www.paulreverehouse.org* 🎫 *$3.50, $5.50 with Pierce-Hichborn House* ⏲ *Mid-April–Oct. 9:30–5:15, Nov.–mid-April 9:30–4:15. Closed Mondays Jan.–March.* Ⓜ *Haymarket, Aquarium, Government Center.*

Paul Revere Mall (*Prado*). This makes a perfect time-out spot from the Freedom Trail. Bookended by two landmark churches—Old North and St. Stephen's—the mall is flanked by brick walls lined with bronze plaques bearing the stories of famous North Enders. An appropriate centerpiece for this enchanting cityscape is Cyrus Dallin's equestrian **statue of Paul Revere.** Despite his depictions in such statues as this, the gentle Revere was stocky and of medium height—whatever manly dash he possessed must have been in his eyes rather than his physique. That physique served him well enough, however, for he lived to be 83 and saw nearly all of his Revolutionary comrades buried. ✉ *Bordered by Tileston, Hanover, and Unity Sts., North End* Ⓜ *Haymarket, Aquarium, Government Center.*

Pierce-Hichborn House. One of the city's oldest brick buildings, this structure, just to the left of the Paul Revere House, was once owned by Nathaniel Hichborn, a boatbuilder and Revere's cousin on his mother's side. Built about 1711 for a window maker named Moses Pierce, the Pierce-Hichborn House is an excellent example of early Georgian architecture. The home's symmetrical style was a radical change from the wood-frame Tudor buildings, such as the Revere House, then common. Its four rooms are furnished with modest 18th-century furniture, providing a peek into typical middle-class life. ✉ *29 North Sq., North End* ☎ *617/523–2338* 🎫 *$2, $5.50 with Paul Revere House* ⏲ *Guided* *tours only; call to schedule* Ⓜ *Haymarket, Aquarium, Government Center.*

Rose Kennedy Greenway. The Rose Kennedy Greenway, a winding series of parks marking the path the highway once took through the city, adds much needed flora and fauna to the area. The park's website has a map of its 15 acres; a pleasant stroll through all of them will take you from the North End to Chinatown. ⇨ *See the Sports and Outdoors chapter for more information.* ✉ *North End* 🌐 *www.rosekennedygreenway.org.*

St. Stephen's. Rose Kennedy, matriarch of the Kennedy clan, was christened here; 104 years later, St. Stephen's held mourners at her 1995 funeral. This is the only Charles Bulfinch church still standing in Boston, and a stunning example of the Federal style to boot. Built in 1804, it was first used as a Unitarian Church; since 1862 it has served a Roman Catholic parish. When the belfry was stripped during a major 1960s renovation, the original dome was found beneath a false cap; it was covered with sheet copper and held together with hand-wrought nails, and later authenticated as being the work of Paul Revere. ✉ *401 Hanover St., North End* ☎ *617/523–1230* 🕓 *Open daily 7:30–5. Mass on Sun. at 11, Sat. at 4, Mon.–Fri. at 7:30 am* Ⓜ *Haymarket, Aquarium, Government Center.*

Salem Street. This ancient and constricted thoroughfare, one of the two main North End streets, cuts through the heart of the neighborhood and runs parallel to and one block west of Hanover. Between Cross and Prince streets, Salem Street contains numerous restaurants and shops. One of the best is Shake the Tree, one of the North End's trendiest boutiques, selling stylish clothing, gifts, and jewelry. The rest of Salem Street is mostly residential, but makes a nice walk to the Copp's Hill Burying Ground. ✉ *North End.*

A STICKY SUBJECT

Boston has had its share of grim historic events, from massacres to stranglers, but on the sheer weirdness scale, nothing beats the Great Molasses Flood. In 1919 a steel container of molasses exploded on the Boston Harbor waterfront, killing 21 people and 20 horses. More than 2.3 million gallons of goo oozed onto unsuspecting citizenry, a veritable tsunami of sweet stuff. Some say you can still smell molasses on the waterfront during steamy weather. Smells to us like urban myth!

NEED A BREAK?

Bova's Bakery. The allure of Bova's Bakery, a neighborhood institution, lies not only in its takeaway Italian breads, calzones, and pastries, but also in its hours: 24 a day (the deli closes at 1 am, however). ✉ ***134 Salem St., North End*** ☎ ***617/523–5601*** 🌐 ***www.bovabakeryboston.com.***

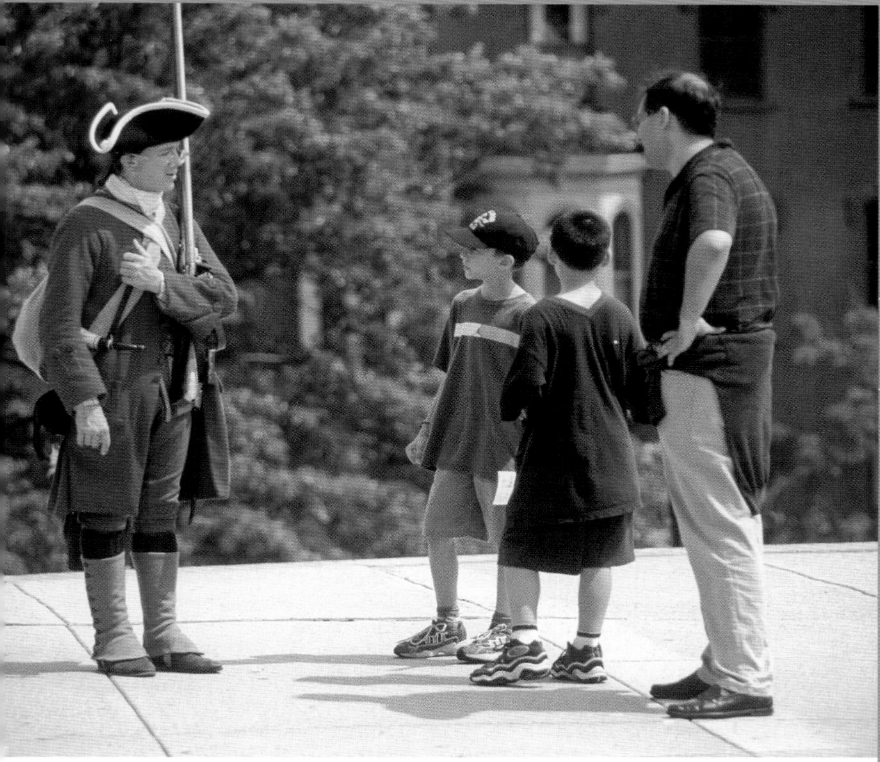

4

CHARLESTOWN

GETTING ORIENTED

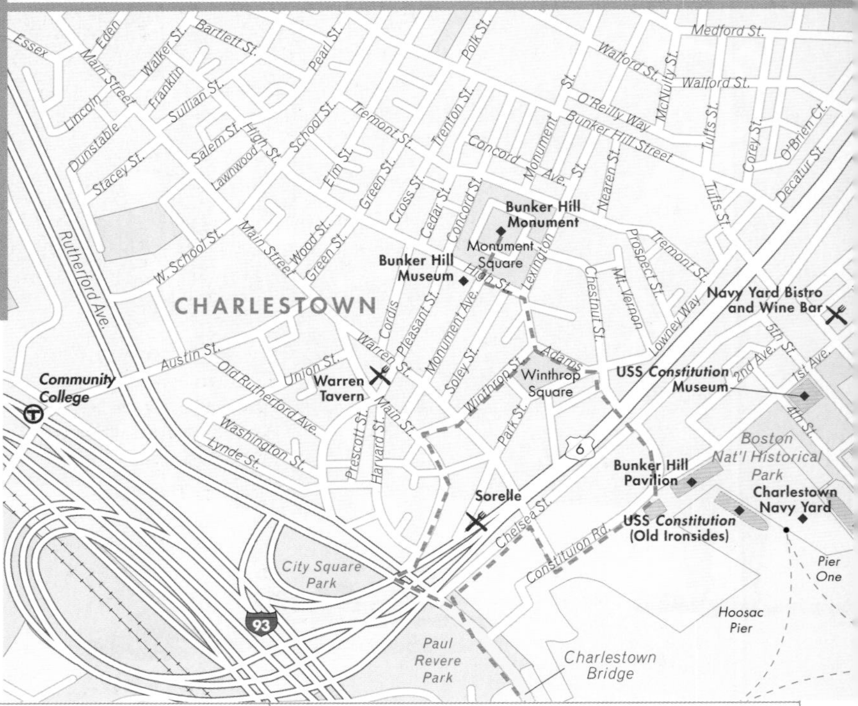

QUICK BITES

American Bakers' Cafe. For coffee, pastries, or a panini at lunchtime, try the Navy Yard's American Bakers' Cafe. ✉ *39 1st Ave., Charlestown* ☎ *617/241–7999.*

Navy Yard Bistro and Wine Bar. Enjoy a cozy dinner at Navy Yard Bistro and Wine Bar. Housed in a National Historic Site in the heart of the Charlestown Navy Yard, this restaurant offers French bistro fare at reasonable prices, with outdoor dining in summer. ✉ *6th St., on corner of 1st Ave., Sixth Street, Charlestown* 🌐 *www.navyyardbistro.com.*

TIMING AND SAFETY

Give yourself two to three hours for a Charlestown walk; the Charlestown Bridge calls for endurance in cold weather. You may want to save Charlestown's stretch of the Freedom Trail, which adds considerably to its length, for a second-day outing. You can always save time backtracking from the route by taking the MBTA water shuttle, which ferries back and forth between Charlestown's Navy Yard and Downtown Boston's Long Wharf.

The Charlestown Navy Yard is generally a safe area, but as always use common sense, as Boston is a big city. Stick to well-lighted streets at night and avoid walking alone.

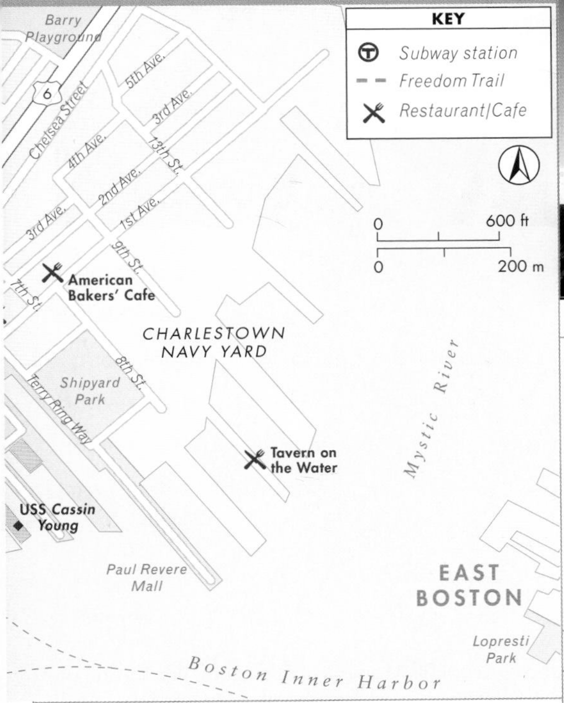

GETTING HERE AND AROUND

The closest subway stop to the Charlestown Navy Yard is North Station (accessible by the Green and Orange lines), about a 15-minute walk. Take Causeway Street northeast and make a left to walk over the Charlestown Bridge. Take a right on Chelsea Street and right again on Warren Street. Constitution Road will be your next left, and from here you can enter the Navy Yard. From Downtown Crossing, take the 93 Bus, which will drop you directly at the Navy Yard. If you are coming from Downtown, try the water shuttle from Long Wharf near the Aquarium. Boats run daily on the hour and half-hour, and the ride is 10 minutes long.

TOP REASONS TO GO

- Climb the 294 steps to the top of the Bunker Hill Monument, and enjoy the views of the city while reliving the battles of the past.
- Tour the USS *Constitution*, and discover why the oldest commissioned warship still afloat in the world is nicknamed "Old Ironsides."

FREEDOM TRAIL SIGHTS

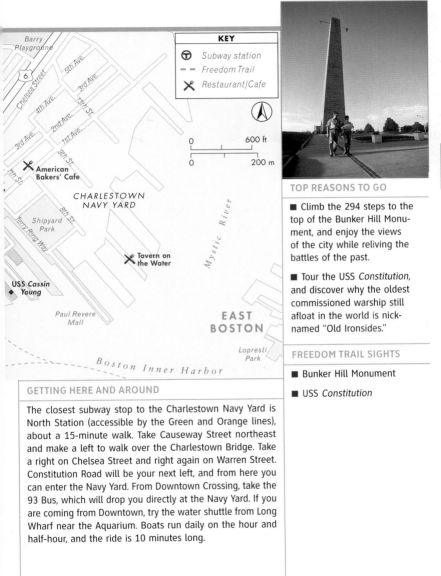

- Bunker Hill Monument
- USS *Constitution*

Sightseeing ★★★
Dining ★★★
Lodging ★
Shopping ★
Nightlife ★★

Boston started here. Charlestown was a thriving settlement a year before colonials headed across the Charles River at William Blaxton's invitation to found the city proper. Today the district's attractions include two of the most visible—and vertical—monuments in Boston: the Bunker Hill Monument, which commemorates the grisly battle that became a symbol of patriotic resistance against the British, and the USS *Constitution,* whose masts continue to tower over the waterfront where it was built more than 200 years ago.

Updated by Kim Foley MacKinnon

The blocks around the Bunker Hill Monument are a good illustration of how gentrification has changed the neighborhoods. Along streets lined with gas lamps are impeccably restored Federal and mid-19th-century town houses; cheek by jowl are working-class quarters of similar vintage but more modest recent pasts. Near the Navy Yard along Main Street is City Square, the beginning of Charlestown's main commercial district, which includes City Square Park, with brick paths and bronze fish sculptures. On Phipps Street is the grave marker of John Harvard, a minister who in 1638 bequeathed his small library to the fledgling Cambridge College, thereafter renamed in his honor. The precise location of the grave is uncertain, but a monument of 1828 marks its approximate site.

TOP ATTRACTIONS

Fodor's Choice ★

Bunker Hill Monument. Three misunderstandings surround this famous monument. First, the Battle of Bunker Hill was actually fought on Breed's Hill, which is where the monument sits today. (The real Bunker Hill is about ½ mile to the north of the monument; it's slightly taller than Breed's Hill.) Bunker was the original planned locale for the battle, and for that reason its name stuck. Second, although the battle is generally considered a colonial success, the Americans lost. It was a Pyrrhic victory for the British Redcoats, who sacrificed nearly half of their 2,200 men; American casualties numbered 400–600. And third: the famous war cry "Don't fire until you see the whites of their eyes" may never have been uttered by American Colonel William Prescott or General Israel Putnam, but if either one did shout it, he was quoting an old Prussian command made necessary by the notorious inaccuracy of the musket. No matter. The Americans did employ a deadly delayed-action strategy on June 17, 1775, and conclusively proved themselves worthy fighters, capable of defeating the forces of the British Empire.

DID YOU KNOW?

The country's first commercial railway was built in 1826 for the express purpose of hauling the granite for the Bunker Hill obelisk from a quarry in Quincy.

Among the dead were the brilliant young American doctor and political activist Joseph Warren, recently commissioned as a major general but fighting as a private, and the British Major John Pitcairn, who two months before had led the Redcoats into Lexington. Pitcairn is believed to be buried in the crypt of Old North Church.

In 1823 the committee formed to construct a monument on the site of the battle chose the form of an Egyptian obelisk. Architect Solomon Willard designed a 221-foot-tall granite obelisk, a tremendous feat of engineering for its day. The Marquis de Lafayette laid the cornerstone of the monument in 1825, but because of a nagging lack of funds, it wasn't dedicated until 1843. Daniel Webster's stirring words at the ceremony commemorating the laying of its cornerstone have gone down in history: "Let it rise! Let it rise, till it meets the sun in his coming. Let the earliest light of the morning gild it, and parting day linger and play upon its summit."

The monument's zenith is reached by a flight of 294 steps. There's no elevator, but the views from the observatory are worth the effort of the arduous climb. A statue of Colonel Prescott stands guard at the base. In the Bunker Hill Museum across the street, artifacts and exhibits tell the story of the battle, while a detailed diorama shows the action in miniature. ✉ *Monument Sq., Charlestown* ☎ *617/242–5641* 🌐 *www.nps.gov/bost/historyculture/bhm.htm* 🎫 *Free* 🕑 *Museum daily 9–5, monument daily 9–4:30* Ⓜ *Community College.*

FAMILY Fodor'sChoice ★ **USS *Constitution*.** Better known as "Old Ironsides," the USS *Constitution* rides proudly at anchor in its berth at the Charlestown Navy Yard. The oldest commissioned ship in the U.S. fleet is a battlewagon of the old school, of the days of "wooden ships and iron men"—when the boat and its crew of 200 succeeded at the perilous task of asserting the sovereignty of an improbable new nation. Every Fourth of July and on certain other occasions, it's towed out for a turnabout in Boston Harbor, the very place its keel was laid in 1797.

The venerable craft has narrowly escaped the scrap heap several times in its long history. The ship was launched on October 21, 1797, as part of the nation's fledgling navy. Its hull was made of live oak, the toughest wood grown in North America; the bottom was sheathed in copper, provided by Paul Revere at a nominal cost. Its principal service was

DID YOU KNOW?

The USS *Constitution* is a bit of an anachronism on the Freedom Trail. Though it is the oldest ship in the Navy, "Old Ironsides" wasn't launched until 1797—well after the American Revolution had been won.

during Thomas Jefferson's campaign against the Barbary pirates, off the coast of North Africa, and in the War of 1812. In 42 engagements its record was 42–0.

The nickname "Old Ironsides" was acquired during the War of 1812, when shots from the British warship *Guerrière* appeared to bounce off the hull. Talk of scrapping the ship began as early as 1830, but it was saved by a public campaign sparked by Oliver Wendell Holmes's poem "Old Ironsides." The ship underwent a major restoration in the early 1990s, and only about 8%–10% of the original wood remains in place, including the keel, the heart of the ship. Today it continues, the oldest commissioned warship afloat in the world, to be a part of the U.S. Navy.

A GOOD WALK

If you choose to hoof it to Charlestown, follow Hull Street from Copp's Hill Burying Ground to Commercial Street; turn left on Commercial and, two blocks later, right onto the bridge. The entrance to the **Charlestown Navy Yard** is on your right after crossing the bridge. Just ahead is the Charlestown Navy Yard Visitors Information Center; inside the park gate are the **USS *Constitution*** and the associated **USS *Constitution* Museum**. From here, the Red Line of the Freedom Trail takes you to the **Bunker Hill Monument**.

The men and women who look after the *Constitution*, regular navy personnel, maintain a 24-hour watch. Sailors show visitors around the ship, guiding them to the top, or spar, deck, and the gun deck below. Another treat when visiting the ship is the spectacular view of Boston across Boston Harbor. Take a few minutes to explore the excellent Navy Yard Visitor Center for an overview before boarding. **TIP→ Instead of taking the T, you can get closer to the ship by taking MBTA Bus 93 to Chelsea Street from Haymarket. Or you can take the Boston Harbor Cruise water shuttle from Long Wharf to Pier 4.** ✉ *Charlestown Navy Yard, 55 Constitution Rd., Charlestown* ☎ *617/242–7511* 🌐 *www.history.navy.mil/ussconstitution* *Free* ⏲ *Apr. 1–Sept., Tues.–Sun. 10–6; Oct., Tues.–Sun. 10–4; Nov.–Mar., Thurs.–Sun. 10–4; last tour at 3:30* Ⓜ *North Station.*

NEED A BREAK?

Pier 6. For a meal on the waterfront, try Pier 6 (in the old digs of Tavern on the Water) in the Charlestown Navy Yard. It's got outstanding harbor views and the requisite New England seafood dishes. ✉ ***1 8th St., Pier 6, Charlestown*** ☎ ***617/242–8040.***

Warren Tavern. After a blustery walk at the Navy Yard, get a seat by the fireplace and warm yourself with a hearty chowder and Sam Adams draft at the Warren Tavern. Built in 1780, this restored colonial neighborhood pub was once frequented by George Washington and Paul Revere. It was one of the first buildings reconstructed after the Battle of Bunker Hill, which leveled Charlestown. ✉ ***2 Pleasant St., Charlestown*** ☎ ***617/241–8142*** 🌐 ***www.warrentavern.com.***

WORTH NOTING

Charlestown Navy Yard. A National Park Service Historic Site since it was decommissioned in 1974, the Charlestown Navy Yard was one of six established to build warships. For 174 years, as wooden hulls and muzzle-loading cannons gave way to steel ships and sophisticated electronics, the yard evolved to meet the Navy's changing needs. Here are early-19th-century barracks, workshops, and officers' quarters; a ropewalk (an elongated building for making rope, not open to the public), designed in 1834 by the Greek Revival architect Alexander Parris and used by the Navy to turn out cordage for more than 125 years; and one of the oldest operational naval dry docks in the United States. The USS *Constitution* was the first to use this dry dock, in 1833. In addition to the ship itself, check out the *Constitution* Museum, the collections of the Boston Marine Society, and the USS *Cassin Young*, a World War II destroyer typical of the ships built here during that era. At the entrance of the Navy Yard is the **Charlestown Navy Yard Visitors Information Center,** with exhibits on ships and a fun little shop. A 10-minute movie about the Navy Yard runs every 15 minutes in a small theater. ✉ *55 Constitution Rd., Charlestown* ☎ *617/242–5601* 🌐 *www.nps.gov/bost/historyculture/cny.htm* 🕓 *Visitor information center Sept.–June, daily 9–5; July and Aug., daily 9–6* Ⓜ *North Station; MBTA Bus 92 to Charlestown City Sq. or Bus 93 to Chelsea St. from Haymarket; or Boston Harbor Cruise water shuttle from Long Wharf to Pier 4.*

NEED A BREAK?

Sorelle. Walking the Freedom Trail is exhausting. Whether Charlestown is your stopping or ending point, take a breather at Sorelle, a hot little bakery with three locations, delicious sandwiches, and refreshing iced coffees. ✉ ***100 City Sq., Charlestown*** ☎ ***617/242-5980*** 🌐 ***www.sorellecafe.com.***

USS *Cassin Young*. From a later date than the *Constitution,* this destroyer saw action in Asian waters during World War II. It served the Navy until 1960. Currently in dry dock for repairs, you can still walk beside it and take in its size. ✉ *Charlestown Navy Yard, 55 Constitution Rd., Charlestown* ☎ *617/242–5601* 🌐 *www.nps.gov/bost/historyculture/usscassinyoung.htm* 🎟 *Free* 🕓 *Call for information.* Ⓜ *North Station; MBTA Bus 92 to Charlestown City Sq. or Bus 93 to Chelsea St. from Haymarket; or Boston Harbor Cruise water shuttle from Long Wharf to Pier 4.*

USS *Constitution* Museum. Artifacts pertaining to the USS *Constitution* are on display—firearms, logs, and instruments. One section takes you step by step through the ship's most important battles. Old meets new in a video-game battle "fought" at the helm of a ship. Kids will love to climb into hammocks and maybe even scrub the decks in interactive exhibits. ✉ *Adjacent to USS Constitution, Charlestown Navy Yard, Charlestown* ☎ *617/426–1812* 🌐 *www.ussconstitutionmuseum.org* 🎟 *Suggested donation $5* 🕓 *Apr.–Oct., daily 9–6; Nov.–Mar., daily 10–5* Ⓜ *North Station; MBTA Bus 92 to Charlestown City Sq. or Bus 93 to Chelsea St. from Haymarket; or Boston Harbor Cruise water shuttle from Long Wharf to Pier 4.*

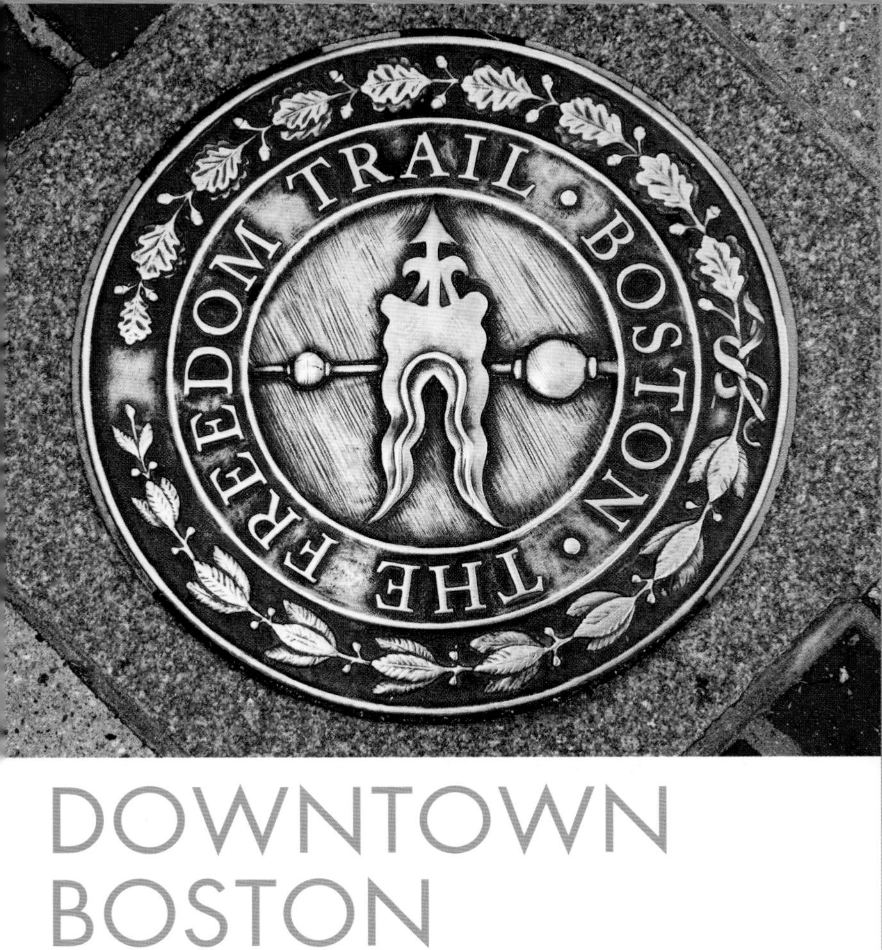

DOWNTOWN BOSTON

GETTING ORIENTED

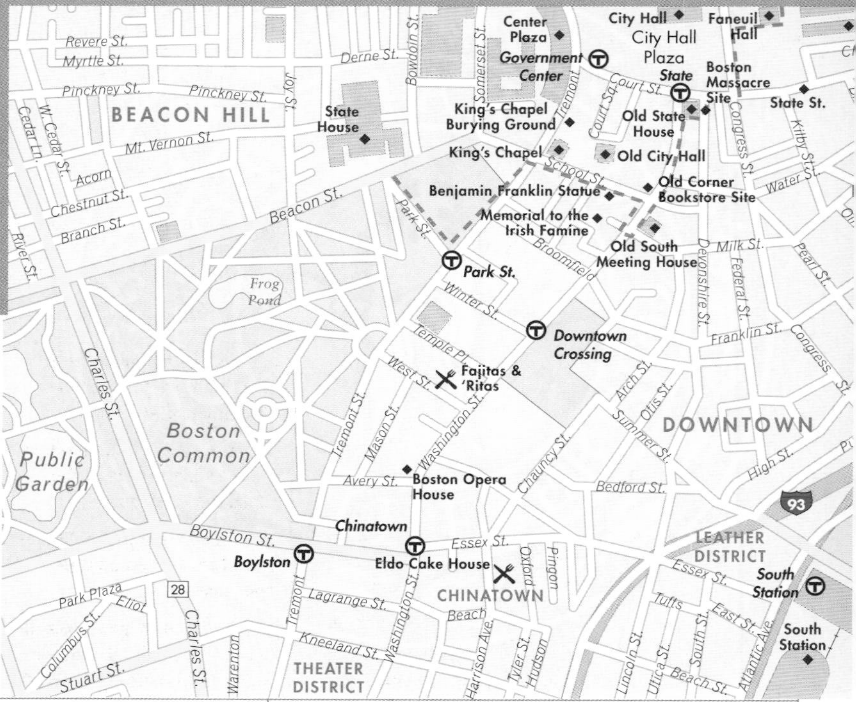

GETTING HERE AND AROUND	TIMING AND SAFETY
Downtown Boston is easily accessible by the T; take the Orange Line to Downtown Crossing, the Blue Line to Aquarium, or the Red Line to South Station or Downtown Crossing. If you are in a car, a garage is your best bet; the **Interpark Garage** (✉ *270 Atlantic Ave.*) is near the New England Aquarium. The Children's Museum is a bit farther away: either walk from South Station or park nearby at the **Stanhope Garage** (✉ *338 Congress St.*).	This section of Boston has a generous share of attractions, so it's wise to save a full day for visiting Downtown, spending the bulk of it at the New England Aquarium or the Children's Museum. There are optimum times to catch some sights: dusk for a romantic stroll along the waterfront at Rowes Wharf, and at 2 pm on sunny days for the only time visitors can access the observation deck at the top of the U.S. Custom House (now a Marriott). But there's no need to visit the aquarium at a special hour—feedings and trainings happen several times a day. Downtown is a safe area, but the Financial District empties out after 6 pm, so choose well-lighted streets when walking alone at night.

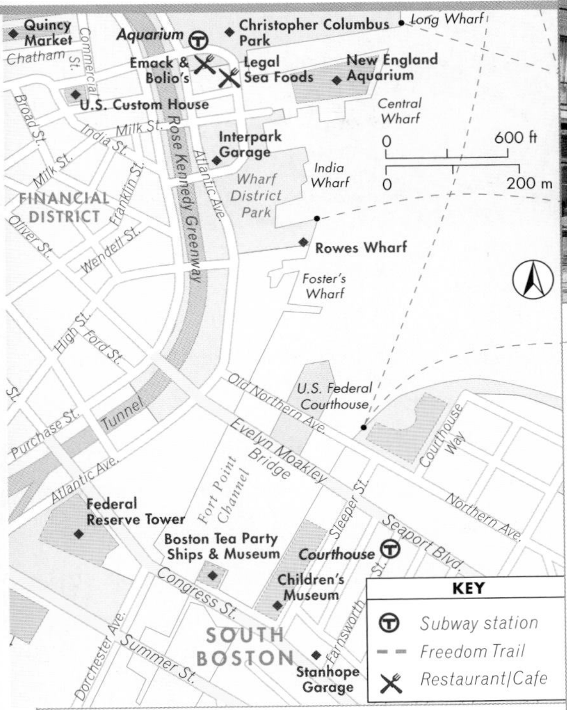

5

QUICK BITES

The quintessential Boston fish haunt, **Legal Sea Foods** (✉ *255 State St.*) is at Long Wharf, steps from the New England Aquarium and other Downtown attractions. Stop in for a bowl of its famous clam chowder—just the thing to take the chill off a cool fall day. For dessert, step right around the corner to **Emack & Bolio's** (✉ *255 State St.*) for homemade ice cream with a rock-and-roll vibe.

DID YOU KNOW?

The Boston Tea Party occurred on Atlantic Avenue near Congress Street. The area was once a wharf—further evidence of Boston's relentless expansion into the harbor. There isn't much to see here now; look for the historical marker commemorating the event on the corner of Congress and Purchase streets.

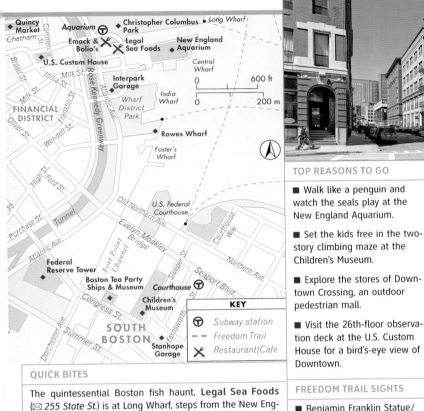

TOP REASONS TO GO

- Walk like a penguin and watch the seals play at the New England Aquarium.
- Set the kids free in the two-story climbing maze at the Children's Museum.
- Explore the stores of Downtown Crossing, an outdoor pedestrian mall.
- Visit the 26th-floor observation deck at the U.S. Custom House for a bird's-eye view of Downtown.

FREEDOM TRAIL SIGHTS

- Benjamin Franklin Statue/ Boston Latin School
- First Public School Site
- King's Chapel and Burying Ground
- Old Corner Bookstore Site
- Old South Meeting House
- Park Street Church

Sightseeing ★★★★
Dining ★★★★
Lodging ★★★★
Shopping ★★★★★
Nightlife ★★★

Boston's commercial and financial districts—the area commonly called Downtown—are concentrated in a maze of streets that seem to have been laid out with little logic; they are, after all, only village lanes that happen to be lined with modern 40-story office towers. Just as the Great Fire of 1872 swept the old Financial District clear, the Downtown construction in more-recent times has obliterated many of the buildings where 19th-century Boston businesspeople sat in front of their rolltop desks. A number of the historic sites that remain tucked among the skyscrapers join together to make up a fascinating section of the Freedom Trail.

Updated by Kim Foley MacKinnon

The area is bordered by State Street on the north and by South Station and Chinatown on the south. Tremont Street and the Common form the west boundary, and the harbor wharves the eastern edge. Locals may be able to navigate the tangle of thoroughfares in between, but visitors are far better off carrying a map.

Washington Street (aka Downtown Crossing) is Downtown's main commercial thoroughfare. It's a pedestrian street once marked by two venerable anchors of Boston's mercantile district, Filene's Basement (now closed) and Jordan Marsh (now Macy's). The block reeks of history—and sausage carts. Street vendors, flower sellers, and gaggles of teenagers, businesspeople, and shoppers throng the pedestrian mall.

Downtown is also the place for some of Boston's most idiosyncratic neighborhoods. The Leather District directly abuts Chinatown, which is also bordered by the Theater District (and the buildings of Tufts Medical Center) farther west, and to the south, the red light of the once-brazen Combat Zone flickers weakly in a pair of adjacent strip clubs. The Massachusetts Turnpike and its junction with the Southeast Expressway cut a wide swath through the area, isolating Chinatown from the South End.

Kids are entertained and educated at the Children's Museum.

TOP ATTRACTIONS

FAMILY **Boston Tea Party Ships & Museum.** After a lengthy renovation, the museum reopened in the summer of 2012 at the Congress St. Bridge where Griffin's Wharf was and the actual spot where the Boston Tea Party took place on December 16, 1773. Visitors can check out *The Beaver II*, a historic reproduction of one of the ships forcibly boarded and unloaded the night Boston Harbor became a teapot, along with a reproduction of the *Eleanor*, another of the ships (the third ship, the *Dartmouth*, is slated to be built in 2014). The museum is big on interaction. Actors in period costumes greet patrons, and after assigning them a colonial persona, ask a few people to heave boxes of tea into the water. Inside, there are 3D Holograms, talking portraits, and even the Robinson Half Tea Chest, one of two original tea chests known to exist. Outside, you can explore replicas of the ships, meet re-enactors, or drink a cup of tea in Abigail's Tea Room, which has one of the best views around. ✉ *Fort Point Channel at Congress St. Bridge, Downtown* 🌐 *www.bostonteapartyship.com* 🎟 *$25 (check website for discounts)* ⏲ *Daily 10–5* Ⓜ *South Station.*

FAMILY Fodor's Choice ★ **Children's Museum.** Most children have so much fun here that they don't realize they're actually learning something. Creative hands-on exhibits demonstrate scientific laws, cultural diversity, and problem solving. Some of the most popular stops are also the simplest, like the bubble-making machinery and the two-story climbing maze. At the Japanese House you're invited to take off your shoes and step inside a two-story silk merchant's home from Kyoto. The "Boston Black" exhibit stimulates dialogue about ethnicity and community, and children can play at a Cape Verdean restaurant and the African Queen Beauty Salon. In the toddler PlaySpace, children under three can run free in a safe environment. There's also a full schedule of special exhibits, festivals, and performances. ✉ *308 Congress St., Downtown* ☎ *617/426–6500* 🌐 *www.bostonkids.org* 🎟 *$14, Fri. 5–9 $1* ⏲ *Sat.–Thurs. 10–5, Fri. 10–9* Ⓜ *South Station.*

FAMILY Fodor's Choice ★ **New England Aquarium.**
See highlighted listing in this chapter.

WORTH NOTING

Benjamin Franklin Statue/Boston Latin School. This stop on the Freedom Trail commemorates the famous revolutionary and inventor. His likeness also marks the original location of Boston Latin School, the country's oldest public school, which still molds young minds, albeit from the Fenway neighborhood today. Franklin attended Boston Latin with three other signers of the Declaration of Independence—Samuel Adams, John Hancock, and Robert Treat Paine—but he has the dubious distinction of being the only one of the four not to graduate. ✉ *School St. at City Hall Ave., Downtown* ☎ *617/357–8300* 🌐 *www.thefreedomtrail.org* Ⓜ *Park.*

Boston Massacre Site. Directly in front of the **Old State House** a circle of cobblestones (on a traffic island) marks the site of the Boston Massacre. It was on the snowy evening of March 5, 1770, that nine British regular soldiers fired in panic upon a taunting mob of more than 75 Bostonians. Five townsmen died. In the legal action that followed, the defense of the accused soldiers was undertaken by John Adams and Josiah Quincy, both of whom vehemently opposed British oppression but were devoted to the principle of fair trial. All but two of the nine regulars charged were acquitted; the others were branded on the hand for the crime of manslaughter. Paul Revere lost little time in capturing the "massacre" in a dramatic engraving that soon became one of the Revolution's most potent images of propaganda. ✉ *Devonshire and Court Sts., Downtown* 🌐 *www.cityofboston.gov/freedomtrail/bostonmassacre.asp* Ⓜ *State.*

Boston Opera House. Originally the B. F. Keith Memorial Theatre in the days of vaudeville, this venue was designed in Beaux-Arts style by Thomas Lamb and modeled after the Paris Opera House. The theater shut its doors in 1991, but a multimillion-dollar restoration completed in 2004 brought theater and dance performances back to the Opera House. ✉ *539 Washington St., Downtown* ☎ *617/259–3400* 🌐 *bostonoperahouseonline.com* Ⓜ *Boylston.*

Chinatown. Boston's Chinatown may seem small, but it's said to be the third largest in the United States, after those in San Francisco and Manhattan. Beginning in the 1870s, Chinese immigrants started to trickle in, many setting up tents in a strip they called Ping On Alley. The trickle increased to a wave when immigration restrictions were lifted in 1968. As in most other American Chinatowns, the restaurants are a big draw; on Sunday many Bostonians head to Chinatown for dim sum. Today the many Chinese establishments—most found along

NEW ENGLAND AQUARIUM

✉ Central Wharf between Central and Milk Sts., 1 Central Wharf, Downtown ☎ 617/973–5200 🌐 www.neaq.org 🎟 $24.95, IMAX $9.95 ⏲ July–early Sept., Sun.–Thurs. 9–6, Fri. and Sat. 9–7; early Sept.–June, weekdays 9–5, weekends 9–6 Ⓜ Aquarium, State.

TIPS

- If you are planning to see an IMAX show as well as check out the aquarium, buy a combo ticket; you'll save $5 for the adult ticket.
- Also, buy the combo ticket if you'd like to do the whale-watch and the aquarium; you'll save $12 if you purchase them together.
- Save yourself the torture of waiting in long weekend lines, and purchase your tickets ahead of time online. You can skip ahead of the crowd and pick up your tickets at the will-call window, or print them out at home.

This aquarium challenges you to imagine life under and around the sea. Its glass-and-steel exterior is constructed to mimic fish scales and seals bark outside. Inside the main facility you'll see penguins, sea otters, sharks, and other exotic sea creatures—more than 30,000 animals, with 800 different species.

Highlights

In the semi-enclosed outdoor space of the New Balance Foundation Marine Mammal Center, visitors enjoy the antics of northern fur seals and sea lions while gazing out at Boston Harbor.

The real showstopper, though, is the newly renovated, four-story, 200,000-gallon ocean-reef tank, one of the largest of its kind in the world. Ramps winding around the tank lead to the top level and allow you to view the inhabitants from many vantage points. Up top, the new Yawkey Coral Reef Center features a seven-tank exhibit gallery that gives a close-up look at animals that might not be easily seen on the reef. Don't miss the five-times-a-day feedings; each lasts nearly an hour and takes divers 24 feet into the tank.

The aquarium has one of the largest exhibits of jellyfish in the country (some grown in the museum's labs.)

Get up close to sharks and rays at the Trust Family Foundation Shark and Ray Touch Tank. The Blue Planet Action Center is a hands-on educational experience where visitors can see shark and lobster nurseries.

At the Edge of the Sea exhibit children can pick up starfish and other creatures. Whale-watch cruises leave from the aquarium's dock from April to October, and cost $45. The 6½-story-high IMAX theater takes you on a 3-D virtual trip from the bottom of the sea to the depths of outer space.

TWO WAYS TO EXPLORE DOWNTOWN

FOR KIDS

Two of the best museums in Boston for children are Downtown: the Children's Museum and the New England Aquarium. Kiddies can run wild in the two-story climbing maze at the Children's Museum and then get up close and personal with seals, penguins, and other marine animals at the aquarium. Both venues are great for rainy day entertainment. End this kid-tastic day with a cherry on top at the Emack and Bolio's ice-cream shop across from the aquarium.

FOR GROWN-UPS

Stop by the King's Chapel to immerse yourself in history and music during one of the regular Tuesday concerts at 12:15 pm. You could easily spend a couple of hours shopping in Downtown Crossing or taking a leisurely walk along the harbor front at Rowes Wharf. While you're there, sample one of the more than 40 different scotches at the Rowes Wharf Bar in the Boston Harbor Hotel. Need an idea for date night? Why not take in a show at the Opera House and savor a late-night dinner for two in Chinatown.

Beach and Tyler streets and Harrison Avenue—are interspersed with Vietnamese, Korean, Japanese, Thai, and Malaysian eateries. A three-story pagoda-style arch at the end of Beach Street welcomes you to the district. ✉ *Bounded (roughly) by Essex, Washington, Marginal, and Hudson Streets, Chinatown* Ⓜ *Chinatown.*

NEED A BREAK?

Eldo Cake House. Never considered bean paste for dessert or eaten a Chinese-style pork bun? Expand your horizons at Eldo Cake House, which has both sweet and savory pastries. ✉ ***36 Harrison Ave., Downtown*** ☎ ***617/350–7977.***

Christopher Columbus Park (*Waterfront Park*). It's a short stroll from the Financial District to a view of Boston Harbor. This green space bordering the harbor and several of Boston's restored wharves is a pleasant oasis with benches and an arborlike shelter. Lewis Wharf and Commercial Wharf (north of the park), which long lay nearly derelict, had by the mid-1970s been transformed into condominiums, offices, restaurants, and upscale shops. Long Wharf's Marriott hotel was designed to blend in with the old seaside warehouses. There are sprinklers, a playground, and even free Wi-Fi. In September the park is home to the Boston Arts Festival. ✉ *Bordered by Atlantic Ave., Commercial Wharf, and Long Wharf, Downtown* 🌐 *www.foccp.org* Ⓜ *Aquarium.*

Federal Reserve Tower. On Atlantic Avenue, across from South Station, is this striking aluminum-clad building, designed in 1976 by Hugh Stubbins and Associates. The tower is mainly used for offices, and is not open to the public. ✉ *600 Atlantic Ave., Downtown* Ⓜ *South Station.*

King's Chapel. Both somber and dramatic, King's Chapel looms over the corner of Tremont and School streets. Its distinctive shape wasn't achieved entirely by design; for lack of funds, it was never topped with the steeple that architect Peter Harrison had planned. The first chapel on this site was erected in 1688, when Sir Edmund Andros, the royal

King's Chapel is missing a steeple, which was never built due to lack of funds.

governor whose authority temporarily replaced the original colonial charter, appropriated the land for the establishment of an Anglican place of worship. This rankled the Puritans, who had left England to escape Anglicanism and had until then succeeded in keeping it out of the colony.

It took five years to build the solid Quincy-granite structure. As construction proceeded, the old church continued to stand within the rising walls of the new, the plan being to remove and carry it away piece by piece when the outer stone chapel was completed. The builders then went to work on the interior, which remains essentially as they finished it in 1754; it's a masterpiece of proportion and Georgian calm. The pulpit, built in 1717 by Peter Vintoneau, is the oldest pulpit in continuous use on the same site in the United States. To the right of the main entrance is a special pew once reserved for condemned prisoners, who were trotted in to hear a sermon before being hanged on the Common. The chapel's bell is Paul Revere's largest and, in his judgment, his sweetest sounding. For a behind-the-scenes look at the bell ("bell")or crypt ("bones"), buy a ticket at the chapel entance. ✉ *Tremont St. at School St., Downtown* ☎ *617/227–2155* 🌐 *www.kings-chapel.org* 🎟 *Self-guide tour, free; Bells and Bones tour, $8 for both or $5 for one.* ⏲ *Labor Day–Memorial Day Mon–Sat. 10–4; Sun. 1:30–4. Year-round music program Tues. 12:15–1; services Sun. at 11, Wed. at 12:15* Ⓜ *Park St., Government Center.*

King's Chapel Burying Ground. Legends linger in this oldest of the city's cemeteries. Glance at the handy map of famous grave sites (posted a short walk down the left path) and then take the path to the right from the entrance and then left by the chapel to the gravestone (1704) of Elizabeth Pain, the model for Hester Prynne in Nathaniel Hawthorne's *The Scarlet Letter.* Note the winged death's head on her stone. Also buried here is William Dawes Jr., who, with Dr. Samuel Prescott, rode out to warn of the British invasion the night of Paul Revere's famous ride. Other Boston worthies entombed here, famous for more conventional reasons, include the first Massachusetts governor, John Winthrop, and several generations of his descendants. The prominent slate monument between the cemetery and the chapel tells (in French) the story of the Chevalier de Saint-Sauveur, a young officer who was part of the first French contingent that arrived to help the rebel Americans in 1778. He was killed in a riot that began when hungry Bostonians were told they couldn't buy the bread the French were baking for their men, using the Bostonians' own wheat—an awkward situation only aggravated by the language barrier. The chevalier's interment here was probably the occasion for the first Roman Catholic Mass in what has since become a city with a substantial Catholic population. ✉ *Tremont St. at School St., Downtown* ☎ *617/227–2155* 🌐 *www.cityofboston.gov/freedomtrail/kingschapel.asp* 🕓 *Daily 9–5* Ⓜ *Park St., Government Center.*

NEED A BREAK?

Fajitas & 'Ritas. Fajitas & 'Ritas, is a fun stop for a quick dose of Tex-Mex or a liter of frozen margaritas. Service is quick and prices are low. ✉ ***25 West St., Downtown*** ☎ ***617/426–1222*** 🌐 ***www.fajitasandritas.com.***

Leather District. Opposite South Station and inside the angle formed by Kneeland Street and Atlantic Avenue is a corner of Downtown that has been relatively untouched by high-rise development: the old Leather District. It's probably the best place in Downtown Boston to get an idea of what the city's business center looked like in the late 19th century. This was the wholesale supply area for raw materials in the days when the shoe industry was a regional economic mainstay; a few leather firms are still here, but most warehouses now contain expensive loft apartments. ✉ *Bordered by Kneeland St., Atlantic Ave., and Lincoln St., Downtown* Ⓜ *South Station.*

Memorial to the Irish Famine. A reminder of the rich immigrant past of this most Irish of American cities consists of two sculptures by artist Robert Shure, one depicting an anguished family on the shores of Ireland, the other a determined and hopeful Irish family stepping ashore in Boston. ✉ *Plaza outside Borders, Washington St. near School St., opposite Old South Meeting House, Downtown* Ⓜ *State, Downtown Crossing.*

Old City Hall. Just outside this site sits Richard S. Greenough's bronze statue (1855) of Benjamin Franklin, Boston's first portrait sculpture. Franklin was born in 1706 just a few blocks from here, on Milk Street, and attended the Boston Latin School, founded in 1635 near the City Hall site. (The school has long since moved to Louis Pasteur Avenue, near the Fenway.) As a young man, Franklin emigrated to Philadelphia, where he lived most of his long life. Boston's municipal government settled into the new City Hall in 1969, and the old Second Empire building now houses business offices. ✉ *41–45 School St., Downtown* 🌐 *www.oldcityhall.com* Ⓜ *State.*

Boston's Old City Hall is surrounded by modern buildings.

Old Corner Bookstore Site. Through these doors, between 1845 and 1865, passed some of the century's literary lights: Henry David Thoreau, Ralph Waldo Emerson, and Henry Wadsworth Longfellow—even Charles Dickens paid a visit. Many of their works were published here by James T. "Jamie" Fields, who in 1830 had founded the influential firm Ticknor and Fields. In the 19th century the graceful, gambrel-roof early-Georgian structure—built in 1718 on land once owned by religious rebel Anne Hutchinson—also housed the city's leading bookstore. Today, somewhat sadly, the building is home to a fast-food joint. ✉ *1 School St., Downtown* 🌐 *www.cityofboston.gov* Ⓜ *State.*

Old South Meeting House. This is the second-oldest church building in Boston, and were it not for Longfellow's celebration of the Old North in "Paul Revere's Ride," it might well be the most famous. Some of the fiercest of the town meetings that led to the Revolution were held here, culminating in the gathering of December 16, 1773, which was called by Samuel Adams to confront the crisis of three ships, laden with dutiable tea, anchored at Griffin's Wharf. The activists wanted the tea returned to England, but the governor would not permit it—and the rest is history. To cries of "Boston Harbor a teapot tonight!" and John Hancock's "Let every man do what is right in his own eyes," the protesters poured out of the Old South, headed to the wharf with their waiting comrades, and dumped 18,000 pounds' worth of tea into the water.

One of the earliest members of the congregation was an African slave named Phillis Wheatley, who had been educated by her owners. In 1773 a book of her poems was printed (by a London publisher), making her the first published African American poet. She later traveled to London, where she was received as a celebrity, but died in poverty at age 31.

The church suffered no small amount of indignity in the Revolution: its pews were ripped out by occupying British troops, and the interior was used for riding exercises by General John Burgoyne. A century later it escaped destruction in the Great Fire of 1872, only to be threatened with demolition by developers. Interestingly, it was the first successful preservation effort in New England. The building opened as an independent, nonprofit museum in 1877 and contains the last remaining example of a two-tiered gallery in a New England meetinghouse.

WORD OF MOUTH

"What I really like about the Custom House is that the views are totally different from the views you get at the Prudential Skywalk Observatory. Here, you can easily spot historic sites, from the dome of Old State House, to Faneuil Hall, to North End, to Old North Church, to the USS *Constitution*, to Bunker Hill. It also has a lovely view of Boston Harbor. And since it is outdoors, you don't have to worry about glass reflection when taking photos." —yk

The Voices of Protest exhibit celebrates Old South as a forum for free speech from Revolutionary days to the present. ✉ *310 Washington St., Downtown* ☎ *617/482–6439* 🌐 *www.oldsouthmeetinghouse.org* 🎟 *$6* 🕘 *Apr.–Oct., daily 9:30–5; Nov.–Mar., daily 10–4* Ⓜ *State, Downtown Crossing.*

Old State House. This colonial-era landmark has one of the most recognizable facades in Boston, with its State Street gable adorned by a brightly gilded lion and unicorn, symbols of British imperial power. The original figures were pulled down in 1776. For proof that bygones are bygones, consider not only the restoration of the sculptures in 1880 but also that Queen Elizabeth II was greeted by cheering crowds on July 4, 1976, when she stood on the Old State House balcony (from which the Declaration of Independence was first read in public in Boston and which overlooks the site of the Boston Massacre).

This was the seat of the colonial government from 1713 until the Revolution, and after the evacuation of the British from Boston in 1776 it served the independent Commonwealth until its replacement on Beacon Hill was completed in 1798. John Hancock was inaugurated here as the first governor under the new state constitution.

Like many other colonial-era landmarks, it fared poorly in the years that followed but when demolition was threatened in 1880, the Bostonian Society organized a restoration, after which the Old State House reopened with a permanent collection that traces Boston's Revolutionary War history. Just outside the Old State House, at 15 State Street, is a visitor center run by the National Park Service; it offers free brochures and also has restrooms. ✉ *206 Washington St., at State St., Downtown* ☎ *617/720–1713* 🌐 *www.revolutionaryboston.org/revboston/visit/* 🎟 *$8.50* 🕘 *Daily 9–5, Memorial Day through Labor Day until 6* Ⓜ *State.*

CLOSE UP

Tours Worth Trying

On Location Tours. On Location Tours (formerly Boston Movie Tours) takes you to Boston's television and movie hot spots like the South Boston of *The Departed*, the *Ally McBeal* building, the tavern from *Good Will Hunting*, the *Cheers* bar, and Fenway Park, home of the Red Sox and location for movies like *Field of Dreams* and *Fever Pitch*. Guides share filming secrets and trivia from movies like *Legally Blonde* and *Mystic River* along with the best celeb spots in town. The "theater-on-wheels" bus tour takes two to three hours, depending on traffic ($38). ☎ *212/683–2027 to purchase tickets* 🌐 *onlocationtours.com/tour/boston-tv-movie/*.

Boston Women's Heritage Trail. Boston Women's Heritage Trail has seven self-guided walks that highlight remarkable women who played an integral role in shaping the history of Boston and the nation as patriots, intellectuals, abolitionists, suffragists, artists, and writers. In addition, there are six mini-trails in various Boston neighborhoods and several themed trails, such as a women artist trail in the Back Bay. View maps of the organization's website. Guided tours available upon request. ☎ *617/522–2872* 🌐 *www.bwht.org*.

Rowes Wharf. Take a Beacon Hill redbrick town house, blow it up to the *n*th power, and you get this 15-story Skidmore, Owings & Merrill extravaganza from 1987, one of the more welcome additions to the Boston Harbor skyline. From under the complex's gateway six-story arch, you can get great views of Boston Harbor and the yachts docked at the marina. Water shuttles pull up here from Logan Airport—the most intriguing way to enter the city. A windswept stroll along the HarborWalk waterfront promenade at dusk makes for an unforgettable sunset on clear days. ✉ *Atlantic Ave. south of India Wharf* Ⓜ *Aquarium*.

South Station. The colonnaded granite structure is the terminal for all Amtrak trains in and out of Boston as well as commuter trains originating from the west and south of the city. Next door on Atlantic Avenue is the terminal for Greyhound, Peter Pan, and other bus lines. Behind the station's grand 1900s facade a major renovation project has created an airy, modern transit center. Thanks to its eateries, coffee bars, newsstand, flower stand, and other shops, waiting for a train here can actually be a pleasant experience. ✉ *Atlantic Ave. and Summer St., Downtown* Ⓜ *South Station*.

State Street. During the 19th century State Street was headquarters for banks, brokerages, and insurance firms; although these businesses have spread throughout the Downtown District, "State Street" still connotes much the same thing as "Wall Street" does in New York. The early commercial hegemony of State Street was symbolized by Long Wharf, built in 1710 and extending some 1,700 feet into the harbor. If today's Long Wharf doesn't appear to be that long, it's not because it has been shortened but because the land has crept out toward its end. State Street once met the water at the base of the Custom House; landfill operations were pursued relentlessly through the years, and the old coastline is now as much a memory as such colonial State Street landmarks as Governor Winthrop's 1630 house and the Revolutionary-era Bunch of Grapes Tavern, where Bostonians met to drink and wax indignant at their treatment by King George.

U.S. Custom House. This 1847 structure resembles a Greek Revival temple that appears to have sprouted a tower. This is the work of architects Ammi Young and Isaiah Rogers—at least, the bottom part is. The tower was added in 1915, at which time the Custom House became Boston's tallest building. It remains one of the most visible and best loved structures in the city's skyline. To appreciate the grafting job, go inside and look at the domed rotunda. The outer surface of that dome was once the roof of the building, but now the dome is embedded in the base of the tower.

The federal government moved out of the Custom House in 1987 and sold it to the city of Boston, which, in turn, sold it to the Marriott Corporation, which has converted the building into hotel space and time-share units, a move that disturbed historical purists. You can now sip a cocktail in the hotel's Counting Room Lounge after 6 pm, or visit the 26th-floor observation deck for a fee. The magnificent Rotunda Room sports maritime prints and antique artifacts, courtesy of the Peabody Essex Museum in Salem. ✉ *3 McKinley Sq., Downtown* ☎ *617/310–6300* Ⓜ *State, Aquarium.*

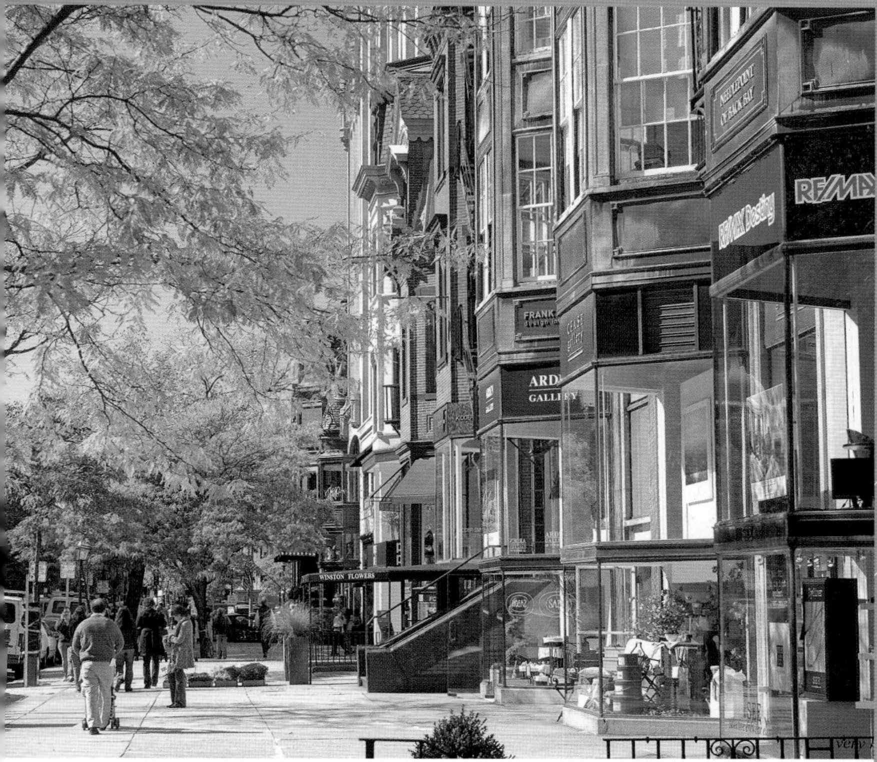

6

BACK BAY AND THE SOUTH END

GETTING ORIENTED

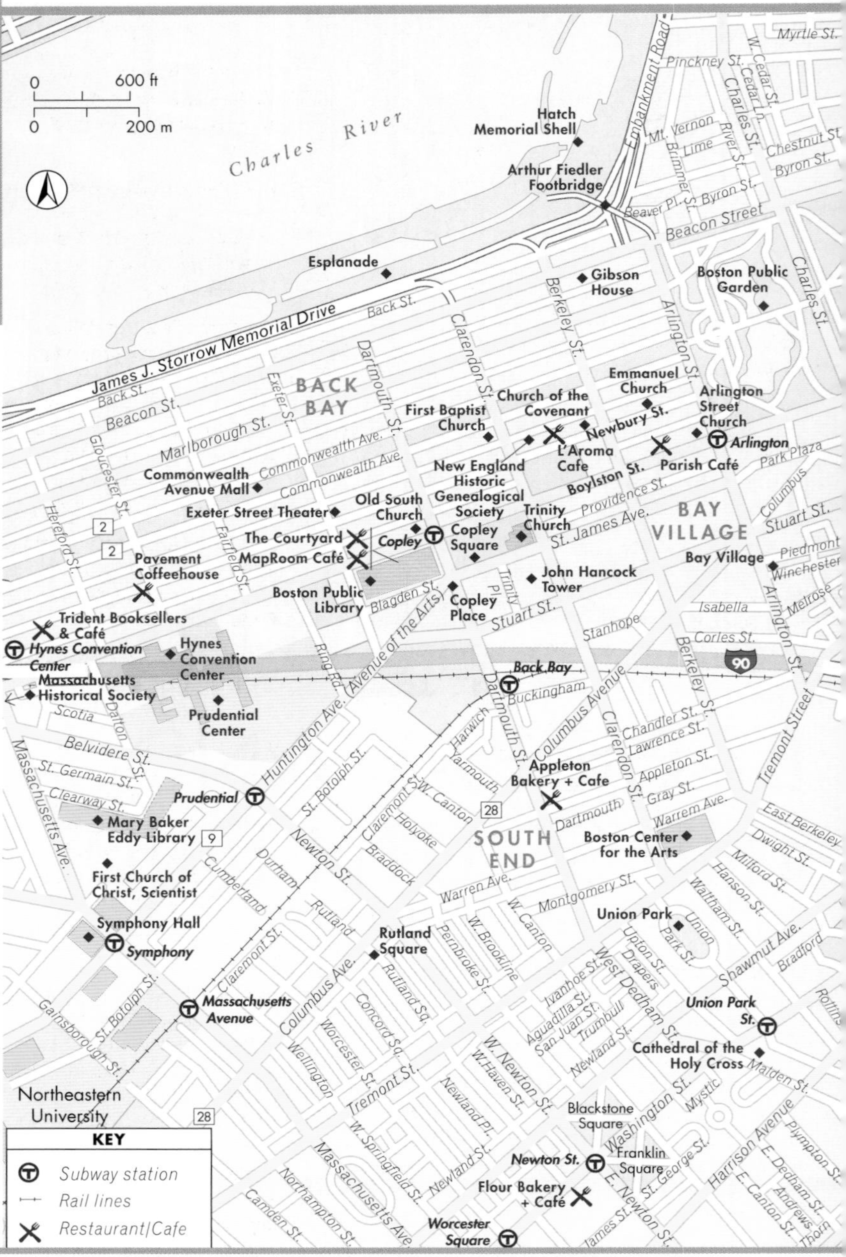

GETTING HERE AND AROUND

There are myriad parking garages in Back Bay. Take the Orange Line to the Back Bay station or the Green Line to Copley for the heart of the shopping areas. The Arlington stop on the Green Line is the most convenient to the Public Garden.

The South End is easily accessible by the T; take the Orange Line to Back Bay and head south on Dartmouth Street to Columbus Avenue, or jump off the Silver Line at Union Park Street or East Berkley Street to access the neighborhood.

TIMING

If you're not looking to max out your credit cards, then you can hurry past the boutiques and cover the Back Bay in about two hours. Allow at least half a day for a leisurely walk with frequent stops on Newbury Street and the shops at Copley Place and the Prudential Center. The reflecting pool at the Christian Science Church is a great time-out spot. Around the third week of April, magnolia time arrives, and nowhere do the flowers bloom more magnificently than along Commonwealth Avenue. In May the Public Garden bursts with color, thanks to its flowering dogwood trees and thousands of tulips. To stay oriented, remember that the north–south streets are arranged in alphabetical order, from Arlington to Hereford.

A few hours is perfect for exploring the South End; add a few more hours for a show at the Boston Center of the Arts or to dine at one of the many excellent restaurants in the area.

NEWBURY QUICK BITES

L'Aroma Cafe. Shopping on Newbury can really wear you (and your wallet) out, so stop in at L'Aroma Cafe for a steaming latte, fresh salad, housemade pizza, or plate of quiche. For its designer address, the prices are reasonable, and the Italian pastries to die for. ✉ *85 Newbury, between Berkeley and Clarendon* ☎ *617/412–4001* 🌐 *www.laromacafe.com/index-2.html.*

TOP REASONS TO GO

- Join the throngs of students, locals, and visitors window-shopping on Newbury Street.
- Admire the architecture, revel in the artistry, and even enjoy an excellent lunch at the Boston Public Library—all without taking out a single book.
- Visit the Public Garden on a sunny, late-spring day and take in the scenery from your seat on the Swan Boats. Don't forget to check out the bronzed statues of the ducklings from Robert McCloskey's Boston classic *Make Way for Ducklings.*
- Enjoy a play, concert, or art installation at the "people's" art-and-culture complex, the Boston Center for the Arts.
- Shop Columbus Avenue and Tremont Street for the perfect additions to your home decor.
- Walk the streets around Rutland Square, Union Park, and Bay Village. Architecture buffs will love the Victorian and Italianate row houses harking back to the neighborhood's 19th-century roots.

SOUTH END QUICK BITES

Appleton Bakery + Cafe. After a morning of gallery hopping in the South End, stop in for a bite at Appleton Bakery + Cafe. All the bakery goods are made fresh daily, and the breakfast burrito has many fans. ✉ *123 Appleton St., at Dartmouth St.* ☎ *617/859–8222* 🌐 *www.appletoncafe.com.*

Sightseeing
★★★★
Dining
★★★★
Lodging
★★★★
Shopping
★★★★★
Nightlife
★★★★★

In the folklore of American neighborhoods, the Back Bay stands with New York's Park Avenue and San Francisco's Nob Hill as a symbol of propriety and high social standing. Before the 1850s it really was a bay, a tidal flat that formed the south bank of a distended Charles River. The filling in of land along the isthmus that joined Boston to the mainland (the Neck) began in 1850, and resulted in the creation of the South End.

THE BACK BAY

Updated by Kim Foley MacKinnon

To the north a narrow causeway called the Mill Dam (later Beacon Street) was built in 1814 to separate the Back Bay from the Charles. By the late 1800s, Bostonians had filled in the shallows to as far as the marshland known as the Fenway, and the original 783-acre peninsula had been expanded by about 450 acres. Thus the waters of Back Bay became the neighborhood of Back Bay.

Heavily influenced by the then-recent rebuilding of Paris according to the plans of Baron Georges-Eugène Haussmann, the Back Bay planners created thoroughfares that resemble Parisian boulevards. The thorough planning included service alleys behind the main streets to allow provisioning wagons to drive up to basement kitchens. (Now they're used for waste pickup and parking.)

Today the area retains its posh spirit, but mansions are no longer the main draw. Locals and tourists alike flock to the commercial streets of Boylston and Newbury, to shop at boutiques, galleries, and the usual mall stores. Many of the bars and restaurants have patio seating and bay windows, making the area the perfect spot to see and be seen while indulging in ethnic delicacies or an invigorating coffee. The Boston Public Library, Symphony Hall, and numerous churches ensure that high culture is not lost amid the frenzy of consumerism.

DID YOU KNOW?

Boston Public Garden's iconic boats have a secret. Creator Robert Paget first crafted the swans to hide the foot-propelled paddle wheel mechanism and cover the boat captain. Launched in 1877, the swans still ply the garden's lagoon.

The Boston Public Library is a stunning cathedral of books.

TOP ATTRACTIONS

FAMILY
Fodor's Choice ★

Boston Public Garden. Although the Boston Public Garden is often lumped together with Boston Common, the two are separate entities with different histories and purposes and a distinct boundary between them at Charles Street. The Common has been public land since Boston was founded in 1630, whereas the Public Garden belongs to a newer Boston, occupying what had been salt marshes on the edge of the Common. By 1837 the tract was covered with an abundance of ornamental plantings donated by a group of private citizens. The area was defined in 1856 by the building of Arlington Street, and in 1860 the architect George Meacham was commissioned to plan the park.

The central feature of the Public Garden is its irregularly shaped pond, intended to appear, from any vantage point along its banks, much larger than its nearly 4 acres. Near the Swan Boat dock is what has been described as the world's smallest suspension bridge, designed in 1867 to cross the pond at its narrowest point.

The Public Garden is America's oldest botanical garden, and has the finest formal plantings in central Boston. The beds along the main walkways are replanted for spring and summer. The tulips during the first two weeks of May are especially colorful, and there's a sampling of native and European tree species.

The dominant work among the park's statuary is Thomas Ball's equestrian **George Washington** (1869), which faces the head of Commonwealth Avenue at the Arlington Street gate. This is Washington in a triumphant pose as liberator, surveying a scene that, from where he

TWO WAYS TO EXPLORE BACK BAY

ART AND ARCHITECTURE

Art and architecture buffs should first stop at the Boston Public Library. Constructed in the Renaissance Revival style, it houses murals by John Singer Sargent; sculpture by Louis Saint-Gaudens; and immense bronze doors by Daniel Chester French, sculptor of the Lincoln Memorial; and a book or two. Next, take in Trinity Church, a Romanesque Revival gem designed by Henry Hobson Richardson, complete with paintings by William Morris and John LaFarge. Visit the Church of the Covenant to view the largest collection of liturgical stained-glass windows by Louis Comfort Tiffany. The First Church of Christ, Scientist melds the 19th and 20th centuries with a Renaissance Revival basilica next to an office building by I. M. Pei. Complete your tour with a stop outside the modern John Hancock Tower, also by I. M. Pei, which at 790 feet is the tallest building in New England.

SHOPPER'S PARADISE

Between Copley Place and Prudential Center, Boylston Street and Newbury Street, there's a store for every shopper. Visit Newbury Street for high-end designer boutiques (think Chanel, Burberry, and Armani) and streetside cafés for watching the other conspicuous consumers. Boylston Street is home to retailers like Crate&Barrel and Apple, as well as numerous bars and restaurants. The Prudential Center mall fronts on Boylston and is anchored by Saks Fifth Avenue, Lord & Taylor, and, luckily for neighborhood residents, a Shaw's supermarket. You can walk through the Prudential Center to reach Copley Place, another chichi mall home to the likes of Neiman Marcus, Louis Vuitton, and Tiffany; there's a Gap, too, for those who must have some new jeans. If you haven't found what you're looking for after an afternoon here, it just might not exist.

stood with his cannons at Dorchester Heights, would have included an immense stretch of blue water. Several dozen yards to the north of Washington (to the right if you're facing Commonwealth Avenue) is the granite-and-red-marble **Ether Monument,** donated in 1866 by Thomas Lee to commemorate the advent of anesthesia 20 years earlier at nearby Massachusetts General Hospital. Other Public Garden monuments include statues of the Unitarian preacher and transcendentalist William Ellery Channing, at the corner opposite his Arlington Street Church; Edward Everett Hale, the author (*The Man Without a Country*) and philanthropist, at the Charles Street Gate; and the abolitionist senator Charles Sumner and the Civil War hero Colonel Thomas Cass, along Boylston Street.

The park contains a special delight for the young at heart; follow the children quack-quacking along the pathway between the pond and the park entrance at Charles and Beacon streets to the *Make Way for Ducklings* bronzes sculpted by Nancy Schön, a tribute to the 1941 classic children's story by Robert McCloskey. ✉ *Bounded by Arlington, Boylston, Charles, and Beacon Sts., Back Bay* Ⓜ *Arlington.*

Swan Boats. The pond has been famous since 1877 for its foot-pedal-powered (by a captain) Swan Boats, which make leisurely cruises during warm months. The pond is favored by ducks and swans, and for the modest price of a few boat rides you can amuse children here for an hour or more. ☎ *617/522–1966* 🌐 *www.swanboats.com* 🎟 *Swan Boats $3 adults; $1.50 children* ⏲ *Swan Boats mid-Apr.–June 20, daily 10–4; June 21–Labor Day, daily 10–5; day after Labor Day–mid-Sept., weekdays noon–4, weekends 10–4.*

Fodor's Choice ★ **Boston Public Library.** This venerable institution is a handsome temple to literature and a valuable research library. The Renaissance Revival building was opened in 1895; a 1972 addition emulates the mass and proportion of the original, though not its extraordinary detail; this skylighted annex houses the library's circulating collections.

You don't need a library card to enjoy the magnificent art. The murals at the head of the staircase, depicting the nine muses, are the work of the French artist Puvis de Chavannes; those in the book-request processing room to the right are Edwin Abbey's interpretations of the Holy Grail legend. Upstairs, in the public areas leading to the fine-arts, music, and rare-books collections, is John Singer Sargent's mural series on the *Triumph of Religion,* shining with renewed color after its cleaning and restoration in 2003.The corridor leading from the annex opens onto the Renaissance-style **courtyard**—an exact copy of the one in Rome's Palazzo della Cancelleria—around which the original library is built. A covered arcade furnished with chairs rings a fountain; you can bring books or lunch into the courtyard, which is open all the hours the library is open, and escape the bustle of the city. Beyond the courtyard is the main entrance hall of the 1895 building, with its immense stone lions by Louis Saint-Gaudens, vaulted ceiling, and marble staircase. The corridor at the top of the stairs leads to **Bates Hall,** one of Boston's most sumptuous interior spaces. This is the main reference reading room, 218 feet long with a barrel-arch ceiling 50 feet high. ✉ *700 Boylston St., at Copley Sq., Back Bay* ☎ *617/536–5400* 🌐 *www.bpl.org* ⏲ *Mon.–Thurs. 9–9, Fri. and Sat. 9–5; Sun. 1–5 (Oct.–June). Free guided art and architecture tours Mon. at 2:30; Tues. and Thurs. at 6; Wed., Fri. and Sat. at 11* Ⓜ *Copley.*

NEED A BREAK?

Courtyard. You can take a lunch break at the Courtyard or the MapRoom Café, adjoining restaurants in the Boston Public Library. Breakfast and lunch are served in the 1895 map room, and the main restaurant, which overlooks the courtyard, is open for lunch and afternoon tea. The Courtyard is open weekdays 11:30–2:30 for lunch and Wednesday–Friday 2–4 for tea. The MapRoom Café is open Monday–Saturday 9–5. ✉ ***700 Boylston St., at Copley Sq., Back Bay*** ☎ ***617/859–2251*** 🌐 ***www.thecateredaffair.com/bpl/courtyard.***

Trinity Church. In his 1877 masterpiece, architect Henry Hobson Richardson brought his Romanesque Revival style to maturity; all the aesthetic elements for which he was famous come together magnificently—bold polychromatic masonry, careful arrangement of masses, sumptuously carved interior woodwork—in this crowning centerpiece of Copley Square. A full appreciation of its architecture requires an understanding of the logistical problems of building it here. The Back

DID YOU KNOW?

In 1885 architects ranked Trinity Church as one of America's 10 most important buildings. Today, the Richardsonian Romanesque structure is the only one of those original ten on the American Institute of Architects "Ten Most Significant Buildings in the United States."

Bay is a reclaimed wetland with a high water table. Bedrock, or at least stable glacial till, lies far beneath wet clay. Like all older Back Bay buildings, Trinity Church sits on submerged wooden pilings. But its central tower weighs 9,500 tons, and most of the 4,500 pilings beneath the building are under that tremendous central mass. The pilings are checked regularly for sinkage by means of a hatch in the basement.

NAME CHANGE

One of Back Bay's main thoroughfares, Huntington Avenue, which stretches from Copley Square past the Museum of Fine Arts, has technically been renamed the Avenue of the Arts. However, old habits die hard, particularly with Bostonians; everyone still calls it Huntington.

Richardson engaged some of the best artists of his day—John LaFarge, William Morris, and Edward Burne-Jones among them—to execute the paintings and stained glass that make this a monument to everything that was right about the pre-Raphaelite spirit and the nascent aesthetic of Morris's Arts and Crafts movement. LaFarge's intricate paintings and ornamented ceilings received a much-needed overhaul during the extensive renovations completed in 2005. Along the north side of the church, note the Augustus Saint-Gaudens statue of Phillips Brooks—the most charismatic rector in New England, who almost single-handedly got Trinity built and furnished. Shining light of Harvard's religious community and lyricist of "O Little Town of Bethlehem," Brooks is shown here with Christ touching his shoulder in approval. For a nice respite, try to catch one of the Friday organ concerts beginning at 12:15. **TIP→ The 11:15 Sunday service is usually followed by a free guided tour.** ✉ *206 Clarendon St., Back Bay* ☎ *617/536–0944* 🌐 *trinitychurchboston.org* 🎫 *Entrance free, guided and self-guided tours $7* ⏲ *Sept.–June Mon., Fri., and Sat. 9–5, Tues.–Thurs. 9–6, Sun. 1–6; services Sun. at 7:45, 9, and 11:15 am and 6 pm. Tours take place several times daily; call to confirm times. Last admission 30 min prior to closing. Hrs change slightly in the summer* Ⓜ *Copley.*

WORTH NOTING

Arlington Street Church. Opposite the Park Square corner of the Public Garden, this church was erected in 1861—the first to be built in the Back Bay. Though a classical portico is a keynote and its model was London's St. Martin-in-the-Fields, Arlington Street Church is less picturesque and more Georgian in character. Note the Tiffany stained-glass windows. During the year preceding the Civil War the church was a hotbed of abolitionist fervor. Later, during the Vietnam War, this Unitarian-Universalist congregation became famous as a center of peace activism. ✉ *351 Boylston St., Back Bay* ☎ *617/536–7050* 🌐 *www.ascboston.org* ⏲ *Sunday services at 11* Ⓜ *Arlington.*

Back Bay Mansions. If you like nothing better than to imagine how the other half lives, you'll suffer no shortage of old homes to sigh over in Boston's Back Bay. Most, unfortunately, are off-limits to visitors, but there's no law against gawking from the outside. Stroll Commonwealth,

CLOSE UP

The Houses of the Back Bay

The Back Bay remains a living museum of urban Victorian–residential architecture. The earliest specimens are nearest to the Public Garden (there are exceptions where showier turn-of-the-20th-century mansions replaced 1860s town houses), and the newer examples are out around the Massachusetts Avenue and Fenway extremes of the district. The height of Back Bay residences and their distance from the street are essentially uniform, as are the interior layouts, chosen to accord with lot width. Yet there's a distinct progression of facades, beginning with French academic and Italianate designs and moving through the various "revivals" of the 19th century. By the time of World War I, when development of the Back Bay was virtually complete, architects and their patrons had come full circle to a revival of the Federal period, which had been out of fashion for only 30 years when the building began. If the Back Bay architects had not run out of land, they might have gotten around to a Greek Revival revival.

The Great Depression brought an end to the Back Bay style of living, and today only a few of the houses are single-family residences. Most have been cut up into apartments, then expensive condominiums; during the boom years of the late 1990s some were returned to their original townhouse status. Interior details have experienced a mixed fate: they suffered during the years when Victorian fashions were held in low regard and are undergoing careful restoration now that the aesthetic pendulum has reversed itself and moneyed condo buyers are demanding period authenticity. The original facades have survived on all but Newbury and Boylston streets, so the public face of the Back Bay retains much of the original charm and grandeur.

An outstanding guide to the architecture and history of the Back Bay is Bainbridge Bunting's *Houses of Boston's Back Bay* (Harvard, 1967). A few homes are open to the public.

Beacon, and Marlborough streets for the best views. For details on lectures, films, and other events offered in some of these respected institutions, see the free, biweekly *Improper Bostonian* and the *Boston Globe*'s "g" section.

Boylston Street. Less posh than Newbury Street, this broad thoroughfare is the southern commercial spine of the Back Bay, lined with interesting restaurants and shops. ✉ *Back Bay.*

Commonwealth Avenue Mall. The mall that extends down the middle of the Back Bay's Commonwealth Avenue, which serves as the green link between the Public Garden and the public parks system, is studded with statuary. One of the most interesting memorials, at the Exeter Street intersection, is a portrayal of naval historian and author Samuel Eliot Morison seated on a rock as if he were peering out to sea. The **Boston Women's Memorial,** installed in 2003, sculpted by Meredith Bergmann, is between Fairfield and Gloucester streets. Statues of Abigail Adams,

Lucy Stone, and Phillis Wheatley celebrate the progressive ideas of these three women and their contributions to Boston's history.

A dramatic and personal memorial near Dartmouth Street is the **Vendome Monument,** dedicated to the nine firemen who died in a 1972 blaze at the Back Bay's Vendome Hotel, which, now office space, is across the street. The curved black-granite block, 29 feet long and waist high, is etched with the names of the dead. A bronze cast of a fireman's coat and hat are draped over the granite. ✉ *Commonwealth Ave. between Arlington St. and Massachusetts Ave., Back Bay* Ⓜ *Arlington, Copley*.

Copley Square. Every April thousands find a glimpse of Copley Square the most wonderful sight in the world: this is where the runners of the Boston Marathon end their 26.2-mile race. A square now favored by skateboarders (much to the chagrin of city officials), the civic space is defined by three monumental older buildings. One is the stately, bowfront 1912 **Fairmont Copley Plaza Hotel,** which faces the square on St. James Avenue and serves as a dignified foil to its companions, two of the most important works of architecture in the United States: Trinity Church—Henry Hobson Richardson's masterwork of 1877—and the Boston Public Library, by McKim, Mead & White. The John Hancock Tower looms in the background. To honor the runners who stagger over the marathon's finish line, bronze statues of the Tortoise and the Hare engaged in their mythical race were cast by Nancy Schön, who also did the much-loved *Make Way for Ducklings* group in the Boston Public Garden. ✉ *Bounded by Dartmouth, Boylston, and Clarendon Sts. and St. James Ave., Back Bay* Ⓜ *Copley*.

Emmanuel Church. Built in 1860, this Back Bay Gothic Episcopal church is popular among classical music lovers—every Sunday morning at 10, from September to May, as part of the liturgy, a Bach cantata is performed; guest conductors have included Christopher Hogwood and Seiji Ozawa. ✉ *15 Newbury St., Back Bay* ☎ *617/536–3355* 🌐 *www.emmanuelboston.org* 🕑 *Service Sun. at 10 am* Ⓜ *Arlington*.

Esplanade. Near the corner of Beacon and Arlington streets, the Arthur Fiedler Footbridge crosses Storrow Drive to the 3-mile-long Esplanade and the **Hatch Memorial Shell.** The free concerts here in summer include the Boston Pops' immensely popular televised Fourth of July performance. For shows like this, Bostonians haul lawn chairs and blankets to the lawn in front of the shell; bring a take-out lunch from a nearby restaurant, find an empty spot—no mean feat, so come early—and you'll feel right at home. An impressive stone bust of the late maestro Arthur Fiedler watches over the walkers, joggers, picnickers, and sunbathers who fill the Esplanade's paths on pleasant days. Here, too, is the turn-of-the-20th-century **Union Boat Club Boathouse,** headquarters for the country's oldest private rowing club. ✉ *Back Bay* 🌐 *www.esplanadeassociation.org*.

Exeter Street Theater. This massive Romanesque structure was built in 1884 as a temple for the Working Union of Progressive Spiritualists. Beginning in 1914, it enjoyed a long run as a movie theater; as the *AIA Guide to Boston* points out, "it was the only movie theater a proper

Boston woman would enter, probably because of its spiritual overtones." Today, it's home to a school. ✉ *26 Exeter St., at Newbury St., Back Bay* 🌐 *www.fst.org/exeter.htm* Ⓜ *Copley.*

First Baptist Church. This 1872 structure, at the corner of Clarendon Street and Commonwealth Avenue, was architect Henry Hobson Richardson's first foray into Romanesque Revival. It was originally erected for the Brattle Square Unitarian Society, but Richardson ran over budget and the church went bankrupt and dissolved. In 1882 the building was bought by the Baptists. The figures on each side of its soaring tower were sculpted by Frédéric Auguste Bartholdi, the sculptor who designed the Statue of Liberty. The friezes represent four points at which God enters an individual's life: baptism, communion, marriage, and death. The trumpeting angels at each corner have earned First Baptist its nickname, "Church of the Holy Bean Blowers." If you phone ahead for an appointment on a weekday, you may be given an informal tour. ✉ *110 Commonwealth Ave., Back Bay* ☎ *617/267–3148* 🌐 *www.firstbaptistchurchofboston.org* 🎟 *Free* 🕓 *Office hours: Tues.–Fr. 10–1; services Sun. at 11 am* Ⓜ *Copley.*

6

NEED A BREAK?

Pavement Coffeehouse. This is a basement spot with solid coffee and espresso drinks, snacks, and Wi-Fi access. ✉ ***286 Newbury St., Back Bay*** ☎ ***617/859–9515*** Ⓜ ***Hynes.***

Parish Café. To try the creations of some of the best local chefs without paying four-star restaurant prices, stop by Parish Café. For $12 to $20 you can get a sandwich designed by the top culinary minds in Boston. The bar is open until 2 am daily, with food service until 1 am, a rare thing in Boston. ✉ ***361 Boylston St., Back Bay*** ☎ ***617/247–4777*** 🌐 ***www.parishcafe.com*** Ⓜ ***Arlington.***

First Church of Christ, Scientist. The world headquarters of the Christian Science faith mixes the traditional with the modern—marrying Bernini to Le Corbusier by combining an old-world basilica with a sleek office complex designed by I. M. Pei. Mary Baker Eddy's original granite First Church of Christ, Scientist (1894) has since been enveloped by a domed Renaissance Revival basilica, added to the site in 1906, and both church buildings are now surrounded by the offices of the Christian Science Publishing Society, where the *Christian Science Monitor* is produced, and by Pei's complex of church-administration structures completed in 1973. You can hear all 13,290 pipes of the church's famed Aeolian-Skinner organ during services. ✉ *175 Huntington Ave., Back Bay* ☎ *617/450–2000* 🌐 *www.tfccs.com* 🎟 *Free* 🕓 *Services Sun. at 10 am and 5 pm. Tours Thurs.–Sat. noon–5, Tues. noon–4, Wed. 1–4, and Sun. 11–3* Ⓜ *Hynes, Symphony.*

Gibson House. Through the foresight of an eccentric bon vivant, this house provides an authentic glimpse into daily life in Boston's Victorian era. One of the first Back Bay residences (1859), the Gibson House is relatively modest in comparison with some of the grand mansions built during the decades that followed; yet its furnishings, from its 1795 Willard clock to the raised and gilded wallpaper to the multipiece faux-bamboo bedroom set, seem sumptuous to modern eyes. Unlike other Back Bay houses, the Gibson family home has been preserved with all its Victorian fixtures and furniture intact. The house serves as the meeting place for the New England chapter of the Victorian Society in America; it was also used as an interior for the 1984 Merchant-Ivory film *The Bostonians*. **TIP→ Though the sign out front instructs visitors not to ring the bell until the stroke of the hour, you will have better luck catching the beginning of the tour if you arrive a few minutes early, but not more than 10.** ✉ *137 Beacon St., Back Bay* ☎ *617/267–6338* 🌐 *www.thegibsonhouse.org* 🎟 *$9* 🕒 *Tours Wed.–Sun. at 1, 2, and 3 and by appointment* Ⓜ *Arlington.*

John Hancock Tower. In the early 1970s, the tallest building in New England became notorious as the monolith that rained glass from time to time. Windows were improperly seated in the sills of the blue rhomboid tower, designed by I. M. Pei. Once the building's 13 acres of glass were replaced and the central core stiffened, the problem was corrected. Bostonians originally feared the Hancock's stark modernism would overwhelm nearby Trinity Church, but its shimmering sides reflect the older structure's image, actually enlarging its presence. The tower is closed to the public. ✉ *200 Clarendon St., Back Bay* Ⓜ *Copley.*

Mary Baker Eddy Library for the Betterment of Humanity. One of the largest single collections by and about an American woman is housed at this library within Christian Science Plaza, along with two floors of exhibits celebrating the power of ideas and providing educational experiences and context to Mary Baker Eddy's life, ideas, and achievements, from the nineteenth century to today.

The library is home to the fascinating **Mapparium,** a huge stained-glass globe whose 30-foot interior can be traversed on a footbridge. You can experience a sound-and-light show in the Mapparium and learn about the production of the *Christian Science Monitor* in the Monitor Gallery. The Quest Gallery explores Mary Baker Eddy's life and encourages others to think about their own personal quests, and the Hall of Ideas showcases the ideas of the world's greatest thinkers in a virtual fountain. ✉ *200 Massachusetts Ave., Back Bay* ☎ *617/222–3711* 🌐 *www.marybakereddylibrary.org* 🎟 *Hall of Ideas and 3rd-fl. library free, exhibits $6* 🕒 *Tues.–Sun. 10–4* Ⓜ *Prudential.*

Massachusetts Historical Society. The first historical society in the United States (founded in 1791) has paintings, a library, and a 12-million-piece manuscript collection from 17th-century New England to the present. Among these manuscripts are the Adams Family Papers, which comprise more than 300,000 pages from the letters and diaries of generations of the Adams family, including papers from John Adams and John Quincy Adams. Casual visitors are welcome, but if you'd like to examine the papers in depth, call ahead. The society also offers a variety of programs and special exhibits. ✉ *1154 Boylston St., Back Bay* ☎ *617/536–1608* 🌐 *www.masshist.org* 🎟 *Free* 🕒 *Gallery hours: weekdays 10–4, Sat. 10–4. Library hours: weekdays 9–4:45 (Tues. until 7:45 pm), Sat. 9–4.* Ⓜ *Hynes.*

Shoppers take a break at a Newbury Street café.

Newbury Street. Eight-block-long Newbury Street has been compared to New York's 5th Avenue, and certainly this is the city's poshest shopping area, with branches of Chanel, Brooks Brothers, Diane von Furstenberg, Burberry, and other top names in fashion. But here the pricey boutiques are more intimate than grand, and people live above the trendy restaurants and ubiquitous hair salons, giving the place a neighborhood feel. Toward the Massachusetts Avenue end, cafés proliferate and the stores get funkier, ending with Newbury Comics and Urban Outfitters. ✉ *From Arlington St. to Mass Ave., Back Bay* Ⓜ *Hynes, Copley.*

New England Historic Genealogical Society. Are you related to Miles Standish or Priscilla Alden? The answer may lie here. If your ancestors were pedigreed New Englanders—or if you're just interested in genealogical research of any kind—you can trace your family tree with the help of the society's collections. The society dates from 1845, and is the oldest genealogical organization in the country. ✉ *101 Newbury St., Back Bay* ☎ *888/296–3447* 🌐 *www.americanancestors.org* 🎟 *$15 fee to use facility* ⏲ *Tues.,Thurs.–Sat. 9–5, Wed. 9–9* Ⓜ *Copley.*

NEED A BREAK?

Trident Booksellers & Café. Folks gather at the two-story Trident Booksellers & Café to review literary best sellers, thumb through the superb magazine selection, and munch on homemade desserts, sandwiches, and soups. It's open from 8 am until midnight daily. ✉ ***338 Newbury St., Back Bay*** ☎ ***617/267–8688*** 🌐 ***www.tridentbookscafe.com*** Ⓜ ***Hynes.***

Old South Church. Members of the Old South Meeting House, of Tea Party fame, decamped to this new site in 1873, a move not without controversy. In an Italian Gothic style inspired by the sociologist John

Ruskin and an interior decorated with Venetian mosaics and stained-glass windows, the "new" structure could hardly be more different from the plain meetinghouse they vacated. The sanctuary is free and open to the public seven days a week. *645 Boylston St., Back Bay 617/536–1970 www.oldsouth.org Mon.–Fri. 8–7, Sat. 10–4. Services Sun. at 9 and 11 am and 6 pm, jazz services Thurs. at 6 M Copley.*

Prudential Center. The only rival to the John Hancock's claim on Boston's upper skyline is the 52-story Prudential Tower, built in the early 1960s when the scale of monumental urban redevelopment projects had yet to be challenged. The Prudential Center, which replaced the railway yards that blocked off the South End, now dominates the acreage between Boylston Street and Huntington Avenue. Its enclosed shopping mall is connected by a glass bridge to the more upscale Copley Place. As for the Prudential Tower itself, the architectural historian Bainbridge Bunting made an acute observation when he called it "an apparition so vast in size that it appears to float above the surrounding district without being related to it." Later modifications to the Boylston Street frontage of the Prudential Center effected a better union of the complex with the urban space around it, but the tower itself floats on, vast as ever. **Prudential Center Skywalk,** a 50th-floor observatory atop the Prudential Tower, offers panoramic vistas of Boston, Cambridge, and the suburbs to the west and south—on clear days, you can even see Cape Cod. *800 Boylston St., Back Bay 800/746–7778, 617/859–0648 for Skywalk www.prudentialcenter.com Skywalk $15 Mon.–Sat. 10–9, Sun. 11–6; Skywalk Nov.–Feb. daily 10–8, Mar.–Oct. daily 10–10 M Prudential Center, Copley Station.*

Hynes Convention Center. The Hynes Convention Center hosts conferences, trade shows, and conventions. It's connected to the Prudential Center, where visitors can find a branch of the Greater Boston Visitors Bureau in the center court of the mall. *617/954–2000 www.massconvention.com.*

Symphony Hall. While Boston's Symphony Hall—the home of the Boston Symphony Orchestra and the Boston Pops—is considered among the best in the world for its sublime acoustics, it's also worth visiting to enjoy its other merits. The stage is framed by an enormous organ facade and an intricate golden proscenium. Above the second balcony are 16 replicas of Greek and Roman statues, which, like the rest of the hall, marry the acoustic and aesthetic by creating niches and uneven surfaces to enhance the acoustics of the space. Although acoustical science was a brand-new field of research when Professor Wallace Sabine planned the interior, not one of the 2,500 seats is a bad one—the secret is the box-within-a-box design. *301 Massachusetts Ave., Back Bay 888/266–1200 box office, 617/638–9390 tours www.bso.org Free walk-up tours Oct.–May, Wed. at 4 and some Sat. at 2 M Symphony.*

NEED A BREAK?

Flour Bakery + Café. A good spot to refuel on a budget is Flour Bakery + Café, a perennial candidate for Boston's best sandwiches and stuffed bread. Also superb are the fresh pizzas, dinner specials, and delicious pastries. You may end up taking home one of their cookbooks as a sweet keepsake.

✉ 1595 Washington St., South End ☎ 617/267-4300 🌐 www.flourbakery.com Ⓜ Back Bay/South End.

THE SOUTH END

The South End lost many residents to the Back Bay in the late 19th century, but in the late 1970s, middle-class professionals began snapping up town houses at bargain prices and restoring them. Solidly back in fashion now, the South End's redbrick row houses in various states of refurbished splendor now house a mix of ethnic groups, the city's largest gay community, and some excellent shops.

Today a large African American community resides along Columbus Avenue and Mass Ave. (short for Massachusetts Avenue), which marks the beginning of the predominantly black neighborhood of Roxbury. Boston's gay community also has a strong presence in the South End, with most of the gay-oriented restaurants and businesses on Columbus Avenue and Tremont Street between East Berkeley Street and Mass Ave. If you like to shop, you'll have a blast in this area, which focuses on home furnishings and accessories, with a heavy accent on the unique and handmade. At the northern tip of the South End, where Harrison Avenue and Washington Street lead to Chinatown, are several Chinese supermarkets. South of Washington Street is the burgeoning "SoWa" District, home to a growing number of art galleries, many of which have relocated here from pricey Newbury Street. From May through October, the excellent SoWa Open Market on Sundays is a great excursion, packed with artists, food trucks, and a farmers' market.

TOP ATTRACTIONS

Rutland Square. Reflecting a time when the South End was the most prestigious Boston address, this slice of a park is framed by lovely Italianate bowfront houses. ✉ *Rutland Sq. between Columbus Ave. and Tremont St.*

Union Park. Cast-iron fences, Victorian-era town houses, and a grassy area all add up to one of Boston's most charming mini-escapes. ✉ *Union Park St. between Shawmut Ave. and Tremont St.* 🌐 *www.upna.org.*

WORTH NOTING

Bay Village. This pocket of early-19th-century brick row houses, near Arlington and Piedmont streets, is a fine, mellow neighborhood (Edgar Allan Poe was born here). Its window boxes and short, narrow streets make the area seem a toylike reproduction of Beacon Hill. Note that, owing to the street pattern, it's nearly impossible to drive to Bay Village, and it's easy to miss on foot. ✉ *Bounded (roughly) by Arlington, Stuart, Charles, and Marginal Sts.* 🌐 *www.bayvillage.net.*

Boston Center for the Arts. Of Boston's multiple arts organizations, this nonprofit arts-and-culture complex is the one that is closest to "the people." Here you can see the work of budding playwrights, check out

CLOSE UP

Prestige Lost

Not long after its conception in the mid-1800s, the South End, somewhat unfairly, lost its elite status to the Back Bay. The literature of the time documents this exodus: the title character in William Dean Howells's *The Rise of Silas Lapham* abandoned the South End to build a house on the water side of Beacon as material proof of his arrival in Boston society. In *The Late George Apley,* John P. Marquand's Brahmin hero tells how his father decided, in the early 1870s, to move the family from his South End bowfront to the Back Bay—a consequence of his walking out on the front steps one morning and seeing a man in his shirtsleeves on the porch opposite. Regardless of whether Marquand exaggerated Victorian notions of propriety (if that was possible), the fact is that people such as the Apleys did decamp for the Back Bay, leaving the South End to become what a 1913 guidebook called a "faded quarter."

rotating exhibits from contemporary artists, or stop in for a curator's talk and other special events. The BCA houses six performance spaces, a community music center, the Mills Art Gallery, and studio space for some 40 Boston-based contemporary artists. ✉ *539 Tremont St., South End* ☎ *617/426–5000* 🌐 *www.bcaonline.org* 🎫 *Free* 🕙 *Weekdays 9–5; Mills Gallery Wed. and Sun. noon–5, Thurs.–Sat. noon–9* Ⓜ *Back Bay/South End.*

Cathedral of the Holy Cross. This enormous 1875 Gothic cathedral dominates the corner of Washington and Union Park streets. The main church of the Archdiocese of Boston and therefore the seat of Cardinal Archbishop Seán Patrick O'Malley, Holy Cross is also New England's largest Catholic church. ✉ *1400 Washington St., South End* ☎ *617/542–5682* 🌐 *www.holycrossboston.com* 🕙 *Mass Sat. at 4:30 pm, Sun. at 8 am and 11:30 am, Mon.–Sat. at 9 am. Services in Spanish Sun. at 9:30 am, Tues. and Thurs. at 7 pm. Service in Latin Sun. at 11 am* Ⓜ *Back Bay.*

Hynes Convention Center. The Hynes Convention Center hosts conferences, trade shows, and conventions. It's connected to the Prudential Center, where visitors can find a branch of the Greater Boston Visitors Bureau in the center court of the mall. ☎ *617/954–2000* 🌐 *www.massconvention.com.*

7

THE FENWAY

GETTING ORIENTED

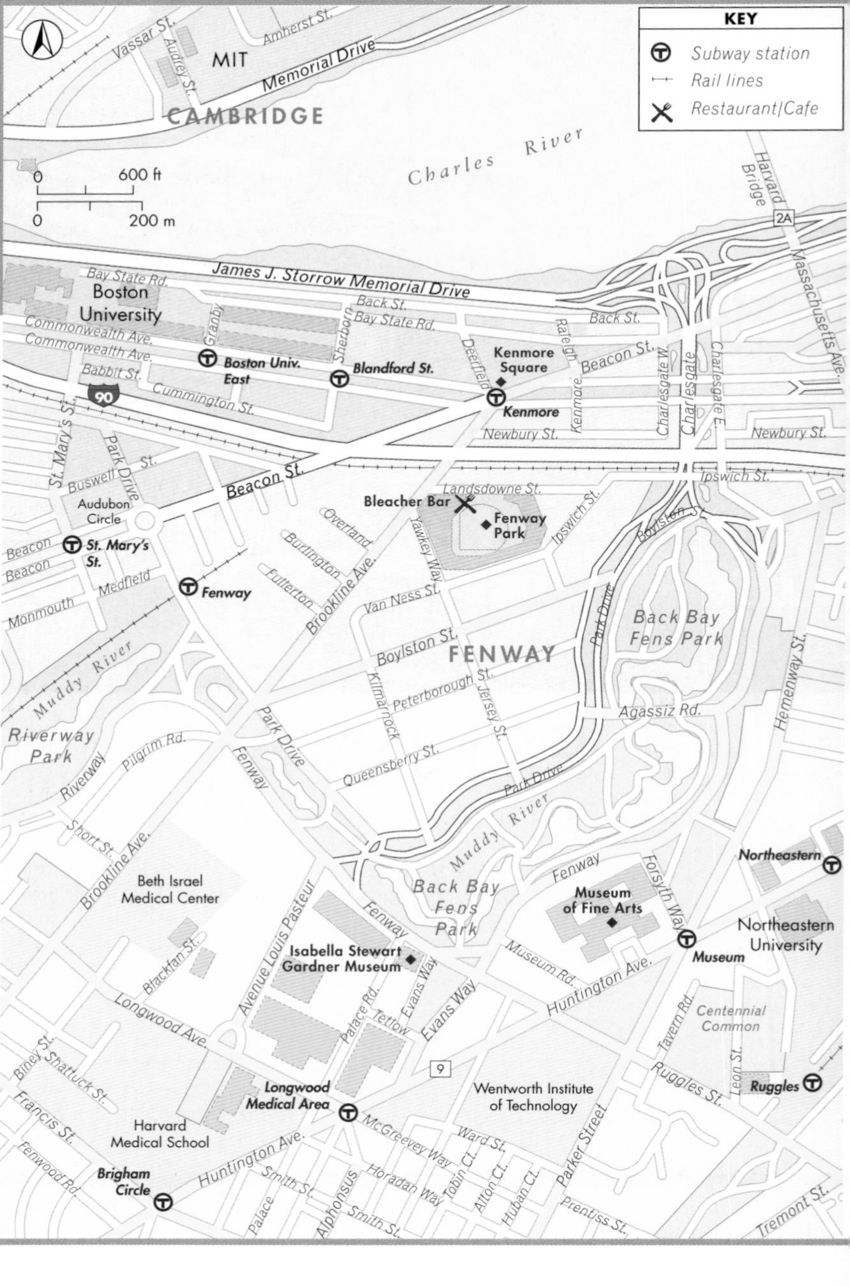

GETTING HERE AND AROUND

The Green Line is the way to go when it comes to getting to the Fenway; get off at the Kenmore or Fenway stops for a short walk to the ballpark. Also know that it *is* possible to drive around this part of town. With a little hunting, on-street parking can usually be found on nongame days; if not, many lots and garages are within reasonable walking distance of Fenway Park.

TIMING AND SAFETY

Although this area can be walked through in a couple of hours, art lovers could spend a week here, thanks to the glories of the MFA and the Isabella Stewart Gardner Museum. (If you want to do a museum blowout, avoid Tuesday, when the Gardner is closed.) To cap off a day of culture, plan for dinner in the area and then a concert at nearby Symphony Hall. Another option, if you're visiting between spring and early fall, is to take a tour of Fenway Park—or better yet, catch a game.

The Fenway and Kenmore Square area is generally safe, and is home to thousands of college students attending Boston University, Wheelock, Simmons, and Emmanuel, to name only a few of the nearby institutions. While the main strips, Beacon Street, Commonwealth Avenue, and Brookline Avenue, can be choked with pedestrians during game day, the marshy area of the Fens is quiet and poorly lighted: avoid walking there alone at night.

QUICK BITES

Nothing beats a dog and a beer at Fenway when you're enjoying the game on a warm summer's night. But even if you don't have a ticket, you can enjoy the same vibe at **Bleacher Bar** (✉ *82A Landsdowne St.*), a hidden-away bar in Fenway Park with a view into center field, and enough historical Red Sox memorabilia to open its own museum.

TOP REASONS TO GO

- Root for the home team (the *only* team in the eyes of Red Sox Nation) at Fenway Park.
- Immerse yourself in masterpieces at the MFA and the Isabella Stuart Gardner Museum.
- Relish the perfect acoustics of a concert at Symphony Hall.

WORD OF MOUTH

"Bring warm clothes. Not sure where you are from, but I have been to Fenway [Park] in May and been freezing. The rest of the country thinks May is mid-Spring, but Boston seems to miss the message some years."

—Gail

FENWAY PARK TOURS

If you can't see the Sox, you can still see the Green Monster up close by going on a tour of the park. The one-hour Fenway walking tours run year-round, and if you go on the day's last tour on a home-game day, you can watch batting practice. Tours run hourly from 9 am to 5 pm (or three hours before game time) and cost $16. ☎ *617/226–6666* ✉ *tours@redsox.com.*

DID YOU KNOW?

Yawkey Way is named for the late Tom Yawkey, who bought the Red Sox in 1933 as a 30th-birthday present for himself and spent the next 43 years pursuing his elusive grail.

Sightseeing
★★★★
Dining
★★★
Lodging
★★★
Shopping
★★
Nightlife
★★★★

The Back Bay Fens marshland gave this section its name, but two quirky institutions give it its character: Fenway Park, which in 2004 saw the triumphant reversal of an 86-year drought for Boston's beloved Red Sox, and the Isabella Stewart Gardner Museum, the legacy of a high-living Brahmin who attended a concert at Symphony Hall in 1912 wearing a headband that read "Oh, You Red Sox." Not far from the Gardner is another major cultural magnet: the Museum of Fine Arts. Kenmore Square, a favorite haunt for Boston University students, adds a bit of funky flavor to the mix.

Updated by Kim Foley MacKinnon

After the outsize job of filling in the bay had been completed, it would have been small trouble to obliterate the Fens with gravel and march row houses straight through to Brookline. But the planners, deciding that enough pavement had been laid between here and the Public Garden, hired vaunted landscape architect Frederick Law Olmsted to turn the Fens into a park. Olmsted applied his genius for heightening natural effects while subtly manicuring their surroundings; today the Fens park consists of irregularly shaped reed-bound pools surrounded by broad meadows, trees, and flower gardens.

The Fens marks the beginning of Boston's Emerald Necklace, a loosely connected chain of parks designed by Olmsted that extends along the Fenway, Riverway, and Jamaicaway to Jamaica Pond, the Arnold Arboretum, and Franklin Park. Farther off, at the Boston–Milton line, the Blue Hills Reservation offers some of the Boston area's best hiking, scenic views, and even a ski lift.

The Daughters of Edward Darley Boit (1882) by John Singer Sargent is one of the 450,000 works of art at the Museum of Fine Arts.

TOP ATTRACTIONS

Fodor's Choice ★ **Fenway Park.** For 86 years, the Boston Red Sox suffered a World Series dry spell, a streak of bad luck that fans attributed to the "Curse of the Bambino," which, stories have it, struck the team in 1920 when they sold Babe Ruth (the "Bambino") to the New York Yankees. All that changed in 2004, when a maverick squad broke the curse in a thrilling seven-game series against the team's nemesis in the series semifinals. This win against the Yankees was followed by a four-game sweep of St. Louis in the finals. Boston, and its citizens' ingrained sense of pessimism, hasn't been the same since. The repeat World Series win in 2007 cemented Bostonians' sense that the universe had finally begun working correctly and made Red Sox caps the residents' semiofficial uniform. ⇨ *See the Fenway Park spotlight in the Sports and the Outdoors chapter for more information.* ✉ *4 Yawkey Way, between Van Ness and Lansdowne Sts., The Fenway* ☎ *877/733–7699 box office, 617/226–6666 tours* 🌐 *www.redsox.com* 🎟 *Tours $16* ⏲ *Tours run daily 9–5, on the hour.* Ⓜ *Kenmore.*

Fodor's Choice ★ **Isabella Stewart Gardner Museum.**
See highlighted listing in this chapter.

Fodor's Choice ★ **Museum of Fine Arts.**
See highlighted listing in this chapter.

DID YOU KNOW?

Isabella Stewart Gardner never believed in insurance, preferring to put her faith in St. George and St. Florian, patron saints protecting against theft and fire. Portraits of both still hang in the entry portal, but the museum now carries insurance.

ISABELLA STEWART GARDNER MUSEUM

280 The Fenway, The Fenway 617/566-1401, 617/566-1088 café www.gardnermuseum.org $15 Museum Wed.-Mon. 11-5, Thurs. 11-9, open some holidays; café Tues.-Fri. 11:30-4, weekends 11-4 M Museum.

TIPS

- If you've visited the MFA in the two days prior to your trip here, there's a $2 admission fee discount.
- A charming quirk of the museum's admission policy waives entrance fees to anyone named Isabella.
- Allot about two hours to tour the museum properly, and note that the collections generally appeal to a "grown-up" audience, so there isn't much for young children here.
- If you're looking for a light lunch after your tour, visit Cafe G near the gift shop.

A young society woman, Isabella Stewart came in 1860 from New York—where ladies were more conspicuous than in Boston—to marry John Lowell Gardner, one of Boston's leading citizens. "Mrs. Jack" promptly set about becoming the most un-Bostonian of the Proper Bostonians. She built the Venetian palazzo to hold her collected arts in a corner of Boston's newest neighborhood with her will stipulating that the building remain exactly as she left it—paintings, furniture, and the smallest object in a hall cabinet—and that is as it has remained. Today, it's one of America's most idiosyncratic treasure houses.

7

Highlights

Gardner's palazzo contains a trove of paintings—including such masterpieces as Titian's *Europa,* Giotto's *Presentation of Christ in the Temple,* and John Singer Sargent's *El Jaleo.* Spanish leather panels, Renaissance fireplaces, and Gothic tapestries accent salons; eight balconies adorn the Venetian courtyard. There's a Raphael Room, Spanish Cloister, Gothic Room, Chinese Loggia, and a Tapestry Room for concerts, where Gardner entertained Henry James and Edith Wharton. An adjacent gallery houses the works of participants in the museum's artist-in-residence program.

On March 18, 1990, the Gardner was the target of a sensational art heist. Thieves disguised as police officers stole 12 works, including Vermeer's *The Concert.* To date, none of the art has been recovered, despite a $5-million reward. Because Mrs. Gardner's will prohibited substituting other works for any stolen art, empty walls identify spots where the paintings once hung.

A Renzo Piano-designed addition to the museum opened in 2012 housing a music hall, exhibit space, classrooms, and conservation labs, where Gardner's works can be repaired and preserved.

MUSEUM OF FINE ARTS

465 Huntington Ave., The Fenway 617/267-9300 www.mfa.org $25 (good for two days in a 10-day period) Sat.–Tues. 10–4:45, Wed.–Fri. 10–9:45. 1-hr tours daily; call for scheduled times Museum.

TIPS

- The year-round cocktail party "MFA First Fridays," from 6 to 9:30—held monthly—has become quite the social event. Stop by to admire the art in a festive atmosphere.
- Be aware that the museum will require you to check any bag larger than 11 inches by 15 inches, even if it's your purse. So save that oversize bag for another day and bring along only the essentials.

Count on staying a while if you have any hope of seeing what's here. Eclecticism and thoroughness, often an incompatible pair, have coexisted at the MFA since its early days. From Renaissance masters to impressionist marvels, African masks and Native American pottery, the collections are shorn of cultural snobbery and shortsighted trendiness.

Highlights

The MFA's collection of approximately 450,000 objects was built from a core of paintings and sculpture from the Boston Athenaeum, historical portraits from the city of Boston, and donations by area universities. The MFA has more than 70 works by John Singleton Copley; major paintings by Winslow Homer, John Singer Sargent, Fitz Henry Lane, and Edward Hopper; and a wealth of American works ranging from native New England folk art and colonial portraiture to New York abstract expressionism of the 1950s and 1960s. Also of particular note are the John Singer Sargent murals adorning the Rotunda. They were unveiled at the museum in 1921 and make for a dazzling first impression on visitors coming through the Huntington Avenue entrance.

American decorative arts are also represented, particularly those of New England in the years before the Civil War. The list goes on: more than thirty galleries contain the MFA's European painting and sculpture collection, dating from the 11th century to the 20th. Contemporary art has a home in the MFA's dramatic I. M. Pei–designed building and the museum also owns one of the world's most extensive collections of Asian art under one roof. Its collection of antique musical instruments is among the finest in the world and with 37 Monets, the MFA has the largest collection of the artist's work outside France.

A GOOD WALK

With Boston's two major art museums on this itinerary, a case of museum fatigue could set in. However, both the Museum of Fine Arts and the Isabella Stewart Gardner Museum are surrounded by the sylvan glades of the Fenway—a perfect oasis and time-out location when you're suffering from gallery overload. From the intersection of Massachusetts and Huntington avenues, with the front entrance of Symphony Hall on your right, walk down Huntington Avenue. On your left is the New England Conservatory of Music and, on Gainsborough Street, its recital center, Jordan Hall. Between Huntington Avenue and the Fenway is the **Museum of Fine Arts (MFA)** and, just around the corner, the **Isabella Stewart Gardner Museum**. If you prefer to pay homage to the Red Sox: from Symphony Hall, go north on Mass Ave., turn left on Commonwealth Avenue, and continue until you reach **Kenmore Square**; from here it's a 10-minute walk down Brookline Avenue to Yawkey Way and **Fenway Park**.

WORTH NOTING

Kenmore Square. Two blocks north of Fenway Park is Kenmore Square, where you'll find fast-food joints, stores, students, and an enormous sign advertising Citgo gasoline. The red, white, and blue neon sign from 1965 is so thoroughly identified with the area that historic preservationists fought, successfully, to save it—proof that Bostonians can be an open-minded lot who don't insist that their landmarks be identified with the American Revolution. The old Kenmore Square punk clubs have given way to a block-long development of chain stores and pricey restaurants, as well as brick sidewalks, gaslight-style street lamps, and tree plantings. In the shadow of Fenway Park between Brookline and Ipswich is **Lansdowne Street,** a nightlife magnet for the young and trendy who have their pick of can't-hear-yourself-think dance clubs and pregame bars. The urban campus of Boston University begins farther west on Commonwealth Avenue, in blocks thick with dorms, shops, and restaurants. ✉ *Convergence of Beacon St., Commonwealth Ave., and Brookline Ave.* Ⓜ *Kenmore.*

8

BOSTON OUTSKIRTS

GETTING ORIENTED

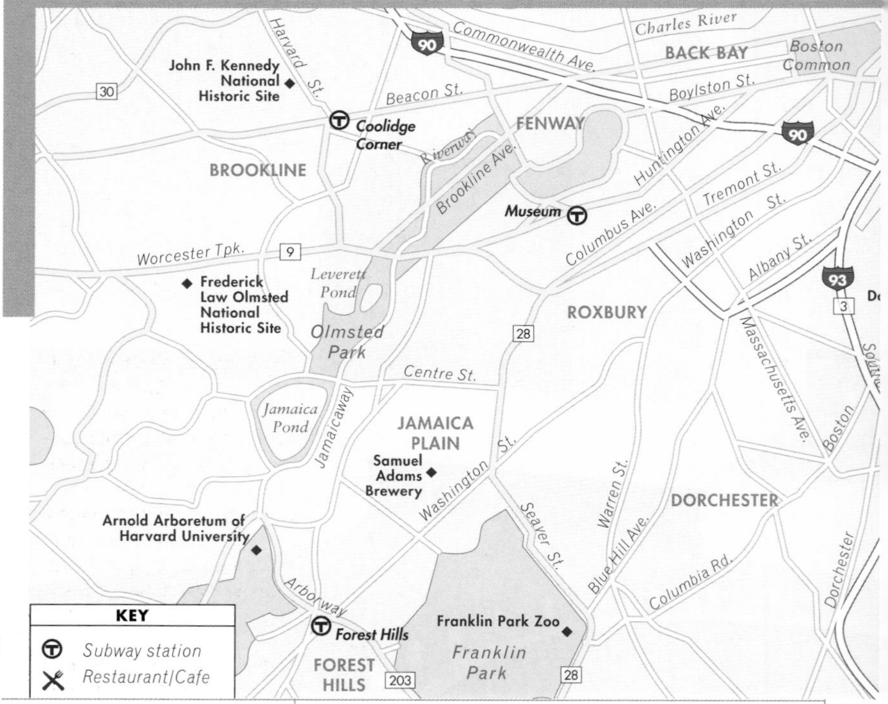

GETTING HERE AND AROUND

While driving to these suburbs is relatively painless, they're not called the "streetcar suburbs" for nothing. To get to South Boston, hop off the Red Line at Broadway. To reach the Arnold Arboretum in Jamaica Plain, take the Orange Line to the end at Forest Hills. Brookline is accessible via the C and D lines of the Green Line.

TOP REASONS TO GO

■ Marvel at the architectural wonder cantilevered over Boston Harbor that houses the Institute of Contemporary Art.

■ Relive the history of Camelot with a visit to the John F. Kennedy Library and Museum.

■ Tour the Samuel Adams Brewery, home to Boston's own award-winning beers. Free samples at the end are the highlight of the tour.

TIMING AND SAFETY

Timing all depends on which areas you decide to explore. Each neighborhood merits a half day, especially factoring in travel time from Boston proper and a leisurely lunch or dinner.

Generally, most of these neighborhoods are safe, particularly in the areas where these attractions reside. But use common sense: stick to well-lighted areas and avoid walking alone late at night.

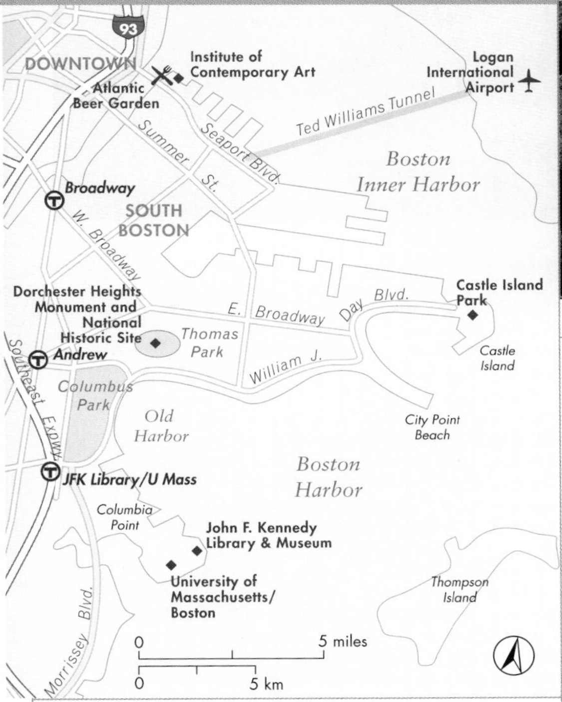

QUICK BITES

Atlantic Beer Garden. If you happen to be visiting the ICA, take a break at the Atlantic Beer Garden. Just steps from the art museum, the bar and restaurant has dozens of flat screens to catch every game, and gorgeous views of the harbor and the ICA from the deck, where you can dine alfresco in summer. ✉ *146 Seaport Blvd.* ☎ *617/357–8000* 🌐 *www.atlanticbeergarden.com.*

A GOOD WALK

A stroll down Brookline's Harvard Street is a great way to spend a few hours if you're in the neighborhood. Browse the bookshelves at **Brookline Booksmith** (✉ *279 Harvard St.*), an excellent local bookstore; or take in an independent film at the **Coolidge Corner Theater** (✉ *290 Harvard St.*). After window-shopping, treat yourself to a few scoops at **J. P. Licks** (✉ *311 Harvard St.*), arguably some of the Boston area's best ice cream.

WORD OF MOUTH

"Sam Adams Brewery: highly recommended. They ask for a $2 donation... The 60-minute tour [came with a] cute souvenir glass and three tastings. I thought my parents would yell at me for taking them to a brewery at 10:30 in the morning, but they enjoyed themselves, so I think they forgot."

—absolutkz

"Spring is the 'showy' time of the year in the [Arnold] Arboretum, but each season reveals wonderful leaves and blooms. Get a map at the visitor center... also see when they are giving free tours."

—cw

8

Sightseeing ★★★
Dining ★★
Lodging ★★
Shopping ★★★
Nightlife ★★

The expansion of Boston in the 1800s was not confined to the Back Bay and the South End. Toward the close of the century, as the working population of the Downtown district swelled and public transportation (first horsecars, then electric trolleys) linked outlying suburbs with the city, development of the "streetcar suburbs" began. These areas answered the housing needs of the rising native-born middle class as well as the second-generation immigrant families already outgrowing the narrow streets of the North and West ends.

Updated by Kim Foley MacKinnon

The landfill project that became South Boston—known as "Southie" and not to be confused with the South End—isn't a true streetcar suburb; its expansion predates the era of commuting. Some of the brick bowfront residences along East Broadway in City Point date from the 1840s and 1850s, but the neighborhood really came into its own with the influx of Irish around 1900, and Irish Americans still hold sway here. Southie is a Celtic enclave, as the raucous annual St. Patrick's Day parade attests.

Among the streetcar suburbs are Dorchester and Jamaica Plain (now part of Boston proper)—rural retreats barely more than a century ago that are now thick with tenements and Boston's distinctive three- and six-family triple-decker apartment houses. Dorchester is almost exclusively residential, tricky to navigate by car, and accessible by the T only if you know exactly where you're going. Jamaica Plain is a hip, young neighborhood with a strong lesbian and ecofriendly population; brunch and a wander through the neighborhood's quirky stores or through the Arnold Arboretum make for a relaxing weekend excursion. Both towns border Franklin Park, an Olmsted creation of more than 500 acres, noted for its zoo. Farther west, Brookline is composed of a mixture of the affluent and students.

SOUTH BOSTON

TOP ATTRACTION

Fodor's Choice ★ **Institute of Contemporary Art.** Housed in a breathtaking cantilevered edifice that juts out over the Boston waterfront, the ICA moved to this site in 2006 as part of a massive reinvention that's seeing the museum grow into one of Boston's most exciting attractions. Since its foundation in 1936, the institute has cultivated its cutting-edge status: it's played host to works by Edvard Munch, Egon Schiele, and Oskar Kokoschka. Early in their careers, Andy Warhol, Robert Rauschenberg, and Roy Lichtenstein each mounted pivotal exhibitions here. Now the ICA is building a major permanent collection for the first time in its history, while continuing to showcase innovative paintings, videos, installations, and multimedia shows. The performing arts get their due in the museum's theater, and the Water Café features cuisine from local seasonal ingredients. In nice weather, you can sit outside and enjoy the views. ✉ *100 Northern Ave., South Boston* ☎ *617/478–3100* 🌐 *www.icaboston.org* 🎫 *$15, free Thurs. 5–9, free for families last Sat. of every month (except Dec.)* ⏲ *Tues. and Wed. 10–5, Thurs. and Fri. 10–9, weekends 10–5. Tours on select weekends at 2 and select Thurs. at 6* Ⓜ *Courthouse.*

WORTH NOTING

Castle Island Park. South Boston projects farther into the harbor than any other part of Boston except Logan Airport, and the views of the Harbor Islands from along Day Boulevard or Castle Island are expansive. At L Street and Day Boulevard is the L Street Beach, where an intrepid group called the L Street Brownies swims year-round, including a celebratory dip in the icy Atlantic every New Year's Day. Castle Island Park is no longer on an island, but **Fort Independence**, when it was built here in 1801, was separated from the mainland by water. The circular walk from the fort around Pleasure Bay, delightful on a warm summer day, has a stunning view of the city's skyline late at night. To get here by the T, take the Red Line to Broadway Station. Just outside the station, catch Bus 9 or 11 going east on Broadway, which takes you to within a block of the waterfront. From the waterfront park you can walk the loop, via piers, around the island. ✉ *Off William J. Day Blvd., South Boston* ☎ *617/727–5290* 🌐 *www.mass.gov/dcr/parks/metroboston/castle.htm* ⏲ *Tours Memorial Day–Labor Day, call for specific tour times.*

8

DORCHESTER

TOP ATTRACTIONS

FAMILY **Franklin Park Zoo.** Lion and tiger habitats, the Giraffe Savannah, and a 4-acre mixed-species area called the Serengeti Crossing that showcases zebras, ostriches, ibex, and wildebeests keep this zoo roaring. The Tropical Forest, with its Western Lowland Gorilla environment, is a big draw, and wallabies, emus, and kangaroos populate the Australian

Arnold Arboretum of Harvard University is an urban oasis just 6 miles from Downtown.

Outback Trail. From May to September butterflies flit and flutter at Butterfly Landing, where docents are on hand to answer questions and give advice on attracting the colorful insects to your own garden. The Children's Zoo entices with sheep, goats, and other beasts. In winter, call in advance to find out which animals are braving the cold. The park, 4 miles from Downtown, is reached by Bus 16 from the Forest Hills (Orange Line) or Andrew (Red Line) T stops; there's plenty of parking. ✉ *1 Franklin Park Rd., Dorchester* ☎ *617/541–5466* 🌐 *www.zoonewengland.com* 🎫 *$17 adults; $11 children ages 2–12* 🕒 *Oct.–Mar., daily 10–4; Apr.–Sept., weekdays 10–5, weekends 10–6.*

John F. Kennedy Library & Museum. Chronicling a time now passing from memory to history, the library-museum is both a center for serious scholarship and a focus for Boston's nostalgia for her native son. The stark, white, prowlike building (another modernist monument designed by I. M. Pei) at this harbor-enclosed site pays homage to the life and presidency of John F. Kennedy and to members of his family, including his wife, Jacqueline, and brother Robert.

The Kennedy Library is the official repository of his presidential papers; the museum displays a trove of Kennedy memorabilia, including re-creations of his desk in the Oval Office and of the television studio in which he debated Richard M. Nixon in the 1960 election. At the entrance, high and dry during the summer months, is the president's 26-foot sailboat; inside, two theaters show a film about his life. The museum exhibits, ranging from the Cuban missile crisis to his assassination, include 20 video presentations. There's also a permanent display on the late Jacqueline Kennedy Onassis, including some samples of her distinctive wardrobe and such personal mementos as a first edition of *One Special Summer*, the book she and her sister wrote and illustrated shortly after a 1951 trip to Paris. A re-creation of the office Robert Kennedy occupied as attorney general from 1961 to 1964 complements "legacy" videos of John's idealistic younger brother. As a somber note in an otherwise gung-ho museum, continuous videos of the first news bulletin of the assassination and the funeral are shown in a darkened hall. Fourth-floor research facilities are open only to serious scholars. The Steven M. Smith Hall provides space for meetings and events; the facility also includes a store and a small café. ✉ *Columbia Point, Dorchester* ☎ *617/514–1600* 🌐 *www.jfklibrary.org* 🎟 *$12* ⏲ *Daily 9–5* Ⓜ *JFK/UMass, then free shuttle bus every 20 mins.*

WORTH NOTING

Dorchester Heights Monument and National Historic Site. In 1776 Dorchester Heights hill commanded a clear view of central Boston, where the British had been under siege since the preceding year. Here George Washington set up the cannons that Henry Knox, a Boston bookseller turned soldier, and later secretary of war, had hauled through the wilderness after their capture at Fort Ticonderoga. The artillery did its job of intimidation, and the British troops left Boston, never to return. The view of Boston from the site is magnificent, particularly if you go during the hours the graceful white tower is staffed, which is admittedly, very rare. Climb its 93 steps and you'll be rewarded with vistas from the Blue Hills to the Harbor Islands, although the lovely park grounds are a destination on their own on a warm day. ✉ *Thomas Park off Telegraph St., near G St., Dorchester* ☎ *617/242–5642* 🌐 *www.nps.gov/bost/historyculture/dohe.htm* 🎟 *Free* ⏲ *Grounds daily. Monument call for schedule* Ⓜ *Broadway, then City Point Bus (9 or 11) to G St.*

8

JAMAICA PLAIN

TOP ATTRACTIONS

Fodor's Choice ★ **Arnold Arboretum of Harvard University.** This 281-acre living laboratory is somewhat incongruously set in a dense urban area. Established in 1872 in accordance with the terms of a bequest from New Bedford merchant James Arnold, it contains more than 4,000 kinds of woody plants, most from the hardy North Temperate Zone. It's a mecca for runners, cyclists, dog walkers, and families. The rhododendrons, azaleas, lilacs, magnolias, and fruit trees are eye-popping when in bloom, and something is always in season from early April through September. In October the park puts on a display in blazing colors. Peters Hill has a grand view of the Boston skyline and local surroundings. The Larz Anderson bonsai collection contains individual specimens imported from Japan that are more than 200 years old. In the visitor center there is a 40-to-1 scale model of the arboretum (with 4,000 tiny trees), plus rotating exhibits. If you visit during May, Lilac Sunday on Mother's Day is an annual celebration of blooming trees, family-friendly activities, and picnicking (the only day it's allowed). The arboretum, 6 miles from Downtown Boston, is accessible by the MBTA Orange Line or Bus 39 from Copley Square to the Custer Street stop in Jamaica Plain (3 blocks away). ✉ *125 Arborway, at Centre St., Jamaica Plain* ☎ *617/524–1718* 🌐 *www.arboretum.harvard.edu* 🎫 *Donations accepted* ⏲ *Grounds daily dawn–dusk; visitor center (which is closed Wed.) Apr.–Oct. daily 11–6, Nov.–Mar. noon–4. Call for walking tours info* Ⓜ *Forest Hills.*

BROOKLINE

TOP ATTRACTION

Frederick Law Olmsted National Historic Site. Frederick Law Olmsted (1822–1903) is considered the nation's preeminent creator of parks. In 1883, at age 61, while immersed in planning Boston's Emerald Necklace of parks, Olmsted set up his first permanent office at Fairsted, an 18-room farmhouse dating from 1810, to which he added another 18 rooms for his design offices. Plans and drawings on display include projects as the U.S. Capitol grounds, Stanford University, and Mount Royal Park in Montréal. You can also tour the design rooms (some now in use as an archive library) where Olmsted and staff drew up their plans; highlights include a 1904 "electric blueprint machine," a kind of primitive photocopier. The 1¾-acre site incorporates many trademark Olmstedian designs, including areas of meadow, wild garden, and woodland; Olmsted believed body and spirit could be healed through close association with nature. The site became part of the National Park Service in 1980; Olmsted's office played an influential role in the creation of this federal agency. ✉ *99 Warren St.* ☎ *617/566–1689* 🌐 *www.nps.gov/frla/index.htm* 🎫 *Free* ⏲ *Grounds open daily, dawn to dusk. Tours June 21–Sep. 15, Wed.–Sun. at 10, 11, 1, 2, 3, and 4. Tours Sep. 16–June 20, Fri.–Sat. at 10, 11, 1, 2, 3, and 4* Ⓜ *Brookline Hills.*

WORTH NOTING

John F. Kennedy National Historic Site. This was the home of the 35th president from his birth on May 29, 1917, until 1921, when the family moved to nearby Naples and Abbottsford streets. Rose Kennedy provided the furnishings for the restored 2½-story, wood-frame structure. You can pick up a brochure for a walking tour of young Kennedy's school, church, and neighborhood. To get here, take the MBTA Green Line to Coolidge Corner and walk north on Harvard Street four blocks. ✉ *83 Beals St.* ☎ *617/566–7937* 🌐 *www.nps.gov/jofi* 🎫 *Free* ⏲ *Mid-May–Oct., Wed.–Sun. 9:30–5, call for tour schedule. In winter, private tours can be arranged* Ⓜ *Coolidge Corner.*

SOMERVILLE

The once sleepy Somerville has come into its own in recent years. Davis Square is a gathering place for Tufts University student, who congregate in its surrounding cafes, clubs, and ethnic restaurants.

9

CAMBRIDGE

GETTING ORIENTED

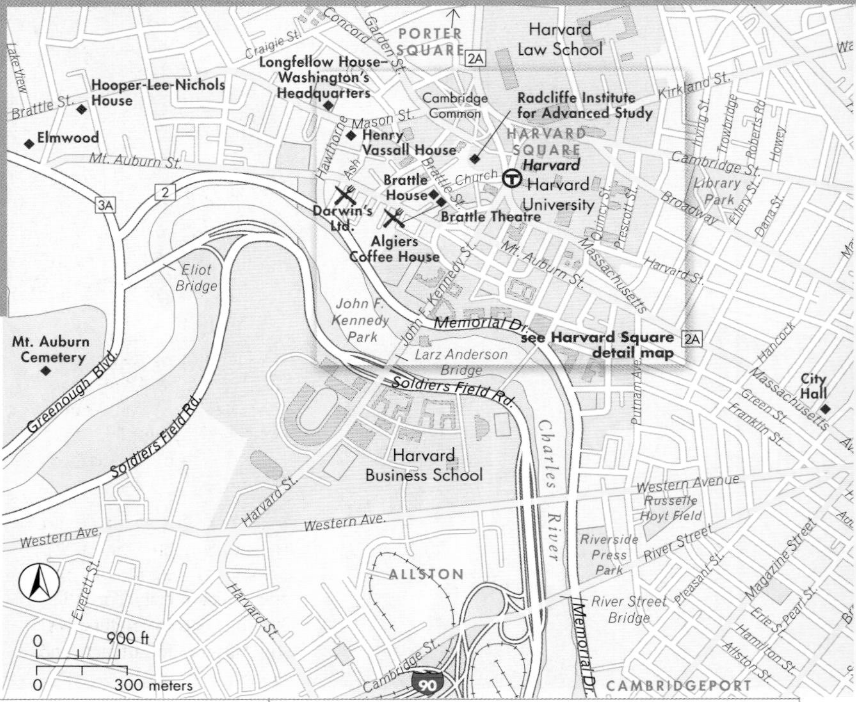

TIMING	GETTING HERE AND AROUND
Harvard Square is worth an afternoon; be sure to take a tour. Most visitors don't go beyond Harvard Square and Harvard Yard, but this is a one-of-a-kind town filled with funky restaurants, independent shops, unique art installations, important historic sites, and a large concentration of independent bookstores. If you plan to explore Harvard's natural history or art museums or explore other Cambridge neighborhoods, give yourself a day or two here. ⇨ *See "It's Hip to Be Square," below, for ideas on where to go.*	Just minutes from Boston, Cambridge is easily reached by taking the Red Line train (otherwise known as the T) outbound to any stop past Charles/MGH station. There are stops at MIT (Kendall Square), Central Square, Harvard Square, Porter Square, Davis Square (actually in Somerville), and Alewife. Harvard Square is the best place to begin any visit to Cambridge, but driving (and parking) here is a small nightmare. Do yourself a favor and take the T. If you insist on driving, suck it up and park in a garage. (Street parking is usually limited to two hours, and most spots are reserved for Cambridge residents.) Driving is less of a pain in other parts of Cambridge, but you're still better off getting around via the T. Try to spend as much time as possible exploring on foot. This is a walking town, and you'll miss a lot of Cambridge's quirkiness if you're moving too fast.

VISITOR INFORMATION

Cambridge Visitor Information Booth. A good place to start is the Cambridge Visitor Information Booth, outside the T station in Harvard Square. Free maps, brochures, historical walking tours, an excellent list of bookstores in the area, and a guide to seasonal events are available. ✉ *Harvard Sq., near MBTA station entrance* ☎ *617/497–1630* 🌐 *www.cambridge-usa.org* ⏲ *Weekdays 9–5, weekends 9–1* Ⓜ *Harvard.*

QUICK BITES

You won't have a hard time finding food in Cambridge; all the major squares are surrounded by interesting independent restaurants. Near Harvard Square try **Mr. Bartley's Burger Cottage** (✉ *1246 Massachusetts Ave.*), a Harvard institution with an extensive (and hilarious) menu that includes dozens of riffs on the humble burger. Casual cafés abound on Brattle Street; good bets include **Tory Row** (✉ *3 Brattle St.*) and **Cardullo's Gourmet Shop** (✉ *6 Brattle St.*), both of which make great sandwiches.

TOP REASONS TO GO

■ Browse the new- and used-book stores, trawl the artsy boutiques, and people-watch in Harvard Square. Take a break at one of the local coffee shops.

■ Do the museum circuit: The Harvard Museums for art; the Semitic Museum for ancient Near Eastern collections; the Peabody and the Natural History Museum for artifacts and culture.

■ Visit MIT to wander the halls, visit its museum, and see Frank Gehry's Seuss-like Stata Center.

■ Breathe the rarefied air of Harvard on an official tour (or an irreverent unofficial one), then return to real life with a burger from Mr. Bartley's.

■ Amble down Brattle Street, visiting the 1700s-era homes of Tory Row (Washington really did sleep here).

MOBILE TOUR

The Cambridge Office for Tourism offers a walking tour for your mobile device on its website 🌐 *www.cambridge-usa.org.*

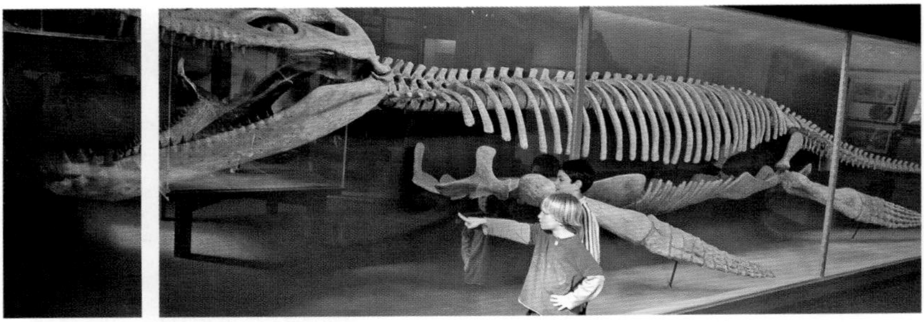

Sightseeing ★★★★
Dining ★★★★★
Lodging ★★
Shopping ★★★★
Nightlife ★★★★★

Updated by Kim Foley MacKinnon

The city of Cambridge takes a lot of hits, most of them thrown across the Charles River by city-proud Bostonians. But Boston's Left Bank—an überliberal academic enclave—is a must-visit if you're spending more than a day or two in the Boston area.

The city is punctuated at one end by the funky architecture of MIT and at the other by the grand academic fortress that is Harvard University. Civic life connects the two camps into an urban stew of 100,000 residents who represent nearly every nationality in the world, work at every kind of job from tenured professor to taxi driver, and are passionate about living on this side of the river.

The Charles River is the Cantabrigians' backyard, and there's virtually no place in Cambridge more than a 10-minute walk from its banks. Strolling, running, or biking is one of the great pleasures of Cambridge, and your views will include graceful bridges, the distant Boston skyline, crew teams rowing through the calm water, and the elegant spires of Harvard soaring into the sky.

No visit to Cambridge is complete without an afternoon (at least) in Harvard Square. It's a hub, a hot spot, and home to every variation of the human condition: Nobel laureates, homeless buskers, trust-fund babies, and working-class Joes. A walk down Brattle Street past Henry Wadsworth Longfellow's house is a joy. Farther along Massachusetts Avenue is Central Square, an ethnic melting pot of people and restaurants. Ten minutes more bring you to MIT, with its eclectic architecture from postwar pedestrian to Frank Gehry's futuristic fantasyland. In addition to providing a stellar view, the Massachusetts Avenue Bridge, spanning the Charles from Cambridge to Boston, is also notorious in MIT lore for its Smoot measurements *(⇨ see "Campus Pranksters" under Massachusetts Institute of Technology)*.

HARVARD SQUARE

In Cambridge all streets point toward Harvard Square. In addition to being the gateway to Harvard University and its various attractions, Harvard Square is home to the tiny yet venerable folk-music club Passim (Bob Dylan played here, and Bonnie Raitt was a regular during her time at Harvard), first-run and vintage movie theaters, concert and lecture venues, and a tempting collection of eclectic, independent shops. Harvard Square is a multicultural microcosm. On a warm day street musicians coax exotic tones from their Andean pan flutes and *erhus*, Chinese stringed instruments, while cranks and local pessimists pass out pamphlets warning against all sorts of end-of-the-world scenarios. You will hear people speaking dozens of languages. In the small plaza atop the main entrance to the Harvard T station known as "the Pit," skaters and punk rockers strut and pose while fresh-faced students impress each other and/or their dates, and quiet clusters study the moves and strategy of the chess players seated outside Au Bon Pain. It's a wonderful circus of humanity.

TOP ATTRACTIONS

Harvard Art Museums. In 2014, the combined collections of the Busch-Reisinger and Fogg museums (which closed in 2008) and the Arthur M. Sackler Museum (which closed in 2013) will be represented under one roof with the umbrella name Harvard Art Museums. Barring any possible delays, Harvard Art Museums are slated to open in late 2014, housed in a new facility designed by architect Renzo Piano. Highlights include American and European paintings, sculptures, and decorative arts from the Fogg Museum; works by German expressionists, materials related to the Bauhaus, and postwar contemporary art from German-speaking Europe from the Busch-Reisinger Museum. The collection will also include ancient Greek and Roman sculpture, Chinese jades, and Islamic ceramics from the Sackler Museum. ✉ *32 Quincy St.* ☎ *617/495–9400* 🌐 *www.harvardartmuseums.org* Ⓜ *Harvard.*

9

NEED A BREAK?

Broadway Marketplace. The Broadway Marketplace is just around the corner from Harvard Yard. Besides the excellent fresh produce, there's a selection of sandwiches and prepared meals; choose one to be heated up and then grab a seat for a quick, delicious (if pricey) bite. Every Thursday (5–7 pm), there's a wine, beer, or liquor tasting, a great way to mingle with locals. ✉ ***468 Broadway*** ☎ ***617/547–2334*** 🌐 ***www.broadwaymarketplace.com.***

FAMILY
Fodor's Choice ★

Harvard Museum of Natural History. Many museums promise something for every member of the family; the vast Harvard Museum complex actually delivers. In 2012, Harvard University created a new consortium, the Harvard Museums of Science & Culture, uniting under one administration several of its most visited public museums. The Harvard Museum of Natural History (which exhibits specimens from the Museum of Comparative Zoology, Harvard University Herbaria, and the Mineralogical and Geological Museum) displays some 12,000 specimens, including dinosaurs, rare minerals, hundreds of mammals and birds, and Harvard's world famous Blaschka Glass Flowers. The museum

DID YOU KNOW?

The Harvard Museum of Natural History's collection includes 21 million specimens, but only a small sample is on display. An active lecture and family program means there's plenty of opportunity to interact with another local species—the Harvard researcher.

combines historic exhibits drawn from the university's vast collections with new and changing multimedia exhibitions such as *New England Forests and Mollusks: Shelled Masters of the Marine Realm*, and the renovated Earth & Planetary Sciences gallery. **TIP→ Check the website for children's events and special engagements, which occur throughout the year.** ✉ *26 Oxford St.* ☎ *617/495–3045* 🌐 *www.hmnh.harvard.edu* 🎫 *$12; free for Massachusetts residents year-round, Sun. 9–noon and Sept.–May, Wed. 3–5. Ticket includes admission to the Peabody Museum* ⏲ *Daily 9–5* Ⓜ *Harvard.*

DID YOU KNOW?

If you have $1,100, you too can get a Harvard Education! The surprisingly affordable Harvard Extension School, part of the university's Faculty of Arts and Sciences, offers a wide range of continuing education courses (some online), taught by honest-to-goodness members of the Harvard faculty. Check the website for details (🌐 *www.extension.harvard.edu*).

FAMILY
Fodor's Choice ★

Harvard Square. Tides of students, tourists, political-cause proponents, and bizarre street creatures are all part of the nonstop pedestrian flow at this most celebrated of Cambridge crossroads.

Harvard Square is where Mass Ave., coming from Boston, turns and widens into a triangle broad enough to accommodate a brick peninsula (above the T station). The restored 1928 kiosk in the center of the square once served as the entrance to the MBTA station (it's now Out of Town News, a fantastic newsstand). Harvard Yard, with its lecture halls, residential houses, libraries, and museums, is one long border of the square; the other three are composed of clusters of banks and a wide variety of restaurants and shops.

On an average afternoon you'll hear earnest conversations in dozens of foreign languages; see every kind of youthful uniform from Goth to impeccable prep; wander by street musicians playing Andean flutes, singing opera, and doing excellent Stevie Wonder or Edith Piaf imitations; and watch a tense outdoor game of pickup chess between a street-tough kid and an older gent wearing a beard and a beret while you slurp a cappuccino or an ice-cream cone (the two major food groups here). An afternoon in the square is people-watching raised to a high art; the parade of quirkiness never quits.

As entertaining as the locals are, the historic buildings are worth noting. Even if you're only a visitor (as opposed to a prospective student), it's still a thrill to walk though the big brick-and-wrought-iron gates to Harvard Yard, past the residence halls and statues, on up to Widener Library.

Across Garden Street, through an ornamental arch, is **Cambridge Common,** decreed a public pasture in 1631. It's said that under a large tree that once stood in this meadow George Washington took command of the Continental Army on July 3, 1775. A stone memorial now marks the site of the "Washington Elm." Also on the Common is the Irish Famine Memorial by Derry artist Maurice Herron, unveiled in 1997 to coincide with the 150th anniversary of "Black '47," the deadliest

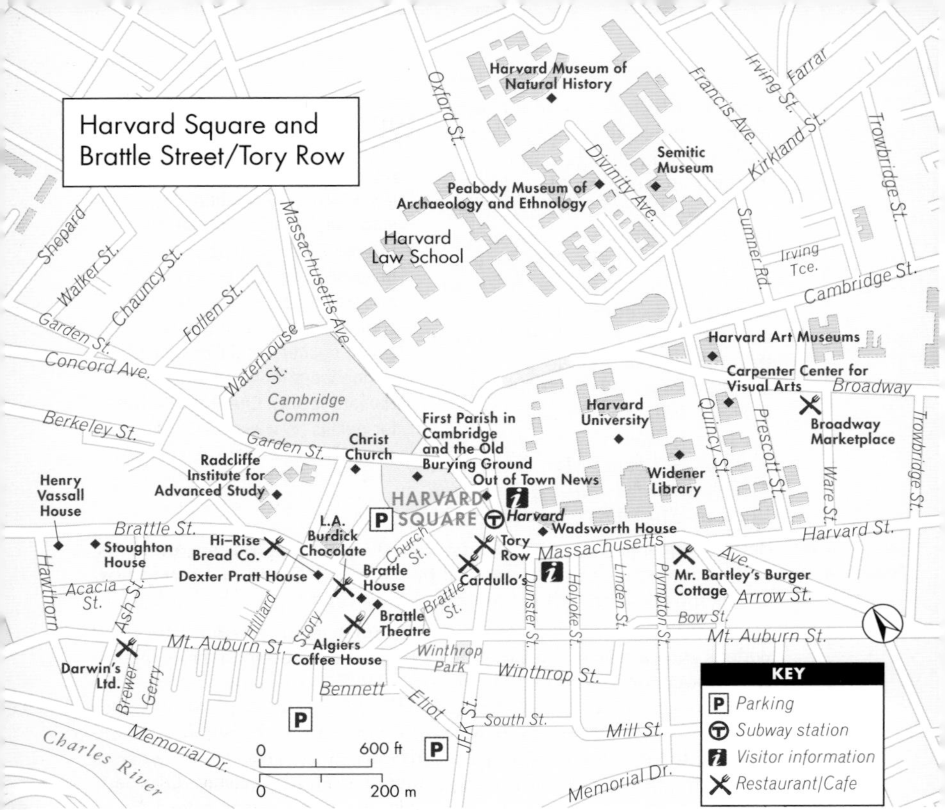

year of the potato famine. It depicts a desperate Irish mother sending her child off to America. At the center of the Common a large memorial commemorates the Union soldiers and sailors who lost their lives in the Civil War. On the far side of the Common (on Waterhouse Street between Garden Street and Massachusetts Avenue) is a fantastic park. ✉ *Boston* 🌐 *www.harvardsquare.com* Ⓜ *Harvard*.

Harvard University. The tree-studded, shady, and redbrick expanse of **Harvard Yard**—the very center of Harvard University—has weathered the footsteps of Harvard students for hundreds of years. In 1636 the Great and General Court of the Massachusetts Bay Colony voted funds to establish the colony's first college, and a year later chose Cambridge as the site. Named in 1639 for John Harvard, a young Charlestown clergyman who died in 1638 and left the college his entire library and half his estate, Harvard remained the only college in the New World until 1693, by which time it was firmly established as a respected center of learning. Local wags refer to Harvard as WGU—World's Greatest University—and it's certainly the oldest and most famous American university.

Although the college dates from the 17th century, the oldest buildings in Harvard Yard are from the 18th century (though you'll sometimes see archaeologists digging here for evidence of older structures). Together

TWO WAYS TO EXPLORE HARVARD SQUARE

HISTORY 101

If you want to revisit the city's Tory beginnings, walk past the **Wadsworth House**, a clapboard house on Massachusetts Avenue that dates from 1726, and enter the dignified hush of the Yard at **Harvard University**. Admire the exterior of **Widener Library** (only students and their guests are allowed inside); it houses one of the largest collections of books, historical materials, and journals in the academic world. Then circle back through the yard, crossing Massachusetts Avenue to view the **First Parish in Cambridge and the Old Burying Ground** on the corner of Church Street. Through the iron railing of the cemetery you can make out a number of tombstones. Buried here are the remains of 17th- and 18th-century Tory landowners, slaves, and soldiers. Continue up Garden Street to **Christ Church**, designed in 1761 and still an active parish. The Cambridge Common, across Garden Street, has a terrific playground in the back corner away from the university (⇨ *see above*); this is a good spot to take a rest.

Retrace your steps along Massachusetts Avenue and cross the street near the First Parish Church. Cut through Harvard Yard, bearing to your left, pass the modern Science Center (a good place for a bathroom break; restrooms are in the basement), and look for the striking Victorian architecture of Memorial Hall. Spend some time milling around the Yard and getting in touch with your inner undergrad.

ARTS ELECTIVES

A big project is currently underway to combine the collections from the Fogg, Busch-Reisinger, and Arthur M. Sackler museums. Slated to open in late 2014, the museums will be housed in a new facility designed by architect Renzo Piano and will be identified as the **Harvard Art Museums**. Highlights will include American and European paintings, sculptures, and decorative arts from the Fogg Museum; works by German expressionists, materials related to the Bauhaus, and postwar contemporary art from German-speaking Europe from the Busch-Reisinger Museum; and examples of ancient Greek and Roman sculpture, Chinese jade, and Islamic ceramics from the Sackler Museum. The nearby **Carpenter Center for the Visual Arts** on Quincy Street offers a strictly contemporary perspective on film and graphic arts. **TIP→ Film lovers: Visit the film archive section on the Harvard website to find film screenings that coincide with your visit.** When you've had your fill of culture, head back to one of the Harvard Square cafés for a snack and serious people-watching.

the buildings chronicle American architecture from the colonial era to the present. **Holden Chapel,** completed in 1744, is a Georgian gem. The graceful **University Hall** was designed in 1815 by Charles Bulfinch. An 1884 statue of John Harvard by Daniel Chester French stands outside; ironically for a school with the motto of "Veritas" ("Truth"), the model for the statue was a member of the class of 1882 and not Harvard himself. **Sever Hall,** completed in 1880 and designed by Henry Hobson Richardson, represents the Romanesque revival that was followed by the neoclassical (note the pillared facade of Widener Library) and

A young academic ponders his studies at Harvard University.

the neo-Georgian, represented by the sumptuous brick houses along the Charles River, many of which are now undergraduate residences. **Memorial Church,** a graceful steepled edifice of modified Colonial Revival design, was dedicated in 1932. Just north of the Yard is **Memorial Hall,** completed in 1878 as a memorial to Harvard men who died in the Union cause; it's High Victorian both inside and out. It also contains the 1,166-seat Sanders Theatre, which serves as the university's largest lecture hall, site of year-round concerts by students and professionals, and the venue for the festive Christmas Revels.

Many of Harvard's cultural and scholarly facilities are important sights in themselves, including the **Harvard Museum of Natural History,** the **Peabody Museum of Archaeology & Ethnology,** and the **Widener Library.** Be aware that most campus buildings, other than museums and concert halls, are off-limits to the general public. ✉ *Bounded by Massachusetts Ave. and Mt. Auburn, Holyoke, and Dunster Sts.* ☎ *617/495–1000* 🌐 *www.harvard.edu* Ⓜ *Harvard.*

Harvard University Events & Information Center. Harvard University Events & Information Center, run by students, includes a small library, a video-viewing area, computer terminals, and an exhibit space. It also distributes maps of the university area and has free student-led tours of Harvard Yard. The tour doesn't include visits to museums, and it doesn't take you into campus buildings, but it provides a fine orientation. The information center is open year-round (except during spring recess and other semester breaks), Monday through Saturday 9 to 5. Tours are offered September through May, every hour between 10 and 4 (except during university breaks). From the end of June through August, guides offer tours every half-hour; however, it's best to call ahead to confirm times. Groups of 20 or more can schedule tours ahead. You can also download a mobile tour if you have a smartphone. ✉ *Holyoke Center, 1350 Massachusetts Ave.* ☎ *617/495–1573* 🌐 *www.harvard.edu/visitors.*

DID YOU KNOW?

One perk of being a university professor with an endowed chair—a position awarded to about a dozen preeminent members of the Harvard faculty—is the official right to graze cattle in Harvard Yard. Not surprisingly, few, if any, ever do.

Peabody Museum of Archaeology and Ethnology. With one of the world's outstanding anthropological collections, the Peabody focuses on Native American and Central and South American cultures. The Hall of the North American Indian is particularly outstanding, with art, textiles, and models of traditional dwellings from across the continent. The Mesoamerican room juxtaposes ancient relief carvings and weavings with contemporary works from the Maya and other peoples. ✉ *11 Divinity Ave.* ☎ *617/496–1027* 🌐 *www.peabody.harvard.edu* 🎫 *$12, includes admission to Harvard Museum of Natural History, accessible through the museum; free for Massachusetts residents on Sun. 9–noon year-round and Wed. 3–5 Sept.–May (excluding commercial groups)* ⏲ *Daily 9–5* Ⓜ *Harvard.*

WORTH NOTING

Carpenter Center for the Visual Arts. This gravity-defying mass of concrete and glass, built in 1963 to contrast with the now-defunct and more traditional Fogg Art Museum next door, is the only building in North America designed by the French architect Le Corbusier. The open floor plan provides students with five stories of flexible workspace, and the large, outward-facing windows ensure that the creative process is always visible and public. The center regularly holds free lectures and receptions with artists on Thursday evenings. At the top of the ramp, the **Sert Gallery** plays host to changing exhibits of contemporary works and has a café. The Main Gallery on the ground floor often showcases work by students and faculty. The **Harvard Film Archive** downstairs screens films nightly, often accompanied by discussions with the filmmakers. ✉ *24 Quincy St.* ☎ *617/495–3251* 🌐 *www.ves.fas.harvard.edu/ccva.html* 🎫 *Galleries free, film screenings $9* ⏲ *Main Gallery Mon.–Sat. 10 am–11 pm, Sun. 1 pm–11 pm; Sert Gallery Tues.–Sun. 1–5. Exhibits closed in the summer* Ⓜ *Harvard.*

Christ Church. This modest yet beautiful gray clapboard structure was designed in 1761 by Peter Harrison, the first architect of note in the colonies. During the Revolution, members of its mostly Tory congregation fled for their lives. The organ was melted down for bullets and the building was used as a barracks during the Siege of Boston. (Step into the vestibule to look for the bullet hole left during the skirmish.) Martha Washington requested that the church reopen for services on New Year's Eve in 1775. The church's historical significance extends to the 20th century: Teddy Roosevelt was a Sunday-school teacher here, and Martin Luther King Jr. spoke from the pulpit to announce his opposition to the Vietnam War. ✉ *Zero Garden St.* ☎ *617/876–0200* 🌐 *www.*

cccambridge.org ⏲ *Visit building any day 8–4. Sun. services at 7:45 and 10:15, with choral evensong at 4 on the first Sun. of month; Wed. services at 12:10* Ⓜ *Harvard.*

WORD OF MOUTH

"We took Basel the dog and headed for Cambridge. There was a big street festival going on to celebrate Oktoberfest. We did a lot of walking, eating and got some great books at the Harvard Book Store."—Icuy

NEED A BREAK?

Out of Town News. Need a news fix? Out of Town News has got you covered. Browse the world at this fascinating international news seller. Peruse the racks at this fabled landmark for international publications in languages from around the world. It's definitely worth a browse. ✉ ***Harvard Sq.*** ☎ ***617/354–1441.***

First Parish in Cambridge and the Old Burying Ground. Next to the imposing church on the corner of Church Street and Mass. Ave., a spooky-looking colonial graveyard houses 17th- and 18th-century tombstones of ministers, early Harvard presidents, and Revolutionary War soldiers. The wooden Gothic Revival church, known locally as "First Church" or "First Parish," was built in 1833 by Isaiah Rogers. The congregation dates to two centuries earlier, and has been linked to Harvard since the founding of the college. ✉ *3 Church St.* ☎ *617/876–7772* 🌐 *www.firstparishcambridge.org* ⏲ *Church weekdays 8–4, Sun. 8–1, service at 10:30. Burying ground daily dawn–dusk* Ⓜ *Harvard.*

Forum. The church sponsors the popular lecture series Forum, featuring well-known authors and academics. ☎ *617/495–2727* 🌐 *www.cambridgeforum.org.*

Semitic Museum. An almost unknown gem, this Harvard institution serves as an exhibit space for Egyptian, Mesopotamian, and ancient Near East artifacts and as a center for archaeological exploration. Who knew that the Sphinx may have had curls? The museum's extensive collection rotates and there are temporary exhibits, so you never know what you might see here. The building also houses the Department of Near Eastern Languages and Civilization, with offices tucked among the artifacts. Note that there is no elevator, though plans are in the works to install one. ✉ *6 Divinity Ave.* ☎ *617/495–4631* 🌐 *www.fas.harvard.edu/~semitic* 🎟 *Free; donations appreciated* ⏲ *Weekdays 10–4, Sun. 1–4* Ⓜ *Harvard.*

Wadsworth House. On the Harvard University side of Harvard Square stands the Wadsworth House, a yellow clapboard structure built in 1726 as a home for Harvard presidents. It served as the first headquarters for George Washington, who arrived on July 2, 1775, to take command of the Continental Army, which he did the following day. The house, closed to the public, now houses general Harvard offices. ✉ *1341 Massachusetts Ave.* 🌐 *www.harvard.edu* Ⓜ *Harvard.*

Widener Library. The Harry Elkins Widener Memorial Library is Harvard University's flagship library. It was named for a young book lover who went down with the Titanic. Holding more than 17 million volumes in more than 70 libraries around the world, the Harvard Library system

CLOSE UP

Old School

Cambridge dates from 1630, when the Puritan leader John Winthrop chose this meadowland as the site of a carefully planned village he named Newtowne. The Massachusetts Bay Colony chose Newtowne as the site for the country's first college in 1636. Two years later, John Harvard bequeathed half his estate and his private library to the fledgling school, and the college was named in his honor. The town elders changed the name to Cambridge, emulating the university in England where most of the Puritan leaders had been educated.

When Cambridge was incorporated as a city in 1846, the boundaries were drawn to include the university area (today's Harvard Square and Tory Row), and the more industrial communities of Cambridgeport and East Cambridge. By 1900 the population of these urban industrial and working-class communities, made up of Irish, Polish, Italian, Portuguese, and French Canadian residents, dwarfed the Harvard end of town. Today's city is much more a multiethnic urban community than an academic village. Visitors in search of any kind of ethnic food or music will find it in Cambridge—the local high school educates students who speak more than 40 different languages at home.

When MIT, originally Boston Tech, moved to Cambridge in 1916, it was the first educational institution that aimed to be more than a trade school, training engineers but also grounding them in the humanities and liberal arts. Many of MIT's postwar graduates remained in the area, and went on to form hundreds of technology-based firms engaged in camera manufacturing, electronics, and space research. By the 1990s manufacturing had moved to the burbs, and software developers, venture capitalists, and robotics and biotech companies claimed the former industrial spaces. This area around Kendall Square is now nicknamed "Intelligence Alley."

is second in size in the United States only to the Library of Congress. Widener Library itself is one of the world's largest individual book repositories: Over 50 miles of bookshelves snake around six stories above and four stories below ground, holding over 3 million volumes. The imposing neoclassical structure was designed by one of the nation's first major African American architects, Julian Abele. In the center of the building stands the private collection of Mr. Widener (including his Gutenberg Bible and Shakespeare First Folio) in a room featuring his original desk. It was his mother's express wish that fresh flowers be placed on the desk, a tradition that continues to this day. The library isn't open to the public; people with a "scholarly need" can apply for admission at the privileges office inside. ✉ *Harvard Yard* ☎ *617/495–2413* 🌐 *www.hcl.harvard.edu/libraries/widener* Ⓜ *Harvard*.

BRATTLE STREET/TORY ROW

Brattle Street remains one of New England's most elegant thoroughfares. Elaborate mansions line both sides from where it meets JFK Street to Fresh Pond Parkway. Brattle Street was once dubbed Tory Row, because during the 1770s its seven mansions, on lands that stretched to the river, were owned by staunch supporters of King George. These properties were appropriated by the patriots when they took over Cambridge in the summer of 1775. Many of the historic houses are marked with blue signs, and although only two (the Hooper-Lee-Nichols House and the Longfellow National Historic Site) are fully open to the public, it's easy to imagine yourself back in the days of Ralph Waldo Emerson and Henry David Thoreau as you stroll the brick sidewalks. Mt. Auburn Cemetery, an exquisitely landscaped garden cemetery, is less than 2 miles down Brattle Street from Harvard Square.

WORD OF MOUTH

"I live in Cambridgeport between Harvard and MIT and walk to Harvard Square all the time. It's a lovely walk by the river. Eat outdoors or in at Henrietta's Kitchen at the Charles Hotel or at Legal Seafoods, or Rialto, all top dining spots. Upstairs on the Square is good also, as is Sandrine's on Holyoke St." —cigalechanta

TOP ATTRACTIONS

Brattle House. This 18th-century, gambrel-roof Colonial once belonged to the Loyalist William Brattle. He moved to Boston in 1774 to escape the patriots' anger, then left in 1776 with the British troops. From 1831 to 1833 the house was the residence of Margaret Fuller, feminist author and editor of *The Dial.* Today it's the office of the Cambridge Center for Adult Education, and is listed on the National Register of Historic Places. ✉ *42 Brattle St.* ☎ *617/547–6789* 🌐 *www.ccae.org* Ⓜ *Harvard.*

NEED A BREAK?

Algiers Coffee House. Algiers Coffee House, upstairs from the Brattle Theatre, is a favorite evening hangout for young actors and artists. Linger over mint tea or a plate of hummus, or enjoy a glass of wine on the second-floor terrace and watch the world go by. ✉ ***40 Brattle St.*** ☎ ***617/492–1557.***

Brattle Theatre. Occupying a squat, barnlike building from 1890, the Brattle Theatre is set improbably between a modern shopping center and a Colonial mansion. The resident repertory company gained notoriety in the 1950s when it made a practice of hiring actors blacklisted as Communists by the U.S. government. For the last half-century it has served as the square's independent movie house, screening indie, foreign, obscure, and classic films, from nouveau to noir; check the website for current offerings and events. ✉ *40 Brattle St.* ☎ *617/876–6837* 🌐 *www.brattlefilm.org* Ⓜ *Harvard.*

Longfellow House-Washington's Headquarters. If there's one historic house to visit in Cambridge, this is it. Henry Wadsworth Longfellow, the poet whose stirring tales of the Village Blacksmith, Evangeline, Hiawatha, and Paul Revere's midnight ride thrilled 19th-century America, once lived in this elegant mansion. One of several original Tory Row homes on Brattle Street, the house was built in 1759 by John Vassall Jr., and George Washington lived here during the Siege of Boston from July 1775 to April 1776. Longfellow first boarded here in 1837 and later received the house as a gift from his father-in-law on his marriage to Frances Appleton, who burned to death here in an accident in 1861.

For 45 years Longfellow wrote his famous verses here and filled the house with the exuberant spirit of his own work and that of his literary circle, which included Ralph Waldo Emerson, Nathaniel Hawthorne, and Charles Sumner, an abolitionist senator. Longfellow died in 1882, but his presence in the house lives on—from the Longfellow family furniture to the wallpaper to the books on the shelves (many the poet's own). The home is preserved and run by the National Park Service; free 45-minute guided tours of the house are offered hourly. The formal garden is the perfect place to relax. **TIP→ Longfellow Park, across the street, is the place to stand to take photos of the house.** The park was created to preserve the view immortalized in the poet's "To the River Charles." ✉ *105 Brattle St.* ☎ *617/876–4491* 🌐 *www.nps.gov/long* 🎫 *Free* 🕑 *Grounds daily dawn to dusk; house May–Oct., Wed.–Sun. 9:30–4:30* Ⓜ *Harvard.*

Mt. Auburn Cemetery. A cemetery might not strike you as a first choice for a visit, but this one is a pleasure. Opened in 1831, it was the country's first garden cemetery, and more than 90,000 people have been buried here—among them Henry Wadsworth Longfellow, Mary Baker Eddy, Winslow Homer, Amy Lowell, Isabella Stewart Gardner, and architect Charles Bullfinch. The grave of engineer Buckminster Fuller bears an engraved geodesic dome. In spring local nature lovers and bird-watchers come out of the woodwork to see the warbler migrations and the glorious blossoms. Brochures, maps, and audio tours are at the entrance. ✉ *580 Mt. Auburn St.* ☎ *617/547–7105* 🌐 *www.mountauburn.org* 🕑 *Grounds open 8–8. Call for information about tours and special events. Office hours: Mon.–Fri. 8:30–4:30; Sat. 8:30 to noon* Ⓜ *Harvard; then Watertown (71) or Waverly (73) bus to cemetery.*

Radcliffe Institute for Advanced Study. The famed women's college, situated around a serene yard, was founded in 1879 and wedded to Harvard University in 1977. It merged with Harvard in 1999, and its name officially changed from Radcliffe College. ✉ *10 Garden St.* 🌐 *www.radcliffe.edu* Ⓜ *Harvard.*

Schlesinger Library. The Schlesinger Library, in Radcliffe Yard, houses more than 50,000 volumes on the history of women in America, including the papers of Harriet Beecher Stowe, Julia Child, Betty Friedan, and other notables. The library is also known for its extensive culinary collections, which contain cookbooks from the 16th century to the present. The library is open to the public, but materials do not circulate. ☎ *617/495–8540.*

9

NEED A BREAK?

Darwin's Ltd. Once beyond the vicinity of Harvard Square, Brattle Street lacks eateries, so before your walk consider stocking up at Darwin's Ltd. on Mt. Auburn, which carries delectable, Cambridge-inspired sandwiches and other "comestibles and caffeinated provisions." ✉ ***148 Mt. Auburn St.*** ☎ ***617/354–5233*** 🌐 ***www.darwinsltd.com.***

WORTH NOTING

Dexter Pratt House. Also known as the "Blacksmith House," this yellow Colonial is now owned by the Cambridge Center for Adult Education. The tree itself is long gone, but this spot inspired Longfellow's

ALL IN GOOD FUN

Harvard's Hasty Pudding Club is well known for its theatricals—its pun-filled burlesque shows and its annual Man and Woman of the Year spectacles have elicited groans from audiences for more than a century. The similarly irreverent *Harvard Lampoon* has been influencing American comedy since the club's inception; early members wrote for the *New Yorker,* while more recently it has proven fertile ground for television comics and writers: the *National Lampoon, Saturday Night Live,* and *The Simpsons* were all spawned by its alumni. The Lampoon Castle (simultaneously located at 44 Bow Street, 14 Linden Street, 17 Plympton Street, and 57 Mt. Auburn Street), replete with hidden doors and secret passages, was built for the club in 1909 by William Randolph Hearst and Boston socialite Isabella Stewart Gardner. The copper ibis on top is reputedly electrified to ward off pranksters from the daily *Harvard Crimson* newspaper, who at the height of the Cold War cut it down and formally presented it to the Soviet Union as a "gift from the students of America." Connections at the State Department had to be called in to retrieve the purloined bird.

lines: "Under a spreading chestnut tree, the village smithy stands." The blacksmith's shop, today commemorated by a granite marker, was next door, at the corner of Story Street. From October to December, the celebrated Blacksmith House Poetry Series runs most Monday nights. Tickets are $3. ✉ *56 Brattle St.* 🌐 *www.ccae.org/events/blacksmith.html* Ⓜ *Harvard.*

NEED A BREAK?

Hi-Rise Bread Company. The Hi-Rise Bread Company, just on the edge of Harvard Square, is a nice stop for a pick-me-up coffee, fresh-baked treat, or fantastic sandwich on homemade bread. It's a great spot for people-watching and the espresso is excellent. ✉ ***1663 Massachusetts Ave.*** ☎ ***617/492–3003.***

L.A. Burdick Chocolates. Chocolate lovers may be seduced by the aromas emanating from L.A. Burdick Chocolates; rich confections or elegant, life-changing hot cocoa may be just the things to restore flagging spirits or weary feet. ✉ ***52 Brattle St.*** ☎ ***617/491–4340*** 🌐 ***www.burdickchocolate.com.***

Elmwood. Shortly after its construction in 1767, this three-story Georgian house was abandoned by its owner, colonial governor Thomas Oliver. Elmwood House was home to the accomplished Lowell family for two centuries. Elmwood is now the Harvard University president's residence, ever since student riots in 1969 drove President Nathan Pusey from his house in Harvard Yard. ✉ *33 Elmwood Ave.* Ⓜ *Harvard.*

Henry Vassall House. Brattle Street's seven houses known as "Tory Row" were once occupied by wealthy families linked by friendship, if not blood. This one may have been built as early as 1636. In 1737 it was purchased by John Vassall Sr.; four years later he sold it to his younger brother Henry. It was used as a hospital during the Revolution, and

CLOSE UP

It's Hip to Be Square

In Cambridge, any commercial area where three or more streets meet in a jumble of traffic and noise has been dubbed a "square." (There are literally hundreds, though most are just simple intersections.) Harvard Square draws the most visitors, but several other neighborhood squares exude their own charms. These are a few of our favorites; if you want to see where real Cantabrigians hang out, head here.

Central Square, at Massachusetts Avenue (known by locals as "Mass Ave."), Prospect Street, and Western Avenue, has Irish pubs, ethnic eats, music clubs, and a row of furniture stores. Cambridge's city government is here, and Ben Affleck and Matt Damon lived in the neighborhood. For good eats, check out the Baraka Café (✉ *80 Pearl St.*) or Green Street (✉ *280 Green St.*). The Central Square T stop is on the Red Line.

Somerville's **Davis Square** is just over the border from northwest Cambridge and easily accessible on the Red Line. This funky neighborhood near Tufts University is packed with great eateries, lively bars, and candlepin bowling. Harvard Square can sometimes feel a little tired after midnight, but there's still a lot of energy here late at night. At the Somerville Theater (✉ *55 Davis Sq.*) you can enjoy cheap first-run movies ($9), excellent popcorn, and even beer and wine with your feature. Check out the hilarious Museum of Bad Art in the basement before or after your flick. The Davis Square T stop is on the Red Line.

Impossibly hip **Inman Square,** at the intersection of Cambridge and Hampshire streets, has a great cluster of restaurants, cafés, bars, and shops. This place is just plain cool. Some highlights include Christina's (✉ *1255 Cambridge St.*), where you can enjoy some wildly inventive ice cream, and Punjabi Dhaba (✉ *225 Hampshire St.*), a perfect stop for cheap-but-good late-night Indian food and outstanding people-watching. Sadly, there's no T service to Inman, but you can get here from Harvard Square or Central Square on foot; it's near the intersection of Hampshire and Cambridge streets.

At **Kendall Square,** near the Massachusetts Institute of Technology (MIT) and the heart of the city's thriving biotech industry, an art-house multiplex shows first-run films. The square is also a stone's throw from the Charles and a short walk from riverside restaurant Dante (✉ *40 Edwin H. Land Blvd.*). The Kendall Square/MIT T stop is on the Red Line.

Porter Square, about a mile northwest of Harvard Square on Mass Ave., has several shopping centers and, within the nearby Porter Exchange, Japanese noodle and food shops. As you walk north (away from Harvard) past the heart of Porter Square, you'll pass pretty much every ethnic eatery imaginable, many of them excellent and far cheaper than Harvard Square restaurants. Standouts include the Cambodian-French fusion Elephant Walk (✉ *2067 Massachusetts Ave.*) and Greek Corner (✉ *2366 Massachusetts Ave.*), but you'll also find Indian, Chinese, Thai, Bangladeshi, Vietnamese, and Himalayan. There are also quite a few unique shops along the way. The Porter Square T stop is on the Red Line.

MIT's Stata Center was designed by Frank Gehry.

the traitor Dr. Benjamin Church was held here as a prisoner. The house was remodeled during the 19th century. It's now a private residence, but from the street you can view the Colonial home with its black-shuttered windows and multiple dormers. ✉ *94 Brattle St.* Ⓜ *Harvard.*

Hooper-Lee-Nichols House. Now headquarters of the Cambridge Historical Society, this is one of two Tory-era homes on Brattle Street fully open to the public. The Emerson family gave it to the society in 1957. Built between 1685 and 1690, the house has been remodeled at least six times, but has maintained much of the original structure. The downstairs is elegantly, although sparsely, appointed with period books, portraits, and wallpaper. An upstairs bedroom has been furnished with period antiques, some belonging to the original residents. Visits are by tour only and run about one hour. A virtual tour of the house is available on the Cambridge Historical Society's website. ✉ *159 Brattle St.* ☎ *617/547–4252* 🌐 *www.cambridgehistory.org* *Donations welcome* ⏲ *Call in advance for tour info* Ⓜ *Harvard.*

KENDALL SQUARE/MIT

Harvard Square may be the center of the "People's Republic of Cambridge," but the Kendall Square neighborhood is the city's hard-driving capitalist core. Gritty industrial buildings share space with sleek office blocks and the sprawling Massachusetts Institute of Technology. Although the MIT campus may lack the ivied elegance of Harvard Yard, major modern architects, including Alvar Aalto, Frank Gehry, I. M. Pei, and Eero Saarinen, created signature buildings here. To reach

MIT, take the Red Line T to Kendall station; if you're headed for the MIT Museum on the western edge of the campus, the Central Square station is more convenient.

TOP ATTRACTIONS

List Visual Arts Center. Local Boston-area artists and art students consider the List Gallery to be the most interesting gallery in town. Founded by Albert and Vera List, pioneer collectors of modern art, this MIT center has three galleries showcasing exhibitions of cutting-edge art and mixed media. Works from the center's collection of contemporary art, such as Thomas Hart Benton's painting *Fluid Catalytic Crackers* and Harry Bertoia's altarpiece for the MIT Chapel, are on view here and around campus. The center's website includes a map indicating the locations of more than 25 of these works. ✉ *20 Ames St., Bldg. E 15* ☎ *617/253–4680* 🌐 *listart.mit.edu* 🎟 *Free* ⏲ *Call ahead for hours* Ⓜ *Kendall/MIT.*

Massachusetts Institute of Technology. This once-tidy engineering school at right angles to the Charles River is growing like a sprawling adolescent, consuming old industrial buildings and city blocks with every passing year. Once dissed as "the factory," particularly by its Ivy League neighbor, Harvard University, MIT mints graduates that are the sharp blades on the edge of the information revolution. It's perennially in the top five of *U.S. News and World Report's* college rankings.

Founded in 1861, MIT moved to Cambridge from Copley Square in the Back Bay in 1916. It has long since fulfilled the predictions of its founder, the geologist William Barton Rogers, that it would surpass "the universities of the land in the accuracy and the extent of its teachings in all branches of positive science." Its emphasis shifted in the 1930s from practical engineering and mechanics to the outer limits of scientific fields.

Architecture is important at MIT. Although the original buildings were obviously designed by and for scientists, many represent pioneering designs of their times. The **Kresge Auditorium,** designed by Eero Saarinen, with a curving roof and unusual thrust, rests on three, instead of four, points. The nondenominational **MIT Chapel,** a circular Saarinen design, is lighted primarily by a roof oculus that focuses natural light on the altar and by reflections from the water in a small surrounding moat; it's topped by an aluminum sculpture by Theodore Roszak. The serpentine **Baker House,** now a dormitory, was designed in 1947 by the Finnish architect Alvar Aalto in such a way as to provide every room with a view of the Charles River. Sculptures by Henry Moore and other notable artists dot the campus. The latest addition is the newly minted Green Center, punctuated by the splash of color that is Sol Lewitt's 5,500-square-foot mosaic floor mural.

The East Campus, which has grown around the university's original neoclassical buildings of 1916, also has outstanding modern architecture and sculpture, including the stark high-rise **Green Building** by I. M. Pei, housing the Earth Science Center. Just outside is Alexander Calder's giant stabile (a stationary mobile) *The Big Sail.* Another Pei work on the East Campus is the **Wiesner Building,** designed in 1985, which houses the **List Visual Arts Center.** Architect Frank Gehry made his mark on the campus with the cockeyed, improbable **Ray & Maria Stata Center,** a complex of buildings on Vassar Street. The center houses computer, artificial intelligence, and information systems laboratories, and is reputedly as confusing to navigate on the inside as it is to follow on the outside. East Campus's **Great Dome,** which looms over neoclassical Killian Court, has often been the target of student "hacks" and has at various times supported a telephone booth with a ringing phone, a life-size statue of a cow, and a campus police cruiser. Nearby, the domed **Rogers Building** has earned unusual notoriety as the center of a series of hallways and tunnels dubbed "the infinite corridor." Twice each winter the sun's path lines up perfectly with the corridor's axis, and at dusk students line the third-floor hallway to watch the sun set through the westernmost window. The phenomenon is known as "MIT-henge."

MIT maintains an information center in the Rogers Building, and offers free tours of the campus weekdays at 11 and 3. Check the schedule, as the tours are often suspended during school holidays. General hours for the information center are weekdays 9–5. ✉ *77 Massachusetts Ave.* ☎ *617/253–4795* 🌐 *www.mit.edu* Ⓜ *Kendall/MIT.*

NEED A BREAK?

Toscanini's Ice Cream. Toscanini's Ice Cream is a well-loved local spot, specializing in all sorts of creative flavors; it has garnered national attention from the likes of the *New York Times* and *People* magazine. Also a good place for coffee, the shop frequently has small art exhibits. From the MIT Museum, it's two blocks up Mass Ave. toward Central Square; look for it on the right. ✉ *899 Main St.* ☎ *617/491–5877* 🌐 *www.tosci.com.*

WORTH NOTING

FAMILY **MIT Museum.** A place where art, science, and technology meet, the MIT Museum boasts the world's largest collection of holograms, though young kids may prefer the moving gestural sculptures of Arthur Ganson. The robot room shows off inventions of MIT's renowned robotics lab and an extensive exhibit on artificial intelligence. Allow an hour or two for a visit and check the schedule for special programs and demonstrations by MIT researchers and inventors. ✉ *265 Massachusetts Ave.* ☎ *617/253–5927* 🌐 *web.mit.edu/museum* 🎫 *$10* ⏲ *Sept.–June, daily 10–5; July and Aug., Fri.–Wed. 10–5, Thurs. 10–7* Ⓜ *Kendall/MIT.*

WHERE TO EAT

Updated by
Victoria Abbott
Riccardi

In a city synonymous with tradition, Boston chefs have spent recent years rewriting culinary history. The stuffy, wood-paneled formality is gone; the endless renditions of *chowdah,* lobster, and cod have retired; and the assumption that true foodies better hop the next Amtrak to New York is also—thankfully—a thing of the past.

In their place, a crop of young chefs have ascended, opening small, upscale neighborhood spots that use local New England ingredients to delicious effect. Traditional eats can still be found (Durgin-Park remains the best place to get baked beans), but many diners now gravitate toward innovative food in understated environs. Whether you're looking for casual French, down-home Southern cooking, some of the best sushi in the country, or Vietnamese banh mi sandwiches, Boston restaurants are ready to deliver. Eclectic Japanese spot o ya and iconic French restaurant L'Espalier have garnered widespread attention, while a coterie of star chefs like Barbara Lynch, Lydia Shire, and Ken Oringer have built mini-empires and thrust the city to the forefront of the national dining scene.

The fish and shellfish brought in from nearby shores continue to inform the regional cuisine, along with locally grown fruits and vegetables, handmade cheeses, and humanely raised heritage game and meats. But don't expect boiled lobsters and baked apple pie. Today's chefs, while showcasing New England's bounty, might offer you lobster cassoulet with black truffles, bacon-clam pizza from a wood-burning oven, and a tomato herb salad harvested from the restaurant's rooftop garden. In many ways, though, Boston remains solidly skeptical of trends. To wit: the cupcake craze and food truck trend hit here later than other cities; the soft frozen yogurt movement has only recently arrived. And over in the university culture of Cambridge, places like East Coast Grill and Raw Bar, Oleana, and Rendezvous espoused the locavore and slow-food movements before they became buzzwords.

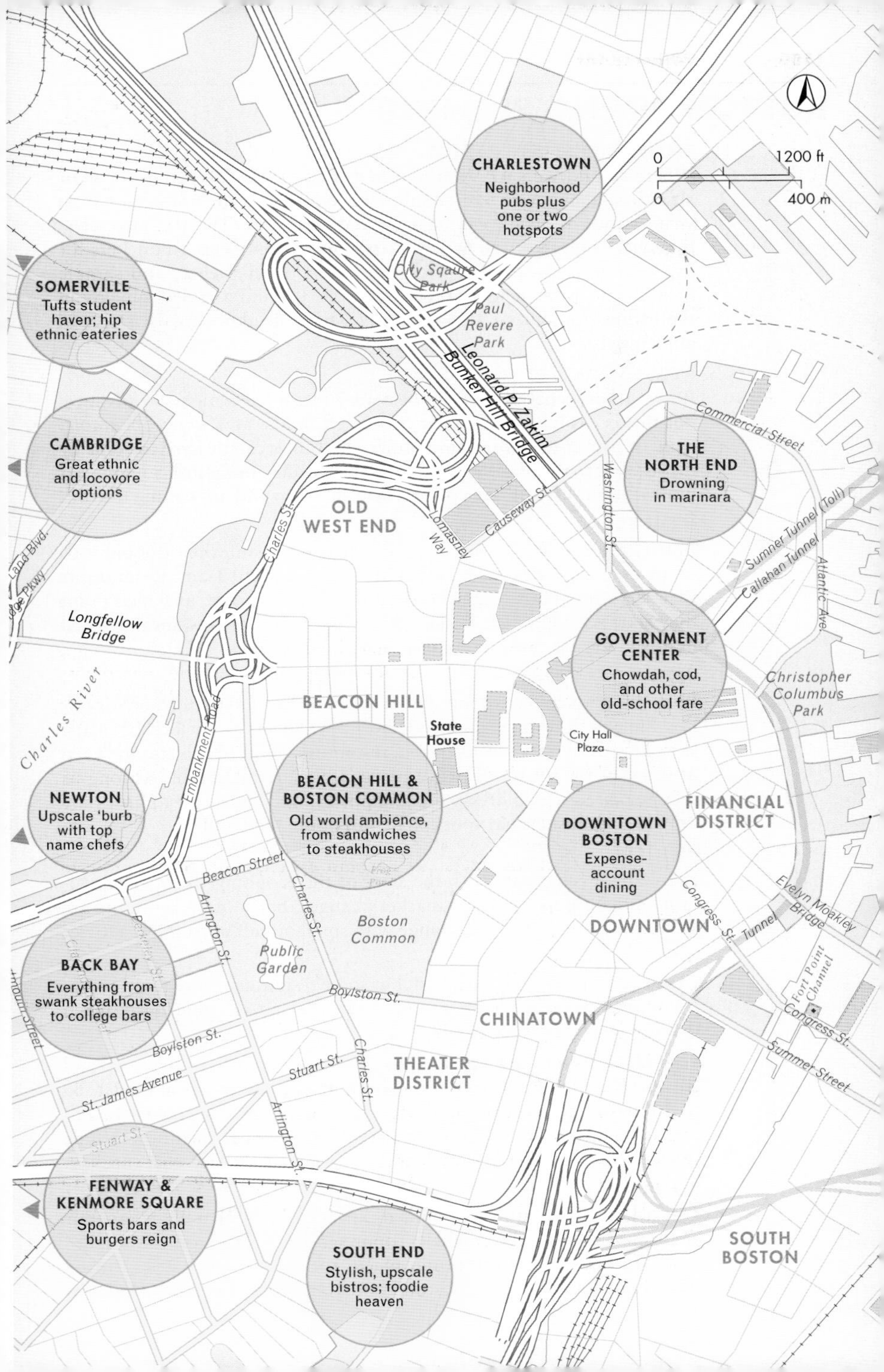

CHARLESTOWN
Neighborhood pubs plus one or two hotspots
SOMERVILLE
Tufts student haven; hip ethnic eateries
CAMBRIDGE
Great ethnic and locovore options
THE NORTH END
Drowning in marinara
GOVERNMENT CENTER
Chowdah, cod, and other old-school fare
BEACON HILL & BOSTON COMMON
Old world ambience, from sandwiches to steakhouses
NEWTON
Upscale 'burb with top name chefs
DOWNTOWN BOSTON
Expense-account dining
BACK BAY
Everything from swank steakhouses to college bars
FENWAY & KENMORE SQUARE
Sports bars and burgers reign
SOUTH END
Stylish, upscale bistros; foodie heaven
0
1200 ft
0
400 m
City Square Park
Paul Revere Park
Leonard P. Zakim Bunker Hill Bridge
Commercial Street
Washington St.
Causeway St.
Lomasney Way
OLD WEST END
Charles St.
Sumner Tunnel (Toll)
Callahan Tunnel
Atlantic Ave.
Longfellow Bridge
Charles River
Embankment Road
BEACON HILL
State House
City Hall Plaza
Christopher Columbus Park
FINANCIAL DISTRICT
Beacon Street
Arlington St.
Charles St.
Boston Common
Public Garden
DOWNTOWN
Congress St. Tunnel
Evelyn Moakley Bridge
Fort Point Channel
Congress St.
Boylston St.
CHINATOWN
Summer Street
Boylston St.
Stuart St.
Charles St.
THEATER DISTRICT
St. James Avenue
Stuart St.
Arlington St.
SOUTH BOSTON

BOSTON DINING PLANNER

EATING OUT STRATEGY

Where should we eat? With hundreds of eateries competing for your attention, it may seem like a daunting question. But fret not—our expert writers and editors have done most of the legwork. The 100-plus selections here represent the best the city has to offer. Search Best Bets for top recommendations by price, cuisine, and experience, and sample local flavor in the neighborhood features. Or find a review quickly in the listings, organized alphabetically within neighborhoods. Delve in and enjoy!

RESERVATIONS

Reservations generally need to be made at least a few nights in advance, but this is easily done by your concierge, online at 🌐 *www.opentable.com*, or by calling the restaurant directly. Tables can be hard to come by if you want to dine between 7 and 9, or on Friday or Saturday night. But most restaurants will get you in if you show up and are willing to wait.

HOURS

Boston's restaurants close relatively early; most shut their doors by 10 or 11 pm, and a few have bars that stay open until 1 am. Restaurants that serve breakfast often do so until 11 am or noon, at which point they start serving lunch. Unless otherwise noted, the restaurants listed in this guide are open daily for lunch and dinner.

WHAT TO WEAR

Boston is a notch or two more reserved in its fashion than New York or Los Angeles. Its dining dress code normally hovers at the level of casual chic. Few of the city's most formal restaurants require jackets, and even at some of the most expensive places jeans are acceptable as long as they're paired with a dressy top and posh shoes. Shorts are appropriate only in the most casual spots. When in doubt, call and ask.

PRICES

Entrée prices fluctuate with the state of the economy. Top-tier restaurants remain impervious to market changes, but more restaurants are accommodating every price range with small or half portions at a lower price.

Credit cards are widely accepted, but some restaurants accept only cash. If you plan to use a credit card, it's a good idea to double-check when making reservations or before sitting down to eat.

TIPPING AND TAXES

Never tip the maître d'. In most restaurants, tip the waiter at least 15% to 20% (to figure the amount quickly, double the 7% tax on the bill and add a little more). Bills for parties of six or more sometimes include service. Tip at least $1 per drink at the bar and $1 for each coat checked.

TOURS

To eat like an Italian, you've got to know your sfogliatelle from your amaretti. Local foodie Michele Topor schools visitors on the "right" kind of olive oil and the primo places to buy Italian pastries during three-hour tours with her Boston Food Tours **North End Market Tour (her**

colleague, Jim Becker, also offers a Chinatown Market Tour, $69 with a dim sum lunch) (✉ *6 Charter St.* ☎ *617/523–6032*), which get off the beaten Hanover Street path. The $54 tour includes a few sample noshes.

CHILDREN

Though it's unusual to see children in the dining rooms of Boston's most elite restaurants, dining with youngsters does not have to mean culinary exile. Many of the restaurants reviewed in this chapter are excellent choices for families and are accordingly marked.

SMOKING

In both Boston and Cambridge, smoking is prohibited in all enclosed public spaces, including restaurants and bars.

USING THE MAPS

Throughout the chapter, you'll see mapping symbols and coordinates (such as ⊕ 3:F2) after property names or reviews. To locate the property on a map, turn to the Boston Dining and Lodging Atlas at the end of this chapter. The first number after the ⊕ symbol indicates the map number. Following that is the property's coordinate on the map grid.

RESTAURANT REVIEWS

Listed alphabetically within neighborhoods.

BOSTON

BEACON HILL AND BOSTON COMMON

Eminently walkable, this is one of Boston's smallest and most historic neighborhoods filled with brick sidewalks, shimmering gas lamps, and 19th-century row houses with brass knockers and flower boxes. On the food front you'll find an appealing blend of fancy and casual restaurants, as well as cafés along the main pedestrian path of Charles Street, where you'll see mothers with strollers, young professionals, and patrician elderly couples, who live right around the corner, all going about their day.

10

$$ MIDDLE EASTERN

✕ **Lala Rokh.** A rotating gallery of Persian art, ranging from miniatures and medieval maps to modern photographs, adorns the walls of this beautifully detailed fantasy of food and art. The cuisine focuses on the Azerbaijanian corner of what is now northwest Iran, including exotically spiced specialties and dishes such as eggplant purée, *pollo* (rice dishes), kebabs, *fesanjoon* (pomegranate-walnut sauce), and lamb stews. The staff obviously enjoys explaining the menu, and the wine list is well selected for foods that often defy wine matches. [$] *Average main: $22* ✉ *97 Mt. Vernon St., Beacon Hill* ☎ *617/720–5511* 🌐 *www.lalarokh.com* ⏲ *No lunch weekends* [M] *Charles/MGH* ⊕ *1:D6.*

$$$$ STEAKHOUSE

✕ **Mooo.** Inside the swanky XV Beacon hotel, lies Mooo, a luxurious, refined dining space in scotch and cream tones that remains civilized despite the restaurant's somewhat goofy name. Chef David Hutton's menu strays toward steak-house fare (hence the title), with dishes driven by local ingredients. Look for a well-rounded list of raw-bar items, iceberg-lettuce salads, and the succulent (and very popular) Kobe beef

BEST BETS FOR BOSTON DINING

With hundreds of restaurants to choose from, how will you decide where to eat? Fodor's writers and editors have selected their favorite restaurants by price, cuisine, and experience in the Best Bets lists below.

Fodor's Choice ★

All Star Sandwich Bar, $, p. 177
Antico Forno, $, p. 154
Area Four, $$, p. 179
Atlantic Fish Co., $$$, p. 162
Clio, $$$$, p. 163
Eastern Standard Kitchen and Drinks, $$, p. 170
Flour Bakery + Café, $, p. 167
Hamersley's Bistro, $$$, p. 167
Hungry Mother, $$$, p. 182
Island Creek Oyster Bar, $$$, p. 170
L'Espalier, $$$$, p. 164
Lumiere, $$$, p. 171
Mistral, $$$$, p. 168
Neptune Oyster, $$$, p. 156
No. 9 Park, $$$$, p. 153
Oleana, $$$, p. 182
Orinoco, $, p. 183
o ya, $$$$, p. 159
Posto, $$, p. 186
Rialto, $$$$, p. 183
Sweet Cheeks, $$, p. 170
Sycamore, $$$, p. 171
Toro, $$$, p. 169
Troquet, $$$$, p. 165
Uni, $$$$, p. 165
West Bridge, $$$, p. 184

By Price

$

All Star Sandwich Bar, p. 177
Antico Forno, p. 154
Flour Bakery + Café, p. 167
Myers + Chang p. **168**
Orinoco, p. 183

$$

Area Four, p. 179
Blue Dragon, p. 158
The Butcher Shop, p. 166
Eastern Standard Kitchen and Drinks, p. 170
Pomodoro, p. 157
Sweet Cheeks, p. 170

$$$

Atlantic Fish Company, p. 162
Hungry Mother, p. 182
Island Creek Oyster Bar, p. 170
Lumiere, p. 171
Oishii Boston, p. 168
Oleana, p. 182
Sycamore, p. 171
Toro, p. 169

$$$$

Clio, p. 163
L'Espalier, p. 164
Grill 23 & Bar, p. 163
Mistral, p. 168
No. 9 Park, p. 153
o ya, p. 159
Rialto, p. 183

By Cuisine

AMERICAN

Bergamot, $$$, p. 185
Eastern Standard Kitchen and Drinks, $$, p. 170
Hamersley's Bistro, $$$, p. 167
Kirkland Tap & Trotter, $$$, p. 185

ASIAN

Myers + Chang, $, p. 168
Fugakyu, $$, p. 173
Oishii Boston, $$$, p. 168
o ya, $$$$, p. 159

FRENCH

L'Espalier, $$$$, p. 164
Lumiere, $$$, p. 171
Mistral, $$$$, p. 168
Troquet, $$$$, p. 165

ITALIAN

Carmen, $$$, p. 154
Rialto, $$$$, p. 183
Sorellina, $$$$, p. 165
Via Matta, $$$, p. 166

SEAFOOD

Atlantic Fish Co., $$$, p. 162
Daily Catch, $, p. 155
Island Creek Oyster Bar, $$$, p. 170
Legal Sea Foods, $$$, p. 158
Neptune Oyster, $$$, p. 156
Summer Shack, $$, p. 165

STEAKHOUSE

Abe & Louie's, $$$$, p. 162
Capital Grille, $$$$, p. 162
Grill 23 & Bar, $$$$, p. 163

By Experience

HISTORICAL INTEREST

Durgin-Park Market Dining Room, $$, p. 153
Union Oyster House, $$$, p. 154

HOT SPOTS

Blue Dragon, $$, p. 158
Myers + Chang, $, p. 168
Posto, $$, p. 186
Scampo, $$$, p. 153
Sycamore, $$$, p. 171
Trade, $$$, p. 162
West Bridge, $$$, p. 184

dumpling appetizer. For entrées, dry-aged sirloins with your choice of sauces, such as Bearnaise, simple meat offerings, and a smattering of seafood selections round out the list. Portions are as exaggerated as the prices, so it's a worthwhile visit, and the wine list, with more than 500 entries, including a few century-old bottles, is an impressive but expensive proposition. Carnivores will be happy to know steak is also available at breakfast (with eggs), lunch, and Sunday brunch. *$ Average main: $46 ✉ 15 Beacon St., XV Beacon Hotel, Beacon Hill ☎ 617/670–2515 🌐 mooorestaurant.com M Park St. ✣ 1:E6.*

$$$$ EUROPEAN Fodor's Choice ★

No. 9 Park. The stellar cuisine at Chef Barbara Lynch's first restaurant continues to draw plenty of well-deserved attention from its place in the shadow of the State House's golden dome. Settle into the plush but unpretentious dining room and indulge in pumpkin risotto with rare lamb or the memorably rich prune-stuffed gnocchi drizzled with bits of foie gras, the latter of which is always offered even if you don't see it on the menu. The wine list bobs and weaves into new territory, but is always well chosen, and the savvy bartenders are of the classic ilk, so you'll find plenty of classics and very few cloying, dessert-like sips here. *$ Average main: $39 ✉ 9 Park St., Beacon Hill ☎ 617/742–9991 🌐 www.no9park.com M Park St. ✣ 1:E6.*

$$$ ITALIAN

Scampo. In the revamped Liberty Hotel—the former site of the infamous Charles Street Jail—this Beacon Hill hot spot has a prison-chic vibe, complete with barred windows and a sign on the wall reminding patrons that "crime doesn't pay." The restaurant's Italian fare, however, is anything but institutional: the house-made mozzarella bar, crusty pizzas, and handmade pastas are all exceptional. Take note of the King Crab Cocktail: thick slices of buffalo mozzarella cheese and slices of avocados mixed with warm buttery Alaskan king crab and drizzled with the house-made mild wasabi aioli. Chef Lydia Shire's creative menu is complemented by a sleek orange bar, curved white-leather booths, and one of the city's most beautiful crowds. *$ Average main: $28 ✉ 215 Charles St., Beacon Hill ☎ 617/536–2100 🌐 www.scampoboston.com M Charles/MGH ✣ 1:D5.*

GOVERNMENT CENTER AND THE NORTH END

GOVERNMENT CENTER

Government Center is home to Faneuil Hall, a tourist magnet, packed with fast-food concessions as well as some more serious alternatives. If you're not on a schedule, and if you've seen enough of Faneuil Hall and want a change of scene, you shouldn't rule out a walk to the North End.

$$ AMERICAN

Durgin-Park Market Dining Room. You should be hungry enough to cope with enormous portions, yet not so hungry you can't tolerate a long wait (or sharing a table with others). Durgin-Park was serving its same hearty New England fare (Indian pudding, baked beans, corned beef and cabbage, and a prime rib that hangs over the edge of the plate) back when Faneuil Hall was a working market instead of a tourist attraction. The service is as brusque as it was when fishmongers and boat captains dined here, but that's just part of its charm. *$ Average main: $19 ✉ 340 Faneuil Hall Market Pl., North Market Bldg., Faneuil Hall ☎ 617/227–2038 🌐 www.arkrestaurants.com/durgin_park.html M Government Center ✣ 1:G5.*

$$$ SEAFOOD **Union Oyster House.** Established in 1826, this is Boston's oldest continuing restaurant, and almost every tourist considers it a must-see. If you like, you can have what Daniel Webster had—oysters on the half shell at the ground-floor raw bar, which is the oldest part of the restaurant and still the best. The rooms at the top of the narrow staircase are dark and have low ceilings—very Ye Olde New England—and plenty of nonrestaurant history. The small tables and chairs (as well as the endless lines and kitschy nostalgia) are as much a part of the charm as the simple and decent (albeit pricey) food. On weekends, especially in summer, make reservations a few days ahead or risk enduring waits of historic proportions. There is valet parking after 5:30 pm Monday through Saturday. One cautionary note: Locals hardly ever eat here. *Average main: $25* *41 Union St., Government Center* *617/227–2750* *www.unionoysterhouse.com* *Haymarket* *1:F5.*

THE NORTH END

As the city's oldest residential area, the North End contains some remarkable Revolutionary War history, including Paul Revere's home, and some really remarkable Italian food. The narrow side streets can be eerily quiet during the day, save for a gathering of grandmothers sitting on lawn chairs outside an apartment building, but then transform into vibrant meeting places come evening, as twenty-something hipsters return home from work and couples of all ages take advantage of the romantic opportunities afforded by the neighborhood's small, rustic restaurants and cannoli-filled cafés.

$ ITALIAN Fodor's Choice ★ **Antico Forno.** Many of the menu choices here come from the eponymous wood-burning brick oven, which turns out surprisingly delicate pizzas simply topped with tomato and fresh buffalo mozzarella. Though its pizzas receive top billing, Antico excels at a variety of Italian country dishes. Don't overlook the hearty baked dishes and handmade pastas; the specialty, gnocchi, is rich and creamy but light. The joint is cramped and noisy, but also homey and comfortable—which means that your meal will resemble a raucous dinner with an adopted Italian family. *Average main: $17* *93 Salem St., North End* *617/723–6733* *www.anticofornoboston.com* *Haymarket* *1:G4.*

$$$$ ITALIAN **Bricco.** A sophisticated but unpretentious enclave of Nouveau Italian, Bricco has carved out quite a following. And no wonder: the handmade pastas alone are argument for a reservation. Simple but well-balanced main courses such as roast chicken marinated in seven spices and a brimming *brodetto* (fish stew) with half a lobster and a pile of seafood may linger in your memory. You're likely to want to linger in the warm room, too, gazing through the floor-to-ceiling windows while sipping a glass of Sangiovese from the Italian and American wine list. *Average main: $40* *241 Hanover St., North End* *617/248–6800* *www.bricco.com* *Reservations essential* *No lunch* *Haymarket* *1:G5.*

$$$ ITALIAN **Carmen.** Here's the kind of undeniably friendly, downright cute hole-in-the-wall that keeps the neighborhood real. With seating for 30, Carmen keeps its capacity crowds happy with glasses of wine and tiny dishes of roasted red pepper and olives at the up-front bar. At tables, meanwhile, diners tuck into comforting specials like homemade pappardelle with creamy mushroom ragu and braised short ribs with

CLOSE UP

A North End "Course Crawl"

The neighborhood is so densely packed with authentic Italian eateries (there are more than 85 lining just a few blocks) that it's nearly impossible to suggest only one. Instead, we recommend embarking on an evening-long "course crawl" to enjoy a variety of the North End's flavors while severely challenging your stomach capacity.

In summer, start with a drink at **Ristorante Fiore** (✉ *250 Hanover St.* ☎ *617/371–1176* ✣ *1:G4*), which has one of the city's best roof decks and a similarly impressive wine list heavy on the Tuscan varietals. Then swing by **Neptune Oyster** (✉ *63 Salem St.* ☎ *617/742–3474* ✣ *1:G5*) for a batch of its namesake crispy oysters served with pistachio aioli as a starter, before crossing the street to **Terramia** (✉ *98 Salem St.* ☎ *617/523–3112* ✣ *1:G4*), where the huge sea-scallop ravioli comes dressed in a lobster mascarpone cream and the gnocchi is accented by white truffle oil.

True Italians make room for *secondi*, or a second, meat-based course. You can't go wrong with **Prezza**'s (✉ *24 Fleet St.* ☎ *617/227–1577* ✣ *1:G4*) wood-grilled veal porterhouse with saffron lobster risotto, or the seared salmon fillet at the broom closet–sized **Pomodoro** (✉ *319 Hanover St.* ☎ *617/367–4348* ✣ *1:G4*).

Before you can succumb to a carbohydrate-stuffed stupor, you need dessert—but most North End restaurants don't serve it. That's because everyone buys cannolis at local bakeries instead. Stop by **Modern Pastry** (✉ *257 Hanover St.* ☎ *617/523–3783* ✣ *1:G4*) *and* **Mike's Pastry** (✉ *300 Hanover St.* ☎ *617/742–3050* ✣ *1:G4*), the two main North End dessert shops, to conduct your own cannoli taste test. Located across Hanover Street from each other, both shops have around-the-clock lines snaking out the door. Modern's cannoli are smaller, more delicate, and flakier than Mike's counterparts, but as for the preference, it's up to you. If you're ricotta-averse, the two bakeries also serve lots of other treats, from gelato to biscotti and marzipan.

Parmesan polenta. Desserts and coffee, however, aren't served. 💲 *Average main: $28* ✉ *33 North Sq., North End* ☎ *617/742–6421* 🌐 *www.carmenboston.com* ✍ *Reservations essential* ⏲ *Closed Mon. No lunch Sun.–Wed., except lunch offered on Wed. from April 1–Dec 31* Ⓜ *Haymarket* ✣ *1:G4.*

$ SEAFOOD ✕ **Daily Catch.** You've just got to love this shoebox-size place—for the noise, the intimacy, the complete absence of pretense, and, above all, the food, which proved so popular, it spawned two other locations (one in Brookline and another in Boston's seaport area). Compact and brightly lighted, this storefront restaurant has been a local staple for 40 years and for good reason. With garlic and olive oil forming the foundation for almost every dish, this cheerful, bustling spot specializes in big skillets of calamari dishes, black squid-ink pastas, and linguine with clam sauce, that all would seem less perfect if served on fine white china versus the actual cooking pan that's placed in front of you with an efficient flourish as soon as it leaves the stove. 💲 *Average*

COFFEE TALK

Café culture is alive and well in the North End. **Caffe Vittoria** (✉ *290–296 Hanover St.* ☎ *617/227–7606* ✣ *1:G4*), established in 1929, is Boston's oldest Italian café. With four levels of seating, three bars that serve aperitifs, and one massive, ancient espresso maker, this old-fashioned café will make you want to lose yourself in these surroundings. At **Caffé Paradiso** (✉ *255 Hanover St.* ☎ *617/742–1768* ✣ *1:G5*) spectacular coffee drinks await, along with the richest gelato in the neighborhood, weighing in at a decadent 14% milk fat (versus the 8% used in traditional versions). **Caffe dello Sport** (✉ *308 Hanover St.* ☎ *617/523–5063* ✣ *1:G4*) is an Italianate version of a sports bar, with two wide screens transmitting live soccer; order espressos, cordials, and gelato. If you're not able to kill a whole afternoon sipping cappuccino, stop by **Polcari's Coffee** (✉ *105 Salem St.* ☎ *617/227–0786* ✣ *1:G4*), selling dried goods by the pound—coffees, teas, herbs, and spices displayed in antique brass bins.

main: $15 ✉ 323 Hanover St., North End ☎ 617/523–8567 ⊕ www.dailycatch.com ✍ Reservations not accepted ▭ No credit cards Ⓜ Haymarket ✣ 1:G4.

$$$ ITALIAN ✕ **Mamma Maria.** Don't let the clichéd name fool you: Mamma Maria is far from a typical red-sauce joint, although some locals find the service lacking. From the handmade wild-mushroom ravioli to the authentic sauces and entrées to some of the best desserts in the North End, you can't go wrong here. The view, meanwhile, is lovely; gaze out onto cobblestone-lined North Square as you finish your pappardelle layered with braised rabbit and a finale of *limoncello* (an Italian lemon-flavored liquor). *[$] Average main: $30 ✉ 3 North Sq., North End ☎ 617/523–0077 ⊕ www.mammamaria.com ⏲ No lunch Ⓜ Haymarket ✣ 1:G4.*

$$$ SEAFOOD Fodor's Choice ★ ✕ **Neptune Oyster.** This *piccolo* oyster bar, the first of its kind in the neighborhood, has only 22 chairs, but the long marble bar adorned with mirrors has extra seating for 15 more patrons, who can watch the oyster shuckers deftly undo handfuls of bivalves to savor by the dozen or on a *plateau di frutti di mare,* a gleaming tower of oysters and other raw-bar items piled over ice that you can order from the slip of paper they pass out listing each day's crustacean options. Dishes change seasonally, but a couple of year-round favorites include the North End Cioppino (fish stew) and the lobster roll that, hot or cold, overflows with meat. Service is prompt even when it gets busy (as it is most of the time). Go early to avoid a long wait. *[$] Average main: $32 ✉ 63 Salem St., North End ☎ 617/742–3474 ⊕ www.neptuneoyster.com ✍ Reservations not accepted Ⓜ Haymarket ✣ 1:G5.*

$$ ITALIAN ✕ **Pizzeria Regina.** This North End institution owned by the Polcari family has been doing what it does best since 1926—creating thin-crusted, brick-oven-charred pizzas with fresh toppings, excellent sauce, and just the right amount of cheese. Beyond two simple salads (garden and Caesar), you won't find other offerings here, just incredibly well made pies, like the Margherita, which contains fresh basil leaves baked into the cheese so they don't burn. The wait can be long, the service brusque,

and the ambience boisterous. But with pizza this good, who cares? *Average main: $20 ✉ 11½ Thatcher St., North End ☎ 617/227–0765 www.pizzeriaregina.com Ⓜ Haymarket ✥ 1:F4.*

$$ ITALIAN **Pomodoro.** This teeny trattoria—just nine tables—is worth the wait, with excellent country Italian favorites such as rigatoni with white beans and arugula, a veal scaloppini with sweet onion balsamic glaze, and a light-but-filling zuppa di pesce. The best choice could well be the classic linguini, accompanied by a bottle of Vernaccia. Pomodoro doesn't serve dessert, but it's easy to find great espresso and pastries in the cafés on Hanover Street. *Average main: $24 ✉ 319 Hanover St., North End ☎ 617/367–4348 Reservations essential No credit cards No lunch weekdays Ⓜ Haymarket ✥ 1:G4.*

$$$$ MODERN ITALIAN **Prezza.** Chef Anthony Caturano pays homage to his Italian grandmother at this warm, convivial eatery by naming it after the tiny Abruzzese village where she was born and then putting a modern twist on the rustic dishes she would have cooked. Favorites include polenta smothered with sausage-meatball-rib sauce; wood-grilled veal porterhouse; and buttery ricotta-stuffed ravioli. An emphasis on garden-fresh ingredients means appetizers, like roasted prosciutto-wrapped figs stuffed with gorgonzola and wood-grilled octopus with white beans, change seasonally. What doesn't change is the friendly service, delicious food, and excellent wine selection (over 8,000 bottles) that's largely Italian. *Average main: $36 ✉ 24 Fleet St., North End ☎ 617/227–1577 www.prezza.com No lunch weekdays Ⓜ Haymarket ✥ 1:G4.*

$$$ ITALIAN **Ristorante Euno.** Unassuming and friendly, Euno is the North End's culinary mouse that roars. The rustic, two-story space used to be a butcher shop, and meat hooks still stud the wall, doubling as coat hangers. Everything from start (a bowl of the buttery olives) to middle (handmade pastas and risottos) to finish (chef's catch of the day) explains why this brick-walled gem is a neighborhood favorite. It's usually full on weekends, but those wise enough to make reservations might snag a table in the romantic downstairs dining room. *Average main: $28 ✉ 119 Salem St., North End ☎ 617/573–9406 www.eunoboston.com No lunch Ⓜ Haymarket ✥ 1:G4.*

$$$ ITALIAN **Terramia Ristorante.** Nearly everything on the menu at this cozy restaurant with a honeyed glow and exposed wooden beams tastes home-cooked and authentic. The simple, regional Italian cuisine includes rich, fresh homemade pastas tossed with equally fresh ingredients and risottos that come perfectly cooked and powerfully flavored. A perennial favorite is the sausage-stuffed veal rolls with mushroom risotto and Fontina cream. The dessert list stops after tiramisu, bread pudding, and a flourless chocolate cake, but who needs more choices than those? Lines can get long on weekends. *Average main: $29 ✉ 98 Salem St., North End ☎ 617/523–3112 www.terramiaristorante.com No lunch Ⓜ Haymarket ✥ 1:G4.*

CHARLESTOWN

English colonists founded this little neighborhood across Boston Harbor before they established Boston. Notable for its historic houses and buildings, including the Bunker Hill Monument and the USS *Constitution*, it also contains a vibrant mix of affordable eateries, mainly along

Main Street and in City Square, that cater to the artists, working families, and young couples who live in the area.

$$$ MOROCCAN

Tangierino. Chef-owner Samad Naamad draws visitors into his enchanting Moroccan fantasy with hearty, spice-driven food, fragrant cocktails, and bi-nightly belly-dancing shows. Indulge in small plates like calamari rubbed with harissa aioli; then enjoy a drawn-out meal of entrées cooked in a tagine (a clay pot used for slow cooking). Tangierino bills itself as the first Moroccan chophouse, meaning those with a taste for the slightly less exotic can partake of meat-and-potato offerings, albeit with Moroccan flair. The downstairs hookah bar, Koullshi, is also owned by Tangierino. *Average main: $28* *83 Main St., Charlestown* *617/242–6009* *www.tangierino.com* *No lunch* *Community College* *1:E2.*

DOWNTOWN BOSTON

Boston's Downtown scene revs up at lunchtime, but the streets get quiet after 5 pm, when everyone goes back to the suburbs. The city center is great for after-hours dining, though, especially in the hideaway restaurants around the former Leather District.

$$ ASIAN FUSION

Blue Dragon. Old Shanghai meets stylish South Boston at TV-star chef Ming Tsai's überpopular Asian gastropub, set in an abandoned triangular diner in the Fort Point neighborhood. The cool younger brother of Tsai's more elegant first restaurant, Blue Ginger, Blue Dragon has all the auspicious feng shui elements intact: wooden furniture; a mirrored waterfall by the tree trunk bar; and a dragon weather vane to elevate the squat white-brick building. Folks regularly form lines around the block in order to slurp up Tsai's East-meets-West cocktails and share succulent braised short-rib pot stickers, lobster *banh mi* (traditional Vietnamese sandwiches made with pâté and pickled vegetables), spicy noodle salads, and tiny teriyaki bison cheeseburgers. Tsai even raided his mother's recipe box to recreate her ever-popular salt-and-pepper shrimp. *Average main: $22 <ADDRESS>* *324 A St., Fort Point Channel* *617/338–8585* *www.ming.com/blue-dragon.htm* *Reservations not accepted* *2:H2* .

$$$ SEAFOOD FAMILY

Legal Sea Foods. What began as a tiny restaurant adjacent to a Cambridge fish market has grown to important regional status, with more than 30 East Coast locations. The hallmark is the freshest possible seafood, whether you have it wood-grilled, in New England chowder, or doused in an Asia-inspired sauce. The jumbo lump crab cakes are divine (no fillers), and the clam chowder is so good it has become a menu staple at presidential inaugurations. For a true taste of New England, don't miss the golden cracker-crowned baked lobster stuffed with shrimp and scallops, one of the most popular entrées on the menu. This location has private dining inside its beautiful, bottle-lined wine cellar. *Average main: $28* *26 Park Sq., Theater District* *617/426–4444* *www.legalseafoods.com* *Open for lunch* *Arlington* *2:D2.*

$$$ FRENCH

Les Zygomates. The French expression for the facial muscles that make you smile is *Les zygomates* and this combination wine bar–bistro inarguably lives up to its name making diners happy with quintessential French bistro fare, like the tiered, ice-packed house platter (*plateau* *maison*) filled with oysters, clams, shrimp, and snow crab claws from the tiny five-seat oyster bar and the unctuous beef short-rib Bourguignon, simply made (with many local ingredients) and simply delicious. The dinner prix-fixe menu beautifully matches the ever-changing wine list, with all wines served by the 2-ounce taste, 6-ounce glass, or bottle. There is also live jazz five nights a week. *Average main: $28 ✉ 129 South St., Downtown ☎ 617/542–5108 🌐 www.winebar.com Reservations essential ⏲ Closed Sun. No lunch Sat. Ⓜ South Station ✣ 2:F2.*

$$$$ FRENCH ✕ **Menton.** Located in the forever up-and-coming Fort Point neighborhood, Barbara Lynch's latest Italian-meets-French eatery, named for a French town near Italy's border, has two luxurious, prix-fixe menus (a four- and seven-course) that have brought critics and food aficionados to the brink of euphoria with sighs of "incredible" and "perfection." And, for good reason. Reflecting what's freshest that day, the four-course menu might begin with a seafood-enriched butter soup, peak with fork-tender veal with escargot, and end with an apricot-garnished sticky bun; the seven-course menu is a bespoke meal composed from the day's list of 15 or so ingredients. If you want to up the ante to your evening, reserve the 12-seat chef's table in the kitchen, an enclosed area with a glass wall offering a sneak peek into the restaurant's inner culinary sanctum. *Average main: $95 ✉ 354 Congress St., Fort Point Channel, Downtown ☎ 617/737–0099 🌐 www.mentonboston.com Reservations essential ⏲ No lunch Ⓜ South Station ✣ 2:H2.*

$$$$ JAPANESE Fodor's Choice ★ ✕ **o ya.** Despite its side-street location and hidden door, o ya isn't exactly a secret: dining critics from the *New York Times*, *Bon Appetit*, and *Food & Wine* have all named this tiny, improvisational sushi spot among the best in the country. Chef Tim Cushman's nigiri menu features squid-ink bubbles, homemade potato chips—even foie gras. Other dishes offer a nod to New England, such as the braised pork with Boston baked beans and grilled lobster with a light shiso tempura. Cushman's wife Nancy oversees an extensive sake list that includes sparkling and aged varieties. *Average main: $36 ✉ 9 East St., Leather District ☎ 617/654–9900 🌐 www.oyarestaurantboston.com ⏲ Closed Sun. and Mon. No lunch Ⓜ South Station ✣ 2:G2.*

$ AMERICAN ✕ **Silvertone.** Devotees of this retro-cool basement restaurant with reasonable prices swear by the no-fuss options such as a truly addictive macaroni and cheese topped with crispy bacon, meat loaf with mashed potatoes, and steak tips. Among the more creative offerings are the appetizers, such as the Caesar salad with honey-chili chicken, and the fish of the day, which might be trout amandine or locally caught bluefish. The wine list is compact but varied and retains one of the lowest mark-ups in the city. Once the after-work crowd pours in, some say the room can become overly loud, the service spotty, and the wait for a table too long. *Average main: $16 ✉ 69 Bromfield St., Downtown ☎ 617/338–7887 🌐 www.silvertonedowntown.com Reservations not accepted ⏲ Closed Sun. No lunch Sat. Ⓜ Park St. ✣ 1:F6.*

$$ ITALIAN ✕ **Sportello.** Barbara Lynch, the queen of Boston's dining scene (⇨ *see also: No. 9 Park, B&G Oysters, The Butcher Shop*) had the foresight to create a culinary triad in the city's burgeoning Fort Point Channel

neighborhood: the posh restaurant Menton, the adjacent below-street-level bar, DRINK, and the upstairs Italian trattoria Sportello, modeled after a diner, with a clean, white, lunch-counter look. Sportello belies its minimalist design with market-fresh fare like deep bowls of truffled gnocchi with peas and plates of spicy smoked pork with roasted onions and farro. There's also an impressive weekend brunch menu. The bakery area has now morphed into a wine bar offering increased seating for 18 more diners and a tantalizing selection of artisanal wines. *$ Average main: $22 ✉ 348 Congress St., Fort Point Channel, Downtown ☎ 617/737–1234 ⊕ www.sportelloboston.com M South Station ⊕ 2:H2.*

CHINATOWN

Boston's Chinatown is the focal point of Asian cuisines of all types, from authentic Cantonese and Vietnamese to Malaysian, Japanese, and Mandarin. Many places are open after midnight, while the rest of the city sleeps or lurks. It's definitely worth the trek, especially if you're trying to track down live-tank seafood prepared in Hong Kong or Chiu Chow style.

$$ CHINESE ✕ **Chau Chow City.** Spread across three floors, this is the largest, glitziest, and most versatile production yet of the Chau Chow dynasty, with dim sum by day and live-tank seafood by night. Overwhelmed? At lunch, order dim sum off rolling carts making their rounds or the clams in black-bean sauce, the sautéed pea-pod stems with garlic, or the honey-glazed shrimp with walnuts. Chau Chow is one of the area's only restaurants that keeps serving well into the wee hours (until 3 am weekdays and 4 am on weekends), making it a staple for late-night diners. Service can be slow and some consider the food overpriced. *$ Average main: $24 ✉ 83 Essex St., Chinatown ☎ 617/338–8158 M Chinatown ⊕ 2:F1.*

WATERFRONT

Tourists flock to Faneuil Hall and the Marketplace almost year-round, so tried-and-true cuisine tends to dominate there. However, some of Boston's most famous seafood restaurants are, naturally, on the waterfront.

$$$ SEAFOOD FAMILY ✕ **Barking Crab Restaurant.** Decked out in cheery Christmas colors of red and green due to a recent renovation, this is, believe it or not, a real, seaside clam shack located smack dab in the middle of Boston with stunning views of the Financial District (and prices to match). An outdoor lobster tent in summer, in winter it retreats indoors to a warmhearted version of a waterfront dive, with chestnuts roasting on a cozy woodstove. Look for the classic New England clambake—chowder, Maine lobster, steamed Cape Cod clams, corn on the cob—or oysters and littlenecks from the raw bar, followed by meaty, golden crab cakes. The "all things local" motto even includes drinks, like unique quaffs from nearby Harpoon Brewery. *$ Average main: $27 ✉ 88 Sleeper St., Northern Ave. Bridge, Waterfront ☎ 617/426–2722 ⊕ www.barkingcrab.com M South Station ⊕ 2:H1.*

$$$$ SEAFOOD ✕ **Legal Harborside.** Paying homage both to the waterfront legend it replaces—Jimmy's Harborside—and its own family-owned roots, Legal Harborside is an intentional one-off, three-floor, 20,000-square-foot

facility unlike any other restaurant in the chain. Level 3 is a rooftop bar and lounge with a sushi menu and copper-fronted fireplace, three walls of windows, and two patios overlooking the waterfront. Level 1 has a fish market, picniclike tables overlooking the marina, and a New England seafood menu. However, it's Level 2, open only for dinner, which tries something different with its experimental menu and fine-dining setting not offered at any other Legal Sea Food. Apps range from the traditional (lobster soup) to the unusual (crispy pig's head and fried clam); filet mignon with Alaskan king crab goes beyond your standard surf and turf dinner entrée, while corn and chorizo add Southwest notes to the butter-poached lobster with mussels. The wine list has 50 varieties carefully selected from vintners whom, like Legal Sea Food, are committed to keeping it all in the family. *Average main: $40* *270 Northern Ave., Liberty Wharf, Waterfront* *617/477–2900* *www.legalseafoods.com/restaurants/boston-legal-harborside* *No lunch on Level 2* *Silver Line Way* *2:H2.*

$$ SEAFOOD FAMILY **Legal Sea Foods.** What better place than the waterfront, only steps from New England Aquarium, cruise ships, and whale-watching boats, to build one of the snazziest branches of the local Legal Sea Foods chain with outdoor seating in the warmer months? In a dining room full of colorful tiles and sea-inspired sculpture, you'll find all the classic and contemporary seafood preparations served in other branches, including fresh oysters, creamy chowders, seafood bisque (there is a light clam chowder for health-conscious diners), crispy fried clams and scallops, wood-grilled fish, and that buttery crumb-topped stuffed lobster. The Vegetarian Box, featuring Thai curried veggies and tofu, is a thoughtful addition for the seafood squeamish. *Average main: $22* *255 State St., Waterfront* *617/742–5300* *www.legalseafoods.com* *Aquarium* *1:H6.*

$$$ EUROPEAN **Meritage.** Set inside the stately Boston Harbor Hotel, Meritage stays focused with its astounding wine list. Chef Daniel Bruce creates scintillating menus to match the cellar's treasures (arranged, appropriately, like a wine list, with headings like "full bodied" and "sparklers"). All menu items are available as small or large plates, and priced at $17 or $34 respectively. With the stunning Rowes Wharf as its backdrop, Meritage has, perhaps, the city's finest waterfront view. Sunday brunch is served. *Average main: $30* *Boston Harbor Hotel at Rowes Wharf, 70 Rowes Wharf, Waterfront* *617/439–3995* *www.meritagetherestaurant.com* *Closed Mon. No lunch* *Aquarium* *1:H6.*

$ SEAFOOD **No Name Restaurant.** Famous for not being famous, the No Name has been serving fresh seafood, simply broiled or fried, since 1917. (For the non-piscivore, they also serve steak, chicken, and kid-friendly chicken fingers.) Once you find it, tucked off New Northern Avenue (as opposed to Old Northern Avenue) between the World Trade Center and the Bank of America Pavilion, you can close your eyes and pretend you're in a little fishing village—it's not much of a stretch. And, the free parking is a bonus. *Average main: $15* *15½ Fish Pier W., off Northern Ave., Waterfront* *617/338–7539* *www.nonamerestaurant.com* *Courthouse* *2:H1.*

10

$$$ MEDITERRANEAN

Trade. After years of anticipation, Jody Adams of Rialto fame has co-opened her second restaurant, Trade, where the Waterfront District crowd slips in for quiet lunches of globally inspired fare, like Asian pork lettuce wraps and plates of soul-warming rigatoni with lamb ragu. Come evening, the boisterous buzz begins and the lofty, white windowed space fills with the young and glamorous eager to unwind over cocktails and plates of smoky pork ribs, seared salmon, and blistered flatbreads (try the tomato four-cheese with arugula) that fly out of the open-hearth pizza oven—perfect for sharing and perfectly delicious. *Average main: $25 540 Atlantic Ave., Waterfront 617/451–1234 trade-boston.com No lunch weekends South Station 2:G1.*

BACK BAY AND THE SOUTH END

BACK BAY

Easily the ritziest section of Boston, Back Bay is where you'll find historic landmarks such as Copley Square and the Boston Public Library rubbing shoulders with stylish boutiques like Valentino and Max Mara. The restaurant scene follows suit with landmark steak houses and seafood spots sharing sidewalk space with more chic, more global options. But don't feel like you have to win the lottery to eat in this area. While lots of fine dining establishments dot the neighborhood, you'll also find plenty of affordable spots including Irish taverns, Thai eateries, and burrito and burger joints.

$$$$ STEAKHOUSE

Abe & Louie's. Go ahead: live the fantasy of the robber baron feasting in a setting of cavernous fireplaces and deep-textured, plush mahogany booths. Abe & Louie's may be a tad Disney-esque in its decor, but its menu lives up to the promise with gorgeous, two-tiered raw platters and juicy rib-eye steaks under velvety hollandaise. Even the linen napkins have little buttonholes for the perfect collar hold. The à la carte Saturday and Sunday brunch has fans raving over the Eggs Benedict Three Ways (with filet mignon, crab, and lobster). *Average main: $42 793 Boylston St., Back Bay 617/536–6300 www.abeandlouies.com Copley 2:A2.*

$$$ SEAFOOD Fodor's Choice ★

Atlantic Fish Co. Designed to look like an ocean vessel with gorgeous wood finishes and nautical artwork, this local seafood restaurant delivers first-class seafood, so fresh that the extensive menus are printed daily to reflect the day's catch served broiled, baked, blackened, fried, grilled, or pan-seared. Unsnap your starched napkin and begin with a platter of chilled seafood (lobster, little necks, oysters, crab, and shrimp), followed by the standout seafood Bolognese (made with ground seafood instead of meat) or any one of the specialties ranging from simple fried Ipswich clams to pan-seared bass in an unctuous lobster cream sauce. The sea bass chowder with bacon is a delectable alternative to the common clam-based versions around town. Steak and chicken are available for culinary landlubbers. *Average main: $31 761 Boylston St., Back Bay 617/267–4000 www.atlanticfishco.com Copley 2:A2.*

$$$$ STEAKHOUSE

Capital Grille. A carnivore's utopia awaits within the clubby, darkwood walls of this beloved steak house favored by those on expense accounts. Adjust your starched napkin and tuck into such staples as lobster and crab cakes, a massive shellfish platter, and succulent meats such as the 24-ounce dry-aged porterhouse. The crowd-watching is as tasty as the food: VIPs in striped suits make deals over dessert, and wives in Manolo Blahnik heels sip martinis. *Average main: $38* ✉ *900 Boylston St., Back Bay* ☎ *617/262–8900* 🌐 *www.thecapitalgrille.com* ⏲ *No lunch weekends* Ⓜ *Hynes* ⊕ *2:A3.*

$$$$ FRENCH Fodor's Choice ★ **Clio.** Years ago, when Ken Oringer opened his snazzy leopard skin–lined hot spot in the tasteful boutique Eliot Hotel, the hordes were fighting over reservations. A 2012 face-lift doubled the size of the bar and made things considerably less formal, save for the food. Opulent offerings like foie gras, Maine lobster, and Kobe sirloin enhanced with flavor-rich foams, emulsions, and bubbles still dominate the menu, along with a few fail-safe options, like crispy chicken and Scottish salmon. A magnet for romantics and die-hard foodies, the place continues to serve some of the city's most fanciful, well-crafted meals. Cocktail aficionados will appreciate the creative and sophisticated bar offerings. *Average main: $39* ✉ *Eliot Hotel, 370 Commonwealth Ave., Back Bay* ☎ *617/536–7200* 🌐 *www.cliorestaurant.com* *Reservations essential* ⏲ *No lunch* Ⓜ *Hynes* ⊕ *3:H2.*

$$$$ ITALIAN **Davio's.** Eating here is like sitting at the grown-up table for the first time. Comfy armchairs and a grand, high-ceilinged dining room give diners a sense of self-importance. Come at lunch, like the rest of the city's power elite, for great pastas (half portions are available) and oversize salads. For dinner, some patrons snag quick, pre-theater bites at the bar while others opt for a more leisurely experience since the kitchen's focus on sophisticated Italian cuisine makes every meal a special occasion. Lucky Pats' ticket holders can enjoy Davio's food at the Patriots Place outpost, near Gillette Stadium, on game day. *Average main: $36* ✉ *75 Arlington St., Back Bay* ☎ *617/357–4810* 🌐 *www.davios.com* ⏲ *No lunch weekends* Ⓜ *Arlington* ⊕ *2:D2.*

$$$ MODERN AMERICAN **Deuxave.** At the corner of two avenues (Commonwealth and Massachusetts), which is how this restaurant got its name (*deux* is French for "two"), you'll find this snazzy, dark-wood enclave serving sophisticated combos of local ingredients, like lobster gnocchi with grapes and walnuts, which sounds odd, but works beautifully. Chef-owner Chris Coombs, who recently opened the steak house Boston Chops, is the culinary mastermind behind this self-described "neighborhood restaurant" that's garnered a following far beyond its Boston zip code. Coombs's juicy spiced duck with lentils and Port, along with his pistachio-crusted lamb are as irresistible as his friendly personality and winning smile. For tipplers, the thoughtfully crafted wine list offers an interesting mix of bottles priced affordably. *Average main: $32* ✉ *375 Commonwealth Ave., Downtown* ☎ *617/517–5915* 🌐 *deuxave.com* Ⓜ *Hynes* ⊕ *3:H2.*

$$$$ STEAKHOUSE **Grill 23 & Bar.** Pinstripe suits, dark paneling, Persian rugs, and waiters in white jackets give this single-location steak house a posh demeanor. The food is anything but predictable, with dishes such as seasonally dressed tartares (steak and tuna) and weekly cuts of all-natural beef like the 14-ounce dry-aged New York sirloin. Seafood specialties such as spicy scallops with mushroom dumplings and baby artichokes give beef sales a run for their money. Desserts, such as the decadent Valrhona chocolate layer cake, rank far above those of the average steak house.

Make sure to leave room. *Average main: $40* *161 Berkeley St., Back Bay* *617/542–2255* *grill23.com* *No lunch* *Back Bay/South End* *2:C2.*

$$
AMERICAN

Joe's American Bar & Grill. Despite its classy Newbury Street address, Joe's dishes up kitschy Fourth of July decor, along with stuffed burgers, clam chowder, and affordable kid-friendly options like pizza and grilled cheese sandwiches served with a complimentary hot fudge sundae. The warm oversize chocolate chip cookie brought to the table in a small black skillet crowned with vanilla ice cream, homemade caramel syrup, and candied pecans, however, is reason enough to stop by. *Average main: $21* *181 Newbury St., Back Bay* *617/536–4200* *www.joesamerican.com* *Copley* *2:B2.*

$$$$
FRENCH
Fodor's Choice ★

L'Espalier. In 2008 L'Espalier left its longtime home in a Back Bay town house, reopening beside the Mandarin Oriental Hotel. The new locale, with its floor-to-ceiling windows and modern decor, looks decidedly different. But chef-owner Frank McClelland's dishes—from caviar and roasted foie gras to garlicky beef tenderloin with braised short ribs and wild mushrooms—are as elegant as ever. In the evening, a three-course prix-fixe, six-course seasonal degustation, and over 10-course chef's journey menu tempt discriminating diners. A budget-minded power lunch as well as à la carte options are available weekday afternoons. Finger sandwiches and sublime sweets are served for weekend tea; the salon menu hits the spot for post-work drinks and nibbles, like a perfectly ripe fromage flight from the city's premier cheese trolley. *Average main: $125* *774 Boylston St., Back Bay* *617/262–3023* *www.lespalier.com* *Reservations essential* *Copley* *2:A2.*

$$$
AMERICAN

Post 390. This hopping "urban tavern" tantalizes diners with creative gastro-pub fare like truffled mushroom flatbread, grilled Atlantic swordfish, lemon-pepper roast chicken, and swoon-worthy cherry-chocolate cake. More than 200 wines, 12 beers on tap, and a host of craft cocktails give tipplers good reason to make frequent visits. The open kitchen, four-sided fireplace, and reasonable prices are inviting enough to turn everyone else into regulars, too, including on Sundays when brunch includes cinnamon roll French toast with banana crème brûlée and pure maple syrup. *Average main: $31* *406 Stuart St., Back Bay* *617/399–0015* *www.post390restaurant.com* *No lunch Sat.* *Back Bay* *2:C2.*

$$
AMERICAN

Sonsie. Café society blossoms along Newbury Street, particularly at Sonsie, where a well-heeled crowd sips coffee up front or angles for places at the bar. Lunch and dinner dishes, such as charcoal duck breast and leg with brown rice and five-spice turnips, are basic bistro fare with an American twist. The restaurant is a terrific place for weekend brunch, when the light pours through the long windows, and is at its most vibrant in warm weather, when the open doors make for colorful people-watching. A downstairs wine room meanwhile offers more intimacy. The late-night menu (nightly until 12:30 am) is perfect for after-hours cravings. *Average main: $23* *327 Newbury St., Back Bay* *617/351–2500* *sonsieboston.com* *Hynes* *3:H2.*

$$$$ ITALIAN

Sorellina. Everything about this upscale Italian spot is oversized, from its space near Copley Square to its portions. The sexy, all-white dining room is filled with well-heeled locals (some live in the gorgeous apartment building above it) who come for the modern twist on basic Italian dishes. Grilled octopus with squid-ink couscous, various versions of carpaccio, and the signature tuna tartare dot the list of starters, while veal saltimbocca with wild mushrooms and truffled whipped potato takes the spotlight. Just save room for dessert: it's always a highlight here. *Average main: $41 1 Huntington Ave., Back Bay 617/412–4600 www.sorellinaboston.com No lunch Copley, Back Bay 2:B2.*

$$ SEAFOOD

Summer Shack. Boston überchef Jasper White has given New England seafood an urban tweak in his boisterous, bright, fun eatery next to the Prudential Center (he also has one in Cambridge), where creamy clam chowder and fried Ipswich clams share menu space with lobster pot stickers and Arctic char with cucumber sauce. In addition to a handful of chicken and meat dishes for those not into seafood, White features the most succulent lobsters in the city (he has a patented process for cooking them), all brought to you by an eager-to-please staff. The entire affair is like one big indoor clambake that begs to be capped off with the delectable, molasses-laced Indian pudding served warm with a scoop of cold vanilla ice cream. *Average main: $19 50 Dalton St., Back Bay 617/867–9955 www.summershackrestaurant.com Hynes 3:H3.*

$$$$ FRENCH FUSION
Fodor's Choice ★

Troquet. Despite boasting what might well be Boston's longest wine list, with nearly 500 vintages (more than 45 of which are available by the glass), plus an unobstructed view of the Common, this French fusion spot flies somewhat under the radar. Still, locals know that Troquet offers all the ingredients for a lovely evening: a quietly elegant dining room, decadent dishes like bacon-wrapped veal sirloin and sticky-toffee pudding, and a knowledgeable yet unpretentious staff. The menu includes by-the-glass wine recommendations after each entrée, so you're sure to sip something delicious and appropriate. *Average main: $37 140 Boylston St., Back Bay 617/695–9463 www.troquetboston.com Closed Sun. and Mon. No lunch Boylston 2:E1.*

$$$ SEAFOOD

Turner Fisheries. On the first floor of the Westin hotel in Copley Square, Turner Fisheries runs a close second to Legal Sea Foods in its traditional appeal. Turner broils, grills, bakes, fries, and steams everything in the ocean, but it also prepares classic and modern sauces, vegetables, and pastas with panache. Any meal should begin with the creamy chowder—the restaurant has won Boston's yearly Chowderfest too many times to contend any more. Round it out with grilled pesto swordfish or one of the city's best-looking mayo-dressed lobster rolls. *Average main: $30 Westin Copley Place Boston, 10 Huntington Ave., Back Bay 617/424–7425 turnersboston.com Reservations essential Closed Sun. Copley 2:B2.*

$$$$ JAPANESE
Fodor's Choice ★

Uni. Downstairs in the swanky Eliot Hotel, Ken Oringer's sleek, 21-seat sashimi bar, Uni, continues to bring raw seafood devotees to their knees. Using no rice in their preparations, two sushi chefs turn succulent morsels of seafood sourced from Tokyo's famed Tsukiji Market and local waters into inventive small bites, like tuna tataki with foie gras and the restaurant's namesake *uni* (sea urchin) with smoked bacon powder. While the menu changes often, safer options include cooked fish tacos and steamed buns stuffed with pork belly. With over 20 varieties of sake and a late-night ramen menu that kicks in at 11 pm (try the pork version in a ruddy pig's foot broth), it's easy to see why this is one of the city's most beloved restaurants. $ *Average main: $42* ✉ *370A Commonwealth Ave.(at Clio in Eliot Hotel), Back Bay* ☎ *617/536–7200* 🌐 *unisashimibar.com* ⏲ *No lunch* Ⓜ *Hynes* ✥ *3:H2.*

$$$ ITALIAN ✕ **Via Matta.** The city's most stylish Italian spot is paradoxically one of its simplest on the culinary front. The kitchen's emphasis is on fresh, intensely flavored ingredients in traditional dishes like monkfish served with ceci beans, olives, *brodetto di pesce* (fish stew), and a citrus herb salad, and a tender lamb loin accompanied by fluffy polenta, *cavalo nero* (black cabbage), smoked almonds, and *verjus* (green juice). Even frequent visitors can enjoy an oft-changing menu, the result of the chef's penchant for seasonal ingredients. The abutting *enoteca* (café)—all mosaic tile and dim lighting—serves daily pizzas, and is the perfect spot for a rendezvous or a nightcap. $ *Average main: $30* ✉ *79 Park Plaza, Back Bay* ☎ *617/422–0008* 🌐 *www.viamattarestaurant.com* ✍ *Reservations essential* ⏲ *Closed Sun. No lunch Sat.* Ⓜ *Arlington* ✥ *2:D2.*

THE SOUTH END

Home to lovely Victorian brownstones, art galleries, and the city's most diverse crowd, the South End is Boston's cultural engine. It's also ground zero for local foodies, who flood the scores of ethnic resto-bars that morph from neighborhood bistros into packed hot spots as the evening progresses. Some of the city's most popular restaurants inhabit the small square between Berkeley Street and Massachusetts Avenue to the west, and Harrison Avenue and Columbus Avenue to the north.

$$$ SEAFOOD ✕ **B&G Oysters.** B&G Oysters' Chef Barbara Lynch (of No. 9 Park, the Butcher Shop, Sportello, and Menton fame) has made yet another fabulous mark on Boston with a style-conscious seafood restaurant that updates New England's traditional bounty with flair. Designed to imitate the inside of an oyster shell, the iridescent bar glows with silvery, candlelighted tiles and a sophisticated crowd. They're in for the lobster roll, no doubt—an expensive proposition at $29, but filled with decadent chunks of meat in a perfectly textured dressing. If you're sans reservation, be prepared to wait: the line for a seat can be epic. Some say the quarters are cramped and the menu is only appropriate for those with deep wallets. $ *Average main: $29* ✉ *550 Tremont St., South End* ☎ *617/423–0550* 🌐 *www.bandgoysters.com* ✍ *Reservations essential* Ⓜ *Back Bay/South End* ✥ *2:D4.*

$$ AMERICAN ✕ **The Butcher Shop.** Chef Barbara Lynch has remade the classic meat market as a polished wine bar–cum–hangout, and it's just the kind of high-quality, low-pretense spot every neighborhood could use. Stop in for a glass of wine and a casual, quick snack of homemade prosciutto and salami or a plate of artisanal cheeses. Or, linger longer over dinner specials like tagliatelle Bolognese and juicy prime rib eye. Reservations are accepted for parties of six or more. $ *Average main: $19* ✉ *552 Tremont St., South End* ☎ *617/423–4800* 🌐 *www.*

thebutchershopboston.com Ⓜ *Back Bay/South End* ✣ *2:D4.*

$$ SPANISH
Estragon. The urbane 1930s decor makes this South End Spanish restaurant feel high-class, but the tapas plates and easy-to-share *raciones* (entrées) make dining here an entirely casual experience. A selection of traditional tapas, such as grilled Spanish sausage on toast and grilled leeks, can easily fill up two people when coupled with entrées like paella (vegetarian or nonvegetarian) or the braised oxtail. Look for a seat on the couches in the back lounge for a more social dining experience. A semiprivate dining area in the front is candlelit and more intimate. *Average main: $24* ✉ *700 Harrison Ave., South End* ☎ *617/266–0443* 🌐 *www.estragontapas.com* ⏲ *Closed Sun. No lunch* Ⓜ *Newton St.* ✣ *2:D5.*

SISTER SISTER

Boston's a small city, so it's no wonder that names are repeated with restaurateurs opening multiple properties. After **Toro**'s success, Ken Oringer welcomed **Coppa** (✉ *253 Shawmut Ave.* ☎ *617/391–0902*), an Italian wine bar with small plates just blocks away. Seth Woods is behind **Metropolis Café** (✉ *584 Tremont St.* ☎ *617/247–2931* ✣ *2:C4*) and **Union Bar and Grille**, which has upscale brasserie vibes while Stephanie Sokolov of **Stephanie's on Newbury** opened **Stephi's on Tremont** (✉ *571 Tremont St.* ☎ *617/236–2063* ✣ *2:C4*), which borrows favorite entrées from its big sib.

$ AMERICAN FAMILY Fodor's Choice ★
Flour Bakery + Café. When folks in the South End need coffee, a raspberry crumb bar—or just a place to sit and chat—they come here. A communal table acts as a gathering spot, around which diners enjoy homemade soups, salads, and sandwiches like a BLT with applewood-smoked bacon. Of course, it's the sweets, like pecan sticky buns and double chocolate cookies that require a trip to Flour, which has proven so popular that owner Joanne Chang has opened three more locations—in the Fort Point Channel neighborhood, Cambridge, and Back Bay. *Average main: $7* ✉ *1595 Washington St., South End* ☎ *617/267–4300* 🌐 *www.flourbakery.com* *Reservations not accepted* Ⓜ *Mass. Ave.* ✣ *2:C5.*

$$ AMERICAN
Franklin Café. This place has jumped to the head of the class by keeping things simple yet effective. (The litmus test: local chefs gather here after work.) Try the turkey meatloaf off the regular menu or the tomato-roasted eggplant offered on the vegetarian and gluten-free menus. The vibe is more that of a bar than a restaurant, so be forewarned that it can get loud. The wait for a table (there are only seven booths and two tables) can be impossible on weekend nights, and desserts are not served. On the upside, food is served until 1:30 am and cocktails until 2 am. *Average main: $18* ✉ *278 Shawmut Ave., South End* ☎ *617/350–0010* 🌐 *www.franklincafe.com* *Reservations not accepted* ⏲ *No lunch* Ⓜ *Back Bay/South End* ✣ *2:D4.*

$$$ FRENCH Fodor's Choice ★
Hamersley's Bistro. Famous for wearing a Red Sox cap, Gordon Hamersley has earned a national reputation, thanks to signature dishes such as spicy halibut and souffléed lemon custard. His devotion to locally sourced ingredients makes dining at his restaurant a joy, no matter what the season. Dishes arrive carefully prepared yet unpretentious,

which explains why he's one of Boston's great chefs. The butter-yellow space has a full bar with two tables for walk-ins, a small dining room, and a larger room that looks into the open kitchen. Brunch is served Sunday. *Average main: $30 ✉ 553 Tremont St., South End ☎ 617/423–2700 🌐 www.hamersleysbistro.com ⏲ No lunch Ⓜ Back Bay/South End ✥ 2:C4.*

$$$$ FRENCH Fodor's Choice ★ ✕ **Mistral.** Polished service and unpretentious dishes, like beef-tenderloin pizza topped with mashed potatoes and white-truffle oil, make Mistral a perennial South End hot spot. Grab a table by the floor-to-ceiling windows or a seat at the buzzing bar—either way, there'll be plenty to see in this airy room with Provençal-theme decor. Boston's fashionable set has been coming here for years, which speaks to chef Jamie Mammano's excellent French-Mediterranean cuisine with favorites like tuna tartare, duck with cherries, and French Dover sole. The menu rarely changes—but no one's complaining. Brunch is served on Sunday. *Average main: $36 ✉ 223 Columbus Ave., South End ☎ 617/867–9300 🌐 mistralbistro.com ⏲ No lunch lunch Ⓜ Back Bay/South End ✥ 2:C3.*

BRUNCH STEALS

Come Sunday, the South End steps out for a morning meal at eateries offering affordable, prix-fixe brunches. At **Union Bar and Grille** (✉ *1357 Washington St.* ☎ *617/423–0555* ✥ *2:D4*) $9.95 buys crumb cake, salmon egg scramble, toast, coffee, and juice. Southwestern **Masa** (✉ *439 Tremont St.* ☎ *617/338–8884* ✥ *2:D3*) offers tapas like plantain empanadas for about $4 and huevos rancheros for less than $10. At **Gaslight** (✉ *500 Harrison Ave.,* ☎ *617/422–0224*) get juice, shortbread, French toast, and coffee for $9.95, which at **Aquitaine** (✉ *569 Tremont St.,* ☎ *617/424–8577*) buys cinnamon buns, juice, coffee, and an omelet with potatoes and toast.

$ CHINESE ✕ **Myers + Chang.** Pink and orange dragon decals cover the windows of this all-day Chinese café, where Joanne Chang (of Flour fame) has returned to her familial cooking roots. Sharable platters of dumplings, wok-charred udon noodles, and stir-fries brim with fresh ingredients from China, Japan, Taiwan, Thailand, and Vietnam. The staff is young and hip, and the crowd follows suit. *Average main: $14 ✉ 1145 Washington St., South End ☎ 617/542–5200 🌐 www.myersandchang.com Ⓜ Back Bay/South End ✥ 2:E4.*

$$$ JAPANESE ✕ **Oishii Boston.** Although the entrance to this superb sushi restaurant may elude you, simply follow the crowds of raw-fish fans streaming into the sleek, gray industrial space, where sushi chef–owner Ting Yen turns succulent morsels of seafood into edible enchantment. From tuna tartare with sesame oil and golden caviar to crunchy tempura oysters, from lobster salad maki to grilled Wagyu beef with shallot-sake sauce, this larger, tonier incarnation of Yen's überpopular 14-seat restaurant Oishii in Chestnut Hill allows him to spread his wings. The vibe is hip and so are the diners. While the delectable nine-course *omakase* (chef's tasting) is quite a splurge ($150), the set lunch specials (*kaiseki*) offer fabulous value. *Average main: $28 ✉ 1166 Washington St.,*

CLOSE UP

Sweet Spots

Some of the tastiest sweets in Boston come from Bread + Butter, a French-inspired bakery in the North End (✉ *64 Cross St.* ☎ *617/248–6900*). Through the store's side window, you can watch owner, Lee Napoli, prepare huge flaky croissants, brown butter pear tarts, and éclairs. Savory offerings include kale and veggie salads, sandwiches stuffed with roast turkey, cheddar, and avocado, along with a nice selection of coffee drinks.

Luscious muffins—including the best-selling "morning glories" (carrot-raisin muffins)—are baked at the South End's **Appleton Bakery** (✉ *123 Appleton St.* ☎ *617/859–8222* ⊕ *2:C3*), which also serves lunch.

Chocolatier and Boston native Larry Burdick spent years in France and Switzerland perfecting his craft before opening **LA Burdick's** (✉ *52–D Brattle St. Cambridge* ☎ *617/491–4340* 🌐 *www.burdickchocolate.com* ⊕ *4:A2*) known for its unbelievably decadent hot chocolate and bite-size gourmet chocolates shaped like mice (complete with almond ears). As you sit at one of the shop's small tables nibbling a macaroon or Linzer torte, you may even forget what country you're in.

Only the iron-willed can walk out of **Sweet** (✉ *49 Massachusetts Ave., Boston* ☎ *617/247–2253* Ⓜ *Hynes*) without a dark chocolate or red velvet cupcake. With four locations, including one in Cambridge, the shops also offer frosting shots for a quick icing fix.

South End ☎ *617/482–8868* 🌐 *www.oishiiboston.com* ⏲ *Closed Mon.* Ⓜ *Washington Street* ⊕ *2:E4.*

$$$ SPANISH Fodor's Choice ★

✕ **Toro.** The opening buzz from chefs Ken Oringer and Jamie Bissonnette's tapas joint still remains—for good reason. Small plates such as grilled corn with aioli and cotija cheese are hefty enough to make a meal, or you can share the paella with a group. An all-Spanish wine list complements the plates. Crowds have been known to wait for more than an hour for dinner. Aim to go for lunch during the week for a less hectic experience. $ *Average main: $30* ✉ *1704 Washington St., South End* ☎ *617/536–4300* 🌐 *www.toro-restaurant.com* ✍ *Reservations not accepted* Ⓜ *Mass. Ave.* ⊕ *2:B6.*

$$ AMERICAN

✕ **Union Bar and Grille.** There's rarely a quiet night at Union, where the bar buzzes with the neighborhood's coolest residents and couples on dates fill the dining room. Despite the show, the menu keeps things down to earth, with golden fried calamari, succulent chicken cooked under a brick (which flattens the bird and makes it super crispy and moist), and iron skillets of warm corn bread served at every table. Brunch is served weekends. $ *Average main: $22* ✉ *1357 Washington St., South End* ☎ *617/423–0555* 🌐 *www.unionrestaurant.com* ⏲ *No lunch* Ⓜ *South End* ⊕ *2:D4.*

THE FENWAY AND KENMORE SQUARE

WORD OF MOUTH

"I really like Eastern Standard. It's a big, high-energy restaurant, and the food is very good and reasonably priced. We go there often, as we always eat there before catching a show at the nearby House of Blues."—sharona

$$ AMERICAN Fodor's Choice ★ **Eastern Standard Kitchen and Drinks.** A vivid red awning beckons patrons of this spacious brasserie-style restaurant. The bar area and red banquettes are filled most nights with Boston's power players (members of the Red Sox management are known to stop in), thirtysomethings, and students from the nearby universities all noshing on raw-bar specialties and comfort dishes such as lamb-sausage rigatoni, rib eye, and burgers. It's a Sunday brunch hot spot, especially on game days (the Big Green Monster is a very short walk away). The cocktail list is one of the best in town, filled with old classics and new concoctions, and in addition to a boutique wine list there is a reserve list for rare beers. A covered, heated patio offers alfresco dining year-round. *Average main: $24 528 Commonwealth Ave., Kenmore Sq. 617/532–9100 www.easternstandardboston.com Kenmore 3:F2.*

$$$ SEAFOOD Fodor's Choice ★ **Island Creek Oyster Bar.** If you're not a fan of oysters, don't let the name of this Hotel Commonwealth restaurant fool you—there's a lot more going on with a menu that's printed fresh daily. Many of the oysters shucked and served here come fresh from the restaurant's own oyster farm in nearby Duxbury Bay; other daily sources can include Maine, Prince Edward Island, and Puget Sound (Washington). Striped bass ceviche and salmon crudo can appear at the raw bar as well. Clams, hand dug on Boston's South Shore, are served both fried and in a classic New England chowder. Fish entrées change daily with what's available and can include day boat cod, sea scallops, and a seafood casserole that serves 1, 2, or 4. Chicken and steak are there for those hankering for land food. Sunday brunch features homemade pastries (walnut sticky buns) and a decadent lobster omelet. *Average main: $27 500 Commonwealth Ave., Kenmore Sq. 617/532–5300 www.islandcreekoysterbar.com No lunch Sat. Kenmore 3:F2.*

$$ SOUTHERN Fodor's Choice ★ **Sweet Cheeks.** Red Sox fans, foodies, and Fenway residents flock to this meat lover's mecca, where Texas-style BBQ is the name of the game. Hefty slabs of dry-rubbed heritage pork, great northern beef brisket, and plump chickens cook low and slow in a jumbo black smoker until saturated with campfire flavor. Owner Tiffany Faison tromped all over the Texas barbecue belt to get her recipes finger-licking right, including the homemade sweet pickles and shaved onion that come with every order, heaped on a tray lined with butcher paper. The baseball-size biscuits served with honey butter are delectable, so don't miss those. Sweet tea and cocktails are served in mason jars, while housemade BBQ sauces (mild, medium, and skull-splittingly hot) sit on the table, along with a tin can of flatware and napkins. (You'll need lots of the latter; with food this good, it's going to get messy!) *Average main: $22 1381 Boylston St., The Fenway 617/266–1300 www.sweetcheeksq.com Fenway 3:E4.*

BOSTON OUTSKIRTS

NEWTON

Artists, writers, doctors, and families populate the leafy, lake-filled suburb of Newton, just seven miles from Downtown Boston, where several big-name chefs have also set down stakes. Lured by lower commercial rents and the ability to live and work in a more bucolic setting—some commute by bike—they are feeding a steady stream of diners hungry for Downtown-quality food at uptown prices

$$$ MODERN FRENCH Fodor's Choice ★

Lumiere. Scrumptious food that balances indulgence with lightness is the name of the game at this elegant New England–style bistro. Relying on local, sustainable seasonal ingredients, the menu frequently changes, however, couples, foodies, and neighborhood folks can't get enough of the creamy corn soup, plump golden scallops in a bright lemon sauce with peas, and spiced chicken, possibly the most succulent in the city. Add a sweet little bar with stellar cocktails, excellent desserts (try the apple tart with sour cream sorbet), and professional, friendly service and it's easy to understand why the accolades and diners continue to pour in. *Average main: $33 ✉ 1293 Washington St., Newton ☎ 617/244–9199 www.lumiererestaurant.com No lunch M West Newton ✣ 3:A4.*

$$$ MODERN AMERICAN Fodor's Choice ★

Sycamore. "Groan-worthy" describes the earthy, market-fresh dishes you'll find at this cozy, brick-walled former butcher shop, which hasn't had a quiet night since it opened in the fall of 2012. Foodies, families, and folks from the neighborhood and beyond can't get enough of dream-team chefs David Punch and Lydia Reichert's culinary homage to New England: house-smoked bluefish pâté, smoky shrimp chowder with local scallops and clams, and last but not least, the whole animal/fish board for two (think duck with rosy breast meat, spiced sausage, and crostini heaped with succulent duck pastrami). Begin with a cocktail from the excellent bar and end with a satisfied smile—made even bigger because area parking is plentiful and mainly free. *Average main: $25 ✉ 755 Beacon St., Newton ☎ 617/244–4445 sycamorenewton.com No lunch M Newton Centre Station ✣ 3:A4.*

JAMAICA PLAIN

This neighborhood is a kind of a mini-Cambridge: multiethnic and filled with cutting-edge artists, graduate students, political idealists, and yuppie families. Recently the area, known for its affordable and unusual ethnic spots, has seen a swell of a more gentrified—but no less creative—sort.

$$ ITALIAN FAMILY

Bella Luna. Tucked away in The Brewery Complex, home to myriad small businesses, including Samuel Adams beer, this restaurant-cum-nightclub offers sci-fi jokes written throughout a spaced-out menu of eccentric pizzas, calzones, and Italian standards. Menu favorites remain, including the "Pizza Menino" (named for the city's mayor), topped with pepperoni, sausage, mushrooms, peppers, and onions, and the "Diedre Delux," dreamed up by a former employee (named Diedre) featuring dried cranberries, caramelized onions, and Gorgonzola cheese. Works by area artists line the walls, and local musicians provide music in the lounge, the Milky Way. (The weekly schedule ranges from salsa to country line dancing.) $ *Average main: $18 ✉ 284 Amory St., Samuel Adams Brewery complex, Jamaica Plain ☎ 617/524–3740 🌐 www.milkywayjp.com ⏲ No lunch Sun.–Fri.* M *Stony Brook ✣ 3:C6.*

$ AMERICAN ✕ **Centre Street Café.** It's impossible not to love J.P.'s hippy cool hangout, where neighborhood residents pack the limited number of tables and local artwork fills the walls. The eclectic menu veers from ethnic inspirations like Asian-inspired Shrimp Nirvana to inventive salads brimming with local produce. There is even the perennial favorite, "Slacker's Breakfast," a choice of four options including three egg dishes and French toast served with fruit and real maple syrup, offered until 3 pm. Lines snake around the block every Saturday and Sunday for the spectacular (and spectacularly filling) brunch. $ *Average main: $13 ✉ 669A Centre St., Jamaica Plain ☎ 617/524–9217 ✍ Reservations not accepted* M *Green St. ✣ 3:C6.*

$ CUBAN ✕ **El Oriental de Cuba.** This light, airy haven with wooden tables and walls full of artwork—featuring tropical fruit, Cuban street life, and magazine covers—serves a large variety of excellent Cuban food, including a restorative chicken soup, a classic Cuban sub, superb rice and beans (opt for the red beans over the black), and sweet "tropical shakes." The menu, written in both English and Spanish begins with breakfast, mainly various preparations of eggs with added ham, chorizo, or cheese. *Tostones* (twice-fried plantains) are beloved during cold New England winters by the city's many Cuban transplants, who will also find such dishes as oxtail, braised beef tongue, and *monfongo* (fried mashed green plantains with pork rinds and garlic oil). $ *Average main: $13 ✉ 416 Centre St., Jamaica Plain ☎ 617/524–6464 🌐 www.elorientaldecuba.com* M *Stony Brook ✣ 3:C6.*

$$$ FRENCH ✕ **Ten Tables.** Jamaica Plain's postage stamp–size, candlelit boîte (there's a sister restaurant in Cambridge) is an enchanting mix of Gallic elegance and chummy neighborhood revelry–both in the atmosphere and the food. Simple but high-quality dishes such as hanger steak with tomato-pepper relish and Sicilian-style fish stew—followed by a carefully chosen "one perfect cheese" plate—seamlessly seal the deal. The $48 tasting menu, $35 if you're a vegetarian or vegan (the latter requires 24-hour advance notice), makes ordering easy. Just be prepared to wait it out for a table, or reserve weeks in advance online, as phones are generally staffed by a recording. The stylish, laid-back bar, where you can enjoy dinner or bar bites, is warmly appointed with reclaimed wood and exposed brick. $ *Average main: $26 ✉ 597 Centre St., Jamaica Plain ☎ 617/524–8810 🌐 tentables.net ✍ Reservations essential ⏲ No lunch* M *Stony Brook ✣ 3:C6.*

BROOKLINE

Going to Brookline is a nice way to get out of the city without really leaving town. Although it's surrounded by Boston on three sides, Brookline has its own suburban flavor, seasoned with a multitude of historic—and expensive—houses and garnished with a diverse ethnic population that supports a string of sushi bars and a small list of kosher restaurants. Most Brookline eateries are clustered in the town's commercial centers: Brookline Village, Washington Square, Longwood, and bustling Coolidge Corner.

CLOSE UP

Boston Classics

Not for nothing did Boston become known as the home of the bean and the cod: simple Yankee specialties—many of them of English origin—and traditional seafood abound.

Boston baked beans are a thick, syrupy mixture of navy beans, salt pork, and molasses cooked for hours. They were originally made by Puritan women on Saturday, so that the leftovers could be eaten on Sunday without breaking the Sabbath by cooking.

You may also want to keep an eye out for Parker House rolls, yeast-bread dinner rolls first concocted at the Parker House Hotel in the 1870s.

Boston cream pie is an addictive simple yellow vanilla cake filled with a creamy custard and iced with chocolate frosting. Many traditional New England eateries (and some steak houses and hotel restaurants) serve a house version. Occasionally you'll find a modernized version, with some creative new element added at trendier restaurants.

The city's beer-drinking enthusiasm is older than the Declaration of Independence—which, incidentally, was signed by Samuel Adams, an instigator of the Boston Tea Party and the man whose name graces the bottles of the country's best-selling craft-brew beer.

$ ECLECTIC **Elephant Walk.** Chef Longteine de Monteiro learned to manage a Cambodian kitchen as the wife of a diplomat, and for a time ran a restaurant in Béziers in southern France. The French-Cambodian menu is separated by region, so you get the best of both worlds. Tease your palate with an exotic assortment of authentic soups and salads, spring rolls that you wrap in fresh lettuce leaves, and a juicy duck breast with Cointreau sauce. The restaurant features extensive vegetarian and gluten-free offerings. The airy atmosphere evokes a British Colonial hotel; the food reminds you of why Phnom Penh was "the Paris of Asia." The desserts, though, are pure Paris. Sunday brunch is served. *Average main: $16* *900 Beacon St., Brookline* *617/247–1500* *www.elephantwalk.com* *St. Mary's* *3:D3.*

$$ JAPANESE **Fugakyu.** The name in Japanese means "house of elegance" and the gracious and efficient service hits the mark, along with the interior's tatami mats, rice-paper partitions, and wooden ships circling a moat around the sushi bar. The extensive menu is both elegant and novel, with thick slabs of super-fresh sashimi, inventive maki rolls, and plenty of cooked items, like panko-crusted pork cutlet and chicken teriyaki for those not into seafood or raw fish. Can't decide what to order? Try the *omakase*, a six-course dinner composed of what's freshest that day ($80). Bento boxes are available at lunch only. *Average main: $20* *1280 Beacon St., Brookline* *617/734–1268* *www.fugakyu.net* *Coolidge Corner* *3:A4.*

$$$ SEAFOOD **Lineage.** Downtown is saturated with decent seafood options, but few hit the mark on inventive fare quite like Lineage. Chef-owner Jeremy Sewall puts the restaurant's central wood-burning stove to good use, and roasts everything from halibut to pork chops. His cousin Mark is a lobsterman, and provides a fresh catch now and then. A number of

CLOSE UP

Top Chef Travels: Ming Tsai's Boston

Ming Tsai has made a name for himself as the premier chef of East-West cuisine. As owner and chef of Wellesley-based Blue Ginger restaurant and Fort Point Channel–based Blue Dragon restaurant, author of five cookbooks, and host of cooking show *Simply Ming*, Ming Tsai artfully showcases the fusion of Eastern and Western culinary techniques.

Q: Where are some of your favorite places to eat in Boston?
A: Uni and Clio. When Clio opened, it took Boston by storm. Clio is fine dining—white tablecloths and the whole nine yards. If my parents were in town and it was a holiday, I'd go to Clio. But Uni is very unconventional. There's no sushi rice, so it's a sashimi bar and 90% of the menu is raw. Ken Oringer gets pristine fish from Japan, and uni (or sea urchin) is one of his signature products.

Q: What other restaurants in Boston do you like?
A: I love Toro, another one of Ken's restaurants. It features some of the best tapas around. The corn on the cob is to die for. For the best sushi, there's Oishii. Chef Ting Yen's dishes are as beautiful as they are delicious. A tried-and-true favorite in Chinatown is Gourmet Dumpling House. I can't go too long without having their Sliced Fish Szechwan style. It's for those not afraid of heat! And Blue Ribbon is an all-time favorite with their authentic Southern BBQ recipes. Also, there's my pal Tiffany Faison's Sweet Cheeks in Fenway—her approach is Texas-style and it's delicious.

Q: Tell us about Blue Ginger. What can people expect when dining there?
A: It's very casual. I mean we have people who come in tuxes and people who come in shorts. It's an open kitchen—the entertainment, action, the feel, the smells are all in the restaurant.

Q: And what about Blue Dragon, your newest venture?

A: The tapas-style menu features an East-West twist on classic pub favorites, like panko-crusted fish-and-chips with black vinegar aioli. There's just one dessert—a spoonable, warm deep-dish chocolate chip cookie with vanilla ice cream and soy caramel drizzle. People seem to talk about that—a lot.

seats at the bar, along with ample space in the oyster-gray dining room, allow diners the option of a casual meal or a comfortable fine-dining experience. Sunday Brunch is available. *Average main: $26* *242 Harvard St., Brookline* *617/232–0065* *www.lineagerestaurant.com* *No lunch* *Coolidge Corner* *3:A4.*

$$ IRISH **Matt Murphy's Pub.** Boston has dozens of Irish pubs, but very few are notable for food—this pub being a welcome exception. Even with a hefty renovation in 2010, this place has maintained its heart, making real poetry out of thick slabs of bread and butter served on wooden boards, giant servings of soup, fish-and-chips presented in a twist of newspaper, and shepherd's pie. Don't miss the house-made ketchup with your French fries or the traditional Irish breakfast consisting of Irish sausage and bacon, potatoes, black and white pudding, beans, and eggs. *Average main: $21* *14 Harvard St., Brookline* *617/232–0188* *No credit cards* *Brookline Village* *3:A6.*

$ AMERICAN **The Publick House.** What started as a simple neighborhood beer bar has reached cultlike status for Brookline-ites and beyond. Serving more than 175 out-of-the-ordinary and artisanal beers, the bar also offers tasty sandwiches, smaller entrées, and main dishes (try the lobster mac and cheese), many of which have beer incorporated into them, such as the steamed mussels (served with golden frites). An adjacent taproom—the Monk's Cell—specializes in Belgian brews. Weekend nights find long lines, but one taste of the city's only "cuisine à la bière" is absolutely worth it. Lunch is available on Saturday and Sunday, and although there are no desserts, you can find an ice cream shop and pastry café across the street. *Average main: $13* *1648 Beacon St., Brookline* *617/277–2880* *Washington Sq.* *3:A4.*

$ INDIAN **Rani.** One of Brookline's more unusual restaurants serves excellent Indian cuisine in the Hyderabadi style, which incorporates northern and southern flavors. Dishes are complex, rich, and layered with sweet and salty. *Murg musalam,* roast chicken in a fragrant brown sauce, is tender and juicy, and any of the tandoori dishes (meats cooked in a clay oven) are designed for beginners. The variety of specialty breads is impressive, and the sleek interior fills up nightly with locals looking for a change of pace from Downtown's more casual Indian buffets. During the day, explore the menu via the daily lunch spread–a selection of the day's freshest offerings. *Average main: $14* *1353 Beacon St., Brookline* *617/734–0400* *www.ranibistro.com* *Coolidge Corner* *3:A4.*

$$ DELI **Rubin's.** Founded in 1928, this award-winning, family-owned kosher Jewish delicatessen is the last one in the Boston area. Fluffy omelets, challah French toast, and fruit blintzes dominate the breakfast menu (served all day), while lunch and dinner offerings range from soups and hearty salads to sandwiches, like the hand-cut pastrami and overstuffed Wall Street number (corned beef, tongue, coleslaw, and Russian dressing) that any New Yorker can respect. You can also try *kasha varnishkes* (buckwheat with bow-tie noodles), hot brisket, and many other high-cholesterol classics. There is even a kid's menu with pasta and red sauce and chicken nuggets. *Average main: $22* *500 Harvard St., Brookline* *617/731–8787* *Closed Sat. No dinner Fri.* *Coolidge Corner* *3:A4.*

$$ SPANISH

Taberna de Haro. Snug and pimento-red inside, this is Boston's first tapas bar to fully capture authentic Spanish cuisine. Kick off dinner with a choice of about 40 hot and cold tapas, including such classics as a tortilla Española, shrimp in garlic oil, braised eggplant, and *jamón Serrano* (Serrano ham). Then, consider one of the select entrées, such as cuttlefish and squid-ink paella, charred rib eye, or grilled lamb chops. The owners have hand-selected an inexpensive all-Spanish wine list with more than 325 varieties, of which 44 are sherry and Manzanilla, including some sweet ones to accompany the traditional Spanish desserts of flan or cheeses with quince paste. An outdoor patio fills up throughout the summer. *Average main: $24* *999 Beacon St., Brookline* *617/277–8272* *www.tabernaboston.com* *Closed Sun. No lunch* *Coolidge Corner* *3:D3.*

$ SOUTHERN

Village Smokehouse. This stalwart Brookline Village BBQ joint has been literally luring customers in by the nose (you can practically smell it from the Brookline Village T stop) since it set up shop 25 years ago. In recent years the vintage plastic checkered tablecloths have been replaced by wooden tables (albeit with red-checkered tops) and more upscale decor. But, the ambience is still a tribute to sauce-drippin' BBQ chicken and ribs, right down to the plastic bibs. Bottom line: expect to get messy. Enjoy! *Average main: $14* *1 Harvard St., Brookline* *617/566–3782* *www.villagesmokehouse.com* *Reservations not accepted* *No lunch Sun.–Thurs.* *Brookline Village* *3:A6.*

$ AMERICAN FAMILY

Zaftigs. Here's something different: a contemporary version of a Jewish delicatessen. How refreshing to have genuinely lean corned beef, a modest slice of cheesecake, low-sugar homemade borscht, and a lovely whitefish-salad sandwich. Believe breakfast is the most important meal? It's served all day, meaning you can skip the hour-long weekend brunch waits and enjoy a plate of the area's best pancakes and stuffed French toast any weekday. Just try to leave room for one of the goodies (cupcakes, Conga bars) in the bakery case. *Average main: $15* *335 Harvard St., Brookline* *617/975–0075* *www.zaftigs.com* *Coolidge Corner* *3:A4.*

WELLESLEY

Wellesley, a western suburb of Boston, is about a 35-minute drive from the city. Or you could jump on the commuter rail's Framingham/Worcester line, which runs between Wellesley and Boston's Back Bay and South Station depots, with trains leaving nearly every hour during the week and every two hours on Saturday.

$$$ ASIAN

Blue Ginger. Chef Ming Tsai's nimble maneuvers in the kitchen have caught the nation's eye via a public TV cooking program, *Simply Ming,* and his five cookbooks. Plan ahead to savor jazzed-up plates of Western-meets-Asian cuisine, including his signature buttery sake-miso marinated sablefish. On evenings and Saturday the no reservations set can drop into the lounge for the chef's Ming's Bings (think slider meets potsticker) and Asian tapas. Weekday lunches include super-fresh salads, hearty sandwiches, and kid-friendly dishes. Some say the prices do not match the food, which can range from spot-on to less than carefully prepared. *Average main: $33* *583 Washington St., Wellesley* *781/283–5790* *www.ming.com* *No lunch weekends* *3:A1.*

CLOSE UP

'Off the Chain' Chains

If you're on the go, you might want to try a local chain restaurant, where you can stop for a quick bite or get some takeout. The places listed here are fairly priced, committed to quality, and use decent, fresh ingredients.

Au Bon Pain. The locally based chain whips up quick salads and sandwiches, fresh-daily croissants and muffins, and has plenty of fruit and juices. It's recently added some appealing snack options, including an apple, blue cheese, and cranberry combo.

B.Good. This chainlet's avocado- and salsa-topped veggie burgers, baked sweet-potato fries, and sesame-ginger chicken salad are redefining fast food in Boston.

Bertucci's. Thin-crust pizzas fly fast from the brick ovens at this Mediterranean spot, where you'll also find a fab vegetable antipasto, pastas, and a gluten-free menu.

Boloco. For quick, cheap, healthful, and high-quality wraps and burritos, this is easily the city's most dependable chain. Boloco's menu also includes smoothies and breakfast options, and its hours are some of the longest in this notoriously early-to-bed city.

Finagle A Bagel. Find fresh, doughy bagels in flavors from jalapeño cheddar to triple chocolate, plus sandwiches and salads. Service is swift and efficient.

UBurger. Better-than-average burgers with toppings that lean toward the gourmet (sautéed mushrooms, blue cheese) and a great chocolate frappe (Boston-ese for milk shake) make this spot the East Coast's answer to California's much-loved In-N-Out.

CAMBRIDGE

10

Among other collegiate enthusiasms, Cambridge has a long-standing fascination with ethnic eateries. Another kind of great restaurant has also evolved here, mixing world-class cooking with a studied informality, particularly around the red-hot Technology Square area near MIT where chefs cook with wood fires and borrow flavors from every continent. For more posh tastes and the annual celebrations that come with college life (or the end of it), Cambridge also has its share of linen-cloth tables.

$
AMERICAN
Fodor's Choice ★

All Star Sandwich Bar. This brightly colored place with about a dozen tables has a strict definition of what makes a sandwich: no wraps. The owners have put together a list of classics, like crispy, overstuffed Reubens and beef on weck, which are served quickly from an open kitchen. Their famous Atomic Meatloaf Meltdown has been highlighted on a number of foodie networks. Not into sandwiches? Soups, salads, a burger, and chili are available, along with a small selection of beer and wine. If pies are more your thing, sister restaurant All-Star Pizza Bar is just across the street. *Average main: $9* *1245 Cambridge St.* *617/868–3065* *www.allstarsandwichbar.com* *Reservations not accepted* *Central/Inman* *4:F2.*

CLOSE UP

Cold Comforts

Bostonians eat more ice cream per capita than anyone else in the United States, according to an oft-repeated—though difficult to verify—factoid. Whether it's actually true, there are a remarkable number of independent, premium ice cream and gelato shops in town, along with a flood of frozen yogurt joints selling sweet and tangy swirls to top with lots of candy and garnishes.

BerryLine. This is the place for superlative soft, tangy frozen yogurt made from real ingredients, like milk, cane sugar, and fresh fruit. Two post-doctoral fellowship student friends—one from MIT and the other from Harvard Medical School—founded this funky local spot with outposts in Porters Square (✉ 1668 Massachusetts Avenue) and Fenway (✉ 1337 Boylston Street). ✉ *3 Arrow Street* ☎ *617/868-3500* 🌐 *www.berryline.com.*

Christina's Homemade Ice Cream. Inman Square dessert mecca Christina's dishes up around 50 ice cream flavors, from honey lavender to cinnamon rice pudding, and an amazingly addictive chocolate mousse. Seasonal flavors, like apple pie, eggnog, and fresh rose, rotate onto the list. ✉ *1255 Cambridge St., Inman Square* ☎ *617/492-7021* 🌐 *www.christinasicecream.com* ✥ *4:F2.*

Emack & Bolio's. Dieting meets decadence at Emack & Bolio's, a half juice/smoothie bar, half ice-cream parlor with several locations including Back Bay (✉ 290 Newbury Street). The flavors here aren't as extreme as the offerings at some competitors, but you'll find rock-solid renditions of favorites like cookie dough and butter pecan. ✉ *255 State St., Waterfront* ☎ *617/367-0220* 🌐 *www.emackandbolios.com* ✥ *2:A2.*

J.P. Licks. This funky local institution has numerous outposts (Boston, Brookline, and Harvard Square). In addition to a stable of ice cream flavors, monthly specials might include gingersnap molasses and s'mores with hard and soft frozen yogurt offerings and superb hot fudge sauce. ✉ *1106 Boylston St., Back Bay* ☎ *857/236-1666* 🌐 *www.jplicks.com* ✥ *3:H2.*

Lizzy's Ice Cream. Barely bigger than a shoebox, this Harvard Square parlor offers more than 50 fabulous flavors like orange-pineapple and Charles River Crunch (a dark-chocolate ice cream with almond toffee nuggets). The frappes and sundaes here are unrivaled. ✉ *29 Church St., Harvard Square* ☎ *617/354-2911* 🌐 *www.lizzysicecream.com* ✥ *4:A2.*

Picco. With a name that's short for Pizza and Ice Cream Company, Picco is perfect for kids and kids at heart. Flavors include coconut-chocolate chip, honey, and Vietnamese cinnamon. It serves real food, too, and there's a rotating list of craft beers from which to choose. ✉ *513 Tremont St., South End* ☎ *617/927-0066* 🌐 *www.piccorestaurant.com* ✥ *2:D3.*

Toscanini's. With flavors such as goat cheese-brownie, burnt caramel, and green tea, this MIT establishment has few equals, especially when it comes to their micro sundae—a small scoop topped with excellent homemade hot fudge and whipped cream—perfect for a guilt-free splurge. ✉ *899 Main St., Central Square* ☎ *617/491-5877* 🌐 *www.tosci.com* ✥ *4:F5.*

$$ MODERN AMERICAN Fodor's Choice ★ **Area Four.** A bonifide hit from day one, everything at this glass-enclosed eatery in the avante-garde Technology Square area is scrumptious–from the morning sticky buns and excellent dark coffee at the café to the clam-bacon pizza in the casual dining room. A central wood-fired oven turns out chewy-crusted pies and small skillets of mac and cheese with croissant crumbs and crackly-skinned chicken over wilted greens. You will find only local, seasonal, and sustainable cooking here. *Average main: $18 ✉ 500 Technology Sq. ☎ 617/758-4444 www.areafour.com Ⓜ Kendall/MIT Station ✣ 4:G5.*

$ MEDITERRANEAN **Baraka Café.** Chef-owner Alia Radjeb Meddeb spent her childhood years in France and Tunisia—a fact reflected sharply in her menu at this tiny, casual eatery that could easily be her home. Imagine chickpea custard with *harissa* (hot sauce) tapenade, spicy lamb and beef sausages, and seven-vegetable couscous served with a flavorful broth. No alcohol is served, but after a few sips of her spiced lemonade with rose petals, you won't care. *Average main: $13 ✉ 80½ Pearl St. ☎ 617/868–3951 www.barakacafe.com Reservations essential No credit cards Closed Mon. No lunch Sun. Ⓜ Central ✣ 4:E5.*

$$ AMERICAN **The Blue Room.** Totally hip, funky, and Cambridge, the brightly colored Blue Room blends a host of cuisines from Moroccan to Mediterranean with fresh, local ingredients. Try the wood-grilled lamb with ratatouille, or the whole roasted catch of the day with salsa verde. On Sunday, you'll find an extraordinary brunch buffet with grilled meats and vegetables, along with regular breakfast fare and scrumptious desserts. Next door, sister property Belly Wine Bar offers wine flights and small bites of Italian-style tapas, cured meats, and cheese. *Average main: $24 ✉ 1 Kendall Sq. ☎ 617/494–9034 www.theblueroom.net No lunch Mon.–Sat. Ⓜ Kendall/MIT ✣ 4:H4.*

$$$ ECLECTIC **Chez Henri.** French with a Latin twist—odd bedfellows, but it works for this cozy red bistro. The dinner menu gets serious, with rum-glazed pork over gingered sweet potato purée and sinfully sweet desserts like chocolate bread pudding. At the snug bar you can sample conch fritters, grilled homemade chorizo, and a pressed Cuban sandwich. The place fills quickly with Cantabrigian locals—an interesting mix of students, professors, and sundry intelligentsia. *Average main: $28 ✉ 1 Shepard St. ☎ 617/354–8980 www.chezhenri.com No lunch. Closed Mon. Ⓜ Harvard ✣ 4:B1.*

10

$$$$ FRENCH **Craigie on Main.** This soulful, white-cloth restaurant is the project of chef-owner Tony Maws, one of Boston's landmark chefs. With a passion for all things fresh, local, and organic, he's in the kitchen most mornings prepping ingredients that likely came from the Harvard or Central Square farmers' markets or another local purveyor. The menu changes daily, so options can range from a Spanish-style octopus to black bass to pork done three ways. Sunday is Chef's Whim Night, meaning that after 9 pm you'll eat four to six courses of whatever Maws feels like cooking for a discounted price ($45 to $57). *Average main: $38 ✉ 853 Main. St. ☎ 617/497–5511 www.craigieonmain.com Closed Mon. Ⓜ Central ✣ 4:F5.*

$$$ MEDITERRANEAN **Dante.** With one of the best patio views of the Charles River, Dante almost resembles a seaside café on the Amalfi coast. Almost. Chef-owner

CLOSE UP

Brain Food

As you wander through Cambridge it's safe to assume that almost every other person on the street attends a nearby institute of higher learning. (Forty percent of the city's population is between the ages of 18 and 29.) Here are a handful of places that cater to poor students:

Darwin's (*148 Mt. Auburn St. 617/354–5233 1629 Cambridge St. 617/491–2999 www.darwinsltd.com 4:A2*). A self-described "shabby-chic deli and café," Darwin's symbolizes both the bohemian Harvard Square of yore and its newer, more gentrified persona. It has nearly 20 sandwiches that cost less than $9 (try The Story, a delicious prosciutto-pesto-fresh mozzarella-tomato combo), very good coffee, locally baked breads, and free Wi-Fi, making it many a student's second home.

Miracle of Science (*321 Massachusetts Ave. 617/868–2866 4:F5*). This funky and casual Central Square restaurant and bar is chock-full of MIT neuroscientists and PhD students at leisure. And no wonder: if anything could drag them away from the lab, it's the Periodic Table of Elements–theme menu with chipotle-tinged turkey chili and several local beers on tap.

Mr. Bartley's Burger Cottage (*1246 Massachusetts Ave. 617/354–6559*). It may just be the perfect cuisine for the student metabolism: a variety of garnished thick burgers with sassy names (many of them celebrities), crispy regular and sweet-potato fries, and onion rings. There's also a great veggie burger, along with comforting fare like baked meatloaf and franks and beans. Soda fountain favorites include thick frappes and the raspberry lime rickey made with fresh limes, raspberry juice, and soda water. During busy times employees hand out menus and take orders on the sidewalk.

Pinocchio's Pizza and Subs (*74 Winthrop St. 617/876–4897 www.pinocchiospizza.net 4:A3*). This hole-in-the-wall's been serving late-night pies to Harvard students for three decades. "Noch's" offers thick, Sicilian-style pizza for little more than two bucks a slice.

Dante DeMagistris culls flavors from that region, and a few others, to present a seafood- and pasta-heavy menu with entrées that focus on hearty portions of protein, such as pan-roasted scallops and a perfectly-cooked pork chop with sweet and sour peppers. Try the chef's tasting menu for seven to nine courses that might include a number of specialties not on the daily menu. *Average main: $27 Royal Sonesta Hotel, 40 Edwin H. Land Blvd. 617/497–4200 www.restaurantdante.com No lunch Lechmere 1:B3.*

$$ AMERICAN

East Coast Grill and Raw Bar. Owner-chef-author Chris Schlesinger built his national reputation on grilled foods and red-hot condiments. The Texas style beef brisket and North Carolina shredded pork are still here, but this restaurant has made an extraordinary play to establish itself in the front ranks of fish restaurants. Spices and condiments are more restrained, and Schlesinger has compiled a wine list bold and flavorful enough to match the highly spiced food. The dining space is completely informal. In addition to Saturday lunch, weekends include a killer Sunday brunch (complete with cornbread-crusted French toast and a do-it-yourself Bloody Mary bar). *Average main: $24 1271 Cambridge St. 617/491–6568 www.eastcoastgrill.net Central 4:F2.*

$$ AMERICAN FAMILY **Full Moon.** Kids will delight in the play kitchen and dollhouse, and parents can cheer that they get to tuck into lovelies such as grilled salmon with sautéed spinach. Meanwhile there's plenty of macaroni and cheese or quesadillas for the young ones. *344 Huron Ave. www.fullmoonrestaurant.com 617/354–6699 4:A1.*

$$ AMERICAN **Green Street.** The tables are small and the service is casual, but the relatively inexpensive New England menu speaks to the young, artistic community that now claims the neighborhood. Wellfleet clam stew with white beans and chorizo is a highlight from the menu, which mostly features modern comfort fare. An emphasis on microbrews and cocktails (the latest owner is a whiz of a bartender) gives this restaurant a relaxed and neighborly bar-scene air. *Average main: $19 280 Green St. 617/876–1655 www.greenstreetgrill.com No lunch Central 4:E5.*

$$$ AMERICAN **Harvest.** Down a cobbled brick passageway in the heart of Harvard Square you'll find this sophisticated shrine to New England cuisine. Chef Mary Dumont's modern interpretation of locally sourced ingredients might yield a meal of braised rabbit over pillowy gnocchi, Scituate lobster in lemongrass broth, and a decadent chocolate cremeux made from Mexican-style Taza Chocolate produced in Somerville (yes, you can tour the factory). The open kitchen makes some noise, but customers at the ever-popular bar don't seem to mind. Outdoor heaters and fireplaces beat back the elements and keep the lush outdoor patio warm and inviting for a surprisingly long stretch of the year. Brunch is served on Sunday. *Average main: $34 44 Brattle St., on walkway 617/868–2255 harvestcambridge.com Harvard 4:A2.*

$$ AFGHAN **The Helmand.** The area's first Afghan restaurant, named after the country's most important river, welcomes you into its cozy Kendall Square confines with Afghan rugs, a wood-burning oven, and exotic, yet extremely approachable food. Standouts, beyond the chewy warm bread, include terrific *aushak* (ravioli stuffed with leeks), *chapendaz* (marinated grilled beef tenderloin served with cumin-spiced hot pepper–tomato purée), and a vegetarian baked pumpkin platter. *Average main: $19 143 1st St. 617/492–4646 helmandrestaurant.com Reservations essential No lunch Lechmere 1:B4.*

$$ AMERICAN **Henrietta's Table.** This cheerful, country-style restaurant in the Charles Hotel was named after the owner's pet pig, Henrietta, whose picture (including one with President and Hillary Clinton) hangs by the entrance area, where a U-shaped bar offers a relaxing spot to enjoy a pre-prandial coffee or cocktail. Chef-owner Peter Davis's passion for working with small area farms, as well as harvesting veggies and honey from the restaurant's rooftop garden and hives, is evident in his fresh, honest, wholesome New England-style dishes, like red flannel hash; creamy Maine crab-corn chowder, and juicy pot roast with mashed potatoes. He even offers that old Yankee standby for dessert: Boston cream pie. *Average*

main: $21 ✉ *One Bennett Street, Harvard Sq.* ☎ *617/661-5005* 🌐 *www.henriettastable.com* ⊕ *1:A3.*

$$$ SOUTHERN Fodor's Choice ★ ✕ **Hungry Mother.** You'll forget you're well above the Mason-Dixon line when you enter this Kendall Square gem, where Virginia-born chef Barry Maiden whips up Southern-inspired comfort food with a hint of French sophistication—and New England ingredients. From fried green tomatoes to cornbread with sorghum butter, from Berkshire pork loin to apple bread pudding, this cozy two-story bistro serves up decidedly soul-warming fare, as well as excellent house-mixed drinks, such as the "No. 43," a concoction of rye, tawny Port, maple syrup, and bitters. $ *Average main: $26* ✉ *233 Cardinal Medeiros Ave., Kendall Square* ☎ *617/499–0090* ⏲ *Closed Mon. No lunch Sat.–Thu.* M *Kendall/MIT* ⊕ *4:H4.*

WORD OF MOUTH

"In the last four to five years, Legal Seafoods has stepped it up. With increased competition, they revamped the menu, added more options, and got back to the original quality that made them "famous." I am a clam chowder fanatic and think theirs is still among the best in Boston. My only complaint now is that they can be a bit overpriced, but it is still worth it."

—Shandy1977

$$$ SEAFOOD FAMILY ✕ **Legal Sea Foods.** All the regional seafood classics, including famed New England chowder, stunningly good crab cakes, and wood-grilled seafood can be found here at the Cambridge outpost of the Legal chain. Just as worthwhile are more modern takes: Italian seafood stew, for example, and blackened rare tuna with sesame-chili vinaigrette. $ *Average main: $25* ✉ *5 Cambridge Center, Kendall Square* ☎ *617/864–3400* 🌐 *www.legalseafoods.com* M *Kendall/MIT* ⊕ *4:H5.*

$ VIETNAMESE ✕ **Le's.** Vietnamese noodle soup called *pho* is the name of the game in this casual eatery (it's set inside the Garage, a small mall in Harvard Square). At less than $10, it's a meal unto itself. Get it filled with chicken, shrimp, or beef, steaming hot in a big bowl. Fresh salads and stir-fries are offered as well. It's all healthy fare, without gloppy sauces, and many of the dishes are steamed. Those approaching from JFK Street can access the restaurant through the main Garage entrance; just head all the way through toward the Dunster Street side at the back. $ *Average main: $8* ✉ *35 Dunster St.* ☎ *617/864–4100* 🌐 *www.lescambridge.com* M *Harvard* ⊕ *4:B2.*

$$$ MEDITERRANEAN Fodor's Choice ★ ✕ **Oleana.** With three restaurants (including Sofra in Cambridge and Sarma in Somerville), and a cookbook to her name, chef-owner Ana Sortun is one of the city's culinary treasures. So is Oleana, which specializes in zesty Eastern Mediterranean *meze* (small plates) plumped up with fresh-picked produce from her husband's nearby Siena Farms. Although the menu changes often, look for the hot, crispy fried mussels starter and the smoky eggplant purée beside tamarind-glazed beef. Lamb gets jacked up with Turkish spices, while duck gets accented with saffron and hazelnuts. In warm weather the back patio garden is a hidden utopia. $ *Average main: $26* ✉ *134 Hampshire St.* ☎ *617/661–*

0505 🌐 www.oleanarestaurant.com ✍ Reservations essential ⏲ No lunch Ⓜ Central ✥ 4:F3.

$ LATIN AMERICAN Fodor's Choice ★

✕ **Orinoco.** It's easy to miss this Latin American restaurant located down an alleyway in Harvard Square. Don't. Owner Andres Banger's dream to bring plates of super-fresh fare from his home country of Venezuala to Cambridge (as well as Brookline and the South End), will reward you with delectable, palm-sized *arepas*, or crispy, hot corn flour pockets stuffed with beans, cheese, and pork; *pabellon criollo*, moist shredded beef with stewed beans, rice, and plantains; and red chili adobo-marinated, charred *pollo* (chicken). Empanadas, hearty salads, and stuffed sandwiches at lunch, along with a selection of wine and beer, round out the affordable menu. When weather permits, ask for a seat on the hidden back patio, a quiet flower- and fountain-filled oasis that makes the rest of the world feel far away. *$ Average main: $17 ✉ 56 JFK St., Harvard Sq. ☎ 617/354–6900 🌐 www.orinocokitchen.com ✍ Reservations not accepted ⏲ Closed Mon. Ⓜ Harvard ✥ 4:A3*

$$ MEDITERRANEAN

✕ **Rendezvous.** In 2005 chef Steve Johnson commandeered a defunct Burger King in Central Square and turned it into a Mediterranean spot committed to locally grown ingredients. (He even has a rooftop garden.) While the dinner menus change frequently, look for locavore options, like apple salad with cheddar and spiced pecans and braised veal-pork meatballs with orecchiette pasta. Exposed brick and a glass ceiling add a touch of casual refinement to the cheery interior, which also includes a bar. (Try the Nehru: saffron gin, lemon, and cardamom.) Sundays, the chef assembles a well-priced $38 three-course prix fixe menu. *$ Average main: $24 ✉ 502 Massachusetts Ave., Central Square ☎ 617/576–1900 🌐 www.rendezvouscentralsquare.com ⏲ No lunch Ⓜ Central Sq. ✥ 4:E5.*

$$$$ ITALIAN Fodor's Choice ★

✕ **Rialto.** The soothing sage and yolk-yellow dining room and its bar have drifted back to their Italian beginnings under the deft helm of chef-owner Jody Adams, one of Boston's most admired kitchen wizards (see Trade), who uses the freshest New England ingredients to prepare her delicate, yet deeply flavored food. While a few signature favorites remain, such as the fisherman's soup and slow-roasted duck (so beloved it inspired one smitten diner to write Adams a poem), her composed salads, pillowy pastas, and entrées, along with a regional Italian menu (that changes every two months) never disappoint. A comprehensive list of Allergy Menus is available for those wishing to avoid alcohol, dairy, gluten, nuts, and animal products. *$ Average main: $37 ✉ Charles Hotel, 1 Bennett St., Harvard Sq. ☎ 617/661–5050 🌐 www.rialto-restaurant.com ⏲ No lunch Ⓜ Harvard ✥ 4:A2.*

$ INDIAN

✕ **Tanjore.** The menu at this regional restaurant reaches from Sindh to Bengal, with some strength in the western provincial foods (Gujarat, Bombay) and their interesting sweet-hot flavors. *Baigan bhurta* is a platter of grilled, mashed eggplant; the rice dishes, chais, and breads are all excellent; and the lunchtime buffet is usually a quick in-and-out affair. The spicing starts mild, so don't be afraid to order "medium." *$ Average main: $15 ✉ 18 Eliot St. ☎ 617/868–1900 🌐 www.tanjoreharvardsq.com Ⓜ Harvard ✥ 4:A3.*

$ AMERICAN ✕ **Tory Row.** A clean, minimalist vibe defines this casual eatery on Harvard Square. Three long black tables surrounded by brushed aluminum bar stools are set at the center of the dining room, encouraging side-by-side seating with strangers; about 10 tables run alongside two walls for the less gregarious. Breakfast and brunch items include steak-and-egg tacos, French toast, and Greek yogurt with fruit; order a mimosa or sangria for a refreshing kick. For lunch and dinner some tasty sandwiches are served, such as turkey meatloaf topped with smoked bacon and served on artisan bread, while baked rigatoni and grilled salmon whet larger appetites. There's a smallish yet varied wine list and craft beer on tap. Service is low-key yet friendly and attentive. *Average main: $16* *3 Brattle St., Harvard Sq.* *617/876–8769* *www.toryrow.us* *Reservations not accepted* *Harvard* *4:A2.*

$$$ EUROPEAN ✕ **UpStairs on the Square.** In the middle of Harvard Square, this multilevel restaurant strikes just the right balance between funky and urbane. The elegant, gold and pink Soirée Dining Room tempts with five- or seven-course tasting menus (which can be vegetarian or vegan upon request), as well as à la carte options like creamy lobster stew and roast duck with blood orange. The festive Monday Club Bar offers a more casual, yet still chic, spot to lunch, brunch, and sup on gourmet pizzas, hanger steak, and impossible-to-resist milk chocolate pecan turtles served slightly cool so they don't melt (they rarely last that long). *Average main: $31* *91 Winthrop St.* *617/864–1933* *www.upstairsonthesquare.com* *Soirée Room: closed Mon. No lunch* *Harvard* *4:A2.*

$$$ MODERN AMERICAN Fodor's Choice ★ ✕ **West Bridge.** Prosecco on tap and serious cocktails may draw area techies, MIT folks, and neighborhood hipsters into this happening, white, window-filled room with exposed ceiling pipes in Kendall Square, but it's the small and large plates of lusty, flavor-rich food that keeps them lingering. The gooey duck egg in a jar served over potato purée with crisp duck skin is a must; also try the roasted cauliflower with hazelnuts and tawny-skinned roast chicken for two. Many menu offering can be tweaked for vegetarians and a broad selection of unusual beers and wines by the glass means every bite will have a great sip to match. *Average main: $26* *1 Kendall Sq., Kendall Sq.* *617/945–0221* *www.westbridgerestaurant.com* *No lunch weekends* *Kendall/MIT* *4:H4.*

$ AMERICAN ✕ **West Side Lounge.** *Understated* is the buzzword at this relaxed but suave bistro, where the food is as comfortable as the setting. A homey, rotating menu complements the room's burgundy tones and cushy seating. The crispy truffle fries are a justified hit—they all but fly out of the kitchen—and the black-pepper mussels release an aromatic cloud of steam when they arrive. Couples on first dates and groups of regulars gather nightly for the well-priced specials and signature cocktails that change with the seasons. Brunch is served Sunday. *Average main: $16* *1680 Massachusetts Ave.* *617/441–5566* *www.westsidelounge.com* *No lunch* *Porter or Harvard* *4:B1.*

SOMERVILLE

Just two miles north of Boston, Somerville is known for its eclectic mix of students, blue-collar families, indie musicians, and immigrants, all of whom help inform the hip restaurant scene here which centers around Davis and Union Squares. In addition to Spanish, Haitian, and Brazilian eateries, you'll find burger joints, BBQ, and tacos, along with a new sort of place—second restaurants from Boston star chefs, eager to share their home cooking with a democratic mix of diners.

$$$ MODERN AMERICAN **Bergamot.** Folks from all over flock to this inviting, votive-lit neighborhood bistro near Cambridge's Inman Square to savor co-owner chef Keith Pooler's magical ways with seasonal New England ingredients. Masterpieces include candy-sweet roasted beets with orange and pistachios, crispy duck confit salad with red wine vinaigrette, and perfectly-cooked local hake over a raft of Swiss chard, golden raisins, and pine nuts. In addition to a well-curated wine list, the classic and modern cocktails are terrific, the service warm and friendly, and the desserts well worth indulging in, whether it's satiny cocoa panna cotta with hazelnut streusel or buttery pear-toffee cake. The nightly three-course prix fixe blackboard menu offers excellent value ($39). *Average main: $27 118 Beacon St., Somerville 617/576–7700 www.bergamotrestaurant.com No lunch 4:D1.*

$$ GERMAN **Bronwyn.** Harkening back to his German heritage, chef-owner Tim Wiechmann and his wife, Bronwyn, the restaurant's namesake, have brought a rib-sticking, yet sophisticated taste of Central and Eastern Europe to Union Square. The menu here includes juicy hand-stuffed pork sausages served with powerfully seasoned sauces, hearty dumplings, noodle dishes (try the chewy pork blood noodles with tender nuggets of pork), and sauerbraten made, not with your average grade of meat, but with Wagyu beef. Small farms supply many ingredients and a designated baker makes the hot pretzels, grainy breads, and desserts (don't miss the Bavarian special of fluffy pan-sautéed pancake batter bits topped with warm fruit sauce). To wash it down, try any of the excellent beers or German, Austrian, or Northern Italian red or white wines. With an outside biergarten and a cozy interior filled with small tables set with medieval manor–like carved wooden chairs, the only thing missing from this Germanic oasis is an Oompah band. *Average main: $22 255 Washington St., Somerville 617/776–9900 www.bronwynrestaurant.com Closed Mon. No lunch 4:G1.*

$$$ AMERICAN **Kirkland Tap & Trotter.** Owner-chef Tony Maws has made a national splash with his fine dining restaurant Craigie on Main, where bistro-style dishes arrive carefully composed with swirls of high-flavor garnishes. Here, he's taking the same high-quality ingredients, but turning them into the sort of rustic, belly-warming dishes he makes for his family at home—succulent beer-braised veal ribs, local swordfish with smoked tomatoes and beans, and creative burgers charred on the kitchen's firewood grill. Communal tables, wood floors, and brick walls contribute to the laid-back vibe, along with a 12-seat bar serving simple, but good cocktails, draft beers, and old-world wines. It's billed as a "neighborhood joint," but given the families, students, and city folk filling the tables, clearly, word has gotten out. *Average*

main: $25 ✉ 425 Washington St., Somerville ☎ 857/259–6585 🌐 www.kirklandtapandtrotter.com ⏲ No lunch ✣ 4:D1.

$$ ITALIAN Fodor's Choice ★ ✕ **Posto.** Don't be fooled into thinking this Davis Square spot is simply an upscale pizzeria. A central wood-burning oven here churns out over a dozen varieties of excellent tomato or "white" bubble-crusted pies (try the "white" gorgonzola, bacon, fig, and caramelized onion pizza), while the kitchen crafts scrumptious starters and mains, like local string bean and pistachio pesto salad, silken tagliatelle cradling tender hunks of braised rabbit in a delicate wine sauce, and succulent swordfish with soft, sweet peppers. The central brick and glass-walled dining room (with sidewalk seating during fair weather) fills nightly. A smaller back room is perfect for young couples and the silver-hair set seeking a bit more privacy or peace and quiet. No matter where you sit, you're in for a terrific meal. [$] *Average main: $22 ✉ 187 Elm St., Somerville ☎ 617/625–0600 🌐 www.postoboston.com ⏲ No lunch ✣ 4:B1.*

BOSTON DINING AND LODGING ATLAS

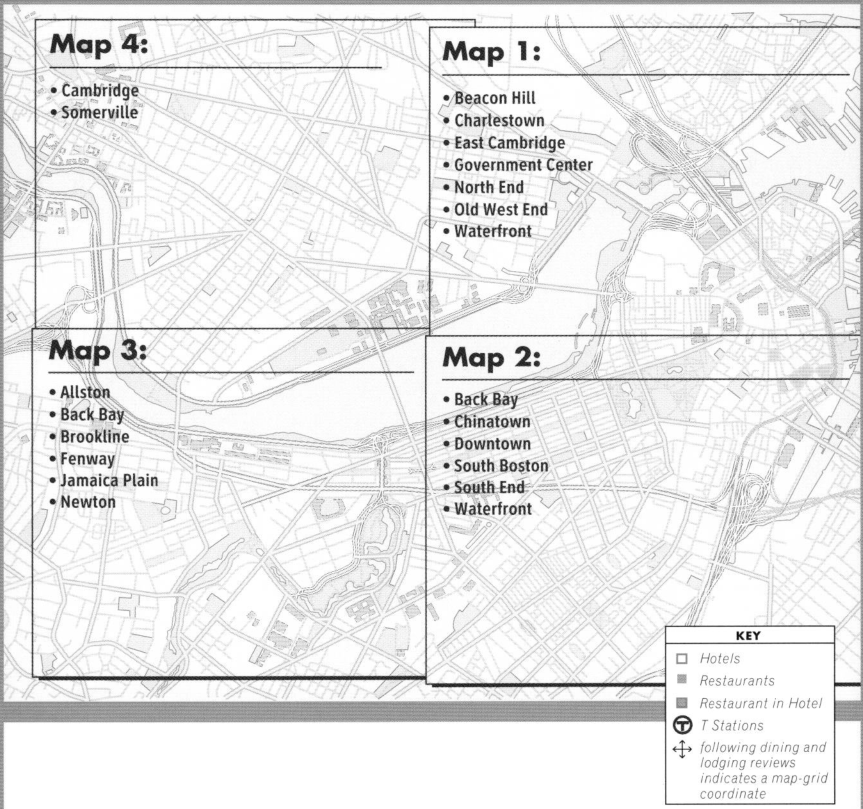
Map 4:
• Cambridge
• Somerville
Map 1:
• Beacon Hill
• Charlestown
• East Cambridge
• Government Center
• North End
• Old West End
• Waterfront
Map 3:
• Allston
• Back Bay
• Brookline
• Fenway
• Jamaica Plain
• Newton
Map 2:
• Back Bay
• Chinatown
• Downtown
• South Boston
• South End
• Waterfront
KEY
Hotels
Restaurants
Restaurant in Hotel
T Stations
following dining and lodging reviews indicates a map-grid coordinate

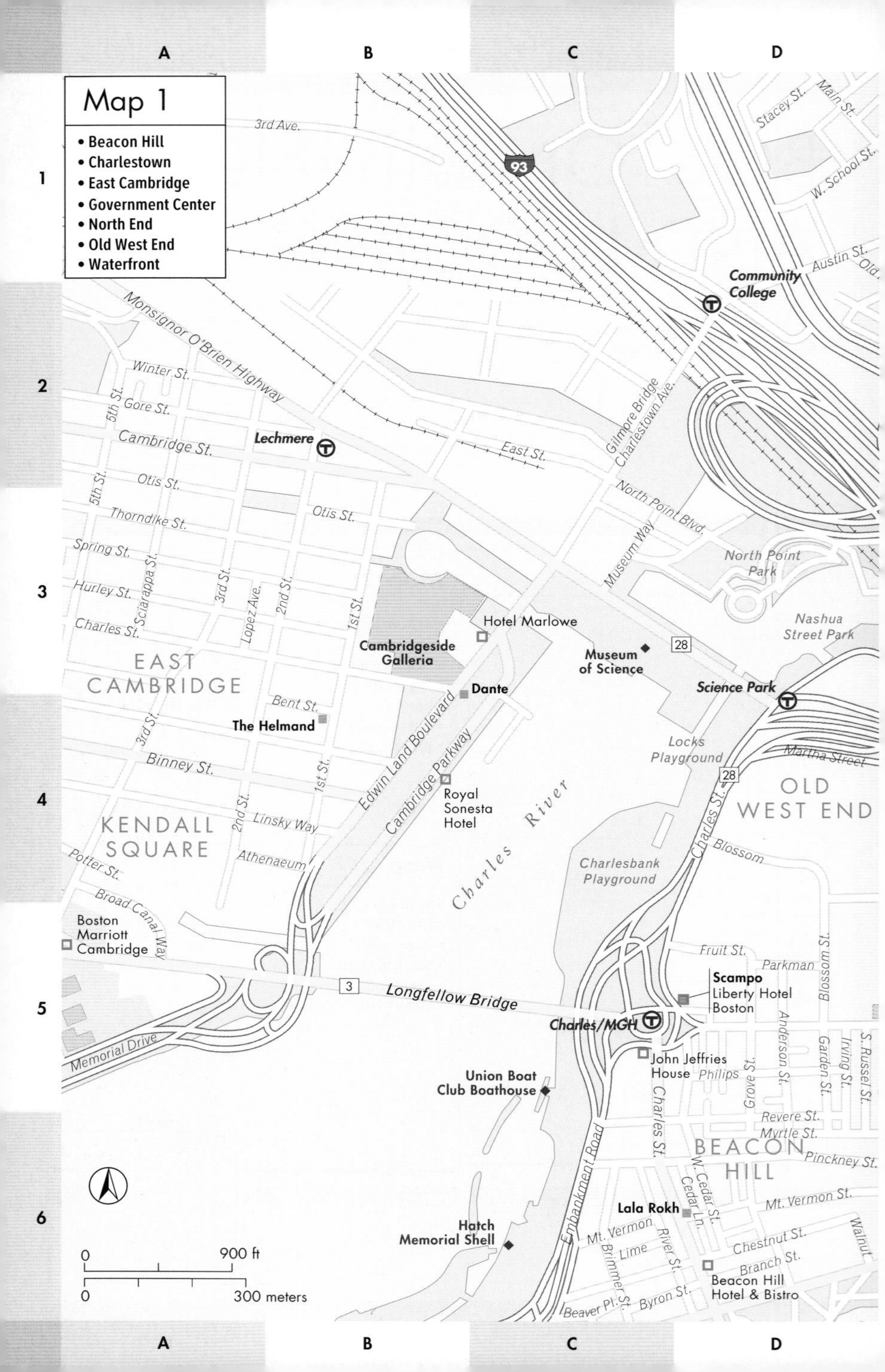
A
B
C
D
1
2
3
4
5
6
Map 1
• Beacon Hill
• Charlestown
• East Cambridge
• Government Center
• North End
• Old West End
• Waterfront
3rd Ave.
93
Stacey St.
Main St.
W. School St.
Austin St.
Old
Community College
Monsignor O'Brien Highway
Winter St.
5th St.
Gore St.
Cambridge St.
Lechmere
East St.
Gilmore Bridge
Charlestown Ave.
Otis St.
Thorndike St.
North Point Blvd.
Spring St.
Museum Way
North Point Park
Hurley St.
Sciarappa St.
3rd St.
Lopez Ave.
2nd St.
1st St.
Charles St.
Hotel Marlowe
Nashua Street Park
Cambridgeside Galleria
28
Museum of Science
EAST CAMBRIDGE
Dante
Science Park
Bent St.
The Helmand
Locks Playground
Martha Street
Binney St.
Edwin Land Boulevard
Cambridge Parkway
OLD WEST END
Royal Sonesta Hotel
Charles River
Linsky Way
KENDALL SQUARE
Athenaeum
Blossom
Potter St.
Charlesbank Playground
Broad Canal Way
Boston Marriott Cambridge
Fruit St.
Parkman
Blossom St.
Scampo
Liberty Hotel Boston
3
Longfellow Bridge
Charles/MGH
Anderson St.
Memorial Drive
John Jeffries House
Philips
Grove St.
Garden St.
Irving St.
S. Russel St.
Union Boat Club Boathouse
Revere St.
Myrtle St.
Embankment Road
BEACON HILL
Pinckney St.
W. Cedar St.
Cedar Ln.
Mt. Vernon St.
Lala Rokh
Hatch Memorial Shell
Mt. Vernon
Lime
Brimmer St.
River St.
Chestnut St.
Walnut
Branch St.
0
900 ft
0
300 meters
Beacon Hill Hotel & Bistro
Beaver Pl.
Byron St.

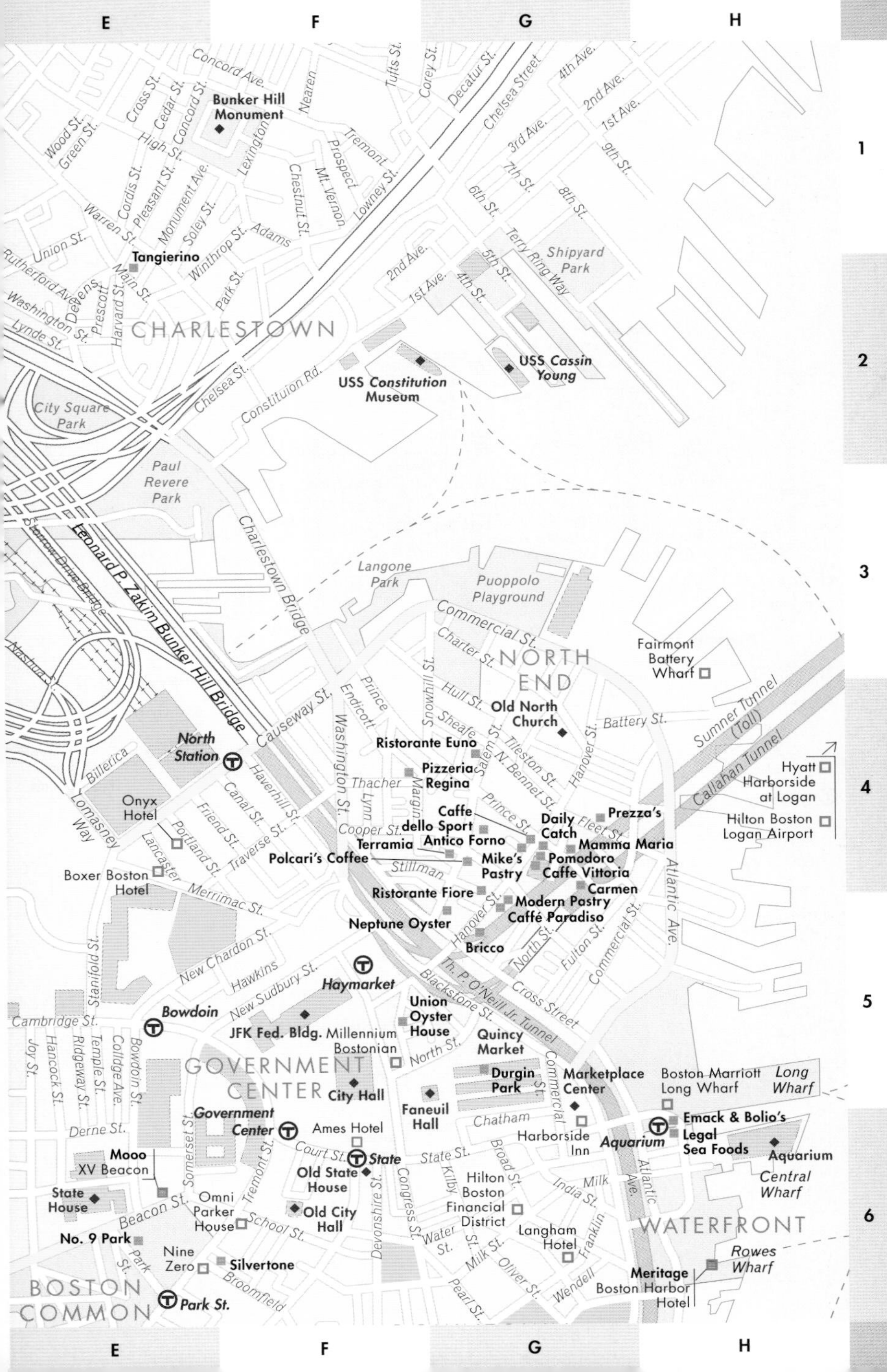
E
F
G
H
1
2
3
4
5
6
CHARLESTOWN
Bunker Hill Monument
Tangierino
USS Constitution Museum
USS Cassin Young
City Square Park
Paul Revere Park
Shipyard Park
Langone Park
Puoppolo Playground
Charlestown Bridge
Leonard P. Zakim Bunker Hill Bridge
Storrow Drive Bridge
NORTH END
Fairmont Battery Wharf
Old North Church
North Station
Onyx Hotel
Boxer Boston Hotel
Ristorante Euno
Pizzeria Regina
Caffe dello Sport
Antico Forno
Terramia
Polcari's Coffee
Mike's Pastry
Daily Catch
Prezza's
Mamma Maria
Pomodoro
Caffe Vittoria
Carmen
Ristorante Fiore
Modern Pastry
Caffé Paradiso
Neptune Oyster
Bricco
Sumner Tunnel (Toll)
Callahan Tunnel
Hyatt Harborside at Logan
Hilton Boston Logan Airport
Haymarket
Bowdoin
JFK Fed. Bldg.
Millennium Bostonian
Union Oyster House
Quincy Market
Durgin Park
Faneuil Hall
Marketplace Center
Boston Marriott Long Wharf
Long Wharf
GOVERNMENT CENTER
City Hall
Government Center
Ames Hotel
State
Old State House
Harborside Inn
Aquarium
Emack & Bolio's
Legal Sea Foods
Central Wharf
Mooo
XV Beacon
State House
Omni Parker House
Old City Hall
Hilton Boston Financial District
Langham Hotel
WATERFRONT
Rowes Wharf
No. 9 Park
Nine Zero
Silvertone
Meritage
Boston Harbor Hotel
BOSTON COMMON
Park St.
Th. P. O'Neill Jr. Tunnel
Cambridge St.
Commercial St.
Atlantic Ave.
Hanover St.
Salem St.
Causeway St.
Chelsea St.
Constitution Rd.
State St.
Court St.
Beacon St.
School St.
Tremont St.
Congress St.
Washington St.

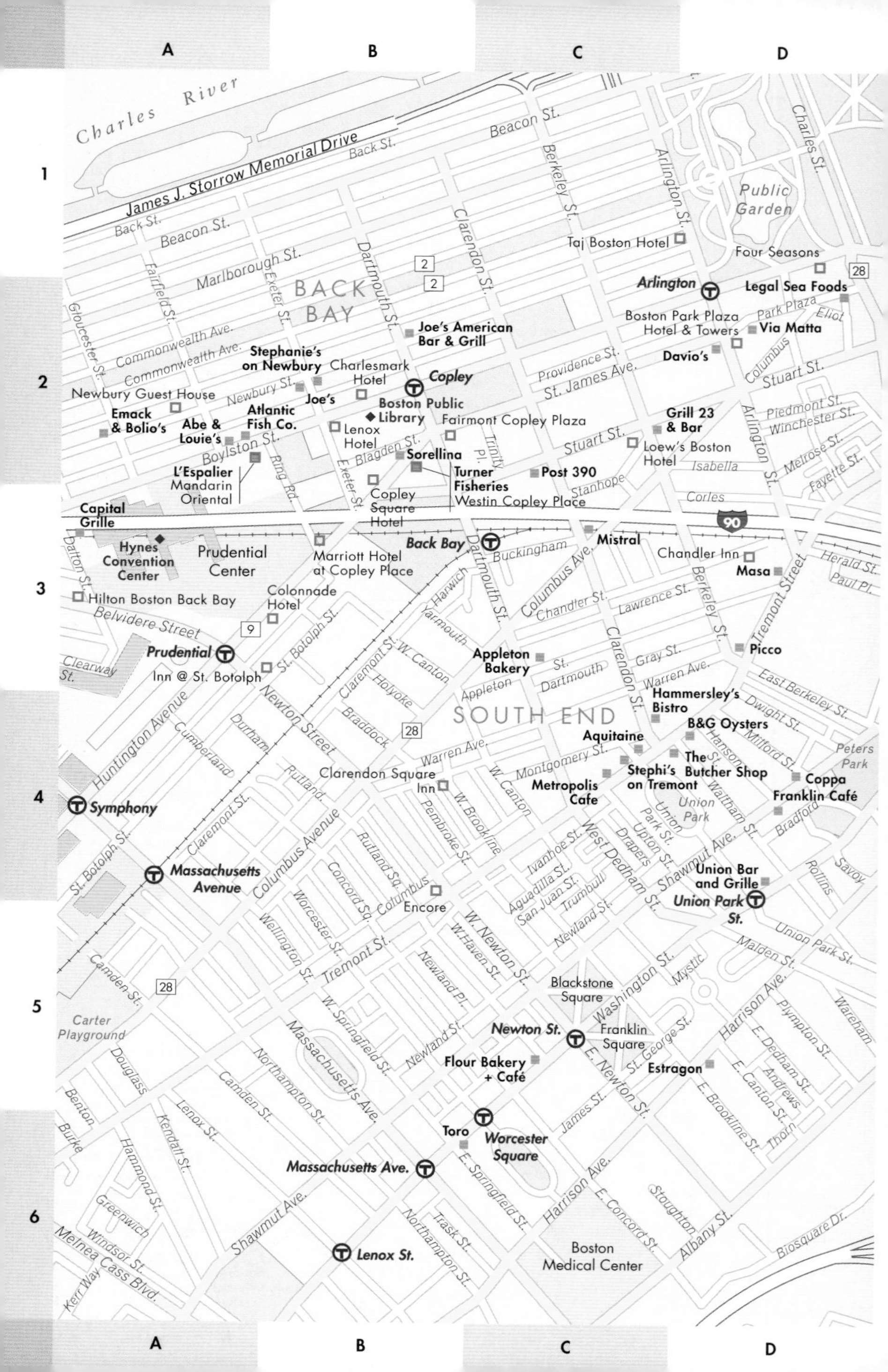
A
B
C
D
1
2
3
4
5
6
Charles River
James J. Storrow Memorial Drive
Back St.
Beacon St.
Marlborough St.
Commonwealth Ave.
Newbury St.
Boylston St.
Gloucester St.
Fairfield St.
Exeter St.
Dartmouth St.
Clarendon St.
Berkeley St.
Arlington St.
Charles St.
Public Garden
BACK BAY
Taj Boston Hotel
Four Seasons
Arlington
Legal Sea Foods
Boston Park Plaza Hotel & Towers
Park Plaza
Eliot
Via Matta
Davio's
Columbus
Stuart St.
Joe's American Bar & Grill
Stephanie's on Newbury
Charlesmark Hotel
Copley
Newbury Guest House
Joe's
Boston Public Library
Emack & Bolio's
Abe & Louie's
Atlantic Fish Co.
Lenox Hotel
Fairmont Copley Plaza
Providence St.
St. James Ave.
Grill 23 & Bar
Piedmont St.
Winchester St.
Loew's Boston Hotel
Isabella
Melrose St.
Fayette St.
Blagden St.
Sorellina
Trinity Pl.
Ring Rd.
L'Espalier
Mandarin Oriental
Turner Fisheries
Westin Copley Place
Post 390
Stanhope
Copley Square Hotel
Corles
Capital Grille
90
28
2
9
Hynes Convention Center
Prudential Center
Marriott Hotel at Copley Place
Back Bay
Buckingham
Mistral
Chandler Inn
Herald St.
Paul Pl.
Masa
Dalton St.
Hilton Boston Back Bay
Colonnade Hotel
Columbus Ave.
Chandler St.
Lawrence St.
Tremont Street
Belvidere Street
Harwich
Yarmouth
Prudential
St. Botolph St.
Appleton Bakery
Picco
Clearway St.
Inn @ St. Botolph
Claremont St.
W. Canton
Holyoke
Appleton
Dartmouth St.
Gray St.
Warren Ave.
East Berkeley St.
Hammersley's Bistro
Dwight St.
Newton Street
Braddock
SOUTH END
Huntington Avenue
Cumberland
Durham
B&G Oysters
Aquitaine
Hanson St.
Milford St.
Peters Park
Warren Ave.
Montgomery St.
The Butcher Shop
Rutland
Clarendon Square Inn
W. Canton
Stephi's on Tremont
Coppa
Metropolis Cafe
Franklin Café
Symphony
W. Brookline
Pembroke St.
Union Park
Union Park St.
Waltham St.
Bradford
Claremont St.
Columbus Avenue
Rutland Sq.
Ivanhoe St.
West Dedham St.
Drapers
Upton St.
Shawmut Ave.
Union Bar and Grille
Rollins
Savoy
Massachusetts Avenue
Concord Sq.
Aguadilla St.
San Juan St.
Trumbull
St. Botolph St.
Worcester St.
Columbus
Encore
W. Newton St.
W. Haven St.
Newland St.
Union Park St.
Wellington St.
Tremont St.
Newland Pl.
Malden St.
Camden St.
Washington St.
Mystic
Blackstone Square
Harrison Ave.
Plympton St.
Wareham
Carter Playground
Massachusetts Ave.
W. Springfield St.
Newland St.
Newton St.
Franklin Square
St. George St.
E. Dedham St.
Douglass
Northampton St.
Flour Bakery + Café
Estragon
Andrews
E. Newton St.
E. Canton St.
Benton
Camden St.
Lenox St.
James St.
E. Brookline St.
Thorn
Burke
Kendall St.
Toro
Worcester Square
Hammond St.
Massachusetts Ave.
E. Springfield St.
Greenwich
Harrison Ave.
E. Concord St.
Stoughton
Shawmut Ave.
Trask St.
Albany St.
Biosquare Dr.
Windsor St.
Northampton St.
Melnea Cass Blvd.
Kerr Way
Lenox St.
Boston Medical Center

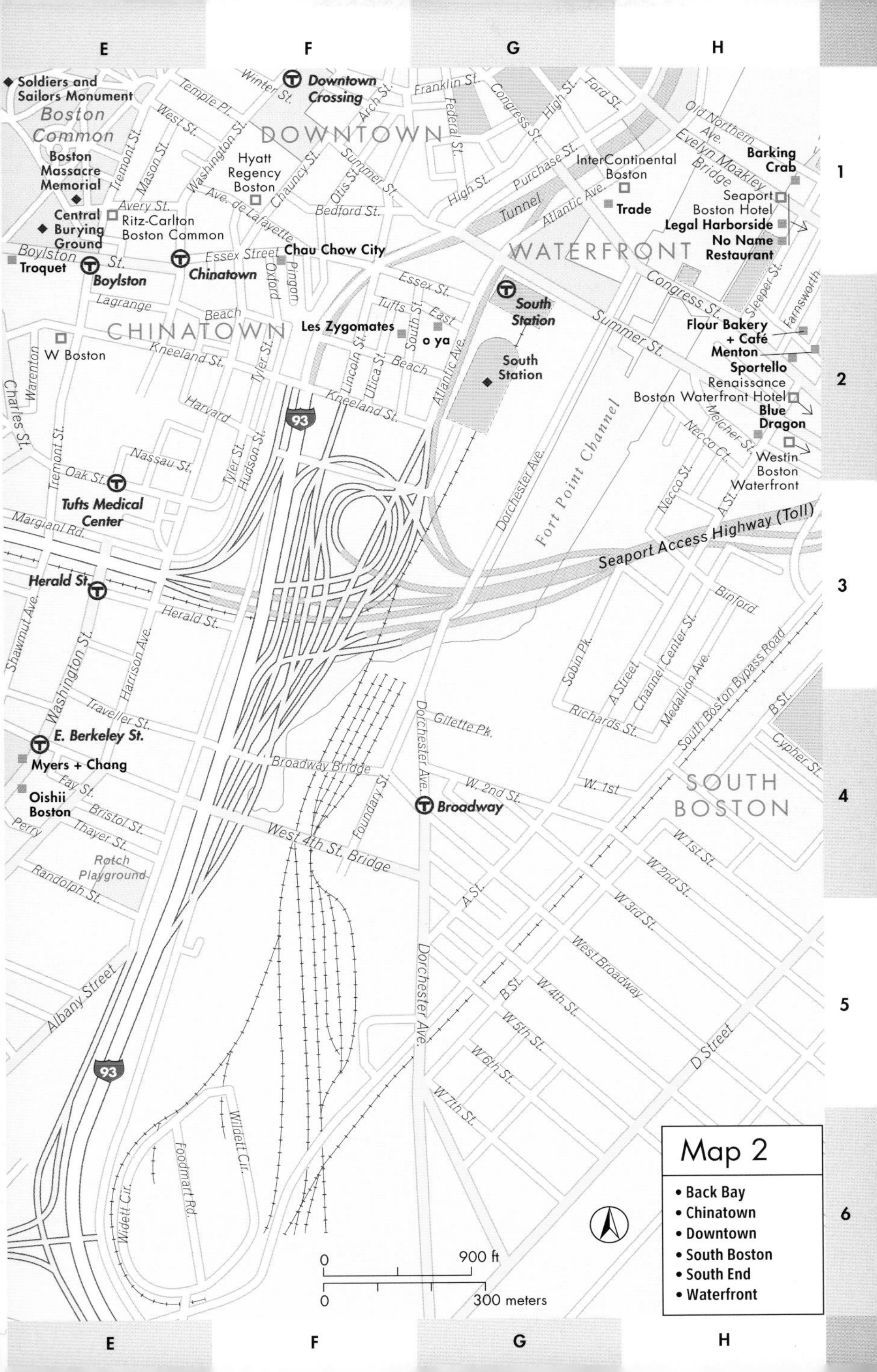
Map 2
• Back Bay
• Chinatown
• Downtown
• South Boston
• South End
• Waterfront
E
F
G
H
1
2
3
4
5
6
DOWNTOWN
CHINATOWN
WATERFRONT
SOUTH BOSTON
Boston Common
Soldiers and Sailors Monument
Boston Massacre Memorial
Central Burying Ground
Troquet
Boylston
Chinatown
Downtown Crossing
Hyatt Regency Boston
Ritz-Carlton Boston Common
Chau Chow City
Les Zygomates
o ya
W Boston
South Station
InterContinental Boston
Trade
Barking Crab
Seaport Boston Hotel
Legal Harborside
No Name Restaurant
Flour Bakery + Café
Menton
Sportello
Renaissance Boston Waterfront Hotel
Blue Dragon
Westin Boston Waterfront
Tufts Medical Center
Herald St.
E. Berkeley St.
Myers + Chang
Oishii Boston
Broadway
Rotch Playground
Fort Point Channel
Seaport Access Highway (Toll)
Tunnel
Temple Pl.
Winter St.
West St.
Tremont St.
Mason St.
Washington St.
Avery St.
Ave. de Lafayette
Chauncy St.
Arch St.
Summer St.
Otis St.
Bedford St.
Franklin St.
Federal St.
Congress St.
High St.
Ford St.
Purchase St.
Atlantic Ave.
Old Northern Ave.
Evelyn Moakley Bridge
Boylston St.
Essex Street
Oxford
Pingon
Lagrange
Beach
Essex St.
Tufts
East
South St.
Kneeland St.
Tyler St.
Lincoln St.
Utica St.
Beach
Harvard
Hudson St.
Nassau St.
Oak St.
Warenton
Charles St.
Marginal Rd.
Herald St.
Shawmut Ave.
Harrison Ave.
Traveller St.
Fay St.
Bristol St.
Thayer St.
Perry
Randolph St.
Albany Street
Broadway Bridge
West 4th St. Bridge
Foundary St.
Dorchester Ave.
Gilette Pk.
W. 2nd St.
W. 1st
Sleeper St.
Farnsworth
Melcher St.
Necco Ct.
Necco St.
A St.
Binford
Sobin Pk.
A Street
Channel Center St.
Medallion Ave.
Richards St.
South Boston Bypass Road
B St.
Cypher St.
W 1st St.
W 2nd St.
W 3rd St.
West Broadway
A St.
B St.
W 4th St.
W 5th St.
W 6th St.
W 7th St.
D Street
Widett Cir.
Foodmart Rd.
93
0
900 ft
300 meters

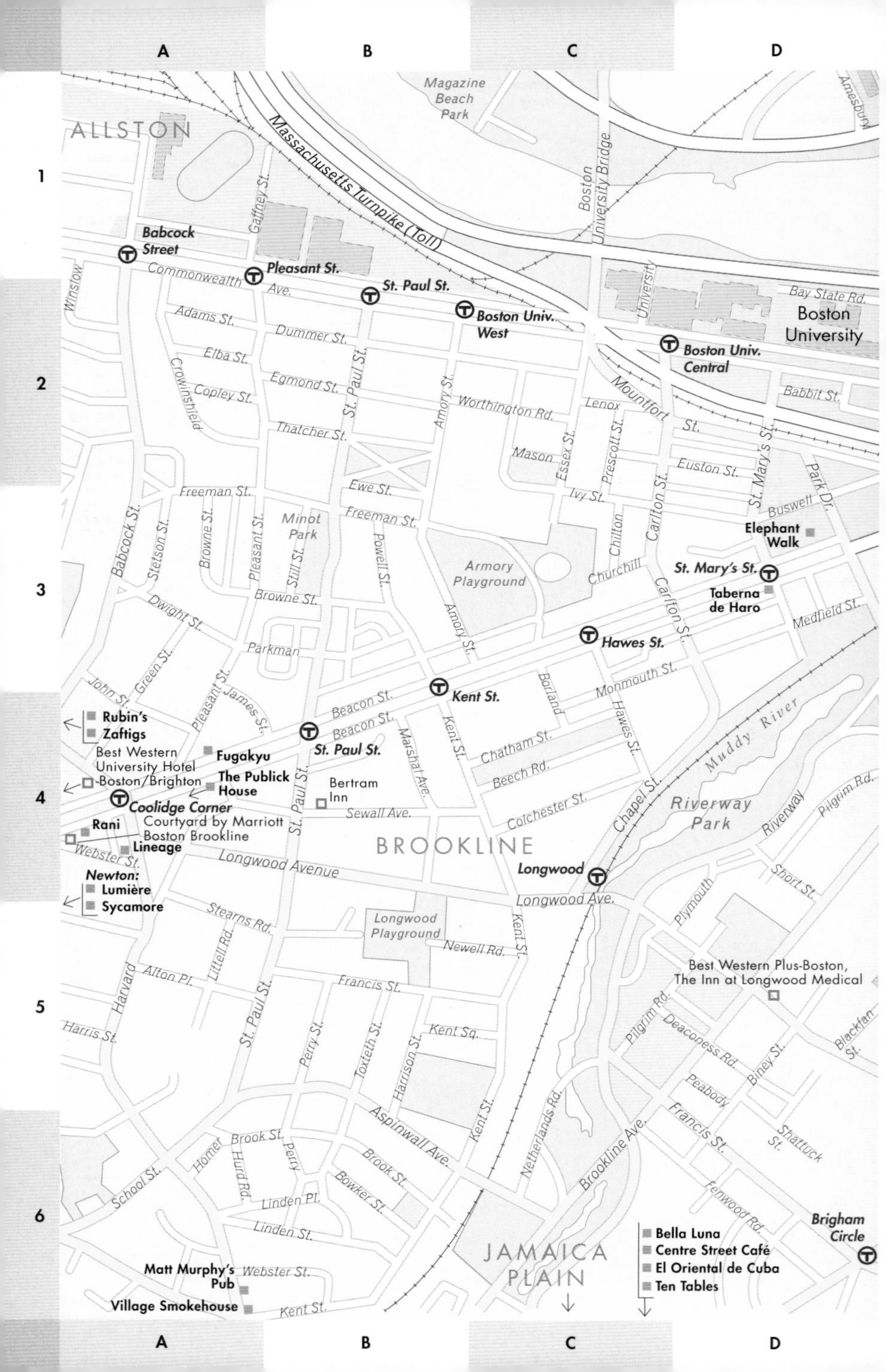

A
B
C
D
1
2
3
4
5
6
ALLSTON
BROOKLINE
JAMAICA PLAIN
Magazine Beach Park
Massachusetts Turnpike (Toll)
Boston University Bridge
Amesbury
Babcock Street
Pleasant St.
St. Paul St.
Boston Univ. West
Boston Univ. Central
Boston University
Bay State Rd.
University
Commonwealth Ave.
Winslow
Gaffney St.
Adams St.
Dummer St.
Elba St.
Egmond St.
Copley St.
Crowinshield
Thatcher St.
St. Paul St.
Amory St.
Worthington Rd.
Lenox
Mountfort St.
Babbit St.
Mason
Essex St.
Prescott St.
Euston St.
St. Mary's St.
Park Dr.
Buswell
Freeman St.
Ewe St.
Freeman St.
Ivy St.
Chilton
Carlton St.
Elephant Walk
Babcock St.
Stetson St.
Browne St.
Pleasant St.
Still St.
Minot Park
Powell St.
Armory Playground
Churchill
St. Mary's St.
Taberna de Haro
Medfield St.
Browne St.
Dwight St.
Parkman
Amory St.
Carlton St.
Hawes St.
Green St.
John St.
Pleasant St.
James St.
Beacon St.
Beacon St.
Kent St.
Borland
Monmouth St.
Muddy River
Rubin's
Zaftigs
Best Western University Hotel Boston/Brighton
Fugakyu
The Publick House
St. Paul St.
Marshal Ave.
Kent St.
Chatham St.
Hawes St.
Beech Rd.
Chapel St.
Riverway Park
Riverway
Pilgrim Rd.
Coolidge Corner
Bertram Inn
Sewall Ave.
Colchester St.
Rani
Courtyard by Marriott Boston Brookline
Lineage
Webster St.
St. Paul St.
Longwood Avenue
Longwood
Short St.
Newton:
Lumière
Sycamore
Longwood Ave.
Plymouth
Stearns Rd.
Longwood Playground
Newell Rd.
Kent St.
Littell Rd.
Alton Pl.
Harvard
Francis St.
Best Western Plus-Boston, The Inn at Longwood Medical
Harris St.
St. Paul St.
Perry St.
Toxteth St.
Harrison St.
Kent Sq.
Pilgrim Rd.
Deaconess Rd.
Biney St.
Blackfan St.
Aspinwall Ave.
Kent St.
Netherlands Rd.
Peabody
Brookline Ave.
Francis St.
Shattuck St.
Brook St.
Homer
Hurd Rd.
Perry
Brook St.
Bowker St.
School St.
Linden Pl.
Linden St.
Fenwood Rd.
Brigham Circle
Matt Murphy's Pub
Webster St.
Village Smokehouse
Kent St.
Bella Luna
Centre Street Café
El Oriental de Cuba
Ten Tables
A
B
C
D

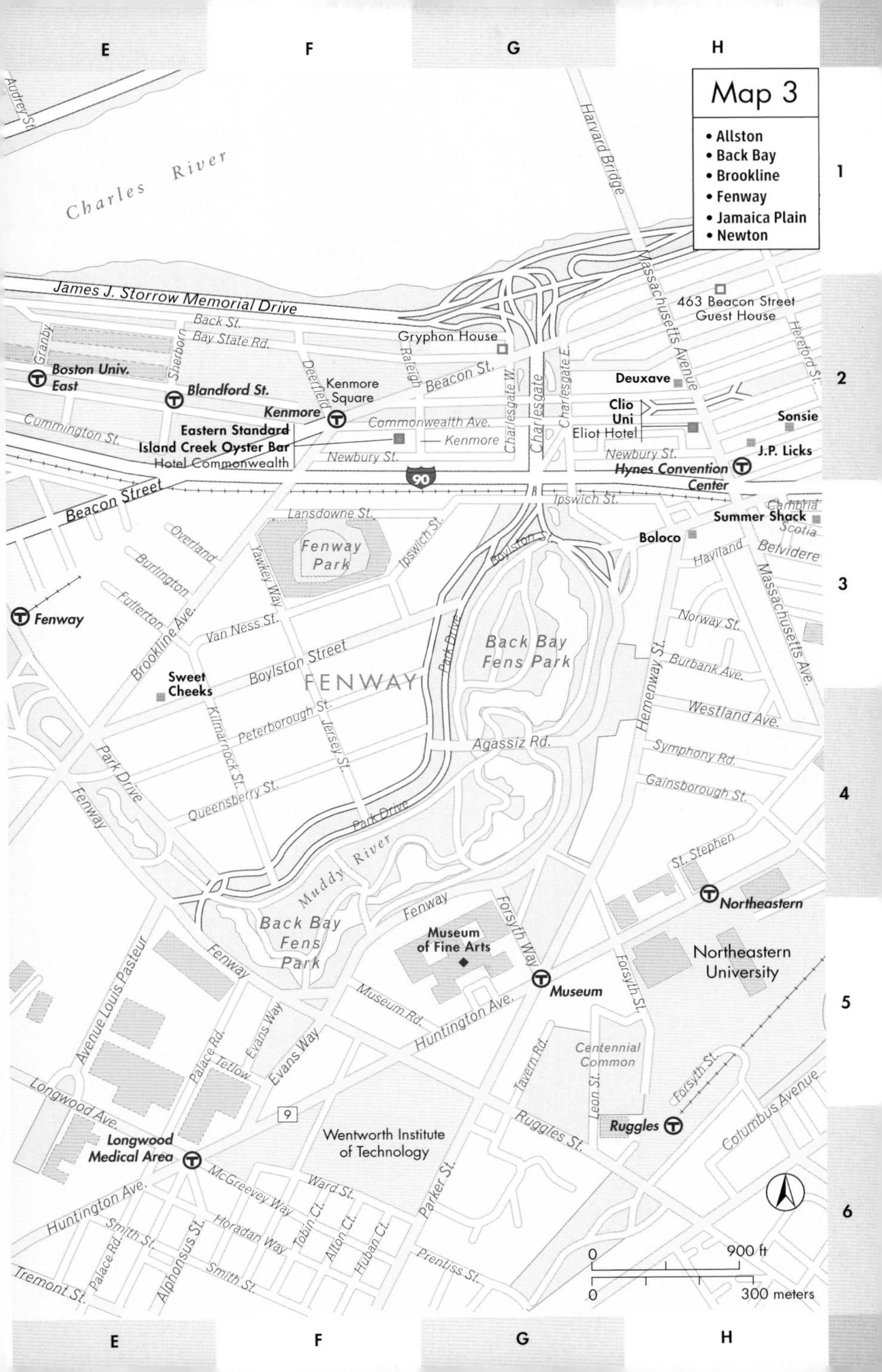

Map 3
• Allston
• Back Bay
• Brookline
• Fenway
• Jamaica Plain
• Newton
E
F
G
H
1
2
3
4
5
6
Charles River
Harvard Bridge
James J. Storrow Memorial Drive
Back St.
Bay State Rd.
Granby
Sherborn
Deerfield
Raleigh
Beacon St.
Gryphon House
463 Beacon Street Guest House
Hereford St.
Massachusetts Avenue
Charlesgate W.
Charlesgate
Charlesgate E.
Boston Univ. East
Blandford St.
Kenmore Square
Kenmore
Deuxave
Clio
Uni
Eliot Hotel
Sonsie
J.P. Licks
Cummington St.
Eastern Standard
Island Creek Oyster Bar
Hotel Commonwealth
Commonwealth Ave.
Kenmore
Newbury St.
Newbury St.
Hynes Convention Center
90
Beacon Street
Lansdowne St.
Ipswich St.
Ipswich St.
Cambria
Summer Shack
Scotia
Boloco
Haviland
Belvidere
Fenway Park
Boylston St.
Overland
Burlington
Fullerton
Yawkey Way
Fenway
Brookline Ave.
Van Ness St.
Norway St.
Massachusetts Ave.
Back Bay Fens Park
Park Drive
Hemenway St.
Burbank Ave.
Sweet Cheeks
Boylston Street
FENWAY
Westland Ave.
Peterborough St.
Kilmarnock St.
Jersey St.
Agassiz Rd.
Symphony Rd.
Gainsborough St.
Park Drive
Fenway
Queensberry St.
Park Drive
Muddy River
St. Stephen
Northeastern
Back Bay Fens Park
Fenway
Museum of Fine Arts
Forsyth Way
Northeastern University
Fenway
Museum
Forsyth St.
Avenue Louis Pasteur
Museum Rd.
Huntington Ave.
Evans Way
Evans Way
Palace Rd.
Tetlow
Centennial Common
Tavern Rd.
Leon St.
Forsyth St.
Longwood Ave.
9
Ruggles St.
Ruggles
Columbus Avenue
Longwood Medical Area
Wentworth Institute of Technology
McGreevey Way
Ward St.
Parker St.
Huntington Ave.
Smith St.
Horadan Way
Tobin Ct.
Alton Ct.
Huban Ct.
Palace Rd.
Alphonsus St.
Smith St.
Prentiss St.
Tremont St.
0
900 ft
0
300 meters

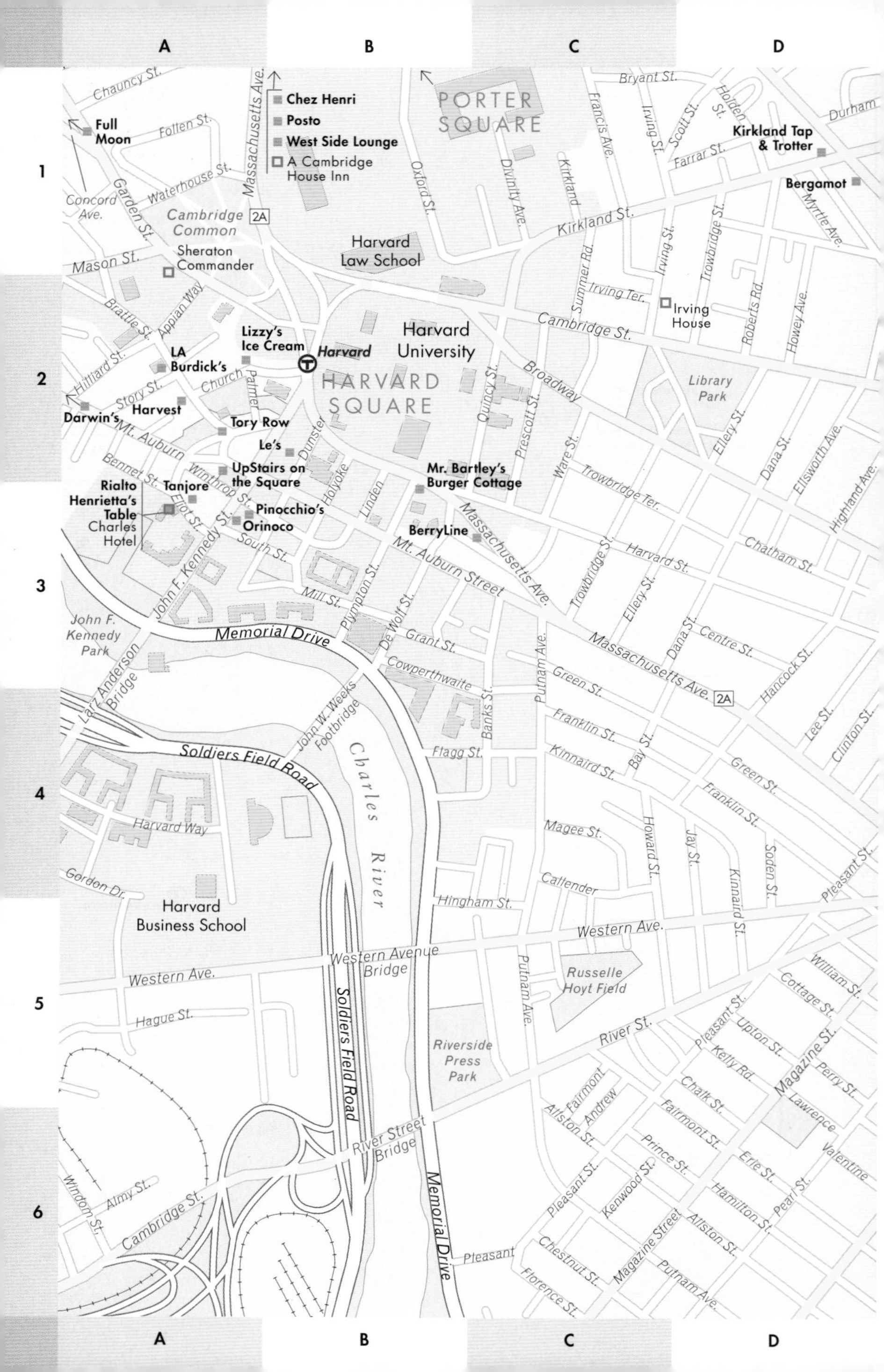
A
B
C
D
1
2
3
4
5
6
Full Moon
Chez Henri
Posto
West Side Lounge
A Cambridge House Inn
PORTER SQUARE
Kirkland Tap & Trotter
Bergamot
Cambridge Common
2A
Sheraton Commander
Harvard Law School
Irving House
Lizzy's Ice Cream
Harvard
Harvard University
HARVARD SQUARE
LA Burdick's
Harvest
Darwin's
Tory Row
Le's
UpStairs on the Square
Mr. Bartley's Burger Cottage
Rialto
Henrietta's Table
Charles Hotel
Tanjore
Pinocchio's
Orinoco
BerryLine
Library Park
John F. Kennedy Park
Harvard Business School
Charles River
Russelle Hoyt Field
Riverside Press Park
Western Avenue Bridge
River Street Bridge
John W. Weeks Footbridge
Larz Anderson Bridge
Chauncy St.
Follen St.
Concord Ave.
Waterhouse St.
Garden St.
Massachusetts Ave.
Mason St.
Brattle St.
Appian Way
Hilliard St.
Story St.
Church
Palmer
Mt. Auburn
Bennet St.
Winthrop St.
Eliot St.
John F. Kennedy St.
South St.
Dunster
Holyoke
Linden
Mill St.
Plympton St.
De Wolf St.
Mt. Auburn Street
Memorial Drive
Grant St.
Cowperthwaite
Banks St.
Flagg St.
Soldiers Field Road
Harvard Way
Gordon Dr.
Western Ave.
Hague St.
Windom St.
Almy St.
Cambridge St.
Oxford St.
Divinity Ave.
Kirkland
Francis Ave.
Bryant St.
Irving St.
Scott St.
Holden St.
Durham
Farrar St.
Kirkland St.
Myrtle Ave.
Summer Rd.
Irving Ter.
Trowbridge St.
Roberts Rd.
Howey Ave.
Cambridge St.
Quincy St.
Prescott St.
Broadway
Ware St.
Trowbridge Ter.
Ellery St.
Dana St.
Ellsworth Ave.
Highland Ave.
Harvard St.
Chatham St.
Centre St.
Hancock St.
Putnam Ave.
Green St.
Franklin St.
Kinnaird St.
Bay St.
Lee St.
Clinton St.
Magee St.
Howard St.
Jay St.
Soden St.
Callender
Hingham St.
Pleasant St.
William St.
Cottage St.
Upton St.
Kelly Rd.
Magazine St.
Perry St.
Chalk St.
Lawrence
Fairmont
Andrew
Allston St.
Fairmont St.
Prince St.
Erie St.
Valentine
Kenwood St.
Hamilton St.
Pearl St.
Magazine Street
Chestnut St.
Florence St.
Pleasant
River St.

Map 4
• Cambridge
• Somerville
E
F
G
H
1
2
3
4
5
6
INMAN SQUARE
CAMBRIDGE
SOMERVILLE
CENTRAL SQUARE
Bronwyn
Christina's
East Coast Grill and Raw Bar
All Star Sandwich Bar
Oleana
Hungry Mother
The Blue Room
West Bridge
Green Street
Rendezvous
Toscanini's
Craigie on Main
Area Four
Baraka Café
Miracle of Science
MIT Museum
Le Méridien Cambridge
Kendall Hotel
Legal Sea Foods
Central
Lincoln Park
John F. Donnelly Field
Edward J. Sennott Park
Massachusetts Insitute of Technology (MIT)
Washington St.
Washington Street
Somerville Ave.
Prospect St.
Webster Ave.
Hampshire St.
Cambridge Street
Broadway
Concord Ave.
Charlestown
Lincoln St.
Main St.
Massachusetts Ave.
Vassar St.
Albany St.
Binney St.
Cardinal Medeiros Ave.
Harvard St.
Bishop Allen Dr.
Green St.
2A
0
900 ft
0
300 meters

Dining

Lodging

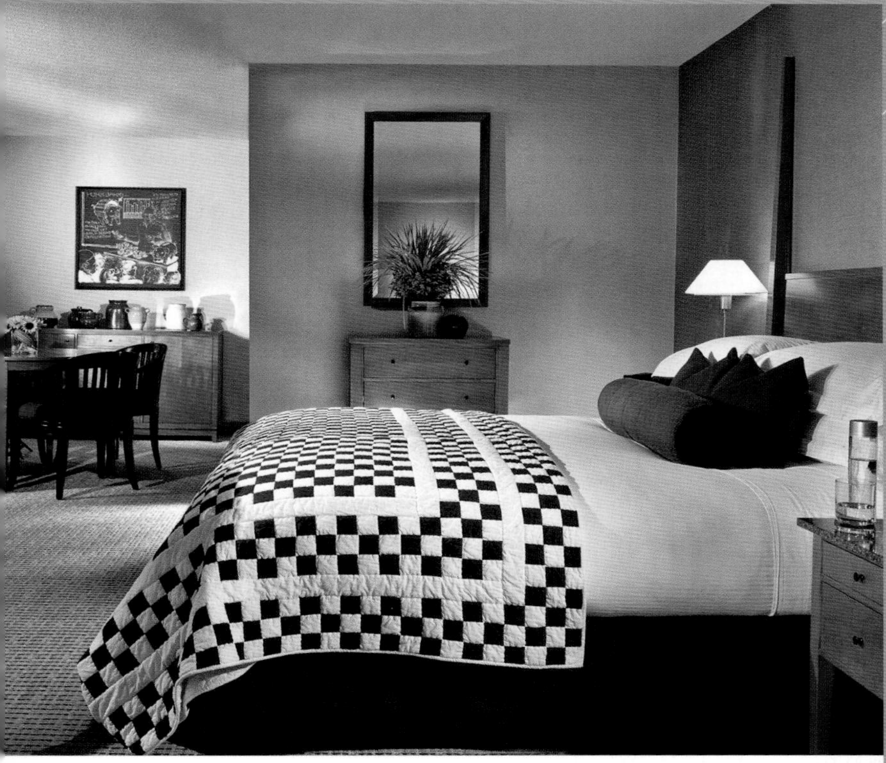

WHERE TO STAY

Updated by Frances Folsom

At one time, great lodging was scarce in Boston. If you were a persnickety blue blood in town to visit relatives, you checked into the Charles or the old Ritz on Newbury. If you were a parent in town to see your kid graduate from one of the city's many universities, you suffered through a stay at a run-down chain. And if you were a young couple in town for a little romance, well, you could just forget it. A dearth of suitable rooms practically defined Boston. Oh, how things have changed.

In the early 2000s, Boston finally got wise to modernization, and a rush of new construction took the local hotel scene by storm. Sleek, boutique accommodations began inviting guests to Cambridge and Downtown, areas once relegated to alumni and business traveler sets. New, mega-luxury lodgings like the Mandarin Oriental and the Taj (the latter, in that old Ritz spot) infiltrated posh Back Bay, while high-end, hipster-friendly spots like the W Boston and Ames are drawing visitors to up-and-coming areas in Downtown. Even mostly residential areas like the South End now draw discerning boarders, thanks to the revamped Chandler and the nearby Inn@St. Botolph.

Speaking of revamped, it seems that nearly every hotel in town just got a face-lift. From spruced up decor (good-bye, grandma's bedspread; hello, puffy white duvets) to hopping restaurant-bars to new spas and fitness centers, Boston's lodgings are feeling the competitive heat and acting accordingly. You don't just get a room anymore—you get an experience.

Many properties have stellar weekend deals, so you may be able to try an upscale Fodor's Choice even if you thought it was out of your budget.

BOSTON LODGING PLANNER

LODGING STRATEGY

Where should we stay? With so many new and improved Boston hotels, it may seem like a daunting question. But fret not—our expert writers and editors have done most of the legwork. The selections here represent the best this city has to offer—from the best affordable picks to the sleekest designer hotels. *Scan "Best Bets" on the following pages for top recommendations by price and experience.* Or find a review quickly in the listings—search by neighborhood, then alphabetically. Happy hunting!

RESERVATIONS

Commencement weekends in May and June book months in advance; prices can be triple the off-season rate, with minimum stays of two to four nights. Leaf-peepers arrive in early October, and fall conventions bring waves of business travelers, especially in the Seaport District. Events such as the Boston Marathon in April and the Head of the Charles in October are busy times for large hotels and small inns alike.

PRICES

The hotel tax in Boston adds 14.95% to your bill; some hotels also tack on energy, service, or occupancy surcharges. Though it's not an absolute necessity, many visitors prefer to bring a car, though parking is another expense then to consider. Almost all lodgings have parking, and most charge for the privilege—anywhere from $15 per day for self-garaging to $35 for valet. When looking for a hotel, don't write off the pricier establishments immediately. Price categories are determined by "rack rates"—the list price of a hotel room, which is usually discounted. Specials abound, particularly in Downtown on weekends. With so many new rooms in Boston, pricing is very competitive, so always check out the hotel website in advance for current special offers.

USING THE MAPS

Throughout the chapter, you'll see mapping symbols and coordinates (such as ✣ 3:F2) after property names or reviews. To locate the property on a map, turn to the Boston Dining and Lodging Atlas at the end of the Where to Eat chapter. The first number after the j symbol indicates the map number. Following that is the property's coordinate on the map grid.

HOTEL REVIEWS

Listed alphabetically within neighborhoods. For expanded hotel reviews, visit Fodors.com.

BOSTON

BEACON HILL AND BOSTON COMMON

If you want calm, serenity, and class, then stay on Beacon Hill. This is one of the poshest neighborhoods in Boston. Its streets are lined with elegant brick buildings holding unique shops and boutique hotels.

WHERE SHOULD I STAY?

NEIGHBORHOOD	VIBE	PROS	CONS
Beacon Hill and Boston Common	Old brick and stone buildings host luxe boutique hotels and B&Bs on the hill or along busy, preppy Charles Street; some skyscraper lodging right on Boston Common.	Safe, quaint area with lamp-lighted streets; chain-free upscale shopping and dining; outdoor fun abounds in the park; good T access.	Street parking is extremely hard to come by; not budget-friendly; close to noisy hospital; hills can be steep.
Downtown Boston	The city's Financial District hums with activity and busy hotels during the week; new boutique lodging is moving in to compete with the big-box chains.	Excellent area for business travelers; frequent low weekend rates; good T and bus access; walking distance to Theater District and some museums.	All but dead at night; expensive garage parking during the day; Downtown Crossing is mobbed at lunchtime and on weekends; poorly marked streets.
The Back Bay	High-priced hotels in the city's poshest neighborhood, home to shops, restaurants, bars, spas, and salons. Commonwealth Avenue is lined with historic mansions.	Easy, central location; safe, beautiful area to walk around at night; ample T access; excellent people-watching.	Rooms, shopping, and eating can be ridiculously expensive; Newbury Street is overcrowded with tourists on weekends.
The South End	Small, funky lodgings in a hip and happening (and gay-friendly) area packed with awesome independent restaurants and shops.	The city's best dining scene; easy T and bus access; myriad parks; walking distance from the Back Bay and Downtown; safe along the main avenues at night.	Some bordering blocks turn seedy after dusk; difficult street parking (and few garages); only a handful of hotel options.
The Fenway and Kenmore Square	A sampling of large and small hotels and inns, plus two hostels; the area is a mix of students, young professionals, and die-hard Sox fans.	Close to Fenway Park (home of the Red Sox); up-and-coming dining scene; less expensive than most 'hoods; accessible by the T.	Impossible street parking on game days (and pricey garages); expect big crowds for concerts and sporting events; some bars are loud and tacky.
Boston Outskirts	Mostly mid-size chain hotels in student neighborhoods full of coffee shops, convenience stores, and rowdy college bars; except for sweet inns in lovely Brookline.	Serviceable airport lodging near Logan; cheap rates on rooms in Brighton and parts of Brookline; easier driving than in Downtown.	No overnight street parking in Brookline; far from Boston center, museums, shopping, and the river; some areas get dicey at night; T rides into the city proper can take an hour.
Cambridge	A mix of grand and small hotels peppers the hip, multi-university neighborhood; expect loads of young freethinkers and efficient (if laid-back) service.	Hallowed academia; verdant squares; good low- and high-cost eating and lodging; excellent neighborhood restaurants; few chain anythings.	Spotty T access; less of a city feel; a few areas can be quiet and slightly dodgy at night; lots of one-way streets make driving difficult.

BEST BETS FOR BOSTON LODGING

Fodor's offers a selective listing of quality lodging experiences in every price range, from the city's best budget beds to its most sophisticated luxury hotels. Here we've compiled our top recommendations by price and experience. The very best properties—in other words, those that provide a particularly remarkable experience in their price range—are designated in the listings with the Fodor's Choice logo.

Fodor's Choice ★

Boston Harbor Hotel at Rowes Wharf, $$$$, p. 203
Charles Hotel, $$$, p. 213
Charlesmark Hotel, $$, p. 206
Eliot Hotel, $$$$, p. 207
Gryphon House, $$$, p. 210
Harborside Inn, $$, p. 203
Hotel Commonwealth, $$$, p. 210
Inn@St. Botolph, $$$, p. 208
Liberty Hotel Boston, $$$$, p. 202
Nine Zero, $$$, p. 205
XV Beacon, $$$$, p. 202

By Price

$

Chandler Inn, p. 210
Encore, p. 210
John Jeffries House, p. 202

$$

Charlesmark Hotel, p. 206

$$$

Charles Hotel, p. 213
Fairmont Copley Plaza, p. 208
Gryphon House, p. 210
Hotel Commonwealth, p. 210
Inn@St. Botolph, p. 208
Le Meridien Cambridge, p. 213
Nine Zero, p. 205
Seaport Boston Hotel, p. 205

$$$$

Boston Harbor Hotel at Rowes Wharf, p. 203
Colonnade Hotel, p. 206
Copley Square Hotel, p. 207
Eliot Hotel, p. 207
Liberty Hotel Boston, p. 202
Mandarin Oriental Boston, p. 209
Renaissance Boston Waterfront Hotel, p. 205
XV Beacon, p. 202

By Experience

BEST GYM

InterContinental Boston, $$$$, p. 204
Ritz-Carlton Boston Common, $$$$, p. 205
Seaport Boston Hotel, $$$, p. 205

BEST HOTEL BAR

Charles Hotel, $$$, p. 213
Copley Square Hotel, $$$$, p. 207
Hotel Commonwealth, $$$, p. 210
InterContinental, $$$$, p. 204
Langham Hotel, $$$, p. 204
Liberty Hotel Boston, $$$$, p. 202

BEST SERVICE

Boston Harbor Hotel at Rowes Wharf, $$$$, p. 203
Boston Park Plaza Hotel & Towers, $$$, p. 206
Four Seasons, $$$$, p. 208
Mandarin Oriental Boston, $$$$, p. 209

BEST HIP HOTELS

Ames Hotel, $$$, p. 202
Charlesmark Hotel, $$, p. 206
Colonnade Hotel, $$$$, p. 206
Copley Square Hotel, $$$$, p. 207
Hotel Marlowe, $$$, p. 213
Inn@St. Botolph, $$$, p. 208
Nine Zero, $$$, p. 205
W Boston, $$$$, p. 206

BEST GRANDES DAMES

Boston Harbor Hotel at Rowes Wharf, $$$$, p. 203
Boston Park Plaza Hotel & Towers, $$$, p. 206
Fairmont Copley Plaza, $$$, p. 208
Omni Parker House, $$$, p. 205
Taj Boston Hotel, $$$, p. 209

Meanwhile, the hip Boston Common shares a vibe of busyness with Boylston and Newbury streets.

$$$ B&B/INN **Beacon Hill Hotel & Bistro.** This home away from home—or, rather, full-service version of home where you hardly have to lift a finger (unless it's to dial room service)—is within walking distance of the Public Garden, Back Bay, Government Center, and the river Esplanade. **Pros:** free Wi-Fi; many nearby shops and restaurants; chef Jason Bonds' decadent Sunday brunch at the ground-floor bistro. **Cons:** neighborhood parking is nonexistent; the rooms are somewhat small. *Rooms from: $325 25 Charles St., Beacon Hill 617/723–7575 www.beaconhillhotel.com 12 rooms, 1 suite Breakfast Arlington, Charles/MGH 1:D6.*

$ B&B/INN **John Jeffries House.** Right next to the Charles/MGH stop, the John Jeffries isn't only easily accessible, it's affordable—a veritable home run in this city. **Pros:** great Beacon Hill location; free Wi-Fi; good value. **Cons:** there's a busy (and noisy) hospital across the street; no spa or gym facilities. *Rooms from: $125 14 David G. Mugar Way, Beacon Hill 617/367–1866 www.johnjeffrieshouse.com 23 rooms, 23 suites Breakfast Charles/MGH 1:C5.*

$$$$ HOTEL Fodor's Choice ★ **Liberty Hotel Boston.** Since it opened in late 2007, the buzz surrounding the chic Liberty—formerly Boston's Charles Street Jail—was at first deafening, with bankers, tech geeks, foreign playboys, and fashionistas all scrambling to call it their own; a few years later, the hype has thankfully died down, though it's still part retreat, part nightclub. **Pros:** Scampo's mouthwatering house-made mozzarella bar; bustling nightlife; proximity to the river and Beacon Hill. **Cons:** loud in-house nightlife; long waits at bars and restaurants. *Rooms from: $699 215 Charles St., Beacon Hill 617/224–4000 www.libertyhotel.com 288 rooms, 10 suites No meals Charles/MGH 1:D5.*

$$$$ HOTEL Fodor's Choice ★ **XV Beacon.** The 1903 Beaux-Arts exterior of one of the city's first small luxury hotels is a study in understated class and elegance. **Pros:** in-room massages; chef Jamie Mammano's steak house, Mooo; free pet stays. **Cons:** some rooms are very small; mattresses are just average; can be expensive on weekends during peak months (May, June, September, October). *Rooms from: $575 15 Beacon St., Beacon Hill 617/670–1500, 877/982–3226 www.xvbeacon.com 63 rooms No meals Government Center, Park St. 1:E6.*

DOWNTOWN BOSTON

This is the place to be whether you're here on business (the closer you are to the Financial District the more business-oriented the hotels become) or pleasure; think High Tea at the Langham Hotel or a stroll through its adjacent park, Post Office Square.

$$$ HOTEL **Ames Hotel.** One of the newest players on the Boston scene, the 114-room Ames is all New England modernity even though it's run by the hip Morgans Hotel Group (think the Delano and Shore Club in Miami). **Pros:** very cool design; cushy beds; limo service. **Cons:** far from South End and Back Bay shopping. *Rooms from: $350 1 Court St., Downtown 617/979–8100, 888/697–1791 www.ameshotel.com 114 rooms No meals State, Government Center 1:F6.*

$$$$ HOTEL Fodor's Choice ★ **Boston Harbor Hotel at Rowes Wharf.** Boston has plenty of iconic landmarks—the "salt and pepper" bridge, Fenway Park, the Public Garden ducklings—but none are as synonymous with überhospitality as the Boston Harbor Hotel, with its 80-foot-tall outdoor archway and rotunda and classic city and harbor views. **Pros:** high-quality Meritage and Sea Grille restaurants; easy walk to Faneuil Hall; water shuttle to Logan Airport. **Cons:** pricey; the spa gets booked up early; less convenient to the Back Bay and South End. *Rooms from: $495 ✉ 70 Rowes Wharf, Downtown/Waterfront ☎ 617/439–7000, 800/752–7077 🌐 www.bhh.com 204 rooms, 26 suites No meals Ⓜ Aquarium, South Station ✣ 1:H6.*

$$$ HOTEL **Boston Marriott Long Wharf.** Families favor this spot that looks like a big brick ship docked in Boston Harbor. **Pros:** next door Tia's bar is a must for outdoor happy hour; good weekend rates (check the Web for deals); great location for first-time visitors. **Cons:** feels like a chain hotel. *Rooms from: $300 ✉ 296 State St., Downtown/Waterfront ☎ 617/227–0800 🌐 www.marriott.com/boston 397 rooms, 15 suites No meals Ⓜ Aquarium on the Blue Line ✣ 1:H5.*

$$ HOTEL **Boxer Boston Hotel.** Steps from the TD Garden and an easy walk from Government Center, Faneuil Hall, and the North End, the nine-floor, 79-room boutique hotel with a crisp, contemporary look is a great value—if you don't mind tiny accommodations. **Pros:** great group rates; free Internet; close to North Station and the T. **Cons:** small rooms and lobby; staff can be indifferent; past guests have complained about hotel being "shopworn." *Rooms from: $220 ✉ 107 Merrimac St., Downtown ☎ 617/624–0202, 877/267–1776 🌐 www.theboxerboston.com 71 rooms, 8 suites No meals Ⓜ North Station ✣ 1:E4.*

$$$$ HOTEL FAMILY **Fairmont Battery Wharf.** One of the growing number of lodgings clustered along Boston's ever-expanding Harborwalk—a pretty pedestrian path that runs from Charlestown to Dorchester—this Fairmont looks more like a gated community than a chain hotel. **Pros:** great water views; access to Harborwalk; close to the North End. **Cons:** far from Newbury Street and South End shopping; 15- to 20-minute walk to nearest T stations. *Rooms from: $499 ✉ 3 Battery Wharf, Downtown ☎ 617/994–9000, 800/257–7544 🌐 www.fairmont.com/battery-wharf-boston 120 rooms, 30 suites Ⓜ Haymarket, North Station ✣ 1:H4.*

$$ HOTEL Fodor's Choice ★ **Harborside Inn.** With rates that are considerably lower than most Waterfront hotels—as low as $119 in the off-season— this hotel with an understated charm is an exceptional value. **Pros:** free Wi-Fi; close to Quincy Market and the New England Aquarium; nearby water taxi. **Cons:** the area might be too touristy for some leisure travelers. *Rooms from: $250 ✉ 185 State St., Downtown/Waterfront ☎ 617/723–7500, 888/723–7565 🌐 harborsideinnboston.com 116 rooms No meals Ⓜ Aquarium ✣ 1:G6.*

$$ HOTEL **Hilton Boston Financial District.** If you're looking for comfortable Downtown lodging, you'll find it at this upscale business hotel with 24-hour fitness and business centers. **Pros:** well maintained; clean and quiet; ideal for business travelers and those with pets. **Cons:** $15 daily Wi-Fi fee; a somewhat corporate vibe. *Rooms from: $259 ✉ 89 Broad*

St., Downtown ☎ *617/556–0006* 🌐 *www.hilton.com* *362 rooms, 66 suites* *No meals* Ⓜ *State* ✥ *1:G6.*

> **WORD OF MOUTH**
>
> "Just got back from a fun weekend in Boston! The Nine Zero was a great hotel for us, very centrally located. We never took a cab or the T and walked everywhere. The rooms are modern and nicely appointed with large bathrooms." —KathyK

$$$ HOTEL **Hyatt Regency Boston.** Picturesque, Downtown Crossing is not, as it is packed with every conceivable kind of discount store and street vendor, but the area hums with activity (of both the low- and high-end variety), and sitting amid all the action is the 22-story Hyatt Regency Boston. **Pros:** good package deals; saunas and whirlpools; good for business travelers. **Cons:** views of office buildings from guest rooms; few chairs around indoor pool; thin walls. $ *Rooms from: $379* ✉ *1 Ave. de Lafayette, Downtown Crossing/Chinatown* ☎ *617/912–1234, 800/233–1234* 🌐 *www.regencyboston.hyatt.com* *498 rooms, 26 suites* *No meals* Ⓜ *Chinatown, Downtown Crossing* ✥ *2:F1.*

$$$$ HOTEL **InterContinental Boston.** Call it the anti-boutique hotel: The 424-room InterContinental, facing both the waterfront and the Rose Kennedy Greenway, consists of two opulent, 22-story towers wrapped in blue glass. **Pros:** upper-floor rooms have great views; cool bathrooms; close to Financial District and South Station. **Cons:** huge function rooms mean lots of conventioneers; far from Newbury Street and South End shopping; guests say the soundproofing could be better. $ *Rooms from: $429* ✉ *510 Atlantic Ave., Downtown/Waterfront* ☎ *617/747–1000, 866/493–6495* 🌐 *www.intercontinentalboston.com* *424 rooms, 38 suites* *No meals* Ⓜ *South Station* ✥ *2:H1.*

$$$ HOTEL **Langham Hotel.** This 1922 Renaissance Revival landmark (the former Federal Reserve Building) strikes an admirable balance between historic, old-world charm and sleek, modern appointments. **Pros:** ideal spot for business travelers; fabulous Sunday brunch and weekend Chocolate Bar at Café Fleuri; the beautiful Post Office Square park adjacent to the Langham is a quiet oasis. **Cons:** Downtown location feels remote on weekends; pricey during the week; expensive valet parking. $ *Rooms from: $395* ✉ *250 Franklin St., Downtown* ☎ *617/451–1900, 800/543–4300* 🌐 *www.boston.langhamhotels.com* *318 rooms, 17 suites* *No meals* Ⓜ *South Station* ✥ *1:G6.*

$$$ HOTEL **Millennium Bostonian Hotel.** Near historic Faneuil Hall, the Bostonian has guest rooms featuring Frette linens, pillowtop mattresses, and the obligatory mammoth TVs—many also have French doors with step-out balconies showcasing city views and the popular North End. **Pros:** North 26's strong cocktails; updated fitness center. **Cons:** some rooms still get street noise; Faneuil Hall can get clogged with tourists; fee for Wi-Fi. $ *Rooms from: $309* ✉ *Faneuil Hall Marketplace, 26 North St., Downtown* ☎ *617/523–3600, 866/866–8086* 🌐 *www.millenniumhotels.com* *187 rooms, 14 suites* *No meals* Ⓜ *Government Center, Haymarket* ✥ *1:F5.*

$$$ HOTEL FAMILY Fodor's Choice ★ **Nine Zero.** Hotel rooms can get a little lonely, and that's why this Downtown spot instated its "guppy love" program; yes, that's right, you get a pet fish on loan. **Pros:** pet- and kid-friendly; lobby wine-tasting every evening (from 5 to 6); Etro bath products. **Cons:** smallish rooms; high parking fees. *Rooms from: $386 ✉ 90 Tremont St., Downtown ☎ 617/772–5800, 866/906–9090 ⊕ www.ninezero.com 185 rooms, 5 suites No meals Ⓜ Park St., Government Center ✣ 1:E6.*

$$$ HOTEL FAMILY **Omni Parker House.** If any hotel says "Boston," it's this one, where JFK proposed to Jackie, and Charles Dickens gave his first reading of "A Christmas Carol"—in fact, you may well see a Dickens impersonator in the lobby, since history tours always include the Parker House on their routes. **Pros:** historic property; near Downtown Crossing on the Freedom Trail. **Cons:** small rooms, some quite dark; thin-walled rooms can be noisy. *Rooms from: $339 ✉ 60 School St., Downtown ☎ 617/227–8600, 800/843–6664 ⊕ www.omniparkerhouse.com 551 rooms, 21 suites No meals Ⓜ Government Center, Park St. ✣ 1:F6.*

$$$ HOTEL **Onyx Hotel.** Sexy, supper-club atmosphere oozes from this eight-year-old contemporary Kimpton Group hotel a block from North Station, making it a favorite of hipsters and hoopsters alike. **Pros:** good location for catching a sporting event or concert at the Garden; near North Station commuter rail and T stop; near several inexpensive restaurants and bars. **Cons:** smallish rooms and bathrooms; small gym; neighborhood can get noisy at night. *Rooms from: $359 ✉ 155 Portland St., Downtown ☎ 617/557–9955, 866/660–6699 ⊕ www.onyxhotel.com 110 rooms, 2 suites No meals Ⓜ North Station ✣ 1:E4.*

$$$$ HOTEL **Renaissance Boston Waterfront Hotel.** Set along the working wharves of Boston Harbor, near the must-visit Institute of Contemporary Art, the Renaissance plays to a watery theme. **Pros:** sleek new lobby Capiz Bar and Lounge; close to the Silver Line (airport transportation) and convention center. **Cons:** some guest-room harbor views are more industrial than scenic; hordes of conventioneers; far from major city attractions. *Rooms from: $449 ✉ 606 Congress St., Downtown/Seaport District ☎ 617/338–4111, 888/796–4664 ⊕ www.renaissanceboston.com 450 rooms, 21 suites No meals Ⓜ World Trade Center ✣ 2:H2.*

$$$$ HOTEL FAMILY **Ritz-Carlton Boston Common.** The Sports Club/LA, the Ritz's mega–fitness center, is the go-to gym for visiting celebs and Poptarts, so you might feel a bit more fabulous—or a whole lot fatter—simply by hanging out here. **Pros:** the Sports Club's very social blu eatery has a great post-gym scene; central location. **Cons:** some complain that guest rooms are too dark and lack "wow" factor; food service is "brutally expensive." *Rooms from: $550 ✉ 10 Avery St., Downtown ☎ 617/574–7100, 800/241–3333 ⊕ www.ritzcarlton.com 150 rooms, 43 suites No meals Ⓜ Boylston St. ✣ 2:E1.*

$$$ HOTEL **Seaport Boston Hotel.** Chances are, if you've ever been to Boston on business, you've already stayed at the Seaport, where guest rooms are among the biggest in the city. **Pros:** on-site Wave Health & Fitness Club; close to a newly developed restaurant scene offering 20 dining options; free Wi-Fi. **Cons:** far from city center. *Rooms from: $369 ✉ World Trade Center, 1 Seaport La., Downtown/Seaport District ☎ 617/385–*

4000, 800/440–3318 ⊕ www.seaportboston.com ⇆ 428 rooms ⊚ No meals Ⓜ World Trade Center ⊕ 2:H1.

$$$$ HOTEL **W Boston.** This 235-room glass tower is fronted by a metal-and-glass "awning" that is outfitted with soft, color-changing neon lights that cast a cheeky glow on passersby, but inside, the nature-inspired decor is modern through and through, with typical W brand touches like a sleek, sceney lobby lounge (complete with falling water display and open fireplace) and a host of room categories such as the standard Wonderful and expanded Wow lodgings. **Pros:** on-site Bliss spa; signature W feather-top beds; fashion scene. **Cons:** fee for Wi-Fi in rooms; area theater and bar crowds can be loud; expensive parking. Ⓢ *Rooms from: $400 ✉ 100 Stuart St., Downtown/Theater District ☎ 617/261–8700 ⊕ www.whotels.com/boston ⇆ 235 rooms ⊚ No meals Ⓜ Boylston, Tufts Medical Center ⊕ 2:E2.*

$$$ HOTEL FAMILY **Westin Boston Waterfront.** The South Boston property is connected to the enormous Boston Convention & Exhibition Center, a magnet for men and women wearing suits and badges. **Pros:** close to the stellar Institute of Contemporary Art; Silver Line to Logan Airport; Westin's signature "heavenly" beds. **Cons:** clusters of meeting-goers; a businesslike chain hotel feel. Ⓢ *Rooms from: $305 ✉ 425 Summer St., Downtown/Seaport District ☎ 617/532–4600 ⊕ www.westinbostonwaterfront.com ⇆ 761 rooms, 32 suites ⊚ No meals Ⓜ South Station, Silver Line ⊕ 2:H2.*

THE BACK BAY AND THE SOUTH END

The Back Bay and the South End are what locals call the "well-heeled" sections of Boston, meaning money talks here—think the likes of Mandarin Oriental or Fairmont Copley Plaza. The streets are lined with upscale, stylish hotels (old and new), boutique hotels, and inns.

THE BACK BAY

$$$ HOTEL **Boston Park Plaza Hotel & Towers.** One of Boston's best locations, this antiques-laden hotel is ideal for those looking for old-world charm. **Pros:** handful of restaurants and bars on the premises; helpful concierge; adjacent to an Exhale spa. **Cons:** rooms are cramped; bathrooms are small; not for hip modernists. Ⓢ *Rooms from: $300 ✉ 50 Park Plaza at Arlington St., Back Bay ☎ 617/426–2000, 800/225–2008 ⊕ www.bostonparkplaza.com ⇆ 941 rooms, 39 suites ⊚ No meals Ⓜ Arlington ⊕ 2:D2.*

$$ HOTEL Fodor's Choice ★ **Charlesmark Hotel.** Hipsters and romantics who'd rather spend their cash on a great meal than a hotel bill have put this late 19th-century former residential row house on the map. **Pros:** fantastic price for the location; free Wi-Fi. **Cons:** some might feel crowded by compact rooms and hallways. Ⓢ *Rooms from: $239 ✉ 655 Boylston St., Back Bay ☎ 617/247–1212 ⊕ www.thecharlesmarkhotel.com ⇆ 40 rooms ⊚ Breakfast Ⓜ Copley ⊕ 2:B2.*

$$$$ HOTEL FAMILY **Colonnade Hotel.** Thanks to a $25-million makeover in 2013 that included a spruced-up facade, new windows, and updated room decor, the Colonnade went from an '80s brass-and-mahogany showcase to a clean, modern environs injected with hues of khaki, chocolate, and chrome. **Pros:** roof-deck pool; across from Prudential Center shopping; good Red Sox packages. **Cons:** Huntington Avenue can get clogged

CLOSE UP

Kid-Friendly Hotels

Almost every Boston hotel allows kids, but a few go out of their way to make little ones feel welcome. The **Fairmont Copley Plaza**'s resident Labrador retriever, Catie Copley, is extra sweet and family-friendly; she's also available on loan for long walks in the park. The **Inn@St. Botolph**'s "Inn-structional" packages are fun for all ages, so bring the kids along to cooking classes (including gelato making—you get to eat it, of course, too!) or ultracool glass-blowing lessons. A stuffed animal is waiting for every child at the **Lenox Hotel**, where the staff puts together myriad kid-focused trips to the Museum of Science and New England Aquarium. At the **Four Seasons**, the Kid-Kation package lineup includes a complimentary toy at check-in, make-your-own ice-cream sundaes, a backpack stuffed with activities and games, and a cookie-making class in the Pastry Shop. If all that sounds exhausting, you could just drop your tot at the **Taj Boston**'s Children's Suite or partake in a pre-planned "Family Connection" package at the **Colonnade Hotel**.

If you're looking for a place for kids to splash around, the **Seaport Hotel** and the **Colonnade** have two of the best pools in the city (Note: The latter becomes a bit of a scene on weekends, so your best bet is an early weekday).

Greater Boston Convention & Visitors Bureau. Request a "Kids Love Boston" brochure from the Greater Boston Convention & Visitors Bureau. The website lists a variety of family-friendly packages that include such extras as complimentary use of strollers and discounts to city attractions. ☎ *617/536–4100, 888/733–2678* 🌐 *www.bostonusa.com.*

with rush-hour traffic; on summer days the pool is packed by 11 am. $ *Rooms from: $479* ✉ *120 Huntington Ave., Back Bay* ☎ *617/424–7000, 800/962–3030* 🌐 *www.colonnadehotel.com* *276 rooms, 9 suites* *No meals* Ⓜ *Back Bay, Prudential Center* ✣ *2:B3.*

$$$$ HOTEL **Copley Square Hotel.** Thanks to an $18-million renovation, the Copley Square Hotel has hurtled into the present with high-tech registration pods, cushy mattresses, and in-room iPod docks—not too shabby for a place that opened in 1891 and has provided respite to a century of celebrities like Babe Ruth, Ella Fitzgerald, and Billie Holiday. **Pros:** free Wi-Fi; free nightly wine tastings; cool bar and club scene. **Cons:** small rooms; rooms facing Huntington Avenue can be noisy; not ideal for older couples seeking peace and quiet. $ *Rooms from: $499* ✉ *47 Huntington Ave., Back Bay* ☎ *617/536–9000* 🌐 *www.copleysquarehotel.com* *143 rooms* *No meals* Ⓜ *Copley, Back Bay* ✣ *2:B2.*

$$$$ HOTEL Fodor's Choice ★ **Eliot Hotel.** One of the city's best small hotels is on posh Commonwealth Avenue, modeled after Paris's epic Champs-Élysées, and it expertly merges the old blue-blood Boston aesthetic with modern flair (like zebra-print rugs mingling with crystal chandeliers); everyone from well-heeled Sox fans to traveling CEOs to tony college parents has noticed. **Pros:** super location; top-notch restaurants; pet-friendly; beautiful rooms. **Cons:** very expensive; some complain of elevator noise. $ *Rooms from: $485* ✉ *370 Commonwealth Ave., Back Bay*

☎ *617/267–1607, 800/443–5468* ⊕ *www.eliothotel.com* *16 rooms, 79 suites* *No meals* Ⓜ *Hynes* ✣ *3:H2.*

$$$ HOTEL FAMILY Fodor's Choice ★ **Fairmont Copley Plaza.** Past guests, including one Judy Garland, felt at home in this decadent, unabashedly romantic hotel that underwent a $20-million renovation in early 2012. **Pros:** very elegant. **Cons:** tiny bathrooms with scratchy towels; charge for Internet access (no charge on Fairmont President's Club level). $ *Rooms from: $369* ✉ *138 St. James Ave., Back Bay* ☎ *617/267–5300, 866/540–4417* ⊕ *www.fairmont.com/copley-plaza-boston* *366 rooms, 17 suites* *No meals* Ⓜ *Copley, Back Bay* ✣ *2:B2.*

$$$$ HOTEL FAMILY **Four Seasons.** This Public Garden–facing spot keeps a surprisingly low profile in Boston—and that's okay by the jeans-clad millionaires and assorted business types who cluster in the glossy lobby or use the Mercedes courtesy car. **Pros:** overlooks the Public Garden; a short walk from Newbury; signature Four Seasons service. **Cons:** pricey during peak times; valet service can be slow. $ *Rooms from: $675* ✉ *200 Boylston St., Back Bay* ☎ *617/338–4400, 800/819–5053* ⊕ *www.fourseasons.com/boston* *196 rooms, 77 suites* *No meals* Ⓜ *Arlington* ✣ *2:D1.*

$ B&B/INN **463 Beacon Street Guest House.** Though there's no sign on the door of this handsome brownstone, international visitors and college students have discovered the rooming house—and quickly warmed to its slightly quirky, old-auntie charm. **Pros:** Newbury Street is three blocks away; the Charles River and Esplanade are one block in the other direction. **Cons:** some rooms have a two-person occupancy limit, and because of the layout, the house isn't appropriate for children under seven. $ *Rooms from: $125* ✉ *463 Beacon St., Back Bay* ☎ *617/536–1302* ⊕ *www.463beacon.com* *20 rooms, 17 with bath* *No meals* Ⓜ *Hynes* ✣ *3:H2.*

$$ HOTEL **Hilton Boston Back Bay.** Rooms at the Back Bay Hilton are relatively spacious, with plush "Serenity" bedding, premium cable channels, Lavazza coffee, and Peter Thomas Roth amenities. **Pros:** oversize showers; good roof-level fitness center; free Wi-Fi in the lobby. **Cons:** fee for Internet in guest rooms; expensive breakfast ("go elsewhere," some reviewers advise). $ *Rooms from: $249* ✉ *40 Dalton St., Back Bay* ☎ *617/236–1100, 888/874–0663* ⊕ *www.hilton.com* *390 rooms, 1 suite* *No meals* Ⓜ *Prudential, Hynes* ✣ *2:A3.*

$$$ B&B/INN FAMILY Fodor's Choice ★ **Inn@St. Botolph.** The posh yet homey 16-room Inn@St. Botolph follows a groundbreaking new hotel model—no front desk, no restaurant, and no valet (there is, however, an office on-site that is staffed 24/7). **Pros:** affordable style; free satellite TV and Wi-Fi; free transit to top area restaurants, where guests also get "preferred" pricing. **Cons:** DIY parking; for those who need handholding, there's no front desk. $ *Rooms from: $379* ✉ *99 St. Botolph St., Back Bay* ☎ *617/236–8099* ⊕ *www.innatstbotolph.com* *16 rooms* *Breakfast* Ⓜ *Prudential* ✣ *2:B3.*

$$$ HOTEL FAMILY **Lenox Hotel.** A good alternative to chain-owned, big-box Back Bay hotels, the family-owned Lenox with top-notch service continues to please a well-groomed clientele. **Pros:** free Wi-Fi; fantastic Copley Square location; historic/architectural charm. **Cons:** bathrooms are small; no minibar; costly parking. $ *Rooms from: $315* ✉ *61 Exeter*

St., Back Bay ☎ 617/536–5300, 800/225–7676 ⊕ www.lenoxhotel.com ⇨ 210 rooms, 4 suites ⑩ No meals Ⓜ Back Bay, Copley ⊕ 2:B2.

$$$$ HOTEL **Loew's Boston Hotel.** Travelers rave about the sleek Loew's Boston Hotel (formerly Back Bay Hotel and Jurys Boston)—"Great staff". . . "Great bar". . . "Great vibe"—see a pattern yet?**Pros:** good restaurant; friendly staff; pet-friendly. **Cons:** bar can be loud; dodgy area at night. *$ Rooms from: $459 ✉ 350 Stuart St., Back Bay ☎ 617/266–7200, 855/495–6397 ⊕ www.loewshotels.com/boston-hotel ⇨ 223 rooms, 3 suites ⑩ No meals Ⓜ Back Bay ⊕ 2:C2.*

$$$$ HOTEL FAMILY **Mandarin Oriental Boston.** With too many amenities to list, the 148-room hotel has helped redefine luxury in town (pay attention, Ritz and Four Seasons) since opening in 2008, and it offers services many guests are calling "out of this world." **Pros:** amazing service; very quiet; good-size rooms. **Cons:** small fitness center; exorbitantly expensive; average views. *$ Rooms from: $600 ✉ 776 Boylston St., Back Bay ☎ 617/535–8888 ⊕ www.mandarinoriental.com/boston ⇨ 136 rooms, 12 suites ⑩ No meals Ⓜ Prudential, Copley ⊕ 2:A2.*

$$ HOTEL **Marriott Hotel at Copley Place.** It's busy-busy, with throngs of tourists and their offspring, but you can't beat the location of this 38-story megahotel. **Pros:** good service; comfortable beds; great location. **Cons:** crowded pool area; chaotic lobby. *$ Rooms from: $279 ✉ 110 Huntington Ave., Back Bay ☎ 617/236–5800, 800/228–9290 ⊕ www.marriott.com ⇨ 1,100 rooms, 47 suites ⑩ No meals Ⓜ Copley, Back Bay ⊕ 2:B3.*

$$ B&B/INN **Newbury Guest House.** A homey feel and personalized service are at the soul of this elegant brownstone at the heart of Boston's most fashionable shopping street. **Pros:** cozy; homey; great location. **Cons:** rooms go quickly year-round; small bathrooms; limited parking. *$ Rooms from: $259 ✉ 261 Newbury St., Back Bay ☎ 617/670–6000, 800/437–7668 ⊕ www.newburyguesthouse.com ⇨ 32 rooms ⑩ Breakfast Ⓜ Back Bay, Hynes, Copley ⊕ 2:A2.*

$$$ HOTEL FAMILY **Taj Boston Hotel.** Standing guard at the corner of fashionable Newbury Street and the Public Garden, the old-school elegant Taj is doing its best to win over the old Ritz fans (it was formerly the landmark Ritz-Carlton Boston), as well as woo new guests, with discounted weekend rates and a soft renovation. **Pros:** white-glove service; great views; proximity to shopping, dining, and the park. **Cons:** occasionally snobby staff; frequently barren restaurant. *$ Rooms from: $399 ✉ 15 Arlington St., Back Bay ☎ 617/536–5700 ⊕ www.tajhotels.com ⇨ 273 rooms, 45 suites ⑩ No meals Ⓜ Arlington ⊕ 2:C1.*

$$$ HOTEL **Westin Copley Place Boston.** If the idea of sleeping in an upscale mall appeals to you, meet your new favorite hotel. **Pros:** great location; wide views; clean, spacious rooms; Heavenly beds. **Cons:** big and busy feeling; pool area is nothing special; some say it's overpriced. *$ Rooms from: $399 ✉ 10 Huntington Ave., Back Bay ☎ 617/262–9600, 888/937–8461 ⊕ www.westincopleyplaceboston.com ⇨ 661 rooms, 142 suites Ⓜ Copley, Back Bay ⊕ 2:B2.*

THE SOUTH END

> **WORD OF MOUTH**
>
> "I usually stayed at the Commonwealth Hotel, which is across the street. I loved the location—lots of good places to eat and shop, walk to Fenway Park, and the T station of the Green Line is right below the hotel, so it's easy to get anywhere in Boston." —Icuy

$ B&B/INN **Chandler Inn.** There's big news at the Chandler: it's almost all new thanks to a 2012 update by big-shot local designers Dennis Duffy and Eric Roseff, who redid 40 of the 56 guest rooms in a fresh, contemporary style and with amenities such as iPod docks, plasma TVs, and marble bathrooms with walk-in glass showers. **Pros:** can't beat the price; friendly staff. **Cons:** area parking is brutally hard to find or expensive; rooms can be noisy. *Rooms from: $175 26 Chandler St., South End 617/482–3450, 800/842–3450 www.chandlerinn.com 56 rooms Breakfast Back Bay 2:D3.*

$$$ B&B/INN **Clarendon Square Inn.** In the heart of the residential South End, this hip property is for travelers who appreciate the intimacy of a B&B and the style and sophistication of an upscale hotel. **Pros:** free Wi-Fi; feels more boutique hotel than B&B; rooftop hot tub. **Cons:** just three rooms means reservations are hard to come by; no elevator; once-free parking now costs $25. *Rooms from: $368 198 W. Brookline St., South End 617/536–2229 www.clarendonsquare.com 3 rooms Breakfast Back Bay 2:B4.*

$ B&B/INN **Encore.** Innkeepers Reinhold Mahler and David Miller who are an architect and creative set designer, respectively, have pooled their creative energies into this South End lodging gem, proving that they know a thing or two about ambience. **Pros:** trendy South End location; free Wi-Fi; Bang & Olufsen sound systems. **Cons:** small breakfast nook; two-night minimums on weekends; no elevator. *Rooms from: $155 116 W. Newton St., South End 617/247–3425 www.encorebandb.com 3 rooms Breakfast Back Bay, Mass. Ave. 2:B4*

THE FENWAY AND KENMORE SQUARE

$$$ B&B/INN Fodor's Choice ★ **Gryphon House.** The staff in this value-packed four-story, 19th-century brownstone is helpful and friendly, and the suites are thematically decorated: one evokes rustic Italy; another is inspired by neo-Gothic art. **Pros:** elegant suites are lush and spacious; gas fireplaces in all rooms; free Wi-Fi. **Cons:** may be too fussy for some; there's no elevator or handicapped access. *Rooms from: $300 9 Bay State Rd., Kenmore Sq. 617/375–9003, 877/375–9003 www.innboston.com 8 suites Breakfast Kenmore 3:G2.*

$$$ HOTEL Fodor's Choice ★ **Hotel Commonwealth.** Luxury and service without pretense makes this hip spot a solid choice—no wonder rumor has it that Bono and the Boss have walked the hallways of the Hotel Commonwealth, as have a host of local celebs and visitors intent on branching out of the Downtown Boston hospitality scene. **Pros:** down bedding; perfect locale for Red Sox fans; happening bar scene at Eastern Standard; free Wi-Fi. **Cons:** area is mobbed during Sox games; small gym. *Rooms from: $399 500 Commonwealth Ave., Kenmore Square 617/933–5000, 866/784–*

CLOSE UP

Lodging Alternatives

Hotels are an obvious lodging choice, but they aren't your only option; there are plenty of other ways to stay in Boston, some with much more affordable rates than your average double room. Bed-and-breakfasts in general often get a bad rap for being too cloying, cutesy, or dusty, but many in the Boston area are updated, clean, and modern, and well worth a look. If you don't need fancy service or amenities, stay in the simplest lodging possible: a hostel.

APARTMENT RENTALS

If you don't mind doing a bit of legwork, you can look into apartment rentals or short-term sublets. This option generally provides a home base that's roomy enough for a family and comes with cooking facilities. Home-exchange directories sometimes list rentals, and many of the B&B agencies *below* also handle apartment, cottage, and house rentals.

BED-AND-BREAKFASTS

Bed & Breakfast Agency of Boston ☎ *617/720–3540, 800/248–9262* ⊕ *www.boston-bnbagency.com.*

Bed & Breakfast Associates ☎ *888/486–6018* ⊕ *www.bnbboston.com.*

Greater Boston Hospitality Bed & Breakfast Service ☎ *617/393–1548* ⊕ *www.bostonbedandbreakfast.com.*

Host Homes of Boston ☎ *617/244–1308, 800/600–1308* ⊕ *www.hosthomesofboston.com.*

HOME EXCHANGES

A home-exchange organization will send you its updated listings of available home swaps via email or printed brochure. It's up to you to make specific arrangements.

HomeLink US ☎ *954/566–2687, 800/638–3841* ⊕ *www.homelink.org/usa.*

Intervac U.S. ☎ *800/756–4663* ⊕ *www.intervacus.com.*

4000 ⊕ *www.hotelcommonwealth.com* *149 rooms, 5 suites* *No meals* Ⓜ *Kenmore* ✣ *3:F2.*

BOSTON OUTSKIRTS

BRIGHTON

$$ HOTEL **Best Western University Hotel-Boston/Brighton.** In a residential neighborhood between Boston University and Boston College, this motel is well priced and fairly quiet. **Pros:** free Wi-Fi; economical option for parents visiting BU or BC students; free parking. **Cons:** no elevator; slow T ride to Downtown. *Rooms from: $230* ✉ *1650 Commonwealth Ave., Brighton* ☎ *617/566–6260, 800/242–8377* ⊕ *www.bostonbw.com* *68 rooms, 6 suites* *Breakfast* Ⓜ *Washington St.* ✣ *3:A4.*

BROOKLINE

$$ B&B/INN **Bertram Inn.** Quiet and old-fashioned is the MO at this antiques-laden inn, which is in walking distance from Cleveland Circle. **Pros:** free Wi-Fi; a breakfast of fresh fruit, pastries, and a warm entrée is served each morning; relaxing living room. **Cons:** no elevator; could be

tidier; 15-minute T ride to Downtown Boston. *Rooms from: $249 92 Sewall Ave., Brookline 617/566–2234, 800/295–3822 www.bertraminn.com 14 rooms Breakfast St. Paul St. 3:B4.*

$$ HOTEL FAMILY **Courtyard by Marriott Boston Brookline.** If you don't mind the anonymity and predictability of a chain hotel—and don't mind staying outside Boston proper—this is a decent choice. **Pros:** kid-friendly with adjoining rooms; 1 mile from Fenway Park and Long Wood Medical Center; roomy bathrooms; free Wi-Fi. **Cons:** staff can be indifferent; dull decor. *Rooms from: $209 40 Webster St., Brookline 617/734–1393, 866/296–2296 www.marriott.com/bosbl 187 rooms, 1 suite No meals Beacon St. 3:A4.*

$$ HOTEL **Best Western Plus - Boston, The Inn at Longwood Medical.** If close proximity to Harvard Medical School or any of its partner hospitals is your top priority, book a room at this Best Western affiliate. **Pros:** helpful staff; medical rate packages; attached to Longwood Galleria Mall and food court. **Cons:** subdued vibe; nothing-special decor; expensive area parking. *Rooms from: $250 342 Longwood Ave., Brookline 617/731–4700, 800/468–2378 www.innatlongwood.com 140 rooms, 15 suites No meals Longwood 3:D5.*

$ HOTEL **Hilton Boston Logan Airport.** Quiet rooms, competitive prices, and an on-airport location make this modern Hilton a good choice for in-and-out visitors to Boston. **Pros:** easy access to Logan Airport; competitive prices. **Cons:** Internet and parking can add up; far from Downtown Boston. *Rooms from: $199 1 Hotel Dr., East Boston 617/568–6700, 800/445–8667 www.hiltonfamilyboston.com 599 rooms, 5 suites No meals Airport 1:H4.*

$$ HOTEL **Hyatt Harborside at Boston Logan International Airport.** Half the rooms at the airport Hyatt have sweeping views of either the city skyline or the ocean; the others overlook planes taking off and landing. **Pros:** close to airport; pool area has skyline views; competent, can-do staff. **Cons:** close to airport; overpriced restaurant (skip it); airport shuttle is frustratingly slow. *Rooms from: $265 101 Harborside Dr., East Boston 617/568–1234, 800/233–1234 www.harborside.hyatt.com 270 rooms No meals Airport 1:H4.*

CAMBRIDGE

Cambridge is much more provincial than Boston given that the hotels in Cambridge have a more intimate feel. Several are on tree-lined streets surrounded by college "yards" or campuses.

$ B&B/INN **A Cambridge House Inn.** This sweet Cambridge spot offers 18 rooms each decorated (some a little too much) with Victorian aesthetics in mind. **Pros:** cozy fireplace lounges; free parking and Wi-Fi; complimentary coffee, tea, and hot chocolate. **Cons:** very quiet area; no elevators. *Rooms from: $150 2218 Massachusetts Ave., Cambridge 617/491–6300, 800/232–9989 www.acambridgehouse.com 33 rooms Breakfast Davis Sq. 4:B1.*

$$$ HOTEL **Boston Marriott Cambridge.** Traveling businesspeople and families like the modern look and efficiency of this 26-story high-rise hotel in Kendall Square, steps from the subway and MIT. **Pros:** top-floor rooms have

stunning views; comfy bed linens; decent cost-saving packages on weekends. **Cons:** zero original charm; smallish pool. *Rooms from: $339 ✉ 2 Cambridge Center, 50 Broadway, Cambridge ☎ 617/494–6600, 888/228–9290 ⊕ www.marriotthotels.com/boscb 433 rooms, 11 suites No meals Ⓜ Kendall/MIT ✥ 1:A5.*

$$$ HOTEL FAMILY Fodor's Choice ★ **Charles Hotel.** It used to be that the Charles was *the* place to stay in Cambridge, and while other luxury hotels have since arrived to give it a little healthy competition, this Harvard Square staple is standing strong. **Pros:** two blocks from the T Red Line to Boston; on-site jazz club and hip Noir bar; outdoor skating rink in winter. **Cons:** luxury comes at a price. *Rooms from: $399 ✉ 1 Bennett St., Cambridge ☎ 617/864–1200, 800/882–1818 ⊕ www.charleshotel.com 249 rooms, 45 suites No meals Ⓜ Harvard ✥ 4:A3.*

$$$ HOTEL **Hotel Marlowe.** If Alice in Wonderland dreamed up a hotel, it might look a bit like the Marlowe—vivid stripes, swirls, and other geometric patterns lend the decor a wild, lively aesthetic. **Pros:** family- and pet-friendly; fun, eclectic atmosphere; free wine tastings. **Cons:** unless you're a Kimpton program member, Wi-Fi comes at a charge; a cab or T ride or walk from central Boston; not for formal decor purists. *Rooms from: $359 ✉ 25 Edwin H. Land Blvd., Cambridge ☎ 617/868–8000, 800/825–7140 ⊕ www.hotelmarlowe.com 236 rooms No meals Ⓜ Lechmere ✥ 1:C3.*

$$ B&B/INN **Irving House.** On a residential street three blocks from Harvard Square, this four-story gray clapboard B&B is a bargain. **Pros:** free Wi-Fi; good location and price; coffee, tea, and pastries are available until 10 pm. **Cons:** parking spaces are first-come, first-served; some rooms with shared baths; four floors are not served by elevator. *Rooms from: $245 ✉ 24 Irving St., Cambridge ☎ 617/547–4600, 877/547–4600 ⊕ www.irvinghouse.com 44 rooms, 29 with bath Breakfast Ⓜ Harvard ✥ 4:C2.*

$$$ HOTEL **Kendall Hotel.** You might think a place in such a high-tech neighborhood would be all stainless steel and chrome; think again: the Kendall Hotel is homey and ultrafriendly, bright-hue and lively—and it's convenient, with a T stop just one block away. **Pros:** quiet rooms; hot buffet breakfast included; free Wi-Fi. **Cons:** to many tchotchkes. *Rooms from: $390 ✉ 350 Main St., Cambridge ☎ 617/577–1300, 866/566–1300 ⊕ www.kendallhotel.com 73 room, 4 suites Breakfast Ⓜ Kendall/MIT ✥ 4:H5.*

$$$ HOTEL **Le Meridien Cambridge.** When the Meridien chain took over the cult favorite geek-chic Hotel at MIT, with its tech-savvy rooms and surroundings, some fans worried the Cambridge spot would lose its charm; but the new owners only amped up the offerings—and added some luxe touches—by displaying cool interactive lobby art from MIT and refurbishing the guest rooms with platform beds, puffy white duvets, flat-screen TVs, and ergonomically designed furniture. **Pros:** walk to many excellent restaurants in Central Square; close to the T (Red Line Central); 24-hour fitness center; free Wi-Fi. **Cons:** pricey high-season rates. *Rooms from: $395 ✉ 20 Sidney St., Cambridge ☎ 617/577–0200, 800/543–4300 ⊕ www.lemeridien.com/cambridge 196 rooms, 14 suites No meals Ⓜ Central, Kendall/MIT ✥ 4:F5.*

$$$ HOTEL FAMILY **Royal Sonesta Hotel.** Right next to the Charles River, the certified-green Sonesta has one of the best city skyline and sunset views in Boston. **Pros:** walk to Museum of Science and T to Downtown Boston; complimentary shuttle to Cambridge area attractions; nice pool. **Cons:** parking is not free. *Rooms from: $379 ✉ 40 Edwin Land Blvd., off Memorial Dr., Cambridge ☎ 617/806–4200, 800/766–3782 www.sonesta.com/boston 379 rooms, 21 suites No meals Lechmere ✢ 1:B4.*

$$$ HOTEL **Sheraton Commander.** The beloved 1927 Harvard Square landmark features classic furnishings with handsome, jewel-colored accents, and cushy leather lounge chairs to serve its mature clientele. **Pros:** free Wi-Fi; helpful, knowledgeable staff; old-school Sunday brunch. **Cons:** small bathrooms; some rooms have views of the parking lot. *Rooms from: $325 ✉ 16 Garden St., Cambridge ☎ 617/547–4800, 800/325–3535 www.sheratoncommander.com 176 rooms No meals Harvard ✢ 4:A1.*

NIGHTLIFE AND THE ARTS

Updated by Fred Bouchard

Boston's cultural attractions are a mix between Old World aesthetics and New World experimentation. At the classical end of the spectrum, revered institutions like the Museum of Fine Arts, the Boston Symphony Orchestra and Boston Pops, and the Isabella Stewart Gardner Museum offer refined experiences. For a less reverential attitude toward the arts, the Institute of Contemporary Art (ICA) features edgy concerts and exhibitions by multimedia and graffiti artists. Many museums, like the MFA, the Gardner Museum, and the ICA also put on unique shows, festivals, and performances in their spaces.

For live shows, head to the compact Theater District to see traveling Broadway revues, national comedy, opera companies, rock bands, and previews of new plays soon headed to New York. Enjoy cocktails at Bina Osteria or the Ritz's Avery Bar, where performers at the nearby Paramount Theater like to unwind after their shows. Or share a quiet chat about the play at Troquet's cozy wine bar.

For a more casual, less costly night out, Boston provides plenty of alternatives. Indie rock and jazz clubs abound, dance clubs and lounges cater to all types of night owls, and bars in every neighborhood blare plasma-screen games—good luck, though, during high season trying to catch games that don't involve the Red Sox, Celtics, Bruins, or Patriots. Scan the crowd over a late-night bite at Miel in the waterfront Inter-Continental Hotel or at the House of Blues on Lansdowne Street for both local and visiting celebrities. Whether it's cheering on the Bruins, Revolution (soccer), Sox, Celtics, or Pats at a watering hole, rocking out at an underground club, or chilling out at an elegant lounge, Boston has cultural amusements for all moods.

NIGHTLIFE PLANNER

COVERS

Cover charges for local acts and club bands generally run $8–$20; big-name acts can be double that. Dance clubs usually charge a cover of $8–$20. Nearly all nightlife spots accept major credit cards; cash-only places are noted.

LAST CALL

Because Boston retains vestiges of its puritanical blue laws, the only places open after the official 2 am closing time for bars and clubs are a few restaurants in Chinatown (at some you can ask for "cold tea" and still get a beer) and a few all-night diners, which won't serve alcohol. Bars may also close up shop early if business is slow or the weather is bad. Blue laws also prohibit bars from offering happy-hour drink specials, although happy-hour food specials abound.

SMOKING

Smoking is banned inside all bars and restaurants.

GETTING INFORMED

The best source of arts and nightlife information is the *Boston Globe*'s "Arts & Entertainment" section (🌐 *www.boston.com/thingstodo*). Also worth checking out are the Thursday "Calendar" section of the *Boston Globe;* the Friday "Scene" section of the *Boston Herald;* and the calendar listings in the many free magazines in drop boxes around town, especially *DigBoston* (🌐 *www.digboston.com*), *Stuff@ Night,* and the *Improper Bostonian*. The *Globe*, *Dig,* and specialized sites as diverse as the thoroughly classical *BostonMusical Intelligencer (🌐 www.classicalscene.org)* and the scruffy indie-rock broadside, the *Boston Hassle*, *(🌐 www.bostonhassle.com)* provide up-to-the-minute information online.

GETTING TICKETS

Boston's supporters of the arts are an avid group; tickets often sell out well in advance. Buy tickets when you make your hotel reservations.

BosTix. This Ticketmaster outlet has two locations that sell half-price tickets for same-day performances and for select advance shows online. Full-price tickets for local attractions like the Boston Duck Tour, Freedom Trail Walking Tours, and New England Aquarium are available. On Friday, Saturday, or Sunday, show up at least a half hour before the booth opens. Booths are in Faneuil Hall and Copley Square. 🌐 *www.bostix.org* ⏲ *Tues.–Sat. 10–6, Sun. 11–4 (both locations).*

Broadway Across America—Boston. This organization brings Broadway shows to Boston in pre- and post-Broadway runs, but by subscription only. Call between 9 am and 5 pm on weekdays. ☎ *866/523–7469* 🌐 *www.broadwayacrossamerica.com.*

Live Nation. This Ticketmaster outlet handles tickets for shows at major Boston venues such as House of Blues, Bank of America Pavilion, Orpheum Theatre, and Paradise Rock Club. Transactions are conducted online. 🌐 *www.livenation.com.*

Ticketmaster. The ticket juggernaut has outlets in local stores (check online for locations), or you can order by phone, but note that Ticketmaster phone charges allow neither refunds nor exchanges. ☎ *800/653–8000 existing orders, 800/745–3000 new orders* 🌐 *www.ticketmaster.com.*

NIGHTLIFE

Boston is a Cinderella city, aglow with delights that for some end all too soon. With the T (subway and bus) making its final runs between midnight and 1 am and taxis sometimes scarce, most nightspots follow accordingly, with "last call" typically by 2 am. Though night owls may be disappointed by the meager late-night options, except in Chinatown, visitors find plenty of possibilities for stepping out on the early side. The martini set may stroll Newbury and Boylston streets in the Back Bay or Downtown, selecting from swank restaurants, lounges, and clubs. Coffee and tea drinkers can find numerous cafés in Cambridge and Somerville, particularly Harvard and Davis squares. Beer enthusiasts often have a viable option on nearly every corner, except in Belmont, where you may have trouble finding a pub to down a pint. For dancing, Lansdowne and Boylston streets near Fenway Park have a stretch of student-oriented hangs, sports bars, brewpubs, and techno clubs. The thriving "lounge" scene in Downtown's cooler hybrid bar-restaurant-clubs provides a mellower, more mature alternative to the student-focused indie clubs. Tourists crowd Faneuil Hall for its pubs, comedy club, and dance spots. The South and North ends, as well as Cambridge and Somerville, cater to the "dinner-and-drinks" set, while those seeking rock clubs should explore Allston, Jamaica Plain, and Cambridge, especially Central Square. College-owned concert halls host homegrown and visiting ensembles nightly. Prominent among these are Harvard University's Sanders Theater, New England Conservatory's Jordan Hall, Berklee's Performance Center, and Boston University's Tsai Performance Center.

BOSTON

BEACON HILL AND THE OLD WEST END

BARS

21st Amendment. Named after the amendment that ended Prohibition, this convivial pub, across from the State House, draws state legislators, lobbyists, and neighborhood regulars, who trade gossip and insider info on notched wooden tables over beer and barbecued chicken salad. Come Sunday night for lively team trivia—and discounted chicken wings. ✉ *150 Bowdoin St., Beacon Hill* ☎ *617/227–7100* 🌐 *www.21stboston.com* Ⓜ *Park St.*

Boston Beer Works. Located near the TD Garden, this BBW branch serves up the same wide array of house-crafted draft beers to Celtics and Bruins fans as its brother spot outside Fenway Park does to thirsty Red Sox fans. It sports six pool tables. ✉ *112 Canal St., Old West End* ☎ *617/896–2337* 🌐 *www.beerworks.net* Ⓜ *North Station.*

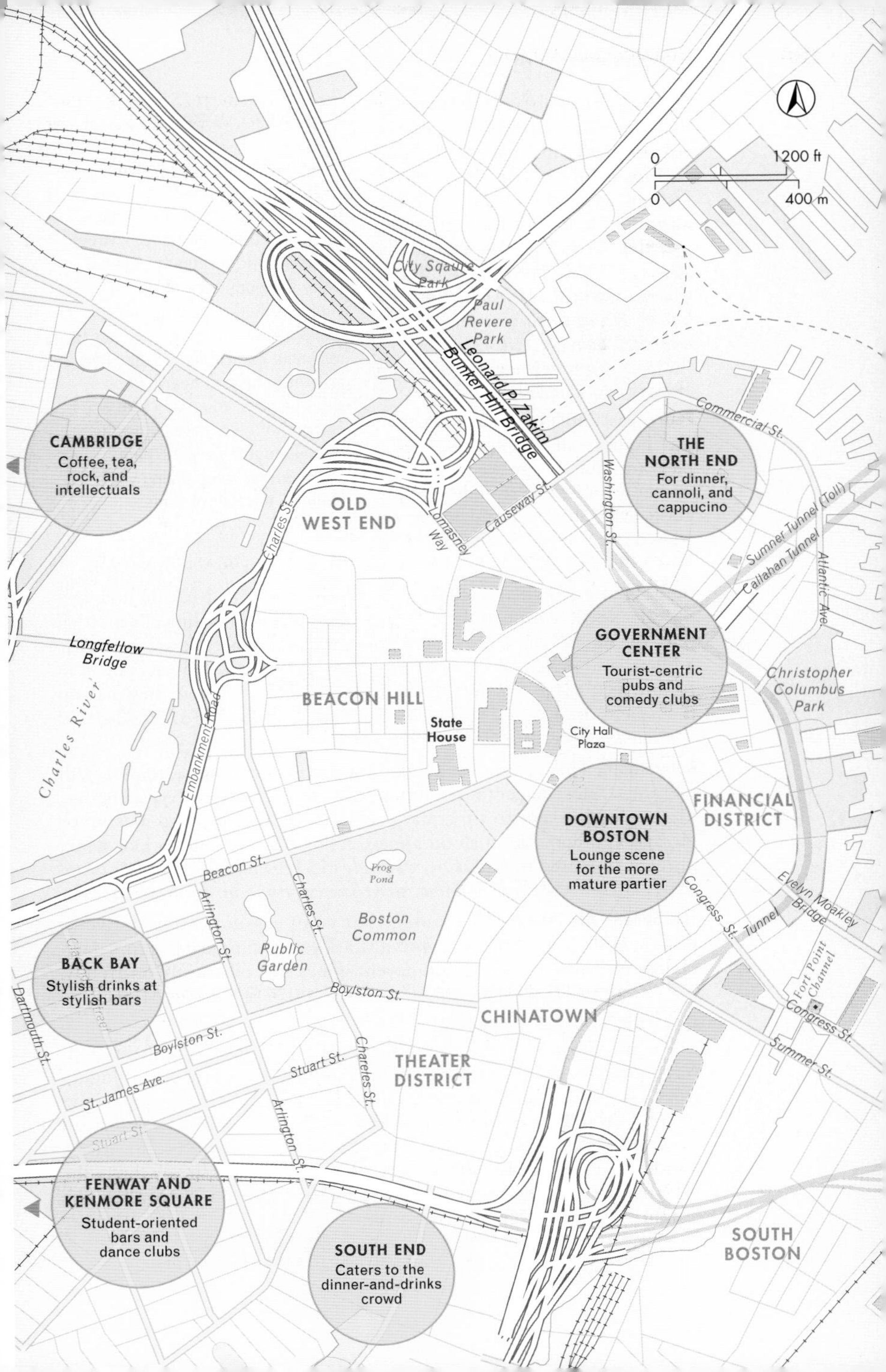

0
1200 ft
0
400 m
City Sqaure Park
Paul Revere Park
Leonard P. Zakim Bunker Hill Bridge
Commercial St.
CAMBRIDGE
Coffee, tea, rock, and intellectuals
THE NORTH END
For dinner, cannoli, and cappucino
OLD WEST END
Charles St.
Lomasney Way
Causeway St.
Washington St.
Sumner Tunnel (Toll)
Callahan Tunnel
Atlantic Ave.
Longfellow Bridge
GOVERNMENT CENTER
Tourist-centric pubs and comedy clubs
Christopher Columbus Park
BEACON HILL
State House
City Hall Plaza
Charles River
Embankment Road
FINANCIAL DISTRICT
DOWNTOWN BOSTON
Lounge scene for the more mature partier
Beacon St.
Frog Pond
Charles St.
Arlington St.
Boston Common
Congress St. Tunnel
Evelyn Moakley Bridge
Public Garden
BACK BAY
Stylish drinks at stylish bars
Dartmouth St.
Boylston St.
Fort Point Channel
CHINATOWN
Congress St.
Boylston St.
Summer St.
Stuart St.
Chareles St.
THEATER DISTRICT
St. James Ave.
Arlington St.
Stuart St.
FENWAY AND KENMORE SQUARE
Student-oriented bars and dance clubs
SOUTH END
Caters to the dinner-and-drinks crowd
SOUTH BOSTON

Cheers. This pub was dismantled in England, shipped to Boston, reassembled, and named the Bull & Finch Pub. It later became the inspiration for the TV show *Cheers*, although it doesn't look anything like the bar in the now-classic TV series. ■ **TIP→ There's a model of the Hollywood set in the upstairs bar.** ✉ *Hampshire House, 84 Beacon St., Beacon Hill* ☎ *617/227–9605* 🌐 *www.cheersboston.com* Ⓜ *Park St., Charles/MGH.*

THE REAL CHEERS

TV's *Cheers* may have ended in 1993, but diehard fans continue to pay their respects at the "original" Bull & Finch Pub on Beacon Street (or its second location in Faneuil Hall). The popularity of the TV show justified recreating the congenial hollow-cube wooden bar to resemble its fictional double, and an atmosphere of hearty good spirit persists. You may claim a certain notoriety here by devouring the double-decker "Giant Norm Burger" and adding your name to the Hall of Fame.

Fours. Just outside the TD Garden, the Four's, all for sports, has a pleasant vibe. It's packed with fans on game and concert nights. Enjoy good fish, chowder, and wings on weekdays. ✉ *166 Canal St., Old West End* ☎ *617/720–4455* 🌐 *www.thefours.com* Ⓜ *North Station.*

Harp. Find a crowded, rollicking atmosphere at this drinking hole just outside North Station and the TD Garden. Although technically an Irish pub, the Harp's three bars serve postgame and concert crowds, sports addicts, and ticketless fans wanting in on the action. Travelers drop in by day, as it's opposite the O'Neill Federal Building (where they pick up their passports). ✉ *85 Causeway St., Old West End* ☎ *617/742–1010* 🌐 *www.harpboston.com* Ⓜ *North Station.*

Ruby Room. This spot in the Onyx Hotel, true to its name, throbs with vibrant scarlet, magenta, shrimp, and vermilion. It's a sexy, seductive, and serpentine spot to sip crafty cocktails (try the ruby red martini or tarragon gimlet) and nosh on appetizers or red menu items like steak, burgers, or seared tuna. ✉ *Onyx Hotel, 155 Portland St., Old West End* ☎ *617/557–9950 hotel* 🌐 *www.rubyroomboston.com* Ⓜ *North Station.*

The Sevens Ale House. This vintage bar is an easygoing alternative to Beacon Hill's tony stuffiness, with its dark tones, simple bar setup, dartboard, well-poured pints, and decent wines. It's pleasantly un-trendy. ✉ *77 Charles St., Beacon Hill* ☎ *617/523–9074* Ⓜ *Charles/MGH.*

GOVERNMENT CENTER

The seat of Boston's city hall and financial center, the Center hosts concerts and circuses on its plaza, shelters popular food trucks serving up sidewalk gourmet, and overlooks those historic brick beehives of activity, Old State House and Faneuil Hall, and the haunting, transparent New England Holocaust Memorial. The Rose F. Kennedy Greenway, a mile-long parkland built over the depressed central artery, links the North End to Chinatown with gardens and trees, and parallels the hotel-rich stretch of the Harborwalk.

BARS

TOP SPORTS BARS

- **Bukowski Tavern,** Back Bay
- **Champions Sports Bar,** Back Bay
- **Fours,** Old West End
- **Harp,** Old West End
- **Fritz Lounge,** South End

Bell in Hand Tavern. The country's oldest continuously operating pub (founded 1795) is named for the occupation of its original owner, town crier Jimmy Wilson. On the edge of Faneuil Hall, this straightforward pub has live music every night of the week downstairs. If you're brave, sing forth at the Tuesday-night karaoke. There are DJs on Friday and Saturday upstairs. ✉ *45–55 Union St., Faneuil Hall* ☎ *617/227–2098* 🌐 *www.bellinhand.com* Ⓜ *Haymarket.*

Black Rose. Very much like a Dublin pub, the Black Rose is decorated with family crests, pictures of Ireland, and portraits of the likes of Samuel Beckett, Lady Gregory, and James Joyce. Its Faneuil Hall location draws as many tourists as locals, but nightly shows, beginning at 9:30, by traditional Irish and contemporary musicians, make it worth braving the crowds. ✉ *160 State St., Faneuil Hall* ☎ *617/742–2286* Ⓜ *Aquarium, State.*

Cheers. This outpost in Faneuil Hall was established in 2001 by popular demand. The owners of the former Bull & Finch in Beacon Hill, which was the inspiration for the show, created an exact reproduction of the TV set, complete with Sam's Red Sox jacket and the photo of the Native-American chief behind the bar. Despite overpriced burgers and seafood, tourists and students pour in. On summer weekends you may catch a solo guitarist. ✉ *Faneuil Hall Marketplace, Government Center* ☎ *617/227–0150* 🌐 *www.cheersboston.com* Ⓜ *Government Center, Haymarket.*

Durgin-Park. Steeped in history since 1828 and serving Yankee classic dishes for nearly as long, Durgin-Park still gets down on weekend evenings, with live cover or jazz bands in the basement Gaslight Pub. ✉ *340 N. Market St., Faneuil Hall* ☎ *617/227–2038* 🌐 *www.arkrestaurants.com/durgin_park.html* Ⓜ *Haymarket.*

Green Dragon Tavern. Less rowdy than its Faneuil Hall neighbors, this now-Irish bar claims to have housed the "Headquarters of the Revolution" and was the inn where silversmith Paul Revere overheard plans for a British assault on Lexington and Concord, prompting his famous ride. Today it's known more for quality Irish music— soloists play in the evenings from 5 to 9 Wednesday through Friday, and bands bring it on nightly beginning at 9. Regular lunch and seafood specials are served by a friendly waitstaff. ✉ *11 Marshall St., Faneuil Hall* ☎ *617/367–0055* 🌐 *www.somerspubs.com* Ⓜ *Haymarket, Government Center.*

Hennessy's. Arguably the best Irish pub in town, Hennessy's guarantees that your drink will be poured by a native Irish bartender (at least during the day) and that there will be a cozy coal fireplace in winter. Expect rowdy crowds for cover bands that play '70s, '80s, and '90s hits; Irish bands play on Saturday afternoons. ✉ *25 Union St., Faneuil*

Hall ☎ *617/742–2121* 🌐 *www.somerspubs.com* Ⓜ *Haymarket, Government Center.*

BOSTON'S BEST IRISH PUBS

- **Burren,** Somerville
- **Doyle's Cafe,** Jamaica Plain
- **Hennessy's,** Faneuil Hall
- **The Plough and the Stars,** Cambridge
- **Druid,** Cambridge

Hong Kong. A rowdy party destination since 1989, the Kong's packed with bachelorette parties, fraternity boys thirsty to share a potent Scorpion Bowl or dollar drinks, party animals hungry for $1 teriyaki skewers and $2 happy-hour apps, and revelers jumping for the dance floor. Often a first or last stop on a bar crawl, the Kong is big on gear and souvenirs, too. ✉ *65 Chatham St., Faneuil Hall* ☎ *617/227–2226* 🌐 *www.hongkongboston.com* Ⓜ *Aquarium, State, Government Center.*

Jose McIntyre's. Satisfy your double craving for a margarita and a Guinness—or Mexican pizza and fish-and-chips at, yup, an Irish-Mexican bar. The eclecticism continues with a dance floor (DJs weekends, jig or salsa?), big screens, and a pool. Caramba, begob! ✉ *160 Milk St., Faneuil Hall* ☎ *617/451–9460* 🌐 *www.josemcintyresboston.com* Ⓜ *Aquarium.*

MUSIC CLUBS

Hard Rock Cafe. This famed chain draws rock music and memorabilia fans to its large space with a double bar—decorated with hundreds of Zildjian cymbals—dance floor, bandstand, restaurant (wall art of signed photos, LPs, guitars, and gear), and private party room. When Cavern Club welcomes name or tribute bands (Doors, Aerosmith, and Pixies) occasionally on weekends, cover may range $10–$20. ✉ *22–24 Clinton St., Faneuil Hall* ☎ *617/424–7625* 🌐 *www.hardrock.com/boston* 🎫 *No cover for drinks/dinner; shows will vary* Ⓜ *Haymarket, Government Center.*

THE NORTH END

BARS

Battery Lounge. This comfy but dazzling waterfront bar in Fairmont Battery Wharf hotel offers two-story glass views of Boston's harbor accompanied by live jazz, 9 pm to midnight Fridays and Saturdays. ✉ *3 Battery Wharf, North End* ☎ *617/994–9000* 🌐 *www.fairmont.com/battery-wharf-boston* Ⓜ *Haymarket.*

Living Room. On the edge of the North End, this upscale bar and lounge is modeled after its name—feel free to stretch out on the lounge's many elegant loveseats and armchairs, or pull up a seat at the bar. Try killer martinis, cocktails, or one of 30 beers, half of them local. On weeknights it's quieter, as friends enjoy tasty half-priced appetizers from 4 to 6, meet for drinks, and watch a game; on weekends, expect a packed house dining until 1 am and DJ dancing until 2. ✉ *101 Atlantic Ave., Waterfront* ☎ *617/723–5101* 🌐 *www.thelivingroomboston.com* Ⓜ *Haymarket, Aquarium.*

CAFÉS AND COFFEEHOUSES

Boston Common Coffee Company. This North End independent outlet of the Boston Common Coffee Company is a café that's more Starbucks than Italian. As if its comfy couches, winter woodstove, free Wi-Fi, and light soups and sandwiches didn't set it apart, it's one of the few cafés in Little Italy that serves a non-espresso "cuppa joe." Also visit BoCoCoCo branches in the Financial District and Downtown Crossing. ✉ *97 Salem St., North End* ☎ *617/725–0040* 🌐 *www.bostoncommoncoffee.com* Ⓜ *Haymarket.*

Fodor's Choice ★ **Caffe Vittoria.** The glorious matriarch of North End cafés, glistening with marble-topped tables, mirrors, and shiny machines lets you glimpse *la dolce vita* on Hanover Street as baristas pump steaming espresso machines from 7 am until midnight. Skip the frenzy at Mike's Pastry next door; relax as you sip a caffe latte or grappa and nibble authentic gelati and pastries like tiramisu, sfogliatelle, and cannoli. It's cash only. ✉ *290–296 Hanover St., North End* ☎ *617/227–7606* 🌐 *www.vittoriacaffe.com* Ⓜ *Haymarket.*

CHARLESTOWN

The historic waterfront along the harbor and Mystic River affords Charlestown sweeping views of the USS *Constitution,* the Navy Yard and Admiralty, and Boston itself, to which Charlestown is linked, by bike paths and Prison Point and Zakim bridges. Bunker Hill's needle monument presides over a quiet, elegant neighborhood, while Main Street and City Square attract visitors to restaurants and taverns.

BARS

Warren Tavern. Massachusetts' oldest watering hole, rebuilt in 1780, was frequented by Paul Revere; even George Washington had a few drinks here. Today its main clientele are tourists and Charlestown professionals. It's an easy stop for a pint en route to the Bunker Hill Monument or historic Navy Yard. Try the house-made potato chips with your ale of choice. There are singers on Wednesdays and Thursdays beginning around 9 pm. ✉ *2 Pleasant St., Charlestown* ☎ *617/241–8142* 🌐 *www.warrentavern.com* Ⓜ *Community College.*

DOWNTOWN AND SOUTH BOSTON

Boston's historic heart beats at the conjunction of Boston Common and the Public Garden: here shoppers and strollers cross paths with students and workers along Tremont and Boylston streets, with Chinatown and the Theater District tucked in between. The Greenway opens up the city center and the bourgeoning Seaport beyond the Fort Point Channel to great benefit and beauty, with gateway boulevards connecting to North Station, South Bay, Long Wharf, and South Station.

BARS

Alley. Several watering holes, packed into one cozy cul-de-sac opposite Boston Common, serve Emerson students, theatergoers, and those wanting late-night action without crisscrossing the city. ✉ *Boylston Pl. off Boylston St., Theater District* Ⓜ *Boylston.*

Sweetwater Tavern. This amiable homebase for Emerson College and New England School of Law students, and late-night denizens of The Alley, offers $5 pints, decent bar food, booming DJs, and live music on weekends. Play trivia, hear comedy, and warble karaoke. During fall, watch college and pro games on big screens. It's open from 11:30 am daily. ✉ *3 Boylston Pl., Downtown/Theater District* ☎ *617/351–2515* 🌐 *www.sweetwatercafeboston.com*

MOST HISTORIC PUBS

- **Bell in Hand Tavern**, Faneuil Hall
- **Doyle's Cafe**, Jamaica Plain
- **Green Dragon Tavern**, Faneuil Hall
- **Last Hurrah**, Downtown
- **Warren Tavern**, Charlestown

Beantown Pub. Right on the Freedom Trail, this is the only pub in Boston where you can enjoy a Sam Adams lager while pondering the grave of that Founding Father himself. It's a fine place to watch multiple sports events, shoot pool, or take snapshots of passing throngs of tourists, students—or yourselves. The standard pub menu, available until 1 am, includes burgers, soups, salads, mains, and sandwiches, many named after local heroes and patriots buried in the Granary Burying Ground (founded 1660) across the street—Mother Goose, Paul Revere, John Hancock, and yes, Mr. Adams (Cajun chicken with Vermont cheddar). ✉ *100 Tremont St., Downtown* ☎ *617/426–0111* 🌐 *www.beantownpub.com* Ⓜ *Park St., Downtown Crossing.*

Bond Restaurant and Lounge. One of the hottest bars in the city, the stylish Bond belies its location in the conservative, tony Langham Boston Hotel with its glittery playground of models and entourages sipping top-shelf cocktails. Private parties revel in the Dom Pérignon Lounge. DJs, from a commanding stone aerie, thump out Top 40 and Euro beats on Friday nights beginning at 10; on Tuesday nights there's a fashion show. Observe the dress code: "dress to impress." ✉ *250 Franklin St., Downtown* ☎ *617/956–8765* 🌐 *www.bondboston.com* Ⓜ *State.*

Drink. Perhaps the most exciting cocktail lounge to open in recent years, Drink is housed in a brick warehouse in the Fort Point Channel area. There's no cocktail menu, so patrons are expected to rely on the knowledgeable bartenders who concoct libations on the spot according to drinkers' preferences. The space has an underground, modern speakeasy feel. Chat with bar manager John Gertsen, a local mixology pioneer, and ask him to make you a "Fort Point." ✉ *348 Congress St., Fort Point, South Boston* ☎ *617/695–1806* 🌐 *drinkfortpoint.com* Ⓜ *South Station.*

Felt. Dress to impress; once past the velvet ropes, you will encounter four floors full of dressed-up, made-up clubgoers, and you may even spot a celebrity at a pool table, on the dance floor, or just enjoying a cocktail. ✉ *533 Washington St., Downtown* ☎ *617/350–5555* Ⓜ *Chinatown, Downtown Crossing, Boylston, Park.*

Franklin Café. Like its sister South End gastropub, Franklin is known equally for its great drinks and its upscale pub food, like the killer roast chicken. Serving dinner until 1:30 am and drinks until 2 am daily, the restaurant's a welcome addition to the quickly gentrifying neighborhood. ✉ *152 Dorchester Ave., South Boston* ☎ *617/269–1003* 🌐 *www.franklincafe.com* Ⓜ *Broadway.*

Good Life. This creative bar mixes exotic martinis and fresh-juice cocktails, and boasts a whopping selection of international vodkas. The menu is broad and healthy. Subterranean Afterlife Lounge draws eclectic crowds for theme nights, with music by the occasional live band and a rotating cast of local DJs spinning for "twerkers" and other dancers. ✉ *28 Kingston St., Downtown* ☎ *617/451–2622* 🌐 *www.goodlifebar.com* Ⓜ *Downtown Crossing.*

Howl at the Moon. Dueling pianos and singers lure in bachelorettes and friends to this *haht pahtee* that's open until 2 am, and they fill requests on the spot for Lady Gaga, Top 40, Elvis, Monkees, Bob Dylan—you name it. ✉ *184 High St., Financial District* ☎ *617/292–4695* 🌐 *www.howlatthemoon.com* Ⓜ *Government Center, South Station.*

J.J. Foley's Bar & Grill. This family-owned, century-old, no-frills Irish pub mixes blue-collar workers with suits from the neighboring Financial District and Downtown Crossing shoppers taking a cider or ale time-out. ✉ *21 Kingston St., Downtown* ☎ *617/695–2529* 🌐 *www.jjfoleysbarandgrill.com* Ⓜ *Downtown Crossing*

Kitty O'Shea's. The bar and fireplace here, as well as the stained-glass windows (and even some of the staffers) were imported from the Emerald Isle, to claim verisimilitude to traditional Irish establishments. On Fridays, a guitarist plays in the early evening. ✉ *131 State St., Downtown* ☎ *617/725–0100* 🌐 *www.kittyosheas.com* Ⓜ *Aquarium, State.*

Last Hurrah. The mahogany club chairs and silver-tray service might make you feel like a Boston Brahmin, even if only for a martini or two. The historic setting and location inside the Omni Parker House right on the Freedom Trail make it an easy stop en route to King's Chapel or Ben Franklin's statue. ✉ *60 School St., Downtown* ☎ *617/227–8600 hotel* Ⓜ *Downtown Crossing, Park.*

Limelight Stage + Studios. Sing privately or go big time: bold karaoke patrons belt out their favorite tunes to the audience, while shy types can rent a "studio" room and croon with friends at this dedicated singers' bar. Linger in the main room and you might catch a local celeb—*American Idol* contestant Ayla Brown, Mayor Menino, and other memorable voices have graced this stage. Expect theatrics, hamming, and a lively crowd. ✉ *204 Tremont St., Downtown/Theater District* ☎ *617/423–0785, 877/557–8271* 🌐 *www.limelightboston.com* 🎫 *Main stage: $5 before 10 pm, $10 after 10 pm; private studios: $10 per person per hr* Ⓜ *Bolston, Park St.*

Lucky's Lounge. This is a subterranean dive with gritty charisma. Live cover bands play at one of its two bars Thursdays and Fridays, and crooners (think Frank Sinatra types) play on the weekends, including for Sunday brunch, to a yuppie-meets-artsy crowd. The hip Rat Pack vibe, large martinis, and fine salads, pizzas, and meatloaf keep lines trailing out the door. The story goes: when its signboard wasn't ready for the 2001 opening, the owners shrugged, "Ah, so what?" and let the place stay nondescript. It's been packed ever since. ✉ *355 Congress St., Fort Point, South Boston* ☎ *617/357–5825* 🌐 *luckyslounge.com* Ⓜ *South Station.*

Ocean Club at Marina Bay. New England's largest summer outdoor dance club spreads over a 62,000-square-foot waterfront property that hosts 1,600 dancers and top-flight international DJs. Advance tickets are required. ✉ *333 Victory Rd., Quincy* ☎ *617/689–0600* 🌐 *oceanclubatmarinabay.com* Ⓜ *North Quincy.*

RumBa. In the InterContinental hotel, RumBa highlights two disparate spirits: rum (more than 70 varieties) and champagne (more than two-dozen types). Slip into the hidden champagne lounge area behind sliding mahogany doors for quieter, secluded celebrations—you must book in advance. Summertime events include Tiki Tuesdays and waterfront DJs. ✉ *510 Atlantic Ave., Downtown* ☎ *617/747–1000* 🌐 *www.intercontinentalboston.com/dining/rumba.aspx* Ⓜ *South Station, Aquarium.*

COMEDY CLUBS

Comedy Connection. This pretty white-and-gold spot, now more than 100 years old, has been the home of Comedy Connection since 2008; it hosts musical acts like Graham Nash and The Dan Band, and comedians like Katt Williams, Aziz Ansari, and Anthony Jeselnik. ✉ *246 Tremont St., in Wilbur Theatre, Theater District* ☎ *617/931–2000* 🌐 *thewilbur.com* Ⓜ *Boylston.*

Dick's Doherty's Comedy Den. Dick Doherty's Comedy Den, tucked away under Howl at the Moon and sharing space with the bar Ultra Down, is the flagship of comic Dick Doherty's comedy-club chain. Shows include stand-up acts, audience-participation improv, hypnotists, and open-mike nights Thursday through Sundays; cover charge is between $15 and $20. ✉ *184 High St., Downtown* ☎ *800/401–2221* 🌐 *dickdoherty.com* Ⓜ *Boylston.*

DANCE CLUBS

Gypsy Bar. With its rich red velvet and crystal chandeliers, Gypsy Bar calls to mind the decadence of a dark European castle. Rows of video screens broadcast the Fashion Network, adding a sexier, more modern touch. Thirtysomething revelers and European students snack on lime-and-ginger-marinated tiger shrimp and sip "See You in Church" martinis (vodka with fresh marmalade) while the trendy dance floor throbs to Top 40 and house music. ✉ *116 Boylston St., Theater District* ☎ *617/482–7799* 🌐 *www.gypsybarboston.com* Ⓜ *Boylston.*

Rumor. This is the place to dance, dance, dance. DJs spin all types of music: house on Tuesday, hip-hop and house on Friday, and house, hip-hop, Latin, and Latin house on weekends. Cover is $10–25. ✉ *100 Warrenton St., Theater District* ☎ *617/422–0045* 🌐 *rumorboston.com* 🎟 *Varies ($10 minimum)* Ⓜ *NE Medical Center.*

Umbria. This five-story Euro-chic townhouse attracts a mature, upscale crowd for its many delights. Above two formal dining rooms—Umbria serving Umbrian specialties and Prime, a steak house and oyster bar—the top three floors host a stylish weekends-only mega-club, with an "ultra-lounge" featuring a vodka bar, table service, and big-name DJs spinning EDM, R&B, techno, and international pop. ✉ *295 Franklin St., Downtown* ☎ *617/338–1000* 🌐 *www.umbriaristorante.com* Ⓜ *South Station.*

CLOSE UP

Blue-Law Blues

Why do Boston bars close so early? Something of the old Puritan ethic of the Massachusetts Bay Colony lingers in the so-called "blue laws" that prohibit sales of alcoholic drinks at bars and restaurants after 1 am on weekdays and 2 am on weekends. The state remains of two minds when it comes to social leniency. The first state to legalize gay marriage was also one of the last to allow liquor sales on Sunday. (Both became legal in 2004.)

Historians surmise that the name "blue laws" goes back to colonial times, when special laws were actually written on blue paper. In 17th-century Boston it was forbidden to walk on the street on Sunday, or to sing, dance, or use a musical instrument at night. Most of these laws have been repealed (though it's still technically illegal to sit on the grass on Boston Common without a proclamation from the mayor). But periodic attempts to push back closing time still meet with heavy opposition from conservative neighborhood groups.

Late-night revelers party on in other ways. Asking for "cold tea" at certain Chinatown restaurants might get you a beer, and at certain Irish bars around town the lights are off, but somebody's home. A modern trend has been to form "private clubs" such as Rise, on Stuart Street, where members pay yearly fees for the privilege of partying (although not drinking) all night. Thankfully, it's no longer illegal to dance until dawn.

Venu. International jet-setters, weekend warriors, and clubby wannabes converge on this outpost evoking Miami's South Beach. It may not be 80 degrees, yet a warm energy sets Venu apart from other dark, techno-industrial clubs. The diverse clientele mixes stylish students with Downtown suits cutting loose. Weekends DJs spin house, Latin, Top 40, and Euro-pop for high-strutters and their entourages. ✉ *100 Warrenton St., Theater District* ☎ *617/338–8061* 🌐 *venuboston.com* Ⓜ *Boylston, Arlington.*

GAY AND LESBIAN

Estate. In the Alley entertainment complex, the Estate offers guest DJs spinning house and dance for amped-up patrons, occasional live acts, belly dancers, and blinks at celebrities. Suite Boston, the in-house "subterranean den," hosts special events such as fashion shows and parties with guest DJs. ✉ *1 Boylston Pl., Downtown/Theater District* ☎ *617/351–7000* 🌐 *www.theestateboston.com* 🎟 *$15–$25.*

Jacque's Cabaret. There's nothing traditional about Jacque's Cabaret, an institution for more than 60 years. Nightly drag-queen shows draw mostly bachelorette parties to gawk while swilling cocktails from paper cups. Downstairs, Jacque's Underground features indie-rock bands on Friday and Saturday, while cabaret acts perform upstairs every night except Tuesday. Because of a long-running licensing dispute, the whole carnival shuts down nightly at midnight. ✉ *79 Broadway, Theater District* ☎ *617/426–8902* 🌐 *www.jacques-cabaret.com* 💳 *No credit cards* Ⓜ *Arlington.*

BACK BAY

Though the name says it, it's hard to believe that this broad street grid running from Boston Public Garden up elegant Beacon Street and Commonwealth Avenue, divided by a statue-filled garden, was until 1830s landfilled dockland. Dominated by the John Hancock Tower and the Prudential, Back Bay is studded with beautiful churches around Copley Square and lively Newbury Street.

SWINGING SINGLES SCENES

- **Felt,** Downtown
- **Rumor,** Theater District
- **Harp,** Old West End
- **Hong Kong,** Faneuil Hall
- **Museum of Fine Arts** (first Friday), The Fenway

BARS

Bukowski Tavern. This narrow barroom has a literary flair and more than 100 brews for your sipping pleasure. A cash-only policy may dissuade travelers, but locals love this funky joint with its slapdash murals, wailing soundtrack, and wall full of personal beer mugs. "Mad dogs" and burgers are cheap (dare you to try the peanut-butter burger!) and the craft drafts and bottles are handpicked. This pub is now cloned in Cambridge at 1281 Cambridge Street. ✉ *50 Dalton St., Back Bay* ☎ *617/437–9999* 🌐 *www.bukowskitavern.net* ▭ *No credit cards* Ⓜ *Hynes.*

Cactus Club. One of the few places in Boston that make a decent margarita, the Cactus Club has a popular outdoor patio for kicking back, sipping frozen drinks, munching tacos, and watching the stylish Back Bay crowds pass by. ✉ *939 Boylston St., Back Bay* ☎ *617/236–0200* 🌐 *www.bestmargaritas.com* Ⓜ *Hynes.*

Champions Sports Bar. This bar calls all sports fans (rabid, yet civilized) with 40 TV screens—including a 12' x 24' whopper where you surely won't miss a play. Visiting-team fans are welcome but may expect to be drowned out by cheers for home teams. Champions is not just about sports and beer (36 taps and scores of bottles): there's a smooth waitstaff, a wine and cocktail list, and linen service. ✉ *Boston Marriott Copley Pl., Copley Pl. Mall, 2nd level, 110 Huntington Ave., Back Bay* ☎ *617/927–5304* 🌐 *www.championsboston.com* Ⓜ *Prudential Center.*

Oak Long Bar & Kitchen. This flagship bar in the 1912 Fairmont Copley Plaza hotel had a centennial stem-to-stern makeover that reconstituted the oak paneling, opened up catbird views over Copley Square, and added sky-high coffered ceilings and a flashy pizza oven. Outdoor seating opens on the Boston Public Library. As you people-watch, peruse a generous menu of signature martinis, single malts, shareable platters, and desserts. ✉ *Fairmont Copley Plaza, 138 St. James Ave., Back Bay* ☎ *617/267–5300* 🌐 *www.fairmont.com/copleyplaza* Ⓜ *Copley.*

Rattlesnake Bar and Grill. Half a block off the Public Garden, this lively bar-resto has *two* patios. In season, both street-side tables and an insiders' rooftop urban canyon lure in Back Bay shoppers and the after-work crowd with friendly service and handcrafted drinks. Brian Poe oversees the Rattlesnake's neo-Tex-Mex cuisine—signature tacos, enchiladas, and wild-boar burritos. ✉ *384 Boylston St., Back Bay* ☎ *617/859–7772* 🌐 *www.rattlesnakebar.com* Ⓜ *Arlington.*

MAKE IT A DATE

- **Bristol Lounge** (for dessert), Back Bay
- **Oak Long Bar & Kitchen**, Back Bay
- **Sonsie**, Back Bay
- **Top of the Hub**, Back Bay

Fodor's Choice ★ **Sonsie.** The crowd spilling through French doors onto the sidewalk café in warm weather consists of trendy cosmopolitans, fun-loving professionals, local sports celebs, and scenesters. Founding owner-chef Bill Poirier's offerings of contemporary Americana have been a Back Bay standout for 20 years. Wine Room, a sleek soft-lit cellar, is a must for oenophiles. The sophisticated jazz-rock soundtrack remains at a civilized volume as you dine, sip, and people-watch. Hungry? There's a weekday lunch, weekend brunch, and daily dinner and late-night menu until 12:30 am. ✉ *327 Newbury St., Back Bay* ☎ *617/351–2500* 🌐 *sonsieboston.com* Ⓜ *Hynes.*

Fodor's Choice ★ **Top of the Hub.** At 52 floors up, this in-the-clouds lounge has incomparable views embracing Boston Harbor, Back Bay, Logan Airport, and the far suburbs. Hip jazz combos swing for starry-eyed dancers, and cheerful servers pour from an extensive drinks (and good wine) list. Bands play nightly from 9 to 1, and during Sunday brunch. There's no cover at the bar, but there's a $24 per person minimum at tables after 8 pm. ✉ *Prudential Tower, 800 Boylston St., 52nd fl., Back Bay* ☎ *617/536–1775* 🌐 *topofthehub.net* Ⓜ *Prudential Center, Hynes.*

CAFÉS AND COFFEEHOUSES

Trident Booksellers & Café. Browse an eccentric collection of books and magazines at this crowded, pleasant café, then have coffee or tea while you read. This is a nice spot for a light meal with a date, solo journal writing or reading, or surfing the Internet with free Wi-Fi. The windows facing Newbury Street (not to mention the patio) are great for people-watching. It's open daily from 8 am until midnight. ✉ *338 Newbury St., Back Bay* ☎ *617/267–8688* 🌐 *www.tridentbookscafe.com* Ⓜ *Hynes.*

MUSIC CLUBS

Red Room @ Cafe 939. By day a Berklee College coffee and snack bar, the Cafe by night opens its tidy, scarlet 150-seat concert space. Run and booked by students, it's an ideal venue for aspiring student bands and indies on the rise. Minimal refreshments are served (no alcohol) in this dedicated concert space, but it shares a foyer with Cactus Club. Cover charges range from zero to $12. ✉ *939 Boylston St., Back Bay* ☎ *617/747–2261* 🌐 *www.cafe939.com* Ⓜ *Hynes.*

THE SOUTH END

Sedate tree-lined streets of newly repointed-brick town houses cast demure impressions, but the South End is a truly "hoppin' hood" with cafés, restaurants, theaters, parks, and recreational enclaves. A stroll along long, narrow Southwest Corridor Park (reclaimed as the Orange Line was built) links walkers from Copley Square (Back Bay Station) to Forest Hills Station, 5 miles away. Along winding lanes of flowering crab trees and community and butterfly gardens, an array of moms with strollers, bikers, dogwalkers, and skateboarders pass tennis courts, summer lawn concerts at Titus Sparrow Park, and kids playing basketball.

BARS

Clerys. Open-windowed, multiroomed Clerys can be your neighborhood bar, Irish pub, dance hall, sports hub, trivia source (Tuesdays), or painting studio (Wednesdays). Expect long lines on weekend nights in this high-traffic club; its several rooms bustle with young professionals and tourists. ✉ *113 Dartmouth St., Back Bay/South End* ☎ *617/262–9874* 🌐 *www.clerysboston.com* Ⓜ *Copley.*

Club Café. This smart multiroom club-cum-restaurant for Boston gays, lesbians, and their straight friends has become livelier than ever going into its 30th year. Behind stylish restaurant 209, the "video lounge" is a relaxed place to dance or watch classic music videos, cult movies, and TV shows. There are trivia, karaoke, Lady Love, and Edge Boston events weekly; Napoleon Cabaret hosts singers nightly. There's never a cover charge, but there are often long lines. ✉ *209 Columbus Ave., South End* ☎ *617/536–0966* 🌐 *www.clubcafe.com* Ⓜ *Back Bay/South End.*

Darryl's Corner Bar & Kitchen. This is a long-time neighborhood soul food and jazz hangout but it looks spiffy, not old. Starters are half price until 6:30 pm. It's reggae night on Tuesdays, and glorified chicken and waffles on Wednesdays. Cover is $3 for live bands and theatergoers receive dining discounts. ✉ *604 Columbus Ave., South End* ☎ *617/536–1100* 🌐 *www.darrylscornerbarboston.com* Ⓜ *Mass Ave.*

Delux Café & Lounge. This unpretentious, cozy bar on a quiet corner attracts old-timers and young professionals with modest drinks and affordable comfort food. The quesadillas are worth the wait for a table. Yellowing posters, dim lights, a '60s soundtrack, and a perennial bartop Christmas tree add to the quirky, retro vibe. Wine list? One red, one white. Entertainment? Talk to the bartender or your friends. It's cash only. ✉ *100 Chandler St., South End* ☎ *617/338–5258* ▭ *No credit cards* Ⓜ *Back Bay/South End.*

Franklin Café. This neighborhood institution is known for great martinis, microbrews on tap, and upscale pub food. There's no placard bearing its name; just look for the martini sign (or the crowd waiting for a dinner table) to know you're there. Note that this is a bar for drinking and socializing, but there's no entertainment here. ✉ *278 Shawmut Ave., South End* ☎ *617/350–0010* 🌐 *www.franklincafe.com* Ⓜ *Back Bay/South End.*

GAY AND LESBIAN

Fritz Lounge. This gay sports bar is popular with the local after-work crowd and the sports teams that Fritz sponsors. Casually dressed gentlemen drop by for the large beer list and steak and eggs during the hopping weekend brunch. ✉ *26 Chandler St., South End* ☎ *617/482–4428* 🌐 *www.fritzboston.com* ▭ *No credit cards* Ⓜ *Back Bay/South End.*

MUSIC CLUBS

Beehive. A jazz-lover's dream deep in the South End, the 'Hive airs professional and up-and-coming acts; often faculty and student bands from Berklee College of Music fill the cavernous brick space with cool charts and lusty solos. Patrons enjoy cocktails and fascinating wines served by a cheerful staff, and dine on Mediterranean appetizer platters, daily special pastas, and comfort entrées. ✉ *541 Tremont St., Back Bay/South End* ☎ *617/423–0069* ⏲ *Closed Mon.* Ⓜ *Back Bay.*

Fodor's Choice ★ **Wally's Café.** A rare gem for jazz and blues fans, Wally's Café was founded in 1947 and is the oldest continuously operating family-owned jazz club in America. Patrons may get to see nostalgic stars like Branford Marsalis or Roy Hargrove dropping by, but the place is internationally renowned for its steady stream of heated performances by local bands and their myriad guests. Wally's diverse crowd attracts regulars from the South End and Roxbury, and music-hungry students, especially from Berklee College of Music. It's open every night of the year and there's no cover. On Mondays it's blues and on Thursdays it's Latin jazz. Daily jam sessions run nightly from 6 to 9: bring your horn! **TIP→ Arrive early if you need a seat. Better yet, forget sitting and blend with the crowd at the bar and stage.** ✉ *427 Massachusetts Ave., South End* ☎ *617/424–1408* 🌐 *www.wallyscafe.com* Ⓜ *Mass Ave., Symphony.*

THE FENWAY

Along the fens unclaimed by Back Bay, where Olmstead's Emerald Necklace winds along museum row, you'll find ball fields, the Kelleher Rose Garden, and extensive, lovingly maintained Victory Gardens in the shadow of Fenway Park and lively upper Boylston Street. Along "Avenue of the Arts" (aka Huntington Avenue) are Symphony Hall, New England Conservatory, Northeastern University, and Museum College of Art. In the middle are Berklee College of Music, Boston Conservatory, and the Massachusetts Historical Society.

BARS

Boston Beer Works. This is a "naked brewery," with all the works exposed—the tanks, pipes, and gleaming stainless-steel and copper kettles used in producing beer. Seasonal brews, in addition to 16 microbrews on tap, draw students, young adults, and tourists alike to the original location (its sibling by the TD Garden is popular, too). The atmosphere is too crowded and noisy for intimate chats, and good luck trying to get in when there's a home game. ✉ *61 Brookline Ave., The Fenway* ☎ *617/536–2337* 🌐 *www.beerworks.net* Ⓜ *Kenmore.*

House of Blues. Around the corner from Fenway Park and girded with bars and restaurants, the city's juggernaut among nightclubs books a wide array of bands into its barnlike music hall nightly. Tickets are $20–$40, with VIP box seats nearly double that. ✉ *15 Lansdowne St., Kenmore Square* ☎ *888/693–2583* 🌐 *www.houseofblues.com* Ⓜ *Kenmore.*

Ramrod & Machine. The granddaddy of Boston gay bars, Ramrod has spawned thriving godsons in Machine (upstairs) and Pool Room (downstairs). There are theme nights with DJs: punk, dance, Latin, Attic. It's open daily, noon to 2 am. ✉ *1254 Boylston St., The Fenway* ☎ *617/266–2986* 🌐 *www.ramrod-boston.com* Ⓜ *Fenway Park.*

BOWLING ALLEYS AND POOL HALLS

Jillian's Boston. Often called the city's best (and certainly biggest) playground for grown-ups, this multistory and multisensory complex dominates the clubby Fenway area with three floors, each with a focal activity and lively bar. Jillian's has 35 pool tables and 12 plasma screens; Lucky Strike Lanes has 16 bowling lanes and an 80-foot video wall blasting sports and music videos; Tequila Rain's dancers go "where it's Spring Break 52 weeks a year." Everything's on until 2 am. ✉ *145 Ipswich St., The Fenway* ☎ *617/437–0300* 🌐 *www.jilliansboston.com* Ⓜ *Kenmore.*

MUSIC CLUBS

Bill's Bar & Lounge. Music, both from DJs and live, plays Thursday through Saturday, including rock, alternative, funk, and punk; on Sunday nights Bill's hosts a reggae dance party. The club is usually mellower than most of its Lansdowne neighbors. Although it's open until 2 am, the live music usually ends by midnight. ✉ *5.5 Lansdowne St.The Fenway* ☎ *617/421–9678* Ⓜ *Kenmore.*

BOSTON OUTSKIRTS

ALLSTON

A haven for students and international culture, this area bristles with music clubs, beer saloons, and ethnic eateries. Union Square, a prime locale, has cheerful, informal restaurants serving foods from Brazil, Colombia, El Salvador, Thailand, Vietnam, Russia, as well as superior Tex-Mex and pizza.

BARS

Sunset Grill & Tap. In the heart of student heaven, the Sunset looks, at first glance, like any neighborhood hangout. But venture inside and you'll be bowled over by its good promise to host the "365-days-a-year beer festival" with a staggering 500 choices of beer, 112 of them on tap. Forget about pallid domestics; try something unpronounceable but appetizing from faraway places—seasonals, cask-conditioned, Belgians. If you're really thirsty, order a "yard"; if curious, order a flight sampler. There are ciders and meads, too. Brewing excellence is matched by fine eats, like steam burgers and curly fries, served until 1 am. ✉ *130 Brighton Ave., Allston* ☎ *617/254–1331* 🌐 *www.allstonsfinest.com* Ⓜ *Harvard.*

MUSIC CLUBS

Brighton Music Hall. This venue connected with Paradise offers nightly double and triple bills. ✉ *158 Brighton Ave., 02134, Allston* ☎ *617/779–0140* 🌐 *crossroadspresents.com/brighton-music-hall* Ⓜ *Harvard Ave.*

Great Scott. Crowds of cool Allston students and greater Boston music fans rock hard until closing at Great Scott, which books an impressive lineup of local and visiting indie rock bands (from 9 pm) and comedy acts (from 7 pm) in live double and triple bills on a varying rotation nearly every night. Check out Friday night's Brit-pop indie-dance night. ✉ *1222 Commonwealth Ave., Allston* ☎ *617/566–9014* 🌐 *www.greatscottboston.com* Ⓜ *Harvard Ave.*

Fodor's Choice ★ **Paradise Rock Club.** This iconic bandbox near Boston University is famed for bringing up big-name talent (think U2 and Dresden Dolls), hosting Coldplay, and nurturing local rock and hip-hop acts. Two tiers of booths provide good sight lines from all angles, even some intimate, out-of-the-way corners. Four bars quench the crowd's thirst, and food is available. Some shows are for 18-plus only. The newer Paradise Lounge next door is a more intimate space to catch local (often acoustic) songsters, literary readings, poetry slams, and other artsy events. Most tickets run $15–$30. ✉ *967–969 Commonwealth Ave., Allston* ☎ *617/562–8800* 🌐 *crossroadspresents.com/paradise-rock-club* Ⓜ *Pleasant St.*

Scullers Jazz Club. Since 1989, this intimate and amiable venue has presented the top names in jazz, Latin, and contemporary, as well as blues, soul, cabaret, and world music. Impresario Fred Taylor continues to welcome jazz greats to Boston, like Harry Connick Jr., Wynton Marsalis, Diana Krall, and Tony Bennett, with performances Wednesday through Saturday nights at 8 and 10; tickets are $20–$50 per show, discounted with dinner in Green Room. Buying tickets in advance is advised. ✉ *Doubletree Guest Suites hotel, 400 Soldiers Field Rd., Allston* ☎ *617/562–4111* 🌐 *www.scullersjazz.com* Ⓜ *BU West, Bus 47, or CT2.*

BARS

JAMAICA PLAIN

Great swaths of green—the Arboretum, Jamaica Pond, and Emerald Necklace stretching miles to the Fenway—set "J.P." apart from other streetcar suburbs. Centre Street runs the cultural gamut with Cuban, Mexican, Indian, Irish, and Dominican restaurants. Cafés and bars are wide open to gays and lesbians and everyone else.

BARS

Fodor's Choice ★ **Doyle's Cafe.** Truly an institution since 1892—and the first pub to put Sam Adams on tap—this friendly, crowded neighborhood Irish pub has become a Boston political landmark. Candidates for offices from Boston City Council to U.S. Senate drop by to eat corned beef and cabbage, sample from 30 tap brews or 60 single-malt scotches, and speechify and "press the flesh." There are non-Irish noshes, too: trout burgers and kale-linguica soup, among others. ✉ *3484 Washington St., Jamaica Plain* ☎ *617/524–2345* 🌐 *www.doylescafeboston.com* 💳 *No credit cards* Ⓜ *Green St., Forest Hills.*

GAY AND LESBIAN

Midway Café. This very popular Jamaica Plain café books a lively mix of nightly rock bands, DJs, and noise artists. There's punk, soul, R&B, and Thursdays a raucous lesbian (straights, too) dance party and "queeraoke." Cover varies nightly. ✉ *3496 Washington St., Jamaica Plain* ☎ *617/524–9038* 🌐 *www.midwaycafe.com* Ⓜ *Green St., Forest Hills.*

CAMBRIDGE

Town meets gown at Harvard Square, and glitz meets neo-tech MIT at booming Kendall Square. As "Mass Ave." (Massachusetts Avenue) bends beyond the Charles, it connects both campuses and Porter Square's ethnic restaurants and jolly scenesters. Inman Square's music spots, Brattle Street's patrician serenity, and the bustle of Cambridgeside's mall and hotel dining rooms enrich the fabric.

BEHIND THE MUSIC SCENE

Boston goes about nurturing young musicians across genres through a feverishly active network of lively small clubs, bars hosting indie and cover bands, college recital and concert halls, bigger mini-arenas, and in-season outdoor concerts. The list of Boston acts that went big time is long and impressive: rock legend Aerosmith and the Cars; punk gods Pixies and Mission of Burma; wildly successful boy bands New Kids on the Block and New Edition; disco diva Donna Summer; and classical cellist Yo Yo Ma. Beantown's youthful energy, bars, and clubs provide fertile ground for developing musical talent, so on your night out you could be catching a glimpse of the "next big thing" in an intimate setting at modest ticket prices.

The ever-dynamic Berklee College of Music deserves credit for drawing hardworking hopefuls to Boston. Among the school's 100 alumni who are Grammy winners are singer/songwriter John Mayer, producer Quincy Jones, and jazz musicians Teri Lyne Carrington, Branford Marsalis, Esperanza Spalding, and Joe Zawinul. The Beehive in the South End taps into the deep talent well by booking jazz shows downstairs in its club space. For intimate folk performances by up-and-comers, connoisseurs head to Harvard Square's Club Passim, where Joan Baez and Joni Mitchell played in their salad days when it was called Club 47. Around the corner, hot rockers hit the big, splashy Sinclair.

In Central Square, places to go are Middle East Restaurant & Nightclub, a favorite three-stage venue of the ska-core pioneers Mighty Mighty Bosstones; and T.T. The Bear's, a well-loved club hosting the infamous annual Rock 'n' Roll Rumble each April as well as sold-out battles of other local bands, signed and unsigned, all year round.

With no shortage of talent, supportive venues, and college students eager to either be or to hear the next great group, Boston's music scenes don't disappoint.

BARS

Alden & Harlow. This elegant subterranean haunt adjacent to Brattle Theater is a fascinating pre- or postmovie dining and hangout spot. ✉ *40 Brattle St., Cambridge* 🌐 *www.aldenharlow.com* Ⓜ *Harvard Square.*

Cambridge Brewing Company. This collegial, cavernous microbrewery has been the haunt of MIT techies since its 1989 founding. Order CBC's Cambridge Amber, Charles River Porter, and Tall Tale Pale Ale fresh in pints, or go for a "tower" (an 83-ounce glass "yard"). In warm weather, try to nab a coveted patio table, a catbird seat for people-watching across bricky Kendall Square. Cheerful staff serve above-average pub food into weekend "beerunches." ✉ *1 Kendall Sq., Bldg. 100, at Hampshire St. and Broadway, Cambridge* ☎ *617/494–1994* 🌐 *www.cambridgebrewing.com* Ⓜ *Kendall/MIT.*

Chez Henri. Enjoy a hip after-work scene at this Franco-Cuban restaurant equidistant from Harvard and Porter squares, home to one of the better Cubano sandwiches north of Miami, and mojitos *muy fuertes* to wash them down. ✉ *1 Shepard St., midway between Harvard and*

Porter Sqs., Harvard Sq., Cambridge ☏ *617/354–8980* 🌐 *chezhenri.com* Ⓜ *Harvard, Porter.*

Dante. The Royal Sonesta Hotel houses Dante, a restaurant whose sleek bar and lounge entice real and aspiring jet-setters with creative cocktails and an expertly created wine list (but no entertainment). Dante hosts parties, including barbecue get-togethers and clambakes that showcase creations by executive chef Dante de Magistris. In warmer months, head outside to the patio for glorious views of the Boston skyline and sailboats on the Charles River. ✉ *Royal Sonesta Hotel, 40 Edwin Land Blvd., Cambridge* ☏ *617/497–4200* 🌐 *www.restaurantdante.com* Ⓜ *Lechmere, Kendall Square.*

TOP LOUNGES

- **Bond Restaurant and Lounge,** Downtown
- **Good Life,** Downtown
- **Living Room,** Waterfront/North End
- **Lucky's Lounge,** South Boston
- **Ruby Room,** Old West End

Druid. You can feel as if you're in Dublin here, with well-poured pints, a dusky atmosphere, and black-and-white pudding on the menu. Located in vibrant Inman Square, Druid welcomes visitors and locals, a mix of Portuguese and Italian Americans, Harvard and MIT students, and young families. There are Irish acoustic music jams Tuesday evenings and Saturday afternoons. ✉ *1357 Cambridge St., Cambridge* ☏ *617/497–0965* 🌐 *www.druidpub.com* Ⓜ *Central, Harvard.*

Grendel's Den. This quintessential grad-student hangout is low-lit and brick-walled. During happy hour, tasty entrées like crab dip, burritos, nachos, and burgers are half priced with a $3-per-person drink (inside only; not on outdoor patio). ✉ *89 Winthrop St., Cambridge* ☏ *617/491–1160* 🌐 *www.grendelsden.com* Ⓜ *Harvard.*

John Harvard's Brew House. A convivial gathering place for the neighboring Ivy Leaguers, John Harvard's Brew House dispenses ales, lagers, pilsners, wheats, and stouts brewed on the premises, just like an English pub. The food is no-frills and hearty. Pizza dough is made with spent-grains from the brewing process. Trivia is on Mondays, and live acoustic and bluegrass music plays Tuesdays through Saturdays. There's no cover. ✉ *33 Dunster St., Cambridge* ☏ *617/868–3585* 🌐 *www.johnharvards.com* Ⓜ *Harvard.*

Middlesex Lounge. The minimalist design of a New York lounge combined with the laid-back friendliness of a neighborhood pub has crafted "Msex" into a cool cross-Charles scene. Rolling settees, movable in varied seating configurations for trivia, games, and nerd nights, are usually cleared by 9 pm, when, Thursday through Saturday, a $10 cover kicks in for DJs spinning crowd-pleasing electronic (EDM) and disco music. Feed on small plates and pressed sandwiches. ✉ *315 Massachusetts Ave., Cambridge* ☏ *617/868–6739* 🌐 *www.middlesexlounge.us* Ⓜ *Central.*

Noir. Cary Grant and Katharine Hepburn would feel at their ease in this nightspot in the Charles Hotel, with its sexy after-hours feel. Sink back into a voluptuous black-leather couch, sip a sultry drink, and cloak yourself in an air of mystery. Wear evening or casual attire. There's a small bites and snack menu. ✉ *Charles Hotel, 1 Bennett St., Cambridge* ☎ *617/661–8010* 🌐 *www.noir-bar.com* Ⓜ *Harvard.*

BEST FOR BEER CONNOISSEURS

- **Boston Beer Works**, The Fenway
- **Bukowski Tavern**, Back Bay
- **Cambridge Brewing Company**, Cambridge
- **The Publick House, Brookline**
- **Sunset Grill & Tap**, Allston

The Plough and the Stars. This genuine Irish pub has doubled as a bohemian oasis for 40 steady years. There's Guinness and Bass on tap, many Irish whiskeys, and light rock, Irish, or country music nearly nightly. Narrow and cozy, the Plough is a comfy, noisy place, a den for locals and students, but a fine place to have lunch alone. The cover charge varies. Fun fact: literary magazine *Ploughshares* was founded here. ✉ *912 Massachusetts Ave., Cambridge* ☎ *617/576–0032* 🌐 *www.ploughandstars.com* Ⓜ *Central, Harvard.*

River Gods. This award-winning bar themes its decor on pagan Celtic lore but emphasizes indie bands and DJs. Situated four blocks from Central Square, it's cluttered with often-changing decorations of namesake gods on every surface. It's also known for its well-priced Irish, American, and vegan food. The rotating roster of DJs includes regulars from WMBR-FM, MIT's wildly eclectic music station. The kitchen closes at 10 pm, but music and dancing go until midnight or 1. ✉ *125 River St., Cambridge* ☎ *617/576–1881* 🌐 *www.rivergodsonline.com* Ⓜ *Central.*

Temple Bar. The chef here emphasizes house-made everything (including condiments). After exploring Cambridge, it's a fine place to enjoy a signature barrel-aged cocktail or espresso martini. If you're hungry, be prepared to be impressed by the Kobe beef sliders. ✉ *1688 Massachusetts Ave., Cambridge* ☎ *617/547–5055* 🌐 *templebarcambridge.com* Ⓜ *Porter, Harvard.*

Toad. Bands, beers, and burgers sum up this amiable little club attached to Christopher's. The bar is maple; the toads are ceramic. Nightly music comes in many a stripe, and usually in double bills. There's never a cover charge. What's not to like? ✉ *1912 Massachusetts Ave., Cambridge* ☎ *617/497–4950 recording* 🌐 *www.toadcambridge.com* Ⓜ *Porter Square.*

West Side Lounge. Hip patrons haunt this low-key bar for its amiable ambience, delicious comfort food, comprehensive cocktail list, and effortless late-night lounging. Try a white-ginger cosmo or prickly pear margarita with creative tapas and wallet-friendly mains. There is no entertainment. ✉ *1680 Massachusetts Ave., Cambridge* ☎ *617/441–5566* 🌐 *www.westsidelounge.com* Ⓜ *Porter, Harvard.*

BOWLING ALLEYS AND POOL HALLS

Flat Top Johnny's. In a mixed commercial and high-tech business park in Kendall Square, Flat Top Johnny's wears its hipster cred on its sleeve. This genuine pool hall (12 tables, no charge) airs alternative rock and

DID YOU KNOW?

Samuel Adams Beer started as a homebrew by Jim Koch. Samuel Adams honors its history with the annual Long-Shots Homebrew contest, where craft brewers submit their creations. The winner's libation is mass-produced and sold in a Samuel Adams variety six-pack.

HOMETOWN BREW

A fun way to get to know a town is to get to know its hometown drinks. And there are few places as closely affiliated with their town of origin as the Samuel Adams Brewery is to Boston.

Samuel Adams beer might seem like it's everywhere, but its producer, the Boston Beer Company, is still considered a craft brewer, with an annual production of less than 2 million barrels per year.

In 1984 founder Jim Koch, unhappy with the low quality of industrially produced beers, decided to try his hand at the family business and introduce new ways of brewing and selling beer based on traditional methods and high-quality ingredients. He named his beer after another man with revolutionary ideas—patriot and statesman Samuel Adams.

Today many quality craft brewers merit attention on Boston's competitive, fanatical beer scene: to name a few, Harpoon Brewery, Boston Beer Works, Trillium Brewing Co., Mystic Brewery, Cisco Brewers, John Harvard's Brew House, Pretty Things, and Buzzards Bay Brewery.

Boston Beer Company's Jamaica Plain facility. You can tour the Boston Beer Company's Jamaica Plain facility, where its research and development into new products is conducted (the bulk of Samuel Adams production is done elsewhere). The entertaining hour-long tour is free to all, and, naturally, includes a tasting (for age 21 or older; ID is checked). Smell and taste the components of brewing: hops, malt, and barley; look at the flavoring process and hear about—perhaps even see—new beers in development. On fair-weather weekends, arrive early to avoid long waits. Tours run continuously all day. ✉ *30 Germania St., Jamaica Plain* ☎ *617/368–5080* 🌐 *www.samueladams.com* Ⓜ *Stony Brook.*

metal, chosen by the tattooed and pierced staff. Artwork by local painters hangs on exposed-brick walls; and the felt on the pool tables is crimson, not green. Bartenders tap from one of Cambridge's finest draft beers selections, and that's saying something. Local band members may hang out here when not gigging and rehearsing. ✉ *1 Kendall Sq., Bldg. 200, Cambridge* ☎ *617/494–9565* 🌐 *www.flattopjohnnys.com* Ⓜ *Kendall/MIT.*

CAFÉS AND COFFEEHOUSES

1369 Coffeehouse. Quirky characters rub elbows with book-writing professors and tweeting students at this Cambridge institution devoted to espresso and cold-brewed iced coffee (also delivered in growlers). Staffers pride themselves on intensive "barista jedi" training, though spiced apple cider is favored in the cool months. Serving pastries galore, daily quiches, cookies, sandwiches, and salads, this café and its Central Square location (✉ 757 Massachusetts Avenue) are packed until 10 pm most nights. The 1369 Coffeehouse was voted Best Coffeehouse 2013 by *Boston Magazine.* ✉ *1369 Cambridge St., Cambridge* ☎ *617/576–1369* 🌐 *www.1369coffeehouse.com* Ⓜ *Bus 69, 83, or 91.*

Café Algiers. This genuine Middle Eastern café serves pita bread, fine hummus, varied salads, exotic teas, and strong coffee—Arabic or

Turkish, in a *briki* (brass or copper pot). Cozy, clustered tables fill both floors and upstairs you can peer at soaring, wood-paneled cathedral ceilings. Service tends toward low-key; visit when you're in the mood to linger over conversation or a novel. ✉ *40 Brattle St., Cambridge* ☎ *617/492–1557* Ⓜ *Harvard.*

Club Passim. Joan Baez, Bob Dylan, Suzanne Vega, Jim Kweskin's Jug Band—thousands of folkies have strummed and warbled their way through Club Passim, one of America's oldest (1958) and renowned Americana and roots music clubs. The cozy brick basement has table service and a counter to buy prepared dishes—Middle Eastern veggie items are yummy. If you travel with your guitar, call about open-mike nights. Classes and workshops at their school around the corner carry on folk traditions. ✉ *47 Palmer St., Cambridge* ☎ *617/492–5300, 617/492–7679 box office* 🌐 *www.clubpassim.org* Ⓜ *Harvard.*

Dado Tea. The New Agey feel here starts with organic teas (coffee, too) and extends to Japanese noodles, dumplings, salads, multigrain wraps, even smoothies. If they're not too crowded, you may linger over free Wi-Fi. **TIP→ The 955 Massachusetts Avenue outpost is more spacious than this one.** ✉ *50 Church St., Cambridge* ☎ *617/547–0950* 🌐 *www.dadotea.com* Ⓜ *Harvard.*

Tealuxe. A "tea bar" with Bombay flair, Tealuxe has nearly 100 different herbal and traditional teas and blends and enticing teatime pastries and goodies—and no coffee. At this favorite hangout, students huddle over textbooks and savor cups of pu-erh, Earl Grey, or ginseng chai at a copper-topped table or window perch. ✉ *0 Brattle St., Cambridge* ☎ *617/441–0077* 🌐 *www.tealuxe.com* Ⓜ *Harvard.*

COMEDY CLUBS

Comedy Studio. Located upstairs at the Hong Kong in Harvard Square, this comedy club schedules platters of silly offerings, including a host of local and touring comedians and, on Tuesdays, a popular magic show. The newly renovated restaurant serves reasonably priced Chinese dishes between smiles. ✉ *1238 Massachusetts Ave., Cambridge* ☎ *617/661–6507* 🌐 *www.thecomedystudio.com* 🎟 *$10–$12* ⏲ *All shows start at 8 pm, Tues.–Sun.* Ⓜ *Harvard.*

ImprovBoston. This Central Square venue flips audience cues into situation comedy, complete with theme song and commercials. Be careful when you go to the restroom—you might be pulled onstage. On some nights performers face off in improv competitions judged by audiences. Shows run Wednesday through Sunday, costing $7 to $16. You may need that beer and wine bar. ✉ *40 Prospect St., Cambridge* ☎ *617/576–1253* 🌐 *www.improvboston.com* Ⓜ *Central.*

MUSIC CLUBS

Cantab Lounge/Third Rail. This place hums every night with live bands cranking out rhythm and blues, soul, funk, rock, or bluegrass. The Third Rail bar downstairs hosts major poetry slams, open-mike readings, and Club Bohemia nights. Its diverse under-40 crowd is friendly and informal. ✉ *738 Massachusetts Ave., Cambridge* ☎ *617/354–2685* 🌐 *www.cantab-lounge.com* 💳 *No credit cards* Ⓜ *Central.*

CLOSE UP

Candlepin Bowling

Pool halls in Boston make a popular winter refuge for teens and university students (though some have age requirements of over 18 or 21). Forget Paul Newman and smoky interiors: Boston likes its billiards halls swanky and well lighted, with polished brass and dark wood. Many of them do double duty as bowling alleys. Be forewarned, however, that in New England bowling is often "candlepin," with smaller balls and different rules.

It was back in 1880 that Justin White trimmed the size of his pins at his Worcester, Massachusetts, bowling hall, giving birth to candlepin bowling, a locally popular pint-size version of tenpin bowling. Now played almost exclusively in northern New England and in the Canadian Maritime Provinces, candlepin bowling is a game of power and accuracy.

Paradoxically, candlepin bowling is both much easier and far more difficult than regular bowling. The balls are significantly smaller, weighing less than 3 pounds. There are no finger holes, and players of all ages and abilities can whip the ball down the alley. But because both the ball and the pins are lighter, it is more difficult to bowl strikes and spares. Players are allowed three throws per frame, and bowlers may hit fallen pins (called wood) to knock down other pins. There has never been a perfect "300" score. The top score is 245. Good players will score around 100 to 110, and novice players should be content with a score of 90.

Among the handful of alleys in and around Boston, many maintain and celebrate their own quirky charm and history.

Boston Bowl. Open 24 hours a day, Boston Bowl attracts a more adult crowd. It has pool tables, a game room, both tenpin and candlestick bowling, and a restaurant and bar. ✉ *820 Morrissey Blvd., Dorchester* ☎ *617/825–3800* 🌐 *www.bostonbowl.com.*

Needham Bowlaway. Founded in 1917, this tiny alley's eight cramped lanes are tucked away down a flight of stairs. Fans say Bowlaway is like bowling in your own basement. The charge is $25 per lane per hour ($20 before noon weekdays). **TIP→ Note that this is a drive-to only destination (no subway station is anywhere nearby).** ✉ *16 Chestnut St., Needham* ☎ *781/449–4060* 🌐 *www.needhambowl.com.*

Sacco's Bowl Haven. The '50s decor here "makes bowling the way it was, the way it is." Run by the fourth generation of the Sacco family, the alleys include a Flatbread Company pizzeria. Its 10 lanes are open all day until midnight and run $25 per hour. ✉ *45 Day St., Somerville* ☎ *617/776–0552.*

Lizard Lounge. Low-key Lizard Lounge is a subterranean nightspot that features experimental and cult bands. Seven nights a week, hear folk, rock, acid jazz, reggae, and pop, and sometimes cabaret, burlesque, or poetry slams (it's poetry Sundays and open-mike Mondays). Martinis are a house specialty. Upstairs, Cambridge Common restaurant serves customized burgers and comfort food (sweet-potato fries, baskets of tater tots, etc.). ✉ *1667 Massachusetts Ave., between Harvard and Por-*

ter Sqs., Cambridge ☎ *617/547–0759* 🌐 *www.lizardloungeclub.com* Ⓜ *Harvard, Porter.*

Middle East Restaurant & Nightclub. This nightclub has balanced its kebab-and-falafel menu with three ever-active performance spaces to carve its niche as one of New England's most eclectic alternative rock venues. National and local acts vie for the large upstairs, tiny corner, and cavernous downstairs rooms. Phenoms like the Mighty Mighty Bosstones got their start here. Music-world celebs drop by when playing town. There's also belly dancing, folk, jazz, country-rock, and dancing at Zu Zu. ✉ *472–480 Massachusetts Ave., Cambridge* ☎ *617/497–0576, 617/864–3278* 🌐 *www.mideastclub.com* Ⓜ *Central.*

Outpost 186. This underground (actually back-alley) arts and performance space hosts experimental and underground music, film, poetry, and graphic arts. Jazz guitarists play during figure drawing classes on Sundays. There's a modest cover charge and few amenities. **TIP→ There's no phone number; watch the online video for directions.** ✉ *186 1/2 Hampshire Street, Inman Sq., Cambridge* 🌐 *www.outpost186.com* Ⓜ *Central.*

Regattabar. Once the go-to club for name jazz acts, Regattabar has lately scaled back its music roster to host private events. Regulars still include top guitarists (John Scofield, Mike Stern, Wayne Krantz, Pat Martino) and local favorites (Mike Bono, Matt Savage). Tickets for shows are $20–$35. The dark 250-seat club with jaunty nautical decor offers reasonably priced fare and drinks. ✉ *Charles Hotel, 1 Bennett St., Cambridge* ☎ *617/661–5000 hotel, 617/395–7757 tickets* 🌐 *www.regattabarjazz.com* Ⓜ *Harvard.*

Ryles Jazz Club. Soft lights, mirrors, and good barbecue set the mood for fine jazz on the ground-floor main stage, host to a steady showcase since the 1960s of new bands, favored locals, and stars like McCoy Tyner and Maynard Ferguson. But Ryles leads a merry double life, because meanwhile, the upstairs dancehall has earned its spurs as a Latin dancers' destination. There's world music Wednesdays and occasionally open-mike poetry. Ryles' ever-popular Sunday jazz brunch requires reservations. The reasonable cover charge varies and there's free parking for patrons. ✉ *212 Hampshire St., Cambridge* ☎ *617/876–9330* 🌐 *www.ryles.com* Ⓜ *Bus 69, 83, or 91.*

Sinclair. Bringing a long-awaited sophisticated rock music and dining venue to Harvard Square, the Sinclair has factory-chic decor, a serious beverage list, creative mixology, and thoughtful comfort cuisine. Its adventurous, near-nightly calendar boasts indie rock, with enticing flings into world and jazz. Accommodating 500, here's a party made to order for grown-ups, academic and streetwise. ✉ *52 Church St., Harvard Sq., Cambridge* ☎ *617/547–5200* 🌐 *www.sinclaircambridge.com* Ⓜ *Harvard Square.*

T.T. the Bear's Place. The nightly live rock roster of this cozy, crowded hangout showcases the area's hot groups, wannabes, and on-the-rise alternative bands in double to quadruple bills. A pillared half wall splits the room conveniently for two fluid camps: dancers/listeners and drinkers/pool players. Monday night is usually acoustic night. Hot shows sell out in advance. ✉ *10 Brookline St., Cambridge* ☎ *617/492–2327* 🌐 *www.ttthebears.com* Ⓜ *Central.*

SALSA CLUBS

Havana Club. At the Greek American Political Club in Central Square, this club has a 5,400-square-foot ballroom dance floor, a rotating cast of DJs and live bands, and (usually) free food such as burritos or nachos. Typically, 300 people show up to dance salsa, creating a lively scene for dancers at any level. Open Friday and Saturday (private functions on other nights), with lessons at 9, Havana Club gets into full swing around 10 pm. ✉ *288 Green St., Cambridge* ☎ *617/312–5550* 🌐 *www.havanaclubsalsa.com* Ⓜ *Central.*

Ryles. This is home to one of the city's friendliest Latin dance scenes. Tuesday through Sunday, newcomers learn salsa moves with experts (arrive early for lessons) then dance the night away (together with friends or the experts). There's also merengue, bachata, and reggaeton. Cover is $10–$15. ✉ *212 Hampshire St., Cambridge* ☎ *617/876–9330* 🌐 *www.ryles.com/dancing.cfm* Ⓜ *Bus 68 or 69.*

SOMERVILLE

Once marginal and blue-collar, crowded Somerville is now popular and hip. Look at Davis Square: a hub for the T and bike paths, the square's alive with cafés, clubs, a big theater, and ethic eateries serving BBQ, sushi, curry, bangers and mash, pad thai, and noodles. It's also a gathering spots for Tufts University students and young thinkers. Union Square's next, as the T pushes beyond Lechmere by 2015.

BARS

Fodor's Choice ★ **Burren.** Your true-emerald Irish music pub pulls in devoted locals and all fans of *craic* (enjoyable environment). Enthusiastic staff and professional bartenders expertly pour Guinness on tap and serve comfort food (fish-and-chips, bangers-and-mash, Irish stew, shepherd's pie). Pleasing decor, a sunny west-facing patio, an old-wood library bar, and slate specials add to the allure of live Irish music—acoustic groups—most nights in both the Front and Back Rooms. Step dancing is on Mondays and international folk is on Wednesdays. There's a minimal cover. ✉ *247 Elm St., Somerville* ☎ *617/776–6896* 🌐 *www.burren.com* Ⓜ *Davis.*

Independent. In Somerville's Union Square, this comfortable neighborhood bar is a good spot to hit for a pint, martini, or hot toddy. Priced right are summertime gin-based cocktails (called Somerville 75, Corpse Reviver, Thyme Daly, Queen Charlotte, and Bees Knees) and quality brews (32 drafts, 60 bottles). ✉ *75 Union Sq., Somerville* ☎ *617/440–6022* 🌐 *www.theindo.com* Ⓜ *Bus 86, 87, 91, CT2.*

Orleans. This bar in Davis Square has floor-to-ceiling windows. The lounge has comfy couches and settees, and a monster screen with Sunday games on. Nightly themes run: pasta Monday, taco Tuesday, trivia Wednesday, wings Thursday, DJ Friday, and karaoke Saturday (after 10 pm). There's a full range of bar and brunch foods. ✉ *65 Holland St., Somerville* ☎ *617/591–2100* 🌐 *www.orleansrestaurant.com* Ⓜ *Davis.*

CAFÉS AND COFFEEHOUSES

Diesel Cafe. This bright and sunny spot with bold local artwork and spacious booths draws in Davis Square hipsters, Tufts students, and gay and lesbian crowds. Luxuriate over crafted salads, soups, and wraps, pastries by Finale, and gourmet coffee from Intelligentsia. Shoot pool at two tables or surf the Internet (Wi-Fi costs $5 per hour). ✉ *257 Elm St., Somerville* ☎ *617/629–8717* 🌐 *www.diesel-cafe.com* Ⓜ *Davis.*

MUSIC CLUBS

Johnny D's Uptown. This is as close as Boston gets to a rural roadhouse: good eats and good music, where every seat is a good seat. The line-up leans into Cajun, country, rockabilly, blues, roots, with a bit of jazz, Latin, and poetry. Come early for Southern and Mediterranean bistro food, or on weekends enjoy the popular jazz brunch both days until 2:30 pm and open blues jam on Sunday afternoons. During Trivia Mondays, hot dogs are a buck-fifty. Those under 21 may visit with a parent or guardian. ✉ *17 Holland St., Somerville* ☎ *617/776–9667 recorded info, 617/776–2004* 🌐 *johnnyds.com* Ⓜ *Davis.*

Somerville Theater. This keystone of Davis Square's growing culture presents films (five screens) and easily 40 concerts a year (Bruce Springsteen and U2 played here). The biggest space for miles around, the 900-seat theater celebrates its centennial this year with special events. In the coffered-ceiling, stone-tiled foyer you may buy beer, wine, popcorn, or Richardson's ice cream to enjoy during the show. ✉ *55 Davis Sq., Somerville* ☎ *617/625–5700* 🌐 *www.somervilletheatreonline.com* Ⓜ *Davis.*

THE ARTS

DANCE

Boston Dance Alliance. This serves as a clearinghouse for local dance information. Visit the alliance's website for upcoming performances and details about Boston dance companies and venues. ✉ *19 Clarendon St., South End* ☎ *617/456–6295* 🌐 *www.bostondancealliance.org* Ⓜ *Back Bay.*

BALLET

Boston Ballet. The city's premier dance company performs at the Boston Opera House. In addition to a world-class repertory of classical and high-spirited modern works, it presents an elaborate signature *Nutcracker* during the holidays. ✉ *19 Clarendon St., South End* ☎ *617/695–6950* 🌐 *www.bostonballet.org* Ⓜ *Back Bay.*

José Mateo's Ballet Theatre. This troupe is building an exciting, contemporary repertory under Cuban-born José Mateo, the resident artistic director-choreographer. Performances, which include an original *Nutcracker,* take place October through April at the **Sanctuary Theatre,** a beautifully converted former church at Massachusetts Avenue and Harvard Street in Harvard Square. ✉ *400 Harvard St., Cambridge* ☎ *617/354–7467* 🌐 *www.ballettheatre.org* Ⓜ *Harvard.*

CONTEMPORARY

Dance Complex. Performances (and classes and workshops) by local and visiting choreographers take place at Odd Fellows Hall, an intimate space that draws a multicultural crowd. Styles range from classical ballet to contemporary and world dance. ✉ *536 Massachusetts Ave., Central Sq., Cambridge* ☎ *617/547–9363* 🌐 *www.dancecomplex.org* Ⓜ *Central.*

FOLK/MULTICULTURAL

Art of Black Dance and Music. The peripatetic, self-producing Art of Black Dance and Music performs the music and dance of Africa, the Caribbean, and the Americas at venues far and wide, like the Reggie Lewis Center and Cambridge Multicultural Arts Center. It also offers lectures, residencies, and workshops at schools and colleges (Roxbury Community College, Boston Conservatory). ✉ *32 Cameron Ave., Somerville* ☎ *617/666–1859* 🌐 *www.abdm.net* Ⓜ *Andrew, then Bus 16 or 17; Ruggles, then Bus 15.*

Cambridge Multicultural Arts Center. Presenting local and visiting arts programs and world, jazz, and dance performances, Cambridge Multicultural Arts Center also has two spacious galleries showcasing international visual arts. ✉ *41 2nd St., Cambridge* ☎ *617/577–1400* 🌐 *www.cmacusa.org* Ⓜ *Lechmere.*

Folk Arts Center of New England. This center promotes participatory international folk dancing and music for adults and children, as well as traditional New England contra dancing at locations throughout greater Boston. Events are outdoors when possible (Copley Square, Watertown, and Newton). ✉ *10 Franklin St., Stoneham* ☎ *781/438–4389 recorded info, 781/438–4387* 🌐 *www.facone.org.*

World Music/CRASHarts. As the metro area's premier presenter of worldwide music and dance, World Music/CRASHarts has a truly global roster featuring exciting contemporary artists in their Boston debuts (like The Bad Plus and Freshlyground), as well as world music icons such as South Africa's Ladysmith Black Mambazo and Ireland's Mary Black. Its annual blockbuster Flamenco Festival packs the Cutler Majestic Theater. Performances unfold at many venues such as Somerville Theatre, Berklee Performance Center, Sinclair, Sanders Theatre, Johnny D's, and Paradise Rock Club. ✉ *720 Massachusetts Ave., Central Sq., Cambridge* ☎ *617/876–4275* 🌐 *www.worldmusic.org* Ⓜ *Central.*

FILM

With its large population of academics and intellectuals, Boston has its share of discerning moviegoers and movie houses, especially in Brookline and Cambridge. Theaters at suburban malls and in Downtown may have better screens, if less adventurous fare. The *Boston Globe* has daily listings in the *G Magazine's* "Living/Arts" section; the *Boston Herald* Friday "Scene" section and the *Improper Bostonian* "Arts" section list films for the week. Movies cost $9–$13. Many theaters have half-price matinees, but may suspend bargain prices during the first week or two of a major film opening.

Boston Public Library. The beautiful and beloved Boston Public Library regularly screens free family, foreign, classic, and documentary films in the Rabb Lecture Hall. Exhibitions and children's activities abound. The Renaissance courtyard hosts summer concerts, and the pretty café is a welcome haven for readers of paperbacks and hardcovers. The exquisite murals of John Singer Sargent and print galleries also merit a walk-through. ✉ *700 Boylston St., Copley Sq., Back Bay* ☎ *617/536–5400* 🌐 *www.bpl.org* Ⓜ *Copley.*

Brattle Theatre. A classic moviegoer's iconic den with 230 seats, Brattle Theatre shows classic movies, new foreign and indie films, theme series, and directors' cuts. Tickets sell out for its annual much-acclaimed Humphrey Bogart festival, scheduled around Harvard's exam period; the Bugs Bunny Film Festival in February; *Trailer Treats,* an annual fundraiser featuring classic and modern movie previews; and DocYard, a stunning series of documentaries. At Christmastime, expect seasonal movies like *It's a Wonderful Life* and *Holiday Inn.* ✉ *40 Brattle St., Harvard Sq., Cambridge* ☎ *617/876–6837* 🌐 *brattlefilm.org* Ⓜ *Harvard.*

Coolidge Corner Theatre. This lovingly restored art deco theater presents an eclectic and exciting bill of world cinema: art films, foreign films, animation and anime fests, documentaries, and classics. An intimate 45-seat screening room also offers experimental films and videos. The independent nonprofit art house also holds book readings, private events, and popular midnight cult movies. ✉ *290 Harvard St., Brookline* ☎ *617/734–2501, 617/734–2500 recorded info* 🌐 *www.coolidge.org* Ⓜ *Coolidge Corner.*

Harvard Film Archive. Screening independent, foreign, classic, and experimental films rarely seen in commercial cinemas, Harvard Film Archive is open to the public Friday through Monday. The 200-seat theater, with pristine film and digital projection, is located in the stunning brick-and-glass Carpenter Visual Arts Center, Le Corbusier's only American building. Tickets are $9. ✉ *Carpenter Center for the Visual Arts, 24 Quincy St., Cambridge* ☎ *617/495–4700* 🌐 *hcl.harvard.edu/hfa* Ⓜ *Harvard.*

Institute of Contemporary Art/Boston. The waterfront location and modern design are reason enough to visit the ICA/B, but its screenings of edgy art flicks, award-winning foreign films, experimental visual media, and documentaries are something else again. ✉ *100 Northern Ave., Waterfront* ☎ *617/478–3100* 🌐 *www.icaboston.org/programs/film* Ⓜ *South Station, Courthouse, World Trade Center.*

Kendall Square Cinema. This cinema's nine screens are devoted to first-run independent and foreign films, and the concession stand offers hip goodies like cappuccino and homemade cookies. Note: 1 Kendall Square stands where Hampshire Street meets Broadway, a 10-minute walk from the Kendall Square T station. A free Galleria Mall shuttle runs from the T by the theater every 20 minutes, Monday through Saturday from 9 am to 7 pm and Sundays from noon to 7. The cinema validates parking in an adjacent garage. ✉ *1 Kendall Sq., Cambridge* ☎ *617/499–1996* 🌐 *www.landmarktheatres.com* Ⓜ *Kendall/MIT.*

Museum of Fine Arts. Cinema has held its rightful place among the arts at the MFA for decades. Film screenings (international, avant-garde,

BIG-PICTURE BOSTON

Hollywood has turned Boston into celluloid gold. Its ethnic enclaves, crooked cops, and notorious love for the Red Sox have all featured prominently in major box-office hits. In addition to recent movies, like 2013's *The Judge, The Equalizer,* and *American Hustle,* here are some films with significant Boston cameos:

The Company Men (2010): With Kevin Costner, Tommy Lee Jones, and Ben Affleck, the story confronts the reality of losing the "good life" to corporate downsizing. Scenes are filmed in Boston and surrounding areas.

The Social Network (2010): Facebook was created by a Harvard University student. Starring Jesse Eisenberg, the film shows a great deal of the stately beauty of the Cambridge campus.

Gone Baby Gone (2007): Ben Affleck's directorial debut follows the case of a missing girl in Dorchester with plenty of South Boston, Dorchester, and Chelsea scenes.

The Departed (2006): Hometown boys Matt Damon and Mark Wahlberg star in this thriller of lies and betrayal between the Irish mob and state police. Visit Chinatown to see where Damon leads Leonardo DiCaprio on a good chase, follow Martin Sheen's ride on the Red Line between South Station and Park Street, or conduct your own clandestine meeting under Dorchester's Neponset Bridge.

Fever Pitch (2005): Drew Barrymore's character falls for Jimmy Fallon's role as a diehard Sox fan. Show your team spirit by visiting the North End (where Fallon's character lives), Boston Common (where Fallon confesses his Sox appeal to Barrymore), and, of course, Fenway Park.

Mystic River (2003): Based on the novel by local author Dennis Lehane, this murder mystery takes place in Southie (South Boston), though some scenes were filmed in Eastie (East Boston). Drive across the Tobin Bridge, a recurring backdrop, or down a pint at Doyle's in Jamaica Plain, where a despondent Tim Robbins gets drunk.

Legally Blonde (2001): The movie that made Reese Witherspoon an A-list star takes place at Harvard Law School, where her character Elle Woods takes on the academic establishment.

Next Stop Wonderland (1998): A nurse (Hope Davis) and a plumber (Alan Gelfant) are slowly drawn to one another in this romantic comedy that includes great scenes of everyday Boston. Tour the New England Aquarium, where Gelfant volunteers, or take the Blue Line to Revere Beach, where the lovebirds finally connect.

Good Will Hunting (1997): Matt Damon is a "Southie"-born genius janitor at MIT. Harvard Square features prominently in scenes where Damon woos Minnie Driver's character. South Boston (particularly the L Street Tavern) is also well represented.

For a movie-theme afternoon, consider a guided walking or bus tour with **Boston Movie Tours** (☎ *800/979-3370*), showcasing spots from *The Departed, Fever Pitch, Good Will Hunting,* and more.

local, exhibition-related) and festivals (like the annual Boston Jewish Film Festival) take place in Remis Auditorium. The new Taste Café and Wine Bar makes an intimate spot for postfilm discussions. ✉ *465 Huntington Ave., TheFenway* ☎ *800/440–6975 box office* 🌐 *www.mfa.org/programs/film* 🎟 *Tickets are $11, though special screenings with guest speakers may run $20–25.* Ⓜ *Museum of Fine Arts, Ruggles.*

MUSIC

For its size, Boston has a great diversity and variety of live music choices. *(⇨ See also Music Clubs in Nightlife, above.)* Supplementing appearances by nationally known artists are performers from the area's many colleges and conservatories, which also provide music series, performing spaces, and audiences. Berklee College of Music has made itself especially visible, with student (and/or faculty) ensembles popping up at formal and informal venues far and wide, especially in summer months, playing mainly jazz, blues, rock, indie, pop, and world music.

Classical music aficionados love the Boston Symphony Orchestra, which performs at Symphony Hall October through early May and at Tanglewood Music Center in Lenox, Massachusetts, from late June through August. A favorite of TV audiences, the Boston Pops presents concerts of "lighter music" from May to July and during December.

Boston also has emerged as the nation's capital of early-music performance. Dozens of small groups, often made up of performers who have one foot in the university and another on the concert stage, play pre-18th-century music on period instruments, often in small churches where the acoustics resemble the venues in which some of this music was first performed.

Boston Early Music Festival. Over 15,000 dyed-in-the-wool early-music devotees visit Boston each mid-June in odd-number years, when the biennial Boston Early Music Festival takes over the city for a week-long cavalcade of performances featuring rebecs, viols, shawms, theorbos, and sackbuts, among others. Types include orchestral, chamber, solo recitals, and operas. Featured in 2013 were Dame Emma Kirkby and Jordi Saval's XXI. ☎ *617/661–1812* 🌐 *www.bemf.org.*

Cambridge Society for Early Music. This group has presented early-music performances since 1980 and deserves much credit for early music's prominence in Boston's musical scene. ☎ *617/489–2062* 🌐 *www.csem.org.*

CONCERT HALLS

Bank of America Pavilion. Up to 5,000 people gather on the waterfront for breathtaking summertime concerts. National pop, folk, and country headliners play the huge white tent from mid-June to mid-September. In chilly months, the scene turns to TD Garden or Comcast Center. ✉ *290 Northern Ave., South Boston* ☎ *617/728–1600* 🌐 *www.bankofamericapavilion.net* Ⓜ *South Station.*

Berklee Performance Center. The main stage for the internationally renowned Berklee College of Music, the "BPC" is best known for its jazz and pop programs, but also hosts folk performers, rock acts, and pop stars such as Andrew Bird, Aimee Mann, and Henry Rollins.

Bargain alert: excellent student and faculty shows and showcases and clinics by famous performers are abundant and cost next to nothing. ✉ *136 Massachusetts Ave., Back Bay* ☎ *617/747–2261 box office* 🌐 *www.berklee.edu/BPC* Ⓜ *Hynes.*

Boston Opera House. The glittering, regilded Boston Opera House hosts plays, musicals, and traveling Broadway shows (long runs for *Wicked, Once)* and also books performers as diverse as Sarah Brightman, B. B. King, and Pat Metheny. The magnificent building, constructed in 1926, also hosts Boston Ballet's iconic holiday sellout, Tchaikovsky's *Nutcracker.* ✉ *539 Washington St., Downtown* ☎ *617/259–3400* 🌐 *www.bostonoperahouseonline.com* Ⓜ *Boylston, Chinatown, Downtown Crossing, Park St.*

Fodor's Choice ★ **Hatch Memorial Shell.** On the bank of the Charles River, this wonderful acoustic shell, 100 feet wide and wood-inlaid, is home to Boston Pops' famous Fourth of July concert and dozens of other free summer concerts and events. Local radio stations air music shows and festivals here from April through October. Friday Flicks, often animated for children, are screened at sunset. ✉ *Off Storrow Dr. at embankment, Beacon Hill* ☎ *617/626–4970* 🌐 *www.mass.gov* Ⓜ *Charles/MGH, Arlington.*

Institute of Contemporary Art/Boston. This institute hosts experimental jazz and world musicians, with some performances in partnership with World Music/CRASHArts or Berklee College of Music. Expect the unexpected—concerts here could contain a mix of disparate instruments, fusions of melody and spoken word, or DJs grooving electronica mash-ups. It's free on Thursdays, with early evening concerts. ✉ *100 Northern Ave., Waterfront* ☎ *617/478–3100* 🌐 *www.icaboston.org/programs/performance* Ⓜ *South Station, Courthouse, World Trade Center.*

Fodor's Choice ★ **Isabella Stewart Gardner Museum.** Renzo Piano's stunning extension and renovation has integrated a new and improved concert space for "Mrs. Jack's" 14th-century Venetian palace. The new Calderwood Hall's starkly striking, acoustically fine red cube hosts young artist showcases. Sunday chamber music includes jazz and contemporary, and an after-hours series on every third Thursday of the month. The museum offers free admission to U.S. military and families, and anyone named Isabella. ✉ *280 The Fenway, The Fenway* ☎ *617/278–5156 box office, 617/566–1401 recorded info* 🌐 *www.gardnermuseum.org* 🎟 *Museum $15; concert tickets extra* Ⓜ *Museum of Fine Arts.*

Museum of Fine Arts. Enjoy jazz, blues, and folk concerts in the outdoor courtyard on Wednesday summer evenings. Otherwise, music happens at Remis Auditorium or the soaring glass courtyard. Choose from four dining venues: upscale restaurant Bravo, New American Cafe in a glass courtyard with Chihuly green-glass frond-totem, Taste (café and wine bar), and the downstairs Garden Cafeteria. First Fridays (free with admission, but secure advance tickets) draw young professionals who dance to DJ music. ✉ *465 Huntington Ave., The Fenway* ☎ *800/440–6975* 🌐 *www.mfa.org/programs/music* Ⓜ *Museum of Fine Arts.*

New England Conservatory's Jordan Hall. One of the world's acoustic treasures, New England Conservatory's Jordan Hall is ideal for solo and string quartet recitals yet spacious enough for chamber and full orchestras. The pin-drop intimacy of this all-wood, 1,000-seat hall is in demand year-round for ensembles visiting and local. Boston Philharmonic and Boston Baroque perform here regularly. Dozens of free faculty and student concerts, jazz and classical, are a best-kept secret. ✉ *30 Gainsborough St., Back Bay* ☎ *617/585–1260 box office* 🌐 *necmusic.edu/calendar_event* Ⓜ *Symphony.*

Orpheum Theatre. A music hall since 1852, The Orpheum Theatre today is a faded yet beloved forum for local and national performers (like Sara Bareilles, Van Morrison, Bonnie Raitt, and the Strokes) who often pack its 2,000 seats. ✉ *1 Hamilton Pl., off Tremont St., Downtown* ☎ *617/482–0106 box office* 🌐 *crossroadspresents.com/orpheum-theatre* Ⓜ *Park St.*

Sanders Theatre. This gilt-wood jewel box of a stage is the preferred venue for many of Boston's classical orchestras and the home of Harvard University's many ensembles. The 180-degree stage design and superb acoustics afford intimacy and crystal projection. A favorite of folk, jazz, and world-music performers, the 1,166-seat Sanders hosts the holiday favorite, *Christmas Revels*, a traditional, participatory Yule celebration. Winston Churchill, Martin Luther King, Leonard Bernstein, and Teddy Roosevelt have lectured at this famed seat of oratory and music. ✉ *Harvard University, 45 Quincy St., Harvard Sq., Cambridge* ☎ *617/496–2222 box office* 🌐 *www.fas.harvard.edu/~memhall/sanders.html* Ⓜ *Harvard.*

Fodor's Choice ★ **Symphony Hall.** One of the world's best acoustical concert halls—some say *the* best—has been home since 1900 to the Boston Symphony Orchestra (BSO) and the Boston Pops. Led by conductor Keith Lockhart, the Pops concerts take place in May and June and around the winter holidays. The hall is also used by visiting orchestras, chamber groups, soloists, and local ensembles. Rehearsals and daytime concerts for students are open to the public, with discounted tickets. ✉ *301 Massachusetts Ave., Back Bay* ☎ *617/266–1492* 🌐 *www.bso.org* Ⓜ *Symphony.*

TD Garden. TD Garden hosts concerts by big-name artists (from Céline Dion to U2), ice shows, and all home games of Bruins hockey and Celtics basketball. ✉ *100 Legends Way, Old West End* ☎ *617/624–1000 event info line* 🌐 *www.tdgarden.com* Ⓜ *North Station.*

Tsai Performance Center. Associated with Boston University, Tsai Performance Center presents many free classical concerts by both student and professional groups. The New England Philharmonic, Alea III, and Boston Musica Viva are regular guests in this exquisitely proportioned and acoustically perfect 500-seat theater. ✉ *685 Commonwealth Ave., Kenmore* ☎ *617/353–6467, 617/353–8725 box office* 🌐 *www.bu.edu/tsai* Ⓜ *Boston University East.*

Chamber Music ⇨ *See Orchestras and Chamber Music.*

CHORAL GROUPS

It's hard to imagine another city with more active choral groups than Boston. Many outstanding choruses are associated with Boston schools and churches.

Renowned Symphony Hall is home to the Boston Symphony Orchestra and Boston Pops.

Boston Cecilia. Founded in 1876, this choral group holds regular concerts at Jordan Hall, Church of the Advent, and All Saints (Brookline); it's especially noted for period-instrument performances of Handel and Bach, and works by undersung contemporary composers. ☎ *617/232–4540* 🌐 *www.bostoncecilia.org.*

Boston Gay Men's Chorus. With an aim to "create a more tolerant society through the power of music," the Boston Gay Men's Chorus has a repertoire that ranges from holiday favorites to show tunes to chamber selections to pop hits. The group performs at Symphony Hall, Jordan Hall, and Cutler Majestic Theatre. ☎ *617/542–7464* 🌐 *www.bgmc.org.*

Cantata Singers. Celebrating its 50th season, Cantata Singers perform choral music from many eras—the Renaissance (e.g., Claudio Monteverdi), Bach, and Mendelssohn to the present (e.g., John Harbison). ☎ *617/868–5885* 🌐 *www.cantatasingers.org.*

Chorus Pro Musica. This dynamic chorus, tackling classics (Bach, Vaughan Williams) and modern works (Rautavaara, Poulenc) under the baton of young music director Jamie Kirsch, presents fall, holiday, and spring concerts at Old South Church or Jordan Hall. ✉ *Administrative office, 645 Boylston St.* ☎ *617/267–7442* 🌐 *www.choruspromusica.org.*

CHURCH CONCERTS

Boston's churches have outstanding music programs. The Saturday *Boston Globe* and *Boston Musical Intelligencer* list performance schedules.

Emmanuel Music. Concerts occur at Emmanuel Church, known as "the Bach church" since 1970 for singing the master's cantatas during Holy Eucharist services on Sundays at 10 am, between September and May.

Concerts, performed by a professional chamber orchestra and chorus, are among Boston's musical gems. Inquire about free Thursday noon concerts in Lindsey Chapel. ✉ *15 Newbury St., Back Bay* ☎ *617/536–3356* 🌐 *www.emmanuelmusic.org* Ⓜ *Arlington.*

Trinity Church. H.H. Richardson's 1877 neo-Romanesque masterwork is the centerpiece of Copley Square and a must-visit on any Back Bay tour. Trinity Boston Foundation presents free half-hour organ or choir recitals on Fridays at 12:15 pm, as well as seasonal choral concerts, in the magnificently textiled and vaulted apse. The church is open daily from 9 to 5. Tours are self-guided ($7) or by group arranged through the church bookstore. Sunday services are at 7:45 am, 9 am, 11:15 am, and 6 pm. ✉ *Trinity Church, 206 Clarendon St., Copley Sq., Back Bay* ☎ *617/536–0944* 🌐 *trinitychurchboston.org* Ⓜ *Back Bay/South End, Copley.*

CONCERT SERIES

Bank of America Celebrity Series. This series presents about 50 signature events annually—renowned orchestras, chamber groups, jazz icons, recitalists, vocalists—at prestigious venues like Symphony Hall, Sanders Theater, Jordan Hall, Pickman Hall, and Berklee Performance Center. In the heady, prestigious mix find cellist Yo-Yo Ma, Sweet Honey in the Rock, saxophonists Wayne Shorter and Sonny Rollins, Israel Philharmonic, and violinist Joshua Bell. Top dance companies perform as well: Alvin Ailey American Dance Theater, Mark Morris Dance Group, and Paul Taylor Dance Company. ✉ *Administrative office, 20 Park Plaza, Suite 1032, Downtown* ☎ *617/482–2595, 617/482–6661 box office* 🌐 *www.celebrityseries.org.*

EARLY-MUSIC GROUPS

Boston Baroque. Founded by conductor Martin Pearlman as "Banchetto Musicale" in 1974, Boston Baroque showcases soloists and guest musicians in precision period-instrument performances of Bach, Handel, Vivaldi, Rameau, and Mozart operas. The holiday-season *Messiah* is a stunner; the 1992 CD version was the first of three Grammy nominations. Performances are held at Jordan Hall and Sanders Theatre in Cambridge; the chamber performances are at more intimate venues. ☎ *617/484–9200* 🌐 *www.bostonbaroque.org.*

Fodor's Choice ★ **Boston Camerata.** Founded in 1954, Boston Camerata has achieved international celebrity, thanks to its passionate commitment and popular recordings. Its loyal cadre of dedicated professional singers and early instrumentalists perform an extensive repertoire of exquisitely detailed medieval, Renaissance, and baroque music—often themed and seasonal—in churches and concert halls worldwide. ☎ *617/262–2092* 🌐 *www.bostoncamerata.org.*

Boston Early Music Festival. This festival is focused on medieval, baroque, and Renaissance music. Throughout the year, concerts, master classes, and lectures take place at churches and concert halls throughout Boston. Every other year in June, a fully staged opera is performed. Past productions have included Conradi's *Ariadne* (1691) and Mattheson's 1710 opera *Boris Goudenow.* ☎ *617/661–1812* 🌐 *www.bemf.org.*

CLOSE UP

Frugal Fun

The nightlife and arts options listed are worth their weight in gold. Yet if you're feeling the pinch, you can be entertained without dropping a dime.

Nosh on gratis appetizers at the **Fritz Lounge** during happy hour on weekdays (of course, you may feel compelled to buy a drink).

See a film at the **Boston Public Library.**

Go baroque—but not broke—with classical and contemporary concerts performed by the Boston University Symphony Orchestra, Alea III, or College of Fine Arts faculty members at the **Tsai Performance Center.**

Head to **Trinity Church** for free Friday organ or choir recitals at 12:15 pm.

Get down to blues and jazz at **Wally's Café**, The **Beehive,** or **939**, where talented students from the Berklee College of Music perform.

Buy a coffee or smoothie, and surf the Web with free Wi-Fi at **Trident Booksellers & Café.**

See art in the making: check out one of the weekend **Boston Open Studios** events (🌐 *www.cityofboston.gov/arts/visual/openstudios.asp*) in neighborhoods throughout the city.

Summer brings even more free activities:

Boston Pops. Bop along with the Boston Pops and other free concerts at the Hatch Memorial Shell June through August. ✉ *Esplanade, 47 David G Mugar Way, Back Bay* ☎ *617/266–1200, 888/266–1200* 🌐 *www.bso.org.*

Esplanade Summer Events. From April through September, the Hatch Shell on the Esplanade is abuzz with free concerts, movie showings, and more—all part of the Esplanade Summer Events. Perennial favorites include the Boston Pops' Fourth of July concert, high-level college and professional orchestral concerts, and "Free Friday Flicks" (at sunset, often animated for kids). ✉ *The Esplanade, Back Bay* ☎ *617/626–4970* 🌐 *www.mass.gov.*

Shakespeare in the Park. On July and August evenings, the Commonwealth Shakespeare Company produces free performances of Shakespeare in the Park on Boston Common or musicals at the Hatch Shell. ☎ *617/426–0863* 🌐 *commshakes.org.*

Summer in the City at Boston Harbor Hotel. Each weeknight of summer, something's happening at Rowes Wharf—music lovers listen to tunes spun by DJs on Monday, soul-bros and sisters enjoy Motown on Tuesday, country fans do their boot-scootin' thing on Wednesday, blues lovers get their blues on Thursday, and cinephiles catch silver screen classics at the waterside on Friday. Boston Harbor Hotel hosts these events along Harborwalk from 6–10 pm. Concerts are staged on a barge anchored behind the hotel. ✉ *70 Rowes Wharf, Waterfront* ☎ *617/439–7000* 🌐 *www.bhh.com.*

Handel & Haydn Society. America's oldest music organization, staging performances since 1815, this group presents almost exclusively European instrumental and choral war-horses, nearly all at Symphony Hall. The group's holiday-season gala of Handel's *Messiah* and a holiday sing-along (at Faneuil Hall) draw faithful regulars. ☎ *617/266–3605 box office, 617/262–1815* 🌐 *www.handelandhaydn.org.*

ORCHESTRAS AND CHAMBER MUSIC

Boston Chamber Music Society. Under artistic directors Marcus Thompson and Ronald Thomas (emeritus), Boston Chamber Music Society performs the classical gamut from Mozart to Mahler to Britten at venues like Harvard's Sanders Theatre and MIT's Kresge Auditorium. ☎ *617/349–0086* 🌐 *www.bostonchambermusic.org.*

Boston Philharmonic. The charismatic Benjamin Zander—whose signature preconcert chats help audiences better understand the blockbuster symphonies they're about to hear—heads up Boston Philharmonic. Performances take place at Harvard's Sanders Theatre, New England Conservatory's Jordan Hall, and Symphony Hall, and include symphonies by Beethoven, Mahler, Shostakovich, and Brahms, plus lots of concertos. ☎ *617/236–0999* 🌐 *www.bostonphil.org.*

Boston Pops. Under the agile baton of Keith Lockhart, Boston Pops (largely Boston Symphony musicians) perform a bracing blend of American standards, movie themes, and contemporary vocal numbers (with top-tier guests) during May and June at Symphony Hall, followed by outdoor concerts on July 3rd and 4th at the Hatch Memorial Shell. Performances also take place at Boston Symphony Orchestra's summer home, Tanglewood in Lenox, Massachusetts, in July and August. The popular outdoor concerts are free and packed; be sure to arrive early with blankets, folding chairs, and a picnic. ☎ *617/266–1492, 888/266–1200 box office* 🌐 *www.bso.org.*

Boston Symphony Orchestra. Founded in 1881, the Boston Symphony is one of America's oldest and most prestigious orchestras. Its season at Symphony Hall runs from September through April. In July and August the music migrates to Tanglewood, the orchestra's beautiful summer home in the Berkshire Mountains in Lenox, Massachusetts. Including tours to Carnegie Hall and China, and the Boston Pops concerts, the BSO presents more than 250 concerts annually. ✉ *301 Massachusetts Ave., Back Bay* 🌐 *www.bso.org* Ⓜ *Symphony.*

Boston Symphony Chamber Players. Composed of principal members of the Boston Symphony Orchestra, Boston Symphony Chamber Players perform throughout the year at various venues around town.

Discovery Ensemble. Youthful, energetic, and full of surprises, Discovery lives up to its name under the dynamic leadership of acclaimed Irish director Courtney Lewis. Only five seasons old, Discovery has—through brilliant mash-ups of classic and modern (Mozart to Ligeti)—developed loyal audiences at Boston's Jordan Hall and Cambridge's Sanders Theatre, and ear-opening collaborations with many area schools. ✉ *Administrative Office, 45 Hodge Rd., Arlington* ☎ *617/800–7588* 🌐 *www.discoveryensemble.org.*

The Boston Ballet puts on both avant-garde and classical performances (like *Swan Lake*, shown).

OPERA

Boston Lyric Opera. At Citi Performing Arts Center's Schubert Theater, the Boston Lyric Opera stages four full productions each season—three classics and a 20th-century work. Recent highlights have included Mozart's *Magic Flute* and Verdi's *Rigoletto.* ✉ *11 Ave. de Lafayette, Downtown* ☎ *617/542–4912, 617/542–6772 audience services office* 🌐 *blo.org* Ⓜ *Boylston.*

Odyssey Opera of Boston. The former Boston Opera Company under new management but with the same excellent conductor, Gil Rose, Odyssey Opera House presents operas at Jordan Hall, which is where the New England Conservatory plays. ✉ *Jordan Hall, 30 Gainsborough St.* ☎ *617/826–1626* 🌐 *www.odysseyopera.org* Ⓜ *Symphony.*

THEATER

In the 1930s Boston had no fewer than 50 performing-arts theaters; by the 1980s the city's Downtown Theater District had all but vanished. Happily, since the 1990s several historic theaters, extensively restored, have reopened to host pre-Broadway shows, visiting artists, comedy, jazz, and local troupes. The glorious renovation of the Opera House in 2004 added new light to the district. Established companies, such as the Huntington Theatre Company and the American Repertory Theatre in Cambridge, stage classic and modern repertory, premiere works by major writers like David Mamet, August Wilson, Tom Stoppard, and Don DeLillo, and pieces by new talents like Lydia Diamond and Diane Paulus.

MAJOR THEATERS

Boston Opera House. The meticulously renovated 2,500-seat, Beaux-Arts building has $35 million worth of gold leaf, lush carpeting, and rococo ornamentation. It features lavish musical productions such as *The Lion King* and Boston Ballet's *The Nutcracker.* ✉ *539 Washington St., Downtown Crossing/Chinatown* ☎ *617/259–3400* 🌐 *www.bostonoperahouseonline.com* Ⓜ *Boylston, Chinatown, Downtown Crossing, Park St.*

Charles Playhouse. The 1839 vintage Charles Playhouse—in its day a church, Prohibition-era speakeasy, and jazz club—has since 1995 hosted the inimitable antics of *Blue Man Group*. This loud, exhilarating trio of deadpan performance artists (who are painted vivid cobalt) pounds drums, shares eureka moments, and sprays sloppy good will. (Warning to first-timers: dress casual, especially if you're sitting down front.) ✉ *74 Warrenton St., Theater District* ☎ *800/982–2787* Ⓜ *Boylston.*

BEST ALFRESCO ARTS EVENTS

- The Boston Pops at the Hatch Memorial Shell
- Summer rock shows at the Bank of America Pavilion
- Shakespeare in the Park on the Boston Common
- Summer concerts at the Museum of Fine Arts' Calderwood Courtyard
- Live music on summer evenings in Copley Square or on the Rose Kennedy Greenway

Citi Performing Arts Center. This performance space complex is dedicated to large-scale productions (at the former Wang Theater) and more intimate shows (at the former Shubert and Colonial theaters). Expect big names (Steely Dan, Diana Ross, Radiolab, Brian Wilson), nationally touring Broadway shows, current comedians, and occasional ballets. ✉ *270 Tremont St., Theater District* ☎ *617/482–9393, 866/348–9738* 🌐 *www.citicenter.org* Ⓜ *Boylston.*

Cutler Majestic Theatre at Emerson College. This theater linked to Emerson's adjacent communications college has a tastefully restored and extravagantly gilt interior, where it hosts a dazzling array of professional and student productions including dance, drama, opera, comedy, and musicals. ✉ *219 Tremont St., Theater District* ☎ *617/824–8000* 🌐 *cutlermajestic.org* Ⓜ *Boylston.*

Huntington Theatre Company. Boston's largest resident theater company consistently performs a high-quality mix of 20th-century plays, new works, and classics under the artistic direction of Peter DuBois and commissions artists to produce original dramas. The Huntington performs at two locations: at the Boston University Theatre and at the Calderwood Theatre Pavilion in the South End. ✉ *Boston University Theatre, 264 Huntington Ave., Back Bay* ☎ *617/266–0800 box office* 🌐 *www.huntingtontheatre.org* Ⓜ *Symphony.*

SMALL THEATERS AND COMPANIES

American Repertory Theater. New director Diane Paulus at the helm is edging the ART into packing sell-out shows and winning Tonys for revivals of *Pippin* and *The Gershwins' Porgy and Bess*. The theater stages experimental, classic, and contemporary plays, often with unusual lighting and stage design, edgy scores, and multimedia effects. It boasts multiple venues. Loeb Drama Center has two theaters; the smaller black-box theater often stages productions by the irreverent Harvard-Radcliffe Dramatic Club. Oberon, a modern theater space with flexible stage design at 2 Arrow Street, engages young audiences in immersive theater, like the "disco-ball and hustle queen" extravaganza, *The Donkey Show*, on Saturday nights. ✉ *64 Brattle St., Harvard Sq., Cambridge* ☎ *617/547–8300* 🌐 *americanrepertorytheater.org* Ⓜ *Harvard.*

Boston Center for the Arts. Comprising more than a dozen quirky resident, emerging, and visiting troupes in six performance areas—two in the Calderwood Pavilion (Roberts, Wimberly), two black-box (Plaza) theaters, and two rehearsals halls—the massive circular brick Cyclorama, built in 1885 to house a 360-degree mural of the Battle of Gettysburg, today hosts concerts, trade events, and beer and wine festivals. The multicultural Company One, gay/lesbian Theatre Offensive, and cutting-edge (Off-Off-Broadway) SpeakEasy Stage Company present shows here year-round. Forty resident visual artists are presented in the Mills Gallery. Hamersley's Bistro and The Beehive share this lively, diverse BCA enclave. ✉ *539 Tremont St., South End* ☎ *617/426–5000* 🌐 *www.bcaonline.org* Ⓜ *Back Bay/South End, Copley.*

Lyric Stage Company Boston. This company mounts a top-notch mix of productions, classic and new, musical and nonmusical. Performances over the years have included *Death of a Salesman, Rich Girl,* and the musical *Into The Woods.* ✉ *YWCA, 140 Clarendon St., 2nd fl., Back Bay* ☎ *617/585–5678* 🌐 *www.lyricstage.com* Ⓜ *Arlington.*

The Publick House. While it makes a great restaurant *(⇨ Where to Eat)*, it makes an even better beer bar, with more than 175 beers on offer. A separate taproom on-site, called the Monk's Cell, specializes in Belgian brews. You'll be asking, "Is it Friday yet?" (But you don't have to wait for the weekend—it's open every day until 2 am). ✉ *1648 Beacon St., Brookline* ☎ *617/277–2880* 🌐 *www.thepublickhousebeerbar.com* Ⓜ *Washington Sq.*

SPORTS AND THE OUTDOORS

FENWAY PARK

(above) Take yourself out to a ballgame at legendary Fenway Park. (lower right) Iconic Sox mark the park walls. (upper right) Flags adorn the epicenter of Red Sox Nation.

For baseball fans a trip to Fenway Park is a religious pilgrimage. The Boston Red Sox have played here since 1912. The oldest Major League Baseball ballpark is one of the last of its kind, a place where the scoreboard is hand-operated and fans endure uncomfortable seats.

For much of the ballpark's history Babe Ruth's specter loomed large. The team won five titles by 1918 but endured an 86-year title drought after trading away the Sultan of Swat. It wasn't enough to lose; the team vexed generations of fans with late-season collapses and post-season bungles. The Sox "reversed the curse" in 2004, defeating the rival Yanks in the American League Championship Series after being down 3–0 in the series (an unheard of comeback in baseball) and sweeping the St. Louis Cardinals in the World Series. The Red Sox won it all again in 2007, against the Colorado Rockies, and yet again against the Cardinals in 2013, the first time since 1918 that the team cinched the series in its hometown. The curse is no more.

FUN FACT

A lone red seat in the right-field bleachers marks the spot where Ted Williams' 502-foot shot—the longest measurable home run hit inside Fenway Park—landed on June 9, 1946.

THE SPORTS GUY

For a glimpse into the psyche of a Red Sox fan read Bill Simmon's book *Now I can Die in Peace.*

THE NATION

The Red Sox have the most rabid fans in baseball. Knowledgeable and dedicated, they follow the team with religious-like intensity. Red Sox Nation has grown in recent years, much to the chagrin of diehards. You may hear the term "pink hat" used to derisively tag someone who is a bandwagon fan (i.e., anyone who didn't suffer with the rest of the "nation" during the title drought).

THE MONSTER

Fenway's most dominant feature is the 37-foot-high "Green Monster," the wall that looms over left field. It's just over 300 feet from home plate and in the field of play, so deep fly balls that would have been outs in other parks sometimes become home runs. The Monster also stops line drives that would have been over the walls of other stadiums, but runners can often leg these hits out into doubles (since balls are difficult to field after they ricochet off the wall).

THE MUSIC

Fans sing "Take Me Out to the Ballgame" during the 7th-inning stretch in every ballpark; but at Fenway, they also sing Neil Diamond's "Sweet Caroline" at the bottom of the 8th. If the Sox win, the Standell's "Dirty Water" blasts over the loudspeakers at the end of the game.

THE CURSE

In 1920 the Red Sox traded pitcher Babe Ruth to the Yankees, where he became a home-run-hitting baseball legend. Some fans—most famously *Boston Globe* columnist Dan Shaughnessy, who wrote a book called *The Curse of the Bambino*—blamed this move for the team's 86-year title drought, but others will claim that "The Curse" was just a media-driven storyline used to explain the team's past woes. Still, fans who watched a ground ball roll between Bill Buckner's legs in the 1986 World Series or saw Aaron Boone's winning home run in the 2003 American League Division Series swear the curse was real.

VISIT THE NATION

13

Not lucky enough to nab tickets ahead of time? Try your luck at Gate E two hours before the game, when a handful of tickets are sold. There's a one-ticket limit, so everyone in your party must be in line. If that doesn't yield results, you can still experience *the Nation*. Head down to the park and hang out on Yawkey Way, which borders the stadium. On game days it's closed to cars and filled with vendors, creating a street-fair atmosphere. Duck into a nearby sports bar and enjoy the game with other fans who weren't fortunate enough to secure seats. A favorite is the **Cask'n Flagon,** at Brookline Avenue and Lansdowne Street, across the street from Fenway. The closest you can get to Fenway without buying a ticket is the **Bleacher Bar** (✉ *82A Lansdowne St.*), which actually has a huge window in the center field wall overlooking the field. If you want to see a game from this unique vantage point, get here early—it starts filling up a few hours before game time.

Updated by Kim Foley MacKinnon

Everything you've heard about the zeal of Boston fans is true; here you root for the home team. You cheer, and you pray, and you root some more. "Red Sox Nation" witnessed a miracle in 2004, with the reverse of the curse and the team's first World Series victory since 1918.

Then in 2007 the Sox proved it wasn't just a fluke with another series win, and yet again in 2013. In 2008 the Celtics ended its 18-year NBA championship drought with a thrilling victory over longtime rivals the LA Lakers. And despite the sting of their Super Bowl losses in 2008 and 2012, the three-time champion New England Patriots are still a remarkable force to be reckoned with.

Bostonians' long-standing fervor for sports is equally evident in their leisure-time activities. Harsh winters keep locals wrapped up for months, only to emerge at the earliest sign of oncoming spring. Once the mercury tops freezing and the snows begin to melt, Boston's extensive parks, paths, woods, and waterways teem with sun seekers and athletes—until the bitter winds bite again in November, and that energy becomes redirected toward white slopes, frozen rinks, and sheltered gyms and pools.

PLANNING

Appalachian Mountain Club. This is a helpful first stop for anyone with questions about the great outdoors. The club's bookstore has maps and guides about hiking and other active pursuits in the Northeast and Mid-Atlantic. The club also runs workshops and organized hiking, paddling, biking, and skiing trips throughout New England. Programs fill up fast, so advance reservations are essential. Fees are higher for nonmembers. A one-year individual membership starts at $50; discounted family, youth, and senior memberships are available. The club office is open weekdays 9 to 5. ✉ *5 Joy St., Beacon Hill* ☎ *617/523–0655* 🌐 *www.outdoors.org* Ⓜ *Park St.*

Department of Conservation & Recreation (*DCR*). Most public recreational facilities, including skating rinks and tennis courts, are operated by the Department of Conservation & Recreation. The DCR provides information about recreational activities in its facilities and promotes the conservation of Massachusetts parks and wilderness areas. ✉ *251 Causeway St., Suite 600, North End* ☎ *617/626–1250* 🌐 *www.mass.gov/dcr.*

SPORTS

Being a sports fan in Boston isn't like being a sports fan anywhere else. There's a sense of obligation to the home team, especially to the Red Sox. And while the offering is spirited and plentiful for spectator sports, Boston also has many opportunities for participatory play as well, from skiing and ice-skating in winter to bicycling, boating, and golfing in warmer months.

BASEBALL

⇨ *See the Fenway Park spotlight at the beginning of this chapter for information on the Boston Red Sox.*

BASKETBALL

Boston Celtics. One of the most storied franchises in the National Basketball Association, the Boston Celtics have won the NBA championship 17 times since 1957, more than any other team in the league. The last title came in 2008, after a solid defeat of longtime rivals (the LA Lakers) ended an 18-year championship dry spell. Basketball season runs from late October to April, and playoffs last until mid-June. ✉ *TD Garden, Old West End* ☎ *866/423–5849, 617/931–2222 Ticketmaster* 🌐 *www.celtics.com.*

BICYCLING

Department of Conservation & Recreation (*DCR*). For other path locations, consult the Department of Conservation & Recreation Website. 🌐 *www.mass.gov/dcr.*

Massachusetts Bicycle Coalition (*MassBike*). This advocacy group works to improve conditions for area cyclists, has information on organized rides, and sells good bike maps of Boston and the state. Thanks to MassBike's lobbying efforts, the MBTA now allows bicycles on subway and commuter-rail trains during nonpeak hours. ✉ *171 Milk St., Suite 33, Downtown* ☎ *617/542–2453* 🌐 *www.massbike.org.*

BIKE PATHS

Dr. Paul Dudley White Bike Path. This 17-mile long path follows both banks of the Charles River as it winds from Watertown Square to the Museum of Science. ✉ *Watertown.*

RENTALS

Back Bay Bicycles. Road bikes rent here for $65 per day (weekly rates are also available)—cash only. ✉ *362 Commonwealth Ave., Back Bay* ☎ *617/247–2336* 🌐 *www.backbaybicycles.com.*

13

Community Bicycle Supply. This South End place rents cycles from April through October. ✉ *496 Tremont St., at E. Berkeley St., South End* ☎ *617/542–8623* 🌐 *www.communitybicycle.com* Ⓜ *Back Bay.*

TOURS

Urban AdvenTours. A variety of themed excursions run throughout Boston and Cambridge, with most covering about 10 to 12 miles. They leave from Urban AdvenTours Atlantic Avenue headquarters and are offered almost every day; in winter, the tours depend on the weather—call to confirm. The main tours cost $50 per person, and tickets are available for purchase through the website. You bring the adrenaline; Urban AdvenTours brings the bikes, helmets, and water. ✉ *103 Atlantic Ave., Downtown* ☎ *617/670–0637* 🌐 *www.urbanadventours.com* Ⓜ *Aquarium Station.*

⇨ *See Massachusetts Bicycle Coalition, Back Bay Bicycles, and Community Bicycle Supply above for information on group rides.*

TOP 5

- Taking in a Red Sox game at Fenway Park.
- Running, walking, or biking along the Charles River or, better yet, sailing on it with Community Boating.
- Seeing magnificent whales and their young close-up on a whale-watch boat tour.
- Exploring the quiet, awe-inspiring trails and shorelines of the Boston Harbor Islands.
- Strolling through the parks and gardens of the Emerald Necklace (including the Boston Common and Public Garden).

BOATING

Except when frozen over, the waterways coursing through the city serve as a playground for boaters of all stripes. All types of pleasure craft, with the exception of inflatables, are allowed from the Charles River and Inner Harbor to North Washington Street on the waters of Boston Harbor, Dorchester inner and outer bays, and the Neponset River from the Granite Avenue Bridge to Dorchester Bay.

Charles River Watershed Association. This association publishes detailed boating information on its Website. ☎ *781/788–0007* 🌐 *www.charlesriver.org.*

Boat Drop Sites. There are several boat drop sites along the Charles.

Clarendon Street ✉ *Back Bay* Ⓜ *Copley, Arlington.*

Hatch Shell ✉ *Embankment Rd., Back Bay* Ⓜ *Arlington, Boylston.*

Pinckney Street Landing ✉ *Back Bay* Ⓜ *Charles/MGH.*

Brooks Street ✉ *Nonantum Rd., Brighton.*

Richard T. Artesani Playground ✉ *Off Soldiers Field Rd., Brighton.*

Charles River Dam, Museum of Science ✉ *Cambridge* Ⓜ *Science Park.*

Watertown Square ✉ *Charles River Rd., Watertown.*

Rowers ready for races during the Head of the Charles Regatta

EVENTS

Head of the Charles Regatta. In mid-October about 300,000 spectators turn out to cheer the more than 7,500 male and female athletes who come from all over the world to compete in the annual Head of the Charles Regatta, which in 2014 marks its 50th anniversary. Crowds line the banks of the Charles River with blankets and beer (although the police disapprove of the latter), cheering on their favorite teams and generally using the weekend as an excuse to party. Limited free parking is available, but the chances of finding an open space close to the race route are slim; take public transportation if you can. During the event, free shuttles run between the start and end point of the race route on both sides of the river. ✉ *Banks of the Charles River, Cambridge* ☎ *617/868–6200* 🌐 *www.hocr.org.*

LESSONS AND RENTALS

Boston University. From May to October, Boston University offers beginner to advanced rowing and sailing programs. ✉ *Dewolfe Boathouse, 619 Memorial Dr., Cambridge* ☎ *617/353–9307 boathouse* 🌐 *www.bu.edu/fitrec* Ⓜ *Boston University Central, Boston University East.*

Charles River Canoe & Kayak Center. From May through mid-November you can rent a canoe, kayak, paddleboat, rowboat, or rowing shell from Charles River Canoe & Kayak Center. The center also offers a variety of canoeing and kayaking classes for all skill levels as well as organized group outings and tours. ✉ *2401 Commonwealth Ave., Newton* ☎ *617/965–5110* 🌐 *www.paddleboston.com.*

Charles River Canoe & Kayak Center's kiosk. From this kiosk you can rent canoes and kayaks on weekends in mid-April and Thursday through

Sunday from May through mid-October. The kiosk is open weekdays only for group appointments. ✉ *Soldiers' Field Rd. near Eliot Bridge, 1071 Soldiers Field Rd., Allston* ☎ *617/965–5110* 🌐 *www.paddleboston.com/boston.php*

Community Boating. Near the Charles Street footbridge on the Esplanade, Community Boating is the host of America's oldest public sailing program. From April through October, $99 nets you a 30-day introductory membership, beginner-level classes, and use of sailboats and kayaks. Full memberships grant unlimited use of all facilities; splash around for 60 days for $209 or all season long for $269. Experienced sailors short on time can opt for a one-day sailboat rental for $79; kayaks rent for $40 per day. ✉ *21 David Mugar Way, Beacon Hill* ☎ *617/523–1038* 🌐 *www.community-boating.org* Ⓜ *Charles/MGH.*

Community Rowing. This organization teaches rowing courses from introductory to competitive adult and youth levels. Private lessons are also available. ✉ *Daly Memorial Skating Rink, 20 Nonantum Rd., Brighton* ☎ *617/779–8267* 🌐 *www.communityrowing.org.*

Jamaica Pond Boat House. From April to October, Courageous Sailing operates out of the Jamaica Pond Boat House and provides lessons and equipment for rowing and sailing on the pond, except when youth classes are in session; call ahead to confirm. One-hour kayak rentals are $12; rowboats $10; and sailboats $15. ✉ *Jamaica Way and Pond St., Jamaica Plain* ☎ *617/522–5061* 🌐 *www.courageoussailing.org/jamaicapond* Ⓜ *Stony Brook, Green.*

FISHING

Efforts to clean up the city's waterways have heightened the popularity of recreational fishing in and around Boston.

MassWildlife Boston Office. Nonresidents can purchase a three-day Massachusetts fishing license for $23.50 at the Wildlife Boston Office, Brookline Town Hall, and some sporting-goods stores around the city. You can also buy one online at MassFishHunt. ✉ *251 Causeway St., North End* ☎ *866/703–1925* 🌐 *www.mass.gov/eea/agencies/dfg/licensing* Ⓜ *North Station.*

FRESHWATER FISHING

Blue Hills Reservation. Houghton's Pond in Blue Hills Reservation is an excellent place to freshwater fish. ✉ *Off Rte. 128, 840 Hillside St., Milton* ☎ *617/698–1802.*

Jamaica Pond. You can freshwater fish in Jamaica Pond. The pond is stocked each year by the Massachusetts Division of Fisheries and Wildlife. ✉ *Jamaica Way and Pond St., Jamaica Plain* 🌐 *www.jamaicapond.com* Ⓜ *Stony Brook, Green.*

Middlesex Fells Reservation. You can fish at Dark Hollow Pond in Middlesex Fells Reservation. ✉ *Off Rte. 93, Main St.* 🌐 *www.fells.org/Visit-Info.html* Ⓜ *Oak Grove Station, Washington.*

Stony Brook Reservation. Turtle Pond in Stony Brook Reservation has excellent fishing. ✉ *Turtle Pond Pkwy., Hyde Park* Ⓜ *Hyde Park, Forest Hills Station.*

SALTWATER FISHING

Locals who want to try saltwater fishing cast their lines from the **John J. McCorkle Fishing Pier** on Castle Island off Day Boulevard in South Boston and **Tenean Beach** and **Victory Road Park** off Morrissey Boulevard in Dorchester.

Boston Harbor Islands National Park Area. This recreational area is known for great fishing, although no public piers are available. Reach the islands by ferry. ☎ *617/223–8666* 🌐 *www.bostonislands.com.*

National Park Service. The NPS is a good source for information about camping, transportation, and the like. ☎ *617/223–8666* 🌐 *www.nps.gov/bost/index.htm*

FOOTBALL

COLLEGE

Boston College Eagles. With the only Division 1A football program in town, the Boston College Eagles play against some of the top teams in the country. ✉ *Alumni Stadium, Chestnut Hill* ☎ *617/552–4622* 🌐 *www.bceagles.com* Ⓜ *Boston College.*

Harvard University Crimson. Built in 1903, Harvard Stadium is the oldest concrete stadium in the country and the home of the Harvard University Crimson. The tongue-in-cheek halftime shows of the Harvard band make any game worth the trip. ✉ *Harvard Stadium, N. Harvard St. and Soldiers Field Rd., Allston* ☎ *617/495–2211* 🌐 *www.gocrimson.com* Ⓜ *Harvard Square.*

NFL

New England Patriots. Boston has been building a football dynasty over the past decade, starting with the New England Patriots come-from-behind victory against the favored St. Louis Rams in the 2002 Super Bowl. Coach Bill Belichick and heartthrob quarterback Tom Brady then brought the team two more championship rings in 2004 and 2005, and have made Patriots fans as zealous as their baseball counterparts. Exhibition football games begin in August, and the season runs through the playoffs in January. The state-of-the-art Gillette Stadium is in Foxborough, 30 miles southwest of Boston. ✉ *Gillette Stadium, Rte. 1, off I–95 Exit 9, Foxborough* ☎ *800/745–3000 Ticketmaster* 🌐 *www.patriots.com* Ⓜ *Gillette Stadium.*

GOLF

Massachusetts Golf Association. This association represents 400 clubs in the state and has information on courses that are open to the public. ✉ *300 Arnold Palmer Blvd., Norton* ☎ *774/430–9100* 🌐 *www.mgalinks.org.*

COURSES

Although you'll need to know someone who knows someone who *is* someone to play at Chestnut Hill's Country Club (which is actually called the Country Club), one of the nation's top-rated private courses, anyone can use the public courses in Boston, which are among the best in the country.

George Wright Golf Course. This hilly course is more challenging than the other Donald Ross–designed course at Franklin Park. It opens for the season starting in April each year. Tee times are necessary on weekends. ✉ *420 West St., Hyde Park* ✣ *From Forest Hills station, take Bus 50, which goes right by the course.* ☎ *617/364–2300* 🌐 *www.cityofbostongolf.com* ⛳ *18 holes. 6600 yards. Par 70. Greens fees: weekends, $45 ($39 for residents); weekdays, $40 ($35 for residents)* Ⓜ *Forest Hills* ☞ *Facilities: Putting green, golf carts, pull carts, rental clubs, pro shop, lessons, restaurant, bar.*

William J. Devine Golf Course at Franklin Park. Donald Ross crafted this course in early 1896. It's open year-round, weather permitting. If you want to play 9 holes instead of 18, you can do so only after 1 pm on weekends. Charges for a golf cart tend to run about $11 to $20 extra per person. The course is part of delightful Franklin Park, which also has picnic facilities and jogging courses. Festivals and other outdoor activities take place all year. ✉ *1 Circuit Dr., Dorchester* ☎ *617/265–4084* 🌐 *www.cityofbostongolf.com* ⛳ *18 holes. 6009 yards. Par 70. Greens fees: $40, weekdays; $45, weekends* Ⓜ *Forest Hills* ☞ *Facilities: Golf carts, pull carts, rental clubs, pro shop, lessons, restaurant.*

HIKING

With the Appalachian Trail just two hours' drive from Downtown and thousands of acres of parkland and trails encircling the city, hikers will not have a lack of options in and around Boston.

FAMILY **Blue Hills Reservation.** A 20-minute drive south of Boston, the Blue Hills Reservation encompasses 7,000 acres of woodland with about 125 miles of trails, some ideal for cross-country skiing in winter, some designated for mountain biking the rest of the year. Although only 635 feet high, Great Blue Hill, the tallest hill in the reservation, has a spectacular view of the entire Boston metro area. It's open daily, and maps are available for purchase at the reservation headquarters or the Blue Hills Trailside Museum. To get there, take Route 93 South to Exit 3, Houghton's Pond. ✉ *695 Hillside St., Milton* ☎ *617/698–1802* 🌐 *www.mass.gov/eea/agencies/dcr/massparks/region-south/blue-hills-reservation.html.*

Boston Harbor Islands National Park Area. Easily accessible from Downtown Boston, the Boston Harbor Islands National Park Area is seldom crowded. The park maintains walking trails through diverse terrain and ecosystems *(⇨ Parks, at the end of this chapter).* 🌐 *www.bostonharborislands.org.*

Middlesex Fells Reservation. Just a few miles north of Boston, the 2,575-acre Middlesex Fells Reservation has well-maintained hiking trails that pass over rocky hills, across meadows, and through wetland areas. Trails range from the quarter-mile Bear Hill Trail to the 6.9-mile Skyline Trail. Mountain bikers can ride along the reservation's fire roads and on a designated loop trail. This sprawling reservation covers area in Malden, Medford, Stoneham, Melrose, and Winchester. To get to the western side of the reservation from Boston, take Route 93 North to Exit 33, and then take South Border Road off the rotary. ☎ *617/727–5380* 🌐 *www.mass.gov/dcr/parks/metroboston/fells.htm.*

DID YOU KNOW?

The Blue Hills Reservation was so named by early European explorers who noticed a bluish hue in the hills. The history of the area's earliest inhabitants, the Native Americans, is told through 16 archaeological sites.

Boston Common becomes an icy wonderland in winter.

Stony Brook Reservation. Excellent hiking footpaths crisscross the 475-acre Stony Brook Reservation, which spans Hyde Park and West Roxbury. ✉ *Turtle Pond Pkwy.* ☎ *617/333–7404* 🌐 *www.mass.gov/dcr/parks/metroboston/stony.htm.*

GROUP HIKES

FAMILY **Blue Hills Trailside Museum.** Managed by the Massachusetts Audubon Society, the Blue Hills Trailside Museum organizes hikes and nature walks. Open Thursday through Sunday and Monday holidays from 10 to 5, the museum has natural-history exhibits and live animals. Admission is $3. The trails are open daily dawn to dusk and are free to explore. Take Route 93 South to Exit 2B and Route 138 North. ✉ *1904 Canton Ave., Milton* ☎ *617/333–0690* 🌐 *www.massaudubon.org.*

Boston Parks & Recreation Department. Rangers lead walks through the Emerald Necklace parks. ✉ *1010 Massachusetts Ave.* ☎ *617/635–4505* 🌐 *www.cityofboston.gov/parks/parkrangers.*

HOCKEY

Boston hockey fans are informed, vocal, and extremely loyal. The stands are packed at Bruins games—especially since winning the Stanley Cup in 2011—despite high ticket prices. Local college hockey teams tend to give spectators plenty to celebrate at a much more reasonable price.

Beanpot Hockey Tournament. Boston College, Boston University, Harvard, and Northeastern teams face off every February in the Beanpot Hockey Tournament at the TD Garden. The colleges in this fiercely contested tournament traditionally yield some of the finest squads in the country. ✉ *TD Garden* 🌐 *www.beanpothockey.com* Ⓜ *North Station.*

Boston Bruins. Beantown's hockey team is on the ice from September until April, frequently on Thursday and Saturday evenings. Playoffs last through early June. ✉ *TD Garden, 100 Legends Way, Old West End* ☎ *617/624–2327* 🌐 *www.bostonbruins.com* Ⓜ *North Station.*

ICE SKATING

Boston Common Frog Pond. Thanks to a refrigerated surface, the Boston Common Frog Pond transforms into a skating park from November to mid-March, complete with a warming hut and concession stand. Admission is $5 for adults; kids 13 and younger skate for free. Skate rentals cost $9 for adults and $5 for kids; lockers are $2. Frog Pond hours are Monday 10 to 4, Tuesday through Thursday and Sunday 10 to 9, and Friday and Saturday 10 to 10. With the gold dome of the State House in the background, it's a spectacular setting. ✉ *Boston Common, enter near Beacon and Walnut Sts., Beacon Hill* ☎ *617/635–2120* 🌐 *www.bostonfrogpond.com* Ⓜ *Park St., Boylston.*

Boston Public Garden. Skaters like to head to the frozen waters of the lagoon at Boston Public Garden, but in 2012 the city posted signs asking people not to skate since it's not regulated; many, however, have ignored the warnings. ✉ *69 Beacon St., Back Bay* 🌐 *www.cityofboston.gov/parks/emerald/public_garden.asp* Ⓜ *Arlington, Boylston.*

Larz Anderson Park. Outside the city, try the skating rink in Larz Anderson Park, at the top of a wooded hill. Admission for Brookline residents is $5; nonresidents pay $8. Skate rentals are $6. The rink is open from December through early March. ✉ *23 Newton St., Brookline* ✣ *From the Forest Hills T station, take Bus 51 toward Cleveland Circle and get off at Clyde and Whitney streets. The park is a five-minute walk away.* ☎ *617/739–7518* 🌐 *www.brooklinema.gov* Ⓜ *Forest Hills.*

Public Ice-skating Rinks. The Department of Conservation & Recreation operates more than 20 public ice-skating rinks; hours and season vary by location. Call for a complete list of rinks and their hours of operation. ☎ *617/626–1250* 🌐 *www.mass.gov/dcr.*

SKATE RENTALS

Beacon Hill Skate Shop. In business for more than 30 years, Beacon Hill Skate Shop rents skates for use in the Frog Pond and Public Garden. A credit card is required; call in advance and they'll have the skates sharpened and ready for you. ✉ *135 Charles St. South, off Tremont St., near Citi Performing Arts Center, South End* ☎ *617/482–7400* 🌐 *www.beaconhillskateshop.com* Ⓜ *Tufts Medical Center.*

RUNNING AND JOGGING

Boston's parks and riverside pathways almost never lack for joggers, even in the worst weather. Paths on both sides of the Charles River are the most crowded and best maintained, particularly along the **Esplanade.** Watch out for in-line skaters and bikers. At **Castle Island** in South Boston, skaters and joggers zip past strolling lovebirds and parents pushing jogging strollers. The tranquil, wooded 1½-mile-long loop around idyllic **Jamaica Pond** is a slightly less crowded option.

EVENTS

Fodor's Choice ★ **Boston Marathon.** Every Patriots' Day (the third Monday in April), fans gather along the Hopkinton–to–Boston route of the Boston Marathon (⇨ *Close-Up box in this chapter*) to cheer on more than 25,000 runners from all over the world. The race ends near Copley Square in the Back Bay. ✉ *Copley Square, Back Bay* 🌐 *www.baa.org* Ⓜ *Copley, Arlington.*

Boston Athletic Association. For information, call the Boston Athletic Association. ☎ *617/236–1652* 🌐 *www.bostonmarathon.org*

Tufts Health Plan 10K for Women. In October, women runners take the spotlight on Columbus Day for the Tufts Health Plan 10K for Women, which attracts about 7,000 participants and 20,000 spectators. Four American records have been set at this race since it began in 1977. There's also a Kids 1K fun run at Boston Common and other family-friendly activities. ✉ *Boston Common* ☎ *888/767–7223 Registration* 🌐 *www.tufts-healthplan.com/tufts10k* Ⓜ *Park, Boylston.*

SKIING

CROSS-COUNTRY

Weston Ski Track. From mid-December to March, the Weston Ski Track provides cross-country skiers and snowshoers with 15 miles of groomed, natural trails and a snowmaking area with a lighted 2-mile ski track. Rentals and basic instruction are available. ✉ *200 Park Rd., Weston* ☎ *617/891–6575* 🌐 *www.skiboston.com.*

DOWNHILL

Berkshires. The Berkshires region in western Massachusetts offers a little bit of Aspen on the East Coast, with tony ski resorts, fine dining, and an upscale atmosphere for those able to take a daylong or weekend ski trip. For details on the various resorts in the Berkshires, go to 🌐 *www.berkshireskiing.com.* ✉ *135 miles west of Boston along I–90 and Rte. 2, Adams* 🌐 *berkshires.org.*

TENNIS

Department of Conservation & Recreation. The Department of Conservation & Recreation maintains more than 25 public tennis courts throughout Boston. These operate on a first-come, first-served basis. Lighted courts are open from dawn to 10 pm; other courts are open from dawn to dusk. ☎ *617/626–1250* 🌐 *www.mass.gov/dcr.*

Charlesbank Park. Some of Boston's most popular lighted courts are those at Charlesbank Park. ✉ *Storrow Dr. opposite Charles St., Beacon Hill* Ⓜ *Science Park*

Marine Park. Marine Park has lighted courts. ✉ *25 Farragut Rd., South Boston* ✣ *From the Andrew T station, take the 10 bus toward City Point via South Bay and get off at Farragut Rd.* Ⓜ *Andrew*

Weider Playground. The courts here are lighted. ✉ *Dale St., Hyde Park* ✣ *From the Forest Hills T station, take the 32 bus toward Cleary Square via Hyde Park Ave. and get off at West St. Walk down West to Gwinnet St. and take a right to go to the park.* 🌐 *www.bostonnatural.org* Ⓜ *Forest Hills*

CLOSE UP

The Boston Marathon

Though it missed being the first U.S. marathon by one year (the first, in 1896, went from Stamford, Connecticut, to New York City), the Boston Marathon is arguably the nation's most prestigious. Why? It's the only marathon in the world for which runners have to qualify; it's the world's oldest continuously run marathon; and it's been run on the same course since it began. Only the New York Marathon compares with it for community involvement. Spectators have returned to the same spot for generations, bringing their lawn chairs and barbecues.

In 2013, a horrific bombing near the finish line killed three people and injured scores of others. The tragic event shocked Boston and the nation, but runners and supporters have sworn to return in even bigger numbers.

Held every Patriots' Day (the third Monday in April), the marathon passes through Hopkinton, Ashland, Framingham, Natick, Wellesley, Newton, Brookline, and Boston; only the last few miles are run in the city proper. The first marathon was organized by members of the Boston Athletic Association (BAA), who in 1896 had attended the first modern Olympic games in Athens. When they saw that the Olympics ended with a marathon, they decided the same would be a fitting end to their own Spring Sports Festival, begun in the late 1880s.

The first race was run on April 19, 1897, when Olympian Tom Burke drew a line in the dirt in Ashland and began a 24.5-mile dash (increased to its current 26.2 miles in 1924) to Boston with 15 men. For most of its history, the race concluded on Exeter Street outside the BAA's clubhouse. In 1965 the finish was moved to the front of the Prudential Center, and in 1986 it was moved to its current location, Copley Square. The race's guardian spirit is the indefatigable John A. Kelley, who ran his first marathon shortly after Warren G. Harding was sworn in as president. Kelley won twice—in 1935 and 1945—took the second-place spot seven times, and continued to run well into his eighties, finishing 58 Boston Marathons in all. Until his retirement in 1992, his arrival at the finish signaled the official end of the race. A double statue of an older Kelley greeting his younger self stands at the route's most strenuous incline—dubbed "Heartbreak Hill"—on Commonwealth Avenue in Newton.

Women weren't allowed to race until 1972, but in 1966 Roberta Gibb slipped into the throngs under a hooded sweatshirt; she was the first known female participant. In 1967 cameras captured BAA organizer Jock Semple screaming, "Get out of my race," as he tried to rip off the number of Kathrine Switzer, who had registered as K. Switzer. But the marathon's most infamous moment was when 26-year-old Rosie Ruiz came out of nowhere to be the first woman to cross the finish line in the 1980 race. Ruiz apparently started running less than 1 mile from the end of the course, and her title was stripped eight days later. Bostonians still quip about her taking the T to the finish.

THE OUTDOORS

BEACHES

Although nearly 20 years of massive cleanup efforts have made the water in Boston Harbor safe for swimming, many locals and visitors still find city beaches unappealing, because much better beaches are a short drive or train ride away. The rocky North Shore—about an hour away—is studded with New England beach towns, each with its favorite swimming spot. Alternatively, if the traffic isn't too awful (and during the summer, that's a big if), you can reach the southern tip of Cape Cod in about an hour. For information on the amazing beaches on the Cape and the nearby islands of Martha's Vineyard and Nantucket (which are reachable by ferry from Boston and several towns on the Cape), pick up a copy of *Fodor's Cape Cod, Nantucket, & Martha's Vineyard* or *Fodor's New England.*

NEAR TOWN

Nantasket Beach. A 45-minute drive from Downtown Boston, Nantasket Beach has cleaner sand and warmer water than most local beaches. Kids love the tidal pools that form at low tide. A 1½-mile promenade makes for great people-watching. Take Route 3A South to Washington Boulevard, Hingham, and follow signs to Nantasket Avenue. **Amenities:** lifeguards; toilets. **Best for:** swimming; walking. ✉ *Rte. 3A, Hull* ☎ *617/727–5290* 🌐 *www.mass.gov/dcr/parks/metroboston/nantask.htm.*

Revere Beach. Just north of the city, Revere Beach, the oldest public beach in America, has faded somewhat since its glory days in the early 20th century when it was a Coney Island–type playground, but it still remains a good spot to people-watch and catch some rays. The sand and water are less than pristine, but on hot summer days the waterfront is still packed with colorful local characters and Bostonians looking for an easy city escape. Most of the beach's former amusements are gone, but you can still catch concerts at the bandstand in summer. **Amenities:** food and drink; lifeguards; showers; toilets. **Best for:** swimming; walking. ✉ *Revere Beach Blvd., Revere* ☎ *781/289–3020* 🌐 *www.mass.gov/dcr/parks/metroboston/revere.htm* Ⓜ *Revere Beach, Wonderland.*

BEACH FOOD

Kelly's Roast Beef. The huge, juicy roast-beef sandwiches served at Kelly's Roast Beef, a local institution since 1951, are the sole reason some Bostonians make the trek to Revere. Other menu favorites include the fried clams and hand-breaded onion rings. It's open from 5 am to 2:30 am Sunday through Thursday, and until 3 am Friday and Saturday. ✉ ***410 Revere Beach Blvd., Revere*** ☎ ***781/284–9129*** 🌐 ***www.kellysroastbeef.com.***

NORTH OF TOWN

Crane Beach on the Crane Estate. The 1,200-acre Crane Beach on the Crane Estate, an hour's drive to the north of Boston in the 17th-century village of Ipswich, has 4 miles of sparkling white sand that serve as a nesting ground for the threatened piping plover, a small shorebird. It's

Sunbathers soak up the rays at Revere Beach.

one of the most stunning beaches in the state. From Rt. 128 North, take Exit 20A and follow Route 1A North for 8 miles. Turn right on Route 133 East and follow for 1 miles. Turn left on Northgate Road and in mile, turn right on Argilla Road and follow for 2 miles to the entrance. Arrive early or come later in the afternoon as the parking lot does fill up and you could be turned away. Admission fees range from $2 to $25, depending on the time of year and whether you arrive on foot or by car. **Amenities:** food and drink; lifeguards; parking (fee); showers; toilets. **Best for:** swimming; walking; sunset. ✉ *Argilla Rd., Ipswich* ☎ *978/356–4354* 🌐 *www.thetrustees.org.*

Singing Beach. In a quiet Cape Ann town 32 miles north of Boston, this beach gets its name from the musical squeaking sound its gold-color sand makes when you step on it. The beach is popular with both locals and out-of-towners in summer. It's also worth a visit in fall, when the crowds have gone home and you'll have the splendid shores all to yourself. There's a snack bar at the beach, but it's worth taking a 10-minute stroll up Beach Street into town to get a cone at Captain Dusty's Ice Cream (✉ *60 Beach St.* ⏲ *Mar.–Oct.*). Because there's no public parking at the beach in season (May–September), the easiest way to get here is by MBTA's Newburyport/Rockport commuter rail line from Boston's North Station to the Manchester stop, which is a 15-minute walk from the beach. From Downtown Boston the train takes 45 minutes and costs $8.75 each way. **Amenities:** food and drink; lifeguards; showers; toilets. **Best for:** swimming; walking. ✉ *Beach St., Manchester-by-the-Sea* ☎ *978/526–2019 summer phone* 🌐 *www.manchester.ma.us/Pages/ManchesterMA_Recreation/singingbeach.*

Plum Island. The well-groomed beaches of Plum Island, located in the Parker River National Wildlife Refuge, are worth the effort of the trek from Boston. The water is clear and blue, but quite cold. You can easily find a secluded spot to sunbathe or bird-watch, a popular activity, but make sure to call in advance in late summer to ask about greenhead flies; they can be vicious here. From I–95 follow Route 113 East (becomes Route 1A South) 3½ miles to Newbury. Then, take a left on Rolfe's Lane and a right on to the Plum Island Turnpike. **Amenities:** parking (fee); toilets. **Best for:** swimming; walking; solitude. ✉ *Plum Island Blvd., Newburyport* ☎ *978/465–5753 (including parking info)* 🌐 *www.fws.gov/refuge/Parker_River/about.html.*

⇨ *For more information on North Shore beaches, see Chapter 15, Side Trips.*

PARKS

Arnold Arboretum. The sumptuously landscaped Arnold Arboretum is open all year to joggers and in-line skaters. Volunteer docents give free walking tours in spring, summer, and fall. ✉ *125 Arborway, Jamaica Plain* ☎ *617/524–1718* 🌐 *www.arboretum.harvard.edu* Ⓜ *Forest Hills.*

FAMILY Fodor's Choice ★ **Boston Harbor Islands National Park Area.** Comprising 34 islands and peninsulas, the Boston Harbor Islands National Park Area is somewhat of a hidden gem for nature lovers and history buffs, with miles of lightly traveled trails and shoreline and several little-visited historic sites to explore. The focal point of the national park is 39-acre Georges Island, where you'll find the partially restored pre–Civil War Fort Warren that once held Confederate prisoners. Other islands worth visiting include Peddocks Island, which holds the remains of Fort Andrews, and Spectacle Island, a popular destination for swimming (with lifeguards). Lovells, Peddocks, Grape, and Bumpkin islands all allow camping with a permit from late June through Labor Day. Peddocks also has yurts available. Pets and alcohol are not allowed on the Harbor Islands. ✉ *Visitor Pavilion, 191 W. Atlantic Ave., Downtown* ☎ *617/223–8666* 🌐 *www.bostonislands.com* Ⓜ *Aquarium.*

Charles River Reservation. Runners, bikers, and in-line skaters crowd the Charles River Reservation at the Esplanade along Storrow Drive, the Memorial Drive Embankment in Cambridge, or any of the smaller and less-busy parks farther upriver. Here you can cheer a crew race, rent a canoe or a kayak, or simply sit on the grass, sharing the shore with packs of hard-jogging university athletes, in-line skaters, moms with strollers, dreamily entwined couples, and intense academics, often talking to themselves as they sort out their intellectual—or perhaps personal—dilemmas. ☎ *617/626–1250* 🌐 *www.mass.gov/dcr/parks/CharlesRiver.*

Hatch Memorial Shell. On the Esplanade, the Hatch Memorial Shell hosts free concerts and outdoor events all summer. ✉ *Esplanade, 47 David G. Mugar Way, Beacon Hill* ☎ *617/626–4970* Ⓜ *Charles/MGH*

FAMILY Fodor's Choice ★ **Emerald Necklace.** The nine large public parks known as Boston's Emerald Necklace stretch 5 miles from the Back Bay Fens to Franklin Park in Dorchester, and include Arnold Arboretum, Jamaica Pond, Olmsted

Park, and the Riverway. The linear parks, designed by master landscape architect Frederick Law Olmsted more than 100 years ago, remain a well-groomed urban masterpiece. Locals take pride in and happily make use of its open spaces and its pathways and bridges connecting rivers and ponds. ⊕ *www.emeraldnecklace.org.*

Emerald Necklace Conservancy. This conservancy maintains a regular calendar of nature walks and other events in the parks. ✉ *125 The Fenway, Fens* ☎ *617/522–2700* ⊕ *www.emeraldnecklace.org* Ⓜ *Museum of Fine Arts, Northeastern*

Boston Parks & Recreation Department. Rangers with the Boston Parks & Recreation Department lead tours highlighting the area's historic sites and surprising ecological diversity. ✉ *1010 Massachusetts Ave.* ☎ *617/635–4505* ⊕ *www.cityofboston.gov/parks/parkrangers*

Harbor Express. Boston Best Cruises offers ferries to the Harbor Islands from Long Wharf (Downtown) or the Hingham Shipyard to Georges Island or Spectacle Island (in summer). High-speed catamarans run daily from May through mid-October and cost $15. Other islands can be reached by the free interisland water shuttles that depart from Georges Island. ☎ *617/770–0400* ⊕ *bostonsbestcruises.com.*

Mt. Auburn Cemetery. Cambridge's historic Mt. Auburn Cemetery is known as one of the best birding spots in the area and also has walking paths, gardens, and unique architecture. You can see the graves of such distinguished New Englanders as Oliver Wendell Holmes, Henry Wadsworth Longfellow, and Mary Baker Eddy. ✉ *580 Mt. Auburn St., Mt. Auburn, Cambridge* ☎ *617/547–7105* Ⓜ *Harvard, then Bus 71 or 73 to Mount Auburn St. at Aberdeen Ave. stop.*

Rose Fitzgerald Kennedy Greenway. After Boston's Central Artery (I–93) was moved underground as part of the Big Dig project, the state transformed the footprint of the former highway into the Rose Fitzgerald Kennedy Greenway, a gorgeous 1½-mile-long ribbon of parks boasting fountains, organically maintained lawns and landscapes, hundreds of trees, and chairs, tables, and umbrellas for the public's use. The Greenway stretches from the North End (New Sudbury and Cross streets) to Chinatown (Kneeland and Hudson streets), curving through the heart of Downtown, just a few blocks from the harbor in most places.

The Conservancy, a non-profit foundation, operates, maintains, and programs the park with more than 350 events each year, including concerts, exercise classes, and farmer's and artisan markets. A mobile food program features more than 20 food trucks and carts operating seasonally in several locations on the Greenway, with the heart of the activity at Dewey Square Park. In 2013, a one-of-a-kind carousel was installed, with 36 seats featuring 14 characters native to the Boston area, including a lobster, rabbit, grasshopper, and falcon. ✉ *Downtown* ☎ *617/292–0020* ⊕ *www.rosekennedygreenway.org* Ⓜ *South Station, North Station, Aquarium, Haymarket.*

SHOPPING

Updated by Frances Folsom

Shopping in Boston is a lot like the city itself: a mix of classic and cutting-edge, the high-end and the handmade, and international and local sensibilities. Though many Bostonians think too many chain stores have begun to clog their distinctive avenues, there remains a strong network of idiosyncratic gift stores, handicrafts shops, galleries, and a growing number of savvy, independent fashion boutiques. For the well-heeled, there are also plenty of glossy international designer shops.

Most stores accept major credit cards and traveler's checks. There's no state sales tax on clothing. However, there's a 6.25% sales tax on clothes priced higher than $175 per item; the tax is levied on the amount in excess of $175.

BOSTON SHOPPING PLANNER

HOURS

Boston's shops are generally open Monday through Saturday from 10 or 11 am until 6 or 7 pm and Sunday from noon to 5. Many stay open until 8 pm one night a week, usually Thursday. Malls are open Monday through Saturday from 9 or 10 am until 8 or 9 pm and Sunday from noon to 6.

GETTING AROUND

Study the T map *(⇨ On the Go map)* before plunging into a shopping tour of Boston or Cambridge. You're almost always better off leaving your car behind than trying to navigate congested city streets and puzzle out parking arcana. Most major shopping neighborhoods are easily accessible on the T: Boston's Charles Street and Downtown Crossing and Cambridge's Harvard, Central, and Porter squares are on the Red Line; Copley Place, Faneuil Hall, and Newbury Street are on the Green Line; the South End is an easy trip on the Orange Line.

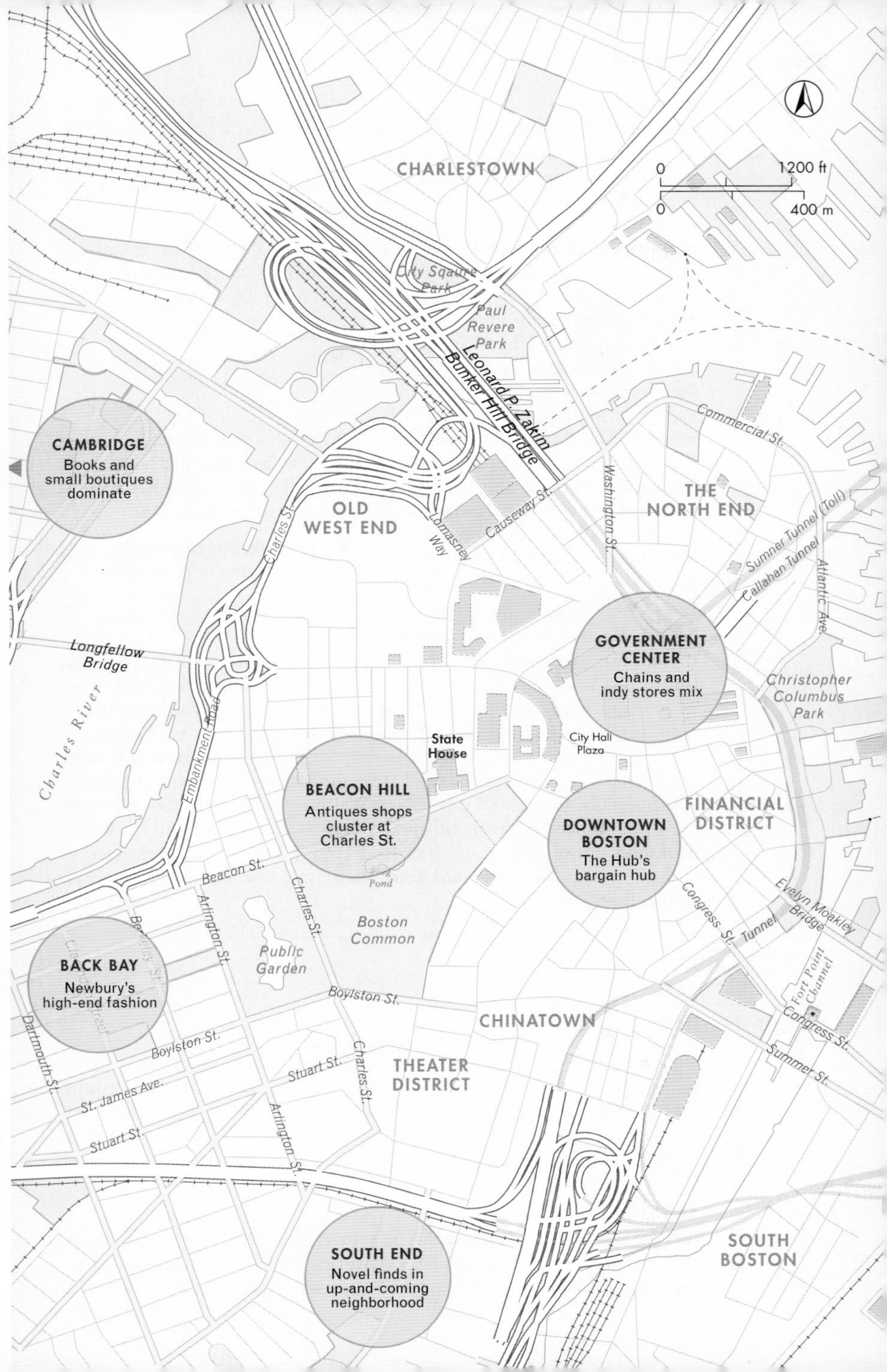
CHARLESTOWN
0
1200 ft
0
400 m
City Square Park
Paul Revere Park
Leonard P. Zakim Bunker Hill Bridge
Commercial St.
CAMBRIDGE
Books and small boutiques dominate
OLD WEST END
Charles St.
Lomasney Way
Causeway St.
Washington St.
THE NORTH END
Sumner Tunnel (Toll)
Callahan Tunnel
Atlantic Ave.
Longfellow Bridge
Charles River
Embankment Road
GOVERNMENT CENTER
Chains and indy stores mix
Christopher Columbus Park
State House
City Hall Plaza
BEACON HILL
Antiques shops cluster at Charles St.
FINANCIAL DISTRICT
DOWNTOWN BOSTON
The Hub's bargain hub
Beacon St.
Frog Pond
Congress St.
Tunnel
Evelyn Moakley Bridge
Boston Common
Charles St.
Arlington St.
Berkeley St.
Public Garden
BACK BAY
Newbury's high-end fashion
Fort Point Channel
Boylston St.
CHINATOWN
Congress St.
Dartmouth St.
Boylston St.
Charles St.
Summer St.
Stuart St.
THEATER DISTRICT
St. James Ave.
Arlington St.
Stuart St.
SOUTH END
Novel finds in up-and-coming neighborhood
SOUTH BOSTON

BLITZ TOURS

Beantown Bahgains. Thriftiness is considered one of the highest moral virtues in New England—even when buying luxury items. At **DSW** you can always find high-end designer shoes for both sexes at decent prices. Several shops full of watches and jewelry at reduced prices (some barely above wholesale) are found along Washington Street. If vintage is your thing, Newbury Street is dotted with consignment shops lined with gently worn Prada, Gucci, Burberry, and their ilk. Look first in **Second Time Around,** or try across the river in Harvard Square at **Oona's.** Both are also known to carry more daring labels such as Chloé and Catherine Malandrino for women, and Ermenegildo Zegna for men.

TOP 5

- Head to Louis Boston for exquisitely made clothing and personalized attention.
- Pick up a Red Sox hat at the T-shirt stand outside Fenway Park on a game day.
- Make an appointment with designer Daniela Corte to buy one of her signature custom-made wrap dresses.
- Pick up a slew of Danish-designed tableware and home decor (that no one else will have!) at Lekker in the South End.
- Hit Charles Street to troll through the dozens of antiques shops.

Books. Boston is a bibliophile's dream. For rare, antique, or just plain unusual books, start at **Ars Libri Ltd.** in the South End, a few blocks away from the Back Bay T stop. From here, head to Newbury Street (turn right on Waltham Street, walk three blocks, and cross Tremont Street, then pick up Clarendon Street to Newbury Street) for a break at the **Trident Booksellers & Café,** one of the city's first bookstore-cafés, almost directly across the street. Alternatively, from Ars Libri follow Waltham to Tremont Street, make a right, and head over the turnpike to reach West Street and the **Brattle Bookshop.** From here, catch the Red Line T into Harvard Square to browse through the **Harvard Book Store** and, just around the corner, **Grolier Poetry Bookshop.**

BOSTON

BEACON HILL

When the British occupied Boston in the 18th century, British soldiers named Beacon Hill "Mount Whoredom" for the houses of ill-repute that lined Charles Street. In the 19th century Beacon Hill became home to the Boston Brahmins and became an upper-class neighborhood. Today the posh shops and homes that line the streets are the most expensive pieces of real estate in the city.

ANTIQUES

A Room With a Vieux Antiques. There's an abundant collection of French antiques from the 19th and 20th centuries here. A restoration department in the back alters furniture to your individual needs. ✉ *20 Charles*

St., Beacon Hill ☎ *617/973–6600* 🌐 *www.aroomwithavieux.com* ⏲ *Closed Sun.* Ⓜ *Charles/MGH.*

Boston Antique Company. This flea market–style collection of dealers has been in business for 32 years and is still going strong. Occupying the lower level of the building, the company contains everything from vintage photos and paintings to porcelain, silver, bronzes, and furniture. ✉ *119 Charles St., Beacon Hill* ☎ *617/227–9810* Ⓜ *Charles/MGH.*

Devonia: Antiques for Dining. Some of the fabulous china sets here are fit for a queen—some really were designed for royalty. Feast your eyes on tens of thousands of pieces of tableware, including, perhaps, the custom-made set of Baccarat once owned by the Sultan of Brunei. ✉ *15 Charles St., Beacon Hill* ☎ *617/523–8313* 🌐 *www.devonia-antiques.com* ⏲ *Closed. Tues.* Ⓜ *Charles/MGH.*

Eugene Galleries. This store is chockablock with prints, etchings, old maps, and books; a 19th-century print of a Boston landmark, for instance, makes for a unique and lasting souvenir. ✉ *76 Charles St., Beacon Hill* ☎ *617/227–3062* 🌐 *eugenegalleries.com* Ⓜ *Charles/MGH.*

Judith Dowling Asian Art. The sophistication here results from spareness and restraint. High-end Asian artifacts include Japanese pottery and scrolls, Buddha figures, painted screens, cabinets, and other furnishings. ✉ *133 Charles St., Beacon Hill* ☎ *617/523–5211* 🌐 *www.judithdowling.com* ⏲ *Closed. Sun.–Wed. (except by appointment)* Ⓜ *Charles/MGH.*

Marika's. Every available inch of space in this jam-packed store, including the walls, is used to display wares. That silver chafing dish might need a polish, and the telephone table may be slightly scratched, but such imperfections keep the prices reasonable. ✉ *130 Charles St., Beacon Hill* ☎ *617/523–4520* Ⓜ *Charles/MGH.*

BEAUTY

The Beauty Mark. The tiny cosmetics boutique has everything to make you look gorgeous, including DuWop lip gloss, Julie Hewitt eye shadow, and St. Tropez self tanner. Manicures, pedicures, and eyelash extensions are available on-site. **■ TIP→ Closed on Sundays.** ✉ *33 Charles St., Beacon Hill* ☎ *617/720–1555* 🌐 *www.thebeautymark.com* ⏲ *Closed Sun.* Ⓜ *Charles/MGH.*

CLOTHING AND SHOES

Cibeline. Local designer Cibeline Sariano handcrafts and designs all her garments, including wrap dresses, blazers, and skirts. ✉ *120 Charles St., Beacon Hill* ☎ *617/742–0244* 🌐 *www.cibelinesariano.com* Ⓜ *Charles/MGH.*

Crush Boutique. This garden-level shop is perfect for everyday work essentials, weekend casual outfits, and even party-girl attire. You'll also find affordable jewelry and handbags to dress up any ensemble. **■ TIP→ Crush's Newbury Street shop (between Fairfield and Gloucester streets) has a more LA vibe to it.** ✉ *131 Charles St., Beacon Hill* ☎ *617/720–0010* 🌐 *www.shopcrushboutique.com* Ⓜ *Charles/MGH.*

Dress. True to its name, this shop owned by two young local women carries a number of great party dresses as well as flattering tees, pretty

CLOSE UP

Major Shopping Districts

Boston's shops and department stores are concentrated in the area bounded by Quincy Market, the Back Bay, and Downtown. There are plenty of bargains in the Downtown Crossing area. The South End's gentrification creates its own kind of consumerist milieus, from housewares shops to avant-garde art galleries. In Cambridge you can find many shops around Harvard and Central squares, with independent boutiques migrating west along Massachusetts Avenue (or "Mass Ave." as most people call it) toward Porter Square and beyond.

BOSTON

Boylston Street. Parallel to Newbury Street is Boylston Street, where a few standout shops such as Pompanoosuc Mills (hand-crafted furnishing) are scattered among the other chains and restaurants.

Charles Street. Pretty Charles Street, running north to south, is crammed beginning to end with top-notch antiques stores such as Judith Dowling Asian Art, Eugene Galleries, and Devonia, as well as a handful of independently owned fashion boutiques whose prices reflect their high Beacon Hill rents. River Street, parallel to Charles Street, is also an excellent source for antiques. Both are easy walks from the Charles Street T stop on the Red Line. Ⓜ *Charles/MGH.*

Copley Place. An indoor shopping mall in the Back Bay, Copley Place includes such high-end shops as Christian Dior and Louis Vuitton. It is anchored by the pricey but dependable Neiman Marcus and the flashy, often overpriced Barneys. ✉ *100 Huntington Ave., Back Bay* ☏ *617/262–6200* 🌐 *www.simon.com/mall/copley-place* Ⓜ *Copley, Back Bay.*

Downtown Crossing. This pedestrian mall has a Macy's, H&M, TJ Maxx—and a big hole in the ground where Filene's Basement used to be. But construction is underway to fill that spot with a multi-use building; the completion date is projected for 2017. ✉ *Washington St. from Amory St. to about Milk St., Downtown* Ⓜ *Downtown Crossing, Park St.*

Faneuil Hall Marketplace. This complex is both huge and hugely popular (drawing 22 million people a year), but not necessarily unique—most of its independent shops have given way to Banana Republic, Urban Outfitters, and other chains. The place has plenty of history, one of the area's great à la carte casual dining experiences (Quincy Market), pushcarts sell everything from apparel to jewelry to candy to Boston souvenirs, and buskers perform crowd-pleasing feats such as break dancing. ✉ *Bounded by Congress St., Atlantic Ave., the Waterfront, and Government Center, Downtown* ☏ *617/523–1300* 🌐 *www.faneuilhallmarketplace.com* Ⓜ *Government Center.*

Newbury Street. Boston's version of LA's Rodeo Drive, all of Newbury Street is a shoppers' paradise, from high-end names such as Brooks Brothers to tiny specialty shops such as the Fish and Bone. Upscale clothing stores, up-to-the-minute art galleries, and dazzling jewelers line the street near the Public Garden. As you head toward Massachusetts Avenue, Newbury gets funkier and the cacophony builds, with skateboarders zipping through traffic and garbage-pail drummers burning licks outside hip boutiques. The big-name stores run from Arlington Street to the

Prudential Center. 🌐 *www.newbury-st.com* Ⓜ *Arlington, Copley, Hynes.*

Prudential Center. A skywalk connects Copley Place to the Prudential Center. The Pru, as it's often called, contains moderately priced chain stores such as Ann Taylor and the Body Shop, and is anchored by Saks Fifth Avenue and Lord and Taylor. ✉ *800 Boylston St., Back Bay* ☎ *800/746–7778* 🌐 *www.prudentialcenter.com* Ⓜ *Prudential.*

South End. Merchants here are benefiting from the ongoing gentrification that has brought high real-estate prices and trendy restaurants to the area. Explore the chic home-furnishings and gift shops that line Tremont Street, starting at Berkeley Street. The MBTA's Silver Line bus runs through the South End. 🌐 *www.south-end-boston.com* Ⓜ *Back Bay.*

CAMBRIDGE

Harvard Square is the place to go for upscale clothes, jewelry, beauty aids, and anything "Harvahd." The best word to describe some of the shops in Central Square—Cheapo Records, Great Eastern Trading Company, and Rodney's Bookstore—is bohemian.

Brattle Street. A handful of chains and independent boutiques are clustered on Brattle Street. ✉ *Behind Harvard Sq., Cambridge* Ⓜ *Harvard.*

CambridgeSide Galleria. Macy's and Sears anchor this basic three-story mall with a food court; it's a big draw for local high-school kids. ✉ *100 CambridgeSide Pl., Kendall Sq., Cambridge* ☎ *617/621–8666* 🌐 *www.cambridgesidegalleria.com* Ⓜ *Lechmere, Kendall/MIT via free shuttle.*

Central Square. This area at the junction of Massachusetts Avenue, Prospect Street, River Street, and Western Avenue has an eclectic mix of furniture stores, used-record shops, ethnic restaurants, and small, hip performance venues. ✉ *East of Harvard Sq., Cambridge* 🌐 *centralsquare.com* Ⓜ *Central.*

Galleria at Harvard Square. Not to be confused with CambridgeSide Galleria, this collection of boutique shops at Harvard Square is matched with a few decent, independently owned restaurants. ✉ *57 JFK St., Cambridge* Ⓜ *Harvard.*

Harvard Square. Harvard Square takes up just a few blocks but holds more than 150 stores selling clothes, books, records, furnishings, and specialty items. (⇨ *Harvard Square Spotlight for more information.)* ✉ *Cambridge* Ⓜ *Harvard.*

Porter Square. This spot in north Cambridge has distinctive clothing stores, as well as crafts shops, coffee shops, natural-food stores, restaurants, and bars with live music. ✉ *West on Mass Ave. from Harvard Sq., Cambridge* Ⓜ *Porter Square.*

DID YOU KNOW?

Charles Street is an antiquer's dream, but it's also Boston's most dog-friendly street. Feel free to shop with your pooch; the area is scattered with water bowls and registers often hide treats. Boutique owners bring their dogs to work.

tops, and shoes from emerging designers. ✉ *70 Charles St., Beacon Hill* ☎ *617/424–7125* 🌐 *www.dressboston.com* Ⓜ *Charles/MGH.*

Helen's Leather Shop. Choose from half a dozen brands of boots (Lucchese, Nocona, Dan Post, Tony Lama, Justin, and Frye); then browse through the leather sandals, jackets, briefcases, luggage, and accessories. ✉ *110 Charles St., Beacon Hill* ☎ *617/742–2077* 🌐 *www.helensleather.com* ⏲ *Closed Tues. May–Oct.* Ⓜ *Charles/MGH.*

Holiday. A stockpile of flirty and feminine getups are the rage here. Cult lines such as Tracy Reese are in regular rotation among the fashionable racks. Keep your eye out for the occasional vintage clutch. ✉ *53 Charles St., Beacon Hill* ☎ *617/973–9730* 🌐 *www.holidayboutique.net* Ⓜ *Charles/MGH.*

Moxie. The selection is always fashion-forward and sophisticated at this home to the season's hottest shoes. ✉ *51 Charles St., Beacon Hill* ☎ *617/557–9991* 🌐 *www.moxieboston.com* Ⓜ *Charles/MGH.*

North River Outfitter. A preppy New Englander's heaven, with walls of Tory Burch tunics, Nantucket red pants, and needlepoint belts. ✉ *126 Charles St., Beacon Hill* ☎ *617/742–0089* 🌐 *www.northriveroutfitter.com* Ⓜ *Charles/MGH.*

Wish. The contemporary women's boutique is home to beloved brands including Diane von Furstenberg, Theory, and Joie. Be sure to stop by in the cooler months—their cashmere selection is otherworldly. ✉ *49 Charles St., Beacon Hill* ☎ *617/227–4441* 🌐 *thewishboston.wordpress.com* Ⓜ *Charles/MGH.*

GIFTS

Black Ink. A wall full of rubber stamps stretches above unusual candles, cookie jars, and other home accessories and gift items. ✉ *101 Charles St., Beacon Hill* ☎ *617/723–3883* 🌐 *www.blackinkboston.squarespace.com* Ⓜ *Charles/MGH.*

The Flat of the Hill. There's nothing flat about this fun collection of seasonal items, toiletries, toys, pillows, and whatever else catches the fancy of the shop's young owner. Her passion for pets is evident—pick up a Fetch & Glow ball and your dog will never again have to wait until daytime to play in the park. ✉ *60 Charles St., Beacon Hill* ☎ *617/619–9977* ⏲ *Closed Mon.* Ⓜ *Charles/MGH.*

Tibet Emporium. More upscale than your average imports store, Tibet Emporium goes beyond the usual masks and quilted wall hangings to offer beautifully delicate beaded silk pillowcases, pashmina wraps in every color imaginable, appliquéd and silk clothing, and finely wrought but affordable silver jewelry. ✉ *103 Charles St., Beacon Hill* ☎ *617/723–8035* Ⓜ *Charles/MGH.*

GROCERS

DeLuca's Market. Here's one neighborhood grocer that delivers the gourmet goods: an international cheese counter, homemade pâtés, fresh produce, and a snacks section that includes a dream team of cookies. ✉ *11 Charles St., Beacon Hill* ☎ *617/523–4343* 🌐 *www.delucasmarket.com* Ⓜ *Charles/MGH.*

Savenor's. If you're looking for exotic game meats, you've come to the right place. Savenor's food market, once Julia Child's favorite butcher, carries buffalo rump, alligator tail, even iguana. There are plenty of tamer choices, too, as well as outstanding cheeses, breads, and treats such as foie gras and smoked salmon. Another location operates in Cambridge. ✉ *160 Charles St., Beacon Hill* ☎ *617/723–6328* 🌐 *www.savenorsmarket.com* Ⓜ *Charles/MGH.*

JEWELRY

Twentieth Century Limited. Every kind of rhinestone concoction imaginable for the bauble babe in your life is here, as well as gently used 20th-century ladies' hats and pocketbooks. ✉ *73 Charles St., Beacon Hill* ☎ *617/742–1031* 🌐 *www.boston-vintagejewelry.com* Ⓜ *Charles/MGH.*

GOVERNMENT CENTER AND THE NORTH END

GOVERNMENT CENTER

The heart of Government Center is the shops at Faneuil Hall Marketplace (*see Major Shopping Districts box*). Over 22 million people come here each year. There's been a marketplace on this spot since Faneuil Hall was built in 1742.

THE NORTH END

This has to be one of Boston's best neighborhoods for shopping. Browse through the Italian green grocers and butcheries inhaling the tantalizing aromas. Or get yourself a little bling at one of the stylish shops lining the crooked streets.

BEAUTY

A Matter of Face. Bliss cosmetics and Paula Dorf tools put this spot on any makeup maven's hit list. ✉ *425 Hanover St., North End* ☎ *617/742–5874* 🌐 *www.amatteroffface.com* ⏲ *Closed Thurs.* Ⓜ *Haymarket.*

CLOTHING AND SHOES

In-Jean-Ius. The name says it all. Citizens of Humanity, Rock & Republic, Paige, and more denim cult favorites reside here. ✉ *441 Hanover St., North End* ☎ *617/523–5326* 🌐 *www.injeanius.com* Ⓜ *Haymarket.*

Shake the Tree. This one-stop shop has an eclectic array of contemporary clothing, bags, jewelry, gifts, and home items. ✉ *67 Salem St., North End* ☎ *617/742–0484* 🌐 *www.shakethetreeboston.com* Ⓜ *Haymarket.*

Twilight. This neatly organized boutique is where you'll find the perfect dress for a date, cocktail party, or wedding. You also can save some cash with Twilight's affordable costume jewelry. ✉ *12 Fleet St., North End* ☎ *617/523–8008* 🌐 *www.twilightboutique.com* Ⓜ *Haymarket.*

HOME FURNISHINGS

Acquire. The bright space boasts the perfect mix of modern and vintage furnishings, including lamps, pillows, pictures, and chairs. ✉ *61 Salem St., North End* ☎ *857/362–7380* 🌐 *www.acquireboutique.com* Ⓜ *Haymarket.*

Boston-area specialty markets nod to the area's rich cultural heritage.

DOWNTOWN BOSTON

Washington Street and Downtown Crossing is where to find bargains. Among the department and clothing stores here is Macy's.

BOOKS

Brattle Book Shop. The late George Gloss built this into Boston's best used- and rare-book shop. Today his son Kenneth fields queries from passionate book lovers. If the book you want is out of print, Brattle has it or can probably find it. The store has been in operation since 1825. ✉ *9 West St., Downtown* ☎ *617/542–0210, 800/447–9595* 🌐 *www.brattlebookshop.com* ⏲ *Closed Sun.* Ⓜ *Downtown Crossing.*

Calamus Bookstore. This friendly, informal store carries not only books but also videos, music, and gifts for the gay, lesbian, bisexual, or transgender shopper. ✉ *92B South St. #B, Leather District* ☎ *617/338–1931* 🌐 *www.calamusbooks.com* Ⓜ *South Station.*

CLOTHING AND SHOES

DSW. Major discounts on high-quality (and big-name) shoes for men and women are what draw much of Boston to this outpost of DSW, also known as Designer Shoe Warehouse. Everything from Nike to Prada can be found at varying discounts—sometimes up to 90% off. ✉ *385 Washington St., Downtown* ☎ *617/556–0052* 🌐 *www.dsw.com* Ⓜ *Downtown Crossing.*

Fodor's Choice ★ **Louis Boston.** Impeccably tailored designs, subtly updated classics, and the latest Italian styles highlight a wide selection of imported clothing and accessories. Visiting celebrities might be trolling the racks along with you as jazz spills out into the street from the adjoining Sam's

SHOP SOUTHIE

You may recognize South Boston or "Southie" from movies like *Good Will Hunting* and *The Departed.* Not to be confused with the South End, this area over the bridge is where you'll hear that thick Boston accent à la Matt Damon and Ben Affleck. The location is primarily known for two things: its large Irish-American population and its beaches. Since 2004, however, it has become one of the city's up-and-coming neighborhoods for great boutiques and top-notch salons. The shift took place under an ambitious redevelopment plan by the mayor. Shops cluster around Summer and East Broadway streets, but there aren't many pit stop places to snack. For great eateries and bars, try Channel Café, Sportello, and Drink on the Fort Point Channel side, also known as South Boston's waterfront and terminal area. The not-to-be missed Institute of Contemporary Art (and its killer gift shop) is over there, too. In addition to elegant Louis Boston (⇨ *Clothing and Shoes, Downtown Boston*), here are some of our top picks in the neighborhood.

CLOTHING

Habit. Find a great denim selection, including James Jeans, Tag Jeans, Citizens, and Hudson along with men's and women's casual chic attire and a few home items here. ✉ *703 E. Broadway, South Boston* ☎ *617/269–1998* 🌐 *www.habitshop.com* Ⓜ *Broadway, Andrew.*

Ku de Ta. Name brands and new designers unite in this store, which offers affordable handbag and jewelry options as well. ✉ *663 E. Broadway, South Boston* ☎ *617/269–0008* 🌐 *www.kudetaboston.com* Ⓜ *Broadway, Andrew* .

BEAUTY

Salon Mario Russo. It may be the most coveted cut in town, but Mario Russo and his expert staff retain a down-to-earth attitude as they provide excellent styling and color services. The manicures are equally good. ✉ *60 Northern Ave., South Boston* ☎ *857/350–3139* 🌐 *www.mariorusso.com* Ⓜ *South Station.*

Sarra. By far the best place to get your brows done, this large studio has a talented staff who takes its time to teach you all the necessary steps to look fabulous. All the products used are available for purchase. ✉ *840 Summer St., South Boston* ☎ *617/269–8999* 🌐 *www.sarraboston.com* 🕒 *Closed Sun.*

Shag. This much-hyped salon delivers with an extremely talented crew that will have you feeling like a rock star by the time you leave. ✉ *840 Summer St., Suite 3, South Boston* ☎ *617/268–2500* 🌐 *www.shagboston.com* 🕒 *Closed Sun.* Ⓜ *Broadway, Andrew.*

Restaurant. ✉ *60 Northern Ave., Downtown* ☎ *617/262–6100* 🌐 *www.louisboston.com* Ⓜ *South Station.*

DEPARTMENT STORES

Macy's. Three floors offer men's and women's clothing and shoes, housewares, and cosmetics. Although top designers and a fur salon are part of the mix, Macy's Boston location doesn't feel exclusive; instead, it's a popular source for family basics. ✉ *450 Washington St., Downtown* ☎ *617/357–3000* 🌐 *www.macys.com* Ⓜ *Downtown Crossing.*

SPECIALTY STORES

Lannan Ship Model Gallery. The 6,000-square-foot space looks like the attic of a merchant seaman: in addition to finished 18th- and 19th-century ship models ($200 to $100,000-plus) and vintage pond yachts, among the treasures are lanterns, navigational instruments, and marine charts, prints, and oils. ✉ *99 High St., Downtown* ☎ *617/451–2650* 🌐 *www.lannangallery.com* 🕓 *Closed Sun.* Ⓜ *South Station.*

BACK BAY AND THE SOUTH END

BACK BAY

This is the neighborhood of the elegant Mandarin Oriental Hotel—so need we say more about the shops you'll find here? Just in case: elegant, chic, modern, stylish.

ANTIQUES

Brodney Antiques & Jewelry. In addition to plenty of porcelain and silver, Brodney claims to have the biggest selection of estate jewelry in New England. ✉ *145 Newbury St., Back Bay* ☎ *617/536–0500* 🌐 *www.brodney.com* 🕓 *Closed Sun.* Ⓜ *Copley.*

ART GALLERIES

Alpha Gallery. Hours vary at this gallery that specializes in 20th-century and contemporary American and European painting, sculpture, and master prints. ✉ *37 Newbury St., Back Bay* ☎ *617/536–4465* 🌐 *www.alphagallery.com* Ⓜ *Arlington.*

Barbara Krakow Gallery. Emerging and established regional and international artists are displayed here. Mediums include contemporary painting, photography, drawing, and sculpture. ✉ *10 Newbury St., 5th fl., Back Bay* ☎ *617/262–4490* 🌐 *www.barbarakrakowgallery.com* 🕓 *Closed Sun. and Mon., and Sat. in July. Closed Aug.* Ⓜ *Arlington.*

Childs Gallery. The large collection of works for sale here includes paintings, prints, drawings, watercolors, and sculpture from the 1500s to the present. ✉ *169 Newbury St., Back Bay* ☎ *617/266–1108* 🌐 *www.childsgallery.com* 🕓 *Closed Sun.* Ⓜ *Copley.*

Copley Society of Art. After more than a century, this nonprofit membership organization continues to present the works of well-known and aspiring New England artists. ✉ *158 Newbury St., Back Bay* ☎ *617/536–5049* 🌐 *www.copleysociety.org* 🕓 *Closed Mon. (by appt. only)* Ⓜ *Copley.*

Gallery NAGA. Contemporary paintings, sculpture, and furniture are displayed in a striking space: the Church of the Covenant. ✉ *67 Newbury St., Back Bay* ☎ *617/267–9060* 🌐 *www.gallerynaga.com* 🕓 *Closed Sun. and Mon. Sept.–June* Ⓜ *Arlington.*

Rolly-Michaux. Only the highest quality of works are here, from the likes of Moore, Calder, Picasso, Chagall, Miró, and Matisse. ✉ *290 Dartmouth St., Back Bay* ☎ *617/536–9898* 🌐 *www.rollymichaux.com* 🕓 *Closed Sun.* Ⓜ *Copley.*

Vose Galleries. Established in 1841, Vose specializes in 19th- and 20th-century American art, including the Hudson River School, Boston School, and American impressionists. The addition of works of contemporary American realism recognizes an area that is often overlooked by the trendier set. ✉ *238 Newbury St., Back Bay* ☎ *617/536–6176* 🌐 *www.vosegalleries.com* ⏲ *Closed Mon.–Sun.* Ⓜ *Copley, Hynes.*

BEAUTY

Bella Santé. As pristine as it is serene, the beautifully designed Bella Santé is well stocked with high-end products and staffed by a well-trained crew. The locker room is stocked with thoughtful amenities such as body creams and just about any hair product you might need. ✉ *38 Newbury St., Back Bay* ☎ *617/424–9930* 🌐 *www.bellasante.com* Ⓜ *Arlington.*

Exhale. This Zen-like sanctuary is deceptively large. The subterranean lower level houses a first-rate spa and yoga studio. Upstairs, you'll find holistic body and skin-care products. ✉ *28 Arlington St., Back Bay* ☎ *617/532–7000* 🌐 *www.exhalespa.com* Ⓜ *Arlington.*

James Joseph Salon. Sleek and modern, yet utterly free of pretense, James Joseph has a fun, talented staff that gives customers exactly the cuts, color, and treatments they ask for. ✉ *30 Newbury St., Back Bay* ☎ *617/266–7222* 🌐 *www.jamesjosephsalon.com* Ⓜ *Arlington.*

The Loft Salon + Day Spa. Stylist Michael Albor is the master of hair color. He'll also sculpt your do into a work of art for events. ✉ *253 Newbury St., Back Bay* ☎ *617/536–5638* 🌐 *www.theloftsalonanddayspa.com* ⏲ *Closed Sun.–Mon.*

Mizu. Renowned hair stylist Charles Maksou calls this futuristic salon home. This very white-walled place offers all the usual treatments, plus a pair of Myvu glasses for watching TV. ✉ *776 Boylston St., Back Bay* ☎ *617/585–6498* 🌐 *www.mizuforhair.com.*

BOOKS

Barnes & Noble. Inside the Prudential Center is a large branch of the popular chain. The diverse bookseller now runs the Harvard Coop. ✉ *800 Boylston St., Back Bay* ☎ *617/247–6959* 🌐 *www.bn.com* Ⓜ *Prudential Center.*

Trident Booksellers & Café. Browse through an eclectic collection of books, tapes, and magazines, then settle in with a snack. It's open until midnight daily, making it a favorite with students. ✉ *338 Newbury St., Back Bay* ☎ *617/267–8688* 🌐 *www.tridentbookscafe.com* Ⓜ *Hynes.*

CLOTHING AND SHOES

Alan Bilzerian. Satisfying the Euro crowd, this store sells luxe men's and women's clothing by such fashion darlings as Yohji Yamamoto and Ann Demeulemeester. ✉ *34 Newbury St., Back Bay* ☎ *617/536–1001* 🌐 *www.alanbilzerian.com* ⏲ *Closed Sun.* Ⓜ *Arlington.*

Anne Fontaine. You can never have too many white shirts—especially if they're designed by this Parisienne. The simple, sophisticated designs are mostly executed in cotton and priced around $160. ✉ *318 Boylston St., Back Bay* ☎ *617/423–0366* 🌐 *www.annefontaine.com* Ⓜ *Arlington, Boylston.*

Betsy Jenney. Ms. Jenney herself is likely to wait on you in this small, personal store, where the well-made, comfortable lines are for women who cannot walk into a fitted size-4 suit—in other words, most of the female population. The designers found here, such as Nicole Miller, are fashionable yet forgiving. ✉ *114 Newbury St., Back Bay* ☎ *617/536–2610* 🌐 *www.betsyjenney.com* Ⓜ *Copley.*

WORD OF MOUTH

"The South End and Charles Street in Beacon Hill have the most independent boutiques (clothing and housewares, etc.). There have also been several stores that have opened in the North End in the last couple of years, mostly clothing boutiques. Newbury Street has a mix of chains and independent stores but is worth checking out as it's the main shopping thoroughfare of the city."—wyatt92

Brooks Brothers. Founded in 1818, Brooks still carries in its nationwide shops the classically modern styles that made it famous—old faithfuls for men such as navy blazers, summertime seersucker, and crisp oxford shirts. Its Newbury Street store offers a similar vibe for women as well. There are also Brooks Brothers shops on State Street and Boylston Street. ✉ *46 Newbury St., Back Bay* ☎ *617/267–2600* 🌐 *www.brooksbrothers.com* Ⓜ *Arlington.*

Calypso. The women's clothing here bursts with bright colors, beautiful fabrics, and styles so fresh you might need a fashion editor to help you choose. ✉ *114 Newbury St., Back Bay* ☎ *617/421–1887* 🌐 *www.calypsostbarth.com* Ⓜ *Copley.*

Chanel. Located at No. 5 in honor of its famous perfume, this branch of the Parisian couture house carries suits, separates, bags, shoes, cosmetics, and, of course, a selection of little black dresses. ✉ *5 Newbury St., Back Bay* ☎ *617/859–0055* 🌐 *www.chanel.com/en_US/fashion.html* Ⓜ *Arlington.*

Daniela Corte. From her sunny Back Bay studio, local designer Corte cuts women's clothes that flatter. Look for gorgeous suiting, flirty halter dresses, and sophisticated formal frocks that can be bought off the rack or be custom tailored. ✉ *211 Newbury St., Back Bay* ☎ *617/262–2100* 🌐 *www.danielacorte.com* Ⓜ *Copley.*

Giorgio Armani. This top-of-the-line Italian couturier is known for his carefully shaped jackets, soft suits, and mostly neutral palette. Two other stores in the national company are elsewhere in Boston—Emporio Armani at the Copley Place Mall and A|X Armani Exchange at 100 Huntington St. ✉ *22 Newbury St., Back Bay* ☎ *617/267–3200* 🌐 *www.armani.com* Ⓜ *Arlington.*

Gretta Luxe. Drop by Copley's sassy little boutique and pick up the latest "it" pieces—from velour hoodies by Juicy Couture to the must-have Stella McCartney design du moment. There are also jewelry, handbags, and other accessories. ✉ *Westin Hotel, Copley Place, 10 Huntington Ave., Back Bay* ☎ *617/536–1959* 🌐 *www.grettaluxe.com* Ⓜ *Copley.*

In the Pink. Don't be caught dead at the Vineyard this year without your Lilly Pulitzer resort wear, available here along with shoes, home decor, and children's clothing. ✉ *133 Newbury St., Back Bay* ☎ *617/536–6423* 🌐 *www.inthepinkonline.com* Ⓜ *Copley.*

John Fluevog Shoes. Many clubgoers have at least one pair of these oh-so-hip shoes in their closets, perhaps because of the company's claim that their Angel soles repel all kinds of nasty liquids "and Satan." ✉ *302 Newbury St., Back Bay* ☎ *617/266–1079* 🌐 *www.fluevog.com* Ⓜ *Copley.*

Jos. A. Bank Clothiers. Like Brooks Brothers, the national chain Joseph Bank is well known to the conservatively well dressed everywhere. ✉ *399 Boylston St., Back Bay* ☎ *617/536–5050* 🌐 *www.josbank.com* Ⓜ *Arlington.*

Kate Spade. Trendsetters go wild for Kate's colorful and classically whimsical handbags, as well as her shoes, PJs, accessories, and travel and cosmetics cases. The Boston shop is open in the evenings, and a Jack Spade is nearby. ✉ *117 Newbury St., Back Bay* ☎ *617/262–2632* 🌐 *www.katespade.com* Ⓜ *Copley.*

Marc by Marc Jacobs. The two-floor boutique carries this designer's younger, casual line with menswear on the first floor and women's on the second. Look, too, for cheap accessories. ✉ *81 Newbury St., Back Bay* ☎ *617/425–0404* 🌐 *www.marcjacobs.com* Ⓜ *Copley.*

CRAFTS

Society of Arts & Crafts. More than a century old, this is the country's oldest nonprofit crafts organization. It displays a fine assortment of ceramics, jewelry, glass, woodwork, and furniture by some of the country's finest craftspeople. ✉ *175 Newbury St., Back Bay* ☎ *617/266–1810* 🌐 *www.societyofcrafts.org* ⏲ *Closed Sun. By appointment only Mon.* Ⓜ *Copley.*

DEPARTMENT STORES

Barneys New York. The hoopla (not to mention the party) generated by this store's arrival was surprising in a city where everything new is viewed with trepidation. But clearly Boston's denizens have embraced the lofty, two-story space because it's filled with cutting-edge lines like Comme des Garçons and Nina Ricci, as well as a few bargains in the second-level Co-op section. ✉ *100 Huntington Ave., Back Bay* ☎ *617/385–3300* 🌐 *www.barneys.com* Ⓜ *Copley.*

Lord & Taylor. Somewhat overstuffed with merchandise, this Boston branch of the popular national chain is a reliable stop for classic clothing by such designers as Anne Klein and Ralph Lauren, along with accessories, cosmetics, and jewelry. ✉ *760 Boylston St., Back Bay* ☎ *617/262–6000* 🌐 *www.lordandtaylor.com* Ⓜ *Prudential Center.*

Neiman Marcus. At its Back Bay location, the flashy Texas-based retailer jokingly referred to by some as "Needless Markup" has three levels of swank designers and a jaw-dropping shoe section, as well as cosmetics and housewares. ✉ *5 Copley Pl., Back Bay* ☎ *617/536–3660* 🌐 *www.neimanmarcus.com* Ⓜ *Back Bay.*

Saks Fifth Avenue. The clothing and accessories at Saks run from the traditional to the flamboyant. It's a little pricey, but this Prudential Center location of the high-end national store is an excellent place to find high-quality merchandise, including shoes and cosmetics. ✉ *The Shops* *at Prudential Center, 800 Boylston St., Back Bay* ☎ *617/262–8500* 🌐 *www.saksfifthavenue.com* Ⓜ *Prudential Center.*

GIFTS

Fresh. You won't know whether to wash with these soaps or nibble on them. The shea butter–rich bars come in such scents as clove-hazelnut and orange-cranberry. They cost $6 to $7 each, but they carry the scent to the end. ✉ *121 Newbury St., Back Bay* ☎ *617/421–1212* 🌐 *www.fresh.com* Ⓜ *Copley.*

HOME FURNISHINGS

Mohr & McPherson. These stores are an exotic visual feast; cabinets, tables, chairs, and lamps from Japan, India, China, and Indonesia, as well as new and antique Oriental rugs, make up the impressive array. Also impressive are the high prices. ✉ *460 Harrison Ave., Back Bay* ☎ *617/210–7900* 🌐 *www.mohr-mcpherson.com* Ⓜ *Mass Ave.*

Showroom. This industrial-looking shop has some of the finest modern furniture in town. Collections from Italian lines Flexform and Cappellini are set up in room-like designs on the floor to give shoppers an accurate visual of their future interior design. ✉ *240 Stuart St., Back Bay* ☎ *617/482–4805* 🌐 *www.showroomboston.com* ⏲ *Closed Sun.* Ⓜ *Arlington.*

JEWELRY

Brodney Antiques & Jewelry. This store sells the most estate jewelry in New England, and its wide selection of platinum filigree diamond rings ensures a steady stream of nervous male customers about to pop the question. ✉ *145 Newbury St., Back Bay* ☎ *617/536–0500* 🌐 *www.brodney.com* ⏲ *Closed Sun.* Ⓜ *Copley.*

Dorfman Jewels. This elegant shop glows with first-class watches, pearls, and precious stones. ✉ *24 Newbury St., Back Bay* ☎ *617/536–2022* 🌐 *www.dorfmanjewelers.com* Ⓜ *Arlington.*

Shreve, Crump & Low. Since 1796, Shreve has specialized in high-end treasures, including gems and handcrafted platinum rings, as well as high-quality antiques. But don't get the impression that you can't afford anything here: one of the store's best-selling items is a $95 ceramic pitcher called "The Gurgling Cod," in honor of the state fish. ✉ *39 Newbury St., Back Bay* ☎ *617/267–9100* 🌐 *www.shrevecrumpandlow.com* Ⓜ *Arlington.*

Small Pleasures. Vintage lovers should not miss the antique and estate jewelry—from Victorian-era tourmaline cocktail rings to mint-condition pocket watches—that fills these cases. The staff is notably helpful and informed. ✉ *Copley Pl., 142 Newbury St., Back Bay* ☎ *617/267–7371* 🌐 *www.small-pleasures.com* ⏲ *Closed. Sun.* Ⓜ *Copley.*

Tiffany & Co. Fine service complements the finest in gems and precious metals—as well as crystal, china, stationery, and fragrances—in this Boston store of the elegant jewelry chain. ✉ *100 Huntington Ave., Copley Pl., Back Bay* ☎ *617/353–0222* 🌐 *www.tiffany.com* Ⓜ *Copley.*

MUSIC STORES

Newbury Comics. This outpost of the renowned pop culture store carries especially good lineups of independent pressings and frequent sales keep prices down. Second and third locations are found on JFK Street in Cambridge and inside the Faneuil Hall Marketplace. ✉ *332 Newbury St., Back Bay* ☎ *617/236–4930* 🌐 *www.newburycomics.com* Ⓜ *Hynes.*

SPECIALTY STORES

The Fish and Bone. This boutique is dedicated to all things cat and dog. Choose from the enormous selection of collars, toys, and food. ✉ *217 Newbury St., Back Bay* ☎ *857/753–4176* 🌐 *www.thefishandbone.com* Ⓜ *Arlington.*

THRIFT SHOPS

The Closet. Chanel purses, Rick Owens jackets, and Hermés bracelets have all graced this jam-packed consignment shop. Its picky choices are your gain. ✉ *175 Newbury St., Back Bay* ☎ *617/536–1919* 🌐 *www.closetboston.com* ⏲ *Closed Mon.* Ⓜ *Arlington.*

Second Time Around. Okay, so $700 isn't all that cheap for a used suit—but what if it's Chanel? Many of the items here, from jeans to fur coats, are new merchandise; the rest is on consignment. The staff makes periodic markdowns, ranging from 20% to 50% over a 90-day period. ✉ *176 Newbury St., Back Bay* ☎ *617/247–3504* 🌐 *www.secondtimearound.net* Ⓜ *Copley.*

SOUTH END

The South End is not what it used to be and that is a good thing. Now housed in what were at one time derelict buildings are upscale shops, restaurants, and bakeries. If you want to bring home a treat for Fido, this is the neighborhood to get it: there are more than 10 chichi pet boutiques here.

ART GALLERIES

Bromfield Art Gallery. A small, cooperative operation, Bromfield mounts month-long shows of its members' work, including oil and acrylic paintings, charcoals, and pastels. ✉ *450 Harrison Ave., South End* ☎ *617/451–3605* 🌐 *www.bromfieldgallery.com* Ⓜ *Tufts Medical Center.*

Samsøn Projects. A truly cross-cultural blend of exhibits, this gallery shows the experimental works of young contemporary artists. ✉ *450 Harrison Ave. @ 29 Thayer St., South End* ☎ *617/357–7177* 🌐 *www.samsonprojects.com* Ⓜ *Tufts Medical Center.*

BOOKS

Ars Libri Ltd. It's easy to be drawn into the rare and wonderful books on display here. The airy space is filled with books on photography and architecture, out-of-print art books, monographs, and exhibition catalogs. ✉ *500 Harrison Ave., South End* ☎ *617/357–5212* 🌐 *www.arslibri.com* Ⓜ *Back Bay.*

CLOTHING AND SHOES

Flock. Browse the collection of organic cotton T-shirts, everyday dresses, and vintage-inspired jewelry at this whimsical, boho-chic boutique. ✉ *274 Shawmut Ave., South End* ☎ *617/391–0222* 🌐 *www.flockboston.com* ⏲ *Closed Mon.* Ⓜ *Back Bay.*

Turtle. If you're not a slave to labels, shop where local, up-and-coming designers showcase their merchandise. ✉ *619A Tremont St., South End* ☎ *617/266–2610* 🌐 *www.turtleboston.com* Ⓜ *Back Bay.*

Uniform. A casual menswear shop with an urban, classic feel. You'll find everything from jackets to socks to shaving needs. ✉ *511 Tremont St., South End* ☎ *617/247–2360* 🌐 *www.uniformboston.com* ⏲ *Closed Mon.* Ⓜ *Back Bay.*

CRAFTS

Gracie Finn's. This trendy South End shop is well stocked with crafts from local artisans; items for sale include pottery, wooden toys, note cards, and luxurious soaps. It's not open in the evenings. ✉ *10 Union Park St., South End* ☎ *617/357–0321* 🌐 *www.graciefinn.com* Ⓜ *Back Bay.*

GIFTS

Coco Baby. From rugs to nightlights to car seats, this store has every baby need covered. Pick up a fun toy or an entire bedroom set. ✉ *1636 Washington St., South End* ☎ *617/247–2229* 🌐 *www.cocobabyboston.com* Ⓜ *Back Bay.*

HOME FURNISHINGS

Hudson. Find carpeting, lighting, seating, vintage items, and just about everything else one needs for a casual yet chic home. ✉ *12 Union Park St., South End* ☎ *617/292–0900* 🌐 *hudsonboston.com* Ⓜ *Back Bay, Prudential.*

Lekker. Dutch design with contemporary panache pervades South Washington Street's coolest home store—the best place to pick up bright oversize pillows, china, tables, Asian cabinets, and sleek, contemporary flatware. ✉ *1313 Washington St., South End* ☎ *617/542–6464* 🌐 *www.lekkerhome.com* Ⓜ *Back Bay.*

THRIFT SHOPS

Fodor's Choice ★ **Bobby from Boston.** For years this hidden gem was kept on the down low—but the word's out. Owner Bobby Garnett's been in the vintage game for decades, and his one-of-a-kind finds are unmatched. The two-room space is mostly menswear, but there are plenty of finds for females, too. ✉ *19 Thayer St., South End* ☎ *617/423–9299* ⏲ *Closed Mon.* Ⓜ *Back Bay, Prudential.*

TOYS

Tadpole. This is a treasure trove of educational games, dolls, trucks, blocks, and every other necessity for a kid's toy chest. Stock up on baby gear and essentials as well. ✉ *58 Clarendon St., South End* ☎ *617/778–1788* 🌐 *www.shoptadpole.com* Ⓜ *Back Bay.*

BOSTON OUTSKIRTS

BROOKLINE

Brookline, four miles west of Boston is easily reached on the MBTA. Its center, Coolidge Corner, is lined with shops selling everything from Russian tchotchkes to ethnic foods.

The Harvard Coop has peddled books to university students since 1882.

ANTIQUES

Autrefois Antiques. Come here to find French country and Italian 18th-, 19th-, and 20th-century furniture, mirrors, and lighting. ✉ *130 Harvard St., Brookline* ☎ *617/566–0113* 🌐 *www.autrefoisantiques.com* Ⓜ *Coolidge Corner.*

CAMBRIDGE

Cross over the Charles River to Cambridge, just as historic as Boston and where Harvard University's historic campus provides a beautiful backdrop for a unique and charming shopping experience.

There's something about Harvard Square that screams sophistication. Maybe it's the area's rich history, with streets and establishments dating back to 1626. Massachusetts Avenue, Brattle Street, and Mt. Auburn Street shape the area and are adorned with various standout boutiques and a handful of chain stores, including Urban Outfitters and Gap. Naturally, a collegiate crowd is drawn to the area, but the stores don't cater to one individual, and the old-meets-new atmosphere makes it a destination for the whole family. On weekends the square holds many festivals, fairs, and events, making it more than your average shopping destination. Also, the stores are open late. If possible, avoid early September, when college students instinctively flock to the region in need of back-to-school everything.

ANTIQUES

Cambridge Antique Market. Off the beaten track, this antique hot-spot has a selection bordering on overwhelming: five floors of goods ranging from 19th-century furniture to vintage clothing, much of it reasonably priced. There are two parking lots next to the building. ✉ *201 Monsignor O'Brien Hwy., Cambridge* ☎ *617/868–9655* 🌐 *www.marketantique.com* ⏲ *Closed Sun.* Ⓜ *Lechmere.*

BOOKS

Grolier Poetry Bookshop. This Harvard Square store, founded in 1927, carries in-print poetry from all eras and from all over the world. ✉ *6 Plympton St., Cambridge* ☎ *617/547–4648* 🌐 *www.grolierpoetrybookshop.org* ⏲ *Closed Sun.–Mon.* Ⓜ *Harvard.*

Fodor's Choice ★ **Harvard Book Store.** The intellectual community is well served here, with a slew of new titles upstairs and used and remaindered books downstairs. The collection's diversity has made the store a favored destination for academics. ✉ *1256 Massachusetts Ave., Cambridge* ☎ *617/661–1515* 🌐 *www.harvard.com* Ⓜ *Harvard.*

Harvard Coop Society. Begun in 1882 as a nonprofit service for students and faculty, the Coop is now managed by Barnes & Noble. In addition to books and textbooks (many discounted), school supplies, clothes, and accessories plastered with the Harvard emblem are sold here, as well as basic housewares geared toward dorm dwellers. ✉ *1400 Massachusetts Ave., Cambridge* ☎ *617/499–2000* 🌐 *www.thecoop.com* Ⓜ *Harvard.*

Raven Used Books. Looking for a stash of scholarly used books? Raven's is a popular place for local students to unload their texts. Another branch is located at 263 Newbury Street. ✉ *52-B JFK St., Harvard Sq., Cambridge* ☎ *617/441–6999* 🌐 *www.ravencambridge.com* Ⓜ *Harvard.*

Schoenhof's. The friendly staff helps patrons navigate through thousands of foreign books, including ones in French, German, Italian, and Spanish. ✉ *76 Mount Auburn St., Cambridge* ☎ *617/547–8855* 🌐 *www.schoenhofs.com* ⏲ *Closed Sun.* Ⓜ *Harvard.*

CLOTHING AND SHOES

Fodor's Choice ★ **Concepts.** Sneaker collectors love having what other people can't find. At Concepts, fanatics will line up around the block when a limited-edition shoe debuts. This store features exclusives by Nike, Jordan, Clarks, Adidas, and others. ✉ *37 Brattle St., Cambridge* ☎ *617/868–2001* 🌐 *www.cncpts.com* Ⓜ *Harvard.*

Mint Julep. Cute dresses, playful skirts, and form-fitting tops make up the selection here. The Cambridge location is a little larger and easier to navigate, but Brookline houses the original. ✉ *6 Church St., Cambridge* ☎ *617/576–6468* 🌐 *www.shopmintjulep.com* Ⓜ *Harvard.*

Passport. You don't need to be a celebrity to get jet-setting style. Passport offers wrinkle-free clothing, foldable ballet flats, headphones, luggage, and everything you need to be a chic traveler. ✉ *43 Brattle St., Cambridge* 🌐 *www.passportboutique.com* ⏲ *Harvard Sq.*

The Tannery. This one of the three stores in the chain carries a bountiful selection of footwear from Frye to Converse. The 39 Brattle Street and

DID YOU KNOW?

Cross through one of Harvard University's gates and go from one of the world's top-ranked schools to one of the Boston area's top-ranked shopping destinations, where indie bookstores, gourmet food, and quirky clothing stores line Harvard Square's redbrick sidewalks. Keep current in the center of the square at Out-of-Town News, where periodicals from all over the world are on sale.

711 Boylston Street locations add in high-end accessories and clothing brands like Helmut Lang and Vena Cava. ✉ *39 Brattle St., Cambridge* ☎ *617/491–1811* 🌐 *www.thetannery.com* Ⓜ *Harvard.*

CRAFTS

Cambridge Artists' Cooperative. The ceramics, weavings, jewelry, and leatherwork here can be pricier than most, but they're all one-of-a-kind or limited edition. ✉ *59A Church St., Cambridge* ☎ *617/868–4434* 🌐 *www.cambridgeartistscoop.com* Ⓜ *Harvard.*

GIFTS

Nomad. Low prices and an enthusiastic staff are just the beginning at this imports store; it carries clothing as well as Indian good-luck *torans* (wall hangings), Mexican *milagros* (charms), mirrors to keep away the evil eye, silver jewelry, and curtains made from sari silk. In the basement you'll find kilims, hand-painted tiles, and sale items. ✉ *1741 Massachusetts Ave., Cambridge* ☎ *617/497–6677* 🌐 *www.nomadcambridge.com* Ⓜ *Porter.*

Tokai Japanese Gifts. Chopstick rests, origami paper, Yukata cotton robes, and high-end kimonos are among the wares here. ✉ *1815 Massachusetts Ave., Cambridge* ☎ *617/864–5922* 🌐 *www.tokaijapanesegifts.com* Ⓜ *Porter.*

GROCERS

Cardullo's. This 50-year-old shop in Harvard Square purveys exotic imports, sandwiches to go, chocolates, breads, olive oils, cheeses, wines, and beer amid impressive clutter. ✉ *6 Brattle St., Cambridge* ☎ *617/491–8888, 800/491–8288* 🌐 *www.cardullos.com* Ⓜ *Harvard.*

HOME FURNISHINGS

Abodeon. New York decorators come to town just to shop this incredible collection of 20th-century modern housewares, both newly produced classic designs and pristine-condition vintage. You might come across a mint 1963 stove, a complete set of Jetson-esque dinnerware, or a Lucite dining set from the early 1970s. As a bonus, the back room contains more than 10,000 hard-to-find records. ✉ *E. 1731 Massachusetts Ave., Cambridge* ☎ *617/497–0137* 🌐 *www.abodeon.com* Ⓜ *Porter.*

RUNNING GEAR

Marathon Sports. Known for its personalized service, Marathon gives advice for choosing the perfect shoe, whether you're a beginning walker or a serious runner. Many marathon runners find their way here before the Boston race each spring. ✉ *1654 Massachusetts Ave., Cambridge* ☎ *617/354–4161* 🌐 *www.marathonsports.com* Ⓜ *Harvard.*

SPECIALTY STORES

Out-of-Town News. Smack in the middle of Harvard Square is a staggering selection of the world's newspapers and magazines. The stand is open daily 6 am to 10:30 pm. ✉ *0 Harvard Sq., Cambridge* ☎ *617/354–1441* Ⓜ *Harvard.*

THRIFT SHOPS

Garment District. This warehouselike building is crammed with vintage, used, and new clothing and accessories. Students crowd the store year-round, and everyone comes at Halloween for that perfect costume.

✉ *200 Broadway, Cambridge* ☎ *617/876–5230* 🌐 *www.garment-district.com* Ⓜ *Kendall/MIT.*

Keezer's. Since 1895 this shop has been many a man's secret weapon for formal wear at an informal price. Pick up new or used suits, tuxedos, ties, shirts, and pants. ✉ *140 River St., Cambridge* ☎ *617/547–2455* 🌐 *www.keezers.com* ⏲ *Closed Sun.* Ⓜ *Central.*

Oona's. Crowded racks of cared-for, secondhand clothing for women and men are reason enough to browse through the multiple rooms of reasonably priced stock. A helpful staff and fun, eclectic vibe just make doing so that much more fun. ✉ *1210 Massachusetts Ave., Cambridge* ☎ *617/491–2654* 🌐 *www.oonasboston.com* Ⓜ *Harvard.*

Poor Little Rich Girl. This shop is a museum of carefully selected vintage designer duds dedicated to big-name brands and trends. ✉ *121 Hampshire St., Cambridge* ☎ *617/873–0809* 🌐 *www.shoppoorlittlerichgirl.com* ⏲ *Closed Tues.* Ⓜ *Kendall/MIT.*

TOYS

FAMILY **The Curious George Store.** Time can really slip away from you in this jungle of kids books and gifts. Decorated with tropical plants, a fake hut, and tot-size chairs, and equipped with puzzles, toys, activity sets, and books of all kinds for all ages, this store is a wonderland for kids and a parent's salvation on a rainy day. ✉ *1 JFK St., Harvard Sq., Cambridge* ☎ *617/498–0062* 🌐 *thecuriousgeorgestore.com* Ⓜ *Harvard.*

FAMILY **Henry Bear's Park.** The specialty at this charming neighborhood store is huggable bears and collectible dolls; it also sells books, toys, and games. ✉ *Porter Sq. Shopping Center, 17 White St., Cambridge* ☎ *617/547–8424* 🌐 *www.henrybear.com* Ⓜ *Porter.*

FAMILY **Stellabella.** Creative toys are the draw here—books and games to stimulate kids' imaginations and get their brains going without relying on TV or violence. No gun or weapon toys are sold. ✉ *1360 Cambridge St., Cambridge* ☎ *617/491–6290* 🌐 *www.stellabellatoys.com* Ⓜ *Central.*

SIDE TRIPS

WELCOME TO SIDE TRIPS

TOP REASONS TO GO

★ **Early American history:** From Plimoth Plantation to Salem, Concord, and Lexington, you can visit colonial-reenactment museums, Revolutionary War battle sites, historic homes, and inns.

★ **Seafaring communities:** Set off on a whale watch from Gloucester, warm yourself after a windy coastal walk in Rockport with clam chowder, and admire the dedicated routine of local fishermen.

★ **Revisit your reading:** Nathaniel Hawthorne's *House of Seven Gables* still stands in Salem. Liberate yourself with a swim in Thoreau's Walden Pond. In Concord, see where both Louisa May Alcott and Ralph Waldo Emerson penned their works.

★ **Cranberry bogs:** The bogs' red, green, gold, and blue colors dot Cape Cod and the Plymouth area.

★ **The *Mayflower II*:** The story of the Pilgrims' Atlantic crossing comes alive in Plymouth.

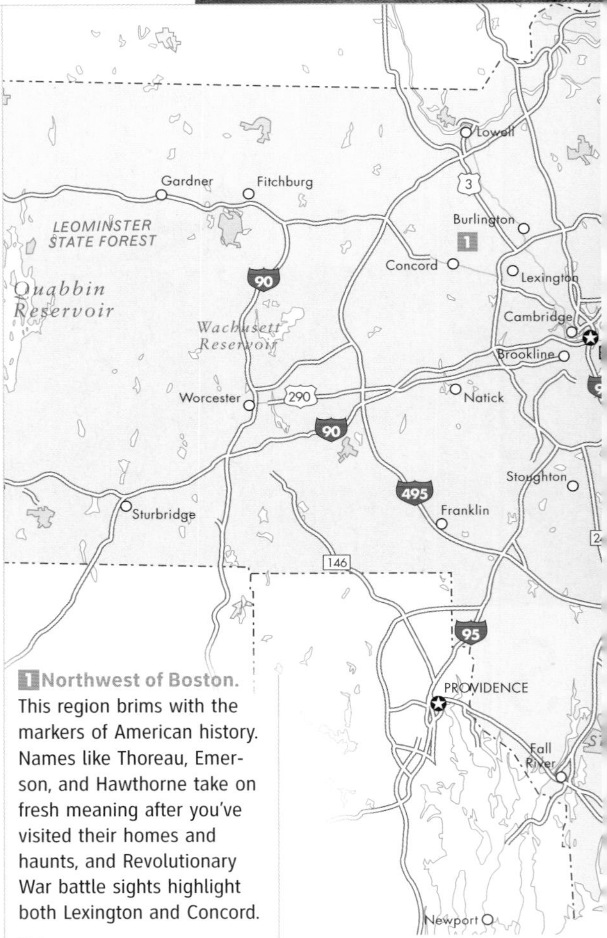

1 Northwest of Boston. This region brims with the markers of American history. Names like Thoreau, Emerson, and Hawthorne take on fresh meaning after you've visited their homes and haunts, and Revolutionary War battle sights highlight both Lexington and Concord.

2 The North Shore. Waterfront towns with classic New England feels dot the Atlantic Coast northeast of Boston. Highlights include seafaring history-steeped communities including Marblehead, Gloucester, and Essex; bewitching Salem; and family-friendly beaches.

3 South of Boston. Gain insights here into what the earliest American settlers experienced. In Plymouth and Plimoth Plantation,

learn how the Pilgrims raised food, built their homes, and survived under harsh conditions. New Bedford's whaling culture and Portuguese heritage come alive on the cobblestone streets along the docks. And don't forget vacation-central Cape Cod!

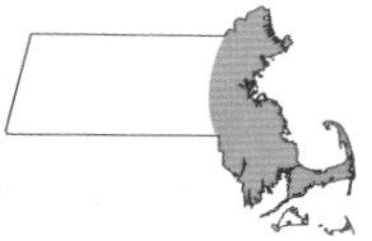

GETTING ORIENTED

Visit Concord and Lexington, to the northwest of Boston, and that history class from high school may suddenly come rushing back to you. The state's coast from Boston to Cape Ann is called the North Shore, visited for its beautiful beaches, quintessential New England seaside communities, and bewitching Salem. South of Boston lies more history in Quincy and Plymouth, and more seaside scenery at Cape Cod.

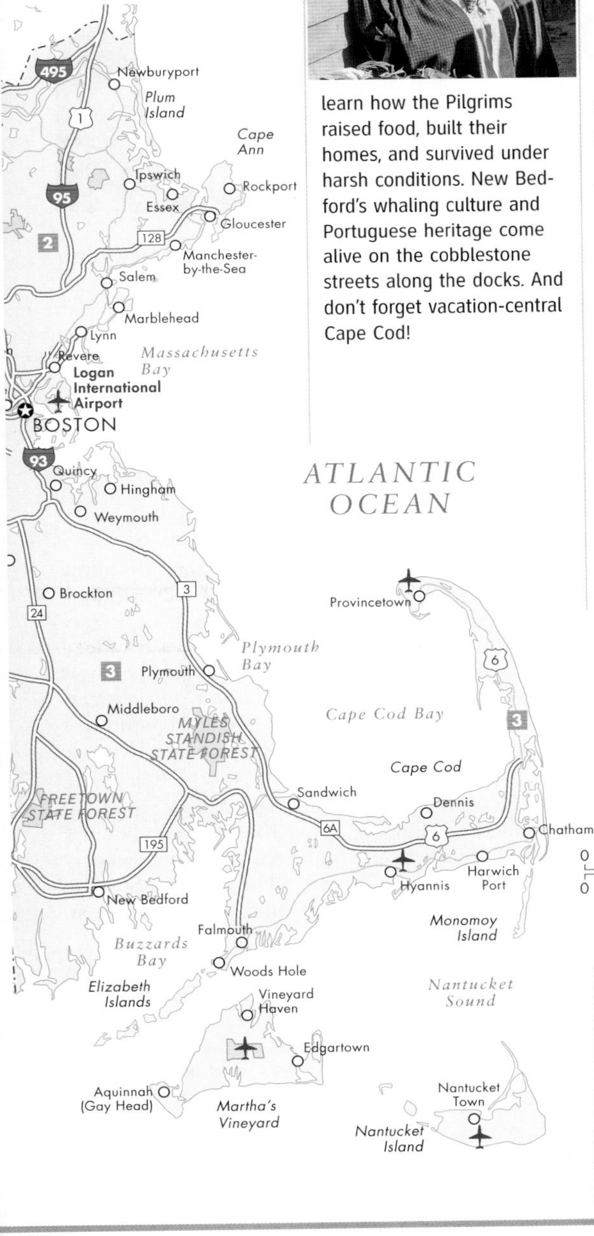

Updated by Frances Folsom

History lies thick on the ground in the towns surrounding Boston—from Pilgrims to pirates, witches to whalers, the American Revolution to the Industrial Revolution. The sights outside the city are at least as interesting as those on Boston's Freedom Trail. When you're ready to trade history lessons for beach fun, Cape Cod to the south and the North Shore to the northeast entice sand-and-sun seekers.

Rich in more than history, the areas surrounding Boston also allow visitors to retrace the steps of famous writers, bask in the outdoors, and browse shops in funky artist communities. The haunts of literary luminaries of every generation lurk throughout Massachusetts. Head to Concord to visit the place where Henry David Thoreau wrote his prophetic *Walden* and where Louisa May Alcott's *Little Women* brightened a grim time during the Civil War. Relive Nathaniel Hawthorne's vision of Puritan-era Salem. Stop in Lowell to see where Jack Kerouac lived before going *On the Road*.

The seaside towns of Massachusetts were built before the Revolution, during the heyday of American shipping. Ipswich's First Period homes (there are more here than anywhere else in the nation) and Newburyport's majestic Federal Style mansions, grand old houses, and bustling waterfronts evoke a bygone world of clipper ships, robust fishermen, and sturdy sailors.

In a more contemporary vein, Boston and its suburbs have become a major destination for food and wine lovers. Internationally acclaimed chefs, including Barbara Lynch, Frank McClelland, and Ming Tsai, draw thousands of devoted, discerning foodies to their restaurants each year. The state's extensive system of parks, protected forests, beaches, and nature preserves satisfies everyone from the avid hiker to the beach bum.

PLANNING

WHEN TO GO

The dazzling foliage and cool temperatures make fall the best time to visit Massachusetts. Summer, especially late in the season when the water is a bit warmer, is ideal for beach vacations. Many towns save their best for winter—inns open their doors to carolers, shops serve eggnog, and lobster boats parade around Gloucester Harbor.

BUDGETING YOUR TIME

Though Massachusetts is small, you can easily spend several weeks exploring it. If you have a few days, head to a town or two north and south of Boston, such as Concord, Plymouth, and Salem. With a week you may want to add on the Berkshires or spend the entire time relaxing on Cape Cod.

GETTING HERE AND AROUND

AIR TRAVEL

BOAT TRAVEL

Though not covered in this chapter, Martha's Vineyard, Nantucket, and Cape Cod are popular getaway destinations from Boston. High-speed ferries provide transportation to Martha's Vineyard and Nantucket. The Bay State Cruise Co. and Boston Harbor Cruises run 90-minute ferry rides between Boston and Cape Cod's Provincetown from May through October; reservations are strongly recommended. For details on what to see and do in these destinations, see *Fodor's Cape Cod, Nantucket, and Martha's Vineyard.*

Bay State Cruise Co. ☎ *877/783–3779* 🌐 *www.baystatecruisecompany.com.*

Boston Harbor Cruises ✉ *Long Wharf, 1 Seaport Ln., Boston* ☎ *617/227–4321, 877/733–9425* 🌐 *www.bostonharborcruises.com.*

CAR TRAVEL

Outside Boston you need a car to explore the state. Expect heavy traffic heading in and out of the city at rush hour, generally from 6 am to 9 am and 4 pm to 7 pm.

From Boston to Lexington, pick up Route 2 West in Cambridge. Exit at Routes 4/225. Turn left on Massachusetts Avenue for the National Heritage Museum. For Lexington's town center, take the Waltham Street–Lexington exit from Route 2. Follow Waltham Street just under 2 miles to Massachusetts Avenue; you'll be just east of the Battle Green. The drive takes about 30 minutes. To continue to Concord, head farther west on Route 2. Or take Interstate 90 (the Massachusetts Turnpike) to Interstate 95 North, and then exit at Route 2, heading west. Driving time is 40–45 minutes from Boston.

The primary link between Boston and the North Shore is Route 128, which follows the coast northeast to Gloucester. To pick up Route 128 from Boston, take Interstate 93 North to Interstate 95 North to Route 128. If you stay on Interstate 95, you'll reach Newburyport. From Boston to Salem or Marblehead, follow Route 128 to Route 114 into Salem or continue to Marblehead. Driving from Boston to Salem takes about 35–40 minutes; to Gloucester or to Newburyport, about 50–60 minutes.

To get to Plymouth, take the Southeast Expressway Interstate 93 South to Route 3 (toward Cape Cod); Exits 6 and 4 lead to downtown Plymouth and Plimoth Plantation, respectively. Allow about one hour.

TRAIN TRAVEL

The MBTA's commuter rail offers service to Newburyport, Ipswich, Rockport, Salem, and Gloucester. Travel times are usually 70 minutes or less.

Massachusetts Bay Transportation Authority ☎ *800/392–6100* ⊕ *www.mbta.com.*

RESTAURANTS

Massachusetts invented the fried clam, and it's served in many North Shore restaurants. Creamy clam chowder is another specialty. Eating seafood in the rough—from paper plates in seaside shacks—is a revered local custom. At country inns you'll find traditional New England dinners: double-cut pork chops, rack of lamb, game, Boston baked beans, Indian pudding, and the dubiously glorified New England boiled dinner (corned beef and cabbage with potatoes, carrots, turnips, and other vegetables).

HOTELS

Although Boston has everything from luxury hotels to charming bed-and-breakfasts, the signature accommodation outside Boston is the country inn; less extravagant and less expensive are B&B establishments, many of them in private homes. Make reservations well in advance if traveling in the summer. Smoking has been banned in all Massachusetts hotels.

TOURS

Brush Hill Tours. Daily July through November and on weekends in May and June, Brush Hill Tours offers motor-coach tours from Boston to Lexington's Battle Green and Concord's Old North Bridge area. Seasonal trips to Salem, Marblehead, and Plymouth are also available. ☎ *781/986–6100, 617/720–6342, 800/343–1328* ⊕ *www.brushhilltours.com.*

Concord Chamber of Commerce. April through November, Concord Chamber of Commerce runs walking tours focusing on the Revolutionary War or the area's rich literary history. Each tour lasts about 1½ hours and departs from the Concord Visitor Center on Sundays, Mondays, and holidays at noon; Fridays at 1 pm; and Saturdays at 11 am and 1 pm. ✉ *58 Main St., Concord* ☎ *978/369–3120* ⊕ *www.concordchamberofcommerce.org* 🎫 *$20.*

Essex River Cruises & Charters. From May to October, Essex River Cruises & Charters organizes narrated cruises of nearby salt marshes and rivers. Call ahead for schedules and reservations. ☎ *978/768–6981, 800/748–3706* ⊕ *www.essexcruises.com.*

Colonial Lantern Tours. Evenings April through November, Colonial Lantern Tours visit the original Plymouth plantation site and historic district. They also conduct a nightly "Ghostly Haunts and Legends" tour

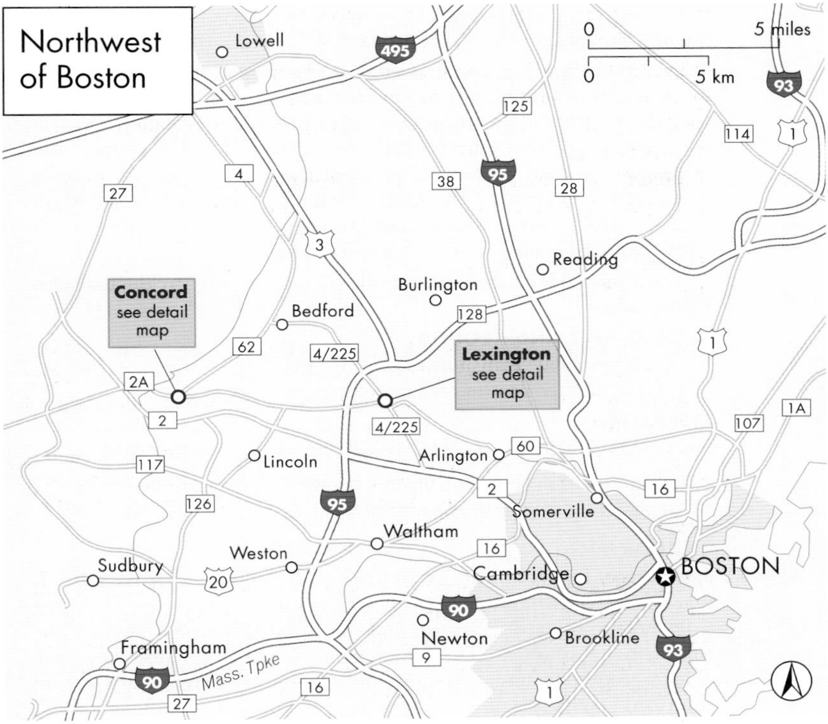

highlighting Plymouth's more macabre history and offer local history and themed holiday tours. Call for reservations and meeting locations. ☎ *774/454–8126* 🌐 *www.lanterntours.com.*

NORTHWEST OF BOSTON

Northwest of the city, Lexington and Concord embody the spirit of the American Revolution. Sites of the first skirmishes of the Revolutionary War, these two quintessential New England towns were also cradles of American literature; several historic homes and small museums here are dedicated to some of the country's first substantial writers—Ralph Waldo Emerson, Nathaniel Hawthorne, Louisa May Alcott, and Henry David Thoreau.

LEXINGTON

16 miles northwest of Boston.

Discontent with the British, American colonials burst into action in Lexington in April 1775. On April 18, patriot leader Paul Revere alerted the town that British soldiers were approaching. The next day, as the British advance troops arrived in Lexington on their march toward Concord, the Minutemen were waiting to confront the redcoats in what became the first skirmish of the Revolutionary War.

These first military encounters of the American Revolution are very much a part of present-day Lexington, a modern suburban town that sprawls out from the historic sites near its center. Although the downtown area is generally lively, with ice-cream and coffee shops, boutiques, and a great little movie theater, the town becomes especially animated each Patriots' Day (April 19 but celebrated on the third Monday in April), when costume-clad groups re-create the Minutemen's battle maneuvers and Paul Revere rides again.

To learn more about the city and the 1775 clash, stop by the **Lexington Visitor Center**.

GETTING HERE AND AROUND

Massachusetts Bay Transportation Authority (MBTA) operates bus service in the greater Boston area and serves Lexington.

ESSENTIALS

Bus Contact **MBTA** ☎ *617/222–3200, 800/392–6100* 🌐 *www.mbta.com.*

Visitor Information **Lexington Visitors Center** ✉ *1875 Massachusetts Ave.* ☎ *781/862–1450* 🌐 *www.lexingtonchamber.org.*

EXPLORING

Battle Green. It was on this 2-acre triangle of land, on April 19, 1775, that the first confrontation between British soldiers, who were marching from Boston toward Concord, and the colonial militia known as the Minutemen took place. The Minutemen—so called because they were able to prepare themselves at a moment's notice—were led by Captain John Parker, whose role in the American Revolution is commemorated in Henry Hudson Kitson's renowned 1900 *Minuteman* statue. Facing downtown Lexington at the tip of Battle Green, the statue's in a traffic island, and therefore makes for a difficult photo op. ✉ *Junction of Massachusetts Ave. and Bedford St.*

Buckman Tavern. While waiting for the arrival of the British on the morning of April 19, 1775, the Minutemen gathered at this 1690 tavern. A half-hour tour takes in the tavern's seven rooms, which have been restored to the way they looked in the 1770s. Among the items on display is an old front door with a hole made by a British musket ball. ✉ *1 Bedford St.* ☎ *781/862–1703* 🌐 *www.lexingtonhistory.org* 🎟 *$7; $12 combination ticket includes Hancock-Clarke House and Munroe Tavern* ⏲ *Apr.–Oct., daily 10–4.*

Hancock-Clarke House. On April 18, 1775, Paul Revere came here to warn patriots John Hancock and Sam Adams (who were staying at the house while attending the Provincial Congress in nearby Concord) of the advance of British troops. Hancock and Adams, on whose heads the British king had put a price, fled to avoid capture. The house, a parsonage built in 1698, is a 10-minute walk from Lexington Common. Inside are the pistols of the British major John Pitcairn, as well as period furnishings and portraits. ✉ *36 Hancock St.* ☎ *781/862–1703* 🌐 *www.lexingtonhistory.org* 🎟 *$7; $12 combination ticket includes Buckman Tavern and Munroe Tavern* ⏲ *Apr.–May, Sat.–Sun. 10–4; June–Oct., daily 10–4.*

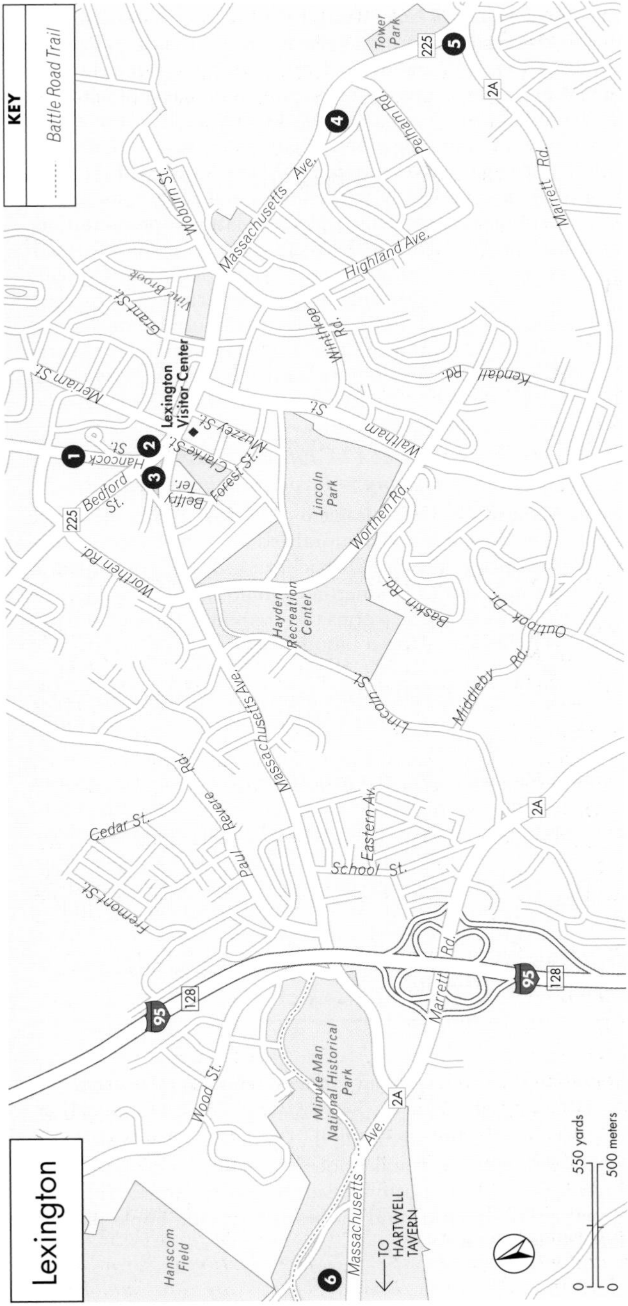

Battle Green 3
Buckman Tavern 2
Hancock-Clarke House 1
Minute Man National Historical Park 6
Munroe Tavern 4
National Heritage Museum 5

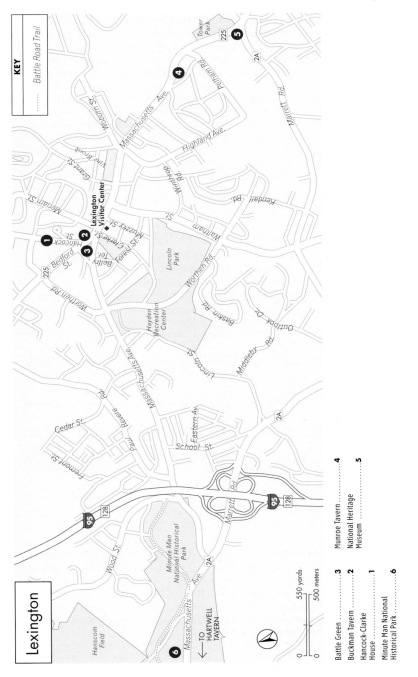

FAMILY **Minute Man National Historical Park.** West of Lexington's center stretches this 1,000-acre, three-parcel park that also extends into nearby Lincoln and Concord *(⇨ Concord, Exploring)*. Begin your park visit at Lexington's **Minute Man Visitor Center** to see its free multimedia presentation, "The Road to Revolution," a captivating introduction to the events of April 1775. Then, continuing along Highway 2A toward Concord, you pass the point where Revere's midnight ride ended with his capture by the British; it's marked with a boulder and plaque, as well as an enclosure where rangers sometimes give educational presentations. You can also visit the 1732 **Hartwell Tavern** (open mid-April through late May, weekends 9:30–5:30, and late May through late October, daily 9:30–5:30), a restored drover's (driver's) tavern staffed by park employees in period costume; they frequently demonstrate musket firing or open-hearth cooking, and children are likely to enjoy the reproduction colonial toys. ✉ *250 North Great Rd.(Hwy. 2A), ¼ mile west of Hwy. 128* ☎ *978/369–6993* 🌐 *www.nps.gov/mima* ⏲ *North Bridge Visitor Center, hrs vary according to season.*

North Bridge Visitor Center ✉ *174 Liberty St.* ☎ *978/369–6993* ⏲ *Apr.–Oct., daily 9–5; Nov., daily 9–4; call for winter hrs.*

Munroe Tavern. As April 19, 1775, dragged on, British forces met fierce resistance in Concord. Dazed and demoralized after the battle at Concord's Old North Bridge, the British backtracked and regrouped at this 1695 tavern 1 mile east of Lexington Common, while the Munroe family hid in nearby woods. The troops then retreated through what is now the town of Arlington. After a bloody battle there, they returned to Boston. Tours of the tavern last about 30 minutes. ✉ *1332 Massachusetts Ave.* ☎ *781/862–1703* 🌐 *www.lexingtonhistory.org* 🎟 *$7; $12 combination ticket includes Hancock-Clarke House and Buckman Tavern* ⏲ *June–Oct., noon–4.*

National Heritage Museum. View artifacts from all facets of American life, put in social and political context. Specializing in the history of American Freemasonry and Fraternalism, the changing exhibits and lectures also focus on local events leading up to April 1775 and illustrates Revolutionary-era life through everyday objects such as blacksmithing tools, bloodletting paraphernalia, and dental instruments, including a "tooth key" used to extract teeth. ✉ *33 Marrett Rd., Hwy. 2A at Massachusetts Ave.* ☎ *781/861–6559* 🌐 *www.monh.org* 🎟 *Donations accepted* ⏲ *Wed.–Sat. 10–4:30.*

CONCORD

About 10 miles west of Lexington, 21 miles northwest of Boston.

The Concord of today is a modern suburb with a busy center filled with arty shops, places to eat, and (recalling the literary history made here) old bookstores. Autumn lovers, take note: Concord is a great place to start a fall foliage tour. From Boston, head west along Route 2 to Concord, and then continue on to find harvest stands and apple picking around Harvard and Stow.

GETTING HERE AND AROUND

The MBTA runs buses to Concord. On the MBTA Commuter Rail, Concord is a 40-minute ride on the Fitchburg Line, which departs from Boston's North Station.

ESSENTIALS

Bus and Train Contact **MBTA** ☎ *617/222–3200, 800/392–6100* 🌐 *www.mbta.com.*

Visitor Information **Concord Visitor Center** ✉ *58 Main St.* ☎ *978/369–3120* 🌐 *www.concordchamberofcommerce.org* ⏲ *Daily 10-4 Mar.–Dec.*

EXPLORING

Boott Cotton Mills Museum. Part of the Lowell National Historic Park complex and about a 10-minute walk northeast from the visitor center is this museum devoted to industrialization. The textile worker's grueling life is shown with all its grit, noise, and dust. You know you're in for an unusual experience when you're handed earplugs—they're for the re-created 1920s weave room, authentic down to the deafening roar of 88 working power looms. Other exhibits at the complex include weaving artifacts, cloth samples, video interviews with workers, and a large, meticulous scale model of 19th-century production. ✉ *115 John St.* ☎ *978/970–5000* 🌐 *www.nps.gov/lowe* 🎟 *$6* ⏲ *Daily 9:30–5.*

15

FAMILY **Concord Museum.** The original contents of Emerson's private study, as well as the world's largest collection of Thoreau artifacts, reside in this 1930 Colonial Revival building just east of the town center. The museum provides a good overview of the town's history, from its original American Indian settlement to the present. Highlights include American Indian artifacts, furnishings from Thoreau's Walden Pond cabin (there's a replica of the cabin itself on the museum's lawn), and one of the two lanterns hung at Boston's Old North Church to signal that the British were coming by sea. **■ TIP→ If you've brought children, ask for a free family activity pack.** ✉ *200 Lexington Rd., entrance on Cambridge Tpke.* ☎ *978/369–9763* 🌐 *www.concordmuseum.org* 🎟 *$10* ⏲ *Jan.–Mar., Mon.–Sat. 11–4, Sun. 1–4; Apr., May, and Sept.–Dec., Mon.–Sat. 9–5, Sun. noon–5; June–Aug., daily 9–5.*

Old Manse. The Reverend William Emerson, grandfather of Ralph Waldo Emerson, watched rebels and redcoats battle from behind his home, which was within sight of the Old North Bridge. The house, built in 1770, was occupied continuously by the Emerson family for almost two centuries, except for a 3½-year period during which Nathaniel Hawthorne rented it. Furnishings date from the late 18th century. Tours run throughout the day and last 45 minutes, with a new tour starting within 15 minutes of when the first person signs up. ✉ *269 Monument St.* ☎ *978/369–3909* 🌐 *www.thetrustees.org/places-to-visit/greater-boston/old-manse.html* 🎟 *$8* ⏲ *Mid-Apr.–Oct., Mon.–Sat. 10–5, Sun. noon–5; Nov.–Mar. Tours Thurs. and Fri. 2, 3, and 4 pm and weekends noon–4:30 (weather permitting).*

Old North Bridge. A half mile from Concord center, at this bridge, the Concord Minutemen turned the tables on the British on the morning of April 19, 1775. The Americans didn't fire first, but when two of their

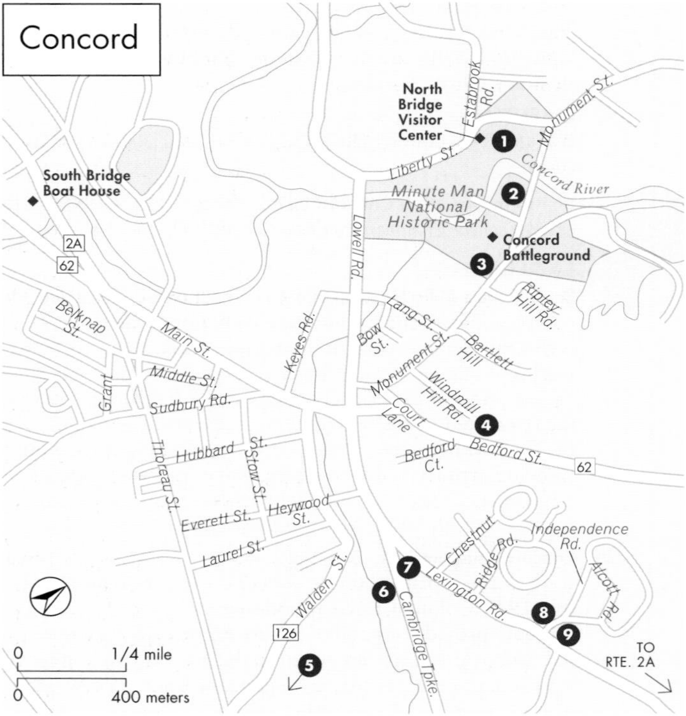

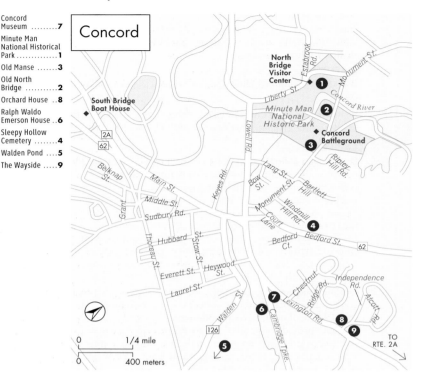

own fell dead from a Redcoat volley, Major John Buttrick of Concord roared, "Fire, fellow soldiers, for God's sake, fire." The Minutemen released volley after volley, and the redcoats fled. Daniel Chester French's famous statue *The Minuteman* (1875) honors the country's first freedom fighters. Inscribed at the foot of the statue are words Ralph Waldo Emerson wrote in 1837 describing the confrontation: "By the rude bridge that arched the flood / Their flag to April's breeze unfurled / Here once the embattled farmers stood / And fired the shot heard round the world." The lovely wooded surroundings give a sense of what the landscape was like in more rural times. ✉ *Concord Center, Near Minute Man Monument* 🌐 *www.nps.gov/mima.*

Orchard House. The dark brown exterior of Louisa May Alcott's family home sharply contrasts with the light, wit, and energy so much in evidence inside. Named for the apple orchard that once surrounded it, Orchard House was the Alcott family home from 1857 to 1877. Here Louisa wrote *Little Women*, based on her life with her three sisters; and her father, Bronson, founded his school of philosophy—the building remains behind the house. Because Orchard House had just one owner after the Alcotts left, and because it became a museum in 1911, many of the original furnishings remain, including the semicircular shelf-desk where Louisa wrote *Little Women.* ✉ *399 Lexington*

Rd. ☎ 978/369–4118 🌐 www.louisamayalcott.org 🎟 $9 ⏲ Apr.–Oct., Mon.–Sat. 10–4:30, Sun. 1–4:30; Nov.–Dec. and Jan. 3–Mar., Sat.–Sun. 11–3, Sat. 10–4:30, Sun. 1–4:30. Half-hour tours begin every 30 mins Apr.–Oct.; call for off-season schedule.

Ralph Waldo Emerson House. The 19th-century essayist and poet Ralph Waldo Emerson lived briefly in the Old Manse in 1834–35, then moved to this home, where he lived until his death in 1882. Here he wrote the *Essays*. Except for artifacts from Emerson's study, now at the nearby Concord Museum, the Emerson House furnishings have been preserved as the writer left them, down to his hat resting on the newel post. You must join one of the half-hour-long tours to see the interior. ✉ *28 Cambridge Tpke., at Lexington Rd. ☎ 978/369–2236 🌐 www.nps.gov/nr/travel/massachusetts_conservation/ralph_waldo_emerson_house.html 🎟 $8 ⏲ Mid-Apr.–mid-Oct., Thurs.–Sat. 10–4:30, Sun. 1–4:30; call for tour schedule.*

Sleepy Hollow Cemetery. In the Author's Ridge section of this cemetery are the graves of American literary greats Louisa May Alcott, Ralph Waldo Emerson, Henry David Thoreau, and Nathaniel Hawthorne. Each Memorial Day Alcott's grave is decorated in commemoration of her death. ✉ *Bedford St. (Hwy. 62) ☎ 978/318–3233 ⏲ Daily dawn–dusk.*

Fodor's Choice ★

Walden Pond. For lovers of early American literature, a trip to Concord isn't complete without a pilgrimage to Henry David Thoreau's most famous residence. Here, in 1845, at age 28, Thoreau moved into a one-room cabin—built for $28.12—on the shore of this 100-foot-deep kettle hole formed by the retreat of an ancient glacier. Living alone for the next two years, Thoreau discovered the benefits of solitude and the beauties of nature. The essays in *Walden*, published in 1854, are a mixture of philosophy, nature writing, and protoecology. The site of the first cabin is staked out in stone. A full-size, authentically furnished replica of the cabin stands about ½ mile from the original site, near the Walden Pond State Reservation parking lot. Even when it's closed, you can peek through its windows. Now, as in Thoreau's time, the pond is a delightful summertime spot for swimming, fishing, and rowing, and there's hiking in the nearby woods. To get to Walden Pond State Reservation from the center of Concord—a trip of only 1½ mile—take Concord's Main Street a block west from Monument Square, turn left onto Walden Street, and head for the intersection of Highways 2 and 126. Cross over Highway 2 onto Highway 126, heading south for ½ mile. ✉ *915 Walden St.(Hwy. 126) ☎ 978/369–3254 🌐 www.mass.gov/dcr/parks/walden 🎟 Free, parking $5 ⏲ Daily 8 am–sunset weather permitting.*

The Wayside. Nathaniel Hawthorne lived at the Old Manse in 1842–45, working on stories and sketches; he then moved to Salem (where he wrote *The Scarlet Letter*) and later to Lenox (*The House of the Seven Gables*). In 1852 he returned to Concord, bought this rambling structure called The Wayside, and lived here until his death in 1864. The home certainly appealed to literary types: the subsequent owner of The Wayside, Margaret Sidney, wrote the children's book *Five Little Peppers and How They Grew* (1881), and before Hawthorne moved in, the

CLOSE UP

Literary Concord

The first wholly American literary movement was born in Concord, the tiny town west of Boston that, quite coincidentally, also witnessed the beginning of the American Revolution.

Under the influence of essayist and poet Ralph Waldo Emerson, a group eventually known as the Transcendental Club (but called the Hedges Club at the time) assembled regularly in Emerson's Concord home. Henry David Thoreau, a fellow townsman and famous proponent of self-reliance, was an integral club member, along with such others as pioneering feminist Margaret Fuller and poet Ellery Channing, both drawn to Concord simply because of Emerson's presence.

Concord also produced beloved authors outside the Transcendentalist movement. These writers include Louisa May Alcott of *Little Women* fame and children's book author Harriet Lothrop, pseudonymously known as Margaret Sydney. Even Nathaniel Hawthorne, whose various temporary homes around Massachusetts constitute a literary trail all their own, resided in Concord during the early and later portions of his career.

The cumulative inkwells of these authors have bestowed upon Concord a literary legacy unique in the United States, both for its influence on literature in general and for the quantity of related sights packed within such a small radius. From Alcott's Orchard House to Hawthorne's Old Manse, nearly all their houses remain standing, well preserved and open for tours.

The Thoreau Institute, within walking distance of a reconstruction of Thoreau's famous cabin in the woods at Walden Pond, is a repository of his papers and original editions. Emerson's study sits in the Concord Museum, across the street from his house. Even their final resting places are here, on Authors Ridge in Sleepy Hollow Cemetery, a few short blocks from the town common. **Concord Bike Tours** (☎ *978/501–7097* 🌐 *www.concordbiketours.com*) will guide you through the sites on two wheels, usually April through November (weather permitting).

Alcotts lived here, from 1845 to 1848. An exhibit center, in the former barn, provides information about the Wayside authors and links them to major events in American history. Hawthorne's tower-study, with his stand-up writing desk, is substantially as he left it. ✉ *455 Lexington Rd.* ☎ *978/318–7863* 🌐 *www.nps.gov* 🎟 *$5* ⏲ *Open by guided tour only, May–Oct.; call for reservations.*

WHERE TO EAT

$$ AMERICAN ✕ **Main Streets Market & Cafe.** Cyclists, families, and sightseers pack into this brick building, which was used to store munitions during the Revolutionary War. Wood floors and blackboard menus add a touch of nostalgia, but the extensive menu includes many modern hits. Breakfast offerings include a quiche and breakfast sandwich of the day. At lunch, the grilled panini are excellent; they also serve flatbread pizza and pub fare. At night heartier offerings dominate the menu, including baked lobster mac and cheese, scallop and shrimp risotto, and a Yankee pot roast dinner. There's a full bar, live music five nights a week,

Retrace Henry David Thoreau's steps at Walden Pond.

and in summer the small alley outside leads to a counter that serves ice cream. It's open late on Friday and Saturday nights. [$] *Average main: $18* ✉ *42 Main St.* ☎ *978/369–9948* 🌐 *www.mainstreetsmarketandcafe.com* ⏲ *No dinner Sun.*

THE NORTH SHORE

The slice of Massachusetts's Atlantic Coast known as the North Shore extends past Boston to the picturesque Cape Ann region just shy of the New Hampshire border. In addition to miles of woods and beaches, the North Shore's highlights include Marblehead, a stunningly classic New England sea town; Salem, which thrives on a history of witches, writers, and maritime trades; Gloucester, the oldest seaport in America; Rockport, rich with crafts shops and artists' studios; and Newburyport, with its redbrick center and clapboard mansions, and a handful of typical New England towns in between. Bustling during the short summer season and breathtaking during the autumn foliage, the North Shore is calmer (and colder) between November and June. Since many restaurants, inns, and attractions operate on reduced hours, it's worth calling ahead off-season.

MARBLEHEAD

17 miles north of Boston.

Marblehead, with its narrow and winding streets, beautifully preserved clapboard homes, sea captains' mansions, and harbor, looks much as it must have when it was founded in 1629 by fishermen from Cornwall and the Channel Islands. One of New England's premier sailing capitals, Marblehead continues to attract boats from along the Eastern seaboard each July during Race Week—first held in 1889. Parking in town can be difficult; lots at the end of Front Street or on State Street by the Landing restaurant are the best options.

TAKE A SEA-FARING TOUR

Yankee Fleet Whale Watching. Aboard every tour, Yankee Fleet Whale Watching performs field research on cetaceans (whales, dolphins, and porpoises). Trips depart daily from April through September; each tour lasts about four hours. Call for reservations. Deep-sea fishing trips are also offered through the fleet. ✉ *121 E. Main St., Gloucester* ☎ *800/942–5464, 855/283–0313* 🌐 *www.yankeefleet.com* 🎫 *$45.*

ESSENTIALS

Visitor Information Marblehead Chamber of Commerce Information Booth ✉ *62 Pleasant St.* ☎ *781/631–2868* 🌐 *www.visitmarblehead.com.*

EXPLORING

The 1768 Jeremiah Lee Mansion. Marblehead's 18th-century high society is exemplified in this mansion run by the Marblehead Museum and historical society. Colonel Lee was the wealthiest merchant and ship owner in Massachusetts in 1768, and although few original furnishings remain, the unique hand-painted wallpaper and fine collection of traditional North Shore furniture provide clues to the life of an American gentleman. Across the street at the main museum (open year-round), the J. O. J. Frost Folk Art Gallery pays tribute the town's talented 19th-century native son; there are also exhibits focusing on the Civil War. ✉ *161 Washington St.* ☎ *781/631–1768* 🌐 *www.marbleheadmuseum.org/LeeMansion.htm* 🎫 *$5* ⏲ *Lee Mansion June–Oct., Tues.–Sat. 10–4; Marblehead Museum Tues.–Sat. 10–4.*

Abbott Hall. The town's Victorian-era municipal building, built in 1876, displays Archibald Willard's painting *The Spirit of '76*. Many visitors, familiar since childhood with this image of the three Revolutionary veterans with fife, drum, and flag, are surprised to find the original in an otherwise unassuming town hall. Also on-site is a small naval museum exploring Marblehead's maritime past. ✉ *188 Washington St.* ☎ *781/631–0000* 🎫 *Free* ⏲ *Call for hrs.*

Fort Sewall. Magnificent views of Marblehead, of the harbor, the Misery Islands, and the Atlantic are best enjoyed from this fort built in 1644 atop the rocky cliffs of the harbor. Used as a defense against the French in 1742 as well as during the War of 1812, Fort Sewall is today open to the public as community parkland. Barracks and underground quarters can still be seen, and Revolutionary War reenactments by members of the modern-day Glover's Marblehead Regiment are staged at the fort annually. ✉ *End of Front St.* ☎ *781/631–1000* 🌐 *www.marblehead.org/index.aspx?NID=1012* 🎫 *Free* ⏲ *Daily sunrise–sunset.*

WHERE TO EAT AND STAY

For expanded hotel reviews, visit Fodors.com.

$ SEAFOOD ✕ **The Landing.** Decorated in nautical blues and whites, this pleasant restaurant sits right on Marblehead harbor, with a deck that's nearly in the water. The restaurant offers classic New England fare like clam

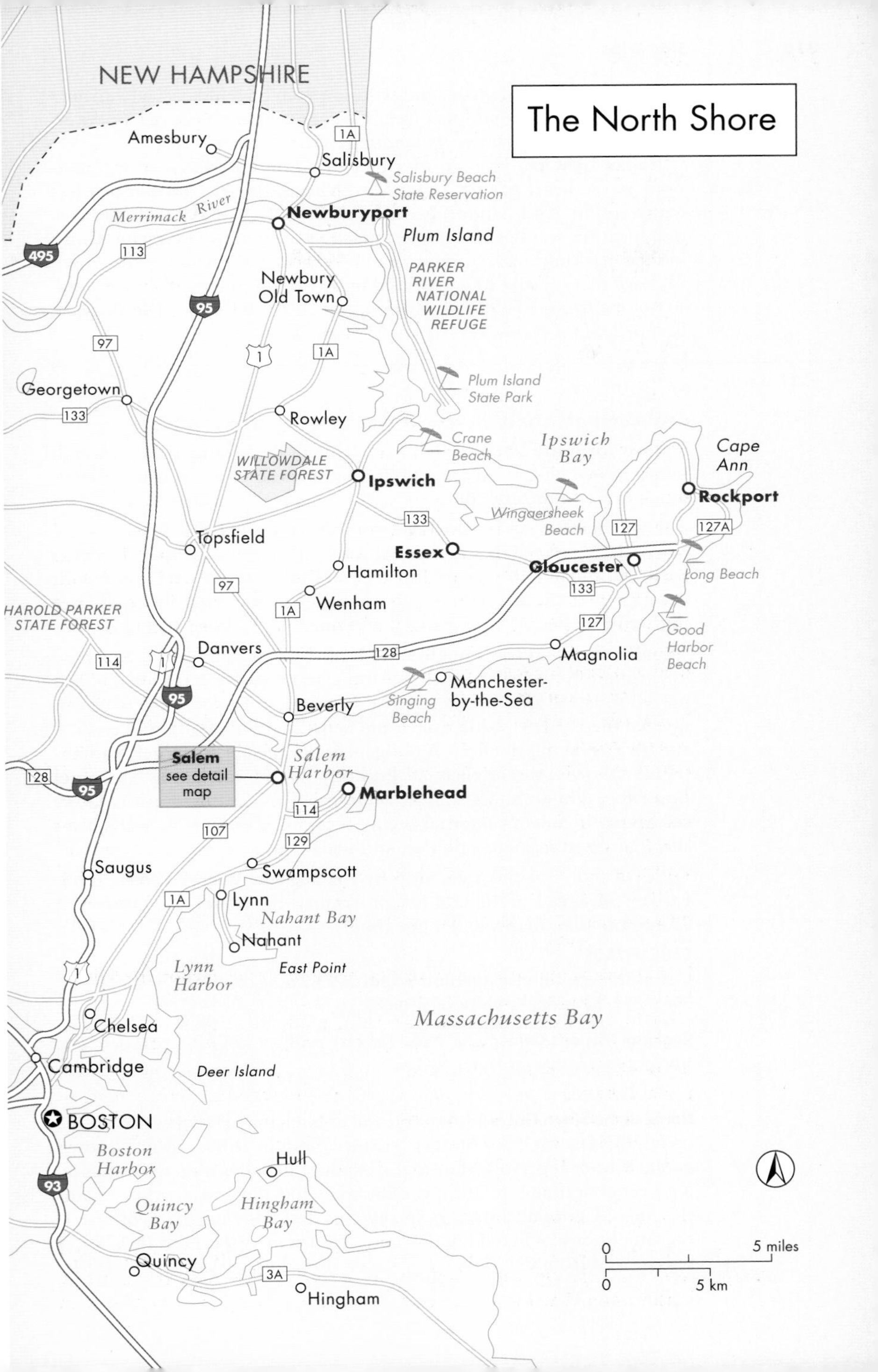

The North Shore
NEW HAMPSHIRE
Amesbury
Salisbury
1A
Salisbury Beach State Reservation
Merrimack River
Newburyport
Plum Island
495
113
PARKER RIVER NATIONAL WILDLIFE REFUGE
Newbury Old Town
95
97
1
1A
Plum Island State Park
Georgetown
133
Rowley
Crane Beach
Ipswich Bay
Cape Ann
WILLOWDALE STATE FOREST
Ipswich
Rockport
Wingaersheek Beach
133
127
127A
Topsfield
Essex
Gloucester
Hamilton
Long Beach
97
133
HAROLD PARKER STATE FOREST
1A
Wenham
127
Good Harbor Beach
Danvers
Magnolia
114
1
128
95
Manchester-by-the-Sea
Singing Beach
Beverly
Salem see detail map
Salem Harbor
128
95
Marblehead
114
107
129
Saugus
Swampscott
1A
Lynn
Nahant Bay
Nahant
East Point
1
Lynn Harbor
Massachusetts Bay
Chelsea
Cambridge
Deer Island
BOSTON
Boston Harbor
Hull
93
Quincy Bay
Hingham Bay
Quincy
3A
Hingham
0
5 miles
0
5 km

chowder and broiled scrod, and serves brunch on Sunday. The pub area has a lighter menu and local feel. *Average main: $12* ✉ *81 Front St.* ☎ *781/639–1266* 🌐 *www.thelandingrestaurant.com.*

$ B&B/INN Fodor's Choice ★ **Harbor Light Inn.** Housed in a pair of adjoining 18th-century mansions in the heart of Old Town Marblehead, this elegant inn features many rooms with canopy beds, brick fireplaces, and Jacuzzis. **Pros:** nice location amid period homes; on-site tavern with pub menu. **Cons:** limited parking; many one-way and narrow streets make this town somewhat confusing to get around in by car and the inn tricky to find. *Rooms from: $149* ✉ *58 Washington St.* ☎ *781/631–2186* 🌐 *www.harborlightinn.com* *20 rooms, 3 apartments.*

SALEM

16 miles northeast of Boston, 4 miles west of Marblehead.

Known for years as the Witch City, Salem is redefining itself. Though numerous witch-related attractions and shops still draw tourists, there's much more to the city. But first, a bit on its bewitched past . . .

The witchcraft hysteria emerged from the trials of 1692, when several Salem-area girls fell ill and accused some of the townspeople of casting spells on them. More than 150 men and women were charged with practicing witchcraft, a crime punishable by death. After the trials later that year, 19 people were hanged and one man was crushed to death.

Though the witch trials might have built Salem's infamy, it'd be a mistake to ignore the town's rich maritime and creative traditions, which played integral roles in the country's evolution. Frigates out of Salem opened the Far East trade routes and generated the wealth that created America's first millionaires. Among its native talents are writer Nathaniel Hawthorne, the intellectual Peabody Sisters, navigator Nathaniel Bowditch, and architect Samuel McIntire. This creative spirit is today celebrated in Salem's internationally recognized museums, waterfront shops and restaurants, galleries, and wide common.

To learn more on the area, stop by the **Regional Visitor's Center**. Innovatively designed in the Old Salem Armory, the center has exhibits, a 27-minute film, maps, and a gift shop.

ESSENTIALS

Visitor Information Destination Salem ✉ *93 Washington St.* ☎ *978/744–3663, 877/725–3662* 🌐 *www.salem.org.*

Regional Visitor's Center ✉ *2 New Liberty St.* ☎ *978/740–1650* 🌐 *www.nps.gov/ner/sama* ⏲ *Daily 9–5.*

EXPLORING

House of the Seven Gables. Immortalized in Nathaniel Hawthorne's classic novel, this site itself is a literary treasure. Built in 1668 and also known as the Turner-Ingersoll Mansion, the house includes a secret staircase, a garret containing an antique scale model of the house, and some of the finest Georgian interiors in the country. Also on the property is the small house where Hawthorne was born in 1804; built in 1750, it was moved from its original location a few blocks away. ✉ *115 Derby*

The House of the Seven Gables inspired Nathaniel Hawthorne's book of the same name.

St. ☎ *978/744–0991* 🌐 *www.7gables.org* 🎫 *$12.50* ⏲ *Nov.–Dec., and mid-Jan.–June, daily 10–5; July–Oct., daily 10–7.*

Fodor's Choice ★ **Peabody Essex Museum.** Salem's world-class museum celebrates maritime art, history, and the spoils of the Asian export trade. Its 30 galleries, housed in a contemplative blend of modern design, represent a diverse range of styles; exhibits include pieces ranging from American decorative and seamen's art to idea studios and photography. While there, be sure to tour the Yin Yu Tang house. This fabulous 200-year-old house dates to the Qing Dynasty (1644–1911) of China. The museum brought it over from China in sections and reassembled it here. ✉ *East India Sq.* ☎ *978/745–9500, 866/745–1876* 🌐 *www.pem.org* 🎫 *$15* ⏲ *Tues.–Sun. 10–5; Mon. holidays 10–5.*

Salem Maritime National Historic Site. Near Derby Wharf, this 9¼-acre site focuses on Salem's heritage as a major seaport with a thriving overseas trade. It includes an orientation center with an 18-minute film; the 1762 home of Elias Derby, America's first millionaire; the 1819 Customs House, made famous in Nathaniel Hawthorne's *The Scarlet Letter*; and a replica of the *Friendship*, a 171-foot, three-mast 1797 merchant vessel. There's also an active lighthouse dating from 1871, as well as the nation's last surviving 18th-century wharves. The West India Goods Store, across the street, is still a working 19th-century store, with glass jars of spices, teas, and coffees. New to the site is the 1770 Pedrick Store House, moved from nearby Marblehead and reassembled right on Derby Wharf; the two-story structure once played a vital role in the lucrative merchant seaside trade. ✉ *193 Derby St.* ☎ *978/740–1650* 🌐 *www.nps.gov/sama* 🎫 *Site free, tours $5* ⏲ *Hrs vary.*

House of the Seven Gables 1
Peabody Essex Museum 2
Salem Maritime National Historic Site 3
Salem Witch Museum 4
Salem Witch Trials Memorial 5

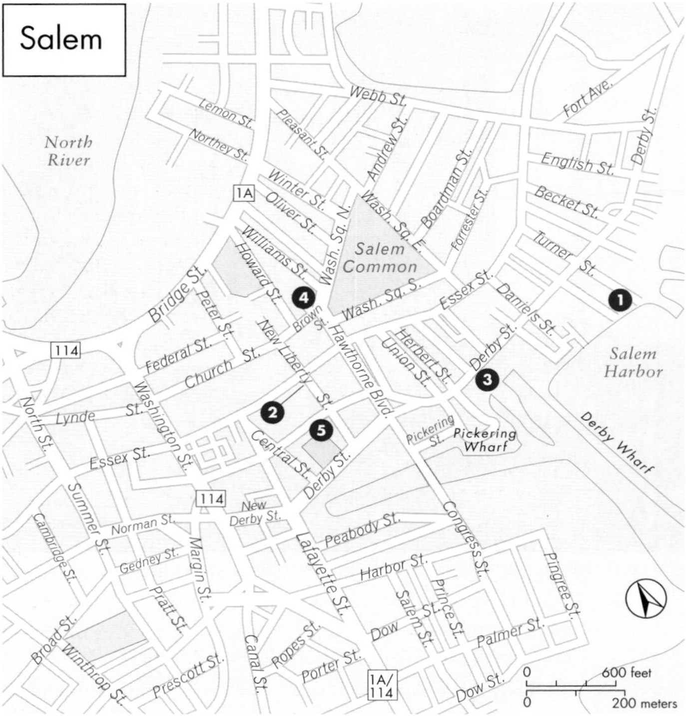

Salem Witch Museum. An informative, if somewhat hokey, introduction to the 1692 witchcraft hysteria, this museum has a short walk-through exhibit, "Witches: Evolving Perceptions," that describes witch hunts through the years. ✉ *19 N. Washington Sq.* ☎ *978/744–1692* 🌐 *www.salemwitchmuseum.com* 🎟 *$9* 🕒 *Daily 10–5; July and Aug., daily 10–7.*

Salem Witch Trials Memorial. Dedicated by Nobel Laureate Elie Wiesel in 1992, this melancholy space—an antidote to the relentless marketing of the merry-witches motif—honors those who died because they refused to confess that they were witches. A stone wall is studded with 20 stone benches, each inscribed with a victim's name, and sits next to Salem's oldest burying ground. ✉ *Off Liberty St. near Charter St.* 🌐 *www.salemweb.com/memorial/memorial.shtml.*

ARTS AND ENTERTAINMENT

THEATER

Cry Innocent: The People versus Bridget Bishop. This show, the longest continuously running play north of Boston, transports audience members to Bridget Bishop's trial of 1692. After hearing historical testimonies, the audience cross-examines the witnesses and must then decide the verdict. Actors respond in character revealing much about the Puritan frame of mind. Each show is different and allows audience members to play their "part" in history. ✉ *Old Town Hall, 32 Derby Sq.* ☎ *978/867–4767* 🌐 *www.cryinnocentsalem.com* 🎟 *$12* 🕒 *July–Oct., showtimes vary.*

CLOSE UP

The First Witch Trial

It was in Danvers, not Salem, that the first witch trial was held, originating with the family of Samuel Parris, a minister who moved to the area in 1680 from Barbados, bringing with him two slaves, including one named Tituba. In 1691 Samuel's daughter, Betty, and niece, Abigail, began having fits. Tituba, who had told Betty and Abigail stories of magic and witchcraft from her homeland, baked a witch cake to identify the witches who were harming the girls. The girls in turn accused Tituba of witchcraft. After three days of questioning, which included beatings from Samuel and a promise from him to free her if she cooperated, Tituba confessed to meeting the devil (in the form of a black hog or dog). She also claimed there were other witches in the village, confirming the girls' accusations against Sarah Good and Sarah Osborne, but she refused to name any others. Tituba's trial prompted the frenzy that led to the deaths of 20 accused witches.

15

WHERE TO EAT AND STAY

For expanded hotel reviews, visit Fodors.com.

$$ SEAFOOD **Finz Seafood & Grill.** This contemporary seafood restaurant on Pickering Wharf treats patrons to prime canal views. Seafood potpie and lobster rolls highlight the lunch menu, while sesame-crusted tuna or steamed lobster are dinner favorites. Nab a seat on the outdoor deck when the weather's fine and eat practically among the boats. There's also live music on Thursday and Friday nights. *Average main: $21* *76 Wharf St.* *978/744–8485* *www.hipfinz.com.*

$ B&B/INN **Amelia Payson House.** Built in 1845, this Greek Revival house is a comfortable bed-and-breakfast near all the historic attractions. **Pros:** spotless; cozy; decorated in period furniture. **Cons:** no children under 14. *Rooms from: $135* *16 Winter St.* *978/744–8304* *www.ameliapaysonhouse.com* *3 rooms* *Closed Dec.–Apr.* *Breakfast.*

$ HOTEL **The Hawthorne Hotel.** Elegantly restored, this full-service landmark hotel celebrates the town's most famous writer and is within walking distance from the town common, museums, and waterfront. **Pros:** lovely, historic lobby; parking available behind hotel; easy walking access to all the town's features. **Cons:** many rooms are small. *Rooms from: $144* *18 Washington Sq. W* *978/744–4080, 800/729–7829* *www.hawthornehotel.com* *93 rooms.*

GLOUCESTER

37 miles northeast of Boston, 8 miles northeast of Manchester-by-the-Sea.

On Gloucester's fine seaside promenade is a famous statue of a man steering a ship's wheel, his eyes searching the horizon. The statue, which honors those who go down to the sea in ships, was commissioned by the town citizens in celebration of Gloucester's 300th anniversary in 1923. The oldest seaport in the nation (with some of the North Shore's best beaches) is still a major fishing port. Sebastian Junger's 1997 book *A Perfect Storm* was an account of the fate of the *Andrea*

Landlubbers can go to sea at Salem's Peabody Essex Museum.

Gail, a Gloucester fishing boat caught in the storm of the century in October 1991. In 2000 the book was made into a movie, filmed on location in Gloucester.

ESSENTIALS

Visitor Information **Cape Ann Chamber of Commerce** ✉ *33 Commercial St.* ☎ *978/283–1601* 🌐 *www.capeannchamber.com.* **Rockport Chamber of Commerce** ✉ *33 Commercial St.* ☎ *978/546–6575* 🌐 *www.rockportusa.com.*

EXPLORING

The Cape Ann Historical Association. Downtown in the Captain Elias Davis 1804 house, this is Gloucester's surprising museum and gallery. It reflects the town's commitment to artists, and has the world's largest collection by maritime luminist Fitz Henry (Hugh) Lane. There's also an excellent exhibit on Gloucester's maritime history. ✉ *27 Pleasant St.* ☎ *978/283–0455* 🌐 *www.capeannmuseum.org* 🎟 *$10* ⏲ *Tues.–Sat. 10–5, Sun. 1–4.*

Hammond Castle Museum. Inventor John Hays Hammond Jr. built this structure in 1926 to resemble a medieval stone castle. Hammond is credited with more than 500 patents, including inventions associated with the organ that bears his name. The museum contains medieval-style furnishings and paintings, and the Great Hall houses an impressive 8,200-pipe organ. From the castle you can see Norman's Woe Rock, made famous by Longfellow in his poem "The Wreck of the Hesperus." ✉ *80 Hesperus Ave., south side of Gloucester off Rte. 127* ☎ *978/283–2080, 978/283–7673* 🌐 *www.hammondcastle.org* 🎟 *$9* ⏲ *May–early June, weekends and mid-June–Oct., daily; call for hrs.*

Rocky Neck. The town's creative side thrives in this neighborhood, the first-settled artists' colony in the United States. Its alumni include Winslow Homer, Maurice Prendergast, Jane Peter, and Cecilia Beaux. ✉ *53 Rocky Neck Ave.* ☎ *978/282–0917* 🌐 *www.rockyneckartcolony.org* 🕙 *Galleries 10–10, May 15–Oct. 15. Call or check website for winter hrs.*

SPORTS AND THE OUTDOORS

BEACHES Gloucester has the best beaches on the North Shore. From Memorial Day through mid-September parking costs $20 on weekdays and $25 on weekends, when the lots often fill by 10 am.

Good Harbor Beach. This beach has calm waters and soft sand, and is surrounded by grassy dunes, making it perfect any time of year. In summer (June, July, and August), it is lifeguard patrolled and there is a snack bar if you don't feel like packing food. The restrooms and showers are clean and wheelchair accessible, and you can pick up beach toys at the concessions. **Amenities:** restrooms, showers, concessions. **Best for:** swimming and playing on the shore. **TIP→ On weekdays parking is plentiful, but the lot fills by 10 am on weekends. In June, green flies can be bothersome.** ✉ *Easily signposted from Rte. 127A* *Parking $20 per car; $25 on weekends and holidays.*

15

Long Beach. Just as its name implies, this soft-sand beach is long, and it's also broad. It draws crowds from the houses that border it, particularly on weekends. Cape Ann Motor Inn is nearby. **Amenities:** None. **Best for:** Families. **TIP→ Very limited parking. Don't even think of parking in neighborhood streets if you don't have a town parking sticker—you will be towed.** ✉ *Off Rte. 127A on Gloucester-Rockport town line.*

Wingaersheek Beach. With white sand and dunes, Wingaersheek Beach is a well-protected cove. The white Annisquam lighthouse is in the bay. The beach is known for its miles of white sand and calm waters. **TIP→ On weekends arrive early. The parking lot generally fills up by midmorning. Amenities: restrooms; food and drink. Best for: families; surfing.** ✉ *Exit 13 off Rte. 128* 🌐 *www.gloucester-ma.gov/index.aspx?nid=299* *Limited parking, $20 per car; $25 on weekends and holidays.*

BOATING **Thomas E. Lannon.** Consider a sail along the harbor and coast aboard the 65-foot schooner Thomas E. Lannon, crafted in Essex in 1996 and modeled after the great boats built a century before. From mid-May through mid-October there are several two-hour sails, including trips that let you enjoy the sunset or participate in a lobster bake. Tickets are $40. ✉ *41 Rogers St., next to Gloucester House restaurant* ☎ *978/281–6634* 🌐 *www.schooner.org.*

WHERE TO EAT AND STAY

For expanded hotel reviews, visit Fodors.com.

$$ AMERICAN ✕ **The Franklin Cafe.** This contemporary nightspot offers bistro-style chicken, roast cod, and steak frites, perfect for the late-night crowd (it's open until midnight). Live jazz is on tap most Tuesday evenings. Look for the signature martini glass over the door. $ *Average main: $20* ✉ *118 Main St.* ☎ *978/283–7888* 🌐 *www.franklincafe.com* 🕙 *No lunch.*

Kids enjoy the white sands of Wingaersheek Beach in Gloucester.

$$ ECLECTIC **Passports.** With an eclectic lunch and dinner menu—hence the name—Passports is a bright and airy café with French, Spanish, and Thai dishes, as well as lobster sandwiches. Early risers can opt for breakfast, which is served only on Sunday mornings. The fried calamari and house haddock are favorites here, and there's always local art hanging on the walls for patrons to buy. Occasionally there are wine tastings. *Average main: $15* *110 Main St.* *978/281–3680.*

$$ RESORT FAMILY **Cape Ann's Marina Resort & Spa.** This year-round hotel less than a mile from Gloucester comes alive in summer. **Pros:** guests get a free river cruise during summer; free Wi-Fi. **Cons:** "resort" is a misnomer—the hotel is surrounded by parking lots; expect motel quality. *Rooms from: $175* *75 Essex Ave.* *978/283–2116, 800/626–7660* *www.capeannmarina.com* *31 rooms* *No meals.*

$$ HOTEL **Cape Ann Motor Inn.** On the sands of Long Beach, this three-story, shingled motel has no-frills rooms except for the balconies and ocean views. **Pros:** exceptional view from every room; kids under five stay free. **Cons:** thin walls; motel quality; summer season can be loud and crowded. *Rooms from: $175* *33 Rockport Rd.* *978/281–2900, 800/464–8439* *www.capeannmotorinn.com* *30 rooms, 1 suite* *Breakfast.*

ROCKPORT

41 miles northeast of Boston, 4 miles northeast of Gloucester on Rte. 127.

Rockport, at the very tip of Cape Ann, derives its name from the local granite formations. Many Boston-area structures are made of stone cut from its long-gone quarries. Today the town is a tourist center with a well-marked, centralized downtown that is easy to navigate and access on foot. Unlike typical tourist-trap landmarks, Rockport's shops sell quality arts, clothing, and gifts, and its restaurants serve seafood or home-baked cookies rather than fast food. Walk past shops and colorful clapboard houses to the end of Bearskin Neck for an impressive view of the Atlantic Ocean and the old, weather-beaten lobster shack known as Motif No. 1 because of its popularity as a subject for amateur painters and photographers.

ESSENTIALS

Visitor Information Rockport Chamber of Commerce *33 Commercial St., Gloucester 978/546–6575 www.rockportusa.com.*

WHERE TO EAT AND STAY

For expanded hotel reviews, visit Fodors.com.

$$ SEAFOOD **Brackett's Ocean View.** A big bay window in this quiet, homey restaurant provides an excellent view across Sandy Bay. The menu includes chowders, fish cakes, and other seafood dishes. *Average main: $18 25 Main St. 978/546–2797 www.bracketts.com Closed Nov.–Mar.*

$$ B&B/INN **Addison Choate Inn.** Just a minute's walk from both the center of Rockport and the train station, this 1851 inn sits in a prime location. **Pros:** proximity to the ocean, shopping, and train station. **Cons:** only one bedroom on the first floor. *Rooms from: $159 49 Broadway 978/546–7543, 800/245–7543 www.addisonchoateinn.com 5 rooms Closed Nov.–Apr. Breakfast.*

$$ HOTEL FAMILY **Bearskin Neck Motor Lodge.** Near the end of Bearskin Neck, this small brick-and-shingle motel offers guests the best of both worlds: a beautiful view of the ocean as well as easy access to shopping. **Pros:** each room has its own balcony and unobstructed view of the Atlantic Ocean; the hotel is located in the thick of restaurant and shops. **Cons:** constant flow of summer tourists on Bear Skin Neck may limit privacy. *Rooms from: $179 64 Bearskin Neck 978/546–6677, 877/507–6272 www.bearskinneckmotorlodge.com 8 rooms Closed early Nov.–late Apr. No meals.*

$ B&B/INN Fodor's Choice ★ **Sally Webster Inn.** This inn with local flavor and within walking range of town activities was named for a member of Hannah Jumper's "Hatchet Gang," teetotalers who smashed up the town's liquor stores in 1856 and turned Rockport into the dry town it remained until as recently as 2007. **Pros:** homey atmosphere in an excellent location with attentive staff. **Cons:** some rooms accessed via stairs. *Rooms from: $140 34 Mt. Pleasant St. 978/546–9251 www.sallywebster.com 7 rooms Breakfast.*

ESSEX

35 miles northeast of Boston, 12 miles west of Rockport.

The small seafaring town of Essex, once an important shipbuilding center, is surrounded by salt marshes and is filled with antiques stores and seafood restaurants.

GETTING HERE AND AROUND

Head west out of Cape Ann on Route 128, turning north on Route 133.

ESSENTIALS

Visitor Information **Escape to Essex** 🌐 *www.visitessexma.com.*

EXPLORING

FAMILY **Essex Shipbuilding Museum.** At what is still an active shipyard, this museum traces the evolution of the American schooner, which was first created in Essex. The museum sometimes offers shipbuilding demonstrations. One-hour tours take in the museum's many buildings and boats, especially the *Evelina M. Goulart*—one of only seven remaining Essex-built schooners. ✉ *66 Main St.(Rte. 133)* ☎ *978/768–7541* 🌐 *www.essexshipbuildingmuseum.org* 🎟 *$7* ⏲ *Mid-May–mid-Oct. Wed.–Sun. 10–5.*

SHOPPING

David Neligan Antiques. For the discerning collector, this shop specializes in high-quality European and English furniture, paintings, decorative art, and more. ✉ *38 Main St.* ☎ *978/768–3910.*

WHERE TO EAT

$$ SEAFOOD FAMILY Fodor's Choice ★ ✕ **Woodman's of Essex.** According to local legend, this is where Lawrence "Chubby" Woodman invented the first fried clam back in 1916. Today this sprawling wooden shack with indoor booths and outdoor picnic tables is *the* place for seafood in the rough. Besides fried clams, you can tuck into clam chowder, lobster rolls, or the popular "downriver" lobster combo. 💲 *Average main: $16* ✉ *121 Main St.(Rte. 133)* ☎ *978/768–2559, 800/649–1773* 🌐 *www.woodmans.com.*

IPSWICH

30 miles north of Boston, 6 miles northwest of Essex.

Quiet little Ipswich, settled in 1633 and famous for its clams, is said to have more 17th-century houses standing and occupied than any other place in America; more than 40 were built before 1725. Information and a booklet with a suggested walking tour are available at the **Ipswich Visitor Information Center.**

ESSENTIALS

Visitor Information **Ipswich Visitor Information Center** ✉ *36 S. Main St. (Rte. 1A)* ☎ *978/356–8540* 🌐 *www.ipswichvisitorcenter.org* ⏲ *Closed Nov.–Apr. Closed May weekdays.*

EXPLORING

Castle Hill on the Crane Estate. This 59-room Stuart-style mansion, built in 1927 for Richard Crane—of the Crane plumbing company—and his family, is part of the Crane Estate, a stretch of more than 2,100 acres along the Essex and Ipswich rivers, encompassing Castle Hill, Crane Beach, and the Crane Wildlife Refuge. Although the original furnishings were sold at auction, the mansion has been elaborately refurnished in period style; photographs in most of the rooms show their original appearance. The Great House is open for one-hour tours and also hosts concerts and other events. Inquire about seasonal programs like

Head to Woodsman's of Essex for classic New England seafood.

fly-fishing or kayaking. If you're looking for an opulent and exquisite overnight stay, book a room at the on-site Inn at Castle Hill. ✉ *Argilla Rd.* ☎ *978/356–4351* 🎫 *Fees vary* ⏲ *Memorial Day–Columbus Day wknd., Wed.–Sat., call for hrs.*

SPORTS AND THE OUTDOORS

FAMILY **Crane Beach.** Crane Beach, one of New England's most beautiful beaches, is a sandy, 4-mile-long stretch backed by dunes and a nature trail. Public parking is available, but on a nice summer weekend it's usually full before lunch. There are lifeguards, a snack bar, and changing rooms. Check ahead before visiting mid-July to early August, when greenhead flies terrorize sunbathers. ■ **TIP→ The Ipswich Essex Explorer bus runs between the Ipswich train station and Crane Beach weekends and holidays from June to September; the $5 pass includes round-trip bus fare and beach admission. Contact the Ipswich Visitor Information Center for information.** ✉ *310 Argilla Rd.* ☎ *978/356–4354* 🎫 *Fees vary* ⏲ *Daily 8–sunset.*

HIKING

FAMILY **Ipswich River Wildlife Sanctuary.** The Massachusetts Audubon Society's Ipswich River Wildlife Sanctuary has trails through marshland hills, where there are remains of early colonial settlements as well as abundant wildlife. Make sure to grab some birdseed and get a trail map from the office. Enjoy bridges, man-made rock structures, and other surprises on the Rockery Trail. ✉ *87 Perkins Row, southwest of Ipswich, 1 mile off Rte. 97, Topsfield* ☎ *978/887–9264* 🌐 *www.massaudubon.org* 🎫 *$4* ⏲ *Hrs vary seasonally.*

WHERE TO EAT

$ SEAFOOD FAMILY Fodor's Choice ★ **Clam Box.** Shaped like a giant fried clam box, this small roadside stand is the best place to sample Ipswich's famous bivalves. Since 1938 locals and tourists have been lining up for clams, oysters, scallops, and onion rings. *$ Average main: $14 ✉ 246 High St.(Rte. 1A) ☎ 978/356–9707 🌐 www.ipswichma.com/clambox ✍ Reservations not accepted ⏲ Closed late Nov.–Feb.*

$ SEAFOOD **Stone Soup Café.** This cheery café provides consistently good food. Excellent breakfasts include omelets, French toast, and assorted pancakes; lunch features chowders, pot roast, or delicious Cuban sandwiches. Its clam chowder took home the town's annual prize six years in a row. Dinner can include lobster bisque, porcini ravioli, or whatever contemporary fare the chef is inspired to cook from the day's farm-stand finds. *$ Average main: $8 ✉ 141 High St., off Rte. 1A ☎ 978/356–4222 ▭ No credit cards ⏲ Closed Mon.–Tues.*

NEWBURYPORT

38 miles north of Boston, 12 miles north of Ipswich on Rte. 1A.

Newburyport's High Street is lined with some of the finest examples of Federal-period (roughly, 1790–1810) mansions in New England. The city was once a leading port and shipbuilding center; the houses were built for prosperous sea captains. Although Newburyport's maritime significance ended with the decline of clipper ships, the town was revived in the 1970s. Today the town bustles with shops, restaurants, galleries, and a waterfront park and boardwalk. The civic improvements have been matched by private restorations of the town's housing stock, much of which dates from the 18th century, with a scattering of 17th-century homes in some neighborhoods.

Newburyport is walker-friendly, with well-marked restrooms and free parking all day down by the water.

A stroll through the **Waterfront Park & Promenade** offers a view of the harbor as well as the fishing and pleasure boats that moor here. A causeway leads from Newburyport to a narrow piece of land known as Plum Island, which harbors a summer colony (rapidly becoming year-round) at one end.

EXPLORING

Custom House Maritime Museum. Built in 1835 in Greek Revival style, this museum contains exhibits on maritime history, ship models, tools, and paintings. *✉ 25 Water St. ☎ 978/462–8681 🌐 www.customhousemaritimemuseum.org 🎫 $7 ⏲ Hrs vary seasonally.*

SPORTS AND THE OUTDOORS

Parker River National Wildlife Refuge. On Plum Island, this 4,662-acre refuge of salt marsh, freshwater marsh, beaches, and dunes is one of the few natural barrier beach–dune–salt marsh complexes left on the Northeast coast. Here you can bird-watch, fish, swim, and pick plums and cranberries. The refuge is a popular place in summer, especially on weekends; cars begin to line up at the gate before 7 am. There's no restriction on the number of people using the beach, but only a limited number of cars are let in; no pets are allowed in the refuge. ✉ *6 Plum Island Tpke.* ☎ *978/465–5753* ⊕ *www.fws.gov/refuge/parker_river* 🎫 *$5 per car, bicycles and walk-ins $2* ⏲ *Daily dawn–dusk. Beach usually closed during nesting season in spring and early summer.*

FAMILY
Fodor's Choice ★
Salisbury Beach State Reservation. Relax at the long sandy beach, launch a boat, or just enjoy the water. From Newburyport center, follow Bridge Road north, take a right on Beach Road, and follow it until you reach State Reservation Road. The park is popular with campers; reservations in summer are made many months ahead to ensure a spot. ✉ *Rte. 1A, 5 miles northeast of Newburyport, Beach Rd., Rte. 1A, Salisbury* ☎ *978/462–4481* ⊕ *www.mass.gov/dcr* 🎫 *Beach free, parking $9.*

NIGHTLIFE

Grog. This lively restaurant and bar hosts blues and rock bands and open-mike sessions several nights a week. Food is served until 11 pm on Friday and Saturday. ✉ *13 Middle St.* ☎ *978/465–8008* ⊕ *www.thegrog.com.*

SHOPPING

Todd Farm Flea Market. A New England tradition since 1971, the Todd Farm Flea Market features up to 240 vendors from all over New England and New York. It's open every Sunday from mid-April through late November, though its busiest months are May, September, and October. Merchandise varies from antique furniture, clocks, jewelry, recordings, and tools to fishing rods, golf accessories, honey products, cedar fencing, vintage toys, and seasonal plants and flowers. Antiques hunters often arrive before the sun comes up for the best deals. ✉ *285 Main St., Rte. 1A, Rowley* ☎ *978/948–3300* ⊕ *www.toddfarm.com* ⏲ *Apr.–Nov., Sun. 5 am–3 pm.*

WHERE TO EAT AND STAY

For expanded hotel reviews, visit Fodors.com.

$$
SEAFOOD
✕ **Glenn's Restaurant & Cool Bar.** A block from the waterfront parking lot, Glenn's offers creative combinations from around the world, with the occasional New England twist. The ever-changing menu might include sesame-crusted yellowfin tuna or house-smoked baby back ribs. There's live jazz or blues on Sunday. 💲 *Average main: $23* ✉ *44 Merrimac St.* ☎ *978/465–3811* ⊕ *www.glennsrestaurant.com* ⏲ *Closed Mon. No lunch.*

$$
B&B/INN
Clark Currier Inn. Once the home of the 19th-century sea captain Thomas March Clark, this 1803 Federal mansion has been beautifully restored. **Pros:** easy to find; close to shopping and the oceanfront; good for couples looking for a peaceful and quiet experience. **Cons:** children under 10 not allowed; rooms can get hot in summer. 💲 *Rooms from: $165* ✉ *45 Green St.* ☎ *978/465–8363* ⊕ *www.clarkcurrierinn.com* *7 rooms, 1 suite* 🍽 *Breakfast.*

SOUTH OF BOSTON

People from all over the world travel south of Boston to visit Plymouth for a glimpse into the country's earliest beginnings. The two main stops are the Plimoth Plantation, which re-creates the everyday life of the

Dip a toe in the ocean at Salisbury Beach.

Pilgrims; and the *Mayflower II,* which gives you an idea of how frightening the journey across the Atlantic must have been. As you may guess, November in Plymouth brings special events focused on Thanksgiving. Farther south, New Bedford recalls the world of whaling.

EN ROUTE

While driving from Boston to Plymouth, you can easily make a stop at **Quincy,** where sites pay tribute to the nation's second and sixth presidents.

Adams National Historic Park. Receive a guided visit of the birthplaces, homes, and graves of Presidents John Adams and his son John Quincy Adams. You also can see the park as part of a trolley tour of the property and family church. ✉ *Carriage house, 135 Adams St., visitor center and bookstore, 1250 Hancock St., Quincy* ☎ *617/770–1175* 🌐 *www.nps.gov/adam* 🎫 *$5* 🕒 *Tours 9–5 daily; last tour at 3:15, mid-Apr.–mid-Nov.*

PLYMOUTH

40 miles south of Boston.

On December 26, 1620, 102 weary men, women, and children disembarked from the *Mayflower* to found the first permanent European settlement north of Virginia (they had found their earlier landing in Provincetown to be unsuitable). Today Plymouth is characterized by narrow streets, clapboard mansions, shops, antiques stores, and a scenic waterfront. To mark Thanksgiving, the town holds activities including historic-house tours and a parade. Historic statues dot the town, including depictions of William Bradford, Pilgrim leader and governor of Plymouth Colony for more than 30 years, on Water Street; a Pilgrim maiden in Brewster Gardens; and Massasoit, the Wampanoag chief who helped the Pilgrims survive, on Carver Street.

ESSENTIALS

Visitor Information **Plymouth Visitor Information Center** ✉ *130 Water St., at Hwy. 44* ☎ *508/747–7533, 800/872–1620* 🌐 *www.visit-plymouth.com* ⏲ *Hrs vary seasonally; check website or call.*

EXPLORING

FAMILY **Mayflower II.** This seaworthy replica of the 1620 *Mayflower* was built in England through research and a bit of guesswork, then sailed across the Atlantic in 1957. As you explore the interior and exterior of the ship, sailors in modern dress answer your questions about both the reproduction and the original ship, while costumed guides provide a 17th-century perspective. Plymouth Rock is nearby. ✉ *State Pier* ☎ *508/746–1622* 🌐 *www.plimoth.org* 🎟 *$10, $35 with Heritage Pass admission to Plimoth Plantation* ⏲ *Late Mar.–Nov., daily 9–5.*

15

National Monument to the Forefathers. The largest freestanding granite statue in the United States, this allegorical monument stands high on a grassy hill. Designed by Hammet Billings of Boston in 1854 and dedicated in 1889, it depicts Faith, surrounded by Liberty, Morality, Justice, Law, and Education, and includes scenes from the Pilgrims' early days in Plymouth. ✉ *Allerton St.* 🌐 *www.visit-plymouth.com.*

FAMILY **Pilgrim Hall Museum.** From the waterfront sights it's a short walk to one of the country's oldest public museums. Established in 1824, Pilgrim Hall Museum transports you back to the time of the Pilgrims' landing with objects carried by those weary travelers to the New World. Included are a carved chest, a remarkably well-preserved wicker cradle, Myles Standish's sword, John Alden's Bible, Native American artifacts, and the remains of the *Sparrow Hawk,* a sailing ship that was wrecked in 1626. ✉ *75 Court St.(Rte. 3A)* ☎ *508/746–1620* 🌐 *www.pilgrimhall.org* 🎟 *$8* ⏲ *Feb.–Dec., daily 9:30–4:30 including Thanksgiving Day.*

FAMILY Fodor's Choice ★ **Plimoth Plantation.** Over the entrance to this popular attraction is the caution: You are now entering 1627. Believe it. Against the backdrop of the Atlantic Ocean, and 3 miles south of downtown Plymouth, this Pilgrim village has been carefully re-created, from the thatch roofs, cramped quarters, and open fireplaces to the long-horned livestock. Throw away your preconception of white collars and funny hats; through ongoing research, the Plimoth staff has developed a portrait of the Pilgrims that's more complex than the dour folk in school textbooks. Listen to the accents of the "residents," who never break out of character. You might see them plucking ducks, cooking rabbit stew, or tending gardens. Feel free to engage them in conversation about their life, but expect only curious looks if you ask about anything that happened after 1627. "Thanksgiving: Memory, Myth & Meaning," an exhibit in the visitor center, offers a fresh perspective on the 1621 harvest celebration that is now known as "the first Thanksgiving." Note that there's not a lot of shade here in summer. ✉ *137 Warren Ave.(Hwy. 3A)* ☎ *508/746–1622* 🌐 *www.plimoth.org* 🎟 *Combination passes for three sites start at $28* ⏲ *Hrs vary seasonally.*

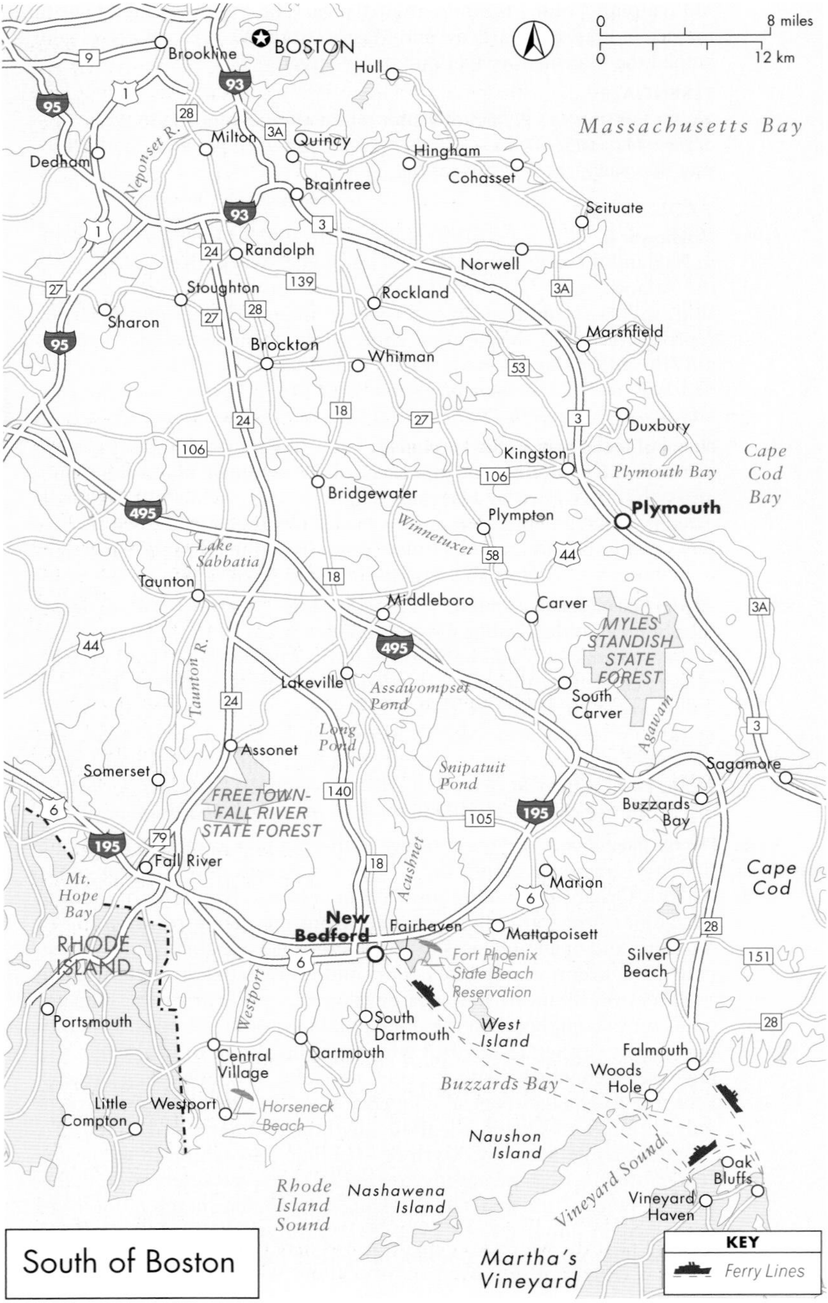

South of Boston

FAMILY **Plymouth Rock.** This landmark rock, just a few dozen yards from the *Mayflower II,* is popularly believed to have been the Pilgrims' stepping-stone when they left the ship. Given the stone's unimpressive appearance—it's little more than a boulder—and dubious authenticity (as explained on a nearby plaque), the grand canopy overhead seems a trifle ostentatious. ✉ *Water St.*

Sparrow House. Built in 1640, this is Plymouth's oldest structure. It is among several historic houses in town that are open for visits. You can peek into a pair of rooms furnished in the spartan style of the Pilgrims' era. The contemporary crafts gallery also on the premises seems somewhat incongruous, but the works on view are of high quality. ✉ *42 Summer St.* ☎ *508/747–1240* 🌐 *www.sparrowhouse.com* 🎟 *House $2, gallery free* ⏲ *Daily 10–5.*

WHERE TO EAT AND STAY

For expanded hotel reviews, visit Fodors.com.

$$ SEAFOOD **Blue-eyed Crab Grille & Raw Bar.** Grab a seat on the outside deck overlooking the water at this friendly, somewhat funky (plastic fish dangling from the ceiling), fresh-fish shack. If the local Island Creek raw oysters are on the menu, go for them! Otherwise start with thick crab bisque full of hunks of floating crabmeat or the steamed mussels. Dinner entrées include seafood stew with chorizo and sweet potatoes and the classic fish-and-chips. Locals come for the brunch specials, too, like grilled shrimp and poached eggs over red-pepper grits, the lobster omelet, and banana-ginger pancakes. $ *Average main: $22* ✉ *170 Water St.* ☎ *508/747–6776* 🌐 *www.blueeyedcrab.com.*

$ HOTEL FAMILY **Best Western Cold Spring.** Walk to the waterfront and downtown Plymouth from this clean, family-friendly two-story motel. **Pros:** free parking; half-mile from Plymouth Rock and *Mayflower II;* some of the best wallet-pleasing rates in the area. **Cons:** basic rooms without much character. $ *Rooms from: $140* ✉ *188 Court St.* ☎ *508/746–2222, 800/678–8667* 🌐 *www.bestwesternmassachusetts.com* *56 rooms* *Breakfast.*

$$ HOTEL **John Carver Inn & Spa.** This three-story colonial-style redbrick building is steps from Plymouth's main attractions. **Pros:** waterfront setting. **Cons:** pool is noisy and often overcrowded; some rooms need updating. $ *Rooms from: $129* ✉ *25 Summer St.* ☎ *508/746–7100, 800/274–1620* 🌐 *www.johncarverinn.com* *74 rooms, 6 suites.*

NEW BEDFORD

45 miles southwest of Plymouth, 50 miles south of Boston.

In 1652 colonists from Plymouth settled in the area that now includes the city of New Bedford. The city has a long maritime tradition, beginning as a shipbuilding center and small whaling port in the late 1700s. By the mid-1800s it had developed into a center of North American whaling. Today New Bedford has the largest fishing fleet on the East Coast. Although much of the town is industrial, the restored historic district near the water is a delight. It was here that Herman Melville set his masterpiece, *Moby-Dick,* a novel about whaling.

DID YOU KNOW?

Plimoth Plantation is about more than Pilgrims. It also honors Native Americans at Wampanoag Site. Visit a traditional house, learn about family life, and chat with Wampanoag people. Note that presenters are not in character as at the plantation site.

CLOSE UP

Thar She Blows

Ships depart regularly for whale-watching excursions from April or May through October, from coastal towns all along the bay. Humpbacks, finbacks, and minkes feed locally in season, so you're sure to see a few—and on a good day you may see dozens. Bring warm clothing, as the ocean breezes can be brisk; rubber-soled shoes are also a good idea.

Boston Harbor Cruises. The high-speed catamarans of Boston Harbor Cruises glide to the whaling banks in half the time of some other cruises, allowing nearly as much whale time in only a three-hour tour. Tours are operated from April to November; call for schedule and reservations. ✉ *1 Long Wharf, next to aquarium, Downtown* ☎ *617/227–4321, 877/733–9425* 🌐 *www.bostonharborcruises.com.*

Cape Ann Whale Watch. This outfit has run whale-watch tours since 1979. ✉ *Rose's Wharf, 415 Main St., Gloucester* ☎ *800/877–5110* 🌐 *www.seethewhales.com.*

Captain Bill's Deep Sea Fishing/Whale Watch. Tours with Captain Bill's Deep Sea Fishing/Whale Watch make use of knowledgeable naturalists from the Whale Center of New England. ✉ *24 Harbor Loop, Gloucester* ☎ *978/283–6995, 800/339–4253* 🌐 *www.captbillandsons.com.*

Capt. John Boats. Several daily whale-watch cruises leave from Plymouth Town Wharf. ✉ *10 Town Wharf, Plymouth* ☎ *508/746–2643* 🌐 *www.captjohn.com.*

New England Aquarium. Daily whale-watching cruises from Central Wharf leave from here. The trip, with an aquarium staff whale expert on board, lasts three to four hours. Tours run from April to October. ✉ *Central Wharf at end of Central St., Downtown, Boston* ☎ *617/973–5206* 🌐 *www.neaq.org* 🎟 *$40.*

15

ESSENTIALS

Visitor Information **New Bedford Office of Tourism** ✉ *Waterfront Visitor Center, Pier 3, 52 Co Op Wharf No. 3* ☎ *800/508–5353, 508/979–1745* 🌐 *www.newbedford-ma.gov/Tourism/DestinationNB/visitorcenter.html.*

EXPLORING

FAMILY **New Bedford Whaling Museum.** Established in 1903, this is the world's largest museum of its kind. A highlight is the skeleton of a 66-foot blue whale, one of only three on view anywhere. An interactive exhibit lets you listen to the underwater sounds of whales, dolphins, and other sea life—plus the sounds of a thunderstorm and a whale-watching boat—as a whale might hear them. You can also peruse the collection of scrimshaw, visit exhibits on regional history, and climb aboard an 89-foot, half-scale model of the 1826 whaling ship *Lagoda*—the world's largest ship model. A small chapel across the street from the museum is the one described in *Moby-Dick*. ✉ *18 Johnny Cake Hill* ☎ *508/997–0046* 🌐 *www.whalingmuseum.org* 🎟 *$14* ⏲ *May–Sept., daily 9-5, Oct.–Apr. Tues.–Sat. 9–4; Sun. 11–4.*

FAMILY **New Bedford Whaling National Historical Park.** The city's whaling tradition is commemorated at this park that takes up 13 blocks of the waterfront

Continued on page 342

A WHALE OF A TALE

by Steve Larese

Cameras have replaced harpoons in the waters north of Cape Cod. While you can learn about New England's whaling history and perhaps see whales in the distance from shore, a whale-watching excursion is the best way to connect with these magnificent creatures—who may be just as curious about you as you are about them.

Once relentlessly hunted around the world by New Englanders, whales today are celebrated as intelligent, friendly, and curious creatures. Whales are still important to the region's economy and culture, but now in the form of ecotourism. Easily accessible from several ports in Massachusetts, the 842-square-mi Stellwagen Bank National Marine Sanctuary attracts finback, humpback, minke, and right whales who feed and frolic here twice a year during their migration. The same conditions that made the Stellwagen Bank area of the mouth of Massachusetts Bay a good hunting ground make it a good viewing area. Temperature, currents, and nutrients combine to produce plankton, krill, and fish to feed marine mammals.

(opposite) Whaling museum custodian and a sperm whale jaw in the 1930s. (top) Hunted to near extinction, humpbacks today number about 60,000, and are found in oceans worldwide.

WHALING IN NEW ENGLAND TIMELINE

mid-1600s	America enters whaling industry
1690	Nantucket enters whaling industry
1820	*Essex* ship sunk by sperm whale
1840s	American whaling peaked
1851	*Moby-Dick* published
1927	The last U.S. whaler sails from New Bedford
1970s	Cape Cod whale-watching trips begin
1986	Ban on whaling by the International Whaling Commission
1992	Stellwagen Bank National Marine Sanctuary established

ON LAND: MARINE AND MARITIME MUSEUMS

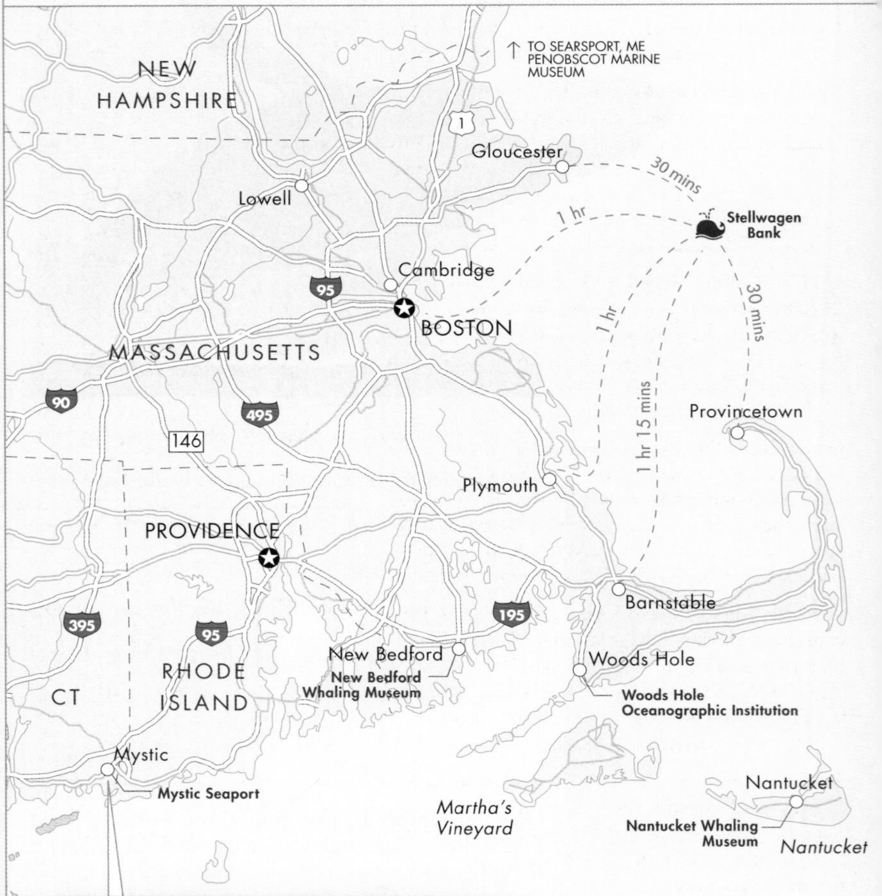

Whaling ships, like the *Charles W. Morgan* at Mystic Seaport, hunted whales for their baleen and oil.

Even landlubbers can learn about whales and whaling at these top New England institutions.

Nantucket Whaling Museum. This former whale-processing center and candle factory was converted into a museum in 1929. See art made by sailors, including masterful scrimshaw—intricate nautical scenes carved into whale bone or teeth and filled in with ink ✉ *Nantucket, Massachusetts* ☎ *508/228–1894* 🌐 *www.nha.org.*

★ **New Bedford Whaling Museum.** More than 200,000 artifacts are collected here, from ships' logbooks to harpoons. A must-see is the 89-foot, half-scale model of the 1826 whaling ship *Lagoda* ✉ *New Bedford, Massachusetts* ☎ *508/997–0046* 🌐 *www.whalingmuseum.org.*

New Bedford Whaling National Historical Park. The visitor center for this 13-block waterfront park provides maps and information about whaling-related sites, including a sea captain's mansion and restored whaling schooner. ✉ *New Bedford, Massachusetts,* ☎ *508/996–4095* 🌐 *www.nps.gov/nebe.*

★ **Mystic Seaport.** Actors portray life in a 19th-century seafaring village at this 37-acre living-history museum. Don't miss the 1841 *Charles W. Morgan,* the world's only surviving wooden whaling ship ✉ *Mystic, Connecticut* ☎ *860/572–5302* 🌐 *www.mysticseaport.org.*

Penobscot Marine Museum. Maine's seafaring history and mostly shore-whaling industry is detailed inside seven historic buildings ✉ *Searsport, Maine* ☎ *207/548–2529* 🌐 *www.penobscotmarinemuseum.org.*

Nantucket Whaling Museum

New Bedford Whaling Museum

Mystic Seaport

THE GREAT WHITE WHALE

Herman Melville based his 1851 classic *Moby-Dick: or, The Whale* on the true story of the *Essex,* which was sunk in 1821 by huge whale; an albino sperm whale called Mocha Dick; and his time aboard the whaling ship *Acushnet.*

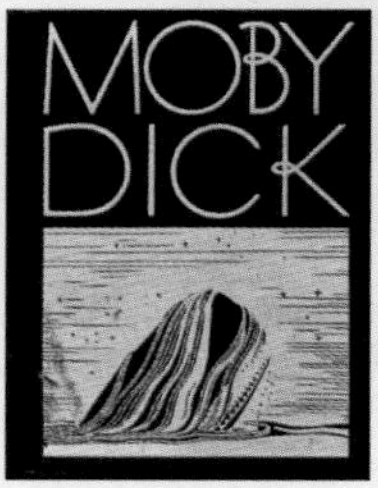

AT SEA: WHALE-WATCHING TOURS

COMMON NORTH ATLANTIC SPECIES

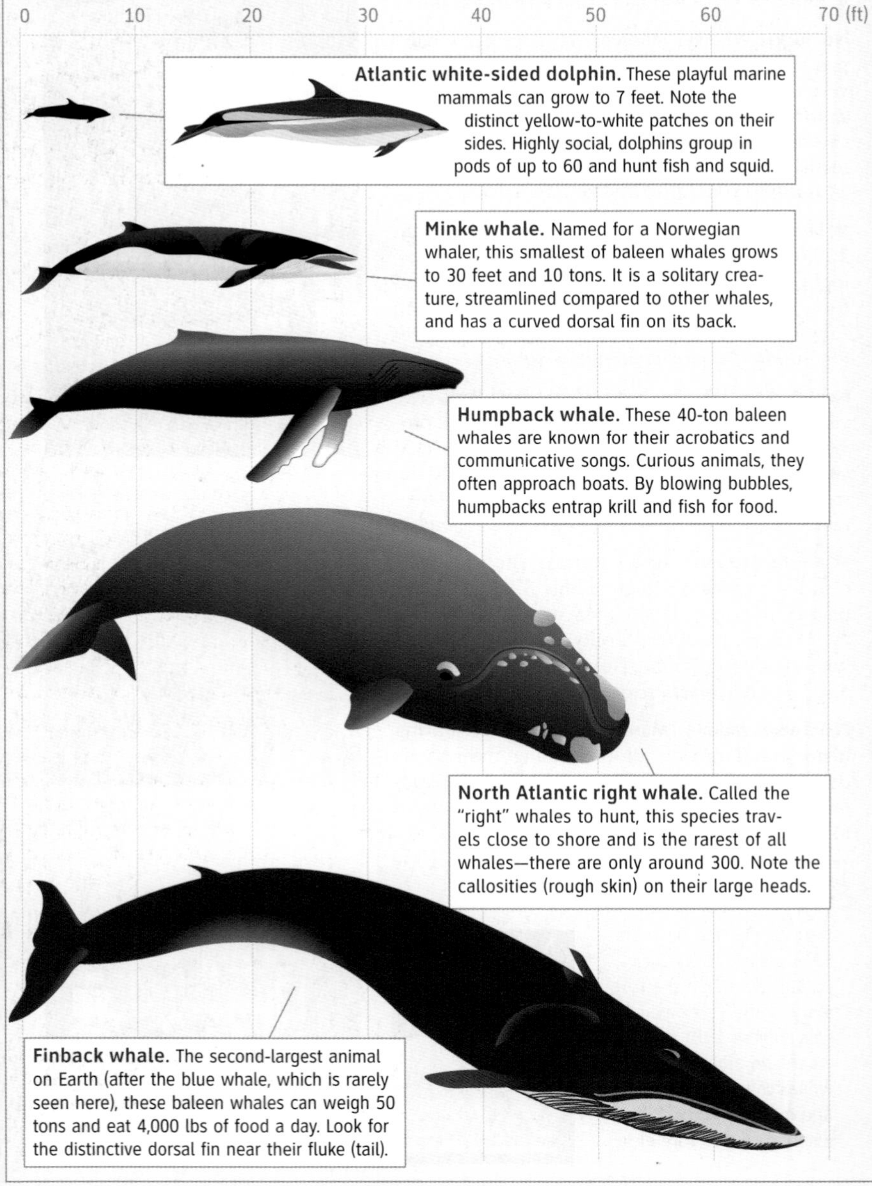

Atlantic white-sided dolphin. These playful marine mammals can grow to 7 feet. Note the distinct yellow-to-white patches on their sides. Highly social, dolphins group in pods of up to 60 and hunt fish and squid.

Minke whale. Named for a Norwegian whaler, this smallest of baleen whales grows to 30 feet and 10 tons. It is a solitary creature, streamlined compared to other whales, and has a curved dorsal fin on its back.

Humpback whale. These 40-ton baleen whales are known for their acrobatics and communicative songs. Curious animals, they often approach boats. By blowing bubbles, humpbacks entrap krill and fish for food.

North Atlantic right whale. Called the "right" whales to hunt, this species travels close to shore and is the rarest of all whales—there are only around 300. Note the callosities (rough skin) on their large heads.

Finback whale. The second-largest animal on Earth (after the blue whale, which is rarely seen here), these baleen whales can weigh 50 tons and eat 4,000 lbs of food a day. Look for the distinctive dorsal fin near their fluke (tail).

SEAWORTHY TRIP TIPS

When to Go: Tours operate April through October; May through September are the most active months in the Stellwagen Bank area.

Ports of Departure: Boats leave from Barnstable and Provincetown on Cape Cod, and Plymouth, Boston, and Gloucester, cutting across Cape Cod Bay to the Stellwagen area. Book tours at least a day ahead in the height of the summer season. Hyannis Whale Watcher in Barnstable, the Dolphin Fleet, Portuguese Princess, Captain John's Whale Watch in Plymouth, the New England Aquarium and Boston Harbor Cruises in Boston are just a few of your options. *See Thar She Blows box in this chapter for more information.*

Cost: Around $40. Check company Web sites for coupons.

What to Expect: All companies abide by guidelines so as not to harass whales. Tours last 3 to 4 hours and almost always encounter whales; if not, vouchers are often given for another tour. Passengers are encouraged to watch the horizon for water spouts, which indicate a surfaced whale clearing its blowhole to breathe air. Upon spotting an animal, the boat slows and approaches the whale to a safe distance; often, whales will approach an idling boat and even swim underneath it.

What to Bring: Plastic bags protect binoculars and cameras from damp spray. Most boats have a concession stand, but pack bottled water and snacks. **TIP→ Kids (and adults) will appreciate games or other items to pass the time in between whale sightings.**

What to Wear: Wear rubber-soled footwear for slick decks. A waterproof outer layer and layers of clothing will help in varied conditions, as will sunscreen, sunglasses, and a hat that can be secured. Most boats have cabins where you can warm up and get out of the wind.

Hyannis Whale Watcher Cruises, Cape Cod Bay

Comforting Advice: Small seat cushions like those used at sporting events may be appreciated. Consider taking motion-sickness medication before setting out. Ginger candy and acupressure wristbands can also help. If you feel queasy, get some fresh air and focus your eyes on a stable feature on the shore or horizon.

Photo Hints: Use a fast shutter speed, or sport mode, to avoid blurry photographs. Most whales will be a distance from the boat; have a telephoto lens ready. To avoid shutter delay on your point-and-shoot camera, lock the focus at infinity so you don't miss that breaching whale shot.

DID YOU KNOW?

Most boats have a naturalist aboard to discuss the whales and their environment. Many companies contribute to population studies by reporting the individual whales they spot. Whale tails, called flukes, are distinct and used like fingerprints for identification.

historic district. The park visitor center, housed in an 1853 Greek Revival building that was once a bank, provides maps and information about whaling-related sites. Free walking tours of the park leave from the visitor center at 10:30, 12:30, and 2:30 in July and August. ✉ *33 William St.* ☎ *508/996–4095* 🌐 *www.nps.gov/nebe* 🎟 *Free* ⏲ *Daily 9–5.*

Rotch-Jones-Duff House & Garden Museum. For a glimpse of upper-class life during New Bedford's whaling heyday, head one-half mile south of downtown to this 1834 Greek Revival mansion. Amid a full city block of gardens, the home housed three prominent families in the 1800s and is filled with elegant furnishings from the era, including a mahogany piano, a massive marble-top sideboard, and portraits of the house's occupants. A free self-guided audio tour is available. ✉ *396 County St.* ☎ *508/997–1401* 🌐 *www.rjdmuseum.org* 🎟 *$6* ⏲ *Mon.–Sat. 10–4, Sun. noon–4.*

WHERE TO EAT

$$ PORTUGUESE ✕ **Antonio's.** Expect the wait to be long and the dining room to be loud, but it's worth the hassle to sample the traditional fare of New Bedford's large Portuguese population at this friendly, unadorned restaurant. Dishes include hearty portions of pork and shellfish stew, *bacalau* (salt cod), and grilled sardines, often on plates piled high with crispy fried potatoes and rice. $ *Average main: $15* ✉ *267 Coggeshall St., near intersection of I–195 and Hwy. 18* ☎ *508/990–3636* 🌐 *www.antoniosnewbedford.com.*

$$ SEAFOOD FAMILY ✕ **Davy's Locker.** A huge seafood menu is the main draw at this spot overlooking Buzzards Bay. Choose from more than a dozen shrimp preparations, or a choice of healthful entrées—dishes prepared with olive oil, vegetables, garlic, and herbs. For landlubbers, chicken, steak, ribs, and the like are also available. $ *Average main: $15* ✉ *1480 E. Rodney French Blvd.* ☎ *508/992–7359* 🌐 *www.davyslockerrestaurant.com.*
Cape Air ✉ *Provincetown* ☎ *866/227–3247, 508/771–6944* 🌐 *www.flycapeair.com.*

Bay State Cruise Company ✉ *Commonwealth Pier, 200 Seaport Blvd, Boston* ☎ *617/748–1428, 877/783–3779* 🌐 *www.baystatecruisecompany.com.*

TRAVEL SMART BOSTON

GETTING HERE AND AROUND

Boston's maze of old and new comes together remarkably well with a little patience. Follow its endless array of narrow, twisting one-way streets radiating from Boston Harbor in the east, and you'll reach the bustle of the Italian-flavored North End. Go west and hit Faneuil Hall, the quaintly named streets of Downtown, and the bricky jungle of Government Center; head southwest toward the Old West End, the "Gah-den"—home of the Celtics and Bruins—and the historic Beacon Hill. The Back Bay's orderly (and alphabetical) grid of streets runs southwest from the base of Beacon Hill, where you'll come upon the retail wonderland of Prudential Center and the artsy, boutique-filled Newbury Street. Beyond that is the Fenway, home to many art museums, the Emerald Necklace's skein of parkland and ponds, and Fenway Park, baseball field of the much-loved Red Sox. To the south spreads the eclectic, trendy South End.

The wide and handsome Charles River serves as a natural dividing line between Boston and its northern neighborhoods and suburbs, including Charlestown and the cities of Cambridge and Somerville. (The Charles is edged with paths to jog, bike, stroll, and gaze at scullers, skylines, and sailing dinghies.) The Fort Point Channel and its picturesque waterside Harbor Walk beneath the spectacularly suspended Zakim Bridge links Downtown with the lively Seaport and Fan Pier districts and South Boston.

Walking is by far the best way to go in this small, finely detailed city. In good weather, bicycling is also catching on (⇨ *see Bike Travel*), as are pedicabs. But the next-best transport within Boston or its near environs is the MBTA system, called "the T" for short. Five "subway" lines—comprising underground trains, aboveground trolleys/light rail, and buses—run through the entire city and outlying suburbs, with additional bus networks filling in some of the gaps. You can ride the T to every major point of interest in the city; you'll probably only need a car to get out of town.

WORD OF MOUTH

After your trip, be sure to rate the places you visited and share your experiences and travel tips with us and other Fodorites in the Travel Talk Forums on 🌐 *www.fodors.com.*

■ TIP→ Ask the local tourist board about hotel and local transportation packages that include tickets to major museum exhibits or other special events.

AIR TRAVEL

Flying times to Boston from New York average 1 hour; it's 1½ hours from Washington, D.C., 2¼ hours from Chicago, 3 hours from Miami, 3½ hours from Dallas, 5½ hours from Los Angeles, 7½ hours from London, 14 hours from Tokyo, and 21 hours from Sydney. Delta, US Airways, and JetBlue run daily shuttle flights from New York and Washington, D.C.

■ TIP→ The Boston Convention and Visitor Bureau's website, 🌐 www.bostonusa.com, has direct links to 19 airlines that service the city. You can book flights here, too.

Airlines and Airports **Airline and Airport Links.com.** Airline and Airport Links.com has links to many of the world's airlines and airports. 🌐 *www.airlineandairportlinks.com.*

Airline Security Issues **Transportation Security Administration.** The TSA has answers to almost every question that might come up. 🌐 *www.tsa.gov.*

AIRPORTS

Boston's major airport, Logan International (BOS), is across the harbor, barely two miles from Downtown, and can be easily reached by taxi, water taxi, or bus/subway via MBTA's Silver or Blue lines. Logan's four passenger terminals are identified by the letters A, B, C, and E. Free airport shuttle buses run between the terminals and airport hotels. Some airlines use different terminals for international and domestic flights; most international flights arrive at Terminal E. A visitor center is in Terminal C. Worcester Regional Airport (ORH), T.F. Green Airport (PVD) in Providence, Rhode Island, and Manchester Boston Regional Airport (MHT) in New Hampshire are about an hour's drive from Boston.

Airport Information **Logan International Airport (Boston)** ✉ *I-90 east to Ted Williams Tunnel* ☎ *800/235-6426* 🌐 *www.massport.com/logan* Ⓜ *Airport.* **Manchester Boston Regional Airport** ✉ *Off I-293/Rte. 101, Exit 2, Manchester, NH, Manchester, New Hampshire* ☎ *603/624-6556* 🌐 *www.flymanchester.com.* **T.F. Green Airport** ✉ *Off I-95, Exit 13, Providence, RI, 2000 Post Rd., Warwick, Rhode Island* ☎ *888/268-7222, 401/691-2471* 🌐 *www.pvdairport.com.*

FLIGHTS

Airline Contacts **Alaska Airlines/Horizon Air** ☎ *800/252-7522* 🌐 *www.alaskaair.com.* **American Airlines** ☎ *800/433-7300* 🌐 *www.aa.com.* **Delta Airlines** ☎ *800/221-1212* 🌐 *www.delta.com.* **JetBlue** ☎ *800/538-2583* 🌐 *www.jetblue.com.* **Southwest Airlines** ☎ *800/435-9792* 🌐 *www.southwest.com.* **Spirit Airlines** ☎ *801/772-7117* 🌐 *www.spiritair.com.* **United Airlines** ☎ *800/864-8331* 🌐 *www.united.com.* **US Airways** ☎ *800/428-4322* 🌐 *www.usairways.com.*

GROUND TRANSPORTATION

BUSES OR SHUTTLE VANS

Several companies offer shared-van service to many Boston-area destinations. Ace American, for instance, provides door-to-door service to several major Back Bay and Downtown hotels. Reservations are not required, because vans swing by all the terminals every 15 minutes. One-way fares are $14.50 ($10 for each additional person.) Easy Transportation runs

NAVIGATING BOSTON

■ Boston is an eminently walkable city, but since its streets were originally laid out as cow paths leading to and from the waterfront, they may be tricky to navigate, so carry a map as you explore.

■ Street numbers are almost always marked with the even numbers on the opposite side from odd numbers. (A notable exception is Beacon Street between the State House and Public Garden).

■ Boston Common and the adjacent Public Garden, Quincy Market, and other tourist focal points in Boston have large maps posted at major intersections to help direct you around the city.

■ The Financial District and Downtown Crossing are part of Downtown. The streets here are laid out with little rhyme or reason and often run only one way.

■ If you find yourself wandering, don't be reluctant to ask passersby for directions. Most residents will be happy to help you get your bearings.

■ The public transportation system, the T, offers easy-to-read navigation guides and maps in every station. It stops at all major points of interest throughout the city, and just beyond the city limits, too.

■ If you decide that you must drive in and around Boston, it's a very good idea to do it with GPS. Most rental agencies offer GPS units as an option, and this is one place in the country where the technology is especially useful.

from the airport to the Back Bay Hilton, Radisson, and Lenox hotels from 7 am to 10 pm. Star Shuttle operates shared vans from the airport to the Marriott Copley Place and Sheraton Copley, every hour on the half hour, from 5:30 am to 11:30 pm. The best deal is Logan Express, with buses from the airport to the suburbs of Braintree, Framingham, Peabody, and Woburn. One-way fares are $12, and accompanied children under 17 ride free.

Contacts **Ace American** ☎ *781/580–9521* 🌐 *www.aceamericancoach.com.* **Easy Transportation** ☎ *617/869–7760* 🌐 *www.easytransportationinc.com.*

Logan Express ☎ *800/235–6426* 🌐 *www.massport.com/logan-airport/To%20and%20From%20Logan/LoganExpress.aspx.* **Star Shuttle** ☎ *617/230–6005* 🌐 *www.starshuttleboston.com.*

RENTAL CARS AND TAXIS

For recorded information about traveling to and from Logan Airport, as well as details about parking, contact the airport's ground-transportation hotline. Traffic in the city can be maddening; it's a good idea to take public transportation to and from the airport.

When driving from Logan to Downtown Boston, the most direct route is by way of the Sumner Tunnel ($3.50 toll inbound; no toll outbound). On weekends, holidays, and after 10 pm weekdays, you can get around Sumner Tunnel backups by using the Ted Williams Tunnel ($3.50 toll inbound; no toll outbound), which will steer you onto the Southeast Expressway south of Downtown Boston. Follow the signs to I–93 northbound to head back into the Downtown area.

Taxis can be hired outside each terminal. Fares to and from Downtown should be about $20, including tip. Taxis must pay an extra toll of $5.25 and a $2.75 airport fee when leaving the airport, which will be tacked onto your bill at the end of the trip. (On the way back to the airport, you'll pay the $2.75 fee again, but not the $5.25 toll.) Major traffic jams, or circuitous routes to avoid them, add to the fare. Avoid hailing rogue taxis: legitimate Boston taxis are white; also check for a medallion plate and a posted photo ID of the driver.

Contacts **Logan Airport Customer Information Hotline** ☎ *800/235–6426.* **Metro Cab** ☎ *617/782–5500* 🌐 *boston-cab.com.* **Town Taxi** ☎ *617/536–5000.*

SUBWAY

The T's Blue (metro or underground train) and Silver (bus) lines run from the airport to Downtown Boston in about 20 minutes. The Blue Line is best if you're heading to North Station, Faneuil Hall, North End/Waterfront, or Back Bay (the Hynes Convention Center, Prudential Center area). Take the Silver Line to South Station, Boston Convention and Exhibition Center, Seaport World Trade Center, Chinatown, Theater District, and South End areas. From North and South stations you can reach the Red, Green, or Orange lines, or commuter rail. The T costs $2.50 for in-town travel if you're paying in cash or $2 if you purchase a CharlieCard (a prepaid stored-value card). ⇨ *See Subway, Train, and Trolley Travel below for more information.* Free 24-hour shuttle buses connect the subway station with all airline terminals. Shuttle Bus 22 runs between the subway and Terminals A and B, and Shuttle Bus 33 runs between the subway and Terminals C and E.

MBTA ☎ *800/392–6100, 617/222–3200, 617/222–5146 TTY* 🌐 *www.mbta.com.*

BICYCLE TRAVEL

Bicycling has finally come of age in Boston. It's common today to see both locals and tourists biking along inner-city streets as well as pedestrian malls and other auto-free zones. Car drivers are becoming more used to having to sharing the road with bicycles, and an increasing number of designated bike lanes are helping make things safer for everyone. Note that helmets are required for anyone 16 or younger.

The city has a fair number of stands for locking your bike. Bicycles can be carried onto most buses and subways (with the exception of the Green Line) during non-peak hours, which are defined as between 7 pm and 7 am and then between 10 am and 4 pm.

BIKE RENTAL

The typical cost for a hybrid bike (with a helmet and lock) is $35 for an 8-hour day. Centrally located bike rental and repair shops include Back Bay Bicycles, Landry's Bikes, and International Bicycle Centers; some bike shops offer guided bike tours. State law requires that all rental companies have helmets available to renters.

TRAILS

The advocacy group MassBike has a website with extensive maps showing bike lanes and bike-friendly trails on its website, as well as more general info for cyclists on its website. There are nearly 50 car-free miles of largely interconnected waterfront pathways that are open to bikes, from Charlestown and the Waterfront to Dorchester and Quincy. Both banks of the Charles River have scenic paths heading westward to Watertown and Newton. Other dedicated bicycle paths, some made from repurposed former rail lines, connect the hub with outer suburbs; the Minuteman Trail, for instance, heads westward from Cambridge for 15 miles, linking Arlington, Lexington, Concord, and Bedford.

HUBWAY

Boston's short-term bike rental program is primarily commuter-oriented, but it can also be a handy and fun way for travelers to cover relatively short distances. Members are able to unlock a bike from a Hubway dock, ride it for up to thirty minutes, and then return it to any other dock. There's no additional charge for any ride that lasts less than 30 minutes, and the docks are in strategic locations throughout the metro area.

Short-term memberships are available for 24 hours ($6), 3 days ($12), and by the month ($20), and you must be 18 or over to join. Sign up online or via one of the kiosks at each dock. Note that the prices don't include a helmet, which isn't mandatory but which is a good idea, or a lock, which isn't necessary if you're taking the bike directly to another dock.

Before taking a bike out, plan your route to the next dock—the Hubway's website and the free Spotcycle app (available for iPhone, Android, and BlackBerry) shows docks' locations, as well as how many bikes and empty spaces are available at each. If you don't manage to return a bike within 30 minutes, an overtime fee will be charged to your credit card. Such fees can be stiff, especially if you've kept the bike longer than an hour.

Bicycle Information

Back Bay Bicycles ✉ *362 Commonwealth Ave., Back Bay* ☎ *617/247–2336* 🌐 *papa-wheelies.com.*

Hubway ☎ *855/448–2929* 🌐 *www.thehubway.com.* **International Bicycle Center** ✉ *89 Brighton Ave., Allston* ☎ *617/783–5804* 🌐 *internationalbike.com.*

Landry's Bicycles ✉ *890 Commonwealth Ave., Allston* ☎ *617/232–0446* 🌐 *www.landrys.com.*

MassBike (*Massachusets Bicycle Coalition*). ✉ *171 Milk St., Downtown Crossing* ☎ *617/542–2453* 🌐 *massbike.org.*

Urban AdvenTours ✉ *103 Atlantic Ave., Waterfront* ☎ *617/670–0637* 🌐 *www.urbanadventours.com.*

BOAT TRAVEL

ARRIVING BY BOAT

Several boat companies make runs between the airport and Downtown destinations. Take the free Shuttle Bus 66 from any terminal to the airport's ferry dock to catch Boston's water taxis.

Rowes Wharf Water Taxi goes from Logan Airport to Rowes Wharf, Downtown, for $10 per person ($17 round-trip). It operates daily from April through October.

Harbor Express water taxis (part of the MBTA system) take passengers from Logan Airport to Long Wharf, Downtown ($10), and to Quincy and Hull on the South Shore ($12). Boats leave approximately every 40–45 minutes from 6:20 am–10:30 pm on weekdays, and from 8:20 am–10:30 pm on weekends.

City Water Taxi has an on-call boat service between the airport and several Downtown locations that operates year-round from 7 am to 10 pm Monday through Saturday and 7 am to 8 pm on Sunday. One-way fares to or from the airport are $10, and round-trip tickets are $17. Service to Charlestown, North Station, and the Black Falcon Cruise Ship Terminal is also available for $20 (one way); if two or more people are traveling together the price drops to $15 per passenger (one way).

GETTING AROUND BY BOAT

MBTA commuter boat service operates weekdays between several Downtown harbor destinations, Charlestown, and quite a few locations on the South Shore. One-way fares range from $8 to $16 depending on the destination. Schedules change seasonally, so call ahead.

Information **City Water Taxi** ☎ *617/422–0392* 🌐 *www.citywatertaxi.com.* **Harbor Express** ☎ *617/770–0040* 🌐 *www.harborexpress.com.* **MBTA** ☎ *617/222–3200* 🌐 *www.mbta.com.* **Rowes Wharf Water Taxi** ☎ *617/406–8584* 🌐 *www.roweswharfwatertaxi.com.*

COMMUTING WITH A VIEW

The Rowes Wharf Water Taxi offers a stunning glimpse of the city's skyline as it makes seven-minute trips across Boston Harbor to and from Logan Airport.

BUS TRAVEL

ARRIVING BY BUS

Greyhound has buses to Boston from all major cities in North America. Besides its main location at South Station, Greyhound has suburban terminals in Newton and Framingham. Peter Pan Bus Lines connects Boston with cities elsewhere in Massachusetts, Connecticut, New Jersey, New York, and Maryland.

Concord Coach runs buses between Boston and Concord, New Hampshire; Portland, Maine; and Bangor, Maine. C&J sends buses up the New Hampshire coast to Newburyport, Massachusetts; Dover, New Hampshire; Durham, New Hampshire; and Portsmouth, New Hampshire. Concord and C&J both leave from South Station (which is connected to the Amtrak station) and Logan Airport. BoltBus offers cheap fares in well-kept buses between Boston, New York City, Philadelphia, and Washington D.C. (express service between Boston and New York City is also available). Megabus also offers low fares, and serves New York City and points south along the East Coast. Both companies leave from South Station.

If you want to travel in style, the LimoLiner provides luxury bus service (with television, movies, high-speed Internet, and food-and-drink service) between Boston's Hilton Back Bay and Manhattan's Hilton New York for $89 each way. This service is open to the general public, not just guests of the Hilton. Reservations are a good idea.

Fares and schedules for all buses except LimoLiner are posted at South Station, at many of the tourist kiosks, and online. Major bus lines now offer Wi-Fi service at no charge. You can usually purchase your tickets online, and major credit cards are accepted for all buses.

Bus Information **BoltBus** ☎ *877/265–8287* 🌐 *www.boltbus.com.* **C&J** ☎ *800/258–7111* 🌐 *www.ridecj.com.* **Concord Coach** ☎ *800/639–3317* 🌐 *www.concordcoachlines.com.* **Greyhound** ☎ *800/231–2222* 🌐 *www.greyhound.com.* **LimoLiner** ☎ *888/546–5469,*

508/436–7425 🌐 *www.limoliner.com.* **Megabus** ☎ *877/462–6342* 🌐 *www.megabus.com.* **Peter Pan** ☎ *800/343–9999* 🌐 *www.peterpanbus.com.*

STATION INFORMATION

South Station ✉ *2 South Station, Atlantic Ave. and Summer St., Downtown* Ⓜ *South Station.*

GETTING AROUND BY BUS

Buses of the Massachusetts Bay Transportation Authority (MBTA) crisscross the metropolitan area and travel farther into suburbia than the subway and trolley lines. Most bus routes run from 5:30 am to 12:30 am.

CharlieCards (prepaid stored-value fare cards) are sold at all subway terminals from ticket agents, who are generally there from 7 am to 7 pm. The hard-plastic cards can be purchased with cash or with debit or credit cards. To pay the bus fare, tap your pass on the fare plate when you enter.

Fares within the city are $2 if paying in cash, or $1.50 if paying with a prepurchased CharlieCard; fares are higher for longer suburban lines. Fare machines accept paper currency but do not return change.

Bus Information MBTA ☎ *617/222–3200, 617/222–5146 TTY* 🌐 *www.mbta.com.*

CAR TRAVEL

Having a car in Boston may be convenient if you're planning day trips outside the city limits, but driving within the city should be avoided, as it's often confusing and stressful. Roads are congested, traffic makes maneuvering difficult, and signage is cryptic (or nonexistent). Parking spaces are often hard to come by, especially during major events like the Boston Marathon and Red Sox games.

If you must drive and you're unfamiliar with the city, it's important to plan your route in advance. Traveling with a GPS unit or smartphone, or renting one with your car rental agency, can be a real help. Boston motorists are notorious for driving aggressively. Pay extra attention to other drivers, and watch out for those using the emergency breakdown lanes (illegal unless posted otherwise), passing on the right, failing to yield, or turning from the wrong lane.

Unlike the rest of the country, the Boston area has many traffic circles, also known as roundabouts. Follow one simple courteous rule, and you'll be fine: cars entering traffic circles must yield to cars already in the circle.

GAS STATIONS

There aren't that many gas stations in Downtown. Try Cambridge Street (behind Beacon Hill, near Massachusetts General Hospital), near the airport in East Boston, along Commonwealth Avenue or Cambridge Street in Allston/Brighton, or off the Southeast Expressway just south of Downtown Boston.

Cambridge service stations can be found along Memorial Drive, Massachusetts Avenue, and Broadway. In Brookline, try Commonwealth Avenue or Boylston Street. Gas stations with 24-hour service can be found at many exits off Route 3 to Cape Cod, suburban Route 128 and Interstate 95, and at service plazas on the Massachusetts Turnpike (Interstate 90). Many offer both full- and self-service.

PARKING

Parking on Boston streets is tricky. Some neighborhoods have strictly enforced residents-only rules, with just a handful of two-hour visitors' spaces; others have meters, which usually cost 25¢ for 15 minutes, with a one- or two-hour maximum. Keep a few quarters handy, as some city meters take nothing else. Newer meters, strategically placed, accept credit cards and issue receipts that you should leave on your dashboard, on the side nearest the street.

The parking police are ruthless—it's not unusual to find a ticket on your windshield five minutes after your meter expires. However, most on-street parking is free after 8 pm in the city and on Sunday. Repeat offenders who don't pay fines may find the "boot" (an immovable steel clamp) secured to one of their wheels.

Major public lots are at Government Center, Quincy Market, beneath Boston Common (entrance on Charles Street), beneath Post Office Square, at Prudential Center, at Copley Place, and off Clarendon Street near the John Hancock Tower. Smaller lots and garages are scattered throughout Downtown, especially around the Theater District and off Atlantic Avenue in the North End. Most are expensive; expect to pay up to $10 an hour or $24 to park all day. The few city garages are a bargain, at about $7–$11 per day. Theaters, restaurants, stores, and tourist attractions often provide customers with one or two hours of free parking (always ask if the establishment validates receipts). Most Downtown restaurants offer valet parking.

ROAD CONDITIONS

Bostonians are notorious for driving erratically and aggressively. These habits, coupled with inconsistent street and traffic signs, one-way streets, and heavy congestion, make it a nerve-wracking city to navigate. Many urban roadways are under construction or are roughly surfaced. Potholes and aboveground manhole covers are common hazards. In general, err on the side of caution, and give yourself a few extra minutes travel time when driving in the city.

ROADSIDE EMERGENCIES

Dial 911 in an emergency to reach police, fire, or ambulance services. If you're a member of the AAA auto club, call its 24-hour help bureau.

EMERGENCY SERVICES

AAA ☎ *800/222–4357* 🌐 *aaa.com.*

RENTING

Rates in Boston begin at about $20 a day for an economy car with air-conditioning, automatic transmission, and unlimited mileage. This doesn't include gas, insurance charges, or the 6.25% tax and $10 surcharge. All major agencies listed *below* have branches at Logan International Airport. Zipcar also has many cars available in the Boston area for its members.

Major Agencies Alamo ☎ *877/222–9075* 🌐 *www.alamo.com.* **Avis** ☎ *800/331–1212* 🌐 *www.avis.com.* **Budget** ☎ *800/527–0700* 🌐 *www.budget.com.* **Hertz** ☎ *800/654–3131* 🌐 *www.hertz.com.* **National Car Rental** ☎ *877/222–9058* 🌐 *www.nationalcar.com.* **Zipcar** ☎ *866/494–7227* 🌐 *www.zipcar.com.*

PEDICAB TRAVEL

Pedicabs, human-powered three-wheeled bicycle rickshaws, are popular modes of transport in the nonwinter months around Boston and Cambridge. These vehicles, which hold two adults easily and three with difficulty, are manned (rarely womanned) by trained cyclists who wear eye-catching shirts, exude good nature and stamina, and have the gift of gab. You can hail one of these three-wheelers on the street or phone for one, with an average wait of ten minutes. Boston patrons most often use them to get from point A to a not-far-away point B; on Red Sox game days, pedicabs swarm towards Fenway Park, often arriving ahead of auto traffic.

There are no fixed fares, since the bikers work for tips; pay your biker (cash only) what you think the ride was worth, though be ready for a sour look if you pay much less than $10 a mile or so. Try to agree on a fee ahead of time. Most pedicabs also offer tours, with minimum fixed fees.

Pedicab Information Boston Pedicab ☎ *617/266–2005* 🌐 *www.bostonpedicab.com.*

Boston Rickshaw ☎ *857/300–0565.*

Cambridge Pedicab ☎ *617/370–3707* 🌐 *cambridge-pedicab.com.*

SUBWAY, TRAIN, AND TROLLEY TRAVEL

The Massachusetts Bay Transportation Authority (MBTA)—known as "the T"—operates subways and buses along five connecting lines, as well as many bus and several rail commuter lines that reach nearby suburbs and cities. Subways and buses operate from about 5:30 am to about 1 am, with limited late-night service. A 24-hour hotline and the MBTA website have specific information on routes, schedules, fares, wheelchair access, and other matters. Free maps are available at the MBTA's Park Street Station information stand, open daily from 7 am to 10 pm. The 🌐 *www.mbta.com* site has a useful trip planner tool.

GETTING AROUND ON THE SUBWAY

"Inbound" trains head into the city center and "outbound" trains head away from it. If you get on the Red Line at South Station, the train heading toward Alewife (Cambridge) is inbound. But once you pass the Park Street station, the train becomes an outbound train. The best way to figure out which way to go is to make note of the destination station, usually listed on the front of the train. So from Downtown the Red Line to Cambridge would be the Alewife train and the Green Line to Fenway would be the Boston College or Cleveland Circle train. Large maps prominently posted at each station show the line(s) that serve it, with each stop marked.

The Red Line originates at Braintree and Quincy Center to the south; the routes join near South Boston at the JFK/UMass stop and continue to Alewife, the northwest corner of Cambridge (near the border with suburban Arlington). The Mattapan high-speed line, also known as the M line, is considered part of the overall Red Line. Originating in Ashmont Station, it transports passengers via vintage yellow trolleys to Mattapan Square. The Green Line operates elevated trolleys that dip underground in the city center. The line originates at Cambridge's Lechmere, heads south, and divides into four routes that end at Boston College (Commonwealth Avenue), Cleveland Circle (Beacon Street, in Brighton), Riverside (Newton at Route 128), and Heath Street (Huntington Avenue in Jamaica Plain). The Blue Line runs weekdays from Bowdoin Square (and weeknights and weekends from Government Center) to the Wonderland Racetrack in Revere, north of Boston. The Orange Line runs from Oak Grove in north suburban Malden to Forest Hills near the Arnold Arboretum.

The Silver Line (a bus line with its own dedicated lanes) has four routes. SL1 connects South Station to Logan Airport; SL2 runs between South Station and the Design Center; SL4 connects Dudley Square and South Station; and SL5 runs between Downtown Crossing and Dudley Square, also stopping in Boylston (SL1 and SL2 are priced like the subway, but SL4 and SL5 are priced like buses, so the fare on these last two lines is only $1.50). Park Street Station (on the Common) and State Street are the major Downtown transfer points.

FARES AND PASSES

T fares are $2.50 for adults paying in cash or $2 with a prepurchased CharlieCard. (Most bus fares are $0.50 cheaper, with the exception of the SL1 and SL2 bus lines, which are priced as if they were part of the subway.) Children age 11 and under ride free. Senior citizens pay $1. Fares on the commuter rail—the Purple Line—vary from $2–11, depending on distance.

Getting a CharlieCard makes it easier to transfer between the subway and the bus, because such transfers are free and you don't need to keep track of individual tickets. Get your CharlieCard from a ticket agent at subway terminals during business hours (7 am to 7 pm); from a machine at the T stations at North Station, South Station, or Back Bay; the CharlieCard office at Downtown Crossing; or online or from some retailers. Check the T's website for more information.

One-day ($11) and seven-day ($18) passes are available for unlimited travel on subways, city buses, and inner-harbor ferries.

Buy passes at any full-service MBTA stations. Passes are also sold at the Boston Common Visitor Information Center (⇨ *Visitor Information*) and at some hotels.

TICKET/PASS	PRICE
Single Fare (subway/ most buses)	$2.50/$2
Unlimited 1-Day Pass	$11
Unlimited 7-Day Pass	$18
Monthly Unlimited Pass	$70

MBTA ☎ *800/392–6100, 617/222–3200, 617/222–5146 TTY* 🌐 *www.mbta.com.*

TAXI TRAVEL

Cabs are available around the clock. You can find them outside most hotels and at designated cabstands around the city, which are marked by signs. Taxis generally line up in Harvard Square, around South Station, near Faneuil Hall Marketplace, at Long Wharf, near Massachusetts General Hospital, and in the Theater District. You can also call or use smartphone apps, such as Hailo or Uber to get a taxi or other hired car.

A taxi ride within the city of Boston costs $2.60 at entry for the first 1/7 mile, and 40¢ for each 1/7 mile thereafter. Licensed cabs have meters and provide receipts. An illuminated rooftop sign indicates an available cab. If you're going to or from the airport or to the suburbs, ask about flat rates. (Be aware that you'll also need to pay a $5.25 toll and a $2.75 airport fee when leaving the airport, and a $2.75 airport fee when traveling to the airport in a cab.) Cabdrivers sometimes charge extra for multiple stops. One-way streets may make circuitous routes necessary and increase your cost.

Trying to hail a cab at around 2 am, when most bars close, can prove difficult, and there will often be a 20- to 30-minute wait if you phone for one. Heading to a cabstand may be your most efficient late-night choice. Avoid the sleek black town cars aggressively offering rides on the street or at airports (aka "rogue taxis")—their drivers sometimes charge more than the agreed-upon rate, and are sometimes even dangerous.

Taxi Companies Independent Taxi Operators Association (ITOA) ☎ *617/426–8700 taxi dispatch* 🌐 *www.itoataxi.com.* **Metro Cab** ☎ *617/782–5500* 🌐 *www.metro-cab.com.* **Town Taxi** ☎ *617/536–5000.*

TRAIN TRAVEL

Boston is served by Amtrak at North Station, South Station, and Back Bay Station. North Station is the terminus for Amtrak's *Downeaster* service from Boston to New Hampshire and Maine. South Station and Back Bay Station, nearby, accommodate frequent Northeast Corridor departures to and arrivals from New York, Philadelphia, and Washington, D.C. Amtrak's pricey, high-speed Acela train cuts the travel time between Boston and New York by an hour, to 3½ hours. South Station and Back Bay Station are the two stops in Boston for Amtrak's *Lake Shore Limited,* which travels daily between Boston and Chicago by way of Albany, Rochester, Buffalo, and Cleveland. Amtrak tickets, schedules, and reservations are available at Amtrak stations, online, by telephone, and through travel agents. Free maps are available at the MBTA's Park Street Station information stand.

Amtrak ticket offices accept all major credit cards, cash, traveler's checks, and personal checks when accompanied by a valid photo ID and a major credit card. You may pay on board with cash or a major credit card, but a surcharge will apply. Amtrak has both reserved and unreserved trains. During peak times, such as a Friday night, get a reservation and a ticket in advance (you may also save money by buying in advance). Trains at nonpeak times are unreserved, with seats assigned on a first-come, first-served basis.

The MBTA runs commuter trains to nearby points south, west, and north. Trains bound for Worcester, Needham, Forge Park, Providence (Rhode Island), and Stoughton leave from South Station and Back Bay Station; those to Fitchburg, Lowell, Haverhill, Newburyport, and Rockport operate out of North Station; those to Middleboro/Lakeville, Kingston/Route 3, Plymouth, and Greenbush depart from South Station.

MBTA commuter-rail stations generally accept only cash. Buy your ticket at the window or in advance, or be ready to pay a $1–2 surcharge in cash when you're on board.

Train Information Amtrak ☎ *800/872–7245* 🌐 *www.amtrak.com.* **Back Bay Station** ✉ *145 Dartmouth St., Back Bay.* **North Station** ✉ *100 Legends Way, Causeway and Friend Sts., North End.* **South Station** ✉ *700 Atlantic Ave., at Summer St., Downtown* Ⓜ *South Station.*

ESSENTIALS

COMMUNICATIONS

INTERNET

Most Downtown hotels offer free or fee-based wireless in their rooms or at least in common areas. Check with your hotel before arriving to confirm.

You'll find that many Internet cafés on Newbury Street and throughout the city offer free Wi-Fi. Most coffee shops, including branches of Pavement, Peets, Starbucks, and Espresso Royale, have free Wi-Fi available to customers. Others may charge a small fee (from $2 and up) depending on the minutes of usage.

Contacts **Cybercafes.** Cybercafes lists more than 4,200 Internet cafés worldwide. *www.cybercafes.com.* **Wi-Fi Free Spot.** Lists hundreds of spots where you can connect to free Wi-Fi around Boston and Massachusetts. *www.wififreespot.com/mass.html.*

DAY TOURS AND GUIDES

Traveling to Boston on a package tour makes it quite convenient for those interested only in hitting the highlights or major historic sites such as the Freedom Trail, Faneuil Hall, the Bunker Hill Memorial, Quincy Market, and Harvard Square. If you're interested in exploring more neighborhoods, a tour will likely not give you time to visit them.

BOAT TOURS

Boston has many waterways that offer stunning views of the city skyline. Narrated sightseeing water tours generally run from spring through early fall, usually until Columbus Day weekend. These trips normally last ¾–1½ hours and cost upwards of $25. Many companies offer whale watches, and sunset or evening cruises with entertainment.

Boston Duck Tours, which give witty narrated land-and-water tours on World War II amphibious vehicles, are very popular. After going by historic sights, the vehicle then dips into the Charles River to offer views of the Boston skyline. These tours, costing $34 for an adult, run through late November (there are also a handful of weekend tours in December). There are departures from Prudential Center; from Huntington Avenue, in front of Shaw's supermarket; from New England Aquarium; and from the Museum of Science.

June through September, you can relive the golden age of sail aboard the *Liberty Clipper,* a replica two-masted gaff-rigged schooner that operates midday harbor tours and romantic sunset cruises from Long Wharf.

Boston Harbor Cruises and Massachusetts Bay Lines have tours around the harbor. Charles Riverboat Company also offers architectural cruises, narrated by experts, that exit the Charles River Basin locks, enter Boston Harbor under the Zakim Bridge, and take in the historic sights of Charlestown as well as the dynamic seaport and waterfront.

Fees and Schedules **Boston Duck Tours** *617/267–3825* *www.bostonducktours.com.* **Boston Harbor Cruises** *1 Long Wharf* *877/733–9425, 617/227–4321* *www.bostonharborcruises.com.* **Charles Riverboat Company** *100 Cambridge Pl., Suite 320, Cambridge* *617/621–3001* *www.charlesriverboat.com.* ***Liberty Clipper*** *67 Long Wharf* *617/742–0333* *www.libertyfleet.com.* **Massachusetts Bay Lines** *60 Rowes Wharf* *617/542–8000* *www.massbaylines.com.*

BUS TOURS

Bus tours, which cost around $25 and run daily from mid-March to early November, cover the main historic neighborhoods in less than four hours. Reserve bus tours at least a day in advance. Boston Private Tours has customized tours in vans or limousines. Brush Hill has more traditional charter bus tours as well as smaller tours, with lots of prepackaged options and add-ons; the 1½-hour narrated tour is popular.

Fees and Schedules **Boston Private Tours** ✉ *707 Main St.* ☎ *978/771–4471* 🌐 *www.bostonprivatetours.com.* **Brush Hill Tours** ✉ *Transportation Bldg., 16 Charles St. S* ☎ *800/343–1328, 781/986–6100* 🌐 *www.brushhilltours.com.*

THEME TOURS

See how the beer's made at the Boston Beer Museum & Samuel Adams Brewery or Harpoon Brewery; hear spine-tingling tales about Boston's famous cemeteries; or tour the offices and printing plant of the *Boston Globe*. Some organizations have special restrictions, such as an age limit for children. To capture the true flavor of Boston's intelligentsia, make a reservation for an art and architecture tour of the Boston Athenaeum, the grande dame of Boston's private libraries. Many tours are free, but you often need to make a reservation at least a few days in advance. It's always a good idea to call ahead to confirm schedules.

Beer Tours **Boston Beer Museum & Samuel Adams Brewery** ✉ *Boston Beer Company, 30 Germania St., Jamaica Plain* ☎ *617/368–5080 tours* 🌐 *www.samueladams.com.*

Harpoon Brewery ✉ *306 Northern Ave., Waterfront* ☎ *617/456–2322* 🌐 *www.harpoonbrewery.com.*

Children's Tours **Boston by Little Feet** ✉ *Meet at Samuel Adams statue in front of Faneuil Hall* ☎ *617/367–2345* 🌐 *www.bostonbyfoot.com/tours/Boston_By_Little_Feet.*

Garden, Parks, and Architecture Tours **Beacon Hill Garden Club Tours** ✉ *Charles and Beacon Sts., Beacon Hill* ☎ *617/227–4392* 🌐 *www.beaconhillgardenclub.org.*

Boston Athenaeum ✉ *10½ Beacon St., Beacon Hill* ☎ *617/227–0270* 🌐 *www.bostonathenaeum.org.* **Boston Park Rangers** ✉ *Parks and Recreation Dept. kiosk in Boston Common* ☎ *617/635–4505* 🌐 *www.cityofboston.gov/parks.*

TROLLEY TOURS

Narrated trolley tours, which usually cost $36 or so, don't require reservations and are more flexible than bus tours; you can hop on and hop off as often as you want. A full trip normally lasts 1½ to 2 hours. All trolleys run daily, though less frequently off-season. Because they're open vehicles, be sure to dress appropriately for the weather.

Old Town Trolley tours, which usually focus on history, includes a tour that's 1½ hours and narrated.

Old Town Trolley ✉ *380 Dorchester Ave., South Boston* ☎ *888/912–8687* 🌐 *www.historictours.com/boston.*

WALKING TOURS

Boston is the perfect city for walking tours, to explore history, literature, the city's ethnic neighborhoods, and other subjects. Most tours cost about $20 and last one to two hours. Guides prefer to keep groups at fewer than 20 people, so always reserve ahead. Several organizations give tours once or twice a day spring through fall and by appointment (if at all) in winter. Others run tours a few days a week, spring through fall. If you'd rather not take a tour using your own two legs, there's also a tour that lets you see the sights on a Segway.

The Women's Heritage Trail, the Freedom Trail, and the Black Heritage Trail can be completed as self-guided tours. Maps for the Women's Heritage Trail are available online and at the Old State House and the National Park Service Visitor Center; the same organization also runs several tours with guides. The Boston Common Visitor Information Center has maps of the Freedom Trail, which is indicated with a red line painted on the ground. The Freedom Trail and the Black Heritage Trail can also be completed with a ranger-led group. The Boston and Cambridge Centers for Adult Education lead in-depth educational tours on many topics, most of them centered on art, architecture, and literature.

Harvard Square is the starting point for free student-led campus tours.

Fees and Schedules **Black Heritage Trail** ☎ *617/725–0022* 🌐 *www.maah.org*. **Boston by Foot** ✉ *290 Congress St., Suite 100* ☎ *617/367–2345* 🌐 *www.bostonbyfoot.com*. **Boston By Segway** ✉ *420 Commercial St., North End* ☎ *866/611–9838, 617/670–4200* 🌐 *bostonbysegway.com*. **Boston Center for Adult Education** ✉ *122 Arlington St.* ☎ *617/267–4430* 🌐 *www.bcae.org*. **Boston Common Visitor Information Center** ☎ *888/733–2678* 🌐 *www.bostonusa.com*. **Cambridge Center for Adult Education** ✉ *42 Brattle St., Cambridge* ☎ *617/547–6789* 🌐 *www.ccae.org*. **Freedom Trail** ☎ *617/357–8300* 🌐 *www.thefreedomtrail.org*. **Harvard Campus Tours** ✉ *Harvard Information Center, 1350 Massachusetts Ave., Cambridge* ☎ *617/495–1573* 🌐 *www.harvard.edu/visitors*. **Historic New England** ✉ *141 Cambridge St.* ☎ *617/227–3956* 🌐 *www.historicnewengland.org*. **National Parks Service Visitor Center** ☎ *617/242–5642* 🌐 *www.nps.gov/bost*. **North End Market Tour** ✉ *6 Charter St.* ☎ *617/523–6032* 🌐 *bostonfoodtours.com*. **Women's Heritage Trail** 🌐 *www.bwht.org*.

GEAR

The first rule of Boston weather: no rules! A chilly, overcast morning can become a sunny, warm afternoon—and vice versa. Try to layer your clothing so that you can remove or add garments as needed for comfort. Rain may appear with little warning, so pack a raincoat and umbrella if you have the room. Boston is a great walking city—despite picturesque but bumpy cobblestone streets, brick walkways, and uneven asphalt—so be sure to bring comfortable shoes. In all seasons, it's often breezier (and colder) along the coast; carry a windbreaker, fleece jacket, or sweatshirt or hoodie when touring the beach or harbor areas.

HOURS OF OPERATION

Banks are generally open weekdays 9 am to 4 or 5 pm, plus Saturday 9 am to noon or 1 pm at some branches. Public buildings are open weekdays 9 to 5.

Although hours vary quite a bit, most museums are open Monday through Saturday 9 or 10 am to 5 or 6 pm and Sunday noon to 5 pm. Some are closed one day a week, usually Monday.

Major pharmacy chains—CVS, Rite-Aid, and Walgreens—are generally open daily between 7 or 9:30 am and 8 or 10 pm; independently owned pharmacies tend to close earlier. Some are open 24/7.

Boston stores are generally open Monday through Saturday 10 or 11 am to 6 or 7 pm, closing later during the holiday-shopping season. Mall shops often stay open until 9 or 10 pm; malls and some tourist areas may also be open Sunday noon–5 or 6 pm.

MONEY

Prices are generally higher in Beacon Hill, the Back Bay, and Harvard Square than other parts of town. You're more likely to find bargains in the North End, Kenmore Square, Downtown Crossing, and Cambridge's Central Square. Many museums offer free admission on one weekday evening, and reduced admissions at all times for children, students, and senior citizens.

ITEM	AVERAGE COST
Cup of Coffee	$2–3
Glass of Wine	$6 and up
Glass / Bottle of Beer	$3.50 and up
Slice of Pizza	$1.50–$3
One-Mile Taxi Ride	$6
Museum Admission (adult)	$9–$21

CREDIT CARDS

Reporting Lost Cards **American Express** ☎ *800/528–4800* 🌐 *www.americanexpress.com*. **Diners Club** ☎ *800/234–6377* 🌐 *www.*

dinersclub.com. **Discover** ☎ *800/347–2683* 🌐 *www.discovercard.com.***MasterCard** ☎ *800/627–8372* 🌐 *www.mastercard.com.* **Visa** ☎ *800/847–2911* 🌐 *www.visa.com.*

RESTROOMS

Public restrooms outside of restaurants, hotel lobbies, and tourist attractions are rare in Boston, but you'll find clean, well-lighted facilities at South Station, Faneuil Hall Marketplace, and the Visitor Information Center on Boston Common.

The Bathroom Diaries. The Bathroom Diaries is flush with unsanitized info on restrooms the world over—each one located, reviewed, and rated. 🌐 *www.thebathroomdiaries.com.*

SAFETY

With their many charming neighborhoods, Boston and Cambridge often feel like small towns. But they're both cities, subject to the same problems plaguing many other urban communities nationwide. Although violent crime is rare, residents and tourists alike sometimes fall victim to pickpockets, scam artists, and car thieves. As in any large city, use common sense, especially after dark. Stay with the crowds and walk on well-lighted, busy streets. Look alert and aware; a purposeful pace helps deter trouble wherever you go. Take cabs or park in well-lighted lots or garages.

Store valuables in a hotel safe or, better yet, leave them at home. Keep an eye (and hand) on handbags and backpacks; do not hang them from a chair in restaurants. Carry wallets in inside or front pockets rather than back pockets. Use ATMs in daylight, preferably in a hotel, bank, or another indoor location with security guards.

Subways and trolleys tend to be safe, but it's wise to stay on your guard. Stick to routes in the main Boston and Cambridge tourist areas—generally, the Downtown stops on all lines, on the Red Line in Cambridge, on the Green Line through the Back Bay, and on the Blue Line around the New England Aquarium. Know your itinerary, and make sure you get on the right bus or train going in the right direction. Avoid empty subway and trolley cars and lonely station hallways and platforms, especially after 9 pm on weeknights. Don't take unmarked taxis or any taxi that lacks a posted photo ID of the driver. The MBTA has its own police officers (who patrol stations and monitor them via video); don't hesitate to ask them for help.

TIP→ Distribute your cash, credit cards, IDs, and other valuables between a deep front pocket, an inside jacket or vest pocket, and a hidden money pouch. Don't reach for the money pouch once you're in public.

TAXES

Hotel room charges in Boston and Cambridge are subject to state and local taxes of up to 14.45%. A sales tax of 7% is added to restaurant and take-out meals, and a sales tax of 6.25% is added to all other goods except nonrestaurant food and clothing valued at less than $175.

TIME

Boston is in the Eastern time zone, 3 hours ahead of Los Angeles, 1 hour ahead of Chicago, 5 hours behind London, and 15 hours behind Sydney. Daylight Savings Time (DST) is observed. DST begins the second Sunday in March, when clocks are set ahead one hour, and ends the first Sunday in November, when clocks are set back an hour (tip for remembrance: "Spring forward, and Fall behind").

TIPPING

In restaurants the standard gratuity is 15% to 20% of your bill. Many restaurants automatically add a 15% to 20% gratuity for groups of six or more.

Tip taxi drivers 15% of the fare, and airport and hotel porters at least $1 per bag. It's also usual to tip chambermaids $1 to $3 daily. Hotel room-service tips vary and may be included in the meal charge. Masseuses and masseurs, hairstylists, manicurists, and others performing personal services generally get a 15% tip. Theater ushers, museum guides, and gas-station attendants generally do not receive tips. Tour guides may be tipped a few dollars for good service. Concierges may be tipped anywhere from $5 to $20 for exceptional service, such as securing a difficult dinner reservation or helping plan a personal sightseeing itinerary.

TIPPING GUIDELINES FOR BOSTON	
Bartender	$1 to $2 per drink
Bellhop	$1 to $5 per bag, depending on the level of the hotel
Hotel Concierge	$5 or more, if he or she performs a service for you
Hotel Doorman	$1 to $2 if he helps you get a cab
Hotel Maid	1$ to $3 a day (either daily or at the end of your stay, in cash)
Hotel Room-Service Waiter	$1 to $2 per delivery, even if a service charge has been added
Porter at Airport or Train Station	$1 per bag
Skycap at Airport	$1 to $3 per bag checked (in addition to any airline-imposed fees)
Taxi Driver	15% to 20%, but round up the fare to the next dollar amount
Tour Guide	10% of the cost of the tour
Valet Parking Attendant	$1 to $2, only when you get your car
Waiter	15% to 20%, with 20% being the norm at high-end restaurants; nothing additional if a service charge is added to the bill
Other	Restroom attendants in more-expensive restaurants expect some small change or $1. Tip coat-check personnel at least $1 to $2 per item checked unless there is a fee, then nothing.

VISITOR INFORMATION

Contact the city and state tourism offices for general information, details about seasonal events, discount passes, trip planning, and attraction information. The National Park Service has an office where you can watch an eight-minute slide show on Boston's historic sites and get maps and directions. The Welcome Center, Boston Common Visitor Information Center, and the Cambridge Tourism Office offer general information.

Contacts Boston Common Visitor Information Center ✉ *148 Tremont St., where Freedom Trail begins, Downtown* ☎ *888/733–2678* 🌐 *www.thefreedomtrail.org/visitor/boston-common.html.* **National Parks Service Visitor Center** ✉ *Faneuil Hall, Downtown* ☎ *617/242–5642* 🌐 *www.nps.gov/bost.* **Cambridge Tourism Office** ✉ *4 Brattle St., Harvard Sq., Cambridge* ☎ *800/862–5678, 617/441–2884* 🌐 *www.cambridge-usa.org.* **Greater Boston Convention and Visitors Bureau** ✉ *2 Copley Pl., Suite 105, Back Bay* ☎ *888/733–2678, 617/536–4100* 🌐 *www.bostonusa.com.* **Massachusetts Office of Travel and Tourism** ✉ *State Transportation Bldg., 10 Park Plaza, Suite 4510, Back Bay* ☎ *800/227–6277, 617/973–8500* 🌐 *www.massvacation.com.*

ONLINE RESOURCES

Boston.com, home of the *Boston Globe* online, has news and feature articles, ample travel information, and links to towns throughout Massachusetts. *The Improper Bostonian,* has nightlife, movie, restaurant, and arts listings. The Bostonian Society answers some frequently asked questions about Beantown history on its website. The iBoston page posts wonderful photographs of buildings that are architecturally and historically important. *WickedLocal* provides a more relaxed (and somewhat irreverent) take on Boston news and information.

All About Boston **Boston.com** 🌐 *www.boston.com.* **Bostonian Society** 🌐 *bostonhistory.org.* **iBoston** 🌐 *www.iboston.org.* **The Improper Bostonian** 🌐 *www.improper.com.* **Wicked Local** 🌐 *www.wickedlocal.com.*

Safety **Transportation Security Administration** (*TSA*). 🌐 *www.tsa.gov.*

INDEX

A

B

PHOTO CREDITS

Front cover: Grant Faint/Photographer's Choice/SuperStock [Description: Swan boats, Public Garden]. 1, Kindra Clineff. 2-3. Chee-Onn Leong/Shutterstock. 5, Tony the Misfit/Flickr. 8-9, Kindra Clineff. 10, Kindra Clineff. 11 (left), Kindra Clineff. 11 (right), ojbyrne/Flickr. 12, Kindra Clineff. 13 (left), Kindra Clineff. 13 (right), Kindra Clineff. 14, joyosity/Flickr. 15 (left), Jorge Salcedo/iStockphoto. 15 (right), Iwan Baan. 18 (top left), Kindra Clineff. 18 (bottom left), Kindra Clineff. 18 (top right), Copyright Tony Rinaldo images. 18 (bottom right), Kindra Clineff. 19 (top left), Kindra Clineff. 19 (bottom left), Kindra Clineff. 19 (top right), Chee-Onn Leong/Shutterstock. 19 (bottom right), Kindra Clineff. 20, Kindra Clineff. 21 (left), Kindra Clineff. 21 (right), Kindra Clineff. 22, Kindra Clineff. 23, NikiSublime/Flickr. 24, Kindra Clineff. 25, Kindra Clineff. 28, Kindra Clineff. 29 (top left), MCS@flickr/Flickr. 29 (bottom left), Classic Vision / age fotostock. 29 (center), A. H. C. / age fotostock. 29 (top right), cliff1066./Flickr. 29 (center right), Classic Vision / age fotostock. 29 (bottom), Kindra Clineff. 30, Kindra Clineff. 31 (top left), Kindra Clineff. 31 (center left), Tony the Misfit/Flickr. 31 (bottom left), Tim Grafft/MOTT. 31 (center bottom), Scott Orr/iStockphoto. 31 (top right), Freedom Trail Foundation. 31 (center right), Kindra Clineff. 31 (bottom right), Kindra Clineff. 32 (top), Kindra Clineff. 32 (bottom), Jim Reynolds/Wikimedia Commons. 33 (top), revjim5000/Flickr. 33 (bottom), Kindra Clineff. Chapter 2: Beacon Hill, Boston Common, and the Old West End: 35, Kindra Clineff. 37, Chee-Onn Leong/Shutterstock. 38, David Eby/Shutterstock. 41, Kindra Clineff. 50, Raymond Forbes / age fotostock. Chapter 3: Government Center and the North End: 53, Kindra Clineff. 55, Biruitorul/Wikimedia Commons. 56, Kindra Clineff. 58, Jorge Salcedo/iStockphoto. 60, Kindra Clineff. 65, Jorge Salcedo/Shutterstock. Chapter 4: Charlestown: 69, Kindra Clineff. 71, Kindra Clineff. 72, Jorge Salcedo/Shutterstock. 74, Kindra Clineff. Chapter 5: Downtown Boston: 77, Stuart Pearce / age fotostock. 79, Marcbela (Marc N. Belanger), [Public Domain], via Wikimedia Commons. 80, Stephen Orsillo/Shutterstock. 81, Danita Delimont / Alamy. 83, Kindra Clineff. 85, Hannu J.A. Aaltonen/Shutterstock. 87, Konstantin L/Shutterstock. Chapter 6: Back Bay and the South End: 91, Heeb Christian/age fotostock. 93, Kindra Clineff. 94, Kindra Clineff. 95, Kindra Clineff. 96, Chee-Onn Leong/Shutterstock. 99, Kindra Clineff. 105, Kindra Clineff. Chapter 7: The Fenway: 109, Israel Pabon/Shutterstock. 111, Kindra Clineff. 112, Museum of Fine Arts, Boston. 113, Museum of Fine Arts, Boston. 114, Isabella Stewart Gardner Museum, Boston. 115, Kindra Clineff. 116, Allie_Caulfield/Flickr. Chapter 8: Boston Outskirts: 119, Frank Siteman/ age fotostock. 121, Kindra Clineff. 122, Iwan Baan. 124, Kindra Clineff.Chapter 9: Cambridge: 127, Steve Dunwell / age fotostock. 129, Kindra Clineff. 130, Ming Vandenberg, www.hmnh.harvard.edu. 132, Harvard Crimson. 136, Kindra Clineff. 144, Jorge Salcedo/Shutterstock. Chapter 10: Where to Eat: 147, Kindra Clineff. 148, Stephi's on Tremont. 174, ˝WGBH/Anthony Tieuli. Chapter 11: Where to Stay: 197, The Charles Hotel. 198, Fairmont Hotels & Resorts. Chapter 12: Nightlife and the Arts: 215, John Coletti / age fotostock. 216, James Cridland/Flickr.237, John Coletti / age fotostock. 250, MCC Dave Kaylor/Wikimedia Commons. 254, Michael Dwyer/Alamy. Chapter 12: Sports and the Outdoors: 257, Kindra Clineff. 258, Chris- Dag/Flickr. 259 (top), Kindra Clineff. 259 (bottom), Kindra Clineff. 260, Kindra Clineff. 263, Kindra Clineff. 267, Kindra Clineff. 268, Kindra Clineff. 273, Kindra Clineff. Chapter 13: Shopping: 277, dk / Alamy. 278, Kindra Clineff. 284, Kindra Clineff. 287, Kindra Clineff. 296, Megapress / Alamy. 298, Danita Delimont / Alamy. Chapter 14: Side Trips: 301, Kindra Clineff. 302, Kindra Clineff. 303 (top), Kindra Clineff. 303 (bottom), Kindra Clineff. 304, Kindra Clineff. 315, Kindra Clineff. 319, Kindra Clineff. 322, Raymond Forbes / age fotostock. 324, Kindra Clineff. 327, Kindra Clineff, 330, Kindra Clineff. 334, Kindra Clineff. 336, Nantucket HistoricalAssociation. 337, Michael S. Nolan / age fotostock. 338, Kindra Clineff. 339 (left), Random House,Inc. 339 (top right), Kindra Clineff, 339 (center right), Penobscot Marine Museum. 339 (bottom right),Kindra Clineff. 341, Jeff Greenberg / age fotostock. Back cover (from left to right): Christopher Penler/Shutterstock; Kindra Clineff; Kindra Clineff. Spine: Samuel Borges Photography/Shutterstock.

NOTES

NOTES

NOTES

NOTES

NOTES

NOTES

ABOUT OUR WRITERS

Victoria Abbott Riccardi is a journalist and author based in Newton, Massachusetts. For the past 17 years she has written on food, wine, nutrition, and travel for a variety of publications including *Bon Appétit, Food & Wine,* and the *New York Times*. In 2003 she wrote the travel memoir *Untangling My Chopsticks: A Culinary Sojourn in Kyoto* (Broadway), a *New York Times* 2003 Notable Book. She also contributed to *Japanese Women Don't Get Old or Fat* (Delacorte Press, 2005); *Culinary Biographies* (Yes Press Inc., 2006); and *The Story of Tea: A Cultural History and Drinking Guide* (Ten Speed Press, 2007). She often blogs at www.victoriariccardi.com about Abner, a honey-brown mouse with discerning taste who likes to nibble on Parisian chocolate, Italian cracker rings, and other gourmet fare. Victoria updated the Where to Eat chapter for this edition.

Boston-based since his years as a Boston College undergrad, **Fred Bouchard** is a die-hard fan of both the Red Sox and the Boston Symphony. He reviews music for *DownBeat Magazine* and the *Boston Musical Intelligencer,* among other publications, and writes about wine and spirits for *Beverage Business*. An inveterate traveler, Fred loves venturing to Europe as often as possible where he is able to indulge his diverse interests including cooking, modern art, photography, and cycling. Fred teaches music journalism and literature at Berklee College of Music in Boston's Back Bay neighborhood. He updated the Experience, Nightlife and the Arts, and Travel Smart chapters.

Born and raised in Cambridge, **Frances Folsom** covers travel, architecture, and antiques for several publications including *American Way,* the *Boston Globe*, and *Antiques and Fine Art Magazine*. Frances is a graduate of Boston State College, where she studied American history. By far her favorite subject to write about is her hometown of Boston. Frances updated the Where to Stay, Shopping, and Side Trips chapters.

Kim Foley MacKinnon is a Boston-based editor, journalist, and travel writer. Over the past decade, her work has appeared in the *Boston Globe, Travel + Leisure* and USA Today, among other publications. Currently, she writes columns for *AAA Horizons* and the Appalachian Mountain Club, and serves as New England food editor for Gayot. Even after two decades living in Boston, Kim never tires of exploring the city. Kim updated the Sports and the Outdoors chapter for this edition, in addition to the Beacon Hill, Boston Common, and the Old West End; Government Center and the North End; Charleston; Downtown Boston; Back Bay and the South End; The Fenway; Boston Outskirts; and Cambridge chapters.

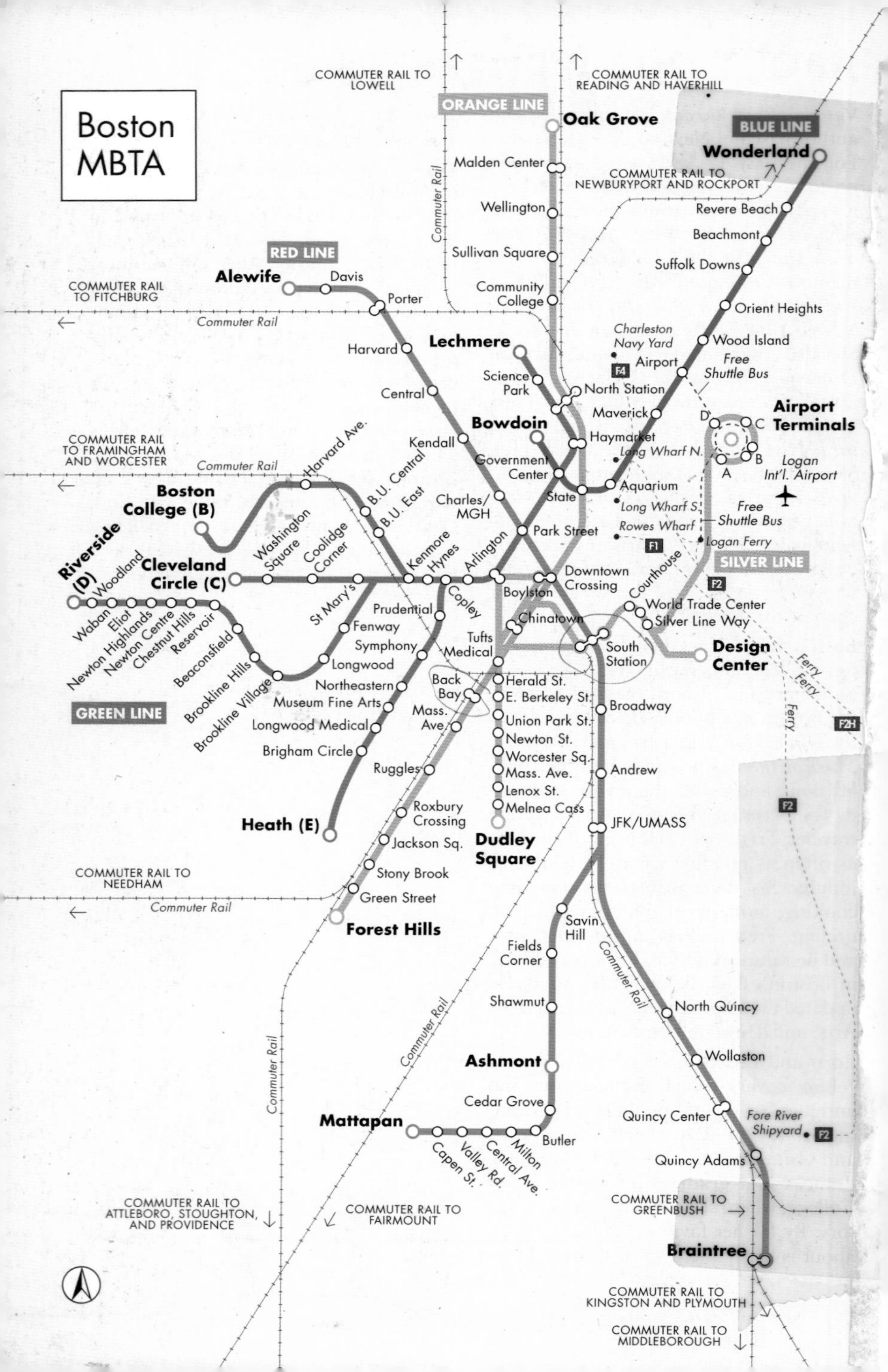
Boston MBTA
COMMUTER RAIL TO LOWELL
COMMUTER RAIL TO READING AND HAVERHILL
ORANGE LINE
Oak Grove
Malden Center
Wellington
Sullivan Square
Community College
BLUE LINE
Wonderland
COMMUTER RAIL TO NEWBURYPORT AND ROCKPORT
Revere Beach
Beachmont
Suffolk Downs
Orient Heights
Wood Island
Airport
Free Shuttle Bus
Maverick
Aquarium
RED LINE
Alewife
Davis
Porter
Harvard
Central
Kendall
Charles/ MGH
Park Street
Downtown Crossing
South Station
Broadway
Andrew
JFK/UMASS
Savin Hill
Fields Corner
Shawmut
Ashmont
Cedar Grove
Butler
Milton
Central Ave.
Valley Rd.
Capen St.
Mattapan
North Quincy
Wollaston
Quincy Center
Quincy Adams
Braintree
COMMUTER RAIL TO FITCHBURG
Commuter Rail
Lechmere
Science Park
North Station
Haymarket
Bowdoin
Government Center
State
Charleston Navy Yard
Long Wharf N.
Long Wharf S.
Rowes Wharf
Logan Ferry
Airport Terminals
Logan Int'l. Airport
Free Shuttle Bus
SILVER LINE
Courthouse
World Trade Center
Silver Line Way
Design Center
Ferry
COMMUTER RAIL TO FRAMINGHAM AND WORCESTER
Boston College (B)
Harvard Ave.
B.U. Central
B.U. East
Washington Square
Coolidge Corner
Cleveland Circle (C)
Riverside (D)
Woodland
Waban
Eliot
Newton Highlands
Newton Centre
Chestnut Hills
Reservoir
Beaconsfield
Brookline Hills
Brookline Village
Longwood
Fenway
St Mary's
Kenmore
Hynes
Copley
Arlington
Boylston
Chinatown
Tufts Medical
Prudential
Symphony
Northeastern
Museum Fine Arts
Longwood Medical
Brigham Circle
Heath (E)
GREEN LINE
Back Bay
Mass. Ave.
Ruggles
Roxbury Crossing
Jackson Sq.
Stony Brook
Green Street
Forest Hills
Herald St.
E. Berkeley St.
Union Park St.
Newton St.
Worcester Sq.
Mass. Ave.
Lenox St.
Melnea Cass
Dudley Square
COMMUTER RAIL TO NEEDHAM
Fore River Shipyard
COMMUTER RAIL TO GREENBUSH
COMMUTER RAIL TO ATTLEBORO, STOUGHTON, AND PROVIDENCE
COMMUTER RAIL TO FAIRMOUNT
COMMUTER RAIL TO KINGSTON AND PLYMOUTH
COMMUTER RAIL TO MIDDLEBOROUGH